STUDIES IN BAPTIST HISTORY A

VOLUME 19

Baptist Identities

International Studies from the Seventeenth

to the Twentieth Century

STUDIES IN BAPTIST HISTORY AND THOUGHT
VOLUME 19

A full listing of all titles in this series
appears at the close of this book

!

ɛ

STUDIES IN BAPTIST HISTORY AND THOUGHT
VOLUME 19

Baptist Identities

International Studies from the Seventeenth

to the Twentieth Century

Edited by

Ian M. Randall, Toivo Pilli and Anthony R. Cross

Foreword by David Bebbington

British Library Cataloguing in Publication Data
A catalogue record for this book is available from the British Library

ISBN-10 1–84227–215–2
ISBN-13 978–1–84227–215–2

Typeset by A.R. Cross
Printed and bound in Great Britain
for Paternoster
by Nottingham Alphagraphics

Series Preface

Baptists form one of the largest Christian communities in the world, and while they hold the historic faith in common with other mainstream Christian traditions, they nevertheless have important insights which they can offer to the worldwide church. *Studies in Baptist History and Thought* will be one means towards this end. It is an international series of academic studies which includes original monographs, revised dissertations, collections of essays and conference papers, and aims to cover any aspect of Baptist history and thought. While not all the authors are themselves Baptists, they nevertheless share an interest in relating Baptist history and thought to the other branches of the Christian church and to the wider life of the world.

The series includes studies in various aspects of Baptist history from the seventeenth century down to the present day, including biographical works, and Baptist thought is understood as covering the subject-matter of theology (including interdisciplinary studies embracing biblical studies, philosophy, sociology, practical theology, liturgy and women's studies). The diverse streams of Baptist life throughout the world are all within the scope of these volumes.

The series editors and consultants believe that the academic disciplines of history and theology are of vital importance to the spiritual vitality of the churches of the Baptist faith and order. The series sets out to discuss, examine and explore the many dimensions of their tradition and so to contribute to their on-going intellectual vigour.

A brief word of explanation is due for the series identifier on the front cover. The fountains, taken from heraldry, represent the Baptist distinctive of believer's baptism and, at the same time, the source of the water of life. There are three of them because they symbolize the Trinitarian basis of Baptist life and faith. Those who are redeemed by the Lamb, the book of Revelation reminds us, will be led to 'fountains of living waters' (Rev. 7.17).

Series Editors

Series Consultant Editors

Contents

Contributors

Austin Bennett Amonette, Assistant Professor of Church History and Theology, Houston Graduate School of Theology, Houston, Texas, USA

John R. Barclay, Secretary Morningside Baptist Church, Edinburgh, Scotland, 1988–96, a member of the Scottish Baptist History Project, and President of the Baptist Union of Scotland 1994–95

William H. Brackney, Professor of Religion and Director, The Program in Baptist Studies, Baylor University 2000–2006, Waco, Texas, USA; Distinguished Professor-Elect of Christian Thought and Ethics, Acadia University and Acadia Divinity College 2006–, Canada

Dennis Bustin, Assistant Professor of History, Atlantic Baptist University, Moncton, New Brunswick, Canada

Sébastien Fath, Groupe de Sociologie des Religions et de la Laïcité, Paris, France

Wayne Flynt, Distinguished University Professor Emeritus, Auburn University, and Professor of History, Samford University, Birmingham, Alabama, USA

Robert Eric Frykenberg, Professor Emeritus of History and South Asian Studies, University of Wisconsin-Madison, Madison, Wisconsin, USA

Erich Geldbach, Professor em. of Ecumenical Studies, Protestant Faculty of the Ruhr-University of Bichum, Germany

Daniel Goodwin, Associate Professor of History, Atlantic Baptist University, Moncton, New Brunswick, Canada

Brian M. Howell, Associate Professor of Anthropology, Department of Sociology and Anthropology, Wheaton College, Wheaton, Illinois, USA

Li Li, Asian Studies Coordinator, Salem State College, Massachusetts, USA

Ken R. Manley, Distinguished Professor of Church History, Whitley College, The University of Melbourne, Australia

D. Densil Morgan, Professor of Theology, Head, School of Arts and Humanities, University of Wales, Bangor, and Warde, Y Coleg Gwyn, the North Wales Baptist College, UK

Henry J. Mugabe, Principal, Baptist Theological Seminary of Zimbabwe, and Visiting Professor of Theology, Baptist Theological Seminary at Richmond, and Divinity School, Wake Forest, USA

Toivo Pilli, Course Leader of Baptist and Anabaptist Studies, International Baptist Theological Seminary, Prague, Czech Republic, and Lecturer in Estonian Church History, Baptist Theological Seminary, Tartu, Estonia

William L. Pitts, Jr, Professor of Religion, Baylor University, Waco, Texas, USA

Ian M. Randall, Lecturer in Church History and Spirituality, Spurgeon's College, London, UK, and Senior Research Fellow, International Baptist Theological Seminary, Prague, Czech Republic

Kenneth B.E. Roxburgh, S. Louis and Ann W. Armstrong Professor and Chair, Department of Religion, Samford University, Birmingham, Alabama, USA

Karen E. Smith, Tutor in Church History and Spirituality at South Wales Baptist College and in Cardiff University, and the Pastor of Orchard Place Baptist Church, Neath, South Wales, UK

Valdis Teraudkalns, Lecturer in Sociology of Religion, Faculty of Theology, University of Latvia, Riga, and Docent in Philosophy, Faculty of Humanities and Law, Rezekne Higher Educational Institution, Rezekne, Latvia

Tadeusz J. Zielinski, Professor of Systematic Theology, the Protestant Department of the Christian Academy of Theology, Warsaw, and Academic Dean, Warsaw Baptist Theological Seminary, Poland

Foreword

'Baptisme', according to the first Particular Baptist confession, drawn up in London in 1644, 'is an Ordinance of the new Testament, given by Christ, to be dispensed onely upon persons professing faith'.[1] That teaching differentiated the seven subscribing churches from their Independent counterparts that, like almost the whole of the remainder of Christendom, practised infant baptism. For the Baptists, to pour water on an uncomprehending baby was to obscure the imperative for people to embrace a personal faith before they could be introduced to the fellowship of believers by the rite of baptism. As Augustus H. Strong, the most systematic of their theologians, put it at the start of the twentieth century, 'Baptists baptize Christians'.[2] So much was clear to them about their identity. But what else was clear? Would they allow others who did not recognise the truth of believer's baptism to join them for communion? Opinion on that question, which had never been unanimous, divided the worldwide Baptist community sharply from the opening of the nineteenth century. Again, would they insist on a certain form of church government? In the seventeenth century, like their Independent cousins, they could not tolerate bishops lording it over God's people, but in the twentieth, as one of the pieces in this collection of essays shows, in Latvia they ordained a bishop of their own. And would they call for any particular form of belief? Many Baptist churches down the centuries required conformity to specified theological convictions, but by the twentieth century large numbers of them condemned any stipulation of doctrinal unanimity as a breach of the 'soul liberty' of the believer. As Bill Leonard has stressed in his book *Baptist Ways*, there has been an enormous variety of expressions of Baptist life and witness, even on matters as central as these.[3] Baptists have differed greatly in their professions of identity.

The religious elements of identity have naturally loomed large in Baptist eyes. What, they have asked, are the essentials for a church that professes to belong to the Baptist faith and order? That can be answered at a theoretical level by providing a checklist of attributes derived from scripture. For all their variety, Baptists have rarely failed to insist, in the abstract, that churches should consist of none but believers. They have rejected the notion that all the people in a particular territory can claim church membership and equally the claim that no qualification at all is required to join a Baptist church. A credible profession of having turned to a personal faith in Jesus Christ is a prerequisite for being accepted into church fellowship. But

---

[1] Article XXXIX, 'The Confession of Faith, of those Churches which are commonly (though falsly) called Anabaptists', in H.L. McBeth, *A Sourcebook for Baptist Heritage* (Nashville, TN: Broadman Press, 1990), p. 50.

[2] A.H. Strong, *Systematic Theology: A Compendium* (Valley Forge, PA: Judson Press, 1962), p. 947.

[3] Bill J. Leonard, *Baptist Ways: A History* (Valley Forge, PA: Judson Press, 2003).

beyond that the religious components of identity have been diverse. Most Baptists have been committed to effort for the spread of the faith, but some have not, believing that this was a task reserved to himself by the Almighty. Most have wanted to assert the principles of religious liberty, but some have endorsed measures adopted by Christian authorities in church and state for the repression of deviance in matters of faith. What is the package of religious characteristics of this kind that are so fundamental that a church cannot be called Baptist without them? How do Baptists differ in their attributes from other confessional groups? What are legitimate innovations within a church before its Baptist credentials are imperilled? Differences of opinion on questions such as these form the substance of many of the essays that follow.

Because Baptist churches are bound to the earth as well as colonies of heaven, their members possess other identities alongside their religious qualities. In particular, Baptists possess national allegiances. Repeatedly there has been an interplay between religious and national identities. Some Baptists have been proud to merge their loyalties as Christians into their versions of patriotism. Others, especially where the state is like the Babylon depicted in scripture, have wanted to keep their citizenship firmly in heaven. Very often, as many of the contributions to this volume reveal, a shift of national identity has been required as churches derived from Christian missions have moved towards self-reliance. Alien nationality can become a liability, especially for church growth, in such circumstances. The task of indigenisation, attaining a fresh degree of integration with the predominant local culture, has been a central aim of sensitive Christian leaders. The separation of Baptists by national loyalties has also formed a perennial theme of denominational history. Analogous divisions have existed over race and language, complicating and sometimes undermining Christian witness. All these topics are represented here.

The papers in this volume arose from the third International Conference on Baptist Studies held in July 2003. It followed others held at Regent's Park College, Oxford, in 1997, and at Wake Forest University, North Carolina, in 2000. Each of the conferences has taken the Baptists as their subject matter but has not been restricted to Baptists as speakers or attenders. This time the event took place at the International Baptist Theological Seminary, near Prague in the Czech Republic, where a wide range of people gathered from many parts of the globe to hear an able series of papers, more than can be represented here. Because of the location of the conference on the eastern side of what was once the iron curtain, there was an awareness of the acuteness of the tensions that can arise over identity. It is not long since Baptists were treated in much of eastern Europe as potential political subversives simply because of their faith. Since the collapse of Communism, they have been trying to assert a profile suited to their new national settings. Furthermore, Baptists do not have a long history in the region and so have sometimes been perceived as a heretical sect. Under these circumstances, issues of identity loom large. Who are the Baptists? These studies should help provide a perspective on the range of characteristics of those who hold that baptism is an ordinance of the New Testament, given by Christ and designed only for those who profess faith.

D.W. Bebbington
September 2005
Baylor University

Introduction

This volume of essays on Baptist identities is one that offers a number of insights into the development and shaping of Baptist life in particular regions. The sum total of what is examined provides a wider, global picture of the Baptist community. In order to emphasise the regional aspects of the studies, part one of the volume contains studies that looks at European Baptist identities, part two has as its focus North America, and part three has studies that range more widely.

In the Part 1, four of the authors analyse features of Baptist experience in the British Isles. The other four deal with Baptist expressions in other countries within Europe—Germany, France, Latvia, and Eastern Europe. The attention given to Britain is appropriate, since until recently the largest Baptist Union to be found in Europe was the Baptist Union of Great Britain (until it was surpassed in size by the Baptist Union of Ukraine) and because Baptist life took shape in England in the early seventeenth century. Dennis Bustin looks at this early period, showing how Hanserd Knollys, who had been a Church of England clergyman but who embraced believer's baptism in the mid-1640s, played a pivotal role in shaping Baptist identity in London. During almost half a century as a Baptist leader, Dennis Bustin argues, Knollys led the Particular (Calvinistic) Baptists 'from the status of a radical sect to a more settled and ordered institution'. Karen Smith's essay has as its focus aspects of the spirituality of English Baptists in the eighteenth century. At a time when work on the history of spirituality is becoming much more common, this study explores 'preparation' as a spiritual discipline, especially preparation for baptism, church membership, the Lord's Supper and death. Karen Smith shows—among other things—that Baptist ecclesiology engendered a high view of the spiritual significance of baptism and the Lord's Supper.

But British Baptists are not found only in England. Historically the Welsh Baptist community has been a strong one. Densil Morgan traces this story, from 1649, taking up in particular the question of the relationship between Baptist identity and national consciousness, an issue which has been crucial for Baptists in many other countries. Whereas Densil Morgan's essay offers an overview, John Barclay's subject is a single Baptist congregation—Morningside Baptist Church, Edinburgh. Scotland, like England, Wales and Ireland, has its own story of Baptist life, but in whatever country Baptists express that life, at its heart is the way that it is expressed within local churches. Hence the importance of local studies—in this case an examination of the 'call of the minister and the character of the church'.

Elsewhere in Europe the German Baptists have, since the early nineteenth century, made an impact in many parts if the continent. Erich Geldbach shows how one of the early German Baptist leaders, Julius Köbner, contributed to the shaping of Baptist identity in such areas as conversion and baptism, scripture, Christ-centredness, the local church, church-state relationships and hymnody. The French Baptists, although always much smaller in numbers than their German counterparts, similarly date from the early nineteenth century. An important factor in terms of their identity in recent decades has been the charismatic movement, and this influence on French Baptist life is examined by Sébastien Fath.

Since the fall of communism in Eastern Europe, there has been a shift eastwards in the centre of gravity of European Baptist life. Toivo Pilli, in another overview essay, surveys Baptist identities in Eastern Europe. He utilises five pairs of polarities which taken together help to provide an understanding of the major features of the Baptist communities in the Eastern European context: Word and Spirit, individual and communal, witness and service, freedom and responsibility, and autonomy and co-operation. Case studies are being undertaken into the history of Baptists in many individual countries in Eastern Europe, and some of these will be published in due course. This volume contains one such study: Valdis Teraudkalns shows the transformations that have taken in Baptist identities in Latvia and the reasons for these transformations.

Part 2 of the collection of essays contains six studies of North American Baptist life, five looking at the USA and one at Canada. Austin Bennett Amonette and Kenneth Roxburgh both analyse important nineteenth-century figures. Alexander Campbell, who is the subject of the essay by Austin Amonette, is best known as the founder of the denomination, the Disciples of Christ, and his eighteen years as a Baptist have been rather neglected. This essay makes good that deficiency. William Bullein Johnson, whose opposition to confessional documents is examined by Kenneth Roxburgh, was a pivotal figure in the founding of the Southern Baptist Convention (SBC). Johnson's views are relevant in the context of contemporary SBC debates about requirements to assent to particular doctrinal statements.

In his essay on the formation of the United Baptist Convention of the Maritime Provinces, Dan Goodwin argues that the three denominations which united to create this new body in 1905–06 all had strong roots in the late eighteenth-century revivals of the Maritime region and that their shared identity enabled, in large part, the union to take place. As with other essays, the Baptist story examined here shows that over time Baptist identity is not completely fixed but neither is it completely fluid: there is a mixture of continuity and discontinuity, but within that early Baptist roots often retain a shaping power.

Having said that, there are also people in the Baptist story who from time to time offer fresh insights and sometimes take Baptist and wider Christian thinking in new directions. Walter Rauschenbush was one such figure. He is rightly viewed, as Reinhold Niebuhr put it, as the real founder of the Social Gospel. However, as Tadeusz Zielinski shows, Rauschenbush was not only a social prophet but also a deeply convinced Baptist who made a significant contribution in the area of Baptist identity. Zielinski is himself Polish, and teaches in Warsaw. He is one of the writers in this volume who looks beyond his own country and culture. Such cross-cultural perspectives are very valuable.

Wayne Flint and Bill Pitts take us to events in the mid-twentieth century and the end of the century. Wayne Flints's topic, Baptist involvement in and responses to the Montgomery, Alabama, bus boycott, explores the deep racial and also class divisions that marked the Baptist community in Montgomery in the 1950s and

1960s. The issue taken up by Bill Pitts is the issue of gender. Significant new opportunities opened up for women in the USA in the 1960s, but this was not always reflected in Baptist churches. This essay illuminates the process by looking at the experience of one church, First Baptist, Waco, which worked through issues of gender and leadership, and then appointed its first women deacons in 1996.

The final six essays, in Part 3, move beyond Europe and North America to other countries. Here we have evidence of the very different ways in which the transmission of Baptist life has taken place, a dynamic which reflects wider Christian movements in mission that have led to the church finding a new global identity.[1] Drawing from his wide experience, Robert Eric Frykenberg tells and sets in context the fascinating and remarkable story of the Naga Baptists. Li Li explores the way in which during the period 1850–1950 Baptists in China moved from a Southern Baptist identity to a Chinese one. In many such situations the Baptist community is empowered by shaping its own indigenous identity.

A contrast to that, however, is offered in the essay by Brian Howell, which looks at how contemporary Baptist congregations in the Philippines have consciously chosen western styles of worship. These Philippine Baptists have not localized their church life. The services are, Brian Howell notes, 'performed largely in English, singing music produced in Alabama or Sydney'. This has been seen as a proper response to global influences within this South-East Asian country. From a similar part of the world, Australasia, Ken Manley explores a related topic: the way in which British and then American influences have played an important part in Australian Baptist life. There has been a desire for an Australian identity, but Baptists have in recent years absorbed a good deal of conservative American Protestant culture. This leads Manley to reflect on the future of Australian Baptist identity.

There are significant parts of the world that are not covered in this volume. Large Baptist communities exist in South America. Russia is a county with a rich Baptist history. In West Africa, countries such as Nigeria and Ghana have seen rapid advances in Baptist life. The Nigerian Baptist community is one of the largest in the world. In this volume, Baptists in Africa are represented by the study Henry Mugabe has undertaken of theological education and the quest for identity in the Baptist Convention of Zimbabwe. Again tensions are explored: long after the end of the foreign missionary era Baptists in Zimbabwe have still found that they cannot engage fully in governing their own institutions because of residual foreign influence.

The final essay was the first paper to be given at the Conference in Prague. It fits well at the end of this volume since it is truly global. William Brackney's study of Baptists, religious liberty and evangelization in the nineteenth century ranges widely. He looks at the English Baptist experience and the missionary links with India, at American Baptist mission in Burma, at African Americans and the significance of African connections, at continental European Baptists and religious freedom, and at

[1] See A.F. Walls, *The Cross-Cultural Process in Christian History* (Edinburgh: T&T Clark, 2002).

developments in China and in South America. This essay, with its analysis of many inter-linking features of Baptist identity across continents and particularly with its emphasis on two major themes in Baptist witness, forms a fitting conclusion to this multi-layered volume on Baptist identities. It is hoped that these studies will stimulate more research and a deepening understanding of the place of Baptist communities in the wider Christian story.

PART 1

European Baptist Identities

CHAPTER 1

Hanserd Knollys and the Formation of Particular Baptist Identity in Seventeenth-Century London[1]

Dennis Bustin

In the autumn of 1609[2] in Cawkwell, Lincolnshire, a rather inconsequential village on the road from Lincoln to Horncastle,[3] near the town of Louth,[4] a young clergyman and his wife Rachel gave birth to a boy. Richard and Rachel Knowles had been married a little over a year and their new son, Hanserd, was a welcome addition to their small family, which also included William, Rachel's son from a previous marriage.[5] Young Hanserd was baptised on 13 November 1609 in Cawkwell by his father Richard.[6] Thus began the life of a man who would become one of the most, if not the most, important member of the Particular Baptist community in London. Hanserd Knollys would play a significant role in the formation of the identity of the Particular Baptists as they emerged in London in the seventeenth century.

---

[1] This theme of Hanserd Knollys' instrumental role in leading the Particular Baptists in forming their identity is central to the author's doctoral dissertation, Dennis Bustin, 'Hanserd Knollys, Particular Baptist Pioneer in Seventeenth-Century England' (PhD dissertation Queen's University at Kingston, 2003). See also Dennis Bustin, *Paradox and Perseverance: Hanserd Knollys, Particular Baptist Pioneer in Seventeenth-Century England* (Studies in Baptist History and Thought, 23; Milton Keynes: Paternoster, forthcoming).

[2] This differs from the date traditionally held for Knollys' birth. The argument supporting this difference is dealt with in detail in, Bustin, 'Knollys: Particular Baptist Pioneer', Appendix 1.

[3] According to the Diocesan return taken in 1563, during this period Cawkwell was a farming area with only three houses and it doubled in size over the next three centuries. The church there evidently served the surrounding farmers and their tenants. Muriel James, *Religious Liberty on Trial: Hanserd Knollys—Early Baptist Hero* (Franklin, TN: Providence House Publishers, 1997), pp. 46-47.

[4] Hanserd Knollys, *The Life and Death of That Old Disciple of Jesus Christ, and Eminent Minister of the Gospel, Mr. Hanserd Knollys* (ed. William Kiffin; London: 1692), hereafter cited as *Life*, p. 1. Pope A. Duncan, *Hanserd Knollys: Seventeenth-Century Baptist* (Nashville, TN: Broadman Press, 1965), p. 8.

[5] For this genealogical information see, Bustin, 'Knollys: Particular Baptist Pioneer', Appendix 1.

[6] Lincolnshire Archives, document Calkwell BT, 1609/10.

The seventeenth century was a significant period in English history. During this time, the people of England experienced unprecedented change and tumult in the political, social, and religious spheres of life. At the same time, the importance of order and the traditional institutions of society were being reinforced. Hanserd Knollys was born during this pivotal period and personified in his life the ambiguity, tension, and paradox of it, openly seeking change while at the same time cautiously embracing order. As a founder and leader of the Particular Baptists in London, he played a pivotal role in helping shape their identity externally in society and internally, as they moved toward becoming more formalised.

Early in his life, Knollys embraced change as he separated from the Church of England, eventually becoming a Particular Baptist. His congregational polity and stance on the importance of the individual believer would lead him to embrace democratic principles and a position of limited religious toleration. Yet throughout his life, as an outsider due to his separatist stand, Knollys diligently sought to demonstrate to his contemporaries that he and his fellow Particular Baptists were neither radical in their beliefs, nor disorderly in their conduct. He sought legitimacy in two ways: first, through aligning himself, in terms of doctrine, with the Reformed position of the Presbyterians and, in terms of polity, with the Independents; second, through distancing himself from more radical religious groups, such as the Levellers, Quakers, and Fifth Monarchists.[7] Even during the period of intense persecution following the Restoration, which Knollys viewed in apocalyptic terms as the end of history, his position was neither revolutionary nor status quo.[8] Finally, as the Glorious Revolution of 1689 brought limited toleration and the Particular Baptists moved toward institutionalisation, Knollys played an essential role, consistently emphasising the separatist distinctives of the Particular Baptists, while, at the same time, stressing the importance of order in the newly emerging denomination. This chapter will examine Hanserd Knollys, a microcosm of the tension and ambiguities of seventeenth-century England, emphasising his importance in helping to shape the identity of the London Particular Baptists, both externally and internally.

The Particular Baptists and their Contemporaries

As the Particular Baptists emerged in the early 1640s in London, they encountered opposition and hostility almost immediately. In the context of the upheaval of the 1640s, society was rife with new ideas and change. The Civil Wars, the radicalisation of Parliament, and the abolition of the Episcopalian Church created ambiguity and openness in English society, politics and religion. Hanserd Knollys

---

[7] This article will not deal with Knollys' responses to these more radical groups. For this see Bustin, 'Knollys: Particular Baptist Pioneer', ch. 4.

[8] I address this period of Knollys' life in more detail in 'Knollys: Particular Baptist Pioneer', chs 5-6 and in my article, 'Papacy, Parish Churches, and Prophecy: The Popish Plot and the London Particular Baptists—A Case Study', *Canadian Journal of History* 38 (December, 2003), pp. 69-81.

arrived in the midst of this shifting environment, returning from New England and docking in London on 24 December 1641.[9] His brief stay in New England had been very difficult. He had met with opposition from John Winthrop and the leaders of the Massachusetts Bay Colony. Forced to leave Boston, he migrated north to the region of Dover, where he once again found himself embroiled in controversy. Eventually this territory also came under the jurisdiction of the Massachusetts leadership, once again forcing Knollys and his family to relocate. Following a brief stay in Long Island, New York, Knollys returned across the ocean.[10] In the words of James Culross, he 'made up his mind that he might as well be knocked about in *Old England*'.[11]

In the political and religious climate of the 1640s, two parties emerged, each seeking to establish a godly reformation of the Church of England. Both the Independents and the Presbyterians had Puritan roots, tracing their doctrine and polity to John Calvin. The major difference between the two related to church government. The Presbyterians, like their Scottish brethren, sought a parish church based upon a hierarchy of Presbyters. The Independents preferred the less structured 'gathered' church and proposed a more congregational, democratic polity.[12] Beyond these two religious groups, in the relative freedom of the 1640s a proliferation of new sects arose, holding to a variety of beliefs and doctrinal positions, many of which were deemed by the majority of Englishmen as being pernicious and heretical. These sects included such groups as the Baptists, Levellers, Diggers, Seekers, and later in the 1650s the Quakers and the Fifth Monarchists.[13]

---

[9] Knollys, *Life*, p. 18.

[10] Knollys' time in New England is dealt with in detail in Bustin, 'Knollys: Particular Baptist Pioneer', ch. 2.

[11] James Culross, *Hanserd Knollys* (London: Alexander & Shepherd, 1895), p. 30. David Cressy assessed that people like Knollys were 'failures in New England, misfits in the godly commonwealth, who departed America in a cloud of scandal and recrimination. The revolution in England afforded them an opportunity to make something of their lives, after making only blunders and enemies in New England.' David Cressy, *Coming Over: Migration and Communication between England and New England in the Seventeenth Century* (Cambridge: Cambridge University Press, 1987), p. 199. However, such an assessment seems to have unfairly embraced and accepted Winthrop's biased position.

[12] See Ernest Sirluck, 'Introduction', in Don M. Wolfe (ed.), *The Complete Prose Works of John Milton* (8 vols; New Haven, CT: Yale University Press, 1953–82), II, chs. 1 and 2; John Morrill, *The Nature of the English Revolution* (New York: Longman, 1993), pp. 69-91. Ian Gentles held that these two factions actually formed as a result of their war views: 'During the ensuing months [while the New Model Army was being established] the war faction would come to be known as the Independents, while the peace party would acquire the label "presbyterian". It should be borne in mind that most MPs did not identify themselves with any political grouping.' Ian Gentles, *The New Model Army in England, Ireland, and Scotland, 1645–1653* (Cambridge, MA: Blackwell, 1992), p. 5.

[13] See Christopher Hill, *The World Turned Upside Down* (London: Penguin Books, 1991 [1972]); and Barry Reay, 'Radicalism and Religion in the English Revolution: An

Prior to removing to New England, Knollys had separated from the Church of England, renounced his ordination, and become an itinerant preacher.[14] Upon his return, he soon joined with the renowned separatist, Independent congregation in London pastored by Henry Jessey.[15] Shortly after the outbreak of war, Knollys threw his lot in with Parliament, entering the service of the Parliamentary Army as a chaplain in 1643.[16] At that time, Knollys probably would have counted himself an Independent, since he had not yet embraced Baptist doctrines.[17] Following his brief experience with the Parliamentary army, he returned to London to teach, disillusioned by the self-serving attitude of the commanders.[18] In early 1644, Knollys and his friend and future fellow Baptist, William Kiffin, initiated a discussion on baptism in the Jacob–Jessey church. In March 1644, Kiffin withdrew and formed his own church.[19] In October 1644, several Baptist churches joined together in signing a confession of faith.[20] Knollys was not among the signatories. At this juncture, Knollys had not fully adopted believer's baptism, but would sometime in late 1644 or early 1645.[21] At this point, he too left the Jacob–Jessey

---

Introduction', in J.F. McGregor and B. Reay (eds), *Radical Religion in the English Revolution* (New York: Oxford University Press, 1984), pp. 1-21.

[14] Knollys, *Life*, pp. 9, 16. Knollys did not give the exact year of his separation from the Church of England. According to Benjamin Stinton, writing shortly after Knollys' death, Knollys left the Church of England in 1636. See *An Account of Some of the Most Eminent & Leading Men among the English Antipaedobaptists*, p. 43. The Stinton Manuscripts are housed at the Angus Library, Regent's Park College, Oxford University.

[15] Murray Tolmie made the statement that Knollys joined the Jessey church after his return in 1641. This could have been true, but the only evidence available concerning his membership comes from 1643/44. Murray Tolmie, *The Triumph of the Saints* (London: Cambridge University Press, 1977), p. 44; W.T. Whitley, 'The Jacob-Jessey Church, 1616–1678', *Transactions of the Baptist Historical Society* 1.4 (January, 1910), p. 254.

[16] Knollys, *Life*, p. 20.

[17] Anne Laurence, *Parliamentary Army Chaplains, 1642–1651* (Suffolk: Boydell Press, 1990), p. 34; Knollys, *Life*, p. 20; Thomas Edwards, *Gangraena: Or a Catalogue and Discovery of many of the Errours, Heresies, Blasphemies and pernicious Practices of the Sectaries of this time...* (London, 1646), Part 1, p. 39. Laurence claimed Knollys was a Baptist. However, his conversion to Baptist beliefs did not occur until 1644 or later. W.T. Whitley, 'Debate on Infant Baptism, 1643', *Transactions of the Baptist Historical Society* 1.4 (January, 1910), pp. 237-45.

[18] Knollys, *Life*, p. 20. This would not end Knollys' career as a chaplain. He would later serve in the New Model Army in 1649 under Whalley. Laurence, *Chaplains*, pp. 52, 55, 58, 143.

[19] Whitley, 'Jacob–Jessey Church', p. 254; Whitley, 'Debate', pp. 237-45; Tolmie, *Triumph*, pp. 44, 55-56.

[20] *The Confession of Faith, Of those Churches which are commonly (though falsly) called Anabaptists* (London: 1644), in William L. Lumpkin, *Baptist Confessions of Faith* (Philadelphia, PA: Judson Press, 1959); hereafter designated *1644 Confession*.

[21] Whitley, 'Debate', pp. 244-45. He had withdrawn from the Jessey church by June 1645 when he returned to baptise Henry Jessey. It is quite fascinating that Knollys, who felt so strongly about baptism and who played such a major role in the formulation of the

church and gathered his own Baptist church in 1645 'in the heart of London' at Great St Helens, next door to an established parish church.[22]

Upon becoming a Particular Baptist, Knollys immediately set about the task of showing his contemporaries that the Particular Baptists were neither pernicious nor heretical. Having attended Cambridge[23] and established himself as a teacher[24] and something of an academic,[25] he was one of very few Particular Baptists with a formal education and, thus, was an obvious champion for their cause. With Presbyterians such as Thomas Edwards, Ephraim Pagett, and Daniel Featley publishing scathing, slanderous works against the 'sectaries' in the mid-1640s,[26] Hanserd Knollys decided to join in the 'print war' on behalf of the Particular Baptists. In this way, he sought to prove the legitimacy of the Particular Baptists to his contemporaries.

During this period, Knollys used his pen in two ways. First, he desired to demonstrate to both the Presbyterians and the Independents that doctrinally the Particular Baptists were Reformed and therefore not significantly different from them. This was necessary due to the rise of other sects during the period, in particular the

---

Particular Baptists doctrine regarding it, never mentioned the time of his conversion to Baptist principles nor of his own baptism in his autobiography.

[22] Knollys, *Life*, p. 23.

[23] Knollys, *Life*, p. 3; James, *Knollys*, p. 55. According to *Alumni Cantabrigienses*, Knollys matriculated on Easter, 1629. James, however, cited the college's annual audit accounts for the date 1627. It would seem that 1627 would be the better option since *Alumni Cantabrigienses* also stated that he was ordained in June 1629, meaning his a stay at Cambridge would have been too brief to be of any significance. John Venn and J. A. Venn, *Alumni Cantabrigienses*, Part I to 1751, vol. III Kaile to Ryves, (Cambridge: Cambridge University Press, 1924), p. 31.

[24] Throughout his life, Hanserd Knollys was involved in education, either as a teacher in a school, as a private tutor or in taking private students in schools he had opened. Knollys, *Life*, pp. 5, 19, 20, 23, 27, 37, 42; 'Genealogical Gleanings in England', in *The New England Historical and Genealogical Register* (Boston, 1895), XLIX, p. 126; Folger Shakespeare Library, Washington. Additional MS 667; *Calendar of State Papers Domestic, Charles II, 1671*, dated 1 January—24 March 1670–71, p. 143; *Calendar of State Papers Domestic, Charles II, 1673–75*, dated 21 December 1673, pp. 66-67.

[25] The works that he published in the 1660s were of an academic nature, in all likelihood related to his teaching. These works included grammatical works, *Grammaticae Graecae compendium* (London, 1664), *Grammaticae Latinae compendium* (London, 1664), *Linguae Hebricae delineatio* (London, 1664), *Radices Hebraicae Omnes, Quae in S. Scriptura, Veteris Testamenti occurrunt* (London, 1664), *Radices simplicium vocum, flexilium maxime, Novi Testamenti* (London, 1664), and *Grammaticae Latinae, Graecae, & Hebricae* (London, 1665), a hermeneutical work, *Miscellanae sacra; or a New Method of considering so much of the history of the Apostles as is contained in Scripture* (London, 1665), and one other academic work, *Rhetoricae adumbratio* (London, 1663).

[26] Edwards, *Gangraena*; Ephraim Pagett, *Heresiography: Or, A Description of the Heretickes and Sectaries of These Latter Times* (London, 1645); Daniel Featley, *The Dippers Dipt. Or, The Anabaptists Duck'd and Plung'd Over Head and Eares* (London, 1645).

General Baptists, who embraced beliefs of free will and universal atonement. Knollys and the Particular Baptists sought to accomplish this through the publication of further confessions. Second, Knollys desired to show both parties the veracity of the two positions, which distinguished the Particular Baptists from them—congregational church government and believer's baptism. Again, the confessions dealt with these beliefs. As well, Knollys and other Particular Baptists participated in public disputations defending their position. However, Knollys' most significant contribution in the 1640s came in the form of two treatises he published, one engaging the Presbyterian John Bastwick concerning congregational government and the other engaging the Independent John Saltmarsh concerning believer's baptism.

Confessions and Disputations

Establishing their Reformed position publicly was of the utmost importance to the Particular Baptists. Clearly, the Particular Baptists had their origins within the Puritan movement, most of the London churches having split from the Independent Jacob–Jessey church over the issue of baptism. Hanserd Knollys himself likely came from a Puritan household. His father Richard had attended Cambridge in the 1580s and would have undoubtedly come under the influence of the Puritan divines there as a student.[27] Certainly those things which he emphasised while bringing up his sons would indicate a Puritan bent.[28] When Knollys himself matriculated at St Catherine's Hall in 1627, Cambridge University was at its peak as a Puritan stronghold.[29] According to James Culross, Knollys studied under the well-known Puritan, Richard Sibbes.[30]

---

[27] Richard matriculated to Trinity and received his degree from Peterhouse, both colleges with an abundance of Puritans on their faculties. Venn and Venn, *Alumni Cantabrigienses*, p. 32. H.C. Porter, *Reformation and Reaction in Tudor Cambridge* (Cambridge: Cambridge University Press, 1958), pp. 207-60. As the work of Patrick Collinson shows, the majority of Bishops and clergy in the Church of England in the early part of the seventeenth century embraced a sort of Calvinism. See Patrick Collinson, *The Elizabethan Puritan Movement* (London: Jonathan Cape, 1967) and *The Religion of the Protestants: The Church in English Society 1559–1625* (New York: Oxford University Press, 1982).

[28] Richard's upbringing included warning Hanserd of the dangers of strong drink and of the importance of keeping one's vows. Knollys, *Life*, pp. 1-2.

[29] The great Puritan divines from Cambridge included William Perkins, Thomas Cartwright, William Ames, Richard Sibbes and Thomas Hooker. Many of the Puritans from Cambridge became influential leaders in New England as well, people such as John Winthrop, John Cotton, John Harvard and Simon Bradstreet, as well as Roger Williams, the great champion of toleration and democratic ideals, a Baptist later a Seeker and the founder of Rhode Island. Porter, *Tudor Cambridge*, pp. 207-60.

[30] Culross, *Knollys*, p. 13. Sibbs was made Master of St Catherine's in 1626. William Haller, *The Rise of Puritanism* (Philadelphia, PA: University of Pennsylvania Press, 1984 [1938]), p. 66.

Thus, it is not surprising that the Particular Baptist confessions drew upon the Puritan tradition. *The Confession of Faith, Of those Churches which are commonly (though falsly) called Anabaptists*, of 1644, which Knollys did not sign, clearly arose as an apologetic document; in the words of B.R. White, the 'Calvinistic Baptists' first public attempt at a corporate defense'.[31] A revision of their confession appeared in 1646.[32] By this point, Hanserd Knollys had joined their ranks as a university-educated clergyman, and very likely played a major role in the composition of this revised statement. This *1646 Confession* softened some of the distinctly Baptist emphasis of the previous one[33] and strengthened the emphasis on Calvinistic theology, perhaps in the hope of finding wider acceptance.

The accusations which they attempted to counter in this revision included the following: that they held to free-will and falling from grace; that they denied election, original sin, children's salvation, the Old Testament, men's propriety in their estates; and that they denounced all who did not practice or believe as they did.[34] The *1646 Confession*, then, contained stronger statements on election (Articles III, V-VI, XXI-XXII), original sin (Article IV), perseverance of the saints (Article XXIII), and against free-will (Article XXIV). As well, it included strong affirmation of the propriety of men's different estates, emphasising the responsibilities of those of higher and wealthier status to care for those beneath them (Article XXXV), and a

---

[31] B.R. White, 'The Origins and Convictions of the First Calvinistic Baptists', *Baptist History and Heritage* 25 (October, 1990), p. 42. Clearly, this confession relied heavily on the 1596 *Separatist Confession*, so Lumpkin, *Baptist Confessions of Faith*, p. 145; B.R. White, *The English Baptists of the Seventeenth Century* (rev. by J.F.V. Nicholson; London: The Baptist Historical Society, rev. edn, 1997), p. 61.

[32] *A Confession of Faith of Seven Congregations or Churches of Christ in London, Which are Commonly (But Unjustly) called Anabaptists* (London: 1646), in Edward Bean Underhill (ed.), *Confessions of Faith and Other Public Documents, Illustrative of the History of the Baptist Churches of England in the 17th Century* (London: Hanserd Knollys Society, 1854); hereafter designated *1646 Confession*.

[33] Changes to the entries on baptism included: Article XXIX stated that baptism is 'to be dispensed upon persons professing faith' whereas in the *1644 Confession* it stated that it was 'to be dispensed *onely* upon persons professing faith' (emphasis added). This omission was in response to Featley's criticism that this entry would be acceptable if the word 'onely' were omitted. Article XL stated that the manner of baptism is 'dipping or plunging the body under water' signifying the 'interest the saints have in the death, burial, and resurrection of Christ'. In the *1644 Confession* it was stated that the manner *'the Scripture holds out to be* dipping or plunging the *whole* body under water' signifying *'first, the washing the whole soule in the bloud of Christ: Secondly,* that interest the Saints have in the death, buriall, and resurrection; *thirdly, together with a confirmation of our faith'* (words in italics removed from the *1646 Confession*). This was again softened in response to Featley's criticism. The argument about immersion turned on the translation of the Greek word βαπτίζω, meaning 'to dip'. Featley countered that the Scriptures did not clearly define baptism as immersion. See Lumpkin, *Baptist Confessions of Faith*, p. 167, notes (a), (c).

[34] *1646 Confession*, p. 21.

statement on liberty of conscience, clearly in response to the Presbyterian attempts in 1645 for uniformity (Article XLVIII).

Public debates also provided a valuable opportunity for the Particular Baptists to represent themselves. One such dispute was arranged for December 1645 between Benjamin Cox, William Kiffin, and Hanserd Knollys on the one side, and Edmund Calamy and other Presbyterians on the other. Following accepted practices of academic debate, they agreed to address, for six hours, the question 'Should the children of believing parents be baptised?' However, citing a threat of violence, the Lord Mayor of London cancelled the debate, leading the Particular Baptists to publish their arguments.[35] Although this dispute never occurred, a year later in 1646, a similar debate took place at Trinity Church, Coventry, between Knollys and Kiffin, and the Rev. John Bryan, DD, Vicar of Trinity Church, and the Rev. Obediah Grew, MA, DD, Vicar of St Michael's Coventry. It is significant that both of their opponents were well-educated ministers within the Established Church. Certainly Knollys' Cambridge education and previous clerical experience made him a valuable asset to the Particular Baptists in these disputations.[36]

Knollys' Publications

Although Knollys unquestionably had an influence in both the confessions and the disputations, his more significant contribution in the 1640s came in his publications. Knollys' polemical writings, *A Moderate Answer unto Dr. Bastwicks Book Called "Independency not God's Ordinance"* and *The Shining of a Flaming Fire In Zion*, produced the clearest presentation of his position on the two major issues which distinguished the Particular Baptists from the Presbyterians—independent, congregational church government and believer's baptism—and the single major aspect in which they diverged from the Independents—believer's baptism. Underlying both of these writings was Knollys' commitment to the authority of conscience informed by the authoritative Scriptures.

The context in which Knollys wrote these works holds as much significance as the content. He published them in the midst of the debate between the Independents and Presbyterians in the Westminster Assembly concerning accommodation for

---

[35] Benjamin Cox, Hanserd Knollys, William Kiffin, *A Declaration Concerning the Publike Dispute Which Should have been in the Publike Meeting-House of Alderman-Bury, the 3d of this instant Moneth of December; Concerning Infants-Baptisme. Together, with some of the Arguments which should then have been propounded and urged by some of those that are falsly called Anabaptists, which should then have disputed* (London, 1645), pp. 2-3.

[36] Arthur S. Langley, 'Seventeenth Century Baptist Disputations', *Transactions of the Baptist Historical Society* 6.3 (July, 1919), p. 224. Of course, these disputes must have been instrumental in the appearance of the revised *1646 Confession* which many have held to have been formulated primarily by Cox and Knollys. Lumpkin, *Baptist Confessions of Faith*, p. 148.

tender consciences.[37] Neither of the two treatises was written in response to a direct attack from an opponent. *A Moderate Answer* was written from the perspective of an outsider, an interested third party. John Bastwick, a staunch Presbyterian, had written his attack against the Independents regarding the proper system of church polity. Bastwick had not addressed the Baptists, nor shown much concern with the issue of accommodation. Instead, he had concentrated on the issue of the gathering of churches and the authority of those individual gathered congregations. Knollys responded, realising that this attack against the Independents contained an implicit attack against the congregational polity of the Particular Baptists. The second treatise, *The Shining of a Flaming Fire*, responded to John Saltmarsh's book *The Smoke In the Temple, Wherein is a Designe for Peace and Reconciliation of Believers of the Several Opinions of these Times about Ordinances, to a Forbearance of each other in Love, and Meeknesse, and Humility* (London; 1646), a work ironically written as a plea for tolerance. Saltmarsh had proposed that the National Church be replaced with a National Covenant based on liberty of çonscience with a view towards unity, not forced uniformity. His approach called for an end to polemics and attacks between differing perspectives and for fellow Christians to attempt to coexist with one another in spite of doctrinal differences. In the process of setting forth this plan for reconciliation, Saltmarsh had critiqued each religious group and its beliefs. With regard to the Baptists, this involved primarily a criticism of their views on and practices of baptism, specifically as to mode (immersion), subjects (believers only), and administrators (any common disciple). Knollys responded to Saltmarsh's statements regarding baptism. So, in both instances, Knollys dealt with only a portion of the works to which he responded.

Bastwick's *Independency Not Gods Ordinance Or a Treatise concerning Church Government, occasioned by the Distractions of these times* (London, 1645), a voluminous tome of two parts totalling 242 pages, contained long and often repetitious arguments. Knollys penned a brief, purposeful response, on the other hand, totalling a mere twenty pages. Bastwick's major point was that presbyterian government dependent upon a common council of presbyters fulfilled God's ordinance. To prove this, he argued four propositions: that there were many congregations of believers in the church of Jerusalem; that these all made but one church; that the apostles and elders ruled this church by a council or presbytery; and that the Jerusalem church and its government provided the pattern for all churches, that every city was to comprise one church and the various officers of that church would comprise a ruling body or council (presbytery).[38] Knollys maintained that Bastwick's examination of Scripture did prove that each city had a presbytery and could ordain elders, that every known New Testament church had elders for officers, that several churches came under the rule of their several elders or presbyters, and that presbyterian government was ordained by God. However, he maintained that

---

[37] Sirluck, *John Milton*, pp. 65-66; Tolmie, *Triumph*, pp. 128-29.
[38] John Bastwick, *Independency Not Gods Ordinance Or a Treatise concerning Church Government, occasioned by the Distractions of these times* (London, 1645), pp. 12-29.

Bastwick failed to prove the kingpin of his whole argument—that such a government depended on a 'Common-counsell, colledge, and court of classicall, or Synodall Presbyters'.[39]

In countering Bastwick's arguments, Knollys showed his training and education, particularly in dealing with the Scriptures and in his mastery of the original languages. In one instance, Bastwick claimed that in 3 John 9, Diotrephes' sin was 'to assume unto himself, and his particular congregation, that power that belonged unto the colledge or councell of Presbyters' thus creating a congregation which was Independent, not ruled by the presbytery. Through a simple rendering of the Greek and examination of Beza's commentary on that verse, Knollys concluded that 'no mention is made of any perticular Congregation' in this verse, but that the command addressed the whole church, and Diotrephes' sin was taking pre-eminence to himself.[40]

One of the key passages, which Bastwick used to support his arguments, was Acts 15—the account of the Council of Jerusalem and its determination of the issue regarding the Gentiles. Knollys pointed out, again using rather simple exegesis, that not only were the apostles and presbyters of Jerusalem present and involved in the decision-making process, but so also were 'the Brethren, even the whole church, the multitude (how many soever the D. can make of them)'.[41] His use of this passage clearly emphasised the role of all members in church government, a central element in the congregational polity of both Baptists and Independents. In *A Moderate Answer*, Knollys displayed a keen mind and ability to debate by clearly summarising Bastwick's own arguments and then very craftily turning them around to prove Independent polity or disprove Presbyterianism.[42] One example of this turning of Bastwick's arguments against him appeared in the section in which Knollys dealt with the question of who had the authority to make the decision about admitting or excommunicating members. He quoted Bastwick as stating that in the case of Paul in Acts 9, the congregation of disciples (not just the presbyters and the apostles, but the 'Brethren') had a say in whether or not he was to be admitted into membership. Thus, the members of the church and not the presbyters alone determined Paul's

---

[39] Knollys, *A Moderate Answer*, pp. 5-6.

[40] Bastwick, *Independency Not Gods Ordinance*, p. 15. Knollys, *A Moderate Answer*, pp. 5-6. The use of Beza was brilliant, for Beza, Calvin's successor in Geneva, carried great weight among the Presbyterians.

[41] Knollys, *A Moderate Answer*, pp. 13-14.

[42] Knollys' familiarity with the conventions of scholarly syllogistic debate was clearly evident in this work. In fact, Knollys was critical of what he believed to be Bastwick's poor debating skills: 'For if the Dr. please to review his Argument, He shall finde, First; that the subject of his Major proposition is left out both in his Minor, and in his Conclusion: The first part of the Doctors Minor should have been this, to witt, But the Apostles in the holy Scripture are called Presbyters, and who ever denyed this; Also the first part of the Doctors conclusion should have been this, from these two premises, to witt; *Ergo*, The Apostles acted as Presbyters which Conclusion is not the thing in Question.' Knollys, *A Moderate Answer*, p. 13.

status. Since this took place in Jerusalem, and since, as 'the Doctor confesseth, yea affirmeth... "that the Mother Church must give an example of government to all the Daughter churches,"' then this established a precedent for congregational decisions on membership.[43]

Although 'moderate' in tone, Knollys' answer to Dr Bastwick's book took a rigid stand against *jure divino* Presbyterianism. At this point (May through July 1645[44]), the official position of the Independent party still inclined toward accommodation, while the Presbyterians resisted such compromise. In contrast, Knollys' firm response to Bastwick took the line that the New Testament did not leave room for compromise, that it contained only one right model, a congregational one. In the New Testament, admission into a church was based upon

> Faith, Repentance, and Baptisme; *and none other*. And whosoever (poor as well as rich, bond as well as free, servants as well as Masters) did make a profession of their Faith in Christ Jesus, and would be baptized with water into the Name of the Father, Sonne, and Holy Spirit, were admitted Members of the Church; but such as did not beleeve, and would not be baptized they would not admit into Church communion. This hath been the practice of some Churches of God in this City.[45]

At this point, Knollys had departed from the position of his Independent brethren and had moved to a Baptist perspective, emphasising believer's baptism as a prerequisite for church membership. Within a very few months of Knollys' debate with Bastwick, the Independents would demand toleration for 'other tender consciences...that they may with the peace of their consciences enjoy'.[46] As dogmatic as Knollys might have appeared, in essence, all that he desired was the liberty to follow his conscience and to expound the word of Scripture that others might also have their consciences awakened.

In a note to Article XLVIII of the 1646 *Confession of Faith*, the London Particular Baptists made the following comment about religious liberty.

> So it is the magistrate's duty to tender the liberty of men's consciences, Eccl. vii. 8, (which is the tenderest thing unto all conscientious men, and most dear unto them, and without which all other liberties will not be worth the naming, much less

---

[43] Bastwick, *Independency Not Gods Ordinance*, pp. 97, 101-02. Knollys, *Moderate Answer*, p. 16.

[44] Thomason transcribed the date on this particular pamphlet of Knollys as 17 July. The dates he gave to Bastwick's work were 21 May and 10 June. Bastwick, *Independency Not Gods Ordinance*, title page. Knollys, *Moderate Answer*, title page.

[45] Knollys, *Moderate Answer*, p. 20 (emphasis added).

[46] Independent minority's proposal to the Westminster Assembly of Divines on 6 November 1645 in *The Papers and Answers of the Dissenting Brethren and Committee of the Assembly of Divines...for Accomodation 1645* (London, 1648).

enjoying) and to protect all under them from all wrong, injury, oppression, and molestation.[47]

Clearly, the Particular Baptists believed that the government's responsibility was to ensure 'liberty of men's consciences'. Such a call took a radical stand. With this statement in mind, as one reads John Saltmarsh's *The Smoke In the Temple*, one might think that Hanserd Knollys would have welcomed this work. Saltmarsh's idea of liberty of conscience was limited to 'the severall godly parties of believers' and that 'the Magistrates sword' should not be used to enforce 'things of pure Gospel mystery' and things of Christian worship.[48] In a word, Saltmarsh sought to bring about unity in the church through humility.

Even though Knollys believed Saltmarsh had written 'out of a sincere desire to receive more light of Truth', he thought it important to refute the thirteen exceptions against the 'Anabaptists' that Saltmarsh had expressed in his *Smoke In the Temple*.[49] By and large in agreement with the general premise of Saltmarsh's book, Knollys limited his response to the criticisms that Saltmarsh had written about Baptists, especially about their view of what Saltmarsh called 'the new Baptism'.[50]

Saltmarsh's thirteen exceptions against the 'new Baptism' could be basically divided into two groups. The first set related to Christ's commissions in Matthew 28.18-19 and Mark 16.16-17 and centred around a discussion concerning water baptism, Spirit baptism, and the names (i.e. Jesus, Holy Spirit, or trinitarian) by which one baptised. The second set related to the issue of gifts and call. The first set of arguments put forth by Saltmarsh tended to be somewhat repetitive and convoluted in their presentation. Knollys quickly discerned this and turned it to his advantage. Saltmarsh saw two types of baptism in the New Testament: water baptism, practised by the apostles in Acts, after the example of John the Baptist and performed in the name of Jesus only; and Spirit baptism, commissioned by Christ in Matthew 28 and Mark 16. Because these passages contained no mention of water, he argued they must have referred to a baptism of Spirit and of gifts.[51]

Knollys aggressively responded to this line of argument using two approaches. First, seeing an element of inconsistency in Saltmarsh's argument, Knollys made Saltmarsh appear to contradict himself. In his first four exceptions, Saltmarsh argued consistently for two types of baptism, water (Acts) and Spirit/gifts (Matthew). Yet in exception ten, he argued that the two types were joined and could not be separated.

---

[47] *1646 Confession*, p. 45.

[48] John Saltmarsh, *Smoke In the Temple, Wherein is a Designe for Peace and Reconciliation of Believers of the Several Opinions of these Times about Ordinances, to a Forbearance of each other in Love, and Meeknesse, and Humility* (London, 1646), pp. 24-26.

[49] Knollys, *Shining of the Flaming Fire*, The Epistle.

[50] Saltmarsh, *Smoke In the Temple*, pp. 14-18. In response to this negative charge of innovation, Knollys stated that Paul's doctrine was called new (Acts 17.19), as was Christ's (Mark 1.27). Knollys, *Shining of the Flaming Fire*, p. 1.

[51] Saltmarsh, *Smoke In the Temple*, pp. 15-17.

Since Knollys had maintained that the Scripture passages commissioned both types of baptism, in his response to the first four exceptions, he used Saltmarsh's tenth exception as a platform for subverting the earlier exceptions.[52] The second approach, which Knollys used to answer Saltmarsh's arguments, was an exegetical one, once more exhibiting his ability and competence in using the original languages. He argued that the Greek verb βαπτίζω simply meant 'to dip in water' and was so used by the Septuagint writers and by the Gospel writers when writing of John the Baptist.[53] In fact, the Gospel of John used this meaning of the word 'without Exception'.[54] Therefore, baptising in the Gospels, particularly in Matthew 28.19, should not be understood as being 'the Baptism of Guifts, nor of Afflictions, nor of any other kinde of Baptizing, but by water'.[55]

The second set of arguments Saltmarsh presented had to do with gifts. He argued that 'common disciples' had not received supernatural, miraculous abilities as gifts, as had the apostles. Therefore they had not the authority to baptise.[56] Ordinances could only be administered by those as 'distinctly, specially, spiritually, powerfully, enabled as the first dispensers'.[57] To this objection, Knollys concurred wholeheartedly, agreeing that the only Christians who should administer the ordinances were those disciples who 'have received such gifts of the Spirit as fitteth or inableth him to preach the Gospel. And those guifts being first tried by, and known to the Church'. But, he countered, Baptist ministers were 'as powerfully inabled as the first Dispenser of Baptism: And we having received Authority from Jesus Christ'.[58]

Although legal toleration would not occur during the 1640s and 1650s, under Oliver Cromwell's Protectorate virtual toleration would. During this time, the Particular Baptists attained a limited level of 'legitimacy' and thus were able to establish themselves and experience significant growth and Hanserd Knollys, as one of their strongest spokesmen and most respected leaders, played a vital role in this effort.

---

[52] Knollys, *Shining of the Flaming Fire*, p. 4.

[53] Knollys, *Shining of the Flaming Fire*, p. 4.

[54] Knollys, *Shining of the Flaming Fire*, p. 4.

[55] Knollys, *Shining of the Flaming Fire*, p. 4. Knollys' purpose for doing this Greek word study was to respond to Saltmarsh's second exception, which stated 'that *baptizing, in Matth. 28:18.* cannot properly, nor in the *word,* and *letter,* be understood of *baptizing* by water.' Knollys, *Shining of the Flaming Fire*, p. 3.

[56] Saltmarsh had given as a distinctive practice of the Baptists that 'whatsoever Disciple can teach the Word, or make out Christ, may Baptize or administer other Ordinances'. Saltmarsh, *Smoke In the Temple*, p. 16.

[57] Saltmarsh, *Smoke In the Temple*, pp. 17-18.

[58] Knollys, *Shining of the Flaming Fire*, p. 9.

Knollys and the Particular Baptists' Move Toward Institutionalisation

In late 1689, Hanserd Knollys turned eighty years old, quite an achievement in the seventeenth century. During those eighty years, Knollys had experienced intolerance and persecution under Archbishop Laud and the Massachusetts Bay Puritans in the 1630s, limited freedom and toleration in the 1640s and 1650s, and renewed intolerance and persecution during the Restoration. However, a far more significant occurrence took place in 1689—the legal toleration of Protestant Dissent. In the final years of the seventeenth century and of Knollys' life, the Particular Baptists entered a new stage as they moved toward institutionalisation in the climate of toleration now afforded them.

On 22 July 1689, a letter went from the leadership of the London churches to Particular Baptist congregations throughout England. Hanserd Knollys, William Kiffin, Benjamin Keach, and several other prominent London pastors, proposed an assembly of Particular Baptist churches from across the land be held in London in September 1689.[59] The churches were to reply to either Kiffin or Knollys.[60] Despite his age, Knollys apparently played an active role in this assembly. This effort by the elder leadership of the Particular Baptists, though indicating the beginnings of institutionalisation, represented in reality for Hanserd Knollys a punctuation of his life's ministry. During his lifetime, Knollys had pastored his London congregation, planted various other churches, participated in itinerant preaching tours, and published or collaborated on nearly thirty works. Throughout his work and writings, particularly his treatises *The World That Now is and the World That is To Come* and *A Gospel Minister's Maintenance Vindicated*, Knollys consistently contributed to the forming identity of the Particular Baptists. Knollys focused on five areas in particular: polity, doctrine, ministry, sacraments/ordinances, and worship.

Polity

Hanserd Knollys arrived at his ecclesiology or doctrine of the church as part of a lifelong journey. In his polity, Knollys emphasised the paradoxical belief of independence and interdependence. At some time after 1633, Knollys 'was convinced of some things about the Worship of God (which I had conformed unto) to be sinful, to wit the Surplice, the Cross in Baptism, and admitting wicked persons to the Lord's Supper',[61] leading him to separate from the Church of England. Separation would not only characterise Knollys' actions throughout his life, but it would

---

[59] *A Narrative of the Proceedings of the General Assembly Of divers Pastors, Messengers, and Ministering Brethren of the Baptized Churches, met together in London from Septemb. 3. to 12. 1689 from divers parts of England and Wales: Owning the Doctrine of Personal Election, and final Perseverance* (London, 1689).

[60] Joseph Ivimey, *A History of the English Baptists* (4 vols; London, 1811–30), I, pp. 478-80.

[61] Knollys, *Life*, p. 9.

become central to his theology of the church. For Knollys, to remain within a corrupt church was tantamount to sin. This theology of separation would become central to the Particular Baptist ideal of independent congregationalism. The true worshipper had no option but separation: 'You cannot enjoy Communion with God, whilst you hold a Communion with Idols, and Image-worshipers.'[62] Thus, separation was vital for a pure church. Self-government and self-determination provided the proper means of insuring continued purity. However, coupled with this ideal was an understanding of the vital nature of the interdependence of individual 'gathered' congregations. While autonomy stood at the heart of the congregational form of church government, at the same time, fellowship and association with others of like mind was vital, though never to the detriment of independence. The efforts made by London Baptists such as Knollys to plant and support new fellowships outside of London during the 1640s and 1650s provided another example of the principle of interdependence. Upon the gathering of a new congregation, he argued, 'the Ministers and Brethren of other Churches being also present, ought to own and acknowledge them to be a Sister Church, by giving them the Right hand of Fellowship; and so commend them by Prayer unto God'.[63]

Doctrine

The theological persuasion of Hanserd Knollys and the Particular Baptists could be described as a moderate form of high-Calvinism, balancing election with an emphasis on evangelism. They emphasised an unquestionably Calvinist and Puritan theology of election with strong importance placed on God's sovereignty, in part to dispel any perception that they were unorthodox.[64] However, the stress on evangelism and on the responsibility of the individual to embrace God's truth and requirements was equally evident. The most obvious reason for this related to the fact that the Particular Baptists gathered their churches. People joined their congregations; they were not born into them as in the parishes of the Established Church. Theirs were believers' churches. It would be crass and simplistic, however, to state that this evangelistic drive was merely for the purpose of expanding their congregations. Rather, the desire for the conversion of others sprang from a concern

---

[62] Hanserd Knollys, *Mystical Babylon Unvailed* (London, 1679), p. 28. See also Hanserd Knollys, *An Exposition of the Whole Book of the Revelation Wherein the Visions and Prophecies of Christ are Opened and Expounded* (London, 1688), p. 125.

[63] Knollys, *The World That Now Is and the World That Is to Come* (London, 1681), Book I, p. 50.

[64] In terms of the more general issues of orthodoxy, such as pertaining to the doctrines of the Trinity, the nature, person, and work of Christ, and the majesty and attributes of God, they were clearly in line with orthodox, historical Christianity. See *Second London Confession*, pp. 9-12, 17-18, 27-34. See also Knollys, *World That Now Is*, Book I, pp. 4-5, 9-10, and *An Exposition of the Whole Book of the Revelation*, pp. 11, 73.

for the spiritual well-being of those they sought to convert. Consider the following quote from Knollys:

> Open your hearts to Christ when he knocks at the Door of your Souls, and calls you to come to him, to receive him, and let him come into your hearts, and dwell in your hearts by his holy Spirit, and sanctifying Grace...not that you can do those things of your selves; I have told you, without Christ you can do nothing... But it is your duty to do them.[65]

Ministry

The lowly status of Baptist preachers made them a ready target for critics. Many of these so-called 'mechanic preachers', who laboured all week and preached on Sunday, were elected by their congregations and often received little or no pay for their pastoral labours.[66] Knollys certainly did not want the ministry to devolve to a position where its integrity was compromised or under question. This concern for the ministry led Knollys to give significant attention to the subject in his writings. Although he certainly supported the priesthood of believers, he also held the office of the minister in high esteem, as a specially appointed office under Christ, and he strongly desired the ordination of godly Particular Baptist ministers. As well, Knollys wanted an educated, professional ministry.[67] Finally, he believed that ministers held authority within their congregations, while at the same time, acted as servants of the church. Knollys emphasised the attributes of the clergy by claiming that 'Pastors and Teachers...that Rule well...ought to be Learned and holy Men, taught of God by his holy Spirit, qualified with Spiritual and Ministerial Gifts and Graces.'[68] Education had always been placed highly in Knollys' scheme of priorities. Knollys and other leaders within the Particular Baptist community paid strong attention to the training of young men for the ministry.[69] At the same time, they also showed concern for the fair treatment of ministers. They held that it was 'very dishonourable to God, and a reproach to our Sacred Religion' for churches to fail to provide 'a due maintenance' for their pastors. In fact, they boldly proclaimed that it was 'a great and crying Sin'.[70]

---

[65] Knollys, *World That Now Is*, Book II, pp. 34-36.

[66] Hill, *World Turned Upside Down*, pp. 28-30.

[67] Hanserd Knollys, *et. al.*, *The Gospel Minister's Maintenance Vindicated. Wherein A Regular Ministry in the Churches, is first Asserted, and the Objections against a Gospel Maintenance for Ministers, Answered* (London, 1689).

[68] Hanserd Knollys, *An Exposition of the Eleventh Chapter of the Revelation* (London, 1679), p. 5.

[69] This concern was first raised in 1675 at a convention of Particular Baptists, where it was proposed that a fund be established to assist in the training and education of young ministers. Thomas P. Dixon, 'The Contribution of the English Baptists to Education, 1660-1820' (PhD dissertation, Vanderbilt University, 1975), pp. 116-17.

[70] Knollys, *et. al.*, *The Gospel Minister's Maintenance Vindicated*, pp. 13-15.

Sacraments/Ordinances

In relation to the sacraments/ordinances, Knollys had a significant role in the discussions in the 1640s that led many to separate from the Jessey church and form Particular Baptist congregations. Though William Kiffin had raised the issue of adult believer's baptism, what Knollys reintroduced to the discussion was the question of the validity of infant baptism.[71] Jessey and some others had been attempting to persuade Hanserd and Anne Knollys to have their newborn son baptised, but they had become uncertain about the scriptural validity of this practice, leading to the discussions that would give birth to many of London's Particular Baptist congregations.[72] Certainly, Knollys became a leading spokesman on this topic for the Particular Baptists as seen above in both the debates and his written treatises. While the Particular Baptists' doctrine of baptism was formulated and settled, for the most part, quite early in their existence, largely because this doctrine clearly set them apart from other Puritans, the same could not be said for the doctrine of communion. Apart from a very definite denial of transubstantiation, Particular Baptists held differing points of view on both the method and meaning of communion. This aspect of Particular Baptist thought continued to be discussed and developed beyond the seventeenth century. Two main issues arose: open versus closed communion, and Zwinglian versus Calvinist interpretations. Knollys himself reflected this ambiguity, usually holding to open communion, yet at times proclaiming a more closed position.[73] The issue of the meaning of the Lord's Supper received little intentional treatment from the Particular Baptists. According to Ernest Payne, Baptists embraced no one interpretation of the presence of Christ in the bread and wine.[74] Along with his Particular Baptist contemporaries, Knollys combined Zwingli's symbolic approach with Calvin's spiritual approach. Knollys stated clearly that Christ instituted his supper to be celebrated 'in *Remembrance* of him…and as a *Memorial* of his Death' (emphasis original).[75] However, the importance of the celebration was not just in the act of remembering what Christ had done on the behalf of sinners, but also in the significant blessing it imparted to the believer. 'Christ giveth his saints spiritual Bread, hidden Manna, New-wine and water of life at his Supper, and in his Ordinances.'[76]

---

[71] Those who joined Spilsbury's congregation had raised this issue in 1638, but it appears that discussion on the issue ended following their exit. Tolmie, *Triumph*, p. 24; 'Kiffin Manuscript' as transcribed in 'Rise of the Particular Baptists in London, 1633–1644', *Transactions of the Baptist Historical Society* 1.1 (January, 1910), p. 231.

[72] Whitley, 'Debate', p. 240.

[73] Knollys, *The Shining of a Flaming Fire*, p. 16.

[74] Ernest Payne, *The Fellowship of Believers: Baptist Thought and Practice Yesterday and Today* (London: Kingsgate Press, 1944), p. 51.

[75] Knollys, *World That Now Is*, Book I, p. 74.

[76] Hanserd Knollys, *An Exposition of the first Chapter of the Song of Solomon* (London, 1656), p. 57.

Corporate Worship

Knollys also gave significant attention to corporate worship in many of his writings. Knollys supported a simple service of worship that followed an orderly pattern.[77] At the heart of the service, in true Puritan style, was the reading and preaching of the word of God, but the service included prayer,[78] prophesying,[79] baptism, the Lord's Supper, and congregational singing as well.[80] In relation to the latter, during the final years of his life, Knollys became involved in a controversy over the public singing of hymns and songs in the worship service, a controversy which separated him from his close friend, William Kiffin, and from the co-pastor of his congregation, Robert Steed.[81] Perhaps due to his age, Knollys took a supporting role in the debate, siding with Benjamin Keach. However, throughout his life, he had been somewhat of a pioneer in regard to hymnody. In books written well before the singing controversy erupted, Knollys had expressed the importance of hymns and of singing in the worship of God. In fact, he claimed to have the 'gift of singing' himself, a gift of musical composition inspired by the Spirit.[82]

Institutionalisation was only in progress at the end of Knollys' life, a fact clearly evident in the continuing debate and lack of consensus in many of these areas at the time of Knollys' death and in the years following. However, without question, Hanserd Knollys was instrumental in helping to bring order and identity to this sect as it began to emerge as a denomination in its own right.

---

[77] Hanserd Knollys, *The Parable of the Kingdom of Heaven Expounded. Or, An Exposition of the first thirteen Verses of the twenty fifth Chapter of Matthew* (London, 1674), pp. 43-44.

[78] The *Second London Confession* stipulated that audible prayer in the presence of others was to be 'in a Known Tongue', an obvious attempt to avoid the excesses of other more ecstatic radical groups such as the Ranters and Quakers. See Chap. XXII, sect. 3, 6, pp. 74, 76.

[79] Knollys did not elaborate on this activity. Suffice it to say that it was to be orderly and judged by others present.

[80] Knollys, *World That Now Is*, Book I, pp. 70-80. Except for the emphasis on congregational singing (more below) this is not dissimilar to the description given in the *Second London Confession*, Chap. XXII, pp. 73-77.

[81] Michael Haykin, *Kiffin, Knollys, and Keach—Rediscovering our English Baptist Heritage* (Leeds: Reformation Today Trust, 1996), pp. 92-93; H. Wheeler Robinson, 'Baptist Church Discipline 1689–1699', *Baptist Quarterly* 1 (1922–23), p. 112.

[82] Hanserd Knollys, 'Courteous Reader', in Katherine Sutton, *A Christian Womans Experiences of the Glorious Working of God's Free Grace. Published for the Edification of others* (Rotterdam, 1663), p. i. Duncan, *Knollys*, p. 55, claimed that Knollys penned the hymns in Sutton's work. (Sutton was almost certainly a member of Knollys' congregation, so J.H.Y. Briggs, 'She-Preachers, Widows and other Women: The Feminine Dimension in Baptist Life since 1600', *Baptist Quarterly* 31.7 [July, 1986], p. 340. See also Ian Mallard, 'The Hymns of Katherine Sutton', *Baptist Quarterly* 20.1 [January, 1963], pp. 23-33.) However, he is mistaken, for they were clearly written by a woman, Sutton herself. Sutton, *A Christian Womans*, p. 40.

Conclusion

In the uncertain and changing climate of seventeenth-century England, Hanserd Knollys played a vital role in shaping the identity of the Particular Baptists, both in terms of how their contemporaries viewed them and of how they viewed themselves. Although in both cases, he sought to emphasise how the Particular Baptists were separate and distinct in their pursuit of truth, at the same time, Hanserd Knollys desired to demonstrate that these distinctions were neither heretical nor disorderly. For nearly fifty years, Hanserd Knollys had been associated with the Particular Baptists. Only he and William Kiffin had remained actively involved in the life of the group from its inception in the 1640s, through the persecutions of the Restoration until the dawn of Toleration in 1689. The continuity and stability which he provided played an instrumental role in leading the Particular Baptists from the status of a radical sect to that of a more settled and ordered institution. One of the last pieces of advice he wrote to his congregation was this: 'The Aim and End of our Zeal must always be the Glory of God, and guided, as I said, by Discretion.'[83]

---

[83] Knollys, 'Last Legacy', in *Life*, p. 50.

CHAPTER 2

Preparation as a Discipline of Devotion in Eighteenth-Century England: A Lost Facet of Baptist Identity?

Karen E. Smith

'Preparation of the heart', or the devotional practice of reflecting on the inward experience of Christian faith, was commonly practised by the Puritans and Separatists and later by their descendants, among them the Baptists. In the eighteenth century, Calvinistic Baptists were regularly reminded of the importance of 'reviewing their experience' and examining their hearts to see if they were right before God. To suggest, however, that preparation as a discipline of devotion might be a lost facet of Baptist identity might seem too broad a claim.

Devotional practice in Baptist life has often been regarded as private and personal. Stressing principles such as the freedom of conscience and the priesthood of believers, and backed up by the biblical injunction 'whenever you pray, go into your own closet and shut the door and pray to your father who is in secret' (Matthew 6.1-7), Baptists have sometimes treated the devotional life of an individual and the public worship of believers together as two separate spheres of activity.

Yet, given the covenant basis of their life together, for eighteenth-century Calvinistic Baptists there was to be no separation of the believer from the community. For early Baptists, church life was very like that of the Separatists, which reflected an insistence on the profession of individual faith and covenant theology as their basis for unity. They believed in the principle of the gathered church and formed congregations which met together and entered into covenant agreements, which signified their desire to 'walk together according to the appointment of Christ'.[1] In short, for early Baptists there was never a sense in which one was merely a believer alone, but one was always bound to Christ and thereby bound inextricably also to those who were within the covenant community and, as such, part of his body, the church.

In recent years covenant language has been used in many different ways. Yet, while in theory one may speak of the 'eternal covenant of grace' as being distinct from the covenant agreement God makes with his church, or the written covenant

---

[1] *Confession of Faith Put forth by the Elders and Brethren Of many Congregations of Christians (baptized upon Profession of their Faith) in London and the Country* (1677), in William L. Lumpkin, *Baptist Confessions of Faith* (Valley Forge, PA: Judson Press, rev. edn, 1969), p. 286.

agreements made by churches, in practice early Baptists did not separate them.[2] There is a real sense in which the people believed their personal commitment to Christ, reflected in God's covenant promise to the church, was expressed through their life together—with one another and with Christ. Perhaps most importantly, covenant was never interpreted in purely individual terms. Devotion to Christ could never be merely personal and private—for as believers who knew and experienced God's covenant love they were, as they often put it, bound together in Christ.

The personal and corporate aspects of devotion were not only interwoven in covenant commitment and expressed in written covenant agreements, but also nurtured and expressed through worship. Indeed, public worship often became a means for expression of private devotion, and private devotion was often to be used for reflection on worship and relationships within the wider community of faith.

The ministry of the Word for instance was intended for public and private use. Sermons were constructed in a way that encouraged private reflection on the Word later. Moreover, hymn singing became a means by which personal faith could find expression in corporate worship. Likewise, participation in the ordinances of baptism and the Lord's Supper was never personal and private but always reflected the deep unity in Christ. Always there was a sense for eighteenth-century Calvinistic Baptists that they were not believers alone but bound together, held together through the covenant bond to Christ and to one another.

This chapter will explore the discipline of preparation, which was viewed by some eighteenth-century Calvinistic Baptists as a life long practice. It will be argued that while preparation has often been associated with a desire for personal assurance of salvation, for many Baptists it was not practised merely as a personal discipline, but was important to their understanding of union with Christ and one another.

After a brief overview of preparation in the Puritan tradition, this chapter will highlight the practice among some English Calvinistic Baptists in the eighteenth century of preparation before baptism and church membership, before the Lord's Supper and preparation for death. It will be suggested that as with any devotional activity rightly practised, preparation was not merely for the assurance or security of the individual, but it was done for God and for others. In keeping with recent historical work, this particular study is regional, and includes amongst its manuscript sources, diaries and sermons, as well as the church records of a group of Calvinistic Baptists in Hampshire and Wiltshire in the eighteenth century. While it may not be argued that all Baptists were alike in their devotional practice, it seems likely that these Baptists reflect the practice of many Calvinistic Baptists in the provinces in the eighteenth century. Hence it will be argued that preparation, as a

---

[2] For four uses of the term covenant, see Paul S. Fiddes '"Walking Together": The Place of Covenant Theology in Baptist Life Yesterday and Today', in W.H. Brackney, Paul S. Fiddes with J.H.Y. Briggs (eds), *Pilgrim Pathways: Essays in Baptist History in Honour of B.R. White* (Macon, GA: Mercer University Press, 1999) pp. 50-58. Fiddes, p. 51, notes the difficulty of separating the uses of the term covenant and suggests that at times 'they are woven together in a harmonious pattern or even into a single multiple-stranded thread'.

devotional practice among Calvinistic Baptists in the eighteenth century, was an integral part and an identifying feature of their life within the community of faith.

The Testimony of the Heart: The Need for Personal Experience

The idea of the 'heart prepared' is often found in Puritan writings.[3] The heart as they understood it was associated with the will or the source of emotion or affection. The idea of the heart was based on biblical usage which was interpreted to mean the 'inner essence' of the whole person, 'the battleground of God and the devil'.[4] The heart or will by nature was not pure, but had to be transformed by grace. While Puritans, as good Calvinists, held to the idea that a person could do nothing on his or her own to acquire grace, they felt a need to constantly search the heart for signs of grace at work. William Perkins, a Puritan theologian, often quoted by eighteenth-century Baptists, wrote:

> Would wee then even from the bottom of our hearts turne to God and become new creatures? Then let us learn to fear God: which is nothing else but this, when a man is persuaded in his own heart and conscience that wheresoever he be, he is in the presence and sight of God, and by reason therof is afraid to sin. This wee must have fully settled in our hearts...[5]

The need to have 'settled hearts' was closely linked to the idea of the discipline of preparation and often Puritan preachers called on their hearers to examine themselves to see if they did in fact know the work of God personally and for themselves. Methods of preaching were developed which aided the hearer in the practice of self-examination. In a treatise on preaching well known to Baptists in the eighteenth century, entitled *The Art of Prophecying* (1606), William Perkins made a distinction between the 'mentall and practicall application' of preaching, and on that basis he developed a method that later was simplified to a triple scheme of doctrine, reasons and uses.[6] Hence, each sermon began with an exposition of doctrine and then followed with an appeal to the understanding. After a discussion of reasons, the sermon concluded with a section on its application which often included questions for self-examination or, as they described it, for the 'improvement' of the hearer. While the first two sections of the sermon provided instruction, the final section was the point at which reason met emotion. Urging each believer in the congregation to

---

[3] See Norman Pettit, *The Heart Prepared: Grace and Conversion in Puritan Spiritual Life* (New Haven, CT: Yale University Press, 1966).

[4] Terrence Erdt, *Jonathan Edwards, Art and the Sense of the Heart* (Amherst, MA: University of Massachusetts Press, 1980), p. 5.

[5] William Perkins, *An Exposition of the Symbole or Creed of the Apostles: According to the Tenour of the Scripture and the Consent of Orthodoxe Fathers of the Church in Workes* (3 vols; Cambridge: John Legatt, 1616), I, p. 223.

[6] William Perkins, *The Art of Prophecying or a Treatise Concerning the Sacred and Onely True Manner and Methode of Preaching* (trans. Thomas Tuke; London: Felix Kyngston, 1617), p. 168.

undergo self-examination, the preacher was to appeal to hearers to apply personally to their own hearts those things they had heard in the public ministry of the Word.

The desire not to be 'hearers' of the Word only, but to see evidence or signs of the work of grace upon one's heart, became closely linked with the doctrine of assurance. For some Calvinists, it seems that for the heart to be prepared meant that one had the assurance that he or she was in a right relationship with God.

The difficulty of looking for the ground of assurance in Calvinistic thought has been discussed and debated at some length. Many would argue that the assurance looked for by later Calvinists must not be ascribed to Calvin himself.[7] In looking at Calvin's understanding of assurance, Zachman has argued that while for Calvin the testimony of a good conscience builds on the foundation of God's witness to us in the gospel and cannot replace the foundation, there is the possibility that the foundation of faith may be reversed and the internal testimony take precedence over the testimony of the Word of God. Indeed, some might argue that the Puritan emphasis on self-examination reflected a tendency to do just that—to put the assurance of faith through the inward testimony of the heart before the foundation of the Word of God.

Of course, whether or not assurance was seen as a requirement of faith and was recognised by all Calvinists is a matter which is of some dispute. Those who have studied the modification of English Calvinism, especially among the Puritans in the seventeenth century, have noted that one of the distinctive marks of their faith and practice was the link which they made between churchmanship and soteriology, particularly as it related to the idea of assurance.[8]

Unlike Calvin who described saving faith as something which was passively received from God, many Puritans seemed to assert that the ability to give signs of an 'effectual calling' could be regarded as an indication that one could be 'assured' of being one of the elect.[9] Believing that the church was properly made up of the elect,

---

[7] Randall C. Zachman, *The Assurance of Faith, Conscience in the Theology of Martin Luther and John Calvin* (Minneapolis, MN: Fortress Press, 1993), p. 7, points out that both Luther and Calvin had a doctrine of limited election which 'restricts the saving efficacy of the reconciliation won in Christ to those who believe in Christ'. He argues, too, that both Luther and Calvin looked for the ground of assurance of faith in the testimony of Jesus Christ alone. But he also maintains that they believed it was the testimony of a 'good conscience' that confirms one's faith and election. Conscience was to submit to the Word of God. The testimony of conscience was not to tell us about the grace of God to us, but to tell us about the sincerity of our response to that grace in faith and love. As Zachman, p. 6, puts it, 'The question that the testimony of a good conscience addresses is not, "Do I have a gracious God?" but rather, "Is my faith in the grace of God sincere or hypocritical?"'

[8] Stephen Brachlow discusses the background to the way Puritan churchmanship was linked to soteriology in his article, 'Puritan Theology and General Baptist Origins', *Baptist Quarterly* 31.4 (October, 1985), p. 183. See also, R.T. Kendall, *Calvin and English Calvinism to 1649* (Studies in Evangelical History and Thought; Carlisle: Paternoster Press, 1997 [1979]).

[9] Brachlow, 'Puritan Theology', p. 184.

the ability to identify particular marks of salvation, naturally, came to be associated with entry into a community of faith.

Precisely when and how this practice developed is not known. It has been argued by some that the early Separatists did not require applicants for membership to be 'tested', but rather merely to give a confession, which amounted to an intellectual understanding of faith. Edmund S. Morgan has written that the idea of requiring members to give an account of their experience developed among non-separating Puritans in Massachusetts and then spread back to England.[10]

My purpose here is not to explore the doctrine of assurance or to debate whether all Puritans or other Calvinists felt that assurance was necessary. What should be noted, however, is that often those who have linked the idea of self-examination or preparation of the heart with assurance have viewed it from the point of individual personal salvation. Even those who have linked the idea of election to churchmanship have sometimes seemed to suggest that all that mattered was knowing who was of the elect so that the visible church could be identified as being the church. Yet, there is another deeper issue and that is that election into membership of the body of Christ was also related to mystical union with Christ.[11] Writing of Puritan devotion, Gordon Wakefield claimed that many people believe that the normative dogma of reformed Christianity is election, which is often interpreted simply 'that only a few can be saved'. However, he argued that the normative dogma is union with Christ by faith. This seems an important point to make, not only when examining Puritan thought but when looking at some of their descendants, the Baptists. While it is difficult to define or describe, for them this mystical union was understood to be part of covenant relationship with Christ and his body, the church.

Like their Puritan forbears, Calvinistic Baptists affirmed the deep sense of oneness with Christ and one another in the church. To be bound together, knit together in the love of Christ as part of his body, the church brought with it privileges as well as responsibilities. Membership in a visible institutional church did not necessarily mean union with Christ and this was not a relationship to be taken lightly, hence the need for written covenants and, of course, one reason for the discipline of preparation. This emphasis on union with Christ is startlingly clear in the diary entry of a Baptist woman who, in 1734, wrote,

> I find the concerns of others goes very near my soul such as I hope have an interest
> in Christ when I know their temptations, their afflictions or their consolations. I

---

[10] Edmund S. Morgan, *Visible Saints* (New York: Cornell University Press, 1963), pp. 58-63, 92-105, 109-10. He claims that reformed churches required nothing more of prospective members than an outward 'profession of faith', an understanding of basic doctrine, and a visibly 'godly conversation', and that the 'test' of experience only emerged in New England probably about 1634 under John Cotton, and then was taken back to England.

[11] Gordon Wakefield, *Puritan Devotion, Its Place in the Development of English Piety* (London: Epworth Press, 1957), p. 5.

seem to bear an equal share in either, and how can it be otherwise when I look upon them together with myself as part of the purchase of Christ's suffering and so a part of that real body of whom Christ is the head.[12]

The focus on 'union with Christ' is a defining point to make when looking at the discipline of preparation practised by Calvinistic Baptists in the eighteenth century. Cynically, it could be argued that emphasis on self-examination was merely part of a personal concern for one's own salvation or was used as a way of monitoring the membership of the visible church. Yet, underpinned by the theological understanding of real union with Christ and his body, the church, preparation, as a devotional practice, became an important means of binding the individual in a deep union with Christ and with the covenant community of faith.

Preparation for Baptism and Church Membership

Eighteenth-century Calvinistic Baptists believed that preparation often began weeks or months before a person was baptised and received as a member of a congregation. In fact, for these Baptists, membership in a particular 'gathered community' of believers was not a matter of 'joining the church' or merely giving verbal assent to a covenant agreement, but rather was dependent upon the individual's ability to demonstrate a sincere commitment to the Lord Jesus based on his or her knowledge of Scripture and experience of Christ.

Throughout most of the eighteenth century those seeking fellowship with a group of believers were required to express their commitment and trust by standing before the congregation to give a testimony of their 'experience' to them. In many ways the individual self-examination and the review of one's experience before the church were both part of the preparation for baptism and church membership.

While entrance into the church was regarded as distinct from baptism, in practice, they were usually combined. However, no one was to be baptised and received into church membership without having first made a public profession of an 'experience of grace', nor without showing clear signs of living in obedience to the commands set forth in Scripture and exemplified in the life of Christ.

If a new believer expressed a desire to join a church, after conversing with the pastor and other believers, a time was arranged for the person to give an account of his or her experience to the congregation. Once the testimony was heard and approved by the members, the believer was then accepted into the fellowship of the church.

Although the practice of both men and women giving an extemporaneous testimony to the congregation before being accepted in the covenant community was normative among Calvinistic Baptists in the eighteenth century, the point at which

---

[12] Diary of Anne Cater (Cator) Steele, 1 April 1734. The ACS diaries are in 3 vols, 1730–1735/6, 1748/9-1752, and 1753–1760. Read on micro-film in the Angus Library, Regent's Park College, Oxford. Mrs Steele was the stepmother of Anne Steele, the well known Baptist hymn writer.

congregations began to expect applicants for church membership to 'give evidence of their faith' is a matter of dispute. Clearly, the practice of requiring individuals to 'give in their experience' to the congregation was practised among Dissenters in England in the 1650s, since two collections of the accounts of members of Independent congregations were then printed.[13] Among Calvinistic Baptists as early as 1654, the question had been raised at a meeting at Taunton 'whether any are to be received into the church of Christ only upon a bare confession of Christ being come in the flesh and assenting to the doctrine and order laid down by him?' To which the meeting replied: 'they may not be admitted on such terms without a declaration of an experimental work of the spirit upon the heart, through the word of the Gospel and suitable to it, being attended with evident tokens of conversion, to the satisfaction of the administrator [of baptism] and brethren or church concerned in it'.[14] Although the way in which the practice of 'testing' applicants developed is open to question, it is agreed that it evolved out of the need for the 'visible community of saints' to test the inward spiritual state of its believers.

Before giving testimony to an experience of faith, individuals often underwent months, if not years, of soul searching. During this time, individuals were often supported by friends and family members who waited anxiously to see if there were any signs of a 'work of grace' upon their hearts. The long period of preparation is attested to in written conversion narratives which, though they vary in length and style,[15] in general often seem to have followed the pattern set out by the Puritan divine, William Perkins.[16] Perkins outlined conversion in progressive stages, which included the acknowledgement of sin, preparation and assurance, conviction, compunction and submission, fear, sorrow and faith.

---

[13] [H. Walker], *Spiritual Experiences of Sundry Believers* (1652). J. Rogers, *Ohel or Beth-Shemesh, A Tabernacle for the Sun* (1653).

[14] B.R. White (ed.), *Association Records of the Particular Baptists of England, Wales and Ireland to 1660: Volume II. The West Country and Ireland* (3 vols; London: Baptist Historical Society, 1971–74), p. 56.

[15] Some attention has been given to conversion narratives among Puritans in England and New England in the seventeenth century, [e.g., Owen C. Watkins, *The Puritan Experience* (London: Routledge and Kegan Paul, 1972); Patricia Caldwell, *The Puritan Conversion Narrative: The Beginnings of American Expression* (Cambridge: Cambridge University Press, 1983), and Charles Lloyd Cohen, *God's Caress: The Psychology of the Puritan Religious Experience* (Oxford: Oxford University Press, 1986)]. However, apart from studies which have attempted to apply modern psychological theory, little has been done by way of comparing and analysing those which exist in the eighteenth century. Cf. F.W.B. Bullock, *Evangelical Conversion in Great Britain, 1696–1845* (London: Budd and Gilliatt, 1959), and Sydney G. Dimond, *The Psychology of the Methodist Revival, An Empirical and Descriptive Study* (London: Oxford University Press, 1926).

[16] Michael J. Watts, *The Dissenters: Volume I. From the Reformation to the French Revolution* (Oxford: Clarendon Press, 1978), p. 174, says 'the process of conversion expounded by Perkins was upheld by English Evangelicals for three centuries as normative of Christian experience'.

Nearly all the narratives emphasise the significance of the Word as the primary means through which believers were brought to recognition of their total depravity before God. Often, for instance, there were references to having been 'struck' or 'impressed' by a verse of Scripture heard in a sermon which led to a period of self-examination, and then to repentance.[17]

The importance of Scripture in the overall process of the discipline of preparation is readily noted in the testimonies. For instance, a testimony given by one woman to the church meeting in Broughton in Hampshire in 1751 began with a recollection of 'religious converse' and a desire to know how to 'get an interest in Christ'.[18] After noting the impression made on her by several sermons, she then related that she went to God in prayer and 'beg'd him to direct me to knowledge of himself and his ways'.[19] This time of prayer was followed by a period of meditation when she had several passages of Scripture 'bro't to mind' which gave her direction.[20] Later, after a period of trial when she was confronted by the death of two family members and a struggle with illness, she said she had arrived at a sense of 'the burden of sin'.[21]

Often believers recorded having heard the Word read and preached, sometimes over a period of one or more years, before they entered a period of doubt and trial which led to a true and sorrowful repentance. Such was the experience of Sarah Miell.[22] According to her own account of her early experience, when she was nineteen she became aware of her 'lost and undone state as a guilty sinner'.[23] Yet, even though she read her Bible and heard the gospel, she said she was 'afraid to lay hold of any of the promises' and was 'oppressed with a heavy load of guilt'.[24] Then, after a period of struggle in which she seemed to waver between 'hoping and fearing', she was able to 'cast her burden on the Lord' and found, in her words, the 'word and ways of God were my chief delight'.[25]

---

[17] It appears that Calvinistic Baptists, like the Puritans, believed 'the spoken word was the one agency by which, on the plane of nature, the innermost faculties could be reached, and this was why the sermon was regarded as the most effective channel of grace'. Watkins, *The Puritan Experience*, p. 6.

[18] The person giving her testimony was Mrs Steele's niece and she inserted a copy of the testimony in her diary. 14 July 1751, ACS Diary.

[19] 14 July 1751, ACS Diary.

[20] 14 July 1751, ACS Diary.

[21] 14 July 1751, ACS Diary.

[22] Sarah Miell was baptised at Broughton under the ministry of Josiah Lewis. Born at Wilcott in Wiltshire in 1751, she attended the Pewsey church under the care of Joseph Townsend from the age of thirteen to nineteen. She married John Miell, a carter, who was called out to preach by the church in Broughton in Hampshire and later served the congregation at Wallop. See 'Obituary of Mrs. Sarah Miell', *Baptist Magazine* 18 (1826), pp. 134-36, and 'Memoir of the Revd. John Miell', *Baptist Magazine* 18 (1826), p. 111.

[23] *Baptist Magazine* 18 (1826), p.134.

[24] *Baptist Magazine* 18 (1826), p.134.

[25] *Baptist Magazine* 18 (1826), p.134.

These testimonies are all very similar to others which were recorded in the seventeenth and eighteenth century. However, while they reflect the fact that much attention was given to the need to give a clear testimony of an experience of grace upon acceptance into a community of faith, the need to look for evidence of faith did not stop here. That is to say, that even after they had testified to their faith and had been accepted into the church, believers were expected to continue the discipline of preparation as they looked for signs of their election and calling. As noted earlier, this did not mean, of course, that even the knowledge of salvation could be attained by one's own merits. 'The grace of faith', as the *Second London Confession* stated, 'whereby the Elect are enabled to believe to the saving of their souls is the work of the Spirit of Christ in their hearts'.[26] However, while assurance was not the essence of faith, nevertheless, knowledge of it was acquired by those who diligently searched. As the *Second London Confession* put it,

> This infallible assurance doth not so belong to the essence of faith, but that a true Believer, may wait long and conflict with many difficulties before he be partaker of it; yet being enabled by the spirit to know the things which are freely given him of God, he may without extraordinary revelation in the right use of means attain there unto: and therefore it is the duty of everyone, to give all diligence to make their Calling and Election sure...[27]

On the whole, the subject of assurance does not seem to have been a point of discussion among church members and persons were not necessarily barred from membership when, after reviewing their experience, they could not give evidence of assurance.

In the records of one congregation in Salisbury in Wiltshire, there was mention of assurance in relation to the church membership when a woman was received in spite of the fact that she could not claim to have full assurance of her experience of salvation in Christ. According to the church records, one man voted against her acceptance because he asserted that 'assurance was necessary'.[28] However, the rest of the members claimed that absolute assurance, while desirable, was not to be a point on which church membership was granted or denied. Later, when this same man raised the issue of assurance again, the congregation affirmed their belief in the doctrine of assurance of faith, but stated, 'we do not nor could we unchristian a man because he does not always enjoy it nor can we call that the faith of devils (sic) which does not allways (sic) come up to assurance'.[29]

While these eighteenth-century Baptists placed much stress on an individual's ability to give a convincing personal testimony, it seems that they did not necessarily believe that full assurance was a prerequisite to church membership. In

[26] *Second London Confession*, in Lumpkin, *Baptist Confessions*, p. 268.
[27] *Second London Confession*, in Lumpkin, *Baptist Confessions*, pp. 274-75.
[28] Samuel Green's letter to the church, December 1776. *The Salisbury Church Account Books* (*SCB*), 1779–1801;1801–1820 and 1789–1824 (Salisbury, Wiltshire).
[29] Letter from the church in reply to Samuel Green (n.d.). *SCB*.

part this was because they understood that the discipline of preparation as an ongoing task even after persons were baptised and received into membership. Clearly, for these Baptists the emphasis on self-examination as part of the discipline of preparation was not merely to keep people from being baptised or to bar people from membership, but it was to encourage growth in holiness and served as a means of drawing people closer to one another and closer to God as they shared in covenant life together.

Preparation, then, was in many ways a life long task. Children were urged from a young age to begin to look to see if they could find evidence of 'a work of grace upon their heart', and parents watched them eagerly for signs or evidences of faith.[30] The wife of John Shoveller of Portsea, for example, reportedly had 'affectionate expostulations' with her children on 'the evil of sin, on the excellence of religion and on the suitableness of salvation exhibited in the Gospel' and 'with tears copiously effusing from her eyes and a heart full of holy agony she often besought them to be reconciled to God'.[31] Though she buried six children in infancy, it was reported that a seventh 'attained the age of five years, and gave the most indubitable evidence of a work of grace in her heart' before leaving the world 'in a flight of sacred rapture'.[32]

Stories of young children having a religious experience were not unusual. James Janeway's *A Token for Children Being An Exact Account of the Conversion, Holy and Exemplary Lives and Joyful Deaths of Several Young Children* (1676), recounted the experiences of a number of children—the youngest between the age of two and three years old—who were 'admirably affected with the things of God'.[33] Although the validity of such accounts may be questioned, the use of stories to teach a particular moral and ethical conduct was a common practice. Calvinistic theology was grounded on the idea of original sin and the total depravity of mankind. It was believed that every child had inherited the 'seed of sinful Adam' and the sooner their plight was put before them the better. Consequently, parents were encouraged to begin when children were very young to instil in them the need to recognise their sin.

As with adults seeking membership in the congregation, however, when children began to raise questions concerning matters of religion their experience was scrutinised for signs that it was valid and true. When the children were 'tested',

---

[30] For an introduction to the religious education of children during the eighteenth century, see Paul Sangster, *Pity My Simplicity, the Evangelical Revival and the Religious Education of Children 1738–1800* (London: Epworth Press, 1963).

[31] *The Baptist Magazine* 8 (1816), p. 250.

[32] *The Baptist Magazine* 8 (1816), p. 250.

[33] In an account of a child who began showing an interest in religion between the age of two and three, Janeway claimed that one sign of the child's interest in religion was that he could not be satisfied with family prayers alone, but 'he would be oft upon his knees by himself in one corner or other'. James Janeway, *A Token for Children being an exact account of the Conversion, Holy and Exemplary Lives and Joyful Deaths of Several Young Children* (1676), p. 19.

usually those who showed the proper emotional response were believed to be under conviction. After a conversation with her daughter, in November 1731, for example, one woman wrote in her diary that she was aware of the dangers of 'imitation', yet she was convinced of the validity of her daughter's feelings when she saw her in tears.[34] She wrote:

> My child talk'd very moving and affectionate to me about her soul fearing she is not converted. Her expressions seem'd far above her age—had she not wept and been very much concern'd I should have tho't was by imitation—I cried to the Lord on her account.[35]

The desire to test the experience of children highlights the emphasis placed on an 'experience' of faith which seems to have implied not only a knowledge of doctrine, but an emotional expression of their faith.[36] Though it appears that while parents began quite early to look for signs or evidence of an experience of grace, generally young people who sought admission to church membership were in their teens.[37]

Sometimes individuals were admitted into fellowship even when their experience and understanding appeared limited. At Broughton in Hampshire one man was accepted by the church even though there was doubt and hesitancy among the church members. The comment was made, 'tho he did not seem to have a large understanding there appeared to be a work of grace upon his heart and the most was for accepting him so they did'.[38]

However, doubt over the genuineness of the experience of believers could lead the church members to postpone their decision until the person had undergone a waiting period and time for further self-examination and reflection. On one occasion, for example, Mrs Steele recorded in her diary that she had talked to someone who wished to be baptised and while she hoped God had 'been at work upon her soul' she had advised her to

---

[34] 26 November 1731, ACS Diary.

[35] 26 November 1731, ACS Diary.

[36] Sangster, *Pity My Simplicity*, p. 189, has noted in his study of the religious education of children that among Evangelicals, the 'emotions of children were deliberately worked on in order to produce a sense of sin and so conversion'.

[37] For example, Anne Steele was fifteen and her brother, William, sixteen when they were baptised and received into membership of the Broughton church. Alicia Miall, wife of Daniel Miall of Portsea, was fifteen when she was baptised. William Steadman's wife, Sarah, was twenty when she was baptised and joined the Broughton church, and her brother Joseph Webb was seventeen when he was baptised. Occasionally, slightly younger members were accepted such as in the case of Steadman's son who was baptised at the age of fourteen and Mary Webb, later married to Nathaniel Rawlings, pastor at Broughton from 1768–78, who was baptised at the age of twelve. *Baptist Magazine* 4 (1812), p. 475; *Baptist Magazine* 7 (1815), p. 223.

[38] 4 October 1730 ACS Diary.

Wait a little longer and be constant in prayer for more knowledge and faith and also to count the cost of a profession of religion then if it appears to be a work of grace upon her heart it will be no grief of mind to her to wait God's time.[39]

Throughout most of the eighteenth century, even women, who generally were admonished to 'keep silent' in church meetings, were expected to stand before the congregation and give evidence of an 'experimental work of grace' on their hearts. As time went on, however, if the person concerned felt unable to speak freely before the congregation, some congregations gave permission for the believer to read a written statement of personal confession or for the testimony to be given in the form of response to questions.

Although the practice of giving an extemporaneous testimony was generally accepted by all Calvinistic Baptists throughout the century, by the first part of the nineteenth century some congregations began to raise questions about the way in which persons should be received into membership. In 1823, John Saffery[40] wrote a circular letter to the churches in the Western Association speaking against the practice of making individuals 'stand while the task of the inquiry is proceeding, more like a trembling culprit than an encouraged disciple', and questioned the scriptural basis for such a practice, by saying

We may fairly ask what Scripture enjoins this coming before the church, as it is called, for the purpose of interrogation? Is it clearly founded on the practice of apostolic or primitive times? If these remarks should seem to look with an aspect of disapprobation upon established custom, we confess the charge. Though we would not willingly remove an ancient land-mark placed by our predecessors on defencable ground; yet bear with us while we ask again, if it would not be safer to the interest of genuine religion, and more protecting to the purity of the churches to allow of private, official inquiry into the state of the individuals who apply for communion? This may be secured by an interview with your minister and two or three experienced members, in whose report you may safely confide. We know this practice prevails in some of our churches and we hope to see it universal.[41]

Saffery may have been correct in claiming that 'private and official inquiry' was safer to the interest of genuine religion. However, the movement away from the 'established custom' of giving a public extemporaneous testimony before the church meeting was also an indication that the emphasis on corporate community, as had

[39] 4 January 1755, ACS Diary.

[40] John Saffery was born at Hythe near Southampton. His first wife, Elizabeth, was the daughter of Joseph Horsey, pastor of the congregation there. She died on 22 May 1798 at thirty-five years of age and he married Maria Grace Saffery, a hymn writer. He went to Salisbury as pastor in 1790. See, *A List of Particular Baptist Churches in England, 1798*, in John Rippon, *The Baptist Annual Register* 3 (1798–1801), p. 37. Hereafter *BAR*.

[41] [John Saffery], *The Circular Letter of the Several Elders, Ministers and Messengers from the Baptist Churches of the Western Association assembled at Chard on May the 21st and 22nd* (Bristol: n.p., 1823), p. 7.

been known in the eighteenth century, was changing. While they continued to affirm their corporate life together, congregations were confronted by a growing emphasis on individualism which, fostered by the Evangelical Revival experience, seems to have stressed the doctrine of personal salvation above all else. While testimony to a personal experience of grace was part of preparation, the link between preparation and the corporate life of the community began to fade. The call to self-examination for Calvinistic Baptists had been concerned with the individual's growth in holiness and most of all it was vital to their understanding of union with Christ. It was not intended as a means by which the hearer might be manipulated through an emotional appeal, nor simply as an exercise in self-awareness.[42] As already noted, a testimony reflecting signs of careful self-scrutiny provided a connection between the personal and the corporate as persons were required to give evidence that they had 'reviewed their experience' before being accepted into the membership of the covenant community. In the nineteenth century in some churches it was no longer necessary for individuals to give their experience to the whole community. This subtle shift in their understanding of the discipline of preparation may have also signaled a shift in their understanding of life within covenant community.

Preparation for the Lord's Supper

One important instance when the connection between self-examination and preparation was evident was in sermons given prior to the celebration of the Lord's Supper. In effect, preparation before the Supper became synonymous with self-examination and was considered necessary if real union with Christ was to take place. That is to say that as the believer was reminded at the table that all were dead in sin until Christ died to bring life to all who believed, so also those who desired to meet the risen Lord at the table and commune with him as part of the fellowship of his body, the church, were to make themselves ready to do so by dying to sin and the old life. Hence, to prepare meant that one consistently held up thoughts, motives and desires to the light of self-examination, and tried to maintain a careful distinction between earthly and heavenly pleasures.

Since they believed there was little hope of communion or union as the body of Christ without true preparation beforehand, it was customary for Calvinistic Baptists to have special meetings which were held before the Supper in order to encourage believers to look carefully at their own personal discipleship to see if they were 'right walkers' in the Lord. William Steadman, for example, recorded that he preached a sermon on Wednesday prior to the Sunday when the Lord's Supper was to be observed and then wrote, that he 'endeavoured to put in practice myself what I recommended to others on Wednesday evening, namely, self-examination.'[43] Then, after 'as attentive a survey of myself as I am capable of', he wrote of his desire to

---

[42] See G.F. Nuttall, *Richard Baxter and Philip Doddridge: A Study in a Tradition* (London: Oxford University Press, 1951), pp. 13 ff.

[43] Thomas Steadman, *Memoirs of William Steadman* (London: Thomas Ward, 1838), pp. 63-64.

live in obedience to Christ and reflected upon his own personal discipleship by saying,

> I hope I do cordially approve of the way of salvation revealed in the Gospel; and trust in Christ alone for the pardon of my sins, and the justification of my person. I hope I have received him in all his offices as my Prophet, Priest and King. I hope I have the fear of God before mine eyes, and an earnest desire to obey his commands. I hope I do reverence his authority, and wish to deny myself everything that is contrary to his will... In social life and in private I desire to obey him. I hope I do sincerely lament my many, many failings. I hope I have some love for God and his people. But not withstanding these conclusions, I have much reason for humiliation and sorrow. For this month past I have not been so spiritual, nor prayed so often, nor so earnestly, nor improved my time so diligently, nor been so watchful over my words and thoughts, as I had been some time before.[44]

At no time was the emphasis on covenant theology more apparent among Baptists than at the celebration of the Lord's Supper. Observed once a month, like baptism, the Lord's Supper was an ordinance of the church and participation in it not only served as a graphic reminder of Christ's love and sacrifice for their salvation, but it also provided an opportunity to share in communion with Christ and in fellowship with other believers.

Standing in the Puritan, Calvinistic tradition, the Baptists related the Lord's Supper to redemption and not to creation and therefore they emphasised God's gracious act of love and the forgiveness of sin, rather than offering. At the Supper, it was believed that guidance and strength for true Christian living could be received and believers were there united with Christ and with other members of his body. From the sermons and hymns of Baptists in the area during this period, one may find the Supper described as both an opportunity to remember and reflect upon Christ's death, as well as a time when one may 'feed on him by faith'.[45] However, the symbols of bread and wine were not mere reminders, but, when received in faith, they provided an opportunity for real communion with Christ.

The idea of the Lord's Supper as both an opportunity for reflection upon the saving work of Christ and also a time of real communion with him is found in Anne Steele's hymn 'Communion With Christ at his Table', which was first written about 1750. The verses call to mind the believers' own unworthiness and Christ's sacrificial love, and at the same time express a desire for real communion with him.

To Jesus our exalted Lord,
(Dear name, by heaven and earth ador'd!)
Fain would our hearts and voices raise,
A Cheerful song of sacred praise.

---

[44] Steadman, *Memoirs of William Steadman*, pp. 63-64.
[45] The Sermons of William Steele (1684–1769) of Broughton in Hampshire. In the Angus Library. Hereafter WSS.

But all the notes which mortals know
Are weak and languishing and low;
Far, far above our humble songs
The theme of immortal tongues.

Yet while around this board we meet,
And worship at his glorious feet;
O let our warm affections move
In glad returns of grateful love.

Yes, Lord we love and we adore,
But long to know and love thee more;
And while we taste the bread and wine,
Desire to feed on joys divine.

Let faith our feeble senses aid
To see thy wondrous love display'd,
Thy broken flesh, thy bleeding veins,
Thy dreadful agonizing pains!

Let humble penitential woe,
with painful, pleasing anguish flow,
And thy forgiving smiles impart
Life, hope and joy to every heart.[46]

Since the Lord's Supper offered the opportunity both to remember Christ's sacrificial love and to experience communion with him, during the eighteenth century there was much emphasis on 'preparation' before approaching the Lord's table. As individuals reflected upon the sacrificial love of Christ, attention was to be given to their own unworthiness even to seek communion with him. John Kent preached a sermon at Broughton in July 1738 on 1 Corinthians 11.28 where he described self-examination as 'an indispensable duty' of all who wished to partake of the Lord's Supper.[47]

---

[46] Copied by her step-mother, Anne C. Steele into her diary on Sunday 10 March 1750 (ACS Diary) and later published in Anne Steele, *Poems On Subjects Chiefly Devotional and Miscellaneous Pieces, under the name Theodosia* (Bristol, 1780).

[47] John Kent was called out to preach occasionally by the church in Broughton, Hampshire, in 1732. His family lived at Wallop and his father was an elder in the Broughton church. He served as an assistant minister in the Broughton church until September 1787. He died in 1796. See, 'Obituary', in *BAR* 2 (1794–97), p. 505, and Steadman, *Memoirs of William Steadman*, p. 170.

Personal preparation before the Supper was to be taken seriously by the believers. On one occasion, Mrs Steele recorded her time of preparation and her experience at the ordinance with these words:

> I read my experience since my last sitting down at the Lord's table and find and know I have been in a poor and barren frame a great part of the time I now beg I may be prepar'd for the ensueing day and I may be refreshed and quickened by the holy ordinances of God's house. I was sweetly drawn out in my evening duty in love and thankfulness... I heard Mr. Eastman pretty diligently from and this is my commandment that we should believe on the name of his son Jesus Christ and love one another...my desires ran out to God in the ordinance both for my comfort for myself and for others that came with power so he that eateth me so shall he live and I hope I have been fed on Christ...[48]

Preparation and participation in the Lord's Supper was both a time of remembrance and a time of communion with Christ. As John Lacy[49] put it in a hymn he wrote 'For the Lord's Supper':

Now let my thankful tongue repeat,
In songs of sacred peace,
How heav'n did all my foes defeat,
And gave me a release.

Let Christ my gracious King, arise,
And rule my stubborn heart:
Descend dear Jesus, from the skies,
And never let us part.

Open the fountain of thy blood,
Where all my love begins;
Give me to plunge into that flood;
To wash away my sins,

---

[48] ACS Diary,

[49] John Lacy (1700–81) was born at Clatford, near Andover, on 22 May 1700 and moved with his family to Portsea in 1704. He married in 1728 and after that joined the Meeting-house Alley church. He was called out by the congregation to preach in March 1732 and in July 1733 he was given pastoral charge of the congregation. He published: *Conference About Infant Baptism* (1741), *An Answer to a late Anonymous Pamphlet Entitled A Treatise on the Subject and Mode of Baptism* (1743), *Divine Hymns* (Portsea, 1747), a translation of *Bull Unigenitus, with its Rise and Progress* (1753), *The Universal System: or Mechanical Cause of All the Appearances and Movements of the Visible Heavens with a Dissertation on Comets* (1779), and, according to Ivimey, who was for some time a member of his church, he left a paper entitled 'The Duty and Office of Deacons'; Samuel Rowles, *The Christian Soldier Waiting For His Crown* (1781); Joseph Ivimey, *A History of the English Baptists* (4 vols; London, 1811–30), IV, pp. 486-89.

Then come, my friends, here let us join,
Since Jesus is so nigh;
Supported by this bread and wine,
Till we are call'd on high.[50]

Many Calvinistic Baptist congregations throughout the eighteenth century appear to have practised 'closed communion', that is the Lord's Supper was only administered in a covenanted local fellowship to those who had been baptised or formally belonged to it or to those who brought letters of recommendation from their home congregations.

Since participation in the Supper was a sign of real communion and fellowship with Christ and with other believers, those who had been baptised were not usually received into 'full communion' with the members of a community of faith until 'ordinance Sunday' when there was the 'breaking of bread'. Early on, much emphasis had been given to the believer's responsibility as a member to attend. While illness sometimes made absence from the table unavoidable, unexcused absence left one open to the discipline of the church. Moreover, those found with a serious moral fault were barred from communion until they showed evidence of true repentance. On the other hand, sometimes restriction from the table was self-imposed. In 1780 it was recorded in the Lymington church book that 'Mrs. George took her place at the Lord's Table after omitting that duty for several years on account of some difficulties in her own mind'.[51]

There were occasions, of course, when absence was unavoidable. For example, in April 1750 Mrs Steele was prevented from attending the Lord's Supper while she was staying with her daughter who was ill. In her diary she reflected on the fact that she had lost an opportunity for 'communion' with Christ and other believers. Describing her private devotion she wrote,

I had a variety of suitable Scriptures upon my mind this morning and though I am absent from the little flock to whom I belong, yet my mind is with them desiring the same blessings both for myself and for them viz. the assistance of the spirit and communion with God in his ordinance.[52]

Although throughout the eighteenth century most of these churches practised closed communion, by the later part of the period there was a gradual acceptance of open communion, though for the most part they still maintained the practice of closed membership. That is to say that while they were willing to share at the Lord's table with those who held to the practice of infant baptism, they were not prepared to go further and accept them into membership without believer's baptism administered to a candidate after profession of their faith and by immersion. As early as 1780 men

---

[50] John Lacy, *Divine Hymns, Made on the Most Important Points of Christianity* (Portsmouth Common: J. Whitewood, 2nd edn, 1776 [1747]), pp. 22-23.

[51] 4 June 1780. The Lymington Church Book (Hampshire Record Office).

[52] 8 April 1750, ACS Diary.

such as Daniel Turner[53] and Robert Robinson[54] wrote treatises which took a stand in favour of open membership. However, it was a practice which was lamented by many members of the denomination who feared that it signaled a move away from Baptist principles, particularly from believer's baptism.

The practice of open communion did not necessarily indicate an acceptance of infant baptism. However, it did clearly reflect something of the growing sense of a united witness to personal salvation among Evangelicals of all denominations. More importantly, it was a significant reflection of the growing individualism among these Baptists which stressed emphasis on personal rather than corporate 'union with Christ' within a specific body of believers. Along with this shift away from corporate unity in the Lord's Supper it appears that there was a loss of emphasis on the discipline of preparation as well.

Preparation for Death

While preaching a sermon on Job 14.14 in 1724, William Steele, of Broughton in Hampshire, instructed his listeners that the one thing needful for a 'safe preparation for death' was true faith in Jesus Christ.[55] Expounding the meaning of faith in Christ as 'not bear (sic) believing but imbracing him', not 'picking and chusing (sic) articles of faith, but resting in him and him alone for salvation', he wrote that the two things which always preceded true faith were conviction of sin and knowledge of the worth and excellence of Christ. Inseparable from faith, according to him, were love and obedience. Finally, he concluded by saying that by nature all persons were unprepared, and that each person should endeavour to attain a state of preparedness by

---

[53] Daniel Turner (1710–98) was pastor at Reading from 1743 to 1748 and after that at Abingdon from 1748 to 1798. He was born at Black Farm near St Albans on 1 March 1710. Before going to Reading, he kept a boarding school at Hemel Hempstead and was an occasional preacher in Baptist chapels. His wife Ann (née Fanch) died in September 1744 and he later married a Mrs Lucas of Reading. He wrote a number of treatises and hymns. W.T. Whitley, *A Baptist Bibliography* (2 vols; London: Kingsgate Press, 1916–22), I, p. 230; S.L. Copson, 'Turner, Daniel (1710–1798)', *Oxford Dictionary of National Biography* (Oxford: Oxford University Press, 2004), http://www.oxforddnb.com/view/article/27845, accessed 31 January 2006.

[54] Robert Robinson (1735–90) was a hymn writer and well known Baptist minister in Cambridgeshire. In May 1752, he heard the Calvinistic Methodist preacher, George Whitefield. By 1755, Robinson began attending a Methodist congregation in London and in 1758 he moved to Norwich and began preaching among Methodist congregations. In 1759 he rejected infant baptism and joined with the Baptists. He went to Cambridge and began to preach to members of the Stone-yard Baptist congregation. In 1761 he accepted a call to be pastor of the church, apparently on the condition that they would practise open communion. He published a number of treatises. See, K.E. Smith, 'Robert Robinson' in D.M. Lewis (ed.), *The Blackwell Dictionary of Evangelical Biography 1730–1860: Volume II. K–Z* (2 vols; Oxford: Oxford University Press, 1995), p. 947.

[55] WSS: Job 14.14 (2 May 1724).

'seeking after it' through prayer, reading and hearing the Word, meditation and conversation.[56]

The tone and tenor of this sermon was repeated by many other Calvinistic Baptist ministers throughout the eighteenth century. Indeed, the idea of faith in Christ and obedience to the commands set forth in Scripture as the only true preparation for death and hope of eternal life was an all-encompassing theme in Calvinistic Baptist devotion. No occasion was lost to warn hearers of the dangers of not being prepared; illness, disease, poverty or misfortune, and even national disasters, were all seen as a providential means by which people would be warned of the dangers of not believing and would thereby be brought into the community of faith.

Death was frequently seen as a warning of the need to be ready to meet a similar fate, and signs that the deceased had been prepared to die were noted carefully and then drawn to the attention of others. Henry Philips,[57] for instance, described the funeral service of George Spier, a deacon in his church, and noted in the church book how Spier's outward circumstances indicated his spiritual preparedness for death. The last few weeks before he died, according to Philips, he had spent much time in prayer with 'more than the usual emotion' and the 'word of God was sweet to his taste'.[58] Moreover, he had prepared by 'ordering all his affairs well' which included making out a will, selecting trustees and funeral bearers and choosing the hymns, as well as the text for his funeral.

The preoccupation with final preparation for death was taken further in the nineteenth century. In fact, deathbeds took on an important role in evangelical theology as they provided an opportunity to a believer to give a personal (Kenneth

---

[56] WSS: Job 14.14 (2 May 1724).

[57] Henry Philips (1719–89) associated with Methodists in Wales. He is said to have credited his first 'serious impressions' at the age of eighteen to Howel Harris and later attended for about eight years the Established Church at Landowror where Griffith Jones was minister. Philips preached in Whitefield's connexion for a time and then, in 1750, decided to leave the Established Church. He was then baptised and received into membership of the Baptist church at Pen-y-garn and after a time was called out by that congregation to preach and went to Bristol to the academy. After supplying a number of churches including those at Broughton and Whitchurch, he eventually moved to Ireland in 1757 before returning to England in 1763 after his wife's health failed. He served the church at Salisbury for twenty-three years from 1766 until his death in 1789. During that time he also engaged in village preaching and by 1775, according to one source, he preached regularly to as many as 200 hearers. However, he never forgot his Welsh ties and in 1773 he was responsible for sending 300 Welsh Bibles to churches in Wales. Philips died on 20 August 1789 at the age of seventy. His friend, Jonathan Adams, minister of the Independent congregation at Scotts Lane, Salisbury, spoke at his interment, and Joseph Horsey, of Portsmouth, preached in the morning and the afternoon. See 'Obituary Notice', in *BAR* 1 (1790–93), p. 128, and Diary of Jonathon Adams, Independent minister of Scotts Lane Salisbury 'Events from 1772 to the Present Year' (The Wiltshire Record Office).

[58] *SCB*.

Brown has suggested an 'overtly propagandist') testimony to his or her faith.[59] Drawing on the work of David Bebbington and R.J. Helmstadter, Pat Jolland has suggested that the idea of a 'good death' was linked to the evangelical conscience which stressed the doctrine of assurance of faith, usually acquired at conversion rather than baptism. Jolland says:

> The Evangelical model of the good Christian death was widely disseminated through Evangelical journals and tracts, which were intended primarily to provide spiritual edification and example—to save souls by showing people how to live and die well. These were usually designed to demonstrate the earnest piety, upright character, and resigned death of dying 'saints'.[60]

Given the fact that so much attention was given to the actual preparation of the deceased throughout the eighteenth and nineteenth centuries, and that it was so closely connected with the doctrines of the Christian life, it follows that the one particular occasion when this theme was heard most frequently was at the funeral service. Since many of these have been preserved and each was preached on a similar occasion and for a similar purpose, funeral sermons are a good source for exploring the shape of theology throughout the period.[61] The purpose of publishing funeral sermons and inscribing them to family and friends was viewed in some sense as an expression of pastoral care on the part of the minister—a way to offer comfort to the bereaved. However, while this may have been part of the reason for publication, funeral sermons were principally used as a medium for evangelism and as an encouragement to others to continue in the discipline of preparation. In the sermons themselves every attempt was made to encourage believers to examine their own lives, to prepare for a similar fate.

---

[59] Kenneth D. Brown, *A Social History of the Nonconformist Ministry in England and Wales, 1800–1930* (Oxford: Clarendon Press, 1988), p. 14. For details of death-bed testimonies in the nineteenth century, see Linda Wilson, *Constrained by Zeal: Female Spirituality amongst Nonconformists 1825–1875* (Studies in Evangelical History and Thought; Carlisle: Paternoster Press, 2000) pp. 154-69.

[60] Pat Jalland, *Death in the Victorian Family* (Oxford: Oxford University Press, 1996), p. 21. For more on the Nonconformist conscience, see David Bebbington, *The Nonconformist Conscience: Chapel and Politics 1870–1914* (London: George Allen & Unwin, 1982), and *Evangelicalism in Modern Britain: A History from the 1730s to the 1980s* (London: Unwin Hyman, 1989); R.J. Helmstadter, 'The Nonconformist Conscience', in G. Parsons (ed.), *Religion in Victorian Britain: Volume IV. Interpretations* (Manchester: Manchester University Press, 1988), pp. 61-95.

[61] In fact, G.F. Nuttall, 'Calvinism in Free Church History,' *Baptist Quarterly* 22.8 (October, 1968), p. 427, has suggested that while one must watch carefully for the hagiographical nature of funeral sermons, 'they form a source too little used in identifying what at any particular time was an accepted ideal among Christian people'. G. F. Nuttall.

Josiah Lewis[62] in 1778 preached the funeral sermon of the hymn writer, Anne Steele, entitled, 'The Mourners Consolation', on John 14.2-3, the text she had requested.[63] In this address, he appealed to the listeners to prepare themselves. Speaking of the need to be prepared to enter the mansion which Christ himself was preparing, he stated,

> There is room for all in the mansions. For youth, for children, for infants, for men of grey hairs, for the opulent, and the needy, for natives and foreigners, for Calvinists, Lutherans, Baxterians and the friends to a thousand other such unto wch (sic) Christianity has been revealed... Christ is preparing a place for us, but are we preparing for him.[64]

In addition to funeral sermons, preparation for death was encouraged by the testimony of friends and family who gathered at the bedside. The questions of the on-lookers were carefully designed to prompt testimonies that would enable the believer to speak with confidence of the assurance of faith and personal communion with Christ. These testimonies were often written down and printed in order to demonstrate the relevance of religion and to encourage readers to deeper commitment.[65] On the lips of Esther Horsey, wife of Joseph Horsey of Portsea[66] were lines to a well-known hymn which were often quoted on death-beds of the nineteenth century, when she reportedly said, 'Everybody thinks that I lie uneasy but they are mistaken; no, Jesus can make a dying bed feel soft as downy pillows are.'[67]

---

[62] Josiah Lewis, *A Pious Memorial, The Mourner's Consolation, A Discourse Occasioned by the decease of Mrs Anne Steele, of Broughton*, in the Steele family papers, Angus Library. (This handwritten transcript of his sermon appears to have been made by Lewis at the request of Steele's nieces.) Lewis assumed pastoral care of the congregation at Broughton in 1777.

[63] [Josiah Lewis], *The Mourners Consolation*, (1778). Steele family papers in the Angus Library.

[64] [Lewis], *The Mourners Consolation*.

[65] [Lewis], *The Mourners Consolation*.

[66] Joseph Horsey (1737–1802) was born in Somerset in 1737. His father, Richard Horsey, was in the linen manufacturing business in the village of Longload, near Somerton. He was a member of the Baptist church at Yeovil and reportedly allowed Whitefield to preach in his home and orchard when he made a tour there. In 1747 and 1748 both Richard Horsey and his wife died and Joseph was brought up by guardians in Hampshire. He was then apprenticed as a turner with a Mr Todd at Gosport until he was twenty years of age. Around the age of twenty he was baptised and joined the Baptist church at Portsmouth under John Lacy's care. He married Susannah Todd and they had two daughters, Susannah, who later became the wife of John Shoveller of Portsmouth, and Elizabeth, who married John Saffery, who was pastor at Sarum from 1789 to 1825. On 15 May 1782 he was ordained as pastor of the Church at Portsmouth. John Shoveller, *Memoirs of the Late Rev. Joseph Horsey, of Portsea, with Mr. Horsey's Farewell Address to his church....also a funeral sermon delivered at his interment by Daniel Miall to which is added an elegy by Mrs. Saffery* (Portsea, 1803), p. 3.

[67] 'Obituary of Mrs. Esther Horsey', *Baptist Magazine* 2 (1810), p. 341.

Emphasis on 'preparation for death', has naturally been a theme of spiritual writers throughout the centuries and was not peculiar to eighteenth-century Calvinistic Baptists.[68] In fact, the way Calvinistic Baptists viewed attendance at deathbeds and their stress on 'holy dying' may again be traced to Puritan devotion.[69] It has been suggested that attendance at the bedside of a believer by members of the congregation may have indicated something of the Puritan's understanding of the 'priestly nature of the whole society'.[70] If this is true, then for Calvinistic Baptists early on in the eighteenth century preparation may also have been very much linked to their understanding of union in Christ.

Clearly by the nineteenth century this began to change. Instead of emphasising the priestly nature of the whole society, it appears that deathbed testimonies emphasised personal witness. Significantly, by the nineteenth century, as Doreen Rosman has pointed out in her *Evangelicals and Culture*, deathbeds had almost a 'sacramental function' in the evangelical experience as it provided an opportunity to speak of personal union with Christ.[71]

The significance of deathbed testimonies in evangelical experience is highlighted further by the fact that not only were they used as a means by which an individual could witness to a personal experience with Christ, but also they came to be used as a means for evangelisation. Deathbed sagas even found their way into the literature for Sunday Schools.[72] Thomas Tilly of Portsea,[73] for instance, published a book entitled: *A Short Account of the Experience and Happy Death of the Following Sunday School Children; Hester Florance, William Burges, Sarah Stripp, and Margaret Ronun* (1822) and claimed that accounts of deathbed conversations were 'effectual to the conversion of youth as to those of riper years'.[74] Questioned about their faith in the time of adversity, in these accounts each child was able to respond

---

[68] John McManners has provided an account of attitudes toward death in eighteenth century France in his book *Death and the Enlightenment* (Oxford: Oxford University Press, 1981). For a discussion on Puritan attitudes to death see, Wakefield, *Puritan Devotion*, pp. 143-53.

[69] For an informative introduction to the Puritan attitude toward death, see David E. Stannard, *The Puritan Way of Death: A Study in Religion, Culture, and Social Change* (Oxford: Oxford University Press, 1977).

[70] Wakefield, *Puritan Devotion*, p. 146.

[71] Doreen Rosman, *Evangelicals and Culture* (Dover, NH: Croom Helm, 1984), p. 103.

[72] Sangster discusses the way death-beds were used as a way to teach children in *Pity My Simplicity*, pp. 65-69, 151.

[73] Thomas Tilly (1780–1851) was born at Ringwood in Hampshire. In 1801, he moved to Poole and went to a Congregational church. He later married Hannah Veal of Ringwood and they were both baptised at Wimborne in 1803. A tailor by trade, he went to Portsea and later began preaching in churches. See, Robert Grace, 'Memoir of the late Rev. Thomas Tilly, of Forton, Hants', *Baptist Magazine* 53 (1851), pp. 481-90.

[74] Thomas Tilly, *A Short Account of the Experience and Happy Death of the Following Sunday School Children; Hester Florance, William Burges, Sarah Stripp, and Margaret Ronun* (Portsea, 1822), p. 35.

with remarkable clarity and quote Scripture, singing or reciting verses of hymns which reveal an unflagging trust and an unfaltering faith and hope.

It is clear that the deathbed testimony had a significant place amongst eighteenth-century Calvinistic Baptists and later amongst other nineteenth-century Evangelicals. While the nature of the evidence at hand limits the comparison which can be made between this type of testimony and that given before acceptance into church membership, it appears that in the nineteenth century more and more emphasis was placed on individual relationship with Christ. That is to say that, fanned by a growing concern for evangelism, in the nineteenth century 'union with Christ' was often expressed as personal union between a believer and other believers as part of Christ's body, the church.

The effect that this growing individualism in the nineteenth century had on the structures of church life was not immediately evident. In part, this was due to the fact that Calvinistic Baptists, like the rest of Old Dissent, shared with the new Evangelicals a common heritage in Puritanism which was grounded in personal faith informed by the spoken Word and improved by constant self-examination. Moreover, central to both Old Dissent and the New Evangelicals was the biblical emphasis on discipleship lived out in separation from the world. They believed that it was the duty of every believer to strive to live in a way that reflected their commitment to Christ.

Unlike the New Evangelicals, however, holy living and holy dying was not merely an expression of personal discipleship and a response to the gospel, but also, traditionally, for Calvinistic Baptists, it had been fundamental to their understanding of the church as a 'gathered' community of believers who were called out to be 'visible saints'. They were called out by Christ not simply to live as individuals in relationship with Christ, but they were to live in union with him and with the members of his body, the church. This was a life-long task and one which required the practice of daily self-examination and careful attention to the discipline of preparation: a discipline which with the new Evangelicalism of the nineteenth century, alas, was to cease to be a facet of Baptist identity.

CHAPTER 3

Conflicting Commitments? Baptist Identity and Welsh National Consciousness, 1649 to the Present

D. Densil Morgan

In his magisterial treatment of 'the command of God the Creator' in *Church Dogmatics* III/4, Karl Barth writes about the context in which the Christian is enabled to respond in freedom to the sovereign command of his or her Lord. Having referred to the encounter of man and woman and the relationship between parents and children, he proceeds to describe what he calls 'near and distant neighbours', near neighbours being those to whom he or she is bound by ties of speech, location and a common history: 'What we have in view, though we cannot guarantee the clarity or precision of the concept, is a person's own particular people or nation.'[1] 'Who is there', he continues,

> who as an individual and by the divine will and ordinance does not belong to a larger group which forms a more or less recognisable totality both physically by wider blood-relationship and biological particularity, and historically by its past, its present speech and customs, and perhaps a common geographical location?[2]

In other words, what Barth is groping after is a concept of ethnicity or nationality, that which turns a collective into a particular people constituted by ties of a common language, an allocated place and a shared past. This, he claims, is the nexus in which the sovereign Lord, who has freely chosen mankind to share fellowship with himself through the gracious election in Christ, has issued the command to obedience and faith: 'It is *here* that the person is before God and in fellowship.'[3]

For a long time Western Christians, especially those in the more powerful nations, have shied away from developing a concept of ethnicity, often for the soundest of reasons. The shadow of imperialism and nationalism as a destructive force is a long one, and the Christian conscience is necessarily tender when reminded of certain aspects of European history since the late nineteenth century. On the other hand the magisterial nations (if we can call them that) are frequently so secure in their cultural or national identity that they hardly realise its existence and are

---

[1] Karl Barth, *Church Dogmatics* (14 vols; trans and ed. by G.W. Bromiley and T.F. Torrance; Edinburgh: T&T Clark, 1936–77), III/4, p. 286, translation revised.

[2] Barth, *Church Dogmatics* III/4, p. 287.

[3] Barth, *Church Dogmatics* III/4, p. 287, emphasis added and translation revised.

surprised that it can be experienced by others as an oppressive force. In either case, the relation between Christian vocation and national identity needs to be delineated with care and, above all, rooted in a biblically responsible doctrine of creation so that the one informs the other and enriches, rather than threatens, the quality of human life. Those of us for whom Welsh nationhood in the early twenty-first century is, in Barth's phrase, 'the allocated framework in which we are obliged to express our own distinct obedience',[4] need to be as conscious of the dangers of conflicting commitments as we are of the potential for harmonization and fruitful engagement between the gospel and ever changing cultural forms. This is a calling from which my fellow Welsh Baptists—hardly renowned, perhaps, for an insightful understanding of the doctrine of creation—are not exempt.

The Christian cause in Wales goes back to the fifth century AD. It was then, with the withdrawal of Roman rule, that the Celtic people of 'the Isle of Britain' were drawn away from their picaresque druidic paganism and converted to the gospel of Christ. It was at this exact juncture that the Brythonic Celts developed into what the Anglo-Saxons would call the Welsh, though they would call themselves *Cymry*—'fellow countrymen'—and their language, newly emerged from Brythonic, as *Cymraeg*. In other words, Welsh nationhood and the advent of a widespread profession of Christian faith were concurrent; judging from the (admittedly sparse) evidence, Wales seems to have been born in the midst of a mighty religious awakening.

From the sixth century to the early modern period, Wales, like the rest of Europe, was incontrovertibly Christian. What is significant from the point of this chapter is that Wales's self-designation as a people was intertwined with their practice of the Christian faith. From the spirited jeremiad of the craggy monk Gildas *De Excidio Brittonum* (*On the Fall of Britain*) during 'the age of the saints', the exquisitely crafted religious poetry of 'the age of the princes', the warm-hearted patriotism of the Cistercian Order during the twelfth and thirteenth centuries—who proved themselves to be the most loyal supporters of Owain Glyndwr, champion of Welsh independence, during his uprising in 1400—medieval Christianity and a feeling for what it meant to be Welsh seemed bound together as one. The interpenetration of national consciousness and religious faith was complete.

The same was true at the dawning of modernity. It was as patriotic Welshmen that the earliest Protestant Reformers made their pitch, with the former Marian exile, Bishop Richard Davies's *Epistol at y Cymry* (*An Epistle to the Welsh*) (1567) as much a nationalist tract as an apologia for the new religious ways. What Davies began, his younger contemporary William Morgan, bishop of Llandaff and later of St Asaph, brought to fruition. It was his magnificent translation of the Welsh Bible in 1588—the jewel in the Reformers' crown—which gave Wales its cultural soul. It was through men like these that Christianity in its Protestant guise and a (by then) very long-established Welsh nationality, were fused together even more tightly than before.

---

[4] Barth, *Church Dogmatics* III/4, p. 288, translation revised.

The Baptist movement was a child, or perhaps a stepchild, of the Reformation. The Reformers' ideal was for a national church renewed according to the Word of God. Although Wales had been subsumed politically into the English state in 1536, culturally it retained its independence and linguistically remained separate from the English norm. The Puritans' vision was for a far more radical reformation than the Reformers had allowed, placing the catholic form of the church and its episcopal government inherited from the medieval past, under a much more bracing scriptural discipline than the Reformers would have wished. Puritanism was an English import into Wales which only began to effect the larger towns and the border districts during the early- to mid-seventeenth century. Though he spent his time mostly in England, the single notable Welshman to be fired with Puritan zeal, the Separatist martyr John Penry (who suffered the same fate as Henry Barrow and John Greenwood by being hanged for sedition in 1593), gave his life for Wales. His three great treatises, *The Aequity of Humble Supplication* (1587), *An Exhortation unto the Governors...of Her Majesty's Country of Wales* (1588) and *A Supplication unto the High Court of Parliament* (1588) were all pleas for the spiritual renewal of his native land. His final words, in his appeal to Lord Burleigh a week before his execution, are an apt summary of his life's aim:

> I am a poor young man born and bred in the mountains of Wales. I am the first, since the last springing up of the Gospel in this latter age, that publicly laboured to have the blessed seed thereof sown in these barren mountains... And now, being to end my days before I am come to the one half of my years, in the likely course of nature, I leave the success of these my labours unto such of my countrymen as the Lord is to raise up after me.[5]

It took another half century for at least some of his countrymen to take up the Puritan cause, and it was among them that the Baptist movement began.

Hugh Evans, a native of Llan-hir, Radnorshire, and an apprentice clothier in Worcester, was converted to the Baptist position through the ministrations of the General Baptist leader Jeremiah Ives, and was compelled with a desire to share his new-found faith with his compatriots. Conscious that 'his native country of Wales did not receive the proper ministration of the ordinance of God',[6] he returned in 1646 to plant Baptist fellowships, Arminian in theology though closed in their communion, throughout mid-Wales. Three years later John Miles, a more precise dogmatician and more accomplished organizer and previously down from Brasenose College, Oxford, arrived in south Wales intent on planting a Calvinist version of the strict-communion Baptist faith in that area, and succeeded to a much greater extent than Evans did. We know little of Miles' background or his cultural make-up, but being a native of Newton Clifford, Herefordshire, he probably knew Welsh. What we

---

[5] David Williams (ed.), *John Penry: Three Treatises Concerning Wales* (Cardiff: University of Wales Press, 1960), p. xxvi.

[6] Thomas Richards, *A History of the Puritan Movement in Wales* (London: National Eisteddfod Association, 1920), p. 206.

do know is that Miles, 'dour and sphinx-like',[7] was a leader among the Welsh Puritans and during the Commonwealth period had his hands on the reins of power. The Act for the Better Propagation of the Gospel in Wales (1650), the first parliamentary bill since the union of Wales with England in 1536 to treat Wales as a separate entity under the crown, illustrated that the Puritans were conscious of Welsh particulars, but it was an Independent, Walter Cradock, who could appeal with most passion on behalf of Wales. Preaching before Parliament on 21 July 1656, he said:

> Let not poor Wales continue sighing, famishing, mourning and bleeding while you have your days of fasting, rejoicing, thanksgiving and praising God... Is it not a sad case that in thirteen counties there should not be above thirteen (God grant that there be more...) conscientious ministers, who in these times expressed themselves firmly and constantly faithful to the Parliament and formerly preached profitably in the Welsh language twice every Lord's day? Yet praised be our God, some few there are...who are ready and willing to be reckoned among them and be spent for the glory of God and the good of their country.[8]

It was another Independent, Morgan Llwyd, who turned this commitment into prose of the most arresting kind, and by so doing immortalized himself as a writer of genius. It was as a Welshman that he wrote, and the titles of his books, *Llythyr i'r Cymry Cariadus* (*A Letter to the Loving Welsh*) (1653), *Gwaedd yng Nghymru* (*A Cry in Wales*) (1653), *Cyfarwyddyd i'r Cymry* (*The Welshman's Instructor*) (1657), indicates how conscious he was of the national identity of his audience. Although Welsh national consciousness fluctuated during this, and other, periods, it was always present, and the Puritans and Nonconformists, among whom the Baptists were counted, participated fully in its fortunes.

During the seventeenth century that consciousness manifested itself in cultural values and customs rather than in political activity. Unlike Scotland, Wales had no institutions of its own. Owain Glyndwr's dream of a national university had been destroyed along with his own downfall in 1410, while the ancient Welsh legal system had been dismantled with the Act of Incorporation in 1536. There was no longer a Welsh court, the principal families or native aristocracy had gravitated towards London. It was there—the ancient centre of 'the Isle of Britain' still celebrated in Welsh folklore—that the Tudor dynasty, proud of their Welsh roots, had ascended to the throne. With Henry Tudor, a Welshman had become once more the titular head of all of Britain. Why fight for independence if Wales, by stealth, had taken the crown? It was, after all, the crown of *Britain*, not England, Britain being the ancient realm inhabited by the Brythonic Celts long before the advent of the upstart Saxons. The myth was a potent one which would last for centuries. Political unionism, a fierce loyalty to the crown, a warm Welsh patriotism and a distinct

---

[7] Thomas Richards, *Religious Developments in Wales, 1652–62* (London: National Eisteddfod Association, 1923), p. 311.

[8] Thomas Rees, *History of Protestant Nonconformity in Wales* (London: John Snow, 1861), p. 78.

disdain for the English as foreign interlopers to be suffered rather than actively welcomed, would characterise Welsh national sentiment until the late-nineteenth century at least. Add to this the 'Romanism' of the English church, introduced by 'Augustine, that proud friar', which only served to infect the evangelical simplicity and biblical purity of the indigenous British church, and you had a heady mix indeed!

It was partly because of this that Puritanism as a popular movement made little headway in Wales. Despite Penry and Cradock and Llwyd, it was altogether too foreign, too English, to make much of an impact. Cromwell was reviled, and with the restoration of the monarchy Wales sighed with relief. The post-restoration Baptist movement was tiny, insignificant and, for many, decidedly un-Welsh. Welshness was vouchsafed by a newly emboldened Anglican establishment which preserved continuity with the past and embodied the seamless unity of religion and state: *eius religio cuius regio*. Was it not the old, familiar established church, sprung from the ancient British church, which had preserved the gospel in its liturgy and had given the people the Bible in their own tongue? Such was the situation for Baptists and other dissenting Christians, until the eighteenth century at least.

This was not to say that the Welsh Baptist movement, small, select, comprising of a handful of churches restricted to south Wales alone, did not see itself as Welsh, its members being proud of their national characteristics and, once more, loyal to the crown. Their preaching, after all, was Bible-based and utilized the Welsh language to the full, and when they did break into print, their didactic works (such as they were) contributed as much to Welsh literature as they did to evangelism and piety. One of the first Welsh language books to be published in America, Abel Morgan's *Cyd-Gordiad Egwyddorawl o'r Scrythurau* (*A Regular Concordance of the Scriptures*) which emerged from the Welsh Baptist community of the Delaware Valley in 1730, illustrated the vitality of the (in his case emigrant) linguistic culture of the time. In all, the Baptists of the Older Dissent, between 1689 and c.1775, lived a quiet, mildly refined life, contributing unsereptitiously to the culture of the day.

Welsh national consciousness was (and remains) a fluctuating rather than a constant phenomenon. The mid-eighteenth century witnessed its renaissance. Gradually a fresh cultural energy, a rejuvenated appreciation for the glories of the past and a new feeling of pride in all things Welsh asserted itself; it was not unconnected with the Romantic movement and culminated in the creative genius of Edward Williams, 'Iolo Morganwg', stonemason, scholar and polymath, at the century's end. Baptists were not unaffected by this renewal and even contributed towards it in a modest way. There was one work, Joshua Thomas's *Hanes y Bedyddwyr ymhlith y Cymry* (*A History of the Baptists among the Welsh*) (1778) which became a milestone for both Baptist historiography and in the progression of the cultural renewal in Wales. Joshua Thomas is admirable in all respects: kind-hearted, scholarly, assiduous, pious, a supreme wordsmith, a first class historian and completely without guile. His volume marked the coming of age of the Baptist movement in Wales. Here was a despised sect which had survived the vicissitudes of ostracism to become a respectable, if not quite yet venerable, tradition in its own right. Thomas's doctrine of history was sophisticated: an irenic Protestantism infused with a warm evangelicalism which affirmed both the Anglican Church and the Methodist movement which was currently having such a startling effect on the country's religious life. This was not to be expected by the 'high church' precisionists of the Older Dissent. Its patriotic credentials were plain for all to see: 'Of all the nations under heaven, it has been the English who have done the most treachery and harm to the Welsh.'[9] This sole discordant note reflects the unionism and loyalty to the *British* crown so typical of the Welsh tradition since the Tudor period; it was the *English* (among whom Thomas, as minister of the Etnam Street church in Leominster, Herefordshire, had laboured for decades) who had oppressed the native Brythonic people, stolen their land and usurped their status. The English were interlopers who could hardly, by now, be dislodged. But the sovereign Lord had overruled and through the union of Wales and England in 1536, cemented by the Tudors, the Protestant religion had triumphed, the Bible had been given pride of place, evangelical spirituality had become the norm and by now, a patriotic renewal had ensued: 'I am quite convinced that since 1700 Wales has never been in a better state... Through the good pleasure of the wise God, the people and their language are set to flourish even more than they have these thousand years past.'[10]

The confidence of this most humane and judicious historian reflected the spiritual revival which was affecting the Welsh Baptist movement at the time. The seventeen churches which the movement possessed in 1735 had, by 1790, grown to thirty-five, and between 1790 and 1815 it had expanded to over a hundred. By then the thousand or so Baptists who had constituted the movement in the early eighteenth century had increased over ten fold.[11] It was the infusion of spiritual vitality via the Evangelical Revival which transformed the small, sober older dissenting body in which Joshua Thomas had been raised, into the vibrant, populist denomination which would become so remarkably successful during the mid-nineteenth century. There were transitional figures who spanned both eras; the most significant from the standpoint of this chapter was Titus Lewis, pastor, lexicographer and theologian and author of an accomplished historical tome *Hanes Prydain Fawr* (*A History of Great Britain*) (1811). For Lewis, as for virtually all of his co-religionists of the time, Whig sensibilities and a loyalty to the crown went hand in hand with a pronounced Welsh patriotism and a staunch evangelical faith. These commitments were complementary rather than conflicting, part of the seamless robe of Welsh Nonconformist identity preserving continuity with the past and a basis for further growth. It was, though, with the hugely popular revivalist preacher Christmas Evans that the values of the Evangelical Revival wholly replaced the older dissenting mean.

Christmas Evans was no radical. His fawning conservatism subsequent generations have found embarrassing in the extreme: 'It is not the province of

---

[9] Joshua Thomas, *Hanes y Bedyddwyr ymhlith y Cymry* (Caerfyrddin: John Ross, 1778), p. xvi.

[10] Thomas, *Hanes y Bedyddwyr*, pp. xiii, xix.

[11] See D. Densil Morgan, '"Smoke, Fire and Light": Baptists and the Revitalisation of Welsh Dissent', *Baptist Quarterly* 32.5 (January, 1988), pp. 224-32.

Christians', he declared on behalf of his fellow ministers of the Anglesey Association in 1817

> to debate and discuss politics—but to behave humbly towards our superiors... We do not feel the least interest in the great noise about universal suffrage, annual Parliaments, reform of Parliament, abolishing of the tithe and many other things... From agrarian laws and Spencean principles good Lord deliver us. We do cordially hate the political leaven of Cobbett, Tom Paine and other anarchists... How unbecoming, how vain it is for the commoner people to engage in political debates.[12]

T.M. Bassett's retort that it was impossible for lackeyism to sink deeper rather understates the truth.[13] Here was loyalty towards the crown taken to an absurd extreme with self-respect being offered up on the altar of a pietism of the most offensive kind. Be that as it may, Evans was uncontrovertibly Welsh; he spoke little English—the article quoted above must have been translated for him—and that which he did was broken and stilted, yet it was he more than anyone else who sustained a movement which had become genuinely national in scope. The Baptists had broken out of their south Wales heartland in 1776 sending a mission into the north. The first north Wales church was planted in 1779 and from then on the movement had included the whole of Wales in its remit. Evans, who had been born into a poor Presbyterian family in the rural south-west in 1766, had moved north in 1789, to pastor churches first on Caernarfonshire's Lleyn peninsula moving to Anglesey in 1791. His long ministry on the island witnessed spectacular revivalistic growth and by the time that he had left for Caerphilly in the soon-to-be-industrialised valleys of south-east Wales in 1826, the Baptist movement had been wholly transformed. No longer was it small, select, introverted with a high church ethos of Calvinistic exactitude, but a vibrant missionary movement, more interested in expansion and growth than in doctrinal precision and ecclesiastical purism. What is more, its churches were being replicated throughout the land in the industrialised south as well as the rural north, with baptisms more than keeping pace with the explosion in the Welsh population which was occurring at the time. Evans's annual preaching tour, like a medieval pilgrimage which took him on a circuit throughout Wales, helped enormously to establish the Baptists as a unified movement. Districts and associations came to be bound together in a specifically national unit. Evans may have been surprised by the effect (and the effectiveness) of his work but it was he, more than anyone else, who by the first quarter of the nineteenth century had created a single Welsh denomination.[14]

By the time of Christmas Evans's death in 1838 a new Wales had been born and Dissent, or Protestant Nonconformity, was no longer peripheral but central to its

---

[12] *North Wales Gazette*, 27 March 1817.
[13] T.M. Bassett, *Bedyddwyr Cymru* (Abertawe: Gwasg Ilston, 1977), p. 124.
[14] See D. Densil Morgan, 'Christmas Evans and the birth of Nonconformist Wales', *Baptist Quarterly* 34 (1991), pp. 116-124.

existence. The Religious Census of 1851 proved what many had suspected for decades, that the Established Church had lost out to the chapels; the statistics proved that five times as many Welshmen and women attended Nonconformist services than those who harkened to the peal of the bells in the parish church. A new voluntary, popular establishment had been forged independent of the state church. Religious revivalism, endemic since the eighteenth century, had drawn tens of thousands from a formal affiliation to the Anglican way into the orbit of an ever-more populist, radical, egalitarian Dissent. The Baptists, already metamorphosed into an energetic missionary force, were transformed into a vast, truly national religio-cultural movement. By 1866 (the year which saw the creation of the Baptist Union of Wales) there were 558 churches in eleven associations, 66,500 church members and as many as 80,000 adherents, that is, those who although not formally church members would attend regularly at the preaching of the Word. Thirty years later, in 1890, there were 850 Baptist fellowships in Wales, 95,000 members and well over 130,000 adherents,[15] and even then the Baptists were only the third largest Nonconformist denomination; the Congregationalists were larger and the Calvinistic Methodists more extensive still. There is little wonder that Wales, that 'nation of Nonconformists', was revered as being one of the most heavily Christianized countries in all of Europe.

This movement, in all, was assertively Welsh. It was partly because of the utilization of the Welsh language, which was the only language of many of the people, that Nonconformity succeeded as it did. Nineteenth-century Welsh Nonconformity was of the people, by the people and for the people, a hugely popular religious option unencumbered by a socially superior, hierarchical church government which represented the interests of an alien class. It was egalitarian and populist empowering the people by giving them a vital faith and the Bible, in Welsh, as *their* book. Hence the remarkable flowering of biblical, expository and didactic literature which turned Wales into a reading nation as well as a highly Christianized one. Political radicalization soon, and inevitably, followed, and with the widening of the franchise a deep divide opened up between a populist, politically progressive, Welsh-medium Nonconformity on the one hand, and a beleaguered though still socially privileged, Tory, Anglophone Established Church on the other. The Baptist leaders of mid-century would no longer espouse the fawning pietism of a Christmas Evans or suffer the indignities of life as second-class citizens. Assertive Welshness became a badge of their collective identity, and their taking of bardic names—'Cynddelw' (Robert Ellis), 'Nefydd' (William Roberts), 'Lleurwg' (John Rhys Morgan)—and revelling in such cultural forms as the eisteddfod and traditional Welsh poetry, defined their witness and their life.

Yet there were ambiguities, too, which increased as the years went by. For many the use of Welsh was pragmatic rather than principled. As the language of the people

---

[15] For the relevant statistics see D. Densil Morgan (ed.), *Y Fywiol Ffrwd: Bywyd a Thystiolaeth Bedyddwyr Cymru, 1649–1999* (Abertawe: Gwasg Ilston, 1999), pp. 24, 38.

it was an essential means of communication, evangelisation and worship, but because English was the language of government, status and the law, there was an incipient sense of inferiority, of shame even, attached to use of the native tongue. Whereas there were those who took pride in the language as being ancient and dextrous through which a Christian civilisation had manifested itself for a thousand years and more, there were others—Welsh to a man—who were embarrassed by a peasant culture so lacking in prestige. The tensions between Micah Thomas, first principal of the Abergavenny Baptist College, founded in 1807, and some of the college's most influential potential supporters led by John Jenkins, Baptist minister at Hengoed, Glamorganshire, illustrated this clearly. Although Thomas knew Welsh, he thought it rustic and uncouth; he had no particular feeling for Welsh nationality and thought Anglicization not only inevitable but a blessing which would open up Wales to England and the world. Jenkins, the Welsh Baptist movement's most accomplished theologian of his generation, took an enormous pride in the Welsh language, its beauty, rich literature and antiquity, and berated Thomas for outlawing it among his students and refusing it a place on the curriculum.

These tensions illustrated the basic ambivalence which afflicted Welsh opinion at the time. It came to a head in the so-called *Brad y Llyfrau Gleision* (*The Treachery of the Blue Books*), the government report on education in Wales in 1847 in which the English establishment blamed what they regarded as the backwardness of the Welsh people on the twin evils of Nonconformity and the Welsh language. The outcry was fierce but the psychological damage had been done. Despite the pugnacious defence of popular Welsh Nonconformity so ably marshalled by Henry Richard MP, Ieuan Gwynedd and others, a whole generation of ministers, elders and laymen, had been stung. Their feelings of cultural inferiority had been unmasked and they determined that never again would their social 'superiors' be given grounds for decrying their values and their norms. For many it meant rejecting Welsh culture as indeed mediocre and uncouth.

It was during this very time that the Welsh Baptist movement expanded most rapidly and its institutions made sound. The Abergavenny College, removed to Pontypool in 1836, was eventually transferred to Cardiff in 1892 where it flourishes to this day as the South Wales Baptist College. A second ministerial training college at Haverfordwest, Pembrokeshire, was established in 1840 partly to offset the Anglicizing influences of Pontypool. It moved to Aberystwyth in 1894 and amalgamated with Cardiff and Bangor in 1899. The north Wales college had been formed at Llangollen in 1862 and transferred to the university city of Bangor in 1892 where it still serves the Welsh-speaking churches of the Baptist Union of Wales. The Union was instigated in 1866 as an umbrella organisation linking churches and associations and spawning its own sub-organisations, the Baptist Temperance Society, the Sunday Schools Council, the Historical Society and the rest. A vigorous press serviced these various causes including *Seren Gomer* (*The Star of Gomer*), Wales's oldest regular Welsh language periodical (1814), *Yr Athraw* (*The Teacher*) for the use of the Sunday schools (1827), the weekly newspaper *Seren Cymru* (*Star of Wales*) (1851) and the monthly *Y Greal* (*The Grail*) (1852). The burgeoning Welsh Baptist communities in the United States had their own periodical *Y Seren Orllewinol* (*The Star of the West*) between 1846 and 1867. All in all, Baptist life in Wales was thriving as never before, activities being conducted almost exclusively through the medium of Welsh, though the ambiguities mentioned above were constantly present. They would only deepen as the Victorian era progressed.

By the late nineteenth century it was obvious that Wales was undergoing fundamental social and cultural change. Secondary education, along English lines, had already been made compulsory in the 1870s. The establishment in 1872 of what would become the University of Wales not only gave Nonconformist youth the opportunity for higher education long denied them since Oxford and Cambridge had been closed to all but Anglicans, but introduced them to potentially troubling trends of critical thought including Darwinism and the like. Whereas Welsh had been seen as a bulwark against secularising trends, it was clear by the 1890s that the Welsh themselves were keen to share all the benefits of Victorian progress even if this meant—sometimes *because* it meant—embracing English mores. By now the ambivalence which had afflicted Welsh national consciousness since the 'Blue Books' controversy, manifested itself even more sharply: some Nonconformists revelled in the conquests of the British—read *English*—empire upon which the sun would never set, while others became even more tenacious in preserving those linguistic values which the chapel culture had enshrined. This also had implications for the older, dual allegience to Britishness *and* to Wales: the tensions would, for some, become unbearable and they would feel that they would have to choose between the two. With the influx of English migrants into the industrialized valleys of the south and along the seaboard of the north, Baptists, ever an evangelistic folk, needed to cater for changing times. More and more churches in south Wales switched to English—there had been two English-speaking associations since mid-century, Monmouthshire (1857) and Glamorgan and Carmarthen (1860)—but it was only as late as 1921 that the English Assembly of the Baptist Union of Wales was formed.

By then things had changed irrevocably. The Great War had been the great divide. Even before the war there were ominous signs that Welsh Nonconformity, previously remarkable for holding the allegiance of the male working class, was being superseded by the secular ideology of socialism and the Labour movement. The religious revival of 1904 did little to halt this trend. By the 1920s secularism was proceeding apace while Nonconformity, though still massively present throughout Wales, was showing signs of serious strain. In some parts of the country, the north-eastern areas and the valleys of east and mid-Glamorgan, Welsh was being superseded by English and Welsh identity was having to be redefined. Because of the close interconnection of Nonconformity and what many considered to be 'the Welsh way of life', the impact upon religion was profound.[16] For the next

---

[16] See D. Densil Morgan, 'The Welsh Language and Religion', in Geraint H. Jenkins (ed.), *'Let's Do Our Best for the Ancient Tongue': The Welsh Language in the Twentieth Century* (Cardiff: University of Wales Press, 2000), pp. 371-96.

half-century, until the virtual demise of 'Nonconformist Wales' in the 1980s or so, the survival of Welsh seemed to be bound up with the fate of chapel life.[17]

During the twentieth century there were those in the Welsh Baptist churches who exemplified each of the prevailing trends. Political nationalism with its embodiment in Plaid Genedlaethol Cymru (later Plaid Cymru), established in 1925, attracted modest Baptist support, with such revered denominational figures as Lewis Valentine and D. Eirwyn Morgan being actively involved in its campaigns. Valentine, Baptist minister in Llandudno, latterly at Rhos, near Wrexham, was the party's first parliamentary candidate, in Caernarfon, in 1929, while Morgan, a graduate of Regent's Park College, Oxford, and principal of the Bangor Baptist College, stood for the Llanelli constituency in 1951, 1955 and 1959. There were other Baptist ministers and laypeople who were more wary of nationalist claims and preferred to define their national identity less in linguistic than in communitarian or even socialist terms. This was especially true of the English language churches of the south-east. The ethos of the English wing of the Baptist Union of Wales has been less radical and less politically engaged than that of the union as a whole, and with the seismic social changes of recent decades, it has tended to replicate the conventional evangelicalism of mainstream British Christianity than to forge an identity which is uniquely Welsh.

The Christian gospel is incarnational or it is nothing. There is no gospel which does not manifest itself in a specific context, in a time and in a place. The divine does not bypass the flesh, therefore questions of history, culture and identity are inevitable and theologically valid. By allowing a theology of redemption to eclipse a sound doctrine of creation, and even more by narrowing redemption to questions of personal salvation alone, there are Christians who have done an injustice to the truth; which brings us back to where we began. It is only when our personal, or national, or cultural, or ethnic identity reflects the balance of scripture, Old Testament as well as New, that justice will be done. When the great doctrines of the faith—creation, incarnation and a redemption which does not spiritualize historical realities in a docetic fashion—are allowed to control our witness and our thought, will we be in a position to consider matters of identity as contributing to rather than detracting from the integrity of the gospel. A commitment to a land and a history and a people need not conflict with an obedience to the lordship of Christ but rather inform it and be made necessary by it. It was Karl Barth who said about his people, the Swiss: 'We cannot leave the ship, even if it is in sorry straits or sinking.' Rather, we 'must affirm the presuppositions of our [people's] past and in our own place and time take up and genuinely share the problems of its future'.[18] That applies to Wales as much as to anywhere else.

---

[17] I have discussed this in more detail in D. Densil Morgan, '"The Essence of Welshness"?: Some Aspects of Christian Faith and National Identity in Wales c.1900–2000', in Robert Pope (ed.), *Religion and National Identity: Scotland and Wales c.1730–2000* (Cardiff: University of Wales Press, 2001), pp. 139-62.

[18] Barth, *Church Dogmatics*, III/4, p. 295, translation revised.

CHAPTER 4

The Call of the Minister and Character of the Church: Baptist Identity at Morningside Baptist Church, Edinburgh, since 1894

John R. Barclay

Introduction

This short study is an attempt at identifying how one Baptist church in Edinburgh, Scotland—Morningside Baptist Church—has called its ministers since its foundation in 1894, and how these fit in with aspects of Baptist identity. The membership of Morningside has, over the years, reflected the nature of the district in which it is placed, although it draws its congregation from many parts of the city. It has been and is mainly a church with a membership of people from professional work backgrounds. Within the context of Baptist churches in Scotland, and also within England and Wales, those which are self supporting can do their own thing as far as calling a minister is concerned. Many Baptist churches have a constitution and/or trust documents which lay down the procedures to be adopted in the calling of a minister, conditions such as that the minister must be baptised by immersion as a believer and must be an accredited minister or probationer of a Baptist Union. Morningside has no formal constitution. It only has a Foundation Covenant.[1] This does not lay down any requirements for the pastor nor how that person is to be selected. Throughout its history Morningside has kept to its Baptist identity by always requiring the pastor to be baptised by immersion as a believer and to be an accredited minister or probationer of a Baptist Union.

The Priesthood of all Believers

One of the chief characteristics of Baptist identity is the priesthood of all believers. In the calling of ministers to Morningside, in common with churches in the Baptist Union of Scotland and in the Baptist Union of Great Britain, every member has the responsibility of seeking and being guided by the Holy Spirit in the choice of

---

[1] Church minutes. All the references in this paper are to material held at Morningside Baptist Church. The references to minutes up to 1973 are based on typed minutes from the original minute books, as these minute books were damaged by fire in 1973 and are fragile to handle. The page numbers refer to the typed minutes.

minister. Normally this choice is exercised in the church meeting by the members present.

The person who was the founding father of Morningside Baptist Church was the Rev. J. Cumming Brown. He was minister of Leith Baptist Church and saw that there was potential for a Baptist witness in the growing suburb of Morningside in the southern part of Edinburgh. He was especially encouraged when he found out that the Morningside Free Church of Scotland (Presbyterian) building was for sale, as that congregation was moving to a larger building about eighty metres up the road. The Free Church congregation did not want the building to fall into the hands of the 'Romanists', who were looking for premises in Morningside. Cumming Brown resigned from the pastorate of Leith Baptist Church.[2] On 7 October 1894 Morningside Baptist Church was established with sixteen people present, including Cumming Brown and his wife. The meeting then heard Cumming Brown read 1 Timothy 3.1-7, containing the Lord's instructions about the office and character of pastors, and he pointed out the duty of the church to proceed to call one if there was unanimity of mind with regard to it. Two men proposed that Cumming Brown be called to the pastorate. An opportunity was given for other names to be proposed or suggestions made. As there were no other suggestions the name of Cumming Brown was put to the meeting, and was accepted unanimously.[3]

For the calling of the next three pastors, the Revs E.G. Lovell, B.J. Cole and F.M. Hirst, the call decision was made by those present and voting at a church meeting.[4] Voting at these three meetings was by a show of hands.[5] For the call of the Rev. John P. Leng in 1943 it was decided by the church meeting 'that any vote for a call shall be by ballot, and that a two-thirds majority of those present and voting shall carry a decision. For those returning a ballot paper shall be considered as present and voting, but any papers not showing a vote either for or against shall be ignored for all purposes.'[6] Since then the call of all ministers has been done in a similar way. Members could vote whether or not they had heard the minister lead a service and preach. This was altered slightly for the call of the Rev. Andrew Rollinson in 1995, when it was agreed that a member had to have heard him lead worship and preach before they could vote. Attendance at the church meeting was not required.[7]

How does this ability to vote on the very important calling of God's servant by everyone, even if they are not present at the church meeting, fit with the Baptist identity of the supremacy of the church meeting in decision-making for the church? Or is it stressing the priesthood of all believers, so that all can take part? Having been a member in four churches in England, and having contacts with a number of

---

[2] Church Minutes 1894–1905, p. 1.
[3] Church Minutes 1894–1905, p. 3.
[4] Church Minutes 1894–1905, p. 21; Church Minutes January 1913–May 1923, p. 6.
[5] Church Minutes 1894–1905, p. 21; Church Minutes 1913–1923, p. 6; Church Minutes 1923–1928, p. 4.
[6] Church Minutes January 1943–December 1950, p. 1.
[7] Vacancy Committee Minutes 18 April 1994, minute 4.1.

others, I know that in these churches members can only vote if they are present at the relevant church meeting. This is not to say that all churches in the Baptist Union of Great Britain follow that practice.

Vacancy Committee (Pastorate Committee)[8]

In the situation in the United Kingdom, when a church has no pastor and is seeking one, the church sets up a Vacancy Committee to search for a new pastor. In many churches in the Baptist Union of Great Britain (BUGB) the Vacancy Committee is the diaconate. In the BUGB booklet 'Advice for Churches in a Pastoral Vacancy' it is assumed that the deacons, and elders if any, will form the Vacancy Committee. There is a paragraph, which says, 'Occasionally the church feels the need to create a Pastorate Committee. If such is considered desirable all the deacons should serve on that committee, and only a few others should be added.'[9] The Baptist Union of Scotland (BUS) has a similar booklet, *Practical Guide lines for Churches in Seeking a Pastor/Minister*. Many paragraphs are exactly the same as those of the BUGB booklet, but one difference is that the Pastorate Committee (Vacancy Committee) usually consists of either all the deacons plus a number of others, or some deacons plus a number of others. In Scotland it is expected that members of the Vacancy Committee will be drawn from the wider membership.[10]

How has Morningside dealt with who should Consider Possible Pastors?

In 1898 when Cumming Brown announced that he would retire at the end of the following year the church committee met at Cumming Brown's home.[11] As the membership in 1898 was forty-one there was no diaconate so a church committee considered three names brought before it.[12] A call was sent to the Rev. Ernest G. Lovell of Chipping Norton in Oxfordshire, who began his ministry in 1900.[13] Unfortunately Lovell died in 1912 at the age of only forty-five.[14] During his

---

[8] Historically the term Vacancy Committee has been used by both the Baptist Union of Great Britain and the Baptist Union of Scotland. In the latter's booklet, *Practical Guidelines for Churches Seeking a Pastor/Minister* (Glasgow: Baptist Union of Scotland, n.d.), p. 7, the heading given is 'Pastorate Committee (Formerly Vacancy Committee)', while the BUGB's booklet, *Advice for Churches in a Pastoral Vacancy* (Didcot: Baptist Union of Great Britain, n.d.), p. 12, says 'Occasionally the church feels the need to create a Pastorate Committee'. In its 2003 vacancy Morningside continued to use 'Vacancy Committee' in order to avoid confusion with the 'Pastoral Committee'.
[9] *Advice for Churches in a Pastoral Vacancy*, p. 12.
[10] *Practical Guidelines for Churches Seeking a Pastor/Minister*, p. 7.
[11] Church Minutes 1894–1905, p. 20.
[12] Church Minutes 1894–1905, p. 20.
[13] Church Minutes 1894–1905, p. 22.
[14] Church Minutes January 1913–May 1923, p. 1.

ministry the membership had grown from fifty-eight to 247. A Vacancy Committee was then set up to seek a successor, but the church record, deacons' minutes, elders' minutes, and church meeting minutes do not record any details. The Vacancy Committee recommended to the church meeting that the Rev. John McBeath of Cambuslang Baptist Church be invited as pastor. The church meeting unanimously agreed an invitation be sent.[15] There is no mention of John McBeath preaching at Morningside. There is also no further reference to John McBeath, not even a note saying that the invitation was declined. In April 1913, the church meeting considered a further recommendation from the Vacancy Committee that an invitation be sent to the Rev. B.J. Cole of Orangefield Baptist Church, Greenock. The congregation had not heard Cole preach in Morningside, but some of the Vacancy Committee had been sent as a deputation to Orangefield to hear him.[16] Therefore, a very small group of the membership had really made the decision. Does this show the trust the membership had in those who went to Greenock?

In the Spring of 1924, for the call of Rev. F.M. Hirst, who had returned from India having served with the Baptist Missionary Society at Serampore College, the only reference in the minutes is that the Vacancy Committee was unanimous in recommending his name to the church meeting. This recommendation was unanimously accepted by a show of hands.[17] Hirst had the longest pastorate at Morningside, lasting just over eighteen years, until 1942. In the 1930s there were discussions about whether or not there had been a time limit on the call. Some members said that Hirst had been called for five or seven years and that this was in the letter of invitation, however Hirst denied this. There is no reference in the minutes, as the seven years ended in 1931, to any discussion of the matter. The points were raised in 1938 when some elders and deacons felt that Hirst had been there long enough.[18]

Before an invitation was sent to the Rev. John P. Leng of Motherwell Baptist Church, who succeeded Hirst, the church meeting unanimously agreed that the call was for five years.[19] This was obviously a reaction to a long ministry. While there is no record in the minutes of the composition of the Vacancy Committee there is a notebook kept by the church secretary of the minutes of the Vacancy Sub-Committee.[20] From the attendance at the Sub-Committee it can be worked out that there were at least two women (Mrs Rattray and Miss Middleton) serving on it.[21] At that time, Morningside, in common with many Baptist churches, had an all male eldership and diaconate. As a number of Baptist churches in Scotland still have an all male diaconate and/or eldership the addition of others to the Vacancy Committee does

---

[15] Church Minutes 1913–1923, p. 1.

[16] Church Minutes 1913–1923, p. 6.

[17] Church Minutes 1923–1928, p. 4.

[18] Deacons Meeting Minutes November 1927–June 1939, p. 80.

[19] Church Minutes 1943–1950, p. 1.

[20] Vacancy Sub-Committee — notebook begun by Alex McKinlay, church secretary. The pages of the notebook are unnumbered.

[21] Vacancy Sub-Committee Notebook, pp. 2 and 13.

allow women to be chosen. (Incidentally, the eldership at Morningside was abolished in 1946.[22]) In order to get a cross-section of the membership, members were added to the Vacancy Committee.

This pattern of having all the deacons on the Vacancy Committee plus others of the membership continued for the next four calls to the pastorate, those of the Revs A. Campbell Dovey in 1949, T. Kerr Spiers 1957, Peter Webb in 1968, and Peter Bowes in 1975. The complete Vacancy Committee became a committee of twenty-four in 1948, twenty-five in 1957, twenty-four again in 1967, and thirty-one in 1975.[23] This was too large a committee to consider those who might be called to the pastorate. So, as had happened in 1943, a Sub-Committee of seven or eight was appointed from the whole Committee. This Sub-Committee included the church secretary and treasurer. At least two of the Sub-Committee were not deacons. The need to have female representation on the Vacancy Committee began to break down as women became eligible for the diaconate after 1965.[24] It appears from the notebook of the Sub-Committee kept by the church secretary and his successors that the Sub-Committee really did the work. It seems that the full Vacancy Committee endorsed the recommendations of the Sub-Committee.

For the calling of the Rev. T.J. Harkin in 1990 and the Rev. Andrew Rollinson in 1995, it was agreed that the Vacancy Committee would consist of eight deacons, chosen by the deacons from a diaconate of eighteen, and eight members, chosen by the church meeting.[25] The church secretary was an ex-officio member. The church meeting also agreed that the pastorate was open to women candidates, which was unusual for a Baptist church in Scotland.[26] On neither occasion was a woman considered for the pastorate.

Percentage of Votes Required for a Call: Is there a Baptist Position?

At Morningside, up until the calling of F.M. Hirst in 1924, all the calls of the first four ministers were unanimous. It is interesting that before the final decision was made to call Ernest Lovell in 1898 the church heard three ministers on three successive Sundays. At the church meeting in the week after the three men had been heard, the meeting voted on all three. They then dropped the one with the least votes and proceeded to vote on the two remaining candidates, with Ernest Lovell receiving the greater number of votes. The meeting then agreed to send a unanimous call![27] It

---

[22] Church Minutes 1943–1950, p. 20.

[23] Church Minutes 1943–1950, p. 20; Vacancy Committee Sub-Committee Notebook, pp. 23, 47, 60 and 68

[24] The minute book covering the 1960s is currently missing. There is a reference to two women standing for election in church meeting minutes.

[25] Church Meeting 19 January 1989, Item 4, p. 26; and Church Meeting 24 February 1994, Item 4, p. 56.

[26] Church Meeting 20 April 1989, Item 4, p. 34.

[27] Church Minutes 1894–1905, p. 21.

seems that a unanimous call was sought even when the membership had reached over 200.

For the call of John Leng, however, a two-thirds majority of those present and voting was enough for a call.[28] It has already been noted that all the members had a vote. The ballot paper could be returned even if the member was not going to be present at the church meeting. In the event, John Leng received the votes of a majority of 79% of those voting.[29] Campbell Dovey received 80.34%, while Kerr Spiers received 78.7%.[30] The percentage figure for Peter Webb is not available but for Peter Bowes it was 89.7%.[31] For the calls given to Terry Harkin and Andrew Rollinson it was agreed that they had to receive at least 80% of the vote cast.[32] This was a recognition of the fact that to have a third of the voters giving a negative vote was too high a percentage against. Even expecting 80% meant that two out of every ten would have voted against the minister. With both Terry Harkin and Andrew Rollinson they received over 90% support.[33]

Ministers Chosen from within the Church

Twice Morningside has chosen ministers from within the membership. These have served alongside another minister, a 'senior' minister. David Wright, in December 1978, offered his services on a part-time basis as an unpaid ministerial assistant to serve primarily in pastoral work. This offer was welcomed with acclamation at a church meeting.[34] Wright, who had been involved in school social work and as a lecturer, was given time to study for the Cambridge Diploma in Religious Studies. In 1986, as the church was growing, he was invited to become a full-time assistant on a paid basis.[35] He served in this way until 1989, when he went to Tonbridge Baptist Church in Kent in a similar post.[36] Jeremy Balfour, who became the pastor's assistant in 2000, had become a member of Morningside while he was the Parliamentary Officer for the Evangelical Alliance (Scotland). He trained as a lawyer but then gained a degree in theology at London Bible College and as a Baptist minister at the Scottish Baptist College. He began helping Andrew Rollinson in various ways and then became pastor's assistant with the agreement of the church meeting.[37] This seems to be a present day variation of an older way of pastors being

---

[28] Church Minutes 1943–1950, p. 1.

[29] Church Minutes 1943–1950, p. 1.

[30] Church Minutes 1943–1950, p, 24; Church Minutes 14 November 1957.

[31] Information from Christine Rutter, member of the Vacancy Committee and Church Meeting 7 July 1975, p. 96.

[32] Church Meeting 19 January 1989, and Deacons' Conference January 1995.

[33] Church Meeting 1990, and Church Meeting 1995.

[34] Special Church Meeting 21 December 1978, p. 4.

[35] Church Meeting 17 April 1986.

[36] Church Meeting 19 January 1989, Item 3, p. 26.

[37] Church Meeting 17 February 2000, Item 5.

chosen for service in a church.[38] Is this a development of a former Baptist identity?[39] Certainly Morningside has changed its thinking and procedures regarding the calling of ministers from time to time, while retaining a key requirement that the pastor be baptised by immersion as a believer and be an accredited minister or probationer of a Baptist Union.[40]

[38] For this practice, see S.J. Price, *Upton: The Story of One Hundred and Fifty Years* (London: Carey Press, 1935), pp. 69-82 (with thanks to Professor John H.Y. Briggs for this reference).

[39] For historical summaries of the calling of ministers and contemporary studies, see, e.g., *The Doctrine of the Ministry* (London: Baptist Union of Great Britain and Ireland, 1961), and a more recent discussion in Paul S. Fiddes, *Tracks and Traces: Baptist Identity in Church and Theology* (Studies in Baptist History and Thought, 13; Carlisle: Paternoster Press, 2003, 'Authority in Relations between Pastor and People: A Baptist Doctrine of Ministry', pp. 83-106.

[40] There is not space to look more widely at the Baptist Union of Scotland and its procedures for helping churches seek pastors, especially the help given through the Superintendent of the Union (now, in Scotland, Ministry Advisor), who works closely with the Superintendents, now Regional Ministers, in the Baptist Union of Great Britain.

CHAPTER 5

Julius Köbner's Contribution to Baptist Identity

Erich Geldbach

Introduction

The pioneer of Baptists on the European continent, Johann Gerhard Oncken (1800–84), is mentioned in many books, even text books that deal with church history. That he had two strong companions, who exerted equal influence in shaping the Baptist community, is less known. One was the Baptist leader in Berlin, Gottfried Wilhelm Lehmann (1799–1882), who had converted from the Moravians, and the other was Julius Köbner (1806–84), the subject of this study, who was baptized by Oncken in 1836 and served as Baptist minister in Hamburg, Barmen, Kopenhagen and Berlin.

Some biographical data is important. Köbner was born on 6 June 1806 as Salomon Köbner, the son of the rabbi in Odense, Denmark. His parents dedicated him to God to become also a rabbi. From 1810 to 1822 he attended school in Odense where he became familiar with German, English and French. He then learnt a trade as an engraver (*Graveur*), and in 1824 he moved to Lübeck where he had intimate conversations with the pastor of the Reformed Church, Dr Geibel, father of the poet Emanuel Geibel. He apparently was inclined towards accepting Christianity, but did not convert. Instead, he moved to Hamburg where he worked in his trade, but also gave private language lessons and wrote occasional pieces of poetry. One of his students was twenty-two year old Juliane Johanna Wilhelmine v. Schröter, the daughter of a Prussian officer in the service of Denmark. They fell in love and promised to be faithful to each other. A year later, 31 July 1826, Köbner received Christian baptism at the hands of Pastor Mutzenbecher in Hamburg's St Peter's Church. He dropped his first name Salomon in favour of Julius Johannes Wilhelm, the male equivalents of his fiancé's first names. As a next step he asked v. Schröter for his daughter, but the Prussian officer declined, whereupon Köbner wrote a letter to the Danish king to ask for the king's permission to marry Juliane. The marriage took place on 29 December 1826. In 1827 their first child, a son, died only a few weeks after he was born.[1]

---

[1] Cf. the biography of Köbner's daughter Ruth Baresel, *Julius Köbner: Sein Leben* (Kassel: Verlag von J.G. Oncken Nachfolger, 1930), pp. 28-32.

In the ensuing years Köbner made a few inventions as far as the printing press is concerned, but received only honorary recognition and no financial compensation. He also wrote a play entitled 'Denmark's First Sovereign. A National Play in Five Acts. With a Prologue on the Occasion of the 25th. Jubilee of King Frederick VI'. It was printed in Altona, today a suburb of Hamburg, but then a separate city under Danish rule. The play depicts the wise rule of the God-fearing Danish king Frederick III in 1660, who with the help of bishop Swane and mayor Nansen managed to unite the nobility and the peasants. Both pillars of society voluntarily agreed to be taxed so that the country's poor condition was improved. The play was performed several times in the principality of Holstein.

In 1834 Köbner and his wife moved to Hamburg where his brother ran a printing press. Julius had also won first prize in a contest in which he proposed to have orphans work with straw as it was an easy way for children to learn. His wife was asked to put his ideas into practice and to teach orphans in several institutions. These were, apparently, the reasons for the couple's move to Hamburg. In the same year, the first Baptist church in that city was founded when Barnas Sears of Hamilton College, USA, baptized Oncken and a handful of his followers in the River Elbe. It seems that in 1836 it was Köbner's wife Juliane who first came into contact with the small Baptist group and with Oncken himself. At first Köbner refused to attend a service, but later did, and after carefully considering the teaching of conversion and baptism, he was baptized on 26 May 1836 and accepted into church membership. His wife followed a few weeks later, as did three of his siblings. Köbner and Oncken soon became friends; Köbner worked for Oncken as translator of English tracts, proofreader and hymn writer. Oncken, in turn, introduced Köbner to the art of public speaking. Upon Oncken's recommendation Köbner and his wife applied for citizenship in the city of Hamburg.

Köbner soon became very active in the cause of the Baptist movement. On several occasions he was arrested and jailed for illegal religious activities. At the request of the city authorities, Köbner compiled a confession of faith which later became the basis for the official Baptist confession.[2] He also travelled throughout Germany and Denmark. In Denmark he found a circle of people who were open to his teaching. When in the autumn of 1839 he returned with Oncken, the latter baptized eleven people upon their confession of faith. Thus the first Danish Baptist church was established. By that time Köbner was well integrated into the young Baptist movement in continental Europe, working side by side with Oncken and being sent across the country. In August 1844 Oncken ordained Köbner to the ministry. Thus he became one of the formative leaders of the Baptists in Germany and Denmark. What were his contributions to Baptist identity?

---

[2] For details, cf. Günter Balders, *Theurer Bruder Oncken. Das Leben Johann Gerhard Onckens in Bildern und Dokumenten* (Wuppertal/Kassel: Oncken Verlag, 1978) pp. 53-54, 87-90.

Conversion and Baptism

As Köbner converted twice to Christianity, it must be assumed that he did not consider his first conversion adequate after he had learnt of the Baptists. What made Baptists so attractive that he changed his religious affiliation again? The key may be the ideas of conversion and baptism as this was what he respected most after he had come into contact with the small Baptist group in Hamburg. How is a person added to the church is the question which he put to the children in his catechism, and the answer is: '[the person] must be born again, come to a recognition of sin, believe in the gospel and change his or her mind and way of living (*Wandel*)'.[3] The entire process is initiated and brought forth by the Holy Spirit. Köbner is very careful to emphasize God's initiative, for it is the Spirit that creates a new heart and a new will and thus grants an erstwhile spiritually dead person spiritual life. Sin is, therefore, the separation of the human person from God. The Holy One is insulted by the sinfulness of humans, but the Spirit works out a new conviction of the heart that replaces the old way of life. The nature of conversion is that it is worked out by God and that it aims toward God. Thus a believer is a person who holds true that which the Scriptures teach about Christ and his full salvation. When a person's faith grows stronger, he or she will delight in the Lord with 'unspeakable gladness'.[4] The change of mind is, therefore, radical: it goes to the very root (*radix*) of a person. What the person used to hate because of the sinful state, he or she now enjoys, and what that person used to love, i.e. ungodly and worldly behavior, he or she now hates. After such an experience, a person is accepted into the church by water baptism.

Köbner's first contribution to Baptist identity is a distinct theology of conversion. Conversion is not what a person can do by his or her free will. The sinfulness of the human heart and the holiness of God are so far apart that a human cannot, by his or her own volition, approach the Holy One. Rather, God must take the sole initiative and radically change the nature of the human heart. In his exposition of Jacob's struggle, Köbner comes to the conclusion that God condescends. It is not we that struggle with God, even though we are, as individuals, indispensably involved in a struggle, but it is rather God's 'eternal', 'unspeakable' and 'motherly' love that struggles with us.[5] The response of a person is faith, which is initially weak, but becomes stronger as the believer lives a life of godliness. All of this is wrought by God and directed toward his glory and to the person's enjoyment. That a person may now love what he once hated and now hates what he once loved, indicates, however, that the human being is personally involved in the process. Conversion, or re-birth, cannot be declared at an infant's birth. Therefore, infant baptism must be rejected.

This is his second contribution: Köbner developed a definite concept of baptism. Baptism is through immersion and in the name of the Triune God—Father, Son and

---

[3] Julius Köbner, *Leitfaden durch die Bibel für Kinder* (Hamburg: Verlag von J.G. Oncken, 1858), p. 77.

[4] Köbner, *Leitfaden*, pp. 77-78.

[5] At various points I have drawn from Köbner's unprinted sermons.

Holy Spirit. It is a seal of justification and holiness and, therefore, follows immediately after the conversion experience. It is the nature of a seal to show unmistakably that a document has the authorization of the person who signed it. God's document is the new human heart, and God adds his seal to it so that the believer is confirmed in his/her faith. The act of *immersion* is important as it points to the dangerous aspect of water. The very moment when the body is immersed under water baptism is a life-threatening experience. This points to the seriousness of the act of baptism, and Köbner adds that sprinkling cannot convey the seriousness of the situation. Again, the emphasis on seriousness has to do with God's holiness and the radical change of the human heart. For out of the act of immersion emerges a new human being whose body has been buried with Christ in the solemn rite of water baptism. At the same time baptism also incorporates a person visibly into the people of God. God initiates a conversion, grants a new heart, seals this at baptism and thereby adds new members to the body of Christ or to his people.

Free Will and Trinitarian Approach

These two contributions may be interpreted in the fashion of give and take. Köbner became aware of the importance of conversion and baptism through his contacts with Baptists, and he widened the understanding of both through his own approach and thinking. Both contributions, of course, raise the question of free will, which has always been troubling for Baptists. In his catechism for children one of the questions is: 'Is not the human will free so that it can do good or evil?' The answer reads: 'The human will is free, but evil so that of its own, it will choose nothing divinely good.'[6] The human will is totally dependent upon God's action or the working of the Holy Spirit to draw the human person to God and into the fellowship of the church. The believer knows that he/she cannot add anything to his/her salvation, but that Christ did all for him/her. The church is, therefore, a spiritual edifice of living stones. These living stones all know that once they were dead, but are now alive through Christ ,and the preaching of the word which is Christ himself. They responded to the word, to God's call, and are now the bride of Christ. This church first came into being at Pentecost when the Spirit descended upon all its members.

Köbner has a trinitarian approach, usually more implicitly than explicitly even though at times his trinitarianism can be explicit. So, for example, in one of his hymns with three stanzas, which is a prayer at the beginning of a new year; each stanza is addressed to one of the persons of the Trinity.[7] God, the Holy One, the Sovereign Creator, works through his Spirit in the hearts of people and draws them to Christ and into his church. The emphasis on the Holy One, the totally Other,

---

[6] Köbner, *Leitfaden*, p. 24.

[7] Julius Köbner, *Um die Gemeinde. Ausgewählte Schriften von Julius Köbner* (ed. Hermann Gieselbusch; Berlin: Kulturelle Verlagsgesellschaft m.b.H., 1927), p. 28: „*Jahresanfang*": „*Lieber Vater, dir verschreibet / Dieses Häuflein sich auf's Neu [...] Jesu, mit Johannes legen / Wir uns hin an deine Brust. [...] Heil'ger Geist, dir übergeben / Wir den Willen und das Herz.*"

may be interpreted as part of his Jewish upbringing. Köbner found the solution to the question how the One Holy God comes in touch with the people he created in the trinitarian teaching of Christianity: God acts on behalf of Christ through his Spirit and assembles people into Christ's body, the church. Köbner's solution to the questions of free will and the church may be seen as his third and fourth contribution to Baptist identity, and it must be added here that all four distinctives are intimately connected to each other.

Rationalism and View of Scripture

The trinitarian approach is important in one other respect. Köbner thought that he could escape what he referred to as a Christian rationalism. He found this rationalism in, for instance, the controversy between Arminianism and Calvinism. Both parties were, in his opinion, guilty of rationalism because each over-emphasized one aspect of divine truth at the expense of others: a pure Arminian will not entirely give God all the glory because of his own will and work; a pure Calvinist, on the other hand, will not feel any responsibility toward the unconverted and will not, with holy zeal, do mission work. Apparent contradictions in the Bible are not to be rationalized in either direction, so Köbner argued, but are to be seen as coming from God whose wisdom is infinitely higher than our capacity to reach definite conclusions. God's comprehensiveness is not to be explained away in a one-sided fashion. It is of decisive importance, according to Köbner, that heart and head work together and put seemingly contradictory truths into the practice of life. Thus, Baptists need to preach a person's responsibility to be converted. A human person will remain unconverted only because he/she wills to be so. The task of the church is to preach Christ and to tell people to accept Christ's full salvation prayerfully now and so to do the will of God. In other words, the church must tell people to work out their own salvation 'with fear and trembling', and after they have done so, they may be told that it is 'God who is at work in you, both to will and to work for his good pleasure', *das Wollen und das Vollbringen*.[8]

This contribution is what could be referred to as the willingness to keep in tension what cannot be easily understood by the human mind. Behind this appeal is a certain way of looking at Holy Scripture. To be sure, Köbner never used the historical-critical method as it was developed during his day and in his country. That, to him, would have been one kind of rationalism. He rather believed the Bible to be God's word. However, he was not a proto-fundamentalist, because he knew and acknowledged contradictions. The Lord's word is often 'hidden' (*absconditus*), and human words seem to be so much wiser and more glorious. But this is a reflection of God's nature. He is at the same time a *deus absconditus et revelatus*, as Luther put it and as Köbner knew. Köbner emphasized that God's word is Christ, the Lord himself. God's word is not a thing, not even a book, but a person, the God-sent

---

[8] Julius Köbner, *Rationalismus unter den Gläubigen* (n.pl.: n.p., n.d.), p. 8, with reference to Phil. 2.13.

Messiah. This very thought prevented Köbner from becoming a proto-fundamentalist—fundamentalism had not yet been invented. He rightly points out that Holy Scripture is a 'precious plumb line' (*Richtschnur*). A *Richtschnur* is important to construct a building, but it is not the building itself. So also is Holy Scripture the criterion—the ancient church called it the canon—to determine the content of Christianity. This may be an important contribution of Köbner for all Baptists with regard to the basis of the faith.

Christ-Centeredness and Ecumenism

It points to yet another contribution: Köbner's entire theology and witness was Christ-centered. In a sermon note on Hebrews 13.8 ('Jesus Christ yesterday and today and the same throughout eternity') he wrote that Jesus is the only way of salvation. Creation is no salvation, and we humans were not created for creation. We are not our own salvation, and a God without Jesus Christ is no salvation. Christ is our perpetual salvation and must, therefore, be the centre of all preaching. A place of worship is never devoted to the art of rhetoric, but to 'ultimate seriousness'; for it is here that Christ as the word of God is preached and where the word of God raises its voice as a double-edged sword which is directed toward the heart.

That Christ is our salvation today unites all children of God regardless of their religious affiliation. For this reason Köbner can refer to Christ as God's word. This Christ-centeredness also helped him to cope with Christian disunity. All who believe in Christ are part of God's people, and this is why he eagerly participated in early ecumenical attempts as they found expression in the Evangelical Alliance. All three early German Baptist leaders, the 'clover leaves' as they were sometimes called—Oncken, Lehmann and Köbner—were founding members of the Evangelical Alliance in London. Köbner would also try to establish contacts wherever he worked with ministers and Christian brethren of other denominations,[9] but his experiences were often disillusioning as the situation in Germany was very hostile toward 'new' religions. Köbner found himself in prison quite often, and even brethren of the Evangelical Alliance were very critical of the 'separatists'. It is, however, important to note that Köbner and the German Baptists did not withdraw from other Christians, but were open to fellowship. Perhaps, this friendly attitude toward Christians in denominations other than his own is an important contribution to Baptist identity because it may guard Baptists from being too arrogant and self-righteous. It is a reminder that the Baptist denomination is only one of the multiple expressions of the Christian church. It is also important to note that one can be totally committed

---

[9] Numerous references could be added here. Suffice it to point to some: in Ludwigsburg he met Hoffmann and discussed 'interesting matters', letter dated 8 September 1853; there was contact with preacher Ribbeck of the Reformed Church of Elberfeld, letter dated 27 September 1853; his discussions with the founder of the Free Evangelical Churches are well documented in Wolfgang Heinrichs, *Freikirchen—eine moderne Kirchenform. Entstehung und Entwicklung von fünf Freikirchen im Wuppertal* (Gießen: Brunnen Verlag, 2nd edn, 1990).

to one's denomination, as Köbner was, and yet be open to and take an interest in other churches.

Autonomy of the Local Church

Another contribution of Köbner is his concept of the autonomy of the local church. At this point he differed sharply from Oncken, the principal founding father. Oncken's approach to organizing the Baptist movement as it began to grow and spread throughout Germany and Denmark was shaped according to a centralized model. The Hamburg church was the first church, and all others were mission stations of the first church. When Oncken's 'missionaries' had found some people in a certain city or village who professed Christ and wanted to be baptized, he came to perform the baptism. Just as the first church in Hamburg was the 'fruit of mission work of our American brethren', so were the new mission stations the fruits of labour of Oncken and his 'apostles'. They had to report to him about their work and they were paid by him for what they did. Oncken's ideal amounts to an autocratic, or in the language of the church, an episcopal control of an expanding missionary society. The church in Hamburg was the headquarters of that society, and the control was applied to the individual missionaries as well as to the individual mission stations. A Puritan ideal of holiness is the leading concept behind this mechanism of control, discipline, or even excommunication, which Gieselbusch called 'rationalistic morality'.[10]

Köbner's concept was different. He stressed the freedom of an individual and the freedom of an individual church. However, he never opted for an extreme individualism as all are incorporated into the church as the body of Christ. The unity of that body of Christ which, as was shown, is not for him identical with the Baptist denomination, but includes all of God's children, is the divine aim. Therefore, the independence of an individual Christian or an individual church runs counter to the idea of unity of the body of Christ. Köbner contended, however, that the members of the body are all sinners even though they are 'holy'. It is very likely that Köbner, at this point, is indebted to Luther's idea of *simul iustus et peccator*, that the Christian is at the same time justified *and* a sinner. Köbner's conclusion, however, is very different from Luther's: As all church members are sinners, they must in certain cases be necessarily independent from each other, i.e. each Christian and each individual church must be free to follow his/her conscience. The church as a communion of 'saintly sinners' or 'sinful saints' requires the liberty of conscience so that nobody is forced into an opinion which is contrary to his/her conviction. The Baptist idea of liberty of conscience is derived from Köbner's concept of the church. The conference of 1849 passed a resolution upon Köbner's recommendation regarding the rite of confirmation. The assembly agreed with Köbner that Baptists should not have their children confirmed. That was the position of all delegates. Interestingly enough the resolution went on 'that it is our duty to grant them [children] liberty of

---

[10] Köbner, *Um die Gemeinde*, p. XIV.

conscience should they make a decision for confirmation...'.[11] The children at a certain age are considered mature enough to follow their consciences even if it is contrary to the conviction of their parents and the Baptist congregation. The autonomy of the local church is, therefore, based on the liberty that each congregation must have in solving problems that concern conscience. Liberty of conscience demands that the autonomy of the local church be established even if that meant to oppose Oncken.

Church–State Relations

The most important contribution of Köbner to Baptist identity is in the area of church–state relationships. Köbner, in a sweeping and dangerous statement, noted that there was no natural affiliation between Christianity and aristocracy. Such a statement was dangerous because the 'state Churches' of the numerous German territories were firmly in the hands of the aristocracy. Ever since Luther had appealed to the princes to act as principal members of the church for its reform and even accept the position of 'emergency bishops' had German princes been in such a position. Thus, even in the nineteenth century, the King of Prussia was the supreme bishop of the church of his territory. It was different in a city like Hamburg, as it was ruled by the city council, called the Senate. Yet that the Hamburg Senate also controlled the city's churches was an unquestionable fact. Köbner considered this arrangement of church and state incompatible with Holy Scripture. He made use of the Bible to explain his point of view. The state church is in a state of slavery in Egypt and is being used to build pyramids which serve the glory of humans, not the glory of God. Whereas Luther had contended that the church of his day was in Babylonian captivity (*De captivitate Babylonica ecclesiae*), Köbner took it a step further back in holy history and declared that the church of his day was enslaved in Egypt.

How can the church be set free from Egyptian slavery and enter into the promised land? It is here that the particular context of Köbner and the early Baptists in Germany is especially significant. As mentioned before, Köbner had been in prison several times; he and the small flock of Baptists were discriminated against, harassed by ordinary people and the police, persecuted by the authorities, fined in courts and subjected to other forms of reprehensions. Then came the year 1848 and the revolution. A parliament was elected and convened in Frankfurt. It is supposed to have been the most learned of all parliaments ever (which is probably why it was unsuccessful). It drafted a constitution for the country with a remarkable bill of rights. Köbner was overwhelmed by the events. For the first time he was able to commit his thoughts to paper without being censored. It may have been in the early

---

[11] Köbner, *Um die Gemeinde*, p. XLI.

part of 1848 that he wrote a small, but powerful pamphlet which he entitled: 'Manifesto of Free Primitive Christianity to the German People'.[12]

Several points need to be stressed:

1. He called his booklet a 'manifesto'. That word had been used by Karl Marx and Friedrich Engels when they published their 'Communist Manifesto' a few months before Köbner's pamphlet appeared in print. Köbner used the same term, which indicates that he could read the signs of the time and knew how to catch the attention of the public.

2. The criterion for him to present the Christian faith is 'primitive Christianity', that is, the way he saw Christianity realized in the writings of the New Testament. He wanted to go back to the very source of the faith which he could find only in the early realization of the church.

3. Köbner proudly added the word 'free'. His version of New Testament Christianity is no longer enslaved in Egypt, but is liberated.

4. Finally, the manifesto is addressed to the German people. He entered into a conversation with the people, presented his case and appealed to the people to see and judge for themselves. The people are throughout the book addressed as 'you'. The church of his day was often referred to as a *Volkskirche*, a people's church. Even then, as now, participation of the people in 'their' church was very low. Köbner also wanted a church that is directed to all the people, but he wanted this church to be free from state control.

> When almighty God broke the chains of your civil enslavement, that invention also broke down through which it had been successful to tie up your tongue. Today the defenders of your rights are glad to be able to speak political truth. But those among your citizens whose heart beats warmer for God than for political truth are equally glad to proclaim Christian truth, no longer bound by a censor who permitted only a monopolized Churchianity to speak so that it may eternally be hidden from you that Christianity and state-clergydom are as far apart as Christ is from Kaiphas. Your priests wail over the fall of aristocratic absolutism, their invaluable pillar, but the confessors of free primitive Christianity wish you luck for possessing precious civil liberties if you receive them gratefully from God and use them according to his will.[13]

These are the passionate words of the opening paragraph, and nobody could have said it better. The Baptist movement was on the side of the political revolution and democracy; Köbner publicly raised his voice to tell the German people in no uncertain terms where the true confessors of God stand politically. There is no 'natural sympathy' for the principles of aristocracy as well as absolutism on the one

---

[12] This has recently been republished in German in Dietmar Lütz, *Am Sitz der Bundesregierung. Freikirchen melden sich zu Wort* (Berlin: WDL-Verlag, 2004), pp. 249-66, and published in English by Ann McGlasham and William H. Brackney, 'German Baptists and the Manifesto of 1848', *American Baptist Quarterly* 23.3 (September, 2004), pp. 258-80.

[13] Köbner, *Um die Gemeinde*, p. 159.

hand[14] and Christianity on the other. Köbner, therefore, called the revolution a 'wonderful earthquake' which brought down the fifteen hundred-year old rule of a state–church that even the sixteenth-century reformation could not abolish. Now, in 1848, 'religious liberty' and 'separation of church and state' is the battle cry, and the priestcraft of the ruling churches is on the verge of collapse. 'This is the judgement of the Lord, our great God.' God must be praised 'for dissolving the old deception of priestly rule into nothingness'.[15]

Why was Köbner so outspoken at this point? Every ruling state–church, be it Roman or Protestant, will sooner or later turn into a persecuting, inquisitory church, and he listed examples from history as well as from the present. In fact, he told the 'beloved' German people[16] that if Baptists were to list all the persecutions that they had to endure during the last fifteen years, it would fill a large volume. 'And this was the work of Protestant pastors....' This coalition of state-clergydom and the police opened the eyes of some to see that the truth was on the side of the persecuted rather than on the side of the persecutors, and this, Köbner insisted, should make clear to everyone that Baptists 'are committed to the principle of religious liberty.'[17] It is surprising that Köbner had a clear understanding of the meaning of religious liberty. In a footnote earlier in the book[18] he had related that Rhode Island had been the first state where full religious liberty had become the law of the land, and he proudly added that it had been a Baptist, Roger Williams, who had secured it. Köbner, therefore, must have read some books to have this kind of information, but unfortunately to this day we do not know his sources. What we do know, however, is a coherent definition of religious liberty from his pen.

He wrote: 'We do not receive this precious freedom only today from some benevolent state power; we have for the past fifteen years considered it our inalienable right and continuously enjoyed it even at the expense of our earthly possessions and freedom. But we maintain not only our own religious liberty, we demand it for every human being who inhabits the soil of the fatherland, we demand it equally for all, be they Christians, Jews, Mohammedans or whatever. We consider it not only a totally unchristian sin to lay the iron fist of coercion upon any human with regard to his/her way of worshiping God, we also believe that the advantage of each religious party demands a totally equal right of all.'[19] In other words: no one party should enjoy certain privileges from state authorities at the expense of others. 'Let no one be deceived! We shall not have true religious liberty if any religious party remains in connection with the state or if the state concerns itself with religious matters.'[20]

---

[14] Köbner, *Um die Gemeinde*, p. 165.
[15] Köbner, *Um die Gemeinde*, pp. 160-61.
[16] Köbner, *Um die Gemeinde*, p. 161.
[17] Köbner, *Um die Gemeinde*, p. 163.
[18] Köbner, *Um die Gemeinde*, p. 160 n. 2.
[19] Köbner, *Um die Gemeinde*, p. 163.
[20] Köbner, *Um die Gemeinde*, p. 164.

Köbner proceeded to explain to the German people some of the theological reasons for demanding religious liberty. When Jesus Christ said 'My kingdom is not of this world' he meant, according to Köbner, that the spiritual and the political realm should never merge, but be kept apart. The church of Christ can never acknowledge a prince as its earthly head because it trusts the Lord whose throne is in heaven. The church is therefore totally independent from any human authority. He refers to Galatians 1.10 where Paul says: 'Am I now seeking the favour of men or of God? Or am I trying to please men? If I were still pleasing men, I should not be a servant of Christ.' Or he quoted Acts 4.19 and 5.29 to indicate that Christians must obey God rather than men. The passage in Matthew 20.25ff is rightly called the 'basic law' of the church of Christ: 'You know that the rulers of the Gentiles lord it over them, and their great men exercise authority over them. It shall not be so among you; but whoever would be great among you must be your servant, and whoever would be first among you must be your slave.'

This basic law, according to Köbner, establishes the principle of equality or egalitarianism in the church, for Christ is its sole master and all members are brethren and servants. Even though there are ministers in the church, especially elders (bishops) and deacons, they are but brethren elected by their brethren. A caste of ministers who are higher than the laity is alien to the true church.[21] The highest authority in the church is the simple majority of votes. By it, ministers are elected, new members admitted and trespassers disciplined or even excommunicated. The congregation consists of those who know, respect and love each other and enjoy the happiness of true brotherly/sisterly love. But the aim is also to be victorious in the numerous vulnerable and destructive events of life and to learn to hold fast to the inner harmony. This can only be accomplished by leaning on the 'great, eternal, wonderful, holy and gracious God'.[22]

The church is commissioned to bring the world the good news. This must also be done in the new context of a democracy and within the framework of religious liberty. How can this be done? This is a question Köbner asked his readers. In his answer he rejected the traditional way to recruit new members by infant baptism and confirmation. These to him are remnants of the system of serfdom and are expressions of a coercive style of religion. Parents may not act as rulers over their children's religion. A new heart is produced by the only legitimate weapon at the disposal of true Christians: the word of truth.[23] Instead of physical or spiritual force Köbner opts for dialogue as long as both sides are open and honest. If people reject the Christian faith after careful examination, so be it. It is much better than

---

[21] Köbner, *Um die Gemeinde*, p. 166, is very sarcastic when he says that a congregation is not an audience which likes to see the same actor appear fifty-two times a year in the same medieval costume to play the first lover of morality. When the church comes together, it wants to receive a communication as to what love of God and love of humankind means from the richness of the divine documents, 'the treasure box of uncreated wisdom'.

[22] Köbner, *Um die Gemeinde*, p. 167.

[23] Köbner, *Um die Gemeinde*, p. 168.

hypocrisy, in which the outer appearance is different from inner convictions. Membership in the church is thus placed on a voluntary basis. Voluntaryism and religious liberty go hand in glove.

That the masses were turning away from the biblical faith was because the fruits of the hypocrisy of the ruling church were falsely regarded as fruits of biblical faith and that the small band of true believers was an invisible church. In his typically passionate address, Köbner turns to the German people and says: 'We lift our hand to the Almighty and Omnipotent and protest before the people of Germany against the assumption that clergydom, covetousness, Jesuitism, absolutism, reactionary conservatism, keeping people in stupidity, deception etc. are the fruits of biblical faith. The fruits of biblical faith are joy, happiness, purity, self-sacrifice, philanthropy, love of fatherland, love of freedom, love of truth, commitment to science, industry and civilization. Where these are lacking, the faith is only the mask of detestable malice.'[24] Köbner concluded that honesty of heart is what he wants the people to display. If someone has anti-biblical principles, let him speak his convictions freely. Within a civil society it is just as virtuous and reputable to call oneself a humanist or an antichristian as a Christian so that no person is tempted to bear a false name. 'Praise be to God that civil emancipation and equality of all religions has finally come!'

His final appeal reads: 'Now, precious German people, make a decision between hypocrisy and truth, between true Christianity and churchly clergydom, between reasonable biblical conviction of heart and unreasonable castles in the air. May the spirit of Jesus Christ lead you in your inquiry that you may be successful and that you may become like Him who knew neither egoism nor hypocrisy. "If you continue in my word, you are truly my disciples, and you will know the truth, and the truth will make you free... So if the Son makes you free, you will be free indeed" [John 8.31–32.36].'[25]

This powerful tract by Köbner on state-church relations was, of course, revolutionary. It was so revolutionary that he was not only attacked from ministers of the state–church, but the tract was immediately taken off the market and pulped when the reactionary forces again had the upper hand. It must also be said that in the ensuing years Köbner himself seems to have forgotten the power of his diatribe. It had very little influence on the Baptist movement in Germany as the young movement more and more began to lose its counter-cultural appeal and became adjusted to the powers that be. What remained was the principle of separation of church and state.

Other Contributions

Time and again in the history of the church, renewal movements introduced new ways of worship, especially new hymns. Köbner was very much aware that the act

[24] Köbner, *Um die Gemeinde*, p.175.
[25] Köbner, *Um die Gemeinde*, p. 176.

of worship demanded new hymns and he authored numerous hymns himself. He edited several collections of hymns both for Germany and for German immigrants in the USA as well as for Denmark. The Danish hymnal 'Troens Stemme' carried 111 hymns by Köbner, either originally in Danish or translated by him from his German hymnal *Glaubensstimme der Gemeine des Herrn* (*Voice of Faith of the Church of the Lord*).[26] Günter Balders has undertaken extensive research about this topic.[27]

He also contributed to thinking about the education of children: he wrote a *Guide through Holy Scripture for Children* (see n. 3). The book is a catechism and follows divine revelation in its six chapters: Creation, Fall, Promise, Jesus Christ, the Church (*Gemeinde*) and Eternity. When one reads today the questions and answers which the children are supposed to learn, one wonders how this can be anything but learning by mechanical rote memory and mimicry. However, Köbner, in a preface to the teachers, emphasized that understanding and thinking are the aims and that the teacher should always address the heart of the child.[28] The ten commandments are explained in two ways: what they reject and what they positively teach ('*was verbietet*' — '*was gebietet*'). It seems important to stress that the rejection of infant baptism does not imply, as is sometimes thought, a neglect of children. The contrary may be true. Children need the special attention of the congregation and his catechism was intended to help people in the church to introduce children to the faith.

Another issue was the production of a confession of faith: even though the city authorities of Hamburg had requested a confession of faith by the Baptist group and a confession had to be drafted, Köbner would have probably produced one even without the city's insistence. He was very much aware of spreading the gospel through various means, and a confession was one way. Closely related to this was his determination to present the Baptists as an attractive alternative to the state church. He especially felt that the learned and intellectuals of society should be reached. This class within society had left the churches in great numbers, not outwardly, but by way of an 'inner emigration' because they found the prevailing church system superstitious.

As Köbner had called upon the German people to opt for honesty (*Redlichkeit*) in public life so that one's position in society was not dependent upon one's outward form of religious affiliation without an inner conviction, he thought that this would appeal to the educated and he began to compose a lengthy poem on the Christian story which he called 'The Great Song'. Readers today may find that it makes for boring reading and that its literary quality leaves much to be desired. Be that as it may, it must be stressed that Köbner saw the need to reach a certain segment of society and he attempted to do so. For the same reason he wrote a drama about the Waldensians in which he portrayed this medieval group of religious dissenters in much the same way as the Baptists of his day. The persecution then resembles the

---

[26] Cf. Köbner, *Um die Gemeinde*, p. XXIX.
[27] Unfortunately he has not yet put together his research in a book.
[28] Köbner, *Leitfaden*, p. iv.

persecution of Baptists now. He also did a translation of a book by Sören Kiekegaard whom he apparently admired. It was the first time that any writing by this famous Danish theologian-philosopher was available in German. The term *Redlichkeit*—translated as honesty—comes from this Danish compatriot of Köbner.

Conclusion

Köbner made an enormous and a creative contribution to Baptist thought and practice. In his work on issues such as conversion, baptism, free will, church and state, worship and education, he helped to forge a European Baptist identity. He made missionary trips not only into Denmark, but also into Holland. When the Swedish Lutheran pastor from Stockholm, Anders Wiberg, visited Hamburg in 1851, he came to know Köbner who at the time wrote and published his booklet about the church in Baptist thinking. Wiberg was so impressed that he became a Baptist and transplanted Köbner's Baptist distinctives to Sweden. In thinking about Baptist identity, it is important to observe that Baptists are an international people. Köbner's voice was also heard beyond the circles of Baptist life. In his powerful plea for religious liberty he rightly contended that this implied the same rights for 'Christians, Jews, Muslims or whoever lives on the soil of the fatherland'. Köbner shaped a way of being Baptist that was definite, but not narrow.

CHAPTER 6

The Impact of Charismatic Christianity on Traditional French Baptist Identity[1]

Sébastien Fath

In spite of its growth,[2] Evangelical Protestantism is still quite mysterious to many people in France, where, according to Danièle Hervieu-Leger,[3] even Catholicism seems to be leaving the cultural mainstream. The plausibility structures of Evangelical identity are difficult to comprehend, especially at the doctrinal level. But one category among this kind of Protestantism seems to draw more interest: it can be summarized in a formula 'Emotional Protestantism'. This concept defines the Pentecostal and Charismatic identity[4] which is particularly flourishing in France, as in 2006 it represents about two thirds of the 350,000 French Evangelicals. According to some observers, the Pentecostalization of Christianity during the twenty-first century seems as inevitable as the rise of the sun. For Evangelical churches, notably Baptist congregations, this impact cannot be overestimated.

Compared with other Evangelical tendencies, Baptist churches seem to combine a particularly strong confessional identity, a 'heritage'[5] rooted in early English Puritan times,[6] with a plasticity due to their congregationalist emphasis. How has this

---

[1] This text reformulates and develops elements from a paper presented at a conference organized by the University of Strasbourg (Professor Jean-Pierre Bastian), 7-9 November 2002. Its title was 'Les baptistes dans l'Europe latine: entre tradition et émotion, quelles recompositions?' This conference has since been published: J-P. Bastian (ed.), *La recomposition des protestantismes en Europe latine. Entre émotion et tradition* (Geneva: Labor et Fides, 2004).

[2] For a general overview of Evangelical History in France, see S. Fath, *Du ghetto au réseau. Le protestantisme évangélique en France, 1800–2005* (Geneva: Labor et Fides, 2005).

[3] D. Hervieu-Leger, *Catholicisme, la fin d'un monde* (Paris: Bayard, 2003).

[4] For a synthesis, see J-P. Willaime, 'Le pentecôtisme: contours et paradoxes d'un protestantisme émotionnel ', *Archives de Sciences Sociales des Religions* 44.105 (janvier-mars, 1999), pp. 5-28.

[5] H.L. McBeth, *The Baptist Heritage: Four Centuries of Baptist Witness* (Nashville, TN: Broadman Press, 1987).

[6] A doctoral thesis has been completed in French on John Smyth, one of the founders of Baptist identity. See J-E. Stauffacher, 'La vie et l'œuvre de John Smyth, 1570?–1612' (PhD thesis, University of Strasbourg, 1987).

identity interacted with the Pentecostal and Charismatic emphasis?[7]   After situating
the tiny French Baptist identity in its European context, a general focus on
Charismatic influence on Baptist identity will be followed by the case study of
France, where Baptists seem to balance between resistance and acculturation.

French Baptist identity in its European Context

European Baptists are a tiny minority, but, as we know, there are important
variations between Baptists in different countries in Europe.

Southern Europe: Particularly Hard Soil for Baptist Identity

Compared to Eastern Europe, but also to Germany, and (last but not least) to the
United Kingdom, Baptist implantation in southern Europe has been very weak.
There are about 40,000 Baptist adherents in France and Spain (between 12,000 and
14,000 baptized members), about 20,000 in Italy and Portugal, a little more than
3,000 in Belgium, and less than 2,000 in French-speaking Switzerland.[8] Behind
these figures there are contrasting realities. In Spain, Italy and Portugal, Baptists
play a major role within Protestant circles, which are, in themselves, very weak. The
French case is different. In this country, Baptists appear well behind Lutherans and
especially Reformed (Presbyterian) Protestants, even if, in the last forty years,
leaders like André Thobois or Louis Schweitzer have played an important role in the
French Protestant Federation, which is easily the main Protestant network.[9] This
specific situation is important to notice. The fact that in many European countries
Baptists seem to be the most visible Protestant group has had an influence on
French Baptist identity. We could imagine that such a situation would encourage

---

[7] Differences between Charismaticism and Pentecostalism are not always clearly
perceived. We might highlight six distinctives. Charismaticism is much more trans-
confessional than Pentecostalism. It emphazises personal development rather than
ascetism. Average social level also seems higher in charismatic churches than in
Pentecostal ones. Charismatic churches do not consider glossolalia as an absolute
condition for 'baptism of the Spirit'. Its worship mode is also more diverse and
innovative (role of music, participation of women, etc) than the Pentecostal style.
Pentecostalism (Assemblies of God type) also vehiculates a rigid conception of charisma,
rooted in the New Testament, especially the 1 Cor. 12.29-30. On the contrary,
Charismatic movments (especially the last 'waves'), seem to be more open to new
charismas, if the Bible does not condemn them explicitly.

[8] Albert W. Wardin (ed.), *Baptists Around the World* (Nashville, TN: Broadman &
Holman, 1995), pp. 271, 285. These statistics are to be taken as evaluations. Statistics
given by the Baptist World Alliance (BWA) in 2003 (http://www.bwanet.org/fellowship/
member-bodies/member-stats.htm#EUROPE) are similar. We have to take into account
that there are many separatist Baptist churches, who are not linked to the BWA. In
general terms, the insular culture of some Baptist movements does not always open the
door to the statistician.

[9] Nearly 80% of all French Protestants (including half the Baptists) belong to it.

Baptists to play down slightly their denominational distinctives in order to appear as the main regular Protestant representatives on the religious and public scene. In France, on the contrary, the very strong Huguenot identity, and the weight of Lutheran and Reformed churches (about 650,000 members in 2003) nurtured, in Baptist ranks, the desire for distinctiveness. After all, they could never appear to be the main Protestant representatives. So they preferred to emphasize why they were different from other Protestants, and this had a direct impact on their history. What is amazing in French Baptist history is that in spite of very small numbers, French Baptists developed a very robust sense of Baptist identity. Sometimes it seems that they even wanted to teach some of their American sponsors how to be better Baptists! This specific emphasis on Baptist identity in France has to be remembered when we examine the impact of Charismatic tendencies.

European Networks

Another important characteristic of French Baptists in their European context is that they early on developed various links with their Anglo-Saxon forefathers,[10] but also with other European countries, especially the Latin countries. As an example we can mention the Baptist regional conference of Latin countries which took place in Paris between 11 and 14 July 1937. Baptists from Belgium (pastors O. Valet and A. Wémers), from Spain (A. Celma from Barcelona), Portugal (Manuel Cerqueira) and Italy (G.B. Scrajber), gathered with their French counterparts, along with many Anglo-Saxon Baptists,[11] including a pastor named Pope who came, not from the Vatican but from the Antipodes, 'accompanied by several Australian Baptists', as the French observer notes.[12] A German Baptist, Dr Johannes Mundhenk, attended too. We might be less optimistic than Dr Lewis, who rejoiced that between 'these Baptists from various countries, the only differences are in physiognomy and language'.[13] But this conference (which treated subjects like youth, evangelization, women's work and missions) is clear evidence, among others, of early networking. Many other signs confirm this, such as the circulation of Baptist writings between Latin countries. Several French Baptist texts were translated for other Latin European

---

[10] For a closer look at American and English influence on continental Baptists, see I.M. Randall, '"The Blessings of an Enlightened Christianity": North American Involvement in European Baptist Origins', *American Baptist Quarterly* 20.1 (March, 2001), pp. 5-26, and S. Fath, 'A Forgotten Missionary Link: The Baptist Continental Society in France (1831–1836) ', *Baptist Quarterly* 40.3 (July, 2003), pp. 133-51.

[11] Dr Truett (from America), President of the BWA, Dr Rushbrooke (from Britain), Secretary of the BWA, Dr Everett Gill, representing Baptists from Southern USA, and Dr Lewis, who managed the European section of the American Baptist Foreign Mission Society, which supported the Baptist implantation in France for a century.

[12] See the reports of the 'Conférence Régionale Baptiste des Pays Latins', *Le Témoin de la Vérité* 7 (juillet-aout, 1937), p. 110.

[13] Dr Lewis, quoted in the reports of the 'Conférence Régionale', p. 118.

Baptists.[14] After World War II, as Baptist churches increased their number in France, the networking activities developed, finding stimulus in the new European Baptist Federation[15] created in 1949.[16]

French Baptists: A Crossroads Situation

The Baptists' particular ability for building networks, articulated both locally and globally, explains in part why we find a very significant proportion of French Baptists at the head of Evangelical organizations in France. While being partly marginalised by the Reformed and Lutheran 'Big Brothers', Baptists played a crucial role in building Evangelical networks in France. For about forty years, the two people who hold the records for presidencies in Evangelical organizations are two Baptists, Jacques Blocher (1909–86) and André Thobois (b.1924). It seems quite difficult in France to build an Evangelical network without Baptists. This important role might also be rooted in the crossroads situation that characterises Baptists.

This crossroads situation works on a more fundamental level. It is crystal clear that more recent Baptist identity is located at an intersection between the Pentecostal/Charismatic world and the Lutheran and Reformed world. Through their theology, and their confessional heritage, Baptists are deeply connected to the *mainstream* Protestant tradition, especially the Reformed one. But through their congregationalist practice, they opened themselves earlier than others to 'emotional influences' from Pentecostalism.[17] This is why they appear in some ways as a 'denominational test' if we want to explore the tension between a kind of 'pietist/orthodox tradition' and 'emotional/experiential tradition'.[18] If the scenario seems to be that there is a dissolution of Baptist identity in the Charismatic/Pentecostal movement, we can suppose that the whole Evangelical

---

[14] See, e.g., Jean-Baptiste Crétin, *Coleccion de textes que establecen las doctrinas cristianas y condenan las tradiciones de la Iglesia Romana. Traducico del Frances de D. Juan Bautista Cretin, pastor en Lyon* (Madrid: Imprenta de Jose Cruzado, 1871). Reuben Saillens, *Consejos Para un nuevo miembro de la Iglesia* (trad. por AMDL Deberes Cristianis pr. Cantaclaro, El Paso, Texas: Reimpresos por "La Vos Bautista", n.d.). Aimé Cadot, *Lettera amichevole ai membri del clero catholico* (published in Italy around 1890).

[15] For the fiftieth anniversary of the European Baptist Federation, a book was published, B. Green, *Crossing the Boundaries: A History of the European Baptist Federation* (Didcot: Baptist Historical Society, 1999).

[16] A European Baptist Mission was created later in 1954. Founded in Zürich, the first president (1954–67) of its executive committee was Henri Vincent, a French Baptist.

[17] The Baptist practice of congregationalism gives the assemblies a quasi 'total freedom' to adopt a 'charismatic style' without risking hierarchical control, E. Veldhuizen in his doctoral thesis, 'Le renouveau charismatique protestant en France (1968–1988)' (PhD thesis, University of Paris IV Sorbonne, 1995), pp. 402-403.

[18] These two poles are to be understood as idea-types, according to Max Weber's definition. In other words, they are based on a stylization of reality in order to have a better understanding of a complex phenomenon. On an empirical level, however, things are more mixed: for example, emotion does not always oppose itself to orthodoxy.

world might take the same road. On the other hand, if Baptist distinctives remain then we can imagine that there will be a quite stable balance in the Evangelical world between both emotional/experiential and pietist/orthodox Protestantism. It is time now to take a closer look at this tension within Baptist identity.

Charismatic Influence on Baptist Identity: A Sociological Overview

Charismatic influence on Baptist identity cannot be understood in exactly the same way as in Catholicism or Reformed Protestantism. The type of religious organization Baptists developed is indeed very specific. The same winds, through different instruments, will not create the same music. The same Charismatic influences, as well, will produce in Baptist circles different results.

Baptist Identity: Between 'Sect' and 'Church'

What puzzles many French observers (and maybe other Europeans as well) is that Baptist churches do not fit in with the distinction between 'Church' and 'Sect'. For a good part of the French public, if you do not fit into the 'Church' type, characterized by a strong institutional regulation from above and a deep involvement in the world's affairs, it means that you belong to a 'Sect', typified by uncomfortable qualities such as intolerance, disorder and a potential threat to the public order. But a closer look at Baptist identity reveals that Baptist churches cannot be included either in one camp or the other. From the 'Church type', Baptists borrow an articulate relationship to global society, but without the institutional dimension. From the 'Sect type', they borrow a militant and horizontal ecclesial organization, but (usually) without retreating from 'the world' or considering themselves to offer the only way of salvation. In fact, the Baptists seem to be 'go-betweens', close to what we call a 'denomination', or a 'Free Church' in the sense used by Ernst Troeltsch.[19] Working from a model built by the French sociologist Jean-Paul Willaime,[20] we can distinguish between a combination of institution and ritual (which is at work in Catholicism), a combination of institution and ideology, or doctrine (which defines the Reformed Protestant model), and a type based on association and charisma (which could define a group like the Davidian sect in Waco). Looking at the Baptist case invites us to add a fourth type, which combines association and doctrine (ideology). The very nature of a Baptist church is association instead of institution. But association does not mean necessarily the triumph of a charismatic leader. In the Baptist case, it is still ideology or doctrine, as happens in institutional churches like the Reformed church, which builds identity.[21] In more precise terms, this doctrine is

---

[19] Cf. E. Troeltsch, *Die Soziallehren der christlichen Kirchen und Gruppen* (Aalen: Scienta Verlag, 1961 [1st edn, 1912]), pp. 733-37.

[20] J-P. Willaime, *La précarité protestante. Sociologie du protestantisme contemporain* (Paris/Geneva: Labor et Fides, 1992), p. 22.

[21] This fourth type can also fit (more or less) with many other Evangelical denominations.

the result of a social construction, defended by specific mediations such as confessions of faith, conventions, meetings, a denominational press, and pastors' training schools.[22]

Doctrine First

This Baptist emphasis on doctrine is difficult to understand. In the Catholic mindset, a doctrinal base cannot survive without a central institution, a 'Magisterium'. According to this vision, autonomous association means the domination of a charismatic leader. But French Baptist history seems to illustrate that an associative model could survive and develop while being regulated by a strong doctrinal and denominational line. This specificity meant that charismatic validation was supposed to be submitted to doctrinal validation. A young pastor cannot validate his calling by saying 'God gave me the gift, God can heal through me', and so on. He has to frame his theology and his pastoral practice according to Baptist distinctives. The Baptist pastor is supposed to be, first, an authorized interpreter of the Scriptures.[23] 'Be convinced of the Biblical truths, be men of the Book!', the leading French Baptist pastor Reuben Saillens advised young preachers.[24] The cornerstone of this religious system is the proper interpretation of the Bible.[25] As pastor André Thobois[26] wrote in 2002: 'Our piety sets its roots in the Bible. We always go back to it, and we conform to it. This is why we never seek elsewhere the source, the form and the meaning of our piety.'[27]

A Dam against Emotional Streams?

This biblical orientation, often inspired by Calvinism (in its 'soft' or 'hard' versions) usually puts its emphasis on the importance of a proper orthodoxy, of conversion and of daily life lived by faith. God must be believed through a certain frame, and concretely experienced. In the majority of Baptist circles, this experience

---

[22] For more details on this typology, see S. Fath, 'Un modèle associatif idéologique', in *Une autre manière d'être chrétien en France. Socio-histoire de l'implantation baptiste (1810–1950)* (Geneva: Labor et Fides, 2001), pp. 515-30.

[23] For more details on this type of pastor, see Jean-Paul Willaime, *Profession: pasteur. Sociologie de la condition du clerc à la fin du XXe siècle* (Geneva: Labor et Fides, 1986).

[24] R. Saillens' Foreword to Samuel Lortsch, *Félix Neff, l'apôtre des Hautes Alpes, biographie extraite de ses lettres* (Toulouse: Nouvelle Société d'éditions de Toulouse, 1941), p. 13.

[25] See Fath, *Une autre manière d'être chrétien*, pp. 576, 605.

[26] He was president of the French Baptist Federation from 1963 to 1987.

[27] 'Notre piété a ses racines dans la Bible. C'est à elle que nous revenons sans cesse et à laquelle nous nous conformons. C'est pourquoi nous ne cherchons nulle part ailleurs la source, la forme et le sens de notre piété ', in A. Thobois, *Pour que notre piété soit vraie* (Paris: Carnets de Croire et Servir, 2002), p. 17.

does not mean miracles and extraordinary signs (even if these are not rejected). According to the pietistic tradition, the main emphasis is on everyday impregnation of biblical wisdom. Daily meditation on the Scriptures thus appears as the favourite tool every Christian must use to improve his or her communion with the Almighty. It is not surprising, then, that pastors themselves are submitted to this biblical regulation. Members are clearly allowed to contest their pastor if their minister seems to diverge from the biblical orientation favoured by the community. Members are admitted into the local church not only by conversion and baptism, but also if they identify themselves in some ways with the doctrinal orientation of the local church.[28]

In spite of the flexibility provided by the associative structure, this emphasis on doctrinal regulation seems relatively hostile to the Charismatic/Pentecostal emphasis, if we define it as the tendency to favour experience and charisma over and above theology or orthodoxy.[29] But do we find an empirical verification of this global analysis? This is what we will try to see in the last part of this chapter.

French Baptist Identity and the Challenge of Charismatic Influence

Evaluating precisely the Charismatic influence on Baptists—which is just one of many fields in which we observe a 'pentecostalization of Christianity'[30]—is not an easy thing to do. Britain apart,[31] monographs about European Baptists are rare, and the figures given by Baptist Unions do not distinguish between Charismatic Baptists and others. Should we then give up the attempt to make an empirical evaluation of Charismatic influence? Hopefully, the French case can be fruitful, since it seems to be less difficult than some others. Divided into three main 'families' of Baptists,[32]

---

[28] As we know, this identification does not always require subscription to a confession of faith. Many Baptist churches do not have such confessions, or do not consider them as totally normative. But, even then, an implicit acceptance of a common doctrinal base seems to be favoured.

[29] Many observers of Charismatic trends admit that doctrinal regulation is not a priority in these circles. For example, 'while there are many biblically responsive Christians who include themselves in the Charismatic movement, there are many others who need to take stock. There are many Charismatics who should ask themselves in all honesty: "Am I putting my emphasis on the Scriptures and God's living Word or on the jolly times, the feelings, the experiences?"' So, J.F. Mc Arthur, Jr, *The Charismatics: A Doctrinal Perspective* (London: Lamp Press, 1979), p. 206.

[30] J-P. Bastian, 'Les protestantismes latino-américains. Un détour pertinent pour la sociologie des protestantismes', in Y. Lambert *et al*, *Le religieux des sociologues* (Paris, L'Harmattan, 1997), p. 145.

[31] See D. McBain, *Fire Over the Waters: Renewal Among Baptists and Others from the 1960s to the 1990s* (London: Darton, Longman & Todd, 1997).

[32] There are about 40,000 Baptist attenders. About a half belong to the Fédération des Églises Évangéliques Baptistes de France (FEEBF). This Federation has been linked to the Fédération Protestante de France (FPF) since 1916. The other half divides itself between the Association Évangélique d'Églises Baptistes de Langue Française (AEEBF) and the

the movement has been studied in its past,[33] but, most of all, it has been analysed in recent decades through the lenses of the Charismatic wave. Evert Veldhuizen's doctoral thesis on Protestant charismaticism is absolutely crucial.[34] With the help of this work, combined with additional sources from the denominational press, it is quite possible to evaluate how Baptist identity is affected by Pentecostal and Charismatic influences. Three main scenarios seem to occur.

First Scenario: 'Baptist', a Label and no More

The first scenario, which occurs sometimes, is that Charismatic influence is so strong that Baptist identity seems to be no more than a label. If you scratch the glaze, there is nothing left of Baptist distinctives. This situation is quite seldom found in France. Probably a little less than 10% of so-called 'Baptists' fit this scenario. We can find a few examples within the French Baptist Federation. But the main field is the 'Fédération des Églises et Communautés Baptistes Charismatiques' (FECBC). Its founder is Charles Schinkel.[35] He started his ministry as a pastor of the Reformed Church. In the spring of 1977, however, he was excluded from his post at Nuneray (Nord-Normandie) by the regional council of the Reformed Church. The main reasons were his strong Charismatic convictions, but also his denial of pedobaptism.[36] Schinkel found out that he was a 'victim of his Evangelical convictions', believing, for example, that his baptisms were not 'rebaptisms'.[37] As a matter of fact, there were many other motives for his exclusion. One of them was that Schinkel refused to follow a bachelor's degree of theology.[38] According to him,

---

independant Baptist churches. Many of the latter belong to the Communion Évangélique de Baptistes Indépendants (CEBI). Because of more restricted views on ecumenism, the two last French Baptist 'families' do not belong to the French Protestant Federation.

[33] See Fath, *Une autre manière d'être chrétien,* and *Les baptistes en France (1810–1950), Faits, dates et documents* (Cléon d'Andran: Excelsis, 2002). This last book provides additional elements to the main book published in 2001 (biographies, a chronology, documents, maps). For a quick overview in English, see S. Fath, 'Another Way of Being a Christian in France: A Century of Baptist Implantation ', in M.M. Hawkins, Jr (ed.), *Global Baptist History: Papers presented at the Second International Conference on Baptist Studies, Wake Forest University, July 2000, Baptist History and Heritage* 36.1-2 (Winter–Spring, 2001), pp. 159-73. (This will also appear in D. Bebbington and A.R. Cross [eds], *Global Baptist History* [Studies in Baptist History and Thought, 14; Milton Keynes: Paternoster, forthcoming, 2006].)

[34] E. Veldhuizen, 'Le renouveau charismatique protestant en France (1968–1988)' (PhD thesis, University of Paris IV Sorbonne, 1995).

[35] See 'Le parcours de Charles Schinkel', in Veldhuizen, 'Le renouveau charismatique protestant', pp. 186-189.

[36] On this aspect, Evert Veldhuizen, 'Le renouveau charismatique protestant', p. 187, rightly points out that Schinkel adopts the Baptist view on baptism. Schinkel was himself baptized by immersion, and after 1973 he only baptized by immersion.

[37] Veldhuizen, 'Le renouveau charismatique protestant', p. 193.

[38] In French, 'licence de théologie'.

such a degree did not give any value to his pastoral ministry. This revealing detail seems to confirm the typical Charismatic emphasis: the pastor is not first a doctor, an authorized interpreter of the Scriptures. He is first a prophet, whose legitimacy is rooted in his calling, his personal charisma. After being excluded from the Reformed Church (ERF), Schinkel developed a network of Charismatic assemblies around his own community, the Christian community of the Burning Bush. In 1986, this building process led to the creation of a 'Federation of Charismatic Churches and Communities'.[39] The Federation's centre is Louvetot, in Caudebec-en-Caux, Normandy, from where a quarterly magazine is distributed.[40] In 1988 the FECBC comprised about 1,100 members and thirteen assemblies.[41] These statistics have not changed much since then.

Based on a very light structure,[42] this Federation roots its identity not in Baptist distinctives—even if we find some of them present—in spite of the use of the word in the self-definition of this network.[43] The main emphasis by far is on the Charismatic identity.[44] Apart from the baptismal practices and the congregationalist orientation, the views on ministry, the spiritual gifts, and the role of doctrine differ notably from the classic French Baptist identity. Pastors, for example, usually emphasise vertical authority, rooted in their personal charisma, their divine calling, while in the majority of Baptist churches the pastor is supposed to be a *primus inter pares*, taking his authority from the vote of the members. Models given to the members are also never quite taken from Baptist history or actuality, but from the globalized universe of Charismatic Christianity.[45] It is no surprise, then, if 'the use of the "Baptist" adjective causes some trouble in the FEEBF'.[46] Baptist identity, in this case, seems to be just a label. The generic content is simply Charismatic: the regulation of the group operates much more through charisma than through Baptist doctrine or orthopraxy.

---

[39] 'Fédération des Églises et Communautés Baptistes Charismatiques'.

[40] Its title is 'Resurrection Magazine'. Charles Schinkel is its director and among its editors, at the beginning of the 2000s, are Jacky Chlepko, Lucien Clerc, André Habersetzer, Daniel Lhermenault, Daniel Mochamps and Jules Thobois.

[41] Veldhuizen, 'Le renouveau charismatique protestant', p. 404.

[42] See C. Schinkel, 'Une Fédération nouvelle sans être une dénomination de plus', *Actes 2* 64, n.d., p. 3.

[43] As he explained it, Schinkel chose to define his movement as 'baptist' because this word was well-situated among French Protestants. It was easily identifiable.

[44] This explains why Veldhuizen chose to categorize the members of the FECBC among 'independant churches' instead of among Baptist churches.

[45] See, for instance, this remark from Charles Schinkel: 'Brother Carlos Anacondia works in the latin south-american world, close to the French situation... Nevertheless, it works there! The Gospel hits in Argentina. Why is it not the same here?', editorial of *Résurrection Magazine* 97 (mai–juin, 2001), p. 3

[46] Veldhuizen, 'Le renouveau charismatique protestant', p. 423.

Second Scenario: Baptist Identity, an Acculturation Space for Charismatic Tendencies

A second scenario is far more frequent. We find it when Baptist identity works as an acculturation space for Charismatic tendencies. This scenario happens in various proportions, and it works in a double sense: there is reciprocity. While radical Pentecostal or Charismatic elements get acculturated into Baptist procedures, the latter also incorporate (or take into account) various elements of the Charismatic culture (worship style, and so on). About 40% of all Baptist churches are directly involved in this acculturation in various ways. The main field of acculturation is the Baptist Federation (FEEBF), which has been confronted by a kind of quasi- or proto-Pentecostal orientation since the nineteenth century. Before the creation of the Federation, the religious views of Irvingites (those who followed the London-based Scottish preacher, Edward Irving), who are considered sometimes as forerunners of Pentecostalism,[47] had an important impact on the first French Baptists, especially in the North but also around the town of Saint Etienne, from the 1830s to the 1850s. The Welsh Revival, fifty years later (1904–06), also influenced many Baptist churches in the North. The emphasis on 'spiritual gifts' particularly attracted them.[48] When the Pentecostal movement settled in France,[49] early relations at the start of the 1930s led to a kind of mini revival in the North (around Denain) and Picardy, from the 1940s to the end of the 1960s. The Pentecostal influence (Assembly of God style) on many existing Baptist and new Baptist churches was obvious. The pastor Jules Thobois,[50] who experienced the 'baptism of the Spirit' in 1947, was then the main leader of this tendency, emphasizing miracles, prophecy, divine healing and, in general terms, 'spiritual gifts'. It is no surprise, then, that the beginning of the Charismatic influence in the early 1970s had an important impact on the Baptist Federation. This impact, which started a few years after its British equivalent,[51] had been prepared by a long history of contacts with and influences from Pentecostals.

A clear majority of the Baptist churches of the Federation are engaged in a process of acculturation with the Pentecostal/Charismatic culture. Several degrees or types of influence can be pointed out. There are some Baptist churches where the Charismatic

---

[47] See C.G. Strachan, *The Pentecostal Theology of Edward Irving* (London: Darton, Longman & Todd, 1973).

[48] For a detailed study of these early links between Baptists and the Pentecostal (and 'pre-pentecostal') movements, see S. Fath 'Baptistes et pentecôtistes en France, une histoire parallèle?', *Bulletin de la Société de l'Histoire du Protestantisme Français* 146 (juillet–septembre, 2000), pp. 523-67.

[49] The only synthesis available on Pentecostal implantation in France (viewed from an insider) is G.R. Stotts, *Le pentecôtisme au pays de Voltaire* (Craponne: Viens et Vois, 1981).

[50] Jules Thobois (b. 1922) is André Thobois' elder brother.

[51] See D.W. Bebbington, 'The Spirit Poured Out: Springs of the Charismatic Movement', in *Evangelicalism in Modern Britain: A History from the 1730s to the 1980s* (London: Routledge, 2nd edn, 1995), pp. 228-48. According to Bebbington, the Charismatic movement started in Britain in 1963.

emphasis is very militant, as it is in the 'Communauté Chrétienne du Point du Jour' in Paris.[52] Many Baptist churches are moderately Charismatic, such as in Soissons or Saint-Quentin, in Picardy. Some of them exhibit attenuated Pentecostal or Charismatic characteristics, like glossolalia, which were more important three decades ago. We find also churches that are non-Charismatic but which are particularly welcoming to members of this orientation, while adopting a worship style inspired from Charismatic trends. In all these cases, it is important to notice that the structures of the Federation did a great deal to adapt the Charismatic culture to the French Baptist identity. Confronted at the end of the 1940s by the growing claims of 'Pentecostal Baptists', the Baptist Federation issued, in 1952, a 'resolution on the orientation of our churches' which defined clearly the common ground which 'Pentecostal Baptists' and others had to work together. According to Evert Veldhuizen, this resolution stressed an 'intermediate position, acceptable for Pentecostal Baptists and the others'. This document[53] makes a distinction between life experiences and confession of faith. The autonomy of the local assembly is recalled, along with the fact that the Holy Spirit works for the conversion, sanctification, Christian communion, perseverance and equipping of the believer. The manifestation of spiritual gifts is not considered as an obligation, which makes for a clear distinction between Baptists and Pentecostal hardliners. Healing is supposed to be a testimony, and certainly not a way of propaganda. Calling for brotherly communion, this text was meant to welcome the emotional/prophetic tendency without accepting that spiritual gifts or experience could compete with the absolute normativity of the Bible.

This text achieved its purpose. It pacified tensions within Baptist ranks. But the relationships between the tendencies sometimes remained difficult. While some pastors complained about what they considered to be the half-hearted attitude of Baptists towards the charisms, others closed the door to the new Pentecostal wave, which seemed a threat to traditional Baptist identity. But in spite of these local difficulties, the synthesis won, and at the beginning of the twenty-first century the FEEBF remains a welcoming acculturation space between a pietistic/orthodox emphasis and an experiential/emotional emphasis. Several initiatives have been taken to maintain this line. The Baptist press, for instance, is an obvious tool for reshaping the Charismatic question according to the Baptist distinctive.[54] The increasing role of the pastoral school of Massy should also be highlighted. It led all

---

[52] Founded in 1907 as a dependance of the Reformed church of Passy, it was separated from the mother church in 1923. This assembly had Thomas Roberts for pastor from 1936. When Jules Thobois left the North of France for Paris in 1963, he replaced Roberts in what was called the 'Église indépendante de la rue Musset'. This church joined the FEEBF in 1966. With hundreds of members, it became an important center of charismatic influence. See Veldhuizen, 'Le renouveau charismatique protestant', ch. 9, 'Au Point du jour', pp. 236-73.

[53] G. Brabant *et al*, *Résolution sur l'orientation de nos Églises* (Paris: FEEBF, 1952).

[54] See, for instance, the special issue on pastoral ministry (and the question of authority) in *Construire Ensemble* 11 (mars, 1999).

pastors, whatever their tendency, to obtain theoretical and theological training.[55] It seems quite clear that, even if officials from the Federation will not admit it openly, the legitimacy of the pastor/doctor is favoured. The pastor/prophet type is accepted, but is invited to complete his training in order to gain doctrinal and exegetical legitimacy as well. The Federation considers this ongoing training as a necessity in order to preserve a specific Baptist identity.[56]

The results of this acculturation can be seen at different levels. First of all, it seems that the tendency to retreat from social issues,[57] which was a mark of early Pentecostal influence on Baptist churches in the 1950s, has been gradually attenuated. After a brutal rupture over the influence of the Social Gospel (whose main figure was Robert Farelly), most of the 'Pentecostal Baptists' came back, in one way or another, to the former dimension of social involvement. The example of 'social Charismatics'[58] in the Christian community of Lille is significant. Founded in 1975 by David Berly, a young Baptist pastor, this community started two 'Fraternities' ('Fraternités') as early as 1980. Open to inter-religious work, it created a meeting point for homeless people since 1985, and became a 'voice of social evangelism'.[59]

Another sign of acculturation is that Charismatics who belong to the FEEBF seem in many cases to be more interested in doctrine, theology, than their colleagues from 'outside' Baptist life. Confessions of faith do exist, and seem to play a real role in most Charismatic-Baptist churches. They clearly incorporate Baptist specificities.[60]

Thus it is quite obvious that the denominational structures settled by the Federation played an important *de facto* role in controlling Charismatic authority[61] in the church. The emphasis on training, on regular regional and national meetings, means that Charismatic pastors have to adapt to the global Baptist 'frame'. These structures seem to attract many Charismatic communities, which seem sometimes

---

[55] This training school for pastors, which works along with a language school (Les Cèdres) created in 1976, does not provide the total pastoral training. The majority of pastors (or future pastors) previously studied at the Bible Institute of Nogent, or at the Evangelical Faculty of Vaux-sur-Seine (interdenominational). The purpose of Massy is to emphasize practical issues and Baptist distinctives.

[56] Every new pastor has to attend six different training sessions of two or three days each. This training has to be followed for no less than two years. A quarterly, *Les Cahiers de l'école pastorale*, is directly related to the school.

[57] For a close study, see S. Fath, 'Les baptistes dans le Bassin houiller du Nord', in B. Duriez (ed.), *Chrétiens et monde ouvrier, 1937–1970* (Paris: ed. de l'Atelier, 2001), pp. 47-61

[58] Veldhuizen, 'Le renouveau charismatique protestant', pp. 315-25.

[59] Veldhuizen, 'Le renouveau charismatique protestant', p. 324.

[60] It is interesting to compare Jules Thobois, 'Charte charismatique', in *Le Point du Jour* 18 (1982), pp. 1-2 (this confession of faith re-uses the one from the Federation, with some additions), with Charles Schinkel, 'Ce que nous croyons' which is displayed in every issue of *Actes 2*.

[61] We use here 'charismatic authority' in the Weberian sense.

tired of their solitary adventures, especially when the heroic founder disappears. Several Charismatic assemblies have knocked on the Federation's door since the 1980s, expressing their desire for a denominational 'frame' which was then lacking.[62] The case of Boulogne-sur-Mer, detailed by Evert Veldhuizen, is a good example of this integration process: because of missionary work performed by the Mission Intérieure Baptiste since 1984 (Baptist Interior Mission, MIB), a small 'Christian community' was founded in this town. But another Charismatic community, seemingly more radical and more isolated, was already there. It was the 'Eglise chrétienne charismatique de Boulogne-sur-Mer', linked to the FECBC (Charles Schinkel). After the departure of the founder, this assembly did not wait long to merge with the other (created by the Baptist Federation). It seems that the help from the 'communauté chrétienne de Lille' (FEEBF) from 1977 to 1984, the mediation of Daniel Lhermenault, the regional president of the FEEBF, and the impulse of a lay member, Maurice Devos,[63] boosted the process. Denominational structures obviously played a major role in this merging.

Nevertheless, the sky of the acculturation process is not without clouds. Tensions are at work. According to a survey conducted in 1988, there were 2,828 Charismatic members in the FEEBF,[64] that is about the half of the professing members. This proportion has increased a little since then. We might say that in 2003 the Charismatic tendency has become a majority, albeit a small majority, in the Federation. The denominational structures, however, remain under the control of a majority of non-Charismatic leaders. Until 2003, a Charismatic pastor had never been elected to the head of the Federation, which is no accident.[65] What is new is that the annual conference of the FEEBF in June 2003 decided for the first time to choose as president a famous Charismatic leader, Daniel Lhermenault. This important decision says more than long discourses about the actual weight of the Charismatic tendency in the Baptist Federation.

However, if the delicate balance between the tendencies means negotiations and tensions, there is no strong identity crisis at work. Since the famous text of 1952, the internal cohesion of the Federation has not really been challenged, and its Baptist identity remains. We cannot exclude, in the future, a disruption of the existing balance. But for the moment, what we observe in the Federation is acculturation instead of expulsion or invasion.

---

[62] This motivation is not the only one: joining the FEEBF was also sometimes a good strategy in order to escape from the accusation of being a strange 'sect'.

[63] Veldhuizen, 'Le renouveau charismatique protestant', p. 317.

[64] Veldhuizen, 'Le renouveau charismatique protestant', p. 402.

[65] In Britain, charismatics attained earlier to the presidency of the Baptist Union. Douglas McBain, author of *Charismatic Christianity* (London: McMillan, 1997) and himself a charismatic, was President of the Baptist Union in 1998–99. His successor (1999–2000) Michael Bochenski is also a charismatic.

Third Scenario: A Fort Alamo against Charismatics

As we all know, Baptists love diversity. It is no surprise, then, to see that some of them cannot accept the two first scenarios. There is (at least) one other: resistance. Charismatic invasion is considered as a threat, a worldly tendency that has to be fought. Even if the influence of the Charismatic Movement seems overwhelming, resistance is the only proper response, as it was in Fort Alamo. Nearly 50% of French Baptists, including a minority of churches in the FEEBF, a vast majority of churches in the Baptist Association (AEEBF), and almost all independent Baptist churches, share the belief that Pentecostals and Charismatics are to be confronted and opposed because their views on charisms are not biblically balanced. As with the other scenarios, this point of view is of course held worldwide.[66] We have to point out that such a condemnation is now much less aggressive than fifty years ago, in times when Pentecostals seemed to others to be inspired by the Prince of Darkness.[67] But we can still perceive it. On the theological level, such Baptists consider that an actualisation of glossolalia is non-biblical. They are also very sceptical about healings and new worship styles. They emphasise a very strong doctrinal regulation, close to the Fundamentalist tradition, which often belongs to their heritage in various proportions. Spiritual experience is here closely monitored, and submitted to a constant biblical validation through the authorized interpretation these churches favour.

While being very cautious toward Charismatics, we can notice that the press of the Baptist Association has shown a more open view in recent years. But no Baptist church belonging to the Association can be described as Charismatic, or related to specific Charismatic networks working in France. When we look at the independent Baptist world, their view of Charismatics is filled even more with suspicion. The new openness of the Association does not occur here. A look at the internet sites of some independent Baptist churches is revealing. An American missionary, Arthur Sommerville, founded the 'Eglise Baptiste du Centre' in Paris, but a French pastor, Emmanuel Bozzi, now leads it. We can read on its internet site that the Baptist church 'takes a stand against apostasy, the Charismatic movement and the Ecumenical movement'. From the same standpoint, the Baptist church of Montpellier explains that 'our worship style seeks to honour Christ, and we do refuse the new worship style which invaded so many churches in our area. We welcome all who want to hear expository preaching.' In less abrupt terms than those used by the Eglise Baptiste du Centre, we find the same rejection of Charismatic style, and the promotion of a liturgy that canalizes emotion and valorizes

---

[66] For a controversial Baptist look at the Charismatic Movement see, e.g., D. Middlemiss, *Interpreting Charismatic Experience* (London: SCM Press, 1996).

[67] See this document from the AEEBF, 'Les voies habituelles du Saint Esprit', in R. Dubarry, *Pour faire connaissance avec un idéal d'Église* (Valence: Imprimeries réunies, 1953), p. 146-52. 'Baptism of the Spirit' is understood as proceeding from 'the Enemy' (Satan).

transmission of the 'Word of God'.[68] This stance relates typically to an Evangelical tradition (including Fundamentalism, but not only it) that seeks to 'harness' emotional phenomenon found during revival events, in the name of a needed 'domestication' of spiritual experience.[69]

Conclusion

Whatever we think about the charismaticization of Christianity, which affects all Christian identities today, it seems that in the French Baptist case things are quite balanced. The so-called 'charismatic wave' is not overwhelming.[70] Charismatic Baptists who have abandoned Baptist specificities are only about 10% of all French Baptists. Within the 40% who are in an acculturation process with Charismatic influence,[71] only about half of them have adopted clear Charismatic distinctives, while others seem to favour acculturation of Charismatics within a pietist/orthodox orientation. Globally, we can consider that less than a third of French Baptist churches are clearly Charismatic, while others are either negotiating with the Charismatic position, or openly rejecting it. This must lead us to conclude that the reconfiguration of Baptist identity does not go in one direction only, even if the Charismatic trend is obvious. By contrast with the real Fort Alamo, extinction might not be inevitable for those who refuse to surrender to the current Charismatic mood. Instead of a war with a winner and a loser, there is a subtle game of mutual influence. Charismatic emphases transform Baptist identity, but it is also the case that the latter canalizes (or rejects) the Charismatic tendency.

---

[68] http://www.diakrisis.org/churches_Europe.htm#France.

[69] J.D. Hunter, *American Evangelicalism: Conservative Religion and the Quandary of Modernity* (New Brunswick: Rutgers University Press, 1983), p. 100.

[70] In his thesis, Evert Veldhuizen evaluates at only 12,000 people within charismatic ranks within French Protestantism during the 1980s (this might be quite underestimated). Reminder: there are about 1,2 million Protestants in France, including 200,000 Pentecostals.

[71] These figures are relatively close to what can be observed in Britain. According to N. Scotland, 50% of English Baptist churches are influenced by the Charismatic Movement. N. Scotland, *Charismatics and the New Millenium: The Impact of Charismatic Christianity from 1960 into the new Millenium* (London: Guildford, 2000), p. 19.

CHAPTER 7

Baptist Identities in Eastern Europe

Toivo Pilli

Introduction

In the first part of this study an attempt is made to present the formative influences that have shaped Baptist life and belief in Eastern Europe. The main focus will be on the developments in the last fifteen or twenty years as well as on present-day challenges, though some references to earlier history will be made. In the second part of the study five polarities of Baptist values are presented. The argument which is developed is that within the area of these polarities, which offer room for certain creative tensions, Eastern European Baptists are in a process of constantly seeking for a better self-understanding. Rather than concentrating on a given set of principles, this analysis pursues the journey of Eastern European Baptists towards their identities. It would also be possible to say that the first part of the exploration here deals with the 'context', and the second part takes a closer look at the 'text' of Baptist identities in Eastern Europe.

Eastern European Baptists are struggling to find a balance between their vision of the past and their vision of the future; they are facing changes but are encouraged by their tradition. An emphasis is placed in this study on the dynamic element of this process, which is always influenced by local situations and cultural features. Perhaps a simple illustration would help to clarify the point. There is a tradition of seeing Baptists as people who stand for their distinctive truths, sometimes with 'the sword of the Word' in their hands. In this approach, the focus is often on Baptist doctrinal distinctives, and an attempt is made 'to give a definitive answer that represents all Baptists'.[1] However, another image may be more appropriate to describe Eastern European Baptists: they are 'pilgrims', they are 'on a journey'. It is not 'a sword', but 'a walking stick', which is their characteristic feature.

---

[1] R. Stanton Norman, *More Than Just a Name: Preserving Our Baptist Identity* (Nashville, TN: Broadman and Holman Publishers, 2001), p. 3.

Cultural, Religious and Historical Backgrounds to Eastern European Baptist Identities

Cultural and Religious Backgrounds

In looking at the identity issue among Baptists, one immediately recognises the diversity of backgrounds. Distinct histories and cultures have shaped and are shaping Baptist life in different areas of this part of the world that is generically called Eastern Europe. When attempts are made to be more specific in defining the region, terms like 'Slavic Europe', 'Ottoman Europe', 'Balkan Europe', 'Soviet Europe' and others have been used.[2] However, these terms are never all-embracing.[3] Even if only the religious context is observed, the picture is far from uniform: there are Baptists who are living in a Roman Catholic context, like those in Poland and Lithuania; there are Protestant pockets that form a background for Baptist identity, as in Latvia and Estonia; and there are vast areas where Baptist identity is formed in an Orthodox setting. One can also add southern republics of the Former Soviet Union where the background is predominantly Muslim. And it should not be forgotten that there are regions where it would be appropriate to talk about a post-Christian culture, gradually replacing a former Christian paradigm.

These contexts give a specific 'colour' to the identities of religious communities and movements. Baptists are no exception. It is difficult, if not impossible, to talk about a singular and unified identity of Baptists in Eastern Europe. It would be more appropriate to talk rather about 'identities' in the plural than about 'an identity' in the singular. There is a variety of beliefs and practices among Eastern European Baptists. The picture is colourful! Even the use of language indicates variety. For example, Latvian and Georgian Baptists are happy to have 'bishops',[4] Russian and Ukrainian Baptists still use the word 'senior presbyter' to denote their leaders, and in Poland or Armenia one would more likely hear the word 'president' or 'chairman'.

There exists an interrelationship between the wider religious background and the Baptist way of being a Christian. Sometimes Baptists have tried to distance themselves from this background, but sometimes they have been influenced by it more than they have been ready to admit. Yakov Krotov, speaking from Russian Orthodox perspective and questioning both Protestant and Orthodox practices in his country, has suggested that a position of passivity would be characteristic of the Orthodox tradition: 'I am sure that the Russian Orthodox emphasis on passivity is

---

[2] Norman Davies, *Europe: A History* (London: Pimlico, 1997), p. 44.

[3] This paper uses the term 'Eastern Europe' with a certain freedom, concentrating mostly on Slavic speaking areas, but referring occasionally to other areas like the Baltics or the countries in Central Asia.

[4] Valdis Teraudkalns, 'Episcopacy in the Baptist Tradition', in Philip E. Thompson and Anthony R. Cross (eds), *Recycling the Past or Researching History?: Studies in Baptist Historiography and Myths* (Studies in Baptist History and Thought, 11; Milton Keynes: Paternoster, 2005), pp. 280-82, 286-91, sections which deal primarily with Latvia.

Christian.'[5] If Krotov is right, and there is an element of passivity—at least at the theological–philosophical level, if not always at the level of practice—in Slavic-Orthodox spirituality, then the Evangelical position would be in clear contrast to the Orthodox view. Passive spirituality would be foreign to Baptists, who would rather agree in their beliefs and practices with the wider Evangelical conviction that activity not passivity is an essential element of being a Christian.[6] We are what we do! Certainly, beliefs are important, but often with an emphasis on 'living out' these beliefs. Krotov, indeed, tries to find ways to reconcile these two positions, giving credit to both, but it is true that doing-orientated Christianity is often recognised as alien, even threatening and aggressive, in an Orthodox context, especially when differences in ecclesiology and mission emerge.

At the same time Baptists in Slavic areas have borrowed some elements from Orthodoxy. These elements can be seen in Baptist church architecture, in worship music, and also in following the Julian calendar for celebrating Easter. Further, Baptists in Georgia also follow the Eastern church calendar for Pentecost. On Pentecost Sunday all the ministers go to the 'Cathedral Baptist Church'. The Georgian Baptist Bishop stated: 'That day we are consecrating holy oil for the use of all the Baptist churches in Georgia.'[7] In their understanding of salvation, Slavic Baptists have been different from the Western Reformed view which emphasises the juridical aspect of salvation. Instead, they would find inspiration from some aspects of Orthodox soteriology: salvation understood as victory over death; Christ as the one who achieves salvation; the Holy Spirit as the one who applies this to people; an emphasis on sanctification by the power of God; and the belief that people have real choices to accept salvation and to actualise it through love.[8] Although Slavic Baptists have often been described as 'Arminian', it would be more appropriate to investigate their links with the Orthodox theology of salvation. Constantine Prokhorov notes that in contrast to Orthodox believers, Russian Baptists stressed faith more than good works, but they were always far removed from Western Reformed views of salvation.[9]

---

[5] Sharon Linzey (ed.), *Christianity in Russia and Post Communist Europe: Directory 2003* (Pasadena, CA: William Carey Library, 2003), p. 27.

[6] For example, David Bebbington has argued that 'activism' is one characteristic feature of Evangelicalism in Britain. David Bebbington, *Evangelicalism in Modern Britain: A History from the 1730s to the 1980s* (Grand Rapids, MI: Baker Book House, 1989), pp. 10-12.

[7] Malkhaz Songulashvili, e-mail message 17 June 2003.

[8] See Donald Fairbairn, *Eastern Orthodoxy through Western Eyes* (Louisville, KY: Westminster John Knox Press, 2002), p. 86.

[9] Constantine Prokhorov, 'Orthodox and Baptists in Russia: The Early Period', in Ian M. Randall (ed.), *Baptists and the Orthodox Church: On the way to understanding* (Prague: International Baptist Theological Seminary, 2003), p. 111

Some Historical Insights

Though it would be inadequate to define Eastern Europe simply according to former political borders as 'a former socialist-bloc region', nonetheless the socio-political aspect should not be neglected. Recent historical changes in former socialist countries have certainly had an effect on churches. Baptists have gone through dramatic transformational situations during the last fifteen or twenty years. Usually these changes, beginning with *perestroika*, are described as a positive development towards more religious freedom and new opportunities for believers. But these cataclysmic events can also be described as a kind of 'social explosion', causing confusion and sometimes collective shock for many Christians. 'Few persons, inside the churches or within the governments or the military, expected that change could come so quickly.'[10] Sergei Nikolaev, President of the St Petersburg Evangelical Theological Academy, has pointed to the change of values: 'It may be the same city and the same region but the atmosphere and values are new.'[11] Rapid changes in the socio-political context often have a double effect. They create an atmosphere of renewal and open doors for new opportunities, but a quest for stability and for well-proven traditions is often born at the same time. Change can be attractive and fearful at the same time. For example, one Baptist theological educator from Moscow described two concerns in Russian Baptist churches today—awareness of the importance of mission and attempts to maintain traditional worship styles.[12] Evangelism and mission demand changes and flexibility; however, this is counterbalanced by a striving to maintain well-established patterns and a wish not to lose one's traditions and values. It is obvious that there has been a tremendous pressure on Eastern European Baptists to cope with change and to re-interpret their self-understanding in the light of the recent years.

In addition, two comments on the wider history of Eastern European Baptists should be made. First, from the beginning there has been a challenge for Eastern European Baptists to find their own, indigenous way of being Baptist. In the nineteenth century, with the influence of German Baptist mission efforts,[13] the question about the relationship between indigenous identities and German Baptist

---

[10] J. Martin Bailey, *The Spring of Nations: Churches in the Rebirth of Central and Eastern Europe* (New York: Friendship Press, 1991), p. 11.

[11] Sergei Nikolaev, 'The Problems of Euro–Asian Theology for the New Millennium', *Religion in Eastern Europe* 10.2 (April, 2000), p. 2.

[12] Nikolai Kornilov, oral information 4 February 2003.

[13] For a survey of German Baptist mission work in the Eastern part of Europe, see Ian M. Randall, 'Every Apostolic Church a Mission Society: European Baptist Origins and Identity', in Anthony R. Cross (ed.), *Ecumenism and History: Studies in Honour of John H.Y. Briggs* (Carlisle: Paternoster Press, 2002), pp. 289-300, and Richard V. Pierard, 'Germany and Baptist Expansion in nineteenth-Century Europe', in D.W. Bebbington (ed.), *The Gospel in the World: International Baptist Studies* (Studies in Baptist History and Thought, 1; Carlisle: Paternoster Press, 2002), pp. 189-208.

patterns entered the scene.[14] In some cases, conflicts were inevitable. Up to the present time, contextualisation is continuously an important issue. The need to find a 'Baptist way' in conformity with the indigenous theological and historical roots in Eastern Europe has been increasingly voiced. There is a challenge to 'combine the enormous experience of evangelical theology of the west with our native religious quest', says Nikolaev.[15] Secondly, a characteristic feature of Eastern European Baptists is a history of disruptions in the course of their development: persecutions, deportations and severe restrictions. This was true in Tsarist Russia, especially during the times of Konstantin Pobedonostsev, the Procurator of the Holy Synod in 1880–1905. Outstanding Evangelical Christian (Baptist) leaders like Vassili Pashkov and Modest Korff were exiled in 1884.[16] Later, during World War I, new pressures came upon many Baptists in Russia, including Siberia, as they were suspected of being involved in espionage or of 'having close ties to military Germanism'.[17] After a decade of relative freedom from 1918–28, a long and devastating persecution began in the Soviet Union that almost wiped out Baptist structures and leadership.[18] Hans Brandenburg noted: 'Stalin made…the struggle against all religious belief into a state matter.'[19] Similar 'historical disruptions' in the course of Baptist life and development are common across Europe, but are not known elsewhere, for example in America.

Persecution became 'hereditary'[20] for many Baptists in Eastern Europe from the nineteenth century onwards. Many, perhaps the majority, of the Baptist churches

---

[14] Being often dismissed as only a foreign (German) imported 'plant' in Lutheran or Orthodox 'soil', Baptists themselves have tended to emphasise their indigenous character. For example, Estonian Baptist leader Karl Kaups, clearly diminishing German Baptist influences, stated in 1934 that Roman Catholicism and Lutheranism came to Estonia from Germany, and Orthodoxy from Russia, but the 'Estonian Baptist [movement] was born in Estonia and by Estonians themselves'. R. Kaups (ed.), *50 aastat apostlite radadel 1884–1934* [*50 Years in the Ways of the Apostles*] (Keila: E.B.K. Liidu kirjastus, 1934), p. 12. Also, S. Savinsky, writing about the early history of Russian and Ukrainian Baptists, tends to play down the German influence. See S. Savinsky, *Istorija Evangelskih Hristian-Baptistov Ukrainy, Rossii, Belorussii 1867–1917* [*History of Evangelical Christians-Baptists in Ukraine, Russia and Belorussia 1867–1917*] (St Petersburg: Biblija dlja Vseh, 1999), p. 96.
[15] Nikolaev, 'The Problems of Euro–Asian Theology', p. 4. The same need in the field of theological education in Eastern and Central Europe has also been pointed out. See Cheryl Brown and Wesley Brown, 'Progress and Challenge in Theological Education in Central and Eastern Europe', *Transformation* 20.1 (January, 2003), pp. 1-3.
[16] Michael Rowe, *Russian Resurrection: Strength in Suffering: A History of Russia's Evangelical Church* (London: Marshall Pickering, 1994), pp. 29, 32.
[17] Savinsky, *Istorija*, p. 310.
[18] Walter Sawatsky, *Soviet Evangelicals Since World War II* (Kitchener, ON: Herald Press, 1981), pp. 45-48.
[19] Hans Brandenburg, *The Meek and the Mighty* (New York: Oxford University Press, 1977), p. 187.
[20] Walter Sawatsky uses this expression, *Soviet Evangelicals*, p. 27.

developed a spirituality where being persecuted, experiencing suffering for Christ, as well as living with an inward-looking view, were all an inseparable part of their self-understanding. All this was aggravated by being a minority religious group. This approach of Baptists has been called 'a survival theology'.[21] This outlook has been evaluated by Westerners in two opposing ways: one view emphasising the faithfulness of Evangelicals during atheism, and another view emphasising legalism, cultural isolation and an inability to absorb new members.[22] Today, Baptists in the Former Soviet Union region are facing a mixed experience. In some cases they have been given wide opportunities for work and even some support from the government, for example in Ukraine, where significant growth is taking place. However, in many places, especially in Central Asia, Baptists face serious restrictions, which, given the background of growing Islamic influence, may become even more severe than during the Soviet years.

Despite the many difficulties and setbacks they have experienced, Eastern European Baptists, looking back into their longer history in the nineteenth and on into the twentieth centuries, can nonetheless see some positive aspects of persecution. It drew clear lines between Christians and non-Christians, it diminished the number of nominal church members and it made commitment—in addition to the new-birth experience—the basis of entrance to church membership for new converts.

An extra item in the melting pot of Eastern European Baptist identities was added in the Former Soviet Union in 1944 when the All-Union Council of Evangelical Christians and Baptists (AUCECB) was formed.[23] This structure was to bring under one umbrella the Baptists, Evangelical Christians, Pentecostals, and, later, Mennonites. All these movements had their own theological and communal identity. From this perspective, it is easier to understand that the history of Baptists in the Former Soviet Union areas is a history of constantly dealing with an identity-question. Also, the famous split in the Baptist body between the AUCECB and the so called *Initsiativniki* or Reform Baptists in the 1960s can be understood not only as personal or doctrinal conflict, but rather as a clash over the issue of identity. *Initsiativniki* leaders were convinced that concessions to atheistic restrictions were dangerously undermining their identity as believers. They demanded a relaxation of

---

[21] Karl Heinz Walter, 'The Future of Theological Education within the European Baptist Federation', *Religion in Eastern Europe* 21.3 (June, 2001), p. 22.

[22] Mark Elliott and Anita Deyneka, 'Protestant Missionaries in the Former Soviet Union', in John Witte and Michael Bourdeaux (eds), *Proselytism and Orthodoxy in Russia: The New War for Souls* (Maryknoll, NY: Orbis Books, 1999), p. 207.

[23] *Istorija Evangelskih Hristian-Baptistov v SSSR* [*A History of Evangelical Christians-Baptists in the USSR*] (Moskva: VSEHB, 1989), pp. 231-34; H. Leon McBeth, *The Baptist Heritage: Four Centuries of Baptist Witness* (Nashville, TN: Broadman Press, 1987), pp. 812-13. For further background, see Maurice Dowling, 'Baptists in the Twentieth-Century Tsarist Empire and the Soviet Union', in Bebbington (ed.), *Gospel in the World*, pp. 209-32.

state control over Christians and a greater democratisation in church life.[24] The AUCECB leadership and its supporters believed that it was still possible to be a Baptist without being actively involved in evangelism—at least temporarily—or in spite of giving up some democratic principles of church government and leadership. As a result of the split, in addition to external pressures an inner fragmentation and conflict became an inseparable part of Baptist life in the Soviet Union. The tensions that emerged in the 1960s have not found a final solution even today.[25]

However, the different combinations of Baptist distinctives in Eastern Europe often find a common centre in a Christological perspective. Glen Stassen has pointed out the same aspect when studying Baptist identity from a Western point of view.[26] Christ-centered discipleship, as Stassen calls this characteristic, may also serve as a platform for reaching a better mutual understanding between Eastern and Western Baptists (if this distinction is still appropriate). Christology for Eastern Europeans is clearly more than a doctrinal question. It has an emphasis on discipleship, character-formation and life-style. It may even be possible to argue that in a Slavic context Baptists have inherited some elements of Orthodox Christology and the Orthodox understanding of God. Baptists would certainly oppose any suggestion that they support the concept of *theosis,* but they would emphasise becoming similar to Christ, coming closer to Christ. Sometimes this approach may even take mystical dimensions. Ivan (Johann) Kargel, an influencial Evangelical Christian pastor and theologian in Russia, once expressed the motto of his life as 'Learn to know Him!' referring to Philippians 3.10: 'I want to know Christ and the power of his resurrection and the fellowship of sharing his sufferings...'.[27] Even his reflections about the work of the Holy Spirit were definitely Christocentric.[28]

Influenced by the cultural, religious and historical context, Eastern European Baptists cannot simply be characterised by a static system of principles, but rather by a process of trying to find their calling and following Christ in their specific setting. Valdis Teraudkalns, talking about Latvian Baptists, has pointed out that 'Every identity, including a religious one, is not something fixed for ages but fluid.'[29] However, this 'fluidity' is not totally chaotic. There are some constituting elements that function as markers where Baptists are seeking for their identity. Between these markers a creative tension is taking place. In what follows an attempt

---

[24] Michael Bourdeaux, *Religious Ferment in Russia: Protestant Opposition to Soviet Religious Policy* (London: Macmillan/ New York: St Martin's Press, 1968), p. 29.

[25] I.V. Podberezkii, *Byt protestantom v Rossii* [*To be a Protestant in Russia*] (Moskva: Institut religii i prava, 1996), pp. 166-67.

[26] Glen Stassen, 'A Proposal for Baptist Theological Identity', lecture at the conference 'Doing Constructive Theologies in a Baptist Way', International Baptist Theological Seminary, Prague, 20 June, 2003.

[27] Sermon notes compiled by Arpad Arder. The author's personal archive.

[28] Ivan Kargel, *Sobranie sochinenii* [*Collected Works*] (Sankt-Peterburg: Biblija dlja vseh, 2002), pp. 118-20.

[29] Valdis Teraudkalns, 'Echoes of Modernity in the Theologies and Praxis of Churches in Contemporary Latvia', *International Review of Mission* 92 (January, 2003), p. 59.

will be made to analyse the process of Eastern European Baptists seeking their identities and meeting new challenges as the people of God. Five pairs of polarities, or markers, will be applied to the Eastern European context: Word and Spirit; individual and communal; witness and service; freedom and responsibility; and autonomy and co-operation.

Eastern European Baptists Looking for Their Way
Word and Spirit

Baptists have traditionally had a focus on the Word of God. The Word and the Bible are often identical or at least inseparable for Baptists. However, in Eastern Europe the role of the Word took specific forms and was emphasised in specific ways. Early Ukrainian Baptists had their roots in Stundism, a 'Bible Study movement' among Protestant colonists in the south of Ukraine.[30] The study of the Bible was not only a matter of finding theological answers. It increased literacy among so-called Stundo-Baptists, and it had ethical consequences. 'The serious teaching of this book opened the way for a miracle: people quit drinking vodka, smoking, and swearing—they were born again, becoming entirely different people.'[31] An emphasis on ethics, when interpreting the biblical message, is one of the characteristic features of Eastern European Baptists. Further, sermons are used as a means of pastoral guidance. Much of the pastoral work that in the West would take place in a pastor's office or during counselling sessions, is in the East supposed to happen through the sermon. The practice of having three or even more sermons during one worship service is still a norm in several Eastern European Baptist church contexts. One may also want to add to the picture the lack of Bibles, which was a sad reality for many decades. This situation motivated many Baptists to learn long passages of the Bible by heart.

During the last fifteen years theological schools have been mushrooming in Eastern Europe.[32] The main interest of the students is to study the Bible. However, the understanding of the role of the Word and how to interpret it is often rather 'linear' and 'literal'. Karl Heinz Walter, a former General Secretary of the European Baptist Federation, has pointed out the problem: 'it is one thing to study and to teach the Bible and it is another issue to begin to think in theological terms.'[33] It may be helpful to re-examine the relationship between the Word and the Spirit in an Eastern European context and to listen to the theologians of the Western tradition, too. Stanley Grenz has said that the 'reading of the text—and under this rubric we would place all our exegetical efforts—is for the purpose of listening to the voice of

---

[30] Steve Durasoff, *The Russian Protestants: Evangelicals in the Soviet Union: 1944–1964* (Rutherford: Fairleigh Dickinson University Press, 1969), p. 39.

[31] *Bratskii Vestnik* [*Brotherly Herald*] 5 (1947), p. 6, quoted in Durasoff, *Russian Protestants*, p. 41.

[32] Brown and Brown, 'Progress and Challenge', p. 1; Peter Penner, 'Critical Evaluation of Recent Developments in the Commonwealth of Independent States', *Transformation* 20.1 (January, 2003), p. 21.

[33] Walter, 'The Future of Theological Education', p. 23.

Spirit who seeks to speak through scripture to the church in the present... [T]he authority of the Bible is in the end the authority of the Spirit whose instrumentality it is.'[34]

An emphasis on the Word is balanced by the question: what is the role of the Holy Spirit—not only in the process of biblical interpretation, but also in Baptist life? This question has become more frequently asked in Baptist communities in Eastern Europe. The charismatic movement is playing a challenging role here. For example, in the Baltics many Baptists have joined new charismatic churches. 'Baptist churches, a denomination somehow standing at the bridge between the older, more established churches and new Christian groups, have been most affected by this process of seeking a new spirituality.'[35] However, the seeking for a more Spirit-orientated spirituality does not necessarily require finding a new faith community; the process takes place also within Baptist churches. In the theological realm the gifts of the Spirit, and pneumatology in general, as well as pentecostal–charismatic manifestations of faith, pose a challenge for many Eastern European Baptists. In 1994, I witnessed a discussion among several key Eastern European Baptist leaders who tended to exclude charismatic phenomena from Baptist self-understanding; indeed there was even a tendency to demonise these phenomena and to see them as threatening and dangerous. Today, the approach would be more embracing, though probably not unanimously so. Also, in the case of some other issues, such as the role of women in the church, the view taken will depend on how the emphasis falls: a Word-approach, especially focusing on a literal understandings of texts, would tend to exclude women from church ministry, while a Spirit-approach would probably tend to be more inclusive.

Individual and Communal

The individual and communal constitute another pair of healthy tensions for Eastern European Baptists. On the one hand, there is a clear tendency among them—as for many Baptists around the world—to understand faith in individual terms. Religious conversion as well as sanctification are often be understood from this perspective. Wayne Stacy has pointed out that 'Our Baptist proclivity toward individualism has caused us to undervalue the communal aspect of salvation.'[36] In Eastern Europe expressions like 'personal spiritual life' or 'personal quiet time' are used to refer to aspects of Baptist spirituality. There is a strong inclination to interpret baptism and the Lord's Supper from an individual perspective: baptism as a person's witness of his or her faith, and the Lord's Supper as a personal remembrance and celebration of

---

[34] Stanley J. Grenz and John Franke, *Beyond Foundationalism: Shaping Theology in a Postmodern Context* (Louisville, KY: Westminster John Knox Press, 2001), p. 65.

[35] Valdis Teraudkalns, 'New Charismatic Churches in Latvia as Examples of Postmodern Religious Subculture', *International Review of Mission* 90 (October, 2001), pp. 447-48.

[36] R. Wayne Stacy (ed.), *A Baptist's Theology* (Macon, GA: Smyth and Helwys Publishing, 1999), p. 171.

Christ's redemptive work. Eastern European Baptists would widely agree with the emphasis on every individual's responsibility to God in matters of faith and moral life, as expressed in documents prepared by Baptists in the West.[37] Understanding faith as something that happens exclusively between 'God and myself' is not only a consequence of Enlightenment philosophy applied by Baptists, it is also a reaction against the religious background—Orthodox, Roman Catholic or Protestant—that (at least in some areas such as soteriology and worship) focuses more on communal and corporate aspects of faith.

Paradoxically, in Eastern European Baptist life community is not lacking, though it is understood more in practical than in theological terms. One may see it as a dissonance between theology and practice. During the times of atheistic pressure, Baptist communities offered important spiritual—and in many cases practical—support for their members. There was a tradition of having something happening at church every day of the week: attending two worship services on Sunday, participating in different choir rehearsals twice a week, having Bible study evenings on Wednesdays, and prayer meetings on Fridays. For the majority of Baptist church members going to church three or four times a week was—and still is—considered a normal way of being a Baptist in many Eastern European countries. Having statistics of 'attendance' would not be understood by these people, as approximate Sunday morning attendance is close to 80-90% anyway. In the 1960s and 1970s, in Estonian rural areas, the average attendance at Baptist churches by the members was close to 100%. In cities the attendance was lower. In several churches Sunday attendance was higher than church membership numbers.[38] Church is a 'gathering church';[39] church is where people of God come together. Especially during the Soviet years, nominal membership was regarded as something foreign, and church discipline could be applied to those who systematically absented themselves from church gatherings. During the last decade there has been a tendency towards less active participation in church meetings, and, reluctantly, some churches have abandoned Sunday evening services. Some Eastern European Baptists have seen this as giving up familiar and safe patterns of being a church, but others have pointed out the positive side: Christian life should be seen as holistic, taking place not only inside a church building but also in everyday life.

Fellowship was an important means of encouragement and spiritual growth within the setting of persecution. Johannes Dyck has argued that in Kazakhstan, and other parts of Central Asia, the semi-legal youth work of the 1970s was characterised by 'an intensive fellowship phase'. The Baptist leaders growing out of these

---

[37] E.g., see a statement 'Baptist Ideals' prepared in 1964 by nineteen Southern Baptist Convention leaders and scholars. There is a separate section about the worth of an individual, in Walter B. Shurden, *The Baptist Identity: Four Fragile Freedoms* (Macon, GA: Smith and Helwys Publishing, 1993), pp. 104-105.

[38] The Senior Presbyter's reports 1964, 1965, 1970–72. The Archive of the Union of Evangelical Christian and Baptist Churches of Estonia.

[39] Keith G. Jones, *A Believing Church* (Didcot: Baptist Union of Great Britain, 1998), p. 38.

fellowship circles—a kind of *ecclesiola in ecclesia*—today work in Kazakhstan, Kyrgyzstan, Uzbekistan and Tadjikistan. Fellowship was 'a central point of ECB [Evangelical Christian and Baptist] identity' in the Former Soviet Union.[40] However, this fellowship emphasis was practised without much in the way of serious and intentional attempts to reflect on it theologically. Thus urbanisation, social changes and the growing variety of theological influences pose new questions for Eastern European Baptists on this individual–communal axis.

Witness and Service

Since 1989, Eastern European countries became increasingly a mission field for many Protestants, including Baptist mission agencies from the West. Also local Baptists have renewed their evangelistic efforts.[41] An emphasis on witness is nothing new either in Baptist life in general, or in Eastern Europe in particular. However, for many decades in the former socialist-atheistic countries the government authorities' pressure had forced the Baptist witness into church buildings, into private homes and into the framework of personal relationships. Witness came to be understood increasingly as something private. In the 1970s, the Senior Presbyter in Estonia, Robert Võsu, wrote a little manual for church members. The manual was entitled *Personal Evangelism*. It pointed out that personal evangelism does not need special means to be fulfilled, it requires less training and it gives the best results.[42] At the same time, a dichotomy developed in Baptist life: the world became sharply divided into two spheres—a public sphere and a private sphere. Partly because of atheistic pressures, religion was pushed into the private sphere of life. In some regions, there was also the strong influence of Pietism, 'with its narrow view of spirituality as a personal, existential and emotional relationship with God'.[43]

The hope that they could bring evangelism into the public sphere of life never died among Eastern European Baptists. In the 1990s, many of them—supported by their foreign, mostly American partners—enthusiastically rushed to test the effectiveness of mass-evangelism. It seemed that mass-evangelism, with an emphasis on verbal proclamation, could replace individual mission responsibility. Soon, there was an increasing disappointment at the results of mass-evangelism, partly because

---

[40] Johannes Dyck, 'Revival as Church Restoration: Patterns of a Revival among Ethnic Germans in the Central Asia after World War II', *Transformation* 21.3 (July, 2004), p. 176.

[41] Sharon Linzey (ed.), *Christianity in Russia and Post Communist Europe: Directory 2003* (Pasadena, CA: William Carey Library, 2003) lists approximately 3,000 foreign and indigenous Christian organisations working in Eastern and Central Europe. Many of them are involved in different areas of mission work.

[42] Robert Võsu, *Isiklik evangelism* [*Personal Evangelism*], typewritten manuscript (Tallinn, 1971), pp. 6-8. A copy in the Archive of the Union of Evangelical Christian and Baptist Churches of Estonia.

[43] Anne-Marie Kool, 'A Protestant Perspective on Mission in Eastern and Central Europe', *Religion in Eastern Europe* 20.6 (December, 2000), p. 7.

of little discipleship work after the major events and partly because in some cases the local churches were not ready to accept new Christians who had not been raised within the Evangelical-Baptist sub-culture. It seems that mass-evangelism as a method continued longer in the Slavic areas of Eastern Europe, but even there—for example, in present-day Ukraine and Russia—the emphasis is on church planting that focuses on spiritual growth and discipleship. Church planting has also been successful in Albania, Armenia, Moldova and Romania. Many Baptist evangelistic efforts can also be characterised by their emphasis on a proclamation that is balanced by what is offered through practical service and social sensitivity.

An openness to help and to serve has certainly been present in Eastern European Baptist life. Peter Penner has stated that 'Russian evangelicals never separated social ministry from gospel preaching and mission work, as one finds in some discussions on mission in western conservative groups that shape today's Christians in the East.'[44] However, during Communism, Christian practical service was necessarily limited. It was directed predominantly to other church members, and even this was illegal. A famous Baptist leader in Latvia, Peteris Egle, organised a special fund for retired pastors and their widows.[45] This was a kind of social ministry, though inward looking and unofficial. In the Soviet Union, Baptists became known as those who took care of each other. This became a powerful message in the socialist society that theoretically offered the best social care in the world, but practically was able to do very little. But Baptists still had to learn how to address issues of social work in the wider society. With the first signs of political freedom, social ministry was quickly revived in areas like Russia, Ukraine, Romania and elsewhere. According to Petr Mitskevich, the Vice-President of the Russian Baptist Union, Russian Baptists today are involved in several forms of social ministry, including ministry for the deaf, for orphans, and work in the hospitals.[46] In the background there was the wider movement of *miloserdiye* (mercy) in the Slavic areas of the Former Soviet Union during *perestroika*. In 1988–89 *miloserdiye* 'became a "buzz-word" in the Soviet press'.[47] In 1988 believers were allowed to do charitable work in hospitals, as there was a tremendous lack of hospital staff in the Soviet Union. At the end of the 1980s, the chairman of the Council for Religious Affairs remarked somewhat reluctantly and contemptuously, 'If the believers want to carry bed-pans, let them.'[48]

It can be argued that in many cases, especially if social work in Eastern Europe was supported substantially from abroad, it tended to be used as an instrument—sometimes in a rather mechanical way—for opening up opportunities

---

[44] Penner, 'Critical Evaluation', p. 15.

[45] Edgars Mazis, oral information 23 June 2003.

[46] Petr Mitskevich, oral information 6 February 2003.

[47] Michael Bourdeaux, 'The Quality of Mercy: A Once-only Opportunity', in John Witte and Michael Bourdeaux (eds), *Proselytism and Orthodoxy in Russia: The New War for Souls* (Maryknoll, NY: Orbis Books, 1999), p. 189.

[48] Jane Ellis, 'Some Reflections about Religious Policy under Khrachev', in Sabrina P. Ramet (ed.), *Religious Policy in the Soviet Union* (Cambridge: Cambridge University Press, 1993), p. 88.

for the verbal proclamation of the gospel. If this was the case, the value of social work was not in its spirit of servanthood but rather in the potential number of new converts. The verbal aspect of the witness often includes emphasis on doctrinal truths. Nigel Wright, writing from a Western perspective, has been calling for a 'modest approach' in witness, adopting a position of 'modest advocacy' and 'sincere conviction', rather than 'strident dogmatism' and 'aggressive confrontation'.[49] Baptists in Eastern Europe would probably see this approach as a 'western problem'. However, it is also the case that in Slavic areas Evangelicals are increasingly seeing the need to interpret complex issues related to verbal proclamation and practical ministry.

Freedom and Responsibility

Religious liberty, the equality of believers and voluntary church membership, are important values for Baptists. Walter B. Shurden has suggested that freedom, counter-balanced by responsibility, is a key word for understanding Baptist faith and life.[50] However, religious liberty, for example, was not an issue that was focused on in registered Baptist churches in the former socialist countries. This principle was suppressed by the government. It has often been argued that the unregistered Baptists stood for this principle. They suffered persecution and imprisonment because they believed that state authorities should not 'meddle with religion, or matters of conscience'—to use the words of an old Baptist document.[51] But even for the underground Baptists, the issue was first of all to have the practical possibility of evangelism and Christian education for their children; religious liberty was not always seen as a value in itself or as a theologically argued facet of Baptist identity.[52] Many Eastern European Baptists developed a self-understanding that marginalised the wider question of religious freedom.

Today, Baptists in Eastern Europe certainly stand up for their religious rights, and in many cases there has been a need to raise their voices and get help from the wider Baptist community when discriminatory religious laws have been prepared or if religious rights have been restricted. In April 2003, a public prosecutor in the

---

[49] Nigel G. Wright, *New Baptists, New Agenda* (Carlisle: Paternoster Press, 2002), pp. 31-32.

[50] Shurden, *Baptist Identity*, p. 3. Shurden defines 'four freedoms' as essential for Baptist identity: Bible freedom, soul freedom, church freedom, and religious freedom.

[51] *Propositions and Conclusions Concerning True Christian Religion, 1612–14*, in W.L. Lumpkin, *Baptist Confessions of Faith* (Valley Forge, PA: Judson Press, rev. edn, 1969), p. 140.

[52] It is slightly surprising to find that religious freedom was mentioned by an Estonian Baptist theologian Osvald Tärk in the 1980s. Osvald Tärk, 'Meie vendluse põhimõtted' ['Principles of Our Brotherhood'], *Logos* 2 (1983), pp. 6-9. Tärk had received his theological education in the USA, and, in general, Estonian Baptists tended to conform less to Soviet state pressure when compared to the official line of the All-Union Council of the Evangelical Christians-Baptists.

western Uzbek town of Mubarek complained that he constantly received protest letters from various parts of the world supporting local Baptists. 'I am fed up with reading them', he said.[53] However, Eastern European Protestants, Baptists included, as a rule would be more cautious in expressing their protests when the issue of religious liberty concerns other religious groups. Sharon Linzey and Yakov Krotov refer to a case in 1997 when Protestant leaders in Russia proposed an agreement in which they were prepared to restrict the rights of future religious groups on the condition that their own rights would be preserved. According to Linzey and Krotov the bill was changed before being signed into the law, and several rights for Protestants were deleted anyway.[54] If religious freedom is not understood as a universal value there is a contradiction in terms. Baptists are continuously in a process of interpreting the significance and meaning of religious freedom, which cannot be understood as a Baptist privilege, but as a Baptist principle.

There are other questions that may help Eastern European Baptists reflect upon their role in society. What should be the distinctive role of Baptist Unions or individual Baptists, perhaps including a political role, in societies where the tradition of democracy is still very 'young'?[55] What can Baptists, with a heritage of voluntarism, offer in societies where non-governmental initiatives are still weak and state bureaucracy is often oppressive? What position do Baptists attribute to themselves as having a voice in societies where religious liberty is far from being self-evident?

These questions find an answer only in the dialectics of freedom and responsibility. Everett Goodwin wrote, 'One of our greatest gifts, *freedom*, is always in tension with our greatest challenge, *responsibility*. Our history began with this tension, and we still find ourselves in the struggle today.'[56] This is also true in an Eastern European context, although responsibility among Slavic Baptists is often understood as personal responsibility in the areas of sanctification and Christian discipleship. Also, the responsibility of the faith community, or rather of its leaders, for the spiritual life of its members is a part of this understanding—often finding its expression in excercising church discipline. A believer's responsibility as a citizen or a member of an ethnic group is much less spoken of—if at all. 'We do not speak about social justice in our Ukrainian churches', one Ukrainian Baptist said.[57] Recent research has argued that there is a tendency among Lithuanian Baptists to distance themselves from their cultural and ethnic heritage and to see it as alien to Baptist

---

[53] 'Uzbekistan: Prosecutor "Fed Up" with Baptist Appeals', *Forum* 18 (24 April 2003): http://www.forum18.org/Archive.

[54] Linzey (ed.), *Christianity in Russia and Post Communist Europe*, pp. 37, 39.

[55] Tadeusz Zielinski, a Baptist who has been a member of the Polish Parliament, gave the J.D. Hughey Memorial Lectures at the International Baptist Theological Seminary, Prague, in 2002, on 'Baptists and Politics: Historical and Contemporary Reflections'.

[56] Everett Goodwin (ed.), *Baptists in the Balance: The Tension between Freedom and Responsibility* (Valley Forge, PA: Judson Press, 1997), p. 1.

[57] Alexander Cherevko, oral information 10 July 2003.

Christians.[58] Eastern European Baptists are still in the process of finding their way between the polarities of freedom and responsibility. Involvement in politics, which can be seen as a form of social responsibility, is far from being a clear issue. Those from a more pietistic background tend to see politics as something dirty. They refer to abuses of power during socialist times, and to cases of recent corruption. Those who have experienced Reformed or charismatic influences often tend to believe that politics gives them a better chance for Christian witness. However, the tradition of responsibility in society is still rather weak among Eastern European Baptists.

Dealing with social and political responsibility also involves the need to overcome the shadows of the past. One of these shadows is 'an inferiority complex', the common belief that Baptists as a religious minority cannot do much.[59] In some cases there is also a need to find reconciliation and forgiveness. In the history of Eastern European Baptists, as well as heroic faith there have also been cases of compromise. For example, yielding to the heavy state pressure, the official leadership of Soviet Baptists clearly discouraged presbyters from doing mission work, stating that their task was not to be missionaries, but pastors.[60] The Baptists' relationships with atheistic state structures is a sensitive theme in Eastern European Baptist history, but it should not be ignored.

Autonomy and Co-operation

The fifth area of creative tension exists between the autonomy of local churches and a need for wider co-operation. Eastern European Baptists have—very much in the same spirit of the Radical Reformation tradition—seen the local and visible church as the place where God's leading and Christian discipleship takes place. Nevertheless, the need for co-operation, especially for keeping fellowship and doing mission work, was understood in the early stages of their development. German Baptist models in the nineteenth century introduced Baptists in many regions of Eastern Europe to the idea of denominational thinking.[61] During socialist times, the hierarchical model of leadership and strongly centralised denominational structures were imposed. Walter Kolarz has stated that the aim of the Soviet religious policy was to make the churches 'not only as docile as possible but also as centralised as possible'.[62] After the collapse of Communism, the role of local churches increased again.

---

[58] Ruta Lysenkaite, 'The Place of Cultural Heritage in the Context of Contemporary Baptist Identity: A Case Study of Klaipeda Baptist Church' (MTh dissertation, International Baptist Theological Seminary, Prague, 2003).

[59] Anne-Marie Kool, 'A Protestant Perspective on Mission', p. 6.

[60] Sawatsky, *Soviet Evangelicals*, p. 59.

[61] For organisational development of Baptists in Europe in the nineteenth century, see Dale R. Kirkwood (ed.), *European Baptists: A Magnificent Minority* (Valley Forge, PA: International Ministries, [1981]), pp. 96-102.

[62] Walter Kolarz, *Religion in the Soviet Union* (London and New York: Macmillan and St. Martin's Press, 1961), p. 304.

Since 1989, the European Baptist Federation has taken conscious steps to recognize the role and 'spiritual riches' of Eastern European Baptists in the wider European Baptist fellowship and to have partnerships in different areas of ministry.[63] But the tradition continues of seeing a local church or a local denomination as independent and autonomous. This view has, no doubt, positive aspects, but it has sometimes also led to 'collective egoism' or to narrow self-centred thinking. This tension was recognized, for example, by the Estonian Baptist Union leadership who in 1999 stated that the strength of the Union was 'the independent acitivities' of local churches; however, the weakness was that the local churches often used their 'autonomy' as an excuse in order not to be involved in wider projects and not to contribute to the work at an all-union level.[64]

With increasing religious and political freedom at the beginning of the 1990s, separatist ideas developed among many Eastern European Evangelicals. Several denominations that had worked under the umbrella of the AUCECB for many decades preferred to continue independently in Russia and Ukraine. Though the political pressure had largely gone, many so called underground Baptists still found it difficult to co-operate with the churches that formerly belonged to the AUCECB. Eastern European Baptists face a challenge to accept cultural and theological variety in Baptist life and practice and to find better ways to co-operate at different levels—local, denominational and ecumenical. In the area of ecumenical co-operation there is a hesitant attitude. This is partly because minority churches have often derived their identity from their opposition to majority churches; they have developed a kind of 'negative identity'. There is a fear of losing one's identity when co-operating too closely with other churches. Nevertheless, areas like social ministries and relief work offer ground for co-operation. Orthodox theologian Vladimir Feodorov, suggesting that ecumenical trends have recently become weaker in Eastern Europe, argues that there is an urgent task 'that all the Eastern and Central European churches face: arousing in believers the spirit of mercy and love, encouraging charitable activities and interest in social ethics, and introducing these subjects in educational systems at different levels'.[65]

Conclusion

Throughout their history, Baptists in Eastern Europe have been continuously searching for more meaningful expressions of their faith as well as for better self-understanding. Historical experiences of persecution, the recent socio-political and

---

[63] Bernard Green, *Crossing the Boundaries: A History of the European Baptist Federation* (Didcot: Baptist Historical Society, 1999), pp. 136-37, 157.

[64] Liidu hetkeseisu analüüsi kokkuvõte [A Summary of the Present Situation of the Union] (11 May 1999). A copy in the author's personal archive.

[65] Vladimir Fedorov, 'Ecumenical Missionary Needs and Perspectives in Eastern and Central Europe Today: Theological Education with an Accent on Mission as a First Priority in our Religious Rebirth', *International Review of Mission* 92 (January, 2003), http://proquest.umi.com/pqdweb, p. 5.

religious changes in the former socialist region, the consequent new opportunities for Christian work and also the influx of Western theological ideas—all these aspects shape Baptist identities in Eastern European countries. Eastern European Baptists do not represent a unified and static system of ecclesial identity; they are constantly in a dialogue with their cultural-religious-historical context. The questions raised and the answers given in this dialogue vary both in place and in time. This study has argued that the polarities of Word and Spirit, individual and communal, witness and service, freedom and responsibility, and autonomy and co-operation, provide insights into how identities have been shaped in the past and continue to develop in the present. However, in this process Eastern European Baptists are also guided by a vision for the future: to grow closer to Christ and to participate more fully in God's mission in this world. These concepts are not unfamiliar within Orthodoxy, and to an extent such resonance is evidence that there is an element of healthy inter-relationship between 'the context', not least the wider religious context, and 'the text', the identities of Baptist communities in Eastern Europe.

CHAPTER 8

Leaving behind Imagined Uniformity: Changing Identities of Latvian Baptist Churches

Valdis Teraudkalns

Because of individualism and fragmentation, wrestling with identity has become a very important characteristic of modern society. In the process of socialisation people identify with those who are similar to them and define themselves against those who are viewed as the unacceptable other. This last aspect creates a tension between various social identities and some authors trace its origins back to ancient Greek philosophy:

> The passion for the One, the Platonic and above all Neoplatonic mysticism, clouding the trinitarian narrative of the Christian New Testament, is a key piece in the composition of Western identity. To the One are linked the invention and ennoblement of hierarchy as a strategy of submission to the totality.[1]

Due to the complexity of social networks we can speak of identities as changing mental and social constructions. In religion it is even more difficult to say what forms identity. This is true in seeking the core identity of any particular division of Christianity, because after trying to point out some distinctive features we discover that the same characteristics also belong to other Christian traditions. For example, Baptists have often stressed the centrality of the local church as a Baptist way of believing. But some Pentecostal theologians also view local churches as central to their spirituality.[2] The same can be said of believers' baptism — it is not unique to the Baptist tradition. Religious identity is constituted not just by one feature but by the whole set of characteristics dominant in the examined religious group in a particular time and space. If taken apart these features can also be found in other divisions of Christianity. We should be very careful in constructing global religious identities because local expressions of belief can differ greatly from that which, in the religious power discourse, has gained the status of dominant and therefore legitimate tradition. Following the sociologist Manuel Castells, we can talk about legitimising identities introduced by the dominant institutions, resistance identities

---

[1] L.C. Susin, 'A Critique of the Identity Paradigm', *Concilium* 2 (2000), p. 86.
[2] Pentecostal theologian Harold D. Hunter has given one of the sections in his article on Pentecostalism the title 'The local church at the centre'. H.D. Hunter, 'We are the Church: New Congregationalism', *Concilium* 3 (1996), p. 19.

generated by those social actors that are stigmatised by the dominant group, and project identities when social actors build a new identity that redefines their position.[3] Of course, identities that start as resistance groups may pass through the stage of projection and may become dominant. In Baptist churches around the world we can see how the charismatic movement, which started as a marginalised group, grew larger in numbers and moved to a more visible and constructive role, and in some cases has become the majority.

In a European context the question of identities has been raised in connection with a current debate about what it means to be European—who is included and who is excluded. We, as Christians, are inclined to stress the Christian past of Europe (quarrels around the European Constitution shows that), but we need to listen also to voices reminding us of the long-standing Jewish and Muslim presence in Europe.[4]

Multiple Faces of the Changing Context

In Latvia, as in other post-socialist countries, in public discourse we often hear concerns about ethnic, religious and other identities perceived as fixed entities grounded in the romanticised past. History shaped in a way which would fit the needs of dominant social actors becomes an important element in constructing ethnic identity. American Latvian historian Valters Nolledendorfs says, 'History, more precisely a nation's historical consciousness, is one of the cornerstones of national identity.'[5] The problem is that behind the pretension to go back to the historical truth inescapably lies a tendency to domesticate the past according to the historical canons set by the present.

Which identity from the past would Latvian Baptists choose to use as a building block for the future? There are many options because of the diversity that has developed in the Baptist movement. We can find a strict and closed identity whose distinct representative is one of the first Latvian Baptist leaders in the nineteenth century, Jekabs Skuja-Dingse (1820–74). He was even against co-operation with groups that were theologically close to Baptists, such as the Moravians. This was during the same period of time as a more ecumenically-minded group of Baptists managed to get the majority of votes in the Latvian Baptist Congress of 1883 in favour of so-called 'dry Baptists' (those who accepted members into local churches without baptism by immersion),[6] a decision that was implemented in only a few churches. There were American Latvian Baptists, first generation emigrants, who in

---

[3] M. Castells, *The Power of Identity* (Oxford: Blackwell, 1998), p. 8.

[4] See, e.g., Talal Asad's view that 'Europe is ideologically constructed in such a way that Muslim immigrants cannot be satisfactorily represented.' T. Asad, 'Muslims and European identity', in E. Hallam and B.V. Street (eds), *Cultural Encounters: Representing 'Otherness'* (London: Routledge, 2000), p. 11.

[5] V. Nollendorfs, 'Vesturiska apzina, integracija un muzejs' ('Historical Counsciousness, Integration and Museums'), *Diena (The Day)* 15 March 2003, p. 14.

[6] J. Tervits, *Latvijas baptistu vesture (History of Baptists of Latvia)* (Riga: Amnis, 1999), p. 65.

the first half of the twentieth century were influenced by the Social Gospel movement and Socialism, and some of them, for example Pastor Peteris Busmanis (1883–1970), even called Stalin a 'Christian brother'.[7] We also should take into consideration the multi-ethnic character of the Baptist movement. From the region of Liepaja there is information from the end of the 1850s that there were about fifteen members of the German-speaking Baptist church in Memel (now Klaipeda, Lithuania) who were visited by the leadership of the church in Memel and who also started their own meetings. Later, German-speaking churches independent of the 'mother church' in Memel were established in the territory of Latvia (the German Baptist church in Liepaja was founded in 1900, and in Riga in 1875).[8] Over the years, some Latvians belonged to these churches because they did not—for reasons including a preference for German culture and disagreement with the policies of Latvian churches—find a spiritual home in churches where the majority was of the same ethnic group.[9] Due to forced emigration, German churches vanished from the Baltic–German population in 1939. However, new groups of German Baptists appeared in Latvia after the Second World War when people from other Soviet republics viewed the Baltic region as a place easier to emigrate to than the West. But with this emigration German Baptists again ceased to exist. Starting from the end of the nineteenth century there were organised Russian Baptist groups in the territory of Latvia. There is information about a Russian Baptist group existing at the end of 1890s in one of the largest cities of Latvia, Daugavpils. In 1906, Russian Baptist worship services started in the Mathew Church in Riga, the capital of Latvia.[10] In 2005 in the Union of Baptist Churches in Latvia (UBCL) from a total of eighty-six churches there were fourteen Russian and three integrated churches.[11] Several Slavonic Baptist churches exist outside the Union. Fuller integration of Slavonic Baptists within the predominantly Latvian Union of Baptist Churches has always been a difficult task. During the Soviet era of Russification and industrialisation many people from Slavonic republics came to the Baltic region as workers. This created tensions which are still felt in everyday life. Historically these ethnic communities have been kept apart by a different language, different culture and different historical memories. Slavonic Baptists, to a greater extent than Latvians, employ dualistic 'two kingdoms' theology, and therefore their integration in local culture has been even more difficult. We also need to remember that both communities of believers pursued different goals. From the very beginning, it was

---

[7] J. Daugmanis, 'Latviesu begla vestule' ('The Letter of a Latvian Refugee'), *Drauga Vests (Friend's News)* 39 (1945), pp. 12-13. This source quotes Bushmanis' letter to pastor Eglitis in Latvia in 1940.

[8] Tervits, *Latvijas baptistu vesture*, p. 203.

[9] E.g., the first known Latvian Baptist, Fricis Jekabsons (b.1830), who was baptized in the Memel Baptist Church in 1855, became a member of the Riga Zion German Baptist Church.

[10] Tervits, *Latvijas baptistu vesture*, p. 207.

[11] A. Lauva, 'LBDS 2005. g. congress Riga' ('UBCL Congress of the Year 2005'), *Kristiga Balss (Christian Voice)* 3 (2005), p. 59.

important for Latvian Baptists to present their faith as 'genuinely' Latvian. The well-known pastor, Janis Inkis (1872–1958), wrote in 1912, 'Baptist faith is faith found by Latvians themselves; it sprung up in their own land, only later finding support abroad.'[12]

The past has many surprises to offer and anyone who wants to talk about a single Baptist tradition or identity is doomed to encounter difficulties, at least from a historical perspective. However, we can observe that the majority of contemporary Latvian Baptists, like other Eastern European Baptists and also following current trends in the society, are often canonizing just one version of their history. This is understandable because they have developed what the former General Secretary of the European Baptist Federation, Karl Heinz Walter, called 'survival theology.'[13] The result, as noted by the Latvian Baptist Bishop, Janis Tervits (1936–2002), is that 'in our churches we have a tendency to evaluate things through what has been read in 16 to 60 page brochures. Our theology often becomes a brochure theology.'[14] Unfortunately, the majority of religious literature translated from other languages follows the same pattern. A good example is the Latvian edition of the American Southern Baptist book *Survival Kit for New Christians*,[15] which mainly consists of a set of questions arranged in a way that does not leave much space for the reader's own critical reflections. A positive example, by contrast, has been set by the local Lutheran Heritage Foundation in Latvia that continues to publish classical texts from the Reformation period.

References to internationally known Baptist doctrinal documents are often used by local Baptist leadership in a selective way. For example, Baptist Bishop Janis Smits, in his statement on Baptist identity published after a seminar on basic Baptist principles held in Riga in 2005, quotes from the Baptist Confession of Faith of 1689 when he talks about the Bible and its importance, but at the same time states that 'each church is independent'[16] without mentioning the principle of interdependency employed by British Baptists in the seventeenth century and bypassing the emphasis on the universal church found in the 1689 Confession.[17]

---

[12] J. Inkis, 'Jubilejas vienpadsmita diena—Puraciema' ('Eleventh Day of Jubilee in Puraciems'), *Avots* (*The Spring*) 30 (1912), p. 353. For this reason the German role in spreading the Baptist faith was downplayed.

[13] 'Bridging the gap between East and West', *Baptist Times* 23 September 2000, p. 5.

[14] J. Tervits, 'But baptistu draudzes loceklim' ('To Be the Member of the Baptist Church'), *Baptistu Vestnesis* (*Baptist Messanger*) 1 (1999), p. 12.

[15] R.V. Neibors, *Celamaize jauniem kristiesiem* (*Survival Kit for New Christians*) (Riga: Amnis, 1998).

[16] J. Smits, 'Baptistu identitate un pamatatzinas' ('Baptist Identity and Basic Beliefs'), *Baptistu Vestnesis* 2 (2005), p. 1.

[17] In the 1689 Confession the chapter on the church (ch. 26) starts with a paragraph on the universal church as 'brought into being by the internal work of the Spirit and truth of grace' (see the modern translation of the Confession: www.rbc.org.nz/library/1689.htm).

Some of the people who during the Soviet period were religious dissidents were so used to long-term marginalisation and being in opposition that they were not able to accommodate to the new political situation. For example, Janis Rozkalns (a former member of Riga's Golgata Baptist church, who during the Soviet period was expelled from the church after a harsh conflict with the local church authorities),[18] distributed an open letter during the annual Latvian Baptist congress in March 2001 in which he criticised the Latvian Christian Radio (renting a part of the Baptist Union House) for co-operation with Roman Catholics and others viewed by him as heretics.[19] In a similar fashion in his memoirs, the Lutheran pastor Andrejs Kavacis, who used to take part in the opposition movement within the Lutheran church known as 'Regeneration and Renewal', reproduced certain stereotypes connecting the fact that some of his clerical colleagues had changed their mind in favour of women's ordination with possible links of these individuals to free-masonry.[20] The publisher of these memoirs (the publishing house 'Vieda') is known as the producer of books with an ultra-nationalistic, xenophobic and esoteric flavour. However, the views just described come from small minority.

With the collapse of the USSR and the subsequent new level of religious freedom we can observe further transformations of Latvian Baptist identities. During the years of forced uniformity characteristic of the Soviet era, Latvian Baptist identity was presented as a single entity. Compilers of an 'official' Soviet Baptist history book published by the All-Union Council of Evangelical Christians–Baptists spoke about Baptists in Latvia having 'confessional homogeneity'.[21] Compared with Baptists in Russia or the Ukraine, Baptists in Latvia after the Second World War certainly appeared to be a more monolithic group because historically Latvia did not have large communities of Evangelical Christians, Pentecostals or Mennonites. Thus, the number of adherents of other denominations who were forced to join the Union because of repressive Soviet politics was not large.[22] However, we should not downplay the continuous impact of inter-war divisions in the local Baptist movement, as well as the influence of other denominations on the Baptist movement. For example, Vladimirs Molcanovs (1890–1968), who came from an ethnically mixed family and was the pastor at Riga's Agenskalns Baptist Church

---

[18] Tervits, *Latvijas baptistu vesture*, pp. 163, 176-77.

[19] J. Rozkalns, *Atklata vestule* (*Open Letter*) dated 27 February 2001. Unpublished document in the author's archive.

[20] A. Kavacis, *Cilveki vestures vejos* (*People in the Winds of History*) (Riga: Vieda, 2002), p. 148. Persons accused by Kavacis are well-known pastors Modris Plate and Juris Rubenis who have also been members of the group 'Regeneration and Renewal'.

[21] *Istorija jevangeljskih hristijan-baptistov* (*History of Evangelical Christians–Baptists*) (Moscow: AUCECB, 1989), p. 357.

[22] However, in the first years after the Second World War the Baptist Union was joined by several Pentecostal churches, one congregation belonging to 'Blue Cross', one to the Evangelical Christian Church, as well as individuals from Methodist and Moravian churches.

from 1950 to 1968, encouraged private confession. In his theology we can find a mixture of Holiness and Orthodox ideas.

During the Soviet period differences in opinion, even tensions, were not uncommon, but there was little space to publicize them or to debate these matters. In the 1990s, when a totally new political climate started, these divisions became more visible. However, a culture of dialogue, which was non-existent in the Soviet period, is not something which can be created overnight. If we skim over the first issues of the Baptist official publication *Baptistu Draudzem* (in 1995 renamed *Baptistu Vestnesis)* we would not find debates on local church problems where names of individuals would be mentioned or exchange of opinions would take place (as could be found, for example, in the *Baptist Times* in the United Kingdom). Problems are mentioned in more abstract form. For example, from questions addressed by ministers to the General Secretary of the World Baptist Alliance, Denton Lotz, during his visit to Latvia in 1991, we can indirectly find out that pastors were concerned about the rise of the Charismatic Movement and the activities of some American evangelists like Jimmy Swaggart.[23]

Factors Behind the Transformation of Identities

There are several factors to be analysed in order to understand some of the present changes more fully.

Conventionalization and Reactions to It

Conventionalization, a process in which adherents of a religious group accept values and behaviour codes shared by the majority of people in the society, in the long term can be avoided only by closed and strict communities like the Amish in North America. At the same time, unavoidably, more radical segments of the religious group react against conventionalization.

Conventionalization is connected with recognition by the state and wider segments of society. When Latvia regained independence, the Baptists became one of the religious groups that were considered traditional. The term 'traditional religion' is not used in the judicial practice of Latvia; however, indirectly, it is reflected in the existing law on religious organisations which lists Baptists among the religious groups which can provide faith-instruction in state-financed schools. Baptists are one of eight denominations whose clergy can legally issue state-approved marriage certificates. Baptist leaders, together with leaders from other large denominations, are involved in consultations with the government and take part in events of national importance like the ecumenical service on Independence Day, when, according to protocol, the State President and other high ranking officials are present. Recognition by the state, active involvement in ecumenical relationships with

---

[23] 'Baptisti musdienu mainigaja pasaule' ('Baptists in a Modern Changing World'), *Baptistu Draudzem (To Baptist Churches)* 1 (1992), pp. 12-15.

'mainline' churches and the resultant respectability is viewed by Latvian Baptist Edgars Mazis as one of Latvian Baptist distinctives in comparison with other countries. At the same time he is asking whether this status has not weakened Baptist stand for religious freedom of other religious minorities.[24]

Conventionalization is also linked with new social opportunities and, at the same time, boundaries are created by changes in the social composition of the religious movement. As noted by Baptist Bishop, Janis Smits (Latvian Baptists are somewhat unusual among Baptists in having bishops[25]—Smits was elected to this position in 2002, ending his term in 2006), 'we feel comfortable in our Baptist subculture that is mainly constituted by the middle class'.[26] Signs of conventionalization are visualised in the architecture and design of places of worship. In late Victorian England, British Nonconformists were eager to leave behind their reputation of being uncultured. The erection of Gothic buildings and efforts towards improvement of liturgy were part of this transformation process.[27] Similarly we can see how in the nineteenth century Unitarians followed the Anglican fashion of adopting the Gothic style as an indication that Unitarians considered themselves to be as 'established' as other branches of Christianity.[28]

At the end of the nineteenth century, Latvian Baptist meeting halls were built mainly following the style then popular in Germany. A newspaper describes the German Baptist church opened in 1878 in the following way: 'Opposite the entrance stands the pulpit, to the right and left side of it are situated cloak-rooms for baptismal candidates, and in front of the pulpit is a place for performing baptism.'[29] From the outside it was noticeable that this and other church buildings built in that period did not have a tower—a characteristic feature of Catholic and Lutheran church architecture. Later in the twentieth century some Baptist churches had towers with a

---

[24] E. Mazis, 'Latvijas baptistu atskiribas no baptistiem citur pasaule' ('Differences of Latvian Baptists from Baptists in Other Parts of the World'), *Cels* (*The Way*) 56 (2005), pp. 178-81.

[25] See V. Teraudkalns, 'Episcopacy in the Baptist Tradition', in P.E. Thompson and A.R. Cross (eds), *Recycling the Past or Researching History?: Studies in Baptist Historiography and Myths* (Studies in Baptist History and Thought, 11; Milton Keynes: Paternoster, 2005), especially pp. 286-93.

[26] J. Smits, 'Paplasinasim robezas!' ('Let's Extend the Boundaries!'), *Latvijas baptistu draudzu gadagramata 2003. gadam* (*Yearbook of the Baptist Churches of Latvia for 2003*) (Riga: Amnis, 2002), p. 35.

[27] P. Shepherd, *The Making of a Modern Denomination: John Howard Shakespeare and the English Baptists 1898–1924* (Studies in Baptist History and Thought, 4; Carlisle: Paternoster Press, 2001), p. 12.

[28] G. Hague, *The Unitarian Heritage: An Architectural Survey of Chapels and Churches in the Unitarian Tradition in the British Isles* (Sheffield: Unitarian Heritage, 1986), pp. 70-94.

[29] 'Baptistu lugsanu nama iesvetisana' ('Dedication of the Baptist Prayer House'), *Balss* (*The Voice*) 8 November 1878, pages are unnumbered.

spire.[30] In some Baptist worship halls (for example in Aizviki) 'altar' paintings appeared. This trend was characteristic of areas where the Baptist movement was chronologically older; for example, in Liepaja district where out of thirteen Baptist churches five have altar paintings.[31] At the beginning, a table at the front of the meeting hall was simply functional: a place for the preacher to put his Bible and hymnbook and lead the worship service. Later the term 'altar table' was applied to it. Nowadays we can see observe also the use of candles, the display of an open Bible and other more 'churchly' attributes.

In the nineteenth century some church members regarded the use of organs and violins (described by opponents as the 'devil's instrument serving amusement') with suspicion.[32] As an expensive instrument organs belonged to the renounced culture of German nobles and their *status quo* religion (Lutheranism). But slowly larger and richer urban churches bought organs and introduced other instruments—some of them associated with the 'world'. In larger churches informal practices have given way to more solemn liturgical traditions. For example, the old tradition that during the annual festivals of local churches all the pastors present sit behind the altar table and are invited to say words of greeting has, in spite of complaints from older clergy, died out in some places.[33] Some pastors, for example Pastor Arturs Skuburs, who used to be the Chair of the Collegium of the Clergy Association, are in favour of using special garments for clergy.[34] Wearing a clerical collar has become widespread among pastors. The same can be said about crosses as symbols in sanctuaries and liturgical gestures used together with words of blessing at the end of worship. There are also local churches where experiments with high-church liturgical practices are taking place. At the same time, Bishop Janis Smits, representing another perspective, states in his summary of the principles of Baptist faith that 'liturgy of worship services, priestly garments...have no basis in the Holy Scriptures'.[35] In many rural churches spontaneous styles of worship, which include testimonies, extemporary prayers and other elements of revivalist practice, have continued. Pastor

---

[30] E.g., in the church buildings in Aizpute (built in 1939) and Talsi (built in 1936), also in Agenskalns Baptist Church in Riga (where the building itself was built in 1916, the spire was added in 1936), but the spire was destroyed after the building was confiscated by the state in 1961. After regaining it in 1989 it is still not restored to the lack of financial resources.

[31] Tervits, *Latvijas baptistu vesture*, p. 306.

[32] F. Cukurs, R. Eksteins and A. Meters (eds), *Dzivibas cels* (*Way of Life*) (ASV [United States of America]: Amerikas Latviesu baptistu apvieniba [Association of Latvian Baptists in America], 1960), p. 134.

[33] J. Tervits, 'But baptistu draudzes loceklim' ('To Be a Member of the Baptist Church'), *Baptistu Vestnesis* 12 (1998), p. 694. Tervits complains that 'we are losing one of the most beautiful Baptist traditions'.

[34] A. Skuburs, 'Par dazam ariskibam baptistu garidznieku kalposana' ('About Some Outer Appearances in the Ministry of Baptist Clergy'), *Baptistu Vestnesis* 6 (1995), pp. 209-11.

[35] J. Smits, 'Baptistu identitate un pamatatzinas' ('Baptist Identity and Basic Beliefs'), *Baptistu Vestnesis* 2 (2005), p. 1.

Peteris Krievs (1915–2000), who was influenced by the Pentecostal and Holiness movements, has expressed this outlook in the following way: 'I am often sadly worried that the worship services of our churches would not turn out to be events where every member of the church knows the next point of the programme and services would not become "pillars of salt"...'.[36] In the last decade, the older currents of the Holiness movement have, in many cases, been transformed by the Charismatic tradition.

The Impact of Global and European Political Transformations

From the 1990s, the process of Latvian integration into various international organisations started. It progressed hand in hand with social and economic transformation. In parts of the society which were not able to adapt so quickly to the new socio-political context, rapid changes created anxiety and fear. For predominantly conservative Eastern European churches, new freedom created a dilemma. On the one hand, churches were delighted about opportunities to worship and to propagate their views, but, on the other hand, they could not accept all the changes that were apparent with the growth of diversity in the social space. This tension clearly appears in *Foundations of the Social Conception of the Russian Orthodox Church,* the document adopted in August 2000 by the Council of the Russian Orthodox Church (Moscow Patriarchate). It recognises that a secular state guarantees the legal status of the church; however, the authors of this document also state, 'introducing the legal principle of freedom of conscience bears witness to the fact that society has lost religious ideas and values'.[37] The theocratic state then becomes the ideal (even if the authors of the document recognise that it cannot be artificially constructed). For the Baptist movement, which traces its origins from the post-Reformation period (and thus has a different history), freedom of religion plays an important role. However, among Baptists we can observe an impulse coming from the Reformed tradition with its aspirations to embody political life-values perceived as Christian. Of course it is part of Christian witness to stand for solidarity with the marginalised, for justice and peace. But there is a danger of pursuing agendas which are based on securing privileges at the expense of others which are viewed as competitors in the market of religious needs, or advocating quick solutions to complex ethical issues (like gender and sexuality) which are matters of debate not only in the wider society but also within the church. As has been noted by the American scholar Sabrina P. Ramet, 'the demands of any religious association to bring laws into harmony with its specific values can be seen only as tending towards theocracy'.[38]

---

[36] Tervits, *Latvijas baptistu vesture*, p. 480.

[37] *Osnovi socialnoj koncepciji Russkoi pravoslavnoj cerkvi* (*Foundations of the Social Conception of the Russian Orthodox Church*) III.6, http://www.russian-orthodox-church.org.ru/sd03r.htm.

[38] S.P. Ramet, *Nihil Obstat: Religion, Politics, and Social Change in East-Central Europe and Russia* (Durham, NC: Duke University Press, 1998), p. 337.

One of the major political events marking the year 2003 in the political landscape of Latvia was a referendum (in September 2003) on joining the European Union. Political developments in Brussels have also been a focus of interest for major European ecumenical organizations and have been widely discussed among Western European Baptists.[39] Working groups of the Church and Society Commission of the Conference of European Churches (CEC) have discussed issues of concern.[40] The draft of the proposed EU Constitution has article 51.1 which states that 'the Union respects and does not prejudice the status under national law of churches and religious associations or communities in the Member States'.[41] In Latvia, both clergy and lay people lack information about EU policies in matters of religion. Views are often based on rumours coming from secondary sources.[42] The situation improved because of the efforts of the Evangelical Alliance of Latvia, which in February 2003 organised a seminar with a representative of the European Evangelical Alliance in the Council of the European Union as a main speaker.[43]

In recent years, a Christian presence in politics in Latvia has become more visible. There are Baptists among the Christian politicians. For example, Ainars Bastiks, the former assistant to the Baptist Bishop, is Children and Family Affairs Minister, who in this post represents the First Party of Latvia. For a short period of time, a member of Riga's Agenskalns Church, Maris Vitols, was Minister of Education and Science, representing the People's Party of Latvia.[44] Christian responsibility for society is incorporated in the Confession of Faith of the Union of Baptist Churches (1998): 'we are proclaiming just, democratic and Christian

---

[39] See, e.g., Tony Peck's (EBF General Secretary), 'Belonging in Europe: Reflections on Current European Baptist Life', *Baptist Ministers' Journal* 291 (July, 2005) p. 17, brief comment on this in his reflections on current Baptist life in Europe. He warns, that 'a gospel "connectedness" in Europe can easily become submerged beneath nationalist anti-European sentiments.'

[40] Readers can easily find current an update on CEC responses to the EU integration and enlargement process by checking the CEC homepage, www.cec-kek.org.

[41] Draft Treaty establishing a Constitution for Europe submitted to the European Council Meeting in Thessaloniki, 20 June 2003, http://european-convention.eu.int/bienvenue.asp?lang=EN.

[42] E.g., Bishop Andrejs Sterns in his report to the Baptist Union's Congress in 2002 relies on information from the local Christian journal *Tiksanas* (*Encounter*) that the 'EU has a special foundation to support the infiltration of homosexual clergymen into the churches'. See *LBDS biskapa A. Sterna zinojums LBDS 2002. gada kongresam* (*Bishop's A. Stern's Report to the Congress of the Union of Baptist Churches of Latvia in 2002*), p. 4 (unpublished).

[43] See http://www.lea.lv/intervija_dzdp.html.

[44] Baptists have also achieved high positions in some other post-Socialist countries. E.g., Baptist lay pastor Alexander Tarchinov, who belongs to the Motherland Party of prime minister Yulia Tymoshenko, has been appointed as the director of the Ukrainian secret service. At the same time he is critical of political parties who use the word 'Christian' ('Baptist Becomes New Secret Service Head', *Baptist Times*, 17 February 2005, p. 4).

development of state social and economic life...'.[45] What easily becomes problematic is the fact that 'Christian development' is subject to a variety of meanings across the political and theological spectrum.

The Generation Gap

Some of the young people who joined Baptist churches after the changes of the early 1990s did not have a Baptist family background and for them the three 'Big Baptist Dont's' (don't smoke, don't drink, don't dance) were open to question. Therefore, it is no surprise that some authors of articles in the Baptist magazine *Baptistu Draudzem* denounced the relaxed attitudes of church young people towards dancing, modern clothing and cosmetics.[46] The editors of the Baptist youth journal *Ej (Go)* were rebuked for publishing extracts from interviews with young people regarding their views about premarital sex and the use of alcohol.[47] These critiques were usually mingled with a sense of living at the beginning of apocalyptic 'dark' times. But, in fact, debates about behavioural codes are nothing new: young people have always been especially subject to the dominant streams of social life. In 1905, the newspaper *Evangelists (Evangelist)* complained that at an outing members of one of the Sunday Schools in Riga had started to dance.[48] Because of the age gap between most pastors and young people (in 2004 the average age of Baptist ministers was forty-five, the same in 1998),[49] these different worlds are difficult to bring together. However, cultural changes have slowly become more and more visible. In the UBCL year book for 1991 there are photographs and some brief information about an Easter event organized in 1990 in Latvia's National Theatre by the Sunday School of the Riga Agenskalns Baptist Church, together with the theatre's actors (one of them, Ilze Rudolfa, being a member of the church)[50]—something which would be difficult to imagine a decade ago.

Another disputed area has been musical style. In the 1970s young Latvian Baptists were influenced by Estonian Christians (Baptists and Methodists) who during that time started to form youth bands. Regular '*Effata* evenings' organised by

[45] *Kristigas dzives kredo (Credo of Christian Life)*, p. 4 (unpublished document).

[46] See, e.g., M. Ceimurs, 'Kadus es velos redzet dievkalpojumos musu jauniesus' ('How I Would Like to See Our Youth'), *Baptistu Draudzem (To Baptist Churches)* 2 (1993), p. 23.

[47] See the respective articles, 'Milet un but miletam' ('To Love and to be Loved'), *Ej (Go)* 2 (1996), p. 7; 'Vai tu sajos Janos lietosi alkoholu?' ('Will You Consume Alcohol in This Jani Festival?'), *Ej* 1 (1996), pages are unnumbered.

[48] 'No Rigas' ('From Riga'), *Evangelists (Evangelist)* 17 (1905), pages are unnumbered.

[49] A. Sterns, 'Garidznieku braliba pedejos piecdesmit gados' ('Brotherhood of Clergy During the Last Fifty Years'), *Latvijas baptistu draudzu gadagramata 2005. gadam (Yearbook of the Baptist Churches of Latvia for 2005)* (Riga: LBDS, 2004), p. 62.

[50] *Latvijas Baptistu draudzu kalendars (Calendar of Latvia's Baptist Churches)* (Riga: LBDS, 1990), p. 80. The photographs are unnumbered in the middle of the book.

the largest Baptist church in Estonia, Oleviste Church in Tallinn, were attended by Latvians.[51] In 1974, under the leadership of Maris Ludviks (who later became a Lutheran pastor), a singing group, 'Maranatha', was organised. Janis Tervits, who then was Baptist Bishop, in his history book writes that this 'group stressed its independence from the order accepted by the local church'.[52] It was not only a clash of worship styles which was at stake here. New worship styles introduced by Baptist youth and younger ministers met with opposition because they challenged the dominant role of the choir. This role developed during the Soviet period when the choir was the only activity allowed in the church (besides preaching). Conductors of choirs became, in some cases, more influential than pastors and other local church workers. Some conductors combined oversight of musical activities with being heavily involved in other dimensions of local church life. The famous Latvian Baptist composer and conductor, Janis Ezerins, was behind reconstruction work done during the Soviet period in the premises of Mathew Church, Riga, which then served as the central Latvian Baptist church.

Nowadays modern forms of worship are becoming more and more widespread. This should be seen not as a part of some kind of foreign influence but as adoption within a local context of modern, globalised youth subcultures. Some churches are trying to lessen the tension by organising separate worship services; for example, on Sundays Riga's Mathew Baptist Church has both a traditional and a more contemporary worship service. Others, like Riga's Agenskalns Church, are designing each main Sunday service differently to avoid the emergence of *de facto* two congregations of one church (the problem that arises when there are two entirely different main services) and also to suit the needs of the participants.

Postdenominationalism

Analysing global religious developments, we can see that signs of a postdenominational era are found in various parts of the world. Alongside individuals and groups who construct strict denominational boundaries, we can also find projects such as the one initiated by Bill Leonard (a church historian from a Southern Baptist background) who, as the basis of the Divinity School at Wake Forest University, USA, has chosen an ecumenical agenda. Its curriculum is based on the conviction that 'various strands of Christian life are perpetually in flux. Evangelicals are seeking out Roman Catholic spirituality. Episcopalians are turning to charismatic practices. Churches are changing their name to hide their denominational affiliation.'[53] Of course, this is a complex process of not only loosening existing confessional ties but also constructing new ones. In the long run, in spite of

---

[51] About '*Effata* evenings', see T. Pilli, 'Union of Evangelical Christians–Baptists of Estonia 1945–1989: Survival Techniques, Outreach Efforts, Search for Identity', *Journal of European Baptist Studies* 1.2 (January, 2001), pp. 41-42.

[52] Tervits, *Latvijas baptistu vesture*, p. 325.

[53] Quoted from 'A Postdenominational Seminary', *Christian Century* 116.25 (1999), pp. 888-89.

different priorities and new lists of problems to be wrestled with, there is no pragmatic escape from issues which have historically divided denominations. As British Baptist theologian Nigel Wright has written, 'fundamental questions of theology never go away. They always abide and must be returned to. Beyond the glow of shared fellowship these are still the hard questions of theological discourse that will raise their heads again in due course. Integral to these questions are questions about the nature of the church itself that lie at the root of so much denominational proliferation.'[54]

The continental European Baptist historical heritage, where over the years the Pietist stress on experiential religion has played an important role, gives additional weight to the current postdenominational disposition of many Latvian Baptists. For these people, consensus about codes of behaviour and expressions of spirituality was more important than dogma. For example, some of the small groups of believers that were organised during the revival in Latvia in the 1920s did not have any clear denominational identity and, depending on the preacher they listened to, they quite readily changed their denominational affiliation.

There is also another reason for downplaying denominationalism. This became evident in the 1980s when public evangelism became possible in Latvia and new churches started to be organised. There were cases when the name 'Baptist' was unknown to the public or had bad connotations as something narrow and therefore sectarian,[55] and as a result some churches or individuals in advertising their activities avoided the Baptist name. Viewers of the Internet home page of the largest Baptist church in Latvia, Mathew Church in Riga, can find something about its denominational belonging only in the sub-section 'history', and, in the vision of the church, any denominational concerns are absent.[56] The Russian-speaking New Evangelical Church in Riga, which joined the Union in 2004, still prefers not to use the Baptist name.

At the same time the wave of postdenominationalism has not created a counter-reaction on the part of the Baptist leadership towards ecumenical relationships. During the Pope's visit in September 1993, Baptist Bishop Janis Eisans, together with other church leaders, took part in a historic worship service in the Lutheran cathedral in Riga. Leaders of various denominations have good personal contacts with each other. However, denominational identity has been an issue frequently raised by the Baptist leadership. For example, Andrejs Sterns, at the Union's Congress in 2002, in his last speech as Bishop stated that

> ecumenical relationships can be a blessing only if we will know how to honour and keep our understanding of Scripture and practical life. If we forget that, we will lose

---

[54] N.G. Wright, *New Baptists, New Agenda* (Carlisle: Paternoster Press, 2002), p. 51.

[55] E.g., in the report on the organizing of a new church in the small town of Ainazi in 1991, we find the phrase that the 'name "Baptist" often created dislike', 'Ainazos' ('In Ainazi'), *Baptistu Draudzem* (*To Baptist Churches*) 1 (1992), p. 6.

[56] www.matejs.lv.

our identity and our mission. It is a big temptation to become inter-confessional. Other churches are not doing that.[57]

Conclusion

This study has spoken of 'imagined uniformity'. There was never one Baptist identity, and conventionalization, political transformations, the generation gap, and postdenominationalism—have increased diversity. The UBCL leadership's attempts to deal with this by way of some uniform practices and also through strengthening the Union's role have not succeeded. The multiple identities have partially to do with the nature of Baptist congregationalism. One Latvian Baptist author said in 1912, 'The Baptist church always has been a separate spiritual state, an independent spiritual republic.'[58] At the same time there is a trend amongst the Baptist leadership that is concerned about laxity. Questions about the Union's role and the limits of the autonomy of the local church are parts of a questionnaire developed for candidates for ordination.[59] The Union has not, however, developed any clear theological principles relating to the interdependence of local churches and their corporate existence in wider associations. The Confession of Faith of the Union of Baptist Churches of Latvia talks about the universal invisible church but underlines only the priority of the local church ('only the church itself determines its life').[60] Too often Baptist identity has been constructed by emphasizing negative aspects of behavior, which then becomes main borderline for being 'in' or 'out'. The construction of a more holistic and positive identity, which would move issues that are part of *adiaphora* to the place they belong, remains an important task for local Baptist leaders and theologians in Latvia.

---

[57] A. Lauva, '2002. gada LBDS congress' ('UBCL Congress of the Year 2002'), *Kristiga Balss (The Christian Voice)* 3 (2002), p. 50.

[58] 'Baptistu nozime latviesu tautas garigas dzives pacelsana pedejos 50. gados' ('Baptist Role in Raising of the Spiritual Life of the Latvian Nation during the last Fifty Years'), *Avots* 20 (1912), p. 233.

[59] See, *LBDS Garidznieku bralibas garidznieku ordinacijas jautajumi (Questionnaire for Ordination of the Clergy Association of the Union of Baptist Churches of Latvia)*, p. 1 (unpublished document, received by the author in 1999).

[60] *Kristigas dzives kredo (Credo of Christian Life)*, pp. 2-3 (unpublished document). According to this document, more is required from the pastor: he has to respect not only the order of the local church but also 'ministerial discipline accepted by the collective labor' (the last phrase is a term coined to describe corporate association life of local churches that have joined the Union).

PART 2

North American Baptist Identities

CHAPTER 9

Alexander Campbell and Baptist Identity: Contributions and Challenges

Austin Bennett Amonette

As the immediate founder of the denomination the Disciples of Christ and the decisive influence behind two additional fellowships, Alexander Campbell (1788–1866) was one of the most important nineteenth-century American Christian leaders. A writer, preacher, teacher, debater, theologian, and churchman, Campbell, who was born in Northern Ireland and educated at the University of Glasgow, Scotland, before moving to North America, was an imposing presence during his lifetime. Ironically, compared with other similar leaders, his legacy has been neglected. For example, no critical biography of Campbell is in print today. After moving to America, although initially a Presbyterian, Campbell became a Baptist, and remained so from 1812 to 1830, a period of time fraught with controversy for Campbell as he developed and refined his theological positions. By 1830 Campbell and what had become his Baptist opponents had reached an impasse, causing Campbell to dissolve his Mahoning Baptist Association, Ohio, thus terminating his relationship with Baptists. Campbell's relatively lengthy Baptist period deserves further examination because in this period he developed several of his distinctive ideas, such as his baptismal theology, anti-clericalism, and limited synergistic congregationalism; and also because it provides a test case for Baptist identity.

C.L. Loos, a younger associate of Campbell and Professor at Campbell's Bethany College, West Virginia, was one of the first historians to analyze the troubled relationship between Campbell and the Baptists, and his interpretation of the events is worth re-examining. Loos's critical argument was that Campbell's Baptist fellowship was, much of the time, 'more formal than real'. He conjectured that Campbell's troubles with his Baptist colleagues began because, on the one hand, they were jealous of his talent and, on the other, great doctrinal differences existed between them. Loos identified three doctrinal differences between Campbell and the Baptists. First, while Baptists were 'strict Calvinists', Campbell was never a Calvinist. Second, Campbell was not a Trinitarian in the same way that the Baptists were because he objected to the use of non-biblical language. Third, while the Baptists adhered to the *Philadelphia Confession of Faith*, Campbell rejected confessions. Because of these three differences, 'a real and lasting union' was 'impossible', Loos concluded. Through his association with the Baptists, Loos argued, Campbell gained two advantages for his future movement: first, it gave him an 'open door' to many churches and people; and second, it provided a 'foundation' of adherents. Loos wrote that, in addition to their jealousy, many Baptists were perturbed that Campbell had persuaded such a great number of them to follow him. Campbell originally thought Baptists to be bigoted and narrow, and he detested the illiteracy among their preachers. Loos opined that he might have brought some prejudice against Baptists with him from Ireland and Scotland. At the end of his life Campbell tearfully confessed to Loos that he 'regretted' his separation from the Baptists.[1]

Loos showed the preoccupation from the earliest Disciples' historiography with Campbell's relationship with the Baptists. Because Campbell adopted an 'anti-sectarian' position, his identification with a 'sect' (the Baptists) was an embarrassment to his own movement, which claimed no direct ecclesiastical ancestors except the primitive church. Furthermore, the somewhat ignominious manner of Campbell's separation from the Baptists—which as a *de facto* excommunication by the Baptists seemed to confirm the caricature of Campbell as a contentious heretic—was a source of consternation to his admirers. Loos, as an eyewitness and participant in the Campbell movement, provided reliable testimony, although, because he was so close to the movement, one may suspect some of his interpretations. He also provided several hypotheses that would be recycled and refined by future historians, such as his opinion that jealousy of Campbell was a factor in his estrangement from the Baptists. This argument is plausible, considering that by the late 1820s Campbell was famous and increasingly well connected; President Andrew Jackson hosted Campbell at the Hermitage in 1827;[2] and in October 1829 Campbell participated in the Virginia Constitutional Convention with James Madison, James Monroe, John Tyler, John Marshall, and John Randolph.[3]

On the other hand, two of Loos' points need further examination. First, Loos' assertion that Campbell had 'never been a Calvinist' is dubious. He must have forgotten or ignored that Campbell was a former Anti-Burgher Seceder Presbyterian who had studied in Scotland. Second, Loos maintained that Campbell's connection with the Baptists was 'more formal than real'. However, on the evidence one can argue that Campbell's connection with the Baptists was 'real', and that, despite the well-documented tension, mutual benefits were gained: the Baptists gained a defender, and Campbell gained a home. Though the relationship was real, it was not sturdy and the tensions proved to be fatal.

Campbell was an active Baptist and he readily identified himself as such in print and in debates for eighteen years, from 1812 to 1830. As a young man he received baptism as a believer from a Baptist preacher, thus breaking with his Presbyterian beliefs; he subsequently led his congregation to join a Baptist association; and he

---

[1] C.L. Loos, 'Introductory Period', in J.H. Garrison (ed.), *The Reformation of the Nineteenth Century* (St. Louis, MO: Christian Publishing, 1901), pp. 53-62.

[2] Eva Jean Wrather, 'Campbell, Alexander', in Carroll Van West (ed.), *The Tennessee Encyclopedia of History and Culture* (Nashville, TN: Rutledge Hill Press, 1998), p. 116.

[3] Robert Richardson, *Memoirs of Alexander Campbell* (2 vols; Nashville, TN: Gospel Advocate Company, 1956 [1868]), II, p. 310.

preached in Baptist churches. Campbell represented the Baptists and articulated a Baptist position at three public debates, with John Walker in 1820, W.L. MacCalla in 1823, and Robert Owen in 1829. From 1823–30 Campbell published a newspaper for Baptists entitled *The Christian Baptist*, in which he both referred to himself as a Baptist and presented Baptist positions.

Not surprisingly, many Baptists doubted Campbell's authenticity as a Baptist. Prominent Baptist historian Robert Semple attacked his sarcastic contentiousness and noted that Campbell had so deviated from orthodox Baptist theology that he had created a 'new sect'. In particular, Campbell's ecclesiology and doctrine of baptism impressed many Baptists as evidence that Campbell had evolved into some non-Baptist variety of Christian expression. The editors of *The Baptist Recorder*, George Waller and Spencer Clack, frequently attacked Campbell in print, while receiving vigorous responses and counterattacks from Campbell. Campbell wrote much about Baptist life and while his language was generally approving, a judgmental and disdainful element was sometimes present, particularly as he described his impression of Baptists before he joined them. Campbell frequently identified himself unequivocally as a Baptist. For instance, he entitled the name of his publication *The Christian Baptist* after discussion with his associate Walter Scott, the famous evangelist. Campbell could not decide what to call the paper. He was partial to the title *The Christian*, but Scott suggested that he name it *The Christian Baptist* so that Baptists would accept it more readily.[4] Campbell disliked using 'Baptist' in the title because he believed that its use would perpetuate the sectarianism that he opposed, but Scott's argument persuaded him on three grounds: Campbell and his partisans were Baptists; the name 'Christian Baptist' was less prejudicial; and the name 'Christian Baptist' gave 'greater currency' to Campbell's ideas.[5] Moreover, Campbell could write statements such as 'since I joined the Baptists'[6] without hesitation or equivocation. In an article entitled 'A Circular Letter', a response to a document signed by, among others, Francis Wayland, Campbell wrote the phrase 'we Baptists' twice: once in the clause 'we Baptists are to march forth' and again in the phrase 'we Baptists in the western states'.[7]

The phrase 'we Baptists' came easily to Campbell: in both the Walker and MacCalla debates Campbell used the phrase. In addition, in those debates he was the defender of the Baptist position. In the Walker debate in 1820, Campbell in his opening speech said that Walker 'challenged the Baptist denomination', probably because Baptist growth 'alarmed the Pedo-baptists'. Thus, from the beginning of the debate Campbell stood as the Baptist defender. He made several subsequent statements that either defended or identified with the Baptist position. In his second speech Campbell said, 'We Baptists affirm that females have a right to Baptism,

---

[4] Gary L. Lee, 'Background of *The Christian Baptist*', in *The Christian Baptist* (Joplin, MO: College Press Publishing, 1983), p. 12.

[5] Richardson, *Memoirs*, II, pp. 49-50.

[6] A. Campbell, 'Address', in *The Christian Baptist* [hereafter *CB*] (ed. and rev. D.S. Burnet; Joplin, MO: College Press Publishing, 1983 [14th 1870]), p. 91.

[7] A. Campbell, 'A Circular Letter', *CB* 1 (5 July 1824), p. 78.

because we are positively informed in the New Testament that men and women were baptized.' In that statement Campbell accomplished two things: first, he identified himself as a Baptist; and, second, he declared his principle of scriptural authority—what appears in the New Testament is normative for faith and practice. In his final speech he said, 'I must return to the "poor Baptists," and take up my abode with them a while longer', indicating that he intended to remain a Baptist for the foreseeable future. Further, in his final speech he provided a rationale for his becoming a Baptist: 'to teach, to believe, to practice nothing in religion for which I cannot produce positive precept, or approved precedent, from the word of God. Assuming this principle, and pursuing it, made me a Baptist, and I continue to practice it unto this day.' His statement indicates that he believed that the Baptists were a group compliant with the religious agenda that he adopted from his time studying Thomas Reid's Common Sense Realism at the University of Glasgow, and that he joined them for that reason. In the preface to the book containing the debate, Campbell again represented the Baptist perspective, writing, 'A Baptist can present, in five minutes, an express command, authorizing his faith and practice, but a Pedo-Baptist...finally fails in the attempt.'[8]

Taken together, all of Campbell's statements in the Walker debate indicate that Campbell's affiliation with the Baptists was real, not merely nominal or formal. In 1822 Campbell felt secure and confident enough as a Baptist to identify himself publicly as one, defend Baptists and their beliefs and practices, provide an eloquent rationale for becoming a Baptist, and boast of the Baptist position. Perhaps Campbell was never so unequivocally a Baptist as he was in the debate with Walker.

Campbell's biographer Robert Richardson related a story that illustrates the increasingly complex relationship between Campbell and the Baptists. In the 1823 debate, MacCalla had attacked Baptist positions, so Campbell's defeat of him was particularly gratifying to the Baptists[9] and their opinion of Campbell improved. Although he had debated with MacCalla as a Baptist, Campbell did not attempt to conceal his idiosyncratic doctrines: in fact, he viewed the debate as an opportunity to educate his fellow Baptist clergy in a superior set of beliefs, particularly his views on Christian union, baptism, and a rationalist approach to the scriptures. Because of the surfeit of praise coming from his fellow Baptists, Campbell felt compelled to address his own doctrines, and he met with a group of Baptist elders (as pastors were called in Campbell's time) to discuss his true beliefs. In the meeting he said, 'Brethren, I fear that if you knew me better you would esteem and love me less. I have as much against you Baptists as I have against the Presbyterians. They err in

---

[8] A. Campbell, *A Debate on Christian Baptism between Mr. John Walker, a Minister of the Secession, and Alexander Campbell* (Indianapolis, IN: Religious Book Service, n.d. [2nd edn, 1822]), pp. 10, 16, 139, vi.

[9] Richardson did not specify who 'the Baptists' were. One of the difficulties of reconstructing the relationship between Campbell and the Baptists is determining the exact meaning of names like 'the Baptists'. Richardson probably meant the Baptists who were present at the debate and those who heard the details secondhand, but he did not specify.

one thing and you in another.' After elder Jeremiah Vardeman (a moderator during the debate) encouraged him to continue, Campbell began to read articles to the assembled Baptists from *The Christian Baptist*, to which the elders responded favourably. Vardeman found no reason to condemn Campbell's orthodoxy based on what Campbell had read to him, and he and the other elders requested that Campbell allow them to help him publicize *The Christian Baptist*.[10]

This encounter illustrates three points about Campbell's relationship with the Baptists prior to 1826. First, Campbell was aware that his Baptist orthodoxy might be suspect among a group of Baptist elders. Perhaps he was using personal rhetoric to soften what he was about to say, but judging from his comment that he 'feared' that the Baptist elders might 'esteem and love' him less, he seemed to be somewhat anxious as to the reaction of the group. Second, Campbell was brash enough to inform a group of Baptist elders that they were as much in error as he believed the Presbyterians to be. This encounter, which occurred during his debate with MacCalla when he was gaining popularity among the Baptists, risked this increased popularity. Third, that he read to them from *The Christian Baptist* indicates the normative position of that publication in Campbell's doctrinal system.

Campbell admitted that his opinion of the Baptists was low before he joined them. His disdain was concentrated on the Baptist ministers. He wrote: 'I had unfortunately formed a very unfavorable opinion of the Baptist preachers as then introduced to my acquaintance, as narrow, contracted, illiberal, and uneducated men.' Then, showing his vacillation, he continued, 'The people, however, called Baptist, were much more highly appreciated by me than their ministry.'[11]

By all accounts, Campbell's Baptist period was uneasy. He was frequently attacked by other Baptists for his heterodoxy. Early in his editorship of *The Christian Baptist*, in September 1824, Campbell wrote of the 'insults and injuries I have received from some Baptists'.[12] He had not been predisposed to dislike the Baptists, though. He wrote: 'I confess, however, that I was better pleased with the Baptist people than with any other community. They read the Bible, and seemed to care for little else in religion than "conversion" and "Bible doctrine."'[13] Among other accusations, Campbell was accused of being a controversialist by his Baptist opponents. Campbell, though, did not view himself in that way, writing later, 'I did not like controversy so well as many have since thought I did.'[14] Despite Campbell's claim, he rarely declined a fight.

Despite the tension that he was experiencing with his fellow Baptists, Campbell believed that he was doing good among them. In August 1828 he wrote, 'I feel myself emboldened to say that my labors have not been in vain; and I do thank God that I have been enabled to persevere in one undeviating course, aiming at the restoration of the ancient order of things, and that he has given me so much success

---

[10] Richardson, *Memoirs*, II, pp. 87-89.
[11] Richardson, *Memoirs*, I, p. 439.
[12] Campbell, 'Address', p. 93.
[13] Richardson, *Memoirs*, I, p. 440.
[14] A. Campbell, 'Concluding Remarks', *CB* 7 (5 July 1830), p. 664.

in my efforts, as to authorize me to look forward with large expectations to a liberal harvest.' Among the proofs that Campbell offered as demonstrating the validity of his labors, he listed that readership and patronage of *The Christian Baptist* had increased, that many readers desired to see the newspaper enlarged, and that many readers had taken an interest in such matters as the name, size, and publication of the newspaper.[15] He promised to continue publishing *The Christian Baptist* for at least another year and concluded that his opponents had been silenced. The key phrase in the passage was 'to look forward with large expectations to a liberal harvest'. Although Campbell did not specify the harvest that Baptists would reap, since he was still a Baptist himself one legitimately can infer that Campbell anticipated a large influx into Baptist churches of people who agreed with him doctrinally. His attitude of anticipation suggests that Campbell intended to remain a Baptist. Ominously for Campbell, his estimation that his opponents had been silenced was premature and too optimistic.

Despite the turmoil in which he found himself, which is outlined below, Campbell desired to remain a Baptist. He wrote: 'I and the church with which I am connected are in "full communion" with the Mahoning Baptist Association, Ohio; and through them, with the whole Baptist society in the United States.' He cited two reasons for his association with the Mahoning Baptists and by extension all American Baptists: first, that his fellow Baptists might protect him from 'far-off and underhand attacks'; second, that he 'may be under the inspection and subject to merited reprehension'. In his relationship with the Baptists, Campbell benefited in two ways: protection from unfair attacks, and review and criticism. He had embraced Baptist Christianity because he found Baptist theology to be compatible in some way with his own theology. However, why did he remain a Baptist, despite significant shifts that were taking place in his thinking? He himself indicated two benefits of remaining a Baptist. Hence, Campbell perceived his association with the Baptists to be a beneficial relationship.

Not only did Campbell perceive the relationship to be beneficial, but he also had no intention of terminating it. In the next section of the same sentence Campbell wrote: 'I do intend to continue in connexion with this people so long as they will permit me to say what I believe, to teach what I am assured of, and to censure what is amiss in their views or practices.' His intention was predicated upon three conditions: to say what he believed, to teach of what he was certain, and to correct what was wrong. His intention to remain a Baptist suggests that he probably considered being a Baptist permanent, and that he did not intend to create a schism among Baptists or establish a new denomination. On the other hand, two points ought to be raised. First, the language of 'intend to continue' was less strong than he might have used. He did not write something like, 'I will always remain with this people.' One's intentions do not always materialize as one envisions. Second, he placed three stringent conditions on his remaining a Baptist. Therefore, while

---

[15] A. Campbell, 'Preface to Volume 6: The Fathers, the Moderns, the Populars, and the Heretics', *CB* 6 (4 August 1828), pp. 462-63.

Campbell was firmly stating his intention to remain a Baptist and was once again readily identifying himself as one, he, perhaps inadvertently, was leaving himself a backdoor exit from his relationship with the Baptists.

In another instance of Campbell's being too optimistic, he naively predicted that future historians would look favorably at the tolerance shown to him by his fellow Baptists. He wrote: 'Mark it well. Their historian, in the year 1900, may say, "We are the only people who would tolerate, or who ever did tolerate, any person to continue as a Reformer or a Restorer amongst us... We constitute the only exception of this kind in the annals of Christianity—nay, in the annals of the world."'[16] On the one hand, Campbell seemed confident that Baptist tolerance would be recognized. On the other hand, he wrote that his imaginary future historian 'may' say—a cautious prediction, suggesting that Campbell himself may not have been sure what the outcome would be. His comments about Baptist life reveal that he was generally content with being a Baptist. He admitted his prejudices and did not spare Baptist ministers and associations his famous sarcasm.[17] He vacillated between caution and over-optimism.

Though Campbell was content as a Baptist until around 1828, his presence in Baptist life irritated many people who were scrupulous about Baptist identity. His Brush Run Church initially joined the Redstone Baptist Association, and Campbell soon aroused suspicion about his Baptist heterodoxy when he preached his notorious 'Sermon on the Law' at the association meeting on 1 September 1816. In the sermon, Campbell followed what he considered to be Pauline logic, and concluded that the law and the gospel were two exclusive entities, and therefore Christians were under no obligation to the law.[18] In particular, Campbell's third conclusion—that nothing necessitates that Christians preach the law to prepare souls for the gospel—contradicted not only Baptist orthodoxy but also much of Protestantism.[19] Campbell's Baptist identity was threatened when he discovered that because of the sermon the Redstone Association considered a heresy trial against him. His solution was to organize a new congregation that would affiliate with another Baptist association, the Mahoning Association, thereby by-passing a confrontation with his enemies in the Redstone Association.[20]

However, his troubles did not vanish with the move to the Mahoning Association. Because of the Mahoning Association's decidedly Campbellian inclination, the Beaver Association, its parent association, passed a resolution to

---

[16] A. Campbell, 'Reply to 'T.T.', *CB* 3 (6 February 1826), p. 217.

[17] Richardson, *Memoirs*, I, p. 440.

[18] A. Campbell, 'Sermon on the Law', http://www.mun.ca/rels/restmov/texts/acampbell/mh1846/SOTL.HTM.

[19] Bruce E. Shields, 'Campbell, Paul, and the Old Testament', http://www.stone-campbelljournal.com/fall99/shields.html.

[20] Richardson, *Memoirs*, II, p. 69.

disfellowship the Mahoning Association in 1829.[21] The Beaver Association also passed resolutions against the Campbell movement ('the Reformers'). The Beaver Anathema, as it was called, contained the following eight resolutions:

1. They, the Reformers, maintain that there is no promise of salvation without baptism.
2. That baptism should be administered to all who say they believe that Jesus Christ is the Son of God, without examination on any other point.
3. That there is no direct operation of the Holy Spirit on the mind prior to baptism.
4. That baptism procures the remission of sins and the gift of the Holy Spirit.
5. That the Scriptures are the only evidence of interest in Christ.
6. That obedience places it in God's power to elect to salvation.
7. That no creed is necessary for the church but the Scriptures as they stand.
8. That all baptized persons have the right to administer the ordinance of baptism.[22]

Obviously Campbell's baptismal theology was the major point of friction, because Resolutions 1, 2, 3, 4 and 8 were all denunciations of it. Resolutions 5 and 7 were condemnations of the Campbellite doctrine of scriptural authority. Resolution 6 illustrated the tension between the Baptists' interpretation of Calvinism and Campbell's. Noticeably absent from the Beaver Anathema was a condemnation of Campbell's ecclesiology.

The Beaver Anathema contained the claim that it was the 'first official declaration of nonfellowship for Mr. Campbell and his followers'.[23] The Beaver Anathema was a catalyst for other associations, such as the Franklin (Kentucky) Association, to pass condemnations of the Campbell movement and reissue the Beaver Anathema.[24] The Franklin Association's condemnation of Campbellism was strong in its opposition to the tone of the movement as well as its theology. Calling Campbellism a 'heresy', the association derided that 'in place of preaching, you may now hear your church covenants ridiculed, your faith, as registered upon your church books, denounced, and yourselves traduced'. Baptists had been subjected to 'strife, schism, and tumult', 'discord', and 'divisions' as a result of Campbell's baleful influence.[25] Baptist associations in Kentucky, Virginia (under the leadership of Robert Semple), and Tennessee passed condemnations of the Campbell movement in swift succession in 1829–30, ranging from the strident to the polite. Some

---

[21] 'Beaver Baptist Association (Pennsylvania) against Campbellism, 1829', in H.L. McBeth, *A Sourcebook for Baptist Heritage* (Nashville, TN: Broadman Press, 1990), p. 243.

[22] Errett Gates, *The Disciples of Christ* (New York: Baker and Taylor, 1905), pp. 161-62.

[23] 'Beaver Association', pp. 243-44.

[24] Winfred Ernest Garrison and Alfred T. DeGroot, *The Disciples of Christ: A History* (St. Louis, MO: Bethany Press, 1948), pp. 193-94.

[25] 'Franklin Baptist Association (Kentucky): Report and Warning about Campbellism, 1830', in McBeth, *Sourcebook*, p. 244.

associations reissued the Beaver Anathema, while others added new denunciations.[26] For instance, in June 1830 the Tate's Creek Association of Kentucky passed the Beaver Anathema with the following four additions: '9. That there is no special call to the ministry; 10. That the law given by God to Moses is abolished; 11. That experimental religion is enthusiasm; 12. That there is no mystery in the Scriptures.'[27] The Tate's Creek Association's addendum to the Beaver Anathema contained four more pointed critiques of Campbellism. The ninth resolution was an attack on Campbell's anti-clericalism; the tenth was a critique of the antinomian position Campbell presented in his 'Sermon on the Law'; the eleventh was an expression of irritation that Campbell had mainly rejected the theology of the Second Great Awakening, which had accounted for so much Baptist growth since 1801; while the twelfth was a criticism of the Baconianism or Common Sense Realism that supported Campbell's doctrine of scriptural authority. Another example was contained within the Beaver Anathema itself: the Appomattox Association of Virginia passed a resolution in which Campbell's writings were said to exert a 'mischievous influence...fomenting envy, strife, and divisions'.[28]

For what was the last issue of *The Christian Baptist* Campbell asked Scott, who was actively evangelizing in Ohio in the aftermath of the Beaver Anathema, for information about his work, and Scott sent Campbell a 'hasty sketch'. Scott wrote that he had been intimidated by having a stick and a sword cane shaken at him as he performed a baptism, that his horse was set loose, and that the hair of her tail was cut off. The Salem church was the epicenter for anti-Campbellite activity, and Scott was forced to avoid that congregation until the people calmed down. He eventually received word from the Salem church that he should never return there.[29] Scott's report was a significant piece of information for two reasons: he provided a firsthand account of being in what amounted to a religious war zone, and he showed the depth of the feeling of those on both sides of the Campbell movement; and the placement of Scott's report in the final issue of *The Christian Baptist* suggests that, though Campbell's relationship with the Baptists was almost over, Baptist relations were still important to him.

Also challenging Campbell's Baptist identity was Robert Semple. Semple wrote a letter to Campbell in December 1825, and Campbell published the letter in the 3 April 1826 edition of *The Christian Baptist*. Campbell introduced Semple to his readers as 'one of the most intelligent, pious, and worthy bishops in Virginia' and the letter itself as 'of importance to myself and to the religious community at large'.[30] The first round of correspondence set the tone for what followed. Semple made two accusations in his letter to Campbell. First, Campbell was a Sandemanian

[26] Garrison and DeGroot, *Disciples of Christ*, pp. 194-96.
[27] Gates, *Disciples of Christ*, pp. 162-63.
[28] 'Beaver Association', p. 244.
[29] A. Campbell and Walter Scott, 'The Beaver Anathema', *CB* 7 (5 July 1830), p. 659.
[30] A. Campbell, Untitled Notice, *CB*, p. 227.

or Haldanian,[31] terms which Semple seems not to have understood in their theological context but by which he meant that Campbell publicly lacked 'forbearance'. Semple famously characterized Campbell as 'in private circles, mild, pleasant, and affectionate; as a writer, rigid and satirical, beyond all the bounds of Scripture allowance'. Contrasting the New Testament with *The Christian Baptist*, Semple scolded Campbell for its severity. Second, selecting Campbell's anti-creedalism and anti-clericalism as particularly unbaptistic, Semple accused Campbell of heterodoxy. Semple wrote to Campbell: 'Your views are generally so contrary to those of the Baptists in general, that if a party was to go fully into the practice of your principles, I should say a new sect had sprung up.'[32] Semple's insinuation that Campbell was flirting with sectarianism was a particularly pointed accusation.

Campbell replied to Semple's letter in the same issue of *The Christian Baptist*. Campbell's too-long and too-detailed reply to Semple creates the impression that Semple's accusations had stung him. First, after a few preliminaries, he addressed Semple's charge that he was a Sandemanian or Haldanian. He professed incredulity that Semple could connect Sandeman and Haldane because they were so temperamentally different: Campbell attempted to defuse Semple's argument by calling Haldane 'mild' and 'charitable'.[33] The problem with Campbell's tactic was that Semple had accused the Haldanians of 'harsh and bitter sarcasms' but not Haldane himself.[34] Campbell admitted that he had been influenced by Sandeman and John Glas, among others; he claimed that Haldane had been less influential than others.[35] He asserted that his 'debt' was small and that other influences had not influenced him as greatly as the Bible.[36] He challenged Semple's use of the term 'forbearance': Campbell claimed that in the Bible 'forbearance' always referred to God's forbearance or to a Christian's forbearance of an injury, but never to differences of opinion. Conceding that some of what he said and wrote 'may appear' to be of a different spirit than the New Testament, Campbell attempted to deflect the

---

[31] Robert Sandeman (1718–71), the son-in-law of John Glas (1693–1773), advocated many positions that the Campbells would eventually espouse, such as literalistic interpretation of the scriptures, the Lord's Supper each Lord's Day, and use of the title 'Church of Christ'. Robert Haldane (1764–1842) was an acquaintance of Campbell when he was studying at the University of Glasgow and became a Baptist. With his brother, James, he advanced Scottish revivalism. For more information see the related articles in William H. Brackney, *Historical Dictionary of the Baptists* (Historical Dictionaries of Religions, Philosophies, and Movements, 25; Lanham, MD: The Scarecrow Press, 1999).

[32] Robert B. Semple, King and Queen Co., Va., to Alexander Campbell, Bethany, Va., 6 December 1825, *CB* 3 (3 April 1826), p. 227.

[33] A. Campbell, 'Reply', *CB* 3 (3 April 1826), p. 228.

[34] Semple to Campbell, *CB*, p. 227.

[35] Campbell, 'Reply', p. 229, wrote that he was 'much prejudiced against his [Haldane's] views and proceedings' when he was in Scotland.

[36] Campbell, 'Reply', p. 229, showed Enlightenment hauteur in his professed method of reading. He wrote, 'I have endeavored to read the scriptures as though no one had read them before me'.

criticism by speculating that if the New Testament writers were to write in his day, the literature that they would produce would be quite unlike the extant New Testament.

What began as a formal correspondence swiftly intensified into a controversy when Spencer Clack, who with George Waller was the editor of *The Baptist Recorder*,[37] wrote a letter to Campbell, telling him that Semple was 'your friend; he loves you, but does not approve of your opinions'. Clack quoted Semple as writing,

> What shall we do with Campbell? He is certainly wise, but not with the wisdom of God, at least not often. He seems to be misled by an ambition to be thought of as a reformer: but he will fail, or I shall miss my guess (as the Yankees say). He may be as learned as Luther, or Calvin, or Melanchthon, but they fell on other days than our friend Alexander. It is one thing to reform Popery, and another to reform the Reformation.

Also, according to Clack, Semple expressed the hope that Campbell would get to the 'right point of the compass'. For his part Clack requested that Campbell compile a summary of his theology so that Clack and others could compare Campbell's theology with their own.[38]

Campbell replied to Clack's letter. By the time of this exchange between the two men in 1827, they already had a mutually antagonistic relationship. Campbell had previously written that *The Baptist Recorder* 'exhibit[ed] a belligerent aspect' toward *The Christian Baptist*.[39] However, in a letter to Campbell, Clack protested that he had 'used mildness in almost everything which I have written either of you or your opinions'.[40] Campbell retorted that he had been 'for more than one year the constant object of vituperation and detraction, of obloquy and misrepresentation' in *The Baptist Recorder*.[41] Clack wrote to Campbell that he wanted to lead him to a 'serious consideration of the importance of cultivating love and union with your brethren'.[42] Campbell responded angrily: 'Did I ask you for advice, brother Clack? Or did I choose you for my preceptor? When I sit for lessons I claim the right of choosing my instructor. And believe me, brother Clack, there are a hundred persons on this continent who would, in my judgment, be more eligible than you.'[43] Clearly an impasse had been reached.

Clack's interposition of himself into the Campbell–Semple correspondence caused more friction for Campbell in a situation that was already precarious: a

---

[37] A. Campbell, 'The Baptist Recorder', *CB* 3 (1 May 1826), p. 239.

[38] Spencer Clack, Bloomfield, Ky., to A. Campbell, Bethany, Va., June 1827, *CB* 5 (5 November 1827), p. 387.

[39] A. Campbell, 'Baptist Recorder', p. 239.

[40] Spencer Clack, Bloomfield, Ky., to A. Campbell, Bethany, Va., May 1827, *CB* 5 (6 August 1827), p. 359.

[41] A. Campbell, 'Reply to the Above—No. 1', *CB* 5 (6 August 1827), p. 360.

[42] Clack to Campbell, *CB*, 387.

[43] A. Campbell, 'Reply to Spencer Clack's 2d Letter—Letter II', *CB* 5 (3 December 1827), p. 396.

respected Baptist had criticized Campbell publicly, and he had to maintain composure. Nevertheless, Campbell counterattacked by creating a list of eleven offences of Clack and Waller. In the same issue of *The Christian Baptist* in which Campbell included his eleven charges against them, Campbell printed a letter that Semple sent to another person, thus reiterating the connection between his fights with Semple and Clack. Semple wrote that he was not fond of controversy, but should he become embroiled in controversy with Campbell, he believed Campbell was 'palpably on the wrong side'. Campbell was a 'champion' and a 'generous combatant'. On the other hand, Semple wrote, 'When I think of Mr. Campbell's talents, conjoined with pleasant manners, and apparently a pious spirit, I am exceedingly grieved that he has been heretofore, and is likely to be hereafter, of so little advantage to the cause. I cannot but hope that he will be brought to a more scriptural and more rational course.'[44] Campbell replied to this same letter in the same issue of *The Christian Baptist*. He contrasted Semple, 'the most competent person in Virginia', with Clack and Waller, who were 'palpably dull'. Campbell expressed appreciation for Semple's wish that he could be more scriptural and rational and asked for Semple's help in the matter. He wrote that Semple could have as much space as he wanted in *The Christian Baptist* to contrast his views with Campbell's because, 'There is no man in America I would rather have for an opponent, if I must have an opponent, than you.'[45] In the letter Campbell showed Semple respect and politeness, which was much different from the defensiveness and sarcasm he showed Clack. Campbell wrote five more open letters to Semple. By 1830 Campbell's preoccupation had subsided. The final reference to Semple in *The Christian Baptist* was in an article that Campbell wrote describing a meeting between the two men. Campbell was pleased with his and Semple's cordial discussion; their uniting in prayer, praise, and worship; and their sharing a meal together. Campbell seemed the most pleased that their public dispute was not repeated in private, and he admired Semple's 'good temper and Christian courtesy'.[46]

Did Campbell influence Baptist identity? Although the data is somewhat obscure compared with Campbell's own Baptist identity, four suggestions are: his rousing success as a debater enlivened Baptist life and created confidence that the Baptist movement was valid *vis à vis* Presbyterianism and socialism; his *Christian Baptist* was a source of doctrinal information for a wide Baptist readership; his preaching was a source of many Baptist conversions; and his challenge to Baptist sensibilities in his debates, writings, and preaching, in which he promulgated doctrines that were heterodox for Baptists, caused a re-evaluation of theology for many Baptists.

Campbell still broods over Baptist memory. His relationship with Baptists illuminates Baptist identity, especially when he is compared to two famous early Baptists, John Smyth and Roger Williams, who both broke with Baptists. Their Baptist periods were short, but in standard Baptist historiography, such as Robert

---

[44] Robert Semple, 'A Letter, Said to Have Been Written by Bishop Semple, from Washington City, to Somebody in Kentucky', *CB* 5 (3 December 1827), pp. 398-99.

[45] A. Campbell, 'To R.B. Semple, of Virginia', *CB* 5 (3 December 1827), p. 399.

[46] A. Campbell, 'Bishop Semple', *CB* 7 (1 March 1830), p. 636.

Torbet's *A History of the Baptists* and H. Leon McBeth's *The Baptist Heritage*, and in a new publication, Bill J. Leonard's *Baptist Ways: A History*, they are remembered as Baptist heroes. Campbell is an interesting counterpoint. He was a Baptist for eighteen years, much longer than either Smyth or Williams. He indicated that he intended to remain a Baptist, but felt compelled to withdraw from Baptist life because, in part, he faced hostility from fellow Baptists. Many Baptists saw Campbell as schismatic, yet John Smyth also split his congregation and might have killed the fledgling Baptist movement. Many remember Campbell as a caustic controversialist, but no American was as contentiously controversial as Roger Williams in his time. Few readers of Baptist history query the Baptist identity of either Smyth or Williams, but few Baptists have been willing to accept Campbell as a real Baptist: among historians, for instance, Torbet and McBeth maligned Campbell, while Leonard virtually ignored him. Why is this? Perhaps because Baptists perceive that Smyth and Williams contributed something positive to Baptist life whereas Campbell was simply a destructive presence. Perhaps the time has arrived for Baptists to forgive Campbell for whatever damage he may have caused, and to acknowledge him as a real Baptist who made Baptist life more robust.

CHAPTER 10

Creeds and Controversies:
Insights from William Bullein Johnson

Kenneth B.E. Roxburgh

Introduction

William Bullein Johnson was one of the most significant Baptist leaders in the Southern states, a 'pivotal figure in the formation of the Southern Baptist Convention' who, more than any other person, shaped 'the structure and nature of the Convention'.[1] Prior to his appointment as President of the SBC in 1845, Johnson had been a key player in various efforts to unite Baptist churches in missionary and educational efforts. For example, Johnson was present at the formation of the Triennial Convention of the United States in 1814,[2] and from 1841–44 served as President of the Convention, immediately prior to the split in 1845.[3] In 1824 he was elected President of the South Carolina State Convention and continued in that position for twenty-seven years, preaching to the Convention on

---

[1] Glenwood Clayton, 'Introduction to Reminiscences', *Journal of the South Carolina Baptist Historical Society* 4 (November, 1978), p. 18. In 'William Bullein Johnson: The First President of the Southern Baptist Convention and his Portrayal of Baptist identity', *Journal of South Carolina Baptist Historical Society* 26 (November 2000), p. 11, Clayton comments that 'his views on the Baptist identity doubtless reflected as well as helped shape and focus Baptist theology of the nineteenth century'.

[2] Luther Rice 'attributed the concept of a national organization to a conversation between himself and William B. Johnson' while Johnson was pastor of the First Baptist Church of Savannah, Georgia, and Rice 'wrote to all societies then formed, urging upon them the importance of the meeting and requesting them to appoint delegates'. James A. Rogers, *Richard Furman: Life and Legacy* (Macon, GA: Mercer University Press, 1985), p. 145. Johnson attended the first meeting in 1814 when only thirty-two people were present, and the final meeting in 1844 at the age of sixty-two when 458 delegates assembled.

[3] Johnson was absent from the Convention from 1820 to 1835. In 1841, in the context of the slavery debate, it has been suggested that Johnson, 'because of his growing reputation as a mediator...was asked to run as a compromise candidate'. See Raymond John Legendre, 'William Bullein Johnson: Pastor, Educator, and Missions Promoter' (DPhil, New Orleans Baptist Seminary, 1988), p. 125.

twelve occasions.[4] In 1831 Johnson became the moderator of the Edgefield Baptist Association and held that position for fifteen years. During this period of time, Johnson served as pastor of churches at Edgefield, SC, and at Euhaw near Beaufort. He founded churches at Greenville, SC, and Columbia, where he was chaplain of South Carolina College. At Anderson, SC, as Chancellor of Johnson Female University (1853–58), he pioneered in higher education for women. As President of the Board of Trustees of Furman Theological Institute, which eventually became the nucleus of the Southern Baptist Theological Seminary in Greenville in 1859, he encouraged theological education among Southern Baptists.[5]

Johnson's experience of Baptist life at association, state and national level led those Southern leaders who met at Augusta in 1845 to follow his lead in preparing a constitution for the newly-fledged body.[6] Johnson's leadership at the convention was recognized, not only when he was appointed President of the Convention, but as he preached the first sermon on 7 May and led the morning devotions the following morning.[7] Johnson was also given the responsibility of issuing an *Address* to the churches on behalf of the Convention. The *Address* was initially written by Johnson and edited by Richard Fuller and T.F. Curtis. One of the most significant comments contained within it stated that the Convention had 'constructed for our basis no new creed; acting in this matter upon a Baptist aversion for all creeds but the Bible'.[8] Tom Nettles described this statement as 'idiosyncratic' and argues that Johnson was 'clearly...out of harmony with his brethren in the South' and that 'those who followed his views were in a vast minority'.[9] Yet, as I will argue, Johnson's views on this issue were well-known to his colleagues and continued to shape the direction of a Convention that, until 1925, did not issue any statement of faith on behalf of its constituents.[10]

---

[4] See the James Pickett Wesberry, *Baptists in South Carolina before the War between the States* (Columbia, SC: R.L. Bryan, 1966), pp. 64-65.

[5] J. Glenwood Clayton, 'The Beginnings of the First Baptist Church', *Journal of the Southern Baptist Historical Society* 14 (November, 1988), p. 18.

[6] Johnson actually came to Augusta with a previously prepared constitution to present to the committee formed for this purpose. James M. Morton, Jr, 'Leadership of W.B. Johnson in the Formation of the Southern Baptist Convention', *Baptist History and Heritage* 5.1 (January, 1970), p. 10.

[7] Robert G. Gardner, *A Decade of Debate and Division: Georgia Baptists and the Formation of the Southern Baptist Convention* (Macon GA:, Mercer University Press, 1995), p. 36.

[8] *Proceedings of the Southern Baptist Convention held in Augusta, Georgia, May 1845* (Richmond, VA, 1845), p. 19.

[9] Tom J. Nettles, 'On the Other Hand: The Decline of Confessions', *Founders Journal* 49 (Summer, 2002), p. 11.

[10] Two earlier brief doctrinal documents were approved by the Convention. In 1914, the *Pronouncement on Christian Union and Denominational Efficiency* set out the Baptist attitude towards the union movement, and in 1919 a committee of the Convention prepared a 'fraternal address' to Baptists in different parts of the world, though this was not approved or adopted by the Convention itself. See discussions of this in James

Baptists, Creeds and Confessions of Faith

It cannot be denied that many Baptists in America used creeds and confessions of faith, often not distinguishing carefully between the two types of documents. Bill Leonard comments that 'in the early days of Baptist experience in America, associations and local churches were frequently, though not always, formed around confessional declarations'.[11] Johnson's aversion to all creeds and confessions of faith did not, then, adequately reflect variations within the Baptist constituency although Lumpkin has reminded us that 'no confession has ever permanently bound individuals, churches, associations, conventions or unions among Baptists'.[12]

Francis Wayland, who succeeded Johnson as President of the Triennial Convention in 1845, published a series of papers in 1857 under the title *Notes on the Principles and Practices of Baptist Churches* in which he stated that 'Baptists Have No Authoritative Confession of Faith, the Absence of Such Confession a Cause of Union Rather Than Division'.[13] More than a century earlier, John Leland maintained that 'for his religious creed he acknowledged no directory but the Bible'.[14] Leland was concerned that a confession might be made into a 'petty Bible',[15] and argued that confessions of faith would 'check any further pursuit after truth'.[16] Johnson clearly identified himself with this particular perspective.

Johnson's Statements on Confessions of Faith

Johnson was among the original nine members of the South Carolina State Convention that was formed in Columbia on 4 December 1821. Johnson was given the responsibility of visiting various churches and one association, to encourage them to join the newly fledged body that had been founded on 'some general principles' and had not yet adopted a 'definitive constitution'. Reflecting on this point in 1848, Johnson stated that 'there is not, in these principles, a single word on

---

Edward Carter, 'The Southern Baptist Convention and Confessions of Faith, 1845–1945' (DTh, Southwestern Baptist Theological Seminary, 1964), p. 3.

[11] William J. Leonard, 'Types of Confessional Documents Among Baptists', *Review and Expositor* 76.1 (Winter, 1979), p. 35.

[12] W.L. Lumpkin, *Baptist Confessions of Faith* (Philadelphia, PA: Judson Press, 1959), p. 17.

[13] Francis Wayland, *Notes on the Principles and Practices of Baptist Churches* (New York, 1857), p. 13.

[14] John Leland in L.F. Green (ed.), *The Writings of the Late Elder John Leland, Including Some Events in His Life written by Himself, with Additional Sketches, Etc.* (New York, 1845), pp. 50-51.

[15] Leland, *Writings*, p. 145. Timothy George comments that 'Baptists have never been *creedalistic* in the sense of placing manmade doctrinal constructs above Holy Scripture', in 'The Priesthood of All Believers and the Quest for Theological Integrity', *Criswell Theological Review* 3.2 (Spring, 1989), p. 287.

[16] Leland, *Writings*, p 114.

the subject of a Standard Confession of Faith'.[17] When the Convention met the
following year and a constitution was adopted, the founders argued that the
'organization and support of a Seminary...under the care of this Convention...will
be conducted...according to the conscientious sentiments of the founders, yet on the
principle of Christian liberty, and in favor of the rights of private judgment'.[18]
Johnson was well aware that churches and associations had often adopted written
confessions of faith but doubted the scriptural warrant for such a practice, and he
made it clear that the phrase 'conscientious sentiments of the founders' of the
Convention had 'no reference to any confession of faith, or standard of orthodoxy for
the Convention or its Seminary'. He stated that the constitution had been the work
of Dr Richard Furman and 'yet it makes no provision for any standard Confession of
Faith, absolutely or relatively'. In 1823, when the Convention met to discuss the
question of organizing a theological institution, he opposed an effort from the
Georgia Baptist Association (later to become the Convention) to adopt the
Philadelphia Confession of Faith as the foundation of the college. In 1824, Johnson
recalled that 'others with myself, opposed its adoption' and the question 'was again
indefinitely postponed' and 'there', comments Johnson 'it found its resting place; and
I thank God for it'.[19] For Johnson, the fact that Professors of Theology at what
became the Furman Theological Institute would be required to teach *Biblical
Theology* and that the Board of Trustees would 'not hesitate to call them to account'
if any question was raised about their teaching. The security of the institution lay
'not in human standards of orthodoxy, but, *Under God*, in the structure of our
organization'.[20] The fact that all the professors would be members of an association
of churches would ensure they could not be 'immoral or heterodox without detection
and removal'.[21] For Johnson, 'it was a new feature in Baptist Theology to talk of
Confessions of Faith as tests of orthodoxy'. [22]

In 1856, writing a series of articles in the *Southern Baptist*, Johnson admitted
that 'Association...usually have an abstract of principles, a creed or confession of
faith...to which every church in the body is required to give its adhesion', although
he stated that in South Carolina there were 'two associations that have not such a
religious standard'.[23] Johnson was concerned that one association had dissolved its
connexion with a church on the ground of her violation of one of the articles of the
abstract of principles. Johnson believed that 'an association can have no authority to
censure a church, much less excommunicate her'.[24] He argued that such occurrences,

---

[17] William B. Johnson, 'To the Baptists of South Carolina...', *Southern Baptist*, 3.24
(18 October, 1848), p. 2.
[18] Johnson, 'To the Baptists', p. 2.
[19] Johnson, 'To the Baptists', p. 2.
[20] Johnson, 'To the Baptists', p. 2.
[21] Johnson, 'To the Baptists', p. 2.
[22] Johnson, 'To the Baptists', p. 2.
[23] One of these was stated to be the Charleston Baptist Association organized in
1850.
[24] Johnson, 'To the Baptists', p. 2.

violating the principle of the independence of the local church, would not occur if churches and associations made 'the scriptures our only standard of faith and practice'.

Johnson, in this series of articles, did not remain unscathed by his opponents. Iveson Lewis Brookes wrote a series of rejoinders to them.[25] He argued that 'every religious denomination, down to the Mormons, profess to base their tenets on the teaching of the Bible'.[26] Although Johnson served on the Board of Trustees of Southern Seminary, 'his advanced age, illnesses, and commitments severely limited…contributions to the efforts'.[27] Yet, although he eventually supported the founding of the seminary, Johnson was unhappy at the strong insistence that many leaders, with a Calvinistic focus, had towards a creed being established for the new school. Johnson believed that this issue would limit the support that would be necessary for the school to succeed.[28]

Johnson's Opposition to Confessional Documents

The concern that Johnson consistently expressed throughout his life regarding confessions of faith was based upon several leading principles.

The Personal Experience of Faith

Johnson maintained that the foundation of Baptist identity was to be found in a faith that was first and foremost personal and not propositional. Indeed, his own encounter with Christ was not one that fitted well with any traditional *Ordo Salutis*. In June 1860, when he was seventy-eight years of age, Johnson published his *Reminiscences*[29] in which he related the early stages of his faith. Johnson was living in Beaufort, SC, with his father and step-mother and in 1803 married a step-niece of his step-mother. In the summer of 1804, the Baptist church in Beaufort experienced a 'deeply interesting revival'.[30] One of the chief influences on his life was a Miss Lydia Turner from London. She was baptized in the Baptist church at Savannah, and

---

[25] Brookes (1793–1865) was a Baptist clergyman, schoolteacher, planter and proslavery apologist.

[26] 'Replies to the Articles of "W" No. VII', *Southern Baptist* 10.49 (5 March 1858), p. 1.

[27] Legendre, 'Johnson', p. 82.

[28] Legendre, 'Johnson', p. 81.

[29] They were published in the *Baptist Courier* from 29 November 1894 to 17 September 1896. They were republished in the *Journal of the South Carolina Baptist Historical Society* 4 (1978) and 5 (1979).

[30] The first pastor, Henry Holcombe, later founded the Baptist church in Savannah where Johnson served as the second pastor and moved to First Baptist, Philadelphia, where the first meeting of the Triennial Convention was held. See website of *The Baptist Church of Beaufort*, www.bcob.org/about_history.htm, consulted on 24 June 2003.

engaged in 'earnest conversation and fervent prayer' for Johnson's conversion.[31] Johnson's conversion was the result of these conversations and two dramatic dreams and visions of Christ. He relates that one evening

> after reading the scriptures and prayer, I retired to bed, and on closing my eyes there appeared before me a form like that of the Lord Jesus with a countenance expressive of distress, indicating that, although *he* died for *my* sins, *I* had not received *him* as *my Savior*. This filled my heart with distress and sorrow. After some time I became more calm and fell asleep. In the morning when I awoke my attention was drawn upward to the right, where I beheld the same form I had the night before. But O how changed! Instead of distress in his countenance, joy beamed forth upon the attendants around him, of whom I seemed to be one, upon whom he looked with a benignant smile and a moral change most happily came over my spirit...and in this happy frame I continued for some weeks.

He confessed that the convictions of sin that he experienced were 'of a gentler kind' but 'no less genuine' than other people.[32] Johnson's experience of conversion may well have seemed suspect to preachers who sought to ensure that their hearers 'achieve proper conversions'.[33] The spiritual encounter that he passed through shaped the emphasis of his life and ministry, as one that was centered upon a personal relationship with Christ, fitting in well with the Separatist Baptist emphasis in the South that stressed personal religious experience.

The revival movement that Johnson encountered in Beaufort was part of a wider movement of the Spirit that broke out in Kentucky in 1800 and swept through the South in the decades that followed, becoming a major impulse for the growth of churches through conversion, and influencing the theological character of pastors and people. Johnson was influenced by his mentor, Richard Furman, who united religious experience[34] with theological reflection.

In 1831, Johnson was pastor of the Baptist church in Edgefield, with a membership of seventy-nine individuals. He joined five other ministers for a camp meeting in Sardis, about ten miles from Edgefield. In a short period of time over 2,000 people were gathering in protracted meetings. Johnson followed this event

---

[31] Legendre, 'Johnson', p. 11, appears to be incorrect in describing her as an 'English evangelist' with the implication that she preached publicly in meetings. Turner was instrumental in leading several individuals to faith in Christ.

[32] William B. Johnson, 'Reminiscences', *Baptist Courier* 26.8 (6 December 1894), p. 1.

[33] Ned Landsman, 'Revivalism and Nativism in the Middle Colonies: The Great Awakening and the Scots Community in East New Jersey', *American Quarterly* 34.2 (Summer, 1982), p. 159.

[34] Furman commented on the Revivals of the early 1800s as 'a very extraordinary work, and I rejoice much that I Have seen it'. See letter cited by John B. Boles, *The Great Revival, 1787–1805: The Origins of the Southern Evangelical Mind* (Lexington, KY: University of Kentucky Press, 1972), p. 77. Boyles, p. 80, comments that Furman 'although eminently orthodox nevertheless appreciated heartfelt religion'.

with special meetings in Edgefield for ten days in August 1831, holding up to four meetings each day. The Edgefield church received forty-five new members and numerous re-dedications[35] as 'a series of revivals swept Edgefield County'.[36] Johnson became a significant leader in this revival movement in South Carolina. Basil Manley, Sr, who was the pastor of the Charleston church, asked Johnson to extend the visits he was making to the Savannah River Baptist Association and preach in Charleston indicating that 'our people are longing for a visit from some of the Revival Ministers'.[37] This revivalist involvement in Johnson's life and ministry greatly influenced the emphasis he gave to personal experience, uniting a fervent faith with a biblical message of salvation through Christ alone.[38]

The Church as a Christocracy

Johnson's stress on the centrality of Christ also became the fundamental feature of his ecclesiology. Johnson used the term 'Christocracy' that expressed 'the true character' of congregational government 'in which his power is manifested in perfect accordance of the freedom of his people'.[39] Johnson further defined a Christocracy as 'that form of government of which Christ is the head, and under which he requires his people to receive all their principles of action from, and to frame all their doings according to, his laws and precepts contained in the Bible'.[40] For Johnson this involved what he called 'democratical' church government 'that is, by the members of the body...in the exercise of a popular vote by the members'.[41] In this way the 'rights of each members are respected' and no other body, either secular or religious, could interfere with the decisions of believers seeking to discern the mind of Christ.

The independence of the local church was a central issue for Johnson. He addressed the question of 'Baptist Usage' in the *Southern Baptist* in 1855 and stated the obvious when he said that 'as far as we know, Baptist Usage is not uniform among the churches'.[42] One area of disagreement among the church that Johnson was aware

---

[35] Johnson, 'Reminiscences', *Baptist Courier* 27.43 (6 August 1896), p. 1, and 27.49 (17 September 1896), p. 1.

[36] J. Glen Clayton, 'South Carolina Shapers of Southern Baptists', *Baptist History and Heritage* 17.3 (July, 1982), p. 18.

[37] Letter from Manley to Johnson cited by Clayton, 'South Carolina Shapers', p. 18.

[38] William G. McLoughlin argues that the impact of Revivalism at this time brought about a change in theology and 'the prevailing world view of southerners' which 'had been Calvinistic, but Calvinism faded fast after 1800', See *Revivals, Awakenings and Reform: An Essay on Religion and Social Change in America, 1607–1977* (Chicago History of American Religion; Chicago, IL: University of Chicago Press, 1978), p. 135.

[39] William B. Johnson, *The Gospel Developed through the Government and Order of the Churches of Jesus Christ*, reprinted in Mark Dever (ed.), *Polity* (Washington DC: Center for Church Reform, 2001), p. 175.

[40] Johnson, 'The Gospel', p. 232.

[41] Johnson, 'The Gospel', pp. 172-73.

[42] William B. Johnson, 'Baptist Usage', *Southern Baptist* 10.31 (7 November 1855), p. 2.

of was in receiving believers who were transferring their membership from one church to another. 'Some' churches, he commented, 'receive applicants for membership by letter, on that certificate only; others, in addition to a letter, require a recital of Christian experience.' For Johnson the basic principle in dealing with such a practical issue was that 'each church of Christ is an independent body, and can have no person, though baptized, forced upon her'.[43] Johnson's own view on this issue arose from a belief that baptism was not an ordinance of the churches but of the kingdom of Christ. Evangelists, he stated, will baptize people into the life of the kingdom, but not into the membership of the church. Therefore, it is the responsibility of the local church to receive that person into its membership, not on the basis of their baptism, but by examining their 'spiritual fitness'. He thus maintained that 'baptism is not the door into any church of Christ. It is the consent of the church alone.'[44]

This emphasis on the independence of the local congregation did not hinder Johnson encouraging fellowship between churches, or the establishment of associations, state and national conventions. However, the purpose of these bodies was limited to specific purposes of extending the kingdom of God through mission and the education of ministers of the gospel. On no account was the association or convention to interfere with the rights of the local church in making decisions about any issue of faith and practice.

The Bible

Johnson expressed a concern that the adoption of confessions of faith tended to undermine the authority of Christ as Lord of the conscience, and that because 'the churches are independent bodies, subject only to Christ, their Head—that His word is the only standard of faith and practice'.[45] He also maintained that confessions of faith were unnecessary encumbrances because the church already possessed the scriptures, a 'perfect and full a standard' of God's will. Why then, turn to the human interpretation which was 'imperfect and limited?'[46]

Writing in the *Southern Baptist* in January 1856, Johnson stated that 'it is difficult to see how among us Baptists, who hold to the sufficiency of the Scriptures, and their paramount authority, it should be considered necessary' to adopt a 'written declaration of the principles of the doctrine of Christ which she believes' as the '*standard of her faith and practices*'. This, he contended, is 'inadmissible' because 'the Bible alone is that standard, and no human compilations or abstracts of principles from the Bible can supplant *that perfect standard*'.[47] He responded to the

---

[43] William B. Johnson, 'The Evangelist, or Preacher of the Gospel', *Southern Baptist* 10.34 (28 November 1855), p. 3.

[44] Johnson, 'The Evangelist', p. 3.

[45] William Johnson, 'Baptist Usage', *Southern Baptist* (7 November 1855), p. 2.

[46] William B. Johnson, *The Gospel Developed through the Government and Order of the Churches of Jesus Christ* (Richmond, VA, 1846), pp. 194, 201.

[47] William B. Johnson, *Southern Baptist*, 10.44 (30 January 1856), p. 2.

affirmation that confessions of faith were compilations based upon scripture by asking 'can man present God's system in a selection and compilation of some of its parts, better than God himself has done it, as a whole in his own book?'[48] Johnson was fully aware that associations did adopt confessions of faith, but argued that 'with so perfect and so full a standard' as the Bible 'why should an imperfect and limited one be adopted?'[49] To Johnson, it was strange that an association of Baptist churches 'that have so strenuously contended for the supremacy and authority of the scriptures' should adopt 'any other religious standard than these holy writings'.[50] The responsibility of churches is in 'humble and fervent prayer' to seek 'the Spirit's aid in all our searching of the oracles of God for knowledge of His will'.[51]

Johnson's confidence in the church being able to discern and decide upon the will of God for their faith and practice was founded on an unwavering commitment to the authority and power of the scriptures and, as the *Second London Confession* of 1688 declared 'the infallible rule of interpretation of Scripture is Scripture itself'.[52] To Johnson, the Bible was the all sufficient source of truth and this led to his opposition to all confessions of faith.

The Purpose of Union with State and National Conventions was Mission and Education

At state and national level, Johnson believed that Baptists came together with the primary purpose of furthering the kingdom of God. In 1821, as a member of the South Carolina State Convention he had committed himself to 'the promotion of the cause and interest of the redeemer'. The *Constitutional Principles* that Johnson shared in preparing stated that churches and associations were joining together as 'a means of vigorous, united exertion in the cause of God' and 'the promotion of evangelical and useful knowledge, by means of religious education; the support of missionary service among the destitute'. This means of working together would not, however, undermine the independence and liberty of the churches because the Convention would not seek to interfere in their life.[53]

Although the initial reason for the separation of Southern churches from the Triennial Convention in 1845 was the issue of slavery, Johnson and other leaders argued that the principle purpose in forming the Southern Baptist Convention was that of 'organizing a plan for eliciting, combining and directing the energies of the

---

[48] Johnson, *Gospel Developed*, p. 233.

[49] William B. Johnson, *Southern Baptist* 11.11 (10 June 1856), p. 1.

[50] Johnson, *Southern Baptists* 11.11 (10 June 1856), p. 1.

[51] Johnson, *Southern Baptists* 11.11 (10 June 1856), p. 1.

[52] Lumpkin (ed.), *Baptists Confessions of Faith*, p. 250. James Leo Garrett reminds Baptists that 'the confessions have always stood in a subordinate relation to the Bible and especially to the New Testament'. 'Biblical Authority According to Baptist Confessions of Faith', *Review and Expositor* 76.1 (Winter, 1979), p. 43.

[53] See Joe M. King, *A History of South Carolina Baptists* (Columbia, SC: The General Board of the South Carolina Baptist Convention, 1964), p. 173.

whole denomination in one sacred effort, for the propagation of the gospel'.[54] When the Baptist Board of Foreign Missions refused to appoint a missionary who was a slaveholder, the new Convention maintained that the Triennial Convention was not following her own constitution which stated that 'such persons as are in full communion with some regular church of our denomination, and who furnish satisfactory evidence of genuine piety, good talents and fervent zeal for the Redeemer's cause, are to be employed as missionaries'.[55] This, they contended, was the reason why they organized a 'Society for the propagation of the Gospel'.[56]

Johnson began his 'Address to the Churches' by stating very clearly that the reason for the division was not on the basis of theology, for both 'Northern and Southern Baptists are still brethren. They differ in no article of the faith. They are guided by the same principles of gospel order.' These 'Principles' are 'conservative; while they are also, as we trust, equitable and liberal' and are 'precisely that of the original union', and thus, he continued, 'we have constructed for our basis no new creed; acting in this matter upon a Baptist aversion for all creeds but the Bible'.[57] This is the context of his famous statement that the basis of the Convention is not a theological statement but a passion for mission, and this held the Convention together through many moments of crisis during the following 130 years. Indeed, 'for the first half century the convention was...often referred to as "the Southern Missionary Convention"'.[58] This meant that churches from different theological perspectives, with varying practices relating to baptism and the administration of the Lord's Supper, could unite for the purpose of mission.

Johnson was asked by the Foreign Mission Board of the new Convention to tour the churches. In this connection, he wrote a letter to various Baptist newspapers.[59] He wrote to encourage churches to arrange special collections of money that could be sent to associations or state conventions, who would then send the monies with their delegates to the meetings of the national convention. This would further the 'principle...for which we have separated.... [t]he supreme authority of the word of God in all points of faith and practice... [n]ot that we love our Northern brethren less, but that we love principle and the Divine Author more...and entered upon the work of propagating the gospel of Christ by the appointment of the Foreign and Domestic Boards'.[60] On this basis, Johnson argued that 'Some' Baptists 'believe in the Calvinistic scheme, and some in the Arminian. Some are hyper-Calvinists, and

---

[54] *Proceedings of the Southern Baptist Convention held in Augusta, Georgia,* (Richmond, VA, 1845), p. 3.
[55] *Proceedings*, p. 12.
[56] *Proceedings*, p. 13.
[57] *Proceedings*, pp. 18-19.
[58] Carter, 'Confessions of Faith', p. 199.
[59] See William B. Johnson, *Alabama Baptist* 16 August 1845, p. 1, cols. 5-6.
[60] Johnson, *Alabama Baptist* 16 August 1845, p. 1.

some are moderate Calvinists' that which unites them is 'His word' that is 'the only standard of faith and practice'.[61]

The Nature of Education as an Unfettered Pursuit of Truth

Throughout his life and ministry Johnson encouraged the work of education. This commitment began during his pastorate in Euhaw, during which Johnson taught for four years (1811–13) at the McNeil Female Academy for 'older and advanced students'.[62] In 1823, he began a period of eight years teaching at the Greenville Female Academy as its first headmaster, where he encouraged 'a thorough and liberal education',[63] seeking to introduce his students to a varied curriculum including philosophy and logic, as well as Latin and Greek, when teaching 'classical languages to young women was unusual, perhaps unique at the time' and 'suggests his beliefs that girls were as intellectually capable as their brothers'.[64] Judith Bainbridge comments that 'Johnson was unusual in his attitude towards female education'. He adopted 'a liberal religious basis not generally shared by his colleagues in the clergy'[65] as he encouraged women students to 'become fitted for the noble studies designed for their occupancy by the common father of all children'.[66]

This commitment to liberal education and academic enquiry also marked his commitment within the South Carolina State Convention as he encountered opposition to ministerial education from other pastors and congregations who were frightened of 'a race of learned but graceless preachers'.[67] Three years later, when he was elected as President of the State Convention, Johnson once again addressed the churches and called them to support a 'classical and theological education for ministers', and in 1826 the Convention established Furman Theological Academy at Edgefield, South Carolina.[68] From 1826 to 1853 Johnson made an enormous

---

[61] William B. Johnson, *Southern Baptist* 7 November 1855. Timothy George infers that when the 'SBC adopted the *Baptist Faith and Message*...the SBC also adopted the Cooperative Program in 1925 thus providing both a confession and financial basis of cooperation'. This was never envisaged by people like Johnson in 1845 and was not the purpose of adopting the *Baptist Faith and Message* in 1925. See Timothy F. George, 'Introduction', John A. Broadus (ed.), *Baptist Confessions, Covenants, and Catechisms* (Nashville, TN: Broadman and Holman, 1996), pp. 12-13.

[62] See Judith T. Bainbridge, *Academy and College: The History of the Woman's College of Furman University* (Macon, GA: Mercer University Press, 2001), p. 8.

[63] See *Baptist Courier* 19.2 (21 April 1887), p. 1.

[64] Bainbridge, *Academy*, pp. 8-9.

[65] Bainbridge, *Academy*, p. 55.

[66] William B. Johnson, *An Address before the Students of Johnson Female Academy delivered on its anniversary, August 1850*, cited in Bainbridge, *Academy*, p. 55.

[67] William B. Johnson, 'Address to the Churches, the State Convention of the Baptist denomination, in South Carolina, to their Constituents, and their Brethren throughout the State', in *Minutes of the State Convention of the Baptists Denomination in South Carolina* (1822), pp. 10-11, cited by Legendre, 'Johnson', p. 59.

[68] Legendre, 'Johnson', pp. 61-63.

contribution to Furman, recognized by Richard Furman, Jr's comment that 'Furman University was due to him more than any other one man'.[69]

In 1847 Johnson was involved in defending the integrity of Furman and two of its Professors against charges of incompetence and heterodoxy made by a former Professor, J.L. Reynolds.[70] J.S. Mims was accused by Reynolds of teaching theological views that were 'at variance with the confessions of faith which have been put forth by the association united in the State Convention, as the exponents of their faith'.[71] The issue surrounded Mims' teaching on 'the doctrine of imputation' to which many students became 'very much opposed' as a result of Mims' exegesis classes.[72] Reynolds maintained that the doctrine of imputation was 'an integral part of the Christian system, presenting the only rational account of the ruined condition of our race, and affording the only means of deliverance from it'.[73]

As President of the Board of Trustees, Johnson responded to Reynolds and stated that 'the Professors of the Furman Theological Institution are both competent and orthodox'.[74] In October 1848, he wrote an article in the *Southern Baptist* and demonstrated that the views of Mims on imputation may have differed from the statements contained in some confessions of faith, but were not contrary to the interpretation of other Baptist scholars on certain biblical passages. Johnson cited a letter from Jesse Hartwell, a former Professor at Furman who had taught there for six years. Hartwell moved to Alabama in 1836, becoming President of the state convention in 1839 and President of the Board of Domestic Missions. From 1844 to 1847, he was a Professor at Howard College in Marion and encountered opposition to his views on imputation and justification.[75] Hartwell told Johnson that he believed 'the views on "Imputation" presented by Prof. Mims to be scriptural and correct' and were the same views he had taught at Furman, and 'I never thought I was heterodox, neither did I conceal my sentiments on this point.... I believe that his sentiments are in accordance with scripture teaching, and we—Baptists—allow no other Creed or Confession as authoritative.'[76] Johnson argued that neither the South Carolina State Convention nor Furman Theological Institute ever adopted a 'Confession of faith framed by man' because 'the Bible alone has been the Standard

---

[69] Legendre, 'Johnson', p. 63.

[70] The controversy generated a series of pamphlets that were gathered together and published in 1848. See *Documents Relating to the Controversy Between Rev. J.L. Reynolds and the Board of Trustees of the Furman Theological Institute of the State of South Carolina* (Charleston, SC, 1848).

[71] J.L. Reynolds, 'Editorial on Furman Theological Institution', *The Baptist Guardian* 15 November 1847, p. 1.

[72] See *Documents*, p. 22.

[73] *Documents*, p. 26.

[74] *Documents*, p. 46.

[75] See Wayne Flynt, *Alabama Baptists: Southern Baptists in the Heart of Dixie* (Tuscaloosa, AL: University of Alabama Press, 1998), p. 59.

[76] Letter of Jesse Hartwell to William B. Johnson, dated 20 September 1848, cited in *Southern Baptist* 3.25 (25 October 1848), p. 2.

for the one and the other... It is a new feature in Baptist Theology to talk of Confessions of Faith as tests of orthodoxy.'[77] In a letter to Mims, Johnson stated that 'in his opinion the doctrine of imputation had been gradually going out of use and that Baptists at least in this state were becoming moderate Calvinists'.[78] In a later letter to Mims, Johnson made it clear that the hyper-Calvinist theology that he believed Reynolds represented would never be popular in South Carolina because 'such views had never been embodied in the Convention Constitution, or the Constitution of the Institution, or prescribed to by the professors or W.B. Johnson'.[79] Johnson expressed his vigorous rejection of both hyper-Calvinism and credalism, confirming his commitment to academic freedom within liberal and theological educational establishments. His commitment to Baptist identity led him to claim that 'the right which I exercise in holding *my* views of divine truth, I cheerfully accord to all others to hold *theirs*'.[80]

Johnson has, at times, been celebrated as a mainline Calvinist in his theology.[81] Yet Johnson seems to distance himself from mainstream Calvinism and, at best, could be described as a moderate Calvinist. For example, within his sermon, *Eternal Misery the Desert of the Sinner*,[82] he refers, on several occasions, to God as being the 'Moral Governor of the Universe', in a manner similar to Hugo Grotius (1583–1645). In a sermon on *Love: Characteristic of the Deity*, Johnson argued that 'the love of God is...represented as the cause of our love to him... [H]is love had devised a plan on which we might be brought to him.' Thus the atonement of Christ was a 'manifestation of the divine love...which should maintain the dignity and preserve the rights of God's moral government.... Taking this view of the atonement then, it will evidently appear, that the love of God is the procuring cause of the atonement, and not the atonement the procuring cause of the love of God.'[83] Johnson did not believe that the atonement of Christ was offered because God was looking for 'the satisfaction of his anger', but rather that 'it represents him as an amiable Father,

---

[77] Letter of William B. Johnson, 'To the Baptists of South Carolina...', *Southern Baptist* 3.24 (18 October 1848), p. 2,
[78] Letter of William B. Johnson to James S. Mims, 25 March 1848, cited by Legendre, 'Johnson', p. 73.
[79] William B. Johnson to J.S. Mims, 6 September 1848, cited in Legendre, 'Johnson', p. 76.
[80] Johnson, *Gospel Developed*, p. 169.
[81] See Tom Nettles, 'A Biographical Sketch of W.B. Johnson', in Basil Manly, Sr (ed.), *Southern Baptist Sermons on Sovereignty and Responsibility* (Harrisonburg, VA: Gano Books, 1984), pp. 33-37. Thomas Ascol, 'Southern Baptists at the Crossroads: Returning to the Old Paths', *Founder's Journal* 19-20 (Winter/Spring 1995), p. 5. Timothy George, 'What Should we Think of Evangelism and Calvinism', *Founder's Journal* 19-20 (Winter/Spring, 1995), p. 53.
[82] William B. Johnson, in William Collier (ed.), *Baptist Preacher Consisting of Monthly Sermons from Living Ministers* (Boston, MA, 1829–1830), number 10 (July, 1830), III, pp. 145-59.
[83] William B. Johnson, 'Love: Characteristic of Deity', in Manly, Sr (ed.), *Sermons on Sovereignty and Responsibility*, pp. 53-55.

and infinitely benevolent moral Governor, who is disposed to manifest his love to rebels, but not in the prostration of the eternal principles of justice and moral law.'[84] Christ did not, then, pay 'the sinner's debt on the principles of pecuniary or commercial justice' but as 'a satisfaction to moral justice'. Thus, 'the atonement of Christ does not deliver any soul from condemnation'[85] and it 'excluded none from its benefits but those who exclude themselves'.[86] Johnson demonstrated a concern for the honor of God as the sovereign and moral governor of the universe, but also for the free agency of humankind who 'exclude themselves by their own act—by their own voluntary opposition to him, and persevering rejection of the only plan by which they can be saved' despite the fact that 'Jesus is freely exhibited to them'.[87] One might even argue that Johnson, far from being a mainline Calvinist, demonstrates indebtedness to the New Haven Divinity of Nathaniel Taylor and Joseph Bellamy, describing the atonement in governmental and moral rather than strictly substitutionary language.[88]

During the latter years of his life, Johnson expressed a concern that the new Southern Seminary would adopt an *Abstract of Principles*, the 'first confessional statement of any type approved for use in a Southern Baptist school'.[89] Although the Professors were required to accept this brief abstract 'as one safeguard against their teaching heresy' , John Broadus, a member of the faculty and second President of the school, indicated that 'in our seminary the student will not be required, at the beginning or the end, to accept any given symbol or doctrine'.[90] Furthermore, James P. Boyce, the first President indicated that the *Abstract of Principles* related to

---

[84] Johnson, 'Love', p. 56.

[85] Johnson, 'Love', p. 56.

[86] William B. Johnson, 'Eternal Misery', in Manly, Sr (ed.), *Sermons on Sovereignty and Responsibility*, p. 159.

[87] Johnson, 'Love', p. 61.

[88] Nathaniel W. Taylor (1786–1858), student of and then theological successor to Timothy Dwight at Yale, was convinced that Calvinism had to interact with the current questions of the day. The Enlightenment made it impossible for Calvinists simply to repeat the old answers without taking into sufficient account the new questions that had been raised. Discussion of individual rights and democratic liberties appeared to render Calvinistic theological and anthropological assumptions anachronistic. Taylor dismissed from the Calvinistic corpus the doctrines of original sin, regeneration, and the bondage of the will. Rather, human beings are born neutral, so that their own conversion and regeneration is self-generated by a self-determining will that possesses 'power to the contrary'. Therefore, humans can overcome sinning if they simply choose to do so. Joseph Bellamy (1719–90), a Congregationalist minister during the Great Awakening. Bellamy also denied original sin and argued that an individual only becomes a sinner by committing the first act. He embraced a governmental theory of the atonement. Bellamy and Taylor both emphasized the idea that God punishes sin rather than sinners. It is his justice, rather than his wrath, that is at issue in the work of Christ.

[89] Leonard, *Types of Confessional Documents*, p. 38.

[90] A.T. Robertson, *Life and Letters of John A. Broadus* (Philadelphia, PA: American Baptist Publication Society, 1901), p. 162.

Baptist principles that were 'universally prevalent' and 'upon no point, upon which the denomination is divided, should the Convention, and through it the Seminary, take a position'.[91]

This indicates that the intellectual freedom which Johnson had relished throughout his life did not entirely diminish and disappear as he withdrew from various spheres of service. When he died, many people gathered to celebrate his life, confident that his ministry had influenced not only his congregations, schools and denomination, but the Southern States that he loved so dearly. His legacy, adhered to tenaciously during his lifetime, was maintained by the Convention for many generations although it has now been rejected in favor of a policy of using confessions of faith, not only as descriptive of Baptist interpretation of the Bible, but prescriptively and as means of hindering an openness to theological investigation and freedom of conscience.[92] For Johnson, this was why he opposed the use of confessions of faith so strongly during his lifetime.

---

[91] James P. Boyce, 'The Two Objections to the Seminary', *Western Recorder* 20 June 1874, p. 2.

[92] For a discussion of the recent controversy over creeds and conventions within the Southern Baptist Convention, see Jeff B. Pool, *Against Returning to Egypt: Exposing and Resisting Credalism in the Southern Baptist Convention* (Macon, GA: Mercer University Press, 1998).

CHAPTER 11

The Meaning of 'Baptist Union' in Maritime Canada, 1846–1906

Daniel Goodwin

In 1946 historian George Levy wrote *The Baptists of the Maritime Provinces: 1753–1946* to help his denomination celebrate its fortieth anniversary as a union of Arminian and Calvinistic Baptists. During the 1905–06 period three denominations—the Convention of Maritime Baptists, the Free Baptists of New Brunswick and the Free Baptists of Nova Scotia—merged to create the United Baptist Convention of the Maritime Provinces. In his chapter on the 'Consummation of Union', Levy cited the often-repeated pragmatic causes to union such as duplication of pastorates, shortages of ministers, and the growing needs of collective foreign mission effort. One less tangible factor leading up to union, according to Levy, was 'the feeling that the...denominations ought to be one'.[1] Although he attempted to suggest that the Regular and Free Baptists of the region gradually became more like each other, Levy did not explore why. What happened in the nineteenth century to soften the denominational boundaries to the point that these three groups were able to see each other as having the same identity? While the practical issues surrounding denomination building are not in doubt, they do beg the question of self-understanding. Why were Calvinistic and Arminian Baptists willing to create a new denomination and leave behind the particular denominations they had laboured to develop? This is the question that concerns this study.

It is the explicit argument of this chapter that Maritime Baptist union was achieved in large measure because religious identity among these groups was forged in the same nineteenth-century context. All three founding denominations had strong roots in the late-eighteenth-century revivals of the Maritime region and remained committed to the new birth, believer's baptism by immersion and the believer's church. In addition, they all experienced a heightened sense of free moral agency that was spread by the emergence of market capitalism and responsible government. This

---

[1] George Levy, *The Baptists of the Maritime Provinces: 1753–1946* (Saint John, NB: Barnes-Hopkins, 1946), p. 269. Other treatments of Maritime Union may be found in Reginald S. Dunn, 'Union of the Regular and Free Baptists of the Maritime Provinces in 1906' (BDiv thesis, Acadia University, 1941); Philip G.A. Griffin-Allwood, 'The Canadianization of Baptists: From Denominations to Denomination' (PhD dissertation, Southern Baptist Theological Seminary, 1986), ch. 3.

in turn led to the modification and decline of Calvinism among the Regular Baptists. Each of the founding groups called upon the authority of the past to make the case for union during a time when a particular interpretation of the 'founders'' wishes proved to be convincing. As all of these Baptists sought to increase their influence by moving toward the Protestant mainstream of Maritime society, they rejected extreme expressions of their traditions including Calvinistic and Arminian primitivism, the belief of instantaneous sanctification, and biblical higher criticism. Consequently, those ministers and churches that might have continued to express radical views were either marginalized or silenced allowing for a more generic Baptist culture to develop in the region. The uniting fervour of the nineteenth century also convinced ministers and laity that cooperation was necessary if Canada was to become fully Christianized. In addition, union was achieved as the Free Baptists of New Brunswick and Nova Scotia ultimately rejected merging with the American Free Will Baptists in favour of the regional union with the Regular Baptists. The powerful combination of these factors helped the Regular Baptists and the Free Baptists of Nova Scotia and New Brunswick to believe that they 'ought to be one'.

The best-known church union in Canadian history is without doubt that of the United Church in Canada in 1925 when the nation's Congregationalists, Methodists, and roughly two-thirds of its Presbyterians joined together. This moment was born out of a long series of studies and negotiations rooted in the notion that a national or even quasi-established church could extend Christian influence much further in Canadian society than if these large denominations remained separate. Leading up to the formation of the UCC, were a series of mergers within the Congregational, Methodist and Presbyterian denominational families that advanced the old world notion that strong national churches would be in the best position to make Canada 'His Dominion'.[2]

In the midst of the uniting church fervour of the nineteenth century, three Baptist groups in Maritime Canada explored the possibilities of church union as well. They included the Regular or Calvinistic Baptists in the three Maritime Provinces, and two Arminian Baptist groups that went through a number of name changes but, for the purposes of this chapter, I will refer to them as the Free Baptists of New Brunswick and the Free Baptists of Nova Scotia. On 10 October 1905, the Regular Baptists and the Free Baptists of New Brunswick declared that the union of the two denominations had been consummated after more than twenty years of sporadic negotiations. The following year, in 1906, the Free Baptists joined what was already the United Baptist Convention of the Maritime Provinces. Although these groups had remained distinct religious bodies until union, their coming together was more of a family reunion than a marriage. In fact, it is the argument of this chapter that Maritime Baptist union was possible, in part, because each group was rooted in the region's religious culture, used the past as an authoritative basis upon which to

---

[2] John Webster Grant, 'Blending Traditions: The United Church of Canada', in *The Churches and the Canadian Experience* (Toronto: Ryerson Press, 1963), pp. 133-44.

argue for union, removed theological extremes in their respective denominations, and experienced common patterns of development in the nineteenth century. Furthermore, the decline of Calvinism among the Regular Baptists and the development of a cooperative spirit rooted in a pragmatism that saw duplication of 'Baptist' work in poor rural areas as a waste of resources also facilitated union negotiations. While other factors were also important, time constraints will not permit a full examination.

All three groups that entered union originated in the revivals that convulsed the region's late-eighteenth and early-nineteenth centuries. Rooted in the revivalistic paradigm of Henry Alline—who almost single-handedly guided the First Great Awakening in Nova Scotia from 1777 to 1783—these three groups drew on a rich spiritual past that stressed conversionism, revivalism, religious experience, and anti-formalism.

In the 1790s, after a number of key Allinite preachers and lay people took their founder's anti-formal religious principles to antinomian extremes, a number of leaders embraced believer's baptism by immersion as a means of washing away the radical outcomes of Allinism and church disorder as a way to guarantee more orthodox belief and practice. By 1809, most of the prominent former Allinite preachers espoused a more controlled approach to church life by embracing Regular Baptist closed communionism that still permitted ecstatic religious experiences but within prescribed boundaries.

Those who rejected the move toward the Calvinsitic position continued to meet 'informally for religious fellowship in upwards of a dozen New Brunswick and Nova Scotia neighbourhoods'. Adhering to the free will theology and open communionism of Henry Alline, 'Christian Conferences' developed in both colonies in the 1830s but refused to take a formal position on the mode and proper candidates for baptism. By the 1840s, however, both the Conferences in New Brunswick and Nova Scotia had embraced believer's baptism by immersion as an official position while still maintaining open communion. These 'Free' Baptists, as they were popularly called, developed much faster in New Brunswick than they did in Nova Scotia in part because the Nova Scotia Free Baptists were influenced by two competing groups from New England which tended to divide their efforts.[3]

While the groups continued to divide over the question of open versus closed communion and free will versus predestination, they nevertheless reflected a common religious heritage of revivalism and conversionism that came to be expressed in outdoor baptismal services. In fact, the Regular and Free Baptists both came to depend heavily upon the spectacle of public baptismal services to make their gospel message visible,[4] and to fuel the flames of revival. Added to their common spiritual heritage was a common formalization process in each denomination that included

---

[3] D.G. Bell, *Henry Alline and Maritime Religion* (Ottawa, ON: Canadian Historical Association, 1993), p. 21.

[4] Daniel C. Goodwin, '"Footprints of Zion's King'", in G.A. Rawlyk (ed.), *Aspects of the Canadian Evangelical Experience* (Montreal and Kingston, ON: McGill-Queen's University Press, 1997), pp. 191-207.

denominational newspapers, Sabbath Schools, temperance societies, home and foreign missions, organizations for women and youth, and a growing interest in higher education. Parallel developments in denominational structures, patterned after other Protestant groups, made each of the Maritime Baptist bodies appear to be even more similar. When their common commitments to evangelism, church extension, revivalism, and the new birth are added to the mix, it is not surprising that some proponents on both sides just believed that it 'should' happen. It was logical. They had been significantly shaped by a common religious culture that they had a hand in creating and they had formalized along common lines in the nineteenth century.

In spite of these striking similarities, they did disagree 'officially' on the question of moral agency in conversion and the communion question. These limits of agreement were expressed clearly in 1845 when the Regular Baptists of Nova Scotia asked the Nova Scotia Free Baptists to consider working side by side in the areas of Sabbath School instruction and the Horton Academy that had been established in 1827. To this request the Free Baptists replied, 'We are not prepared to contribute to your institutions, yet we wish to cultivate good will...with your denomination.'[5] The Nova Scotia Free Baptists who were concentrated in southwestern Nova Scotia, at this juncture, continued to be influenced by American preachers, in part, because of their close geographical proximity to New England and were not willing to cooperate with their Regular Baptist neighbours.

In 1846, the Calvinistic Baptists of Nova Scotia and New Brunswick joined their respective denominational institutions to create a Convention in order to build denominational structures cooperatively. Their growing commitment to foreign missions was a catalyst at this time. The significance of the Convention's creation for this study rests entirely on the notion that all future alliances among Maritime Baptists would be significantly motivated by the desire to extend Christian (read Baptist) influence in the region and beyond. There is no evidence that the Baptist union movement, as it developed, was influenced by any notion of the 'sin of a divided Christendom'. That different groups and stripes of Baptists regarded each other as potential collaborators was a testimony to a common heritage and understanding of the Christian faith, even if Arminian Baptist groups from New England made that common heritage more difficult to recognize.

Between the 1880s and the time of Baptist union in 1905–06, arguments in favour of the merger made use of arguments from history in two compelling ways. The first concerned the general notion of Christian progress so prevalent in the Anglo-American world, and, according to some unionists, so purely preserved in the Baptist expression of the faith. Union advocates relied upon the 'trail of blood' theory that Baptists originated in the ministry of John the Baptist and had a continuous presence throughout Christian history as those who practiced believer's baptism by immersion. Ingram E. Bill from the Calvinistic Baptists made this case in 1886 to his Free Baptist cousins in Fredericton, New Brunswick, noting:

---

[5] Minutes of the Nova Scotia Baptist Association, 1845, p. 20.

The Church record was red with the blood of martyrs. And why? Because they have always stood for the truth. The Baptists have been the true custodians of the ordinance of baptism. Amid all the changes and innovations, they have ever continued to sustain the primitive teachings of the church in this one important and distinctive feature.[6]

Bill also pleaded that since Baptists have 'stood together through all these ages' they 'could not afford to be separated'. They 'belonged to one Baptist family'.[7] This Baptist view of Christian history merged well with the optimism that pervaded late-nineteenth-century Maritime Canada as it experienced growth in industrialization, urbanization, social reform activism and the promise of a newly created nation. The future was bright, and if the Baptists made right decisions it might well be a Baptist future. Ingram Bill's son and namesake spoke for many of his generation when he remarked, 'This movement is in harmony with the spirit of the age. We should throw ourselves into it and secure the many benefits accruing to both sides by the union. If the "Basis" [of Union] is adopted he [God] shall renew his age forty years.'[8]

That the age required the consolidation of resources and the burial of old antipathies was not doubted by those who advocated the union cause. History itself was the convincing teacher and guide for the future. In 1902, Regular Baptist minister and unionist Edward Manning Saunders published his *History of the Baptists of the Maritime Provinces* that contained chapters written by Edwin Crowell and Joseph McLeod in the Free Baptists of Nova Scotia and New Brunswick respectively. Obviously written to foster union sentiment, this volume demonstrated the common New Light or Allinite heritage of each of the Baptist groups in the region in order to support the case that a denominational merger was really destined to be a re-gathering of God's chosen tribes. Saunders went so far as to compare Henry Alline and Joseph Howe, 'each [being]...a democrat through and through, having an underlying passion for the welfare of the people as a whole'. According to Saunders, both men had broken up the tallow ground for future generations, having torn 'down the tyrannies in the religious and civil spheres in Nova Scotia'.[9] If Joseph Howe had been providentially used to bring about responsible government in Nova Scotia, a union of Baptist groups would promote and extend religious democracy in the region. For Saunders, the sense of destiny could not be denied.

J.H. Saunders, writing an article on the heritage of revival for the Regular Baptist readers of the *Messenger and Visitor*, argued as well for the 'liberalizing' and 'progressive' elements of Allinite and Baptist religion that shaped the region. Revival and its accompanying conversions, he noted, 'uplift[ed] the common people and ...put them in power' and laid the foundation for 'free citizenship' on earth as it

---

[6] *Religious Intelligencer* (hereafter *RI*), 10 November 1886.
[7] *RI*, 10 November 1886.
[8] *Messenger and Visitor* (hereafter *MV*), 31 August 1887.
[9] E.M. Saunders, *History of the Baptists of the Maritimes* (Halifax, NS: John Burgoyne, 1902), p. 23. See also the related editorial *MV*, 31 August 1902.

is in heaven.[10] While this mixing of progressive democratic values with evangelical religion in late-nineteenth-century Maritime Canada deserves more study, it is clear that this fusion was a useful tool for convincing reluctant Calvinistic and Free Baptists that church union was a civic as well as a religious duty and to deny union was to deny the providential hand of God in history.

In order to make the case for union even more compelling to local Baptists, efforts were made to write histories of specific churches with a view of demonstrating a common past for congregations with links to the late eighteenth or early-nineteenth centuries.[11] Churches in Yarmouth, Wolfville, Havelock and Isaac's Harbour, to name just a few, had their histories produced with a view to clarifying identity and renewing vision for the future.[12] In 1887, the Free Baptists of Nova Scotia listened to Jacob Porter read a history of their labours with a view to educating his co-constituents about their past as Arminian Baptists. Beginning with New Testament Baptist origins, Porter highlighted early General British Baptists that were Arminian in theology, the common Free Baptist and Calvinistic Baptist participation in eighteenth-century revivals, the importance of Henry Alline, as well as the Free Will Baptists from New England who had been influenced by Alline's theology, to a series of mergers among Nova Scotia's Arminian Baptists in the nineteenth century. Refusing to take a position on whether Nova Scotia Free Baptist should unite with New England Free Will Baptists or other Baptists in the Maritimes, Porter did promote the notion of church unions: 'Have we not found, are we not proving that union is strength, and that union must be in the fellowship of the Spirit?'[13] In response to his question, Porter maintained that such mergers should be pursued only with a strong sense of providential history. Unlike some union advocates, Porter believed that the question of organic union should be considered only with a decided sense of unique denominational identity. Others such as Ingram Bill of the Calvinistic Baptists believed in 1888 that 'the desire for organic union' was greatly increasing due to 'old prejudices' having been removed.[14] What they both shared was a view common to most evangelicals in Victorian Canada. Historian Michael Gauvreau has argued persuasively that evangelical church leaders used the study of history as a key to understanding the faith, stressing 'activity, ethics, and human behaviour over the quest for dogma—the statement of immutable precise categories of belief and knowledge'.[15]

If the written past was a key element in advancing and defining the nature of the union debate, so too was the 'living past'. Indeed, in the 1880s it became essential for unionists in both camps to parade before their constituencies those whose

---

[10] *MV*, 19 November 1902.
[11] *MV*, 19 November 1902; 7 June 1903.
[12] 'Local Church Histories', *Messenger and Visitor*, 4 May 1904.
[13] J. Porter, *RI*, 5 October 1887.
[14] *RI*, 31 October 1888.
[15] Michael Gauvreau, *The Evangelical Century: College and Creed in English Canada from the Great Revival to the Great Depression* (Montreal and Kingston, ON: McGill-Queen's University Press, 1991), p. 73.

ministries stretched back to the first third of the nineteenth century. New Brunswick Free Baptist unionists used George A. Hartley as their living link to the past. Born in 1831 and dying in 1903, two years before union, he was an effective revivalist who baptized more than 1,200 into Free Baptist churches. A moderator of the Conference six times, he published the first theological tract written by a NB Free Baptist. It was entitled *Immortality vs. Annihilation* and published in 1867. In 1891, Hartley was one of several church union advocates in the New Brunswick Free Baptist Conference. It was reported in the *Religious Intelligencer* that the venerable leader 'thought the time had come when we should give a definite expression of our wish and intention on this important question' and continued to be 'favourable to union'.[16] The same article also reminded its readers that 'Father' Edward Weyman had also been 'anxious' for union 'in the last years of his life' and 'felt sure that the venerable man having got to heaven, is still more anxious for it'.[17] Selecting the late Weyman to 'testify' to the benefits of the proposed merger would have provided additional authority to the arguments for union. Born in 1800, Weyman participated in early Allinite meetings in the Millstream area of New Brunswick in the 1820s and participated in the formalization process that created the New Brunswick Free Baptist denomination. Having died in the early stages of serious union discussions his voice nevertheless continued to be heard well after his death.[18]

If the historical voices of Weyman and Hartley were integral in making the case for union among the Free Baptists, the most 'venerable' voice for the Regular Baptists was that of Ingram Bill. Since most of the original 'Fathers' had died by the 1850s,[19] Regular Baptists were forced to rely upon the authority of the aging Ingram Bill, noted in his obituary in 1891 as a 'son of the Fathers'.[20] Born in 1805, Bill was an effective revivalist, denomination builder, newspaper editor, educator, and author of the lengthy history entitled *Fifty Years with the Baptist Ministers and Churches of the Maritime Provinces*.[21] This 'son of the Fathers' carried more authority and experience to the union discussion than any other Regular Baptist leader in the 1880s. Bill had the unique qualities and background necessary to guide the matter. During that decade, Bill worked with a committee of Regular and Free Baptist ministers who traveled from place to place presenting the union platform. Having developed a positive relationship with the Free Baptists of Nova Scotia and New Brunswick, Bill often presented an historical sketch of the Maritime Baptists

---

[16] *RI*, 21 October 1891.

[17] *RI*, 21 October 1891.

[18] See the important entries for Hartley and Weyman in Frederick C. Burnett, *Biographical Directory of Nova Scotia and New Brunswick Free Baptist Ministers and Preachers* (Hantsport, NS: Lancelot Press, 1996), pp. 108-109, 181.

[19] See my '"The Faith of the Fathers": Evangelical Piety of Maritime Regular Baptist Patriarchs and Preachers 1790–1855' (PhD dissertation, Queen's University, 1997), ch. 9.

[20] *Daily Telegraph* (Saint John, NB), 8 August 1891.

[21] *Fifty Years with the Baptist Ministers and Churches of the Maritime Provinces* (Saint John, NB: Barnes, 1880).

drawn from his own book and other sources followed by pleas for church union. So aged and in poor health was Bill in the 1880s that meetings were often scheduled around his availability and not according to the convenience of local churches. During one of those meetings in Yarmouth, Nova Scotia, in July of 1887, it was reported in the *Yarmouth Herald* that 'as it is not likely that Dr. Bill will ever be this way again, the meeting had to be held now in order to have the advantage of the Doctor's presence'.[22] The advantage of Bill's presence was that he alone had the necessary clout to speak to all Maritime Baptist groups on the issue. His credentials were impeccable and his motivations were clear.

An eminently practical man when it came to the finer points of theology, Bill was sometimes criticized for not taking foundational theological issues seriously. For example, Alexander Taylor, a 'Father' of New Brunswick Free Baptists remarked of Bill's efforts:

> How a basis of Union for the two denominations can be found without the intervention of doctrine is something I cannot comprehend…
>
> …the doctrines of Divine Sovereignty and free moral agency should be considered and adjusted before a proper Union can take place.[23]

While Bill's authority to speak on the question of union was not challenged, his vision for a united Baptist effort in the Maritimes overrode any doctrinal considerations. For him, believer's baptism by immersion and congregational church government provided the necessary basis for Baptist cooperation regardless of others' doctrinal peculiarities. Instead of attempting a sort of synthesis that would balance divine sovereignty and human moral agency, he argued for a union based on significant shared theological distinctives, and the reduction of duplication of ministry efforts. Ultimately, Bill's vision became the accepted norm for the UBCMP, though he did not live long enough to see it.

In order for the vision of a Baptist merger to be achieved a number of theological obstacles had to be overcome. In 1886, a committee comprised of Regular and New Brunswick Free Baptists met to formulate a basis of union. On that occasion *The New Hampshire Confession of Faith* of 1833—that the Regular Baptists in southern New Brunswick had adopted in 1880—was brought to the discussion table.[24] The New Brunswick Free Baptists brought their 'Free Christian Baptist Treatise' that was a revision of one prepared by the American Free Will Baptists.[25] Historian Philip Griffin-Allwood has argued that *The New Hampshire Confession* was less overtly Calvinistic than previous statements that had 'emphasized the role of the decrees in

---

[22] As reported in the *RI*, 13 July 1887.
[23] *RI*, 2 January 1885.
[24] For *The New Hampshire Confession* (1833), see W.L. Lumpkin, *Baptist Confessions of Faith* (Valley Forge, PA: Judson Press, 2nd edn, 1969), pp. 361-67.
[25] *A Treatise of the Faith of the Free Christian Baptists in Nova Scotia and New Brunswick* (Saint John, NB: Bailey and Day, 1848).

dividing the elect from the unelect' and stressed instead 'the perseverance of the saints'.[26] The Free Baptist *Treatise* was more decidedly baptistic than previous New Light Baptist statements had been. As committee members of both camps entered into discussion they found much common ground. According to one Regular Baptist correspondent, as the members went through their respective documents section by section,

> There were surprises on both sides. Some tenets, we supposed our F.C. Baptist brethren held, they repudiated. Some they supposed we held, they found we repudiated. On one of two cases, where there appeared to be a substantial difference, mutual explanations showed that there was harmony of belief, notwithstanding. Even in the cases where there was expected to be the widest divergence of belief it was found to be far less wide than was supposed.[27]

During these meetings, the Nova Scotia Free Baptists declined an invitation to participate. Not surprisingly, the questions of perseverance of the saints and open versus closed communion became issues and were modified in the second draft the following year. The 1887 draft removed any implicit references to predestination or closed communion.[28] Historians have made much of the general decline of Calvinism among Anglo-American Protestants in the nineteenth century. Daniel Walker Howe has argued that populist Christianity often responded negatively to Calvinism because it was frequently espoused by those in the upper class.[29] According to Nathan Hatch, Calvinism had a passive dimension related to divine sovereignty that went against the political and economic developments in western democracies, especially the United States. 'The argument against Calvinism pitted enlightenment commonsense against scholastic metaphysics of the educated elite.'[30] It is noteworthy in this regard that one of the few serious reservations about union made by the Regular Baptists came from J.W. Johnstone, son of the former Premier of Nova Scotia, judge, and member of the upper-middle class in Halifax.[31] That the Calvinistic scheme may have been valued more by this Regular Baptist clique in Halifax than its rural cousins is very likely. It should be remembered that the Calvinism embraced by the Regular Baptists, even in 1809, had more to do with establishing church order and accountability in belief and practice than it did with a

---

[26] Philip G.A. Griffin-Allwood, 'Is Confessing an Evangelical Consensus a Hindrance to Pluralism?: An Atlantic Baptist Case Study', unpublished paper, 1990, p. 13. See also Griffin-Allwood's 'The Canadianization of Baptists: From Denominations to Denomination' (PhD dissertation, Southern Baptist Theological Seminary, 1986), ch. 3.

[27] Union Between Baptists and Free Baptists', *MV*, 20 October 1886, p. 4.

[28] George Levy, *The Baptists of the Maritime Provinces 1753–1946* (Saint John, NB: Barnes-Hopkins, 1946), pp. 275-77.

[29] Daniel Walker Howe, 'The Decline of Calvinism: An Approach to its Study', *Comparative Studies in Society and History* 14.3 (June, 1972), pp. 306-27.

[30] Nathan Hatch, *The Democratization of American Christianity* (New Haven, CT: Yale UP, 1989), 171-173.

[31] *MV*, 1 November 1899; Saunders, *Baptists of the Maritimes*, p. 488.

wholesale adoption of Reformed Baptist thought. As liberal politics and a free market system began to exert their cultural influence in the Maritimes by the 1880s, it was obvious that these trends had impacted the region's Baptists as free moral agency came to be accepted regardless of whether one was a Calvinistic or Arminian Baptist. According to 'S' who wrote in the *Religious Intelligencer* in 1884, 'Hyper-Calvinism is largely of the past, as a matter of history; to-day it is a well-known fact of experience that the very high views as to limited atonement and election have undergone a considerable change. It can safely be said that more liberal views prevail approaching to beliefs of Free Baptists.'[32]

In an editorial published in the *Messenger and Visitor* in November of 1899, it was noted that fine doctrinal disputes had become a marginalized, if not a strictly private matter for many in the region's Baptist groups.

> It is probable that the greater number of Baptists hold to the Calvinistic view of Christian doctrine, and the greater number of Free Baptists to the Arminian view. But the distinction between the two views no longer has the significance for church relationship that it once had. The acceptance of Calvinistic doctrine is not now, if it ever was, a condition of admission into a [Regular] Baptist church, and we suppose that no Christian would be in any danger of exclusion from Free Baptist communion because of being a Calvinist.[33]

The abiding concern of both brands of Baptists in the late-nineteenth century was not so much one's theological orientation but rather if one had been converted and baptized. Most other theological points, beyond basic belief and practice, were largely a private matter. Furthermore, the rigid closed communionism of early nineteenth-century Regular Baptists had given way to open communion, at least in practice. This meant 'that if members of other denominations wish to partake of the Lord's Supper in a [Regular] Baptist church, and if, knowing the Baptist position, they are willing to take responsibility of doing so, it is no part of the duty of the minister of the church to deny them the privilege'.[34] By 1900, the impact of classical liberal economic and political thought on Regular Baptists had weakened an already anaemic Calvinism to the point that the theological barriers of belief and communion practice were removed. Consequently, the pursuit of Baptist union was made much easier in the late nineteenth century than it would have been earlier.

As the Regular and Free Baptist denominations in the Maritimes came to view questions of moral agency and communionism to individual consciences and local churches, both groups were adamant that theological deviations outside of this growing Baptist consensus would not be tolerated. For example, the Regular Baptists and Free Baptists of New Brunswick experienced schisms related substantially to the growing generic Baptist middle ground of the late nineteenth

---

[32] 'S', 'Union Question', *RI*, 11 July 1884.
[33] *MV*, 1 November 1899.
[34] *MV*, 1 November 1899. For comments on similar developments in the United States see Henry Vedder, 'Are Baptists Becoming Open Communion', *RI*, 5 January 1898.

century that was characterized by the emergence of denominational structures, respectability or the 'bourgeoisification' of religious practice and the softening of theological distinctives.

The first schism took place in 1861 when eight Regular Baptist churches and at least three ministers in southern New Brunswick left their denomination to form the Particular Dependent Close-Communion Baptists. Holding to what Philip Griffin-Allwood has called the 'Edwardian Evangelical paradigm', these reformed Baptists believed their co-religionists had

> departed from the doctrine and practice of the primitive Churches-sanctioned unholy ministers in their body-interfered with the independence of the Churches-discouraged discipline, by gathering up excluded persons, and, after forming them into societies, received them into the association, thereby encouraging sin, and trifling with God's authority.[35]

They also believed that many Regular Baptist ministers of New Brunswick had been permitted to abandon Calvinistic teaching without censure. While at least one of the ministers who established this new denomination had been marginalized among the Province's Regular Baptists and was seeking recognition as an important Baptist leader, it should be remembered that this ultra-Calvinistic group garnered significant support because there was a sense that that the original 'Faith of the Fathers' had been largely modified among the current generation of denominational leaders. This separate, primitivistic and decidedly Calvinistic group of Baptists siphoned off some of the more traditionally Reformed churches and leaders among the Regular Baptists in New Brunswick and facilitated the decline of Calvinism among the mainstream Regular Baptists in the region. Indeed, this schismatic group demonstrates that some of the more extreme forms of Calvinism, closed communionism, and church discipline were being marginalized by the second half of the nineteenth century, paving the way for a broadly-defined Maritime Baptist culture that left little room for dogmatically held theological extremes. It was this middle ground that came to dominate Regular and Free Baptist life and facilitated union in 1905 and 1906.

The first Free Baptist schism occurred in 1874 and was led by the New Brunswick Free Baptist preacher George Whitefield Orser. He believed that his fellow Arminian Baptists had formalized to the point of departing from the primitive and pure faith of the 'founders.' He wrote,

> [I]n the beginning of the denomination they took the Word of the Lord as their only rule in all things. But as the denomination has advanced, certain things have grown up, and are endorsed by the Conference, that he does not find any warrant for in the Bible. Sabbath Schools and Missions are among these things.[36]

---

[35] *Minutes of the Dependent Close-Communion Baptists*, 1861.
[36] New Brunswick Free Baptist Minutes, 1874, p. 35.

Orser expressed concern that New Brunswick Free Baptists were following the example of 'other denominations', which assuredly included the Regular Baptists, instead of 'revealed truth'.[37] Orser rejected the exchange of a distinctive Allinite language and approach to the faith that had been forged in the late-eighteenth century for an 'undifferentiated evangelicalism' that was in part the result of a 'modernizing' approach to denomination building. He and his followers withdrew from the New Brunswick Free Baptists in 1874.[38] At the time of his death in 1885, 'Orserites', or 'Primitive Baptists' as they became known, boasted approximately forty churches 'in the Upper St. John valley of New Brunswick and Maine, several in Western Nova Scotia, one on Deer Island and one in Lowell Massachusetts'.[39] The significance of this schism for Baptist union was that it removed many of those traditionalists who were unsure of the trappings of denominational structures and the desire of Free Baptist leaders to move their religious tradition into the mainstream of religious and cultural life. Had the 'Orserites' remained with the Free Baptists, the evidence suggests they would have had serious reservations about cooperating with the Calvinistic Baptists who were even more enthusiastic about pouring old wine into new wineskins.

If the 'Orserites' represented a sort of ecclesiastical restorationism, the second schismatic group, the 'holiness Baptists', represented more of a 'spiritual' restorationism. Between 1882 and 1888, the exploration of denominational union was put on hold by the New Brunswick Free Baptists as they encountered a period of debate about the nature of sanctification and its limits. In a sympathetic tone, one Regular Baptist writer noted,

> In view of the dissensions among themselves over the doctrine of instantaneous sanctification, it was thought best not to consider the Basis [of Union]. The fact that the very brethren who helped frame the 'Basis' advised the Conference to delay action is proof of this.[40]

While the region's Baptists had been exposed to the holiness teaching of Phoebe Palmer in 1857 and 1858 and the ministry of American Wesleyan Methodist holiness preachers in the 1860s and 1870s, the teaching of entire sanctification did not take root until Aaron Hartt, son of Samuel Hartt one of the 'Fathers' of the New Brunswick Free Baptists, began to promote the 'second blessing' among his co-religionists. Having experienced 'entire sanctification' at a Methodist camp meeting in New England in 1882, Aaron Hartt held a series of meetings in Woodstock, New Brunswick that began a 'holiness stir' that spread to other pastors and congregations. The Free Baptist minister in Woodstock at that time was G.W. MacDonald who

---

[37] New Brunswick Free Baptist Minutes, 1874, p. 35.

[38] D.G. Bell, 'The Allinite Tradition and the New Brunswick Free Christian Baptists 1830–1875', in Robert S. Wilson (ed.), *An Abiding Conviction: Maritime Baptists and Their World* (Hantsport, NS: Lancelot Press, 1988), p. 65.

[39] Bell, 'The Allinite Tradition', p. 70.

[40] *MV*, 23 November 1887.

recalled twelve years later the intense experience of entire holiness under Hartt's ministry:

> ...after praying and wrestling with God in the hope of making my heart clean by my own struggles, but in vain, my soul gathered strength to lay everything on the altar, and claimed the blessing of perfect love by faith in the cleansing blood. My struggling eased, and my soul rested on the bosom of Jesus as a poor weary child, weary of its loving mother. Such rest, only to be experienced, never fully told. Rest from all the inward warfare caused by remaining evil in my heart, and withal a sense of cleanness, purity and such a deep satisfied assurance of having reached the place where the soul could dwell with God, and that God had perfected His love in me. There was no doubt about it; the Comforter had come. How easy now to pray, to praise; what a constancy of faith; how deep the peace; how bright the hope. Since that memorable night I have never doubted my soul's entire sanctification.[41]

While the Free Baptists had a rich and varied heritage of experiential Christianity, the introduction of this new experience posed problems for some of the leaders of the denomination who regarded the teaching of entire sanctification as 'Methodistic, unscriptural, promised sinless perfection and was a divider of churches'.[42] What made this development so threatening was the status given to those who experienced the second blessing. As George Rawlyk has pointed out, 'If entire sanctification became the litmus test for denominational leadership they realized that their opponents would easily push them aside in any power struggle.'[43] In addition, there was also the fear that any teaching that stressed an unfamiliar and normative religious experience would violate the religious tradition of the Free Baptists. In other words, the meaning given to this post-conversion experience potentially created two types of Christians: those who are fully sanctified and those who were not. Such a distinction went against the growing sense that all believers should be treated equally as seen among the Regular Baptists who relaxed their views on closed communion. The tensions among the New Brunswick Free Baptists over the holiness issue escalated to the point that on 15 October 1888 the Conference

> Resolved that...in heartfelt sorrow, and in the spirit of brotherly kindness, and in the spirit of denominational loyalty, in doing the only thing that now seems to us possible, and just to all our cherished interests, declare that this Elder's Conference is not in sympathy with, and cannot longer fellowship as ministers of this Conference with brethren who teach or preach the doctrine of instantaneous entire sanctification.[44]

---

[41] G.W. MacDonald, *King's Highway*, 15 March 1894.

[42] Laurence K. Mullin, 'The Organization of the Reformed Baptists', paper presented at the Atlantic District of the Wesleyan Church, 10 October 1978, p. 6.

[43] George A. Rawlyk, 'The Holiness Movement and Canadian Maritime Baptists', in George A. Rawlyk and Mark A. Noll (eds), *Amazing Grace: Evangelicalism in Australia, Britain, Canada and the United States* (Grand Rapids, MI: Baker Books, 1993), p. 307.

[44] Free Christian Baptist Conference, *Minutes* (1888), pp. 47-49.

Consequently, several elders and churches were removed from fellowship and later that year formed 'The Reformed Baptist Alliance of Canada'.[45] While the denomination did not capture a significant following in the Maritimes, its formation clearly provided an option for those Regular and Free Baptists who wanted to embrace the doctrine of entire sanctification. The 'schisms' of the New Brunswick Free Baptists are key to the church union story for Maritime Baptists because the Primitive and Reformed Baptists siphoned off those who had serious reservations with the formalization process of denomination building, and those looking for a well-defined theology of a second work of grace. If there were to be a Maritime Baptist union, it would be based in part on denominational structures and a minimally defined Baptist faith. The promoters of union among the New Brunswick Free Baptists understood the implications and problems an 'aberrant' theological position might pose for union. In fact, New Brunswick Free Baptists suspended any serious discussion of union with the Regular Baptists during this period.[46] It would have been almost impossible for a basis of union to be formulated if the concerns of the Primitive and Holiness Baptists had been included.

The Regular Baptists never faced the same kind of schisms that their Free Baptist cousins did in the decades leading up to union. However, they did deal with a serious debate over the nature of biblical criticism and its implications for the use of the Bible in local Baptist churches. How the Regular Baptists chose to deal with this topic helps explain the success of union negotiations? Between 1903 and 1904, Henry F. Waring, minister of the First Baptist Church in Halifax, entered into an exchange with Edward Manning Saunders and others on how 'modern' Baptists should approach the Bible and what assumptions about inspiration, if any, should be taken into consideration. Carried in the pages of the Regular Baptist newspaper the *Messenger and Visitor* and in a number of pamphlets and one book, the debate was sparked by Saunders' response to Waring's lectures to his 'large and intelligent Bible Class'[47] at First Baptist Church, Halifax. As a member of the same church, Saunders sought to challenge Waring's openness to the new biblical scholarship that was sweeping much of North American Protestantism at the time. As the denomination contemplated its own identity and the possibility of joining forces with the region's Free Baptists, its attitude toward critical scholarship became an important issue. The leaders of the Regular Baptists knew that there had been substantial changes to their approach to faith since the 'days of the Fathers', but what were the limits? For example, it was readily acknowledged by S.M. Black, editor of the *Messenger and Visitor*, that the days of highly emotional religion had largely passed to the point that 'The tendency of the present day in religious experience is not to make too much of the emotional element, but to make too little of it.'[48] Having said that, he

---

[45] See E.G. Britten, 'A History of the Reformed Baptist Alliance of Canada' (BDiv thesis, Acadia University, 1964).

[46] Levy, *Baptists of the Maritime Provinces,* pp. 273-74.

[47] H.F. Waring, 'What is the Bible and How Should it be Studied?', *MV*, 23 March 1904.

[48] S.M. Black, 'The Emotional in Religion', *MV*, 23 September 1903.

was quick to point out that while emotion 'has its place...it must not be permitted to crowd out other things of equal importance. It must not usurp the throne of either faith or of reason.'[49] While the Regular Baptist leaders had always been aware of the necessity of considering the affective and the cognitive when reflecting on faith, exactly how they should proceed at the beginning of the twentieth century was not altogether clear.

Waring's approach to the Bible involved using 'common sense, knowledge, [and] spiritual insight' in order to appropriate a fair meaning of the text.[50] Arguing for a high view of scripture, based in part on a study of comparative religious literature, Waring had serious reservations about calling the Bible inerrant.

My method of studying the contents of the Bible is then to begin by seeking the authors' thoughts and from these thoughts to proceed, as best we can, to God's truths. Dr. [E.M.] Saunders' contention was that what might naturally seem to be the authors' meaning, if it were not God's truth could not be the meaning of the passage. Back of this was the assumption that the Bible was inerrant. The difference in the way Dr. Saunders and I approached the study of the contents of the Bible was that the Dr. approached with the assumption that they were inerrant, and I did not.[51]

It would be a mistake to conclude that Waring stated the Bible to be in error, however. He simply did not want to be 'in the difficult position of one who asserts its inerrancy'.[52] With great optimism, Waring maintained that it was possible to come to the true meaning of any text by using biblical criticism, regardless of one's view on the inspiration of the scriptures. In an attempt to come to grips with the issue and excite the passions of newspaper readers, Saunders responded to Waring's unwillingness to embrace inerrancy by showing that such a view had much in common with American Unitarians who rejected inerrancy and biblical authority in favour of rationalism that seemed suspiciously similar to Waring's very reasoned approach. In addition, Saunders collected and printed in the *Messenger and Visitor* damning responses from fellow Regular Baptist ministers and scholars who questioned how biblical authority could be maintained if the Bible was not inerrant. Remarks were included from leading preachers such as I.W. Porter, R. Osgood, W.C. Goucher, J.B. Ganong, and academics such as Calvin Goodspeed of McMaster University.[53] Beyond the local petty squabbles from First Baptist, Halifax, that may have initially sparked this debate, Saunders genuinely believed that a strict use of higher criticism would eventually compromise orthodox beliefs such as the incarnation and the atonement, and he was not alone.[54] In response to the debate that

---

[49] Black, 'The Emotional in Religion'.
[50] Waring, 'What is the Bible', *MV*, 23 March 1904.
[51] H.F. Waring, 'First Questions First', *Messenger and Visitor,* 13 April 1904.
[52] Waring, 'First Questions First'.
[53] E.M. Saunders, 'Some Criticisms of the Article by the Rev. H.F. Waring', *Messenger and Visitor*, 30 March 1904.
[54] Waring's lectures to his Halifax congregation were later published in Henry F. Waring, *Christianity and Its Bible* (Chicago, IL: University of Chicago Press, 1907). See

persisted in the *Messenger and Visitor*, an anonymous author wrote 'A Criticism on Criticism' and declared,

> I cannot understand why some of our ministers wish to place themselves alongside of Bible critics. About twenty years ago we heard a great deal from infidels and atheists, outside of the churches against the Bible. We don't hear much noise from that quarter now, because Satan knows their work is being done within the pale of Christianity. Why this uproar about adjusting the Bible to popular ear...? If the teaching of the Book is to be accepted, we should ask God to adjust the eyes and ears and the heart of the critics as well as the masses by regeneration. We would find little difficulty in getting the masses, if we mean by this term the common people—for they heard Jesus gladly—to reverence and believe the Bible, if these carping scholastic critics would let up their slashing the books which make the Book of Books.

> What good has ever come to a sin-burdened soul from all that ever these destructive critics have ever written, or even higher critics in any class?[55]

While 'Observer' obviously sided with Saunders in the debate, Waring's position was rejected not just on theological or intellectual grounds, but also because higher criticism, it was believed, could not lead to conversions or build up the faith of believers. For 'Observer', the real predicament of people had not really changed over time. The heart needed to be regenerated and any intellectual or practical innovations that did not address that central concern were by definition suspect or irrelevant. That this would be the case is not surprising given the fact that Maritime Baptists sustained their emphasis on the new birth and remained uncommitted to any rigid system of biblical or theological interpretation. It must be remembered that at their founding, the Calvinistic Baptists adopted Regular Baptist polity more for the sake of church structure and accountability than a Reformed systematic approach to theology. That Maritime Regular Baptists were committed to orthodox 'fundamentals' of the faith during this period is without question. They just remained ambivalent about sophisticated approaches to the Bible. This ambiguity clearly made accomplishing Baptist union easier than it would have been if the Calvinistic Baptists were rigidly confessional.

During the years leading up to union, the *Messenger and Visitor* contained some articles on the new theology and its possible implications for the future. The reactions, while cautious, did not include a call for creedal formulations designed to guarantee doctrinal purity. Rather, the call was to a heightened awareness of the historic faith of the 'Fathers' that stressed conversionism and piety. As one writer put it, 'Have we outgrown the faith of our fathers? Are the "old paths" overgrown

---

the following responses: E.J. Grant, *'Christianity and Its Bible': A Critique* (n.pl.: n.p., n.d.); Perry J. Stackhouse, *An Answer to Criticisms of 'Christianity and Its Bible', and a Discussion of the Baptist Position and the Question of Honesty* (Campbellton, NB: Morning Graphic, n.d.).

[55] 'A Criticism on Criticism', *Messenger and Visitor*, 4 May 1904.

[sic]? And is there a new and better way? For ourselves there is not much in the new theories. We have no desires to dictate to any man what he shall believe and teach. The pastors of our churches, as a rule, are loyal to Jesus Christ. The Word of God is their "rule of faith and practice."'[56] Coming close to the 'no creed but the Bible' approach that marked many nineteenth-century sectarian Protestants, Maritime Regular Baptists had a long history of filtering new ways of thinking through the rubric of the unrefined biblicism of the 'Faith of the Fathers'.[57] Such a position resonated in the Free Baptist community as well. For example, Aaron Kinney, a Free Baptist from New Brunswick, wrote in 1884 that 'If, where we differ, we would all confine ourselves to the use of scripture language, every Christian would be satisfied' about the nature of Baptist union.[58] Indeed, it would ultimately be that historic connection to a common tradition among the three uniting Baptist groups that facilitated union in 1905 and 1906.

It would be a mistake to regard the motivations for Baptist union to have been entirely the result of local and regional factors. The nineteenth century was a period of great denomination building and organic unions among Protestants in the Anglo-American world, and these developments did not go unnoticed by Maritime Baptist groups. Presbyterians led the way in Canada by achieving no fewer than thirteen unions between 1817 and 1875 when the Presbyterian Church in Canada came into being.[59] The Methodists in Canada also spawned no fewer than twelve unions in the nineteenth century making it the largest denomination in Canada by 1884.[60] In June 1884, it was noted in the *Religious Intelligencer* that through union 'Methodism [in Canada] has taken a long and strong step forward, and may be expected to accomplish more as a Christian force than before.' The writer continued by noting, 'we may say that it appears very clear that the tendency of the times is strongly towards the consolidation of those Christian bodies which have few and non-essential differences'.[61] The union of major Protestant denominations was a much-debated topic in the late-nineteenth and early-twentieth centuries in the English-speaking world. That Canadian Protestants and Maritime Baptists, in particular, were aware of this trend cannot be doubted.[62] The example set by Presbyterian and Methodist unions in Canada inspired Maritime Free and Regular Baptists to explore cooperation

---

[56] S.M. Black, 'Some Fundamentals', *MV*, 20 May 1903.

[57] See Daniel C. Goodwin, 'The Faith of the Fathers: Evangelical Piety of Maritime Regular Baptist Patriarchs and Preachers 1790–1855' (PhD dissertation, Queen's University, Kingston, Ontario, 1997), ch. 9.

[58] Aaron Kinney, 'Baptist Union', *RI*, 11 July 1884.

[59] John Moir, *Enduring Witness: A History of the Presbyterian Church in Canada* (Toronto, ON: Presbyterian Press, 1996), p. 55.

[60] Neil Semple, *The Lord's Dominion: The History of Canadian Methodism* (Montreal and Kingston, ON: McGill-Queen's University Press, 1996), p. 5.

[61] 'Union', *RI*, 6 June 1884.

[62] John Webster Grant, *The Church in the Canadian Era* (Burlington, ON: Welch Publishing, 1988), pp. 106-107.

as a necessary step toward being a stronger presence for God in the east of Canada.[63]
One Free Baptist commentator observed,

> The Union of Presbyterians and of the Methodists, which not many years ago
> seemed impossible, but which being accomplished has proved so great an
> advantage to them, has probably impressed Baptists that the different branches of
> their family might also be united greatly to the advantage of the peculiar principles
> which they hold in common. The tendency of the times is strongly towards
> consolidation, and that this tendency in Christian bodies is of God has, we think,
> been clearly enough demonstrated in the experience of those that have
> consolidated.[64]

Committed to the belief that the 'tendency of the times' toward close cooperation
was divinely sanctioned, Baptist union advocates were conscious of the need for their
denominations to embrace these changes in order to make Canada, or at least eastern
Canada, 'His Dominion'. Canadian Protestants were known in the Anglo-American
world, according to the *Advertiser* published in London, England, as having 'a good
pre-eminence among Christian nations because of her achievements in church
unions'. The editor of the *Messenger and Visitor* commented that the 'various
branches of the Baptist family will, we think, see that closer union is wiser than
separation'.[65]

There were limits established in the Maritime Baptist discussion of the wider
'union frenzy' of the late nineteenth century, however. During the Synod meetings
of the Anglican Church in Montreal in 1886, a discussion was held about possible
church union with Presbyterians and Methodists and other Protestants as a means of
addressing the 'evils of a divided Christianity'. One Maritime Regular Baptist
correspondent cautioned his readers about the optimism of such thinking noting that
discussions focused upon church government and baptism instead of the foundational
point of the new!birth. That Baptists would be left out of these discussions because
of their view of baptism irritated the correspondent because the 'truth in regard to the
spirituality of the kingdom of Christ is one for which we have been born into this
world to confirm, and under no circumstances may we fail to do so'.[66] In other
words, the key to any discussion about church union or cooperation was not about
structures or forms but about the true nature of the church as a collection of believers
alone. Some pedobaptists, such as the Presbyterians, took issue with the Baptist
position on the sacraments and the nature of the church as a 'barrier to Christian
union'. In an article in the July issue of the *Presbyterian Review* reprinted, in part,
in the *Messenger and Visitor*, C.A. Briggs wrote, 'the Baptist doctrine with one
blow destroys the ministry and the church-rights of all the people of other Christian

---

[63] 'Canadian Methodism', *RI*, 26 January 1883; 'Union', *RI*, 16 February 1883. The
Free Baptists in the Maritimes were especially aware of the Methodist unions and found
potential to enhance efforts in evangelism appealing.
[64] 'Baptist Union', *RI* 26 December 1884.
[65] 'Church Union', *MV*, 22 February 1893.
[66] 'Church Unity', *MV*, 27 October 1886.

rights of all the people of other Christian churches by refusing to recognize the validity of their baptism'.[67] Briggs went on to describe the Baptists as 'intolerant', to which the editor of the *Messenger and Visitor* retorted, 'We are not alarmed at the accusation of intolerance. The truth is the most intolerant thing under heaven. The reason is that it is like its author, who never tolerates error.'[68] The aspirations of Free and Regular Maritime Baptists to participate fully in the Protestant mainstream were countered by distinctive beliefs such as believer's baptism by immersion and a believers' church. Consequently, their enthusiasm for organic union had to be confined to Baptist groups.

The sense of expectation associated with denominational mergers in Canada and beyond played an important part in fuelling the desire for Baptist union in the Maritimes. Readers of the two major Baptist periodicals in the region were exposed to stories of cooperative Baptist work in Britain and the United States.[69] In 1891, the union of the General Baptists (of the New Connexion) and Baptist Union (Particular Baptists) was achieved providing an example of a union that was able to cope with theological diversity while maintaining the distinctives of believer's baptism by immersion and the believers' church. In that same year Maritime Regular Baptists were invited to send delegates to the 'assembly of Baptists of world-wide Anglo-Saxon nations' that was to meet in Edinburgh, Scotland, in October.[70] The invitation was extended by J.H. Shakespeare, the Secretary of the Baptist Union of Great Britain and Ireland, who served a denomination of Baptists that contained both Arminians and Calvinists. Embracing the promise of the twentieth century, he wrote, 'I earnestly trust that this Congress may promote the unity of Baptists throughout the world and give an impetus to the progress of the Denomination through the New Century.'[71]

If British Baptists and global Baptist cooperative efforts provided examples and a sense of urgency toward union among Maritime Baptists, the American connection—much closer to home—provided both encouragement and challenges to the dream of union. For example, when the Regular Baptists and the Free Baptists of New Brunswick considered the possibility of cooperation between 1884 and 1886, the Nova Scotia Free Baptists decided against sending any official delegates to the joint committee: 'We find that the body of our people are not just now prepared for organic union.'[72] Of the three groups that entered union, there is no question the Free Baptists of Nova Scotia were the most influenced by American Baptists. In the spring of 1880, Nova Scotia Free Baptists contemplated their denomination's future. In an open letter to his co-religionists, Burton Minard wrote that 'Ten years sojourn in New England have convinced me that my provincial distrust of our Yankee

---

[67] 'A Barrier to Christian Union', *MV*, 27 July 1887.

[68] 'A Barrier to Christian Union'.

[69] Leon McBeth, *The Baptist Heritage: Four Centuries of Baptist Witness* (Nashville, TN: Broadman Press, 1987), pp. 292-93.

[70] Herbert C. Creed, 'An Ecumenical Baptist Congress', *MV*, 16 January 1901.

[71] Creed, 'An Ecumenical Baptist Congress'.

[72] *RI*, 17 November 1886.

cousins was unfounded. Though different flags float over our heads, the same blood flows in our veins; our ancestors were rocked side by side in the same cradle.'[73] Minard believed incorrectly that the Free Baptists of his province had been started largely by New England Free Will Baptists. That this point was not the case went unnoticed because of the confusing origins of Arminian Baptist work in south-western Nova Scotia in the early nineteenth century. Nevertheless, he argued that union with the American denomination was logical as they held to the same treatise of faith, participated in the same foreign mission efforts, and would benefit greatly from cooperation in publishing, and education.[74] Furthermore, Minard discarded any possible argument rooted in Canadian nationalism, noting, 'There has been much more political agitation and strife among us as a nation since Confederation than there has been for a century, or is ever likely to occur again between us and the United States.'[75] Implicit in Minard's position was the idea that Nova Scotia Free Baptists were quite different from the New Brunswick Free Baptists. This notion was rejected by a columnist in the *Religious Intelligencer* who cited Minard's 'anti-Canadian feeling':

> We have nothing to say about any soreness that may still exist concerning the confederation of the Provinces, but we think it unfortunate that it should be imported into the question of union of Christian denominations essentially one and having their home in sister Provinces.[76]

The Nova Scotia region that was home to most of the province's Free Baptists was also home to some of the most anti-Confederation activity in the new nation that had been formed in 1867.[77] Minard argued that English Canada was far more 'new England in its habits and customs than British, decidedly more democratic in political convictions than monarchical, and...energized more by the spirit of the New World than the Old World'.[78] In other words, those political and religious principles most valued and practiced by Free Baptists in Maritime Canada were of American origin and, on that basis, should justify a merger of Free Baptists to their 'American cousins'. Not wanting to appear anti-patriotic, Minard was quick to assure his readers that 'he who advances the cause of Christ the most efficiently serves his country best'.[79] It is unclear how many of Minard's readers actually agreed with his position that Canada's best interests were served by the region's Free Baptists joining

---

[73] Burton Minard, 'An Open Letter to the Free Baptists of NS, no. 3', *RI*, 26 March 1880.

[74] Minard, 'An Open Letter'.

[75] Minard, 'An Open Letter'.

[76] *RI*, 9 April 1880.

[77] Kenneth G. Pyke, *Nova Scotia and Confederation, 1864-74* (Toronto, ON: University of Toronto Press, 1979).

[78] Burton Minard, 'Open Letter to the Free Baptists of Nova Scotia, no. 4', *RI*, 7 May 1880.

[79] Burton Minard, 'Open Letter to the Free Baptists of Nova Scotia, no. 5', *RI*, 14 May 1880.

American Free Will Baptists because it would strengthen their influence in Canada. However, what is obvious is that the question of religious identity was tied in part to feelings of nationalism as well as international denominationalism.

That Nova Scotia Free Baptists experienced the tensions between nationalism, regionalism, and denominational identity more keenly than Free Baptists in New Brunswick and even Ontario was a result of the province's historic connection to New England. The seaward focus of Nova Scotia's coastal communities meant that they had much in common with their neighbours south of the border. Out-migration from the region to New England also meant that close family ties were maintained and fostered during the nineteenth century. According to historian Alan Brookes, by the 1880s 'the exodus had taken on the characteristics of a mass migration' and he notes that the Maritime Baptist groups were included in this emigration to the United States.[80] With more than a little exaggeration Minard noted the 'emigration of hundreds of thousands from the Maritime Provinces' to New England and that 'enough Free Baptists have left New Brunswick and settled in Boston, Mass., alone to make the largest church worshipping in that city'.[81] Based on his impressionistic evidence, Minard argued that joining the American Free Will Baptists would ensure that displaced Maritime Free Baptists would not be lost to other denominations in the United States.

In response to Minard's pro-American stance, T.H. Siddall, another Free Baptist preacher who served in both Nova Scotia and New Brunswick, made the case for Maritime exceptionalism and argued against the notion that Maritime Canadians and Maritime Free Baptists were a mere extension of American political and religious culture. He asked, 'in religious societies has not history shown that while organizations may be the same in one land as another, yet the current and character of religious life, moulded and fashioned by such organization, may be distinctive, bearing impresses peculiar to the individual nationality?' While conceding that some Free Baptist Churches in Nova Scotia were planted by Free Will Baptist ministers from New England, Siddall highlighted the essential 'British' colonial context in which these churches grew. This influence he noted was to be found in the more 'conservative' approach in 'religious methods' and worship when compared to their American counterparts.[82] Challenging Minard's dubious reading of Nova Scotia's political history, Siddall showed that developments in responsible government reflected a strong British sensibility, insisting, 'the very foundation of our Government is essentially British'.[83]

---

[80] Alan Brookes, 'Out-migration from the Maritime Provinces, 1860–1900: Some Preliminary Considerations', in P.A. Buckner and David Frank (eds), *Atlantic Canada After Confederation: The Acadiensis Reader Vol. 2* (Fredericton, NB: Acadiensis Press, 1985), pp. 39 and 43. See also Patricia A. Thornton, 'The Problem of Out-Migration from Atlantic Canada, 1871–1921: A New Look', *Acadiensis* 15.1 (Autumn, 1985), pp. 3-34.

[81] Burton Minard, 'An Open Letter to the Free Baptists of Nova Scotia, no. 3', *RI*, 23 April 1880.

[82] T.H. Siddall, 'Free Baptist Union, no. 2', *RI*, 16 April 1880.

[83] T.H. Siddall, 'Free Baptist Union, no. 3', *RI*, 21 May 1880.

As Free Baptists in the Maritime Provinces contemplated the possibility of organic union, they were swept up in a morass of competing allegiances. Were they firstly Nova Scotians, New Brunswickers, Maritimers, Canadians, British, or transplanted Americans? What was the relationship between their theology, geographical location and cultural heritage? To date, Canadian religious historians have not studied these tensions closely. However, they provided the context in which three different Baptist groups of the region worked out the implications of their identity for the basis of wider cooperation.

CHAPTER 12

Baptist Identity in the Thought of Walter Rauschenbusch

Tadeusz J. Zielinski

Max Stackhouse, who retrieved and published posthumously one of Rauschenbusch's books, entitled his editorial introduction to that work 'The Continuing Importance of Walter Rauschenbusch'.[1] Indeed, the continuing presence of Rauschenbusch's thought in scholarly periodicals and theological monographs proves his continuing relevance for current religious reflection. However, this German–American thinker is remembered and valued almost exclusively because of his influential remarks on issues from the field of Christian social ethics. He is rightly viewed, as Reinhold Niebuhr put it, as a 'Real founder of the Social Gospel'.[2] But his enduring role as a social prophet who inspires new generations of Christians should not divert our attention from the fact that Rauschenbusch devoted not a little of his time to Baptist denominational concerns. To put it more straightforwardly, Rauschenbusch was a deeply convinced Baptist. His definite position on Baptist identity should allow us to find in him a leading modern exponent of Baptist distinctives which were viewed by him as a safeguard of authentically Christian identity. The following study is devoted to the exposition of Rauschenbusch's main convictions in the area of Baptist identity. After a brief biographical note I will introduce his whole theological vision, and then I will survey what he expounds as the main reasons—as he himself put it—why it is proper to be a Baptist. At the end I will try to address weaknesses of his view of Baptist convictions and then evaluate the foundational aspects of Rauschenbusch's Baptist principles that seem to be relevant for future generations of believers within the Baptist tradition.

---

[1] Walter Rauschenbusch, *Righteousness of the Kingdom* (ed. Max L. Stackhouse; Nashville, TN: Abingdon Press, 1968), p. 7.
[2] Reinhold Niebuhr, *An Interpretation of Christian Ethics* (New York: Harper and Brothers, 1935), p. 2.

Rauschenbusch's Life

The name Rauschenbusch indicates German roots.[3] Born in 1861 in Rochester, New York, in the family of a German Lutheran clergyman who turned Baptist, Walter was brought up in a strictly pietistic atmosphere. He undertook thorough studies both in the United States and Germany. Due to his sympathy with some tenets of historical criticism and nineteenth-century liberal theology, he was not accepted as a candidate for overseas mission. He then decided to take the post of pastor of the 125 member German Baptist Church in the one of most neglected areas of New York city, called 'Hell's Kitchen'. Serving in this working-class area, he encountered the most shocking outcomes of industrialization. When asked about the source of his passion for social involvement he later remarked that it 'did not come from the Church.... It came from outside. It came through personal contact with poverty, and when I saw how men lived all their life long, hard, toilsome lives, and at the end had almost nothing to show for it. How strong men begged for work and could not get it in hard times; how little children died—oh, the children's funerals! They gripped my heart.'[4]

The church's general lack of substantial interest in the social problems of the lower classes radicalised the social element of Rauschenbusch's ministry. *Vis-à-vis* 'unsocial Christians and unchristian Socialists' (Fosdick)[5] Rauschenbusch became a modern trailblazer of Christian social action. Although due to his profound deafness he had to leave his pastoral occupation, he fought his cause as a seminary professor, an advisor to leading politicians (including Theodore Roosevelt, Woodrow Wilson and David Lloyd George), a national speaker, and a profound and attractive writer. Through semi-communal experiments like the Society of Jesus or the Brotherhood of Kingdom, and major ventures such as Baptist Congresses (1881–1915),[6] he spread his concern that Christians should express their piety in solving the daily problems of the weakest and the poorest in society in a structural and thorough way. Attacked by those who labelled him indiscriminately as a liberal theologian, he was valued more outside than inside his own Baptist confessional fold. As he confessed from his deathbed, 'My life has been physically very lonely and often beset by the consciousness of conservative antagonism.'[7] He passed away in 1918 just before the

---

[3] For the full scale biography, see Paul M. Minus, *Walter Rauschenbusch: American Reformer* (New York: Macmillan, 1988). See also Klaus Jurgen Jaehn, *Rauschenbusch: The Formative Years* (Valley Forge, PA: Judson Press, 1976); Dores R. Sharpe, *Walter Rauschenbusch* (New York: Macmillan, 1942); Reinhart Müller, *Walter Rauschenbusch: Ein Beitrag zur Begegnung des deutschen und des amerikanischen Protestantismus* (Leiden: E.J. Brill, 1957).

[4] Harry Emerson Fosdick, 'Introduction: An Interpretation of the Life and Work of Walter Rauschenbusch', in Benson Y. Landis (ed.), *A Rauschenbusch Reader: The Kingdom of God and the Social Gospel* (New York: Harper and Brothers, 1957), p. xvi.

[5] Fosdick, 'Introduction', p. xv.

[6] See the entry on 'Baptist Congress' in William H. Brackney, *Historical Dictionary of the Baptists* (Lanham, MD: Scarecrow Press, 1999), p. 45.

[7] Winthrop S. Hudson (ed.), *Walter Rauschenbusch: Selected Writings* (New York, Paulist Press, 1984), pp. 45-46.

end of the First World War, seeing how his over-optimistic and even utopian dreams of a peaceful and just world-order had fallen apart.[8]

Survey of Rauschenbusch's Theology

In looking at Rauschenbusch's theology it must be stated that central to his thought was the concept of the Kingdom of God. The Kingdom of God was to him a reality that embraced religious and social life. Ethically understood, the Kingdom was viewed by him as the embodiment of the gospel vision of interpersonal relationships. In Rauschenbusch's opinion, the gospel cannot be seen only as an antidote to the supernatural needs of the human person, but it has to be relevant to all aspects of daily existence. Each person needs the whole gospel, and the traditional message preached by Protestant churches presented, in his view, a reduced, limited gospel. According to Rauschenbusch, the old message must be extended, must be intensified, and must embrace social issues also. Therefore, the real, authentic gospel can, in his opinion, rightly be named the 'Social Gospel'.[9] He wrote, 'We want revolution from inside and from outside', and the Social Gospel requires 'more of faith and less of faith'. Personal piety and social involvement were for him, therefore, complementary. Christians cannot limit themselves to an individualistic soteriology, even one supported by charity work.

According to Rauschenbusch, the Kingdom of God, which is the locus of personal piety and social sensitivity, can gradually transform culture, can improve, edify and redeem the whole of social life, drawing into its circle active individuals and institutions. The Kingdom of God starts from individual conversion, and like the mustard seed sown in the soil of society it will flourish, giving shelter to the needy. God in his immanence is the primary mover of the Kingdom, and Jesus of Nazareth, as the incarnation of the Kingdom's new style of life, is the primary example of the human being who is actively sensitive to needy fellow humans. The Christian as the follower of Jesus will promote the cause of embodying Jesus' lifestyle in daily life. The followers of the Nazarene will introduce gradually new forms of interpersonal relationships and in an evolutionary way will transform the surrounding society, dealing with social inequality, unemployment, extreme poverty and warfare. Churches, understood by Rauschenbusch as simple, friendly communities, will then be the main promoters of a way of living that is proper to the Kingdom of God.

---

[8] 'Since 1914 the world is full of hate, and I cannot expect to be happy again in my lifetime', cited by Fosdick, 'Introduction', p. xxi.

[9] On aspects of Rauschenbusch's concept of the Social Gospel, see Vernon Parker Bodein, *The Social Gospel of Walter Rauschenbusch and Its Relation to Religious Education* (New Haven, CT: Yale University Press, 1944). On the Social Gospel movement as such, see Robert T. Handy (ed.), *The Social Gospel in America 1870–1920* (New York: Oxford University Press, 1966).

The *Loci* of Rauschenbusch's Remarks on Baptist Identity

After his pastoral ministry, Rauschenbusch held a professorship of New Testament Theology and Church History in Rochester. His most meaningful achievements in the field of theology were, however, in the area of systematic theology (if we understand that term in a non-Anglo-Saxon sense), and were mainly in the field of Christian social ethics. From this area of thought come his major works: *Christianity and the Social Crisis* (1907), *For God and People: Prayers of the Social Awakening* (1909), *Christianizing the Social Order* (1912), and *Theology for the Social Gospel* (1917).[10] These works were written with real ecumenical acumen and were directed as manifestos to mobilize the whole church catholic, and as a result they do not contain any explicit statements on Baptist identity. Indeed, there is no reference to the Baptist tradition. Hence in looking for Rauschenbusch's remarks on Baptist identity we must look elsewhere, namely to articles in periodicals or to his unpublished papers. Fortunately there is a thorough exposition of his Baptist convictions given in a series of four short articles. He wrote them in 1905 and 1906 for *The Rochester Baptist Journal* under the title 'Why I Am a Baptist'.[11] It must be stated that these articles seem to be the least reprinted and least known of his work. The title serves to signal the narrowness of the content. Here we have particularity, rather than the catholicity which characterizes his best known writings. Nonetheless, here in this twenty-page treatise we can find him at his best, writing—as is usually the case—in dynamic, elegant, essayistic style, using many metaphors and analogies, sharply, brilliantly and eloquently phrasing his thoughts, and most of all strongly moving the hearts of his hearers. Another Baptist, Sydnor Stealey, who once edited this work, rightly said, '[I]t is one of the best statements ever written on our distinctive principles.'[12]

Rauschenbusch's Attempt to Construct a Balanced View of Baptist Identity

Although Rauschenbusch himself was of Baptist extraction he was also a self-committed Baptist. Anyone reading his 'Why I Am a Baptist' article (to which we will later refer as to *WB*) will notice that 'the prophet from Rochester' was proud of

---

[10] Walter Rauschenbusch, *Christianity and the Social Crisis* (New York: Macmillan, 1907); *For God and the People: Prayers of the Social Awakening* (Boston: The Pilgrim Press, 1909); *Christianizing the Social Order* (New York: Macmillan, 1912); and *A Theology for the Social Gospel* (New York: Macmillan, 1917).

[11] Two older reprints of that work are slightly abridged versions: Walter Rauschenbusch, 'Why I Am a Baptist', in Sydnor L. Stealey (ed.), *A Baptist Treasury* (New York: Thomas Y. Crowell, 1958), pp. 163-84; Walter Rauschenbusch, 'Why I Am a Baptist', in Henlee H. Barnette (ed.), *Baptist Leader*, January 1958, pp. 1-10. The newest publication appeared in a full version prepared by Foy Valentine, 'Walter Rauschenbusch, "Why I Am a Baptist"', *Christian Ethics Today* 1.1 (April, 1995), pp. 20-31. All quotations from the work that follow come from the edition of 1995.

[12] Stealey (ed.), *A Baptist Treasury*, p. 163.

his Baptist persuasion. For instance, he is ready to say that the 'democracy of the Baptist churches is something to be proud of';[13] or, elsewhere, 'I am proud to think that our church life is in harmony with that great ideal of government of the people, by the people and for the people, which mankind is slowly toiling to realize.'[14] On several occasions he emphasizes his conviction that Baptist faith is of noble stock. The word 'noble' is an expression that he uses very often to convey something of value. Therefore, for example, when he speaks of Baptist ecclesiology he says that it 'is built on very noble Christian lines'.[15] Speaking about the Baptist approach to state–church relations he shares his conviction that 'Baptists have [a] far nobler and prouder position' and, indeed, were 'pioneers in that principle toward which the civilized nations are slowly drifting'.[16] However, Rauschenbusch is very definite in his opinion that Baptist identity is based not on one more or less important distinctive, but on a whole set of major convictions. So he very forcefully states that '[O]ur Baptist faith…is founded on great principles'.[17]

Rauschenbusch protests against an understanding of Baptist identity which points to the practice of baptism of believers by immersion as the decisive element of Baptist distinction from other Christians. He speaks about—in the plural—Baptist 'principles', or about a 'body of truth'. In his opinion, Baptist identity is worthy of close attention as a set of convictions: 'It is a good thing to raise the question: "Why are you a Baptist?" I wish all our church members had to answer it clearly and fully. It is possible to be a Baptist on small grounds or on large grounds. Some man will say: "I am a Baptist because the Greek word 'baptiso'[18] means 'immerse'." That is quite true, but that is a pretty small peg to hang your religious convictions on.' Therefore, Rauschenbusch supplies us with an illustration: 'A near-sighted child was taken to the zoo and stood in front of the lion's cage. The lion's tail was hanging down through the bars. "But I thought the lion was different", said the child, "it looks like a yellow rope." So there are Baptists who have hitherto discovered only the tail-end of our Baptist ideals and convictions and it is no wonder that they turn out as narrow as the tail they devoutly believe in.' At once Rauschenbusch adds another candid comparison: 'It is possible to play "Nearer, my God to Thee" with one finger on a little reed-organ of four octaves. But it is very different music when the same melody is played with all the resources of a great pipe-organ and all the richness of full harmony.'[19]

It is beyond any doubt, therefore, that our author wants to promote the whole wealth of Baptist convictions, and so he speaks about 'Embracing my Baptist inheritance with heartiness and intelligence.'[20] Concluding these observations on the

---

[13] *WB*, p. 25.
[14] *WB*, p. 25.
[15] *WB*, p. 25.
[16] *WB*, p. 26.
[17] *WB*, p. 24.
[18] This transliteration is original.
[19] All previous 3 quotes from *WB*, pp. 21-22.
[20] *WB*, p. 26.

status of Baptist convictions in the hierarchy of Rauschenbusch's values, we cannot omit the fact that it was crucial to his thinking to view the Baptist position as the radicalization of Protestant principles,[21] and, linked with this, he clearly had a high regard for Protestantism as such. He saw Protestantism as a value worthy of radical practice. In his own words, 'That is one reason why I am a Baptist, because by being a Baptist I am a radical Protestant.'[22]

Having all this in mind, it should be taken into consideration that Rauschenbusch does not turn his pride about Baptist principles into a 'Baptist brag'. He balances his Baptist pride with Baptist self-criticism by submitting straightforward statements that emphasize weaknesses in Baptist practice. Being convinced of the strength of the main tenets of Baptist faith, he notices that Baptists sometimes do not live up to them: 'some [of us] misuse it or misunderstand it, or are inwardly traitors to it'.[23] Elsewhere he is even more critical, saying, 'I do not mean that Baptists have been faultless in their application of these principles; they have sinned and bungled more often that not';[24] or 'We are not a perfect denomination. We are capable of being as narrow and small as anybody.'[25] Referring to ecclesiological concerns, on which he comments at some length in his article, Rauschenbusch dares to say, 'I know well that Baptist churches have not lived up to these magnificent principles. Churches like individuals, are in perpetual danger of backsliding. There are churches that admit almost anybody and exclude scarcely anybody. There are Baptist churches in which a small junta of men rule and democracy has become a mere name. There are Baptist ministers who are more priestly in spirit and temper than the present pope.'[26] In Rauschenbusch's view this is because we do not strive to broaden our hearts and minds: 'Little beliefs make little men. Many Baptists are cut on a small pattern because their convictions are so small.'[27] In such a situation, instead of a lively practice of Baptist convictions we have insufficient and poor substitutes—as he puts it, 'dried plants and stuffed animals as exponents of the Promised Land'.[28]

Rauschenbusch's Four Reasons for Being a Baptist

From the previous remarks we understand that Rauschenbusch wants to be a Baptist on 'large grounds'. He recognizes a whole 'body of truth' on which he can base his Baptist key distinctives. Hence he offers us in the text from the *Rochester Baptist*

---

[21] For elaboration of the notion that the Baptist form of Christianity is the radicalization of Protestantism, see Tadeusz J. Zielinski, 'Baptyzm—kazus radykalnego protestantyzmu' ('Baptists—The Case for Radical Protestantism'), *Mysl Protestancka* 4 (2001), pp. 2-4.
[22] *WB*, p. 28.
[23] *WB*, p. 24.
[24] *WB*, p. 31.
[25] *WB*, p. 31.
[26] *WB*, p. 26.
[27] *WB*, p. 21.
[28] *WB*, p. 21.

Journal an extensive set of convictions that he lists under the headings of four 'Reasons'. So we have 'My first reason' for being a Baptist, 'My second reason', etc.. Now it is appropriate to present all four principles, and after doing so, I will proceed to evaluate them with an attempt to discover the foundational and enduring elements of Baptist identity in Rauschenbusch's thought. The following are Rauschenbusch's four basic tenets of Baptist identity.[29]

The Primacy of Personal Christian Experience

The Baptist version of Christianity is for Rauschenbusch an 'experimental religion'.[30] Christianity is only present where there is a firsthand experience of God. '[N]othing will take the place of personal experience. In the study of the natural sciences the modern method is to put the student into direct contact with nature. The dissection of a single animal will give more knowledge of biology than the best textbooks in which a student reads what others have observed. Baptists believe in advanced methods in religion. They confront the soul with God.'[31] This saving confrontation starts with evangelism and personal conversion, which Rauschenbusch understood in a fairly evangelical sense. Therefore, he says, 'we are an evangelistic body. We summon all to conscious repentance from sin...'.[32] But he does not equate 'experimental religion' with narrow emotionalism or the cult of feelings.[33] Although he values emotion as an element of human experience,[34] yet he has a holistic concept of experience, where there is a place for discipline, rationality and clear conviction ('conscious personal experience'[35]). This is evident in his perception of the category of faith; he goes far beyond the differentiation of *fides qua* and *fides quae* and teaches us that faith 'is a kind of algebraic symbol, expressing the inner religious experience and life in Christ'.[36]

Democracy in Organized Church Life

In his anthropology Rauschenbusch clearly identifies rigid individualism as a source of evil. Sharing the traditional Baptist concern for a properly understood

---

[29] Naming particular tenets from Rauschenbusch's list I use the headings that were added in brackets to his text. They came probably from the pen of Foy Valentine, an editor of the 1995 version of *WB*.

[30] *WB*, p. 21.

[31] *WB*, p. 22.

[32] *WB*, p. 21.

[33] 'I know...that "experience" with very many is a very shallow emotion', *WB*, p. 23.

[34] See Hudson (ed.), *Selected Writings*, p. 34.

[35] *WB*, p. 22. *WB*, p. 23: '[W]e insist on repentance from sin and submission to the will of God.'

[36] *WB*, p. 23.

ecclesiology,[37] he propounds implicitly the idea of the 'gathered church of regenerated ones'. He starts with the statement that 'We are social beings. An isolated individual is...a crippled man',[38] and proceeds to say that the Baptist movement 'tries to create an organization of really Christian people'.[39] From this he derives the principle of closed membership,[40] of democratic forms of church government,[41] and of the institutional separation of church and state, although not the separation of religious and social life: 'Our Baptist churches decline all alliances with the State... Some Baptists seem to think that this separation is based on the idea that the spiritual life has nothing to do with the secular life. I utterly deny that assertion and think it a calamitous heresy.' [42]

Christ-like Life and not Ritual is True Worship and Religion

In his third reason for being a Baptist, Rauschenbusch shares his conviction that Baptists properly understand biblical worship as a way of life and not a ritual. He proceeds to engage in sharp criticism of every kind of religious ceremonialism, and this leads him to an exposition of a strictly non-sacramental view of baptism and the eucharist. As a proud and at the same time critical Protestant, Rauschenbusch describes the negative impact of ritualism and acknowledges the achievements of Protestant Reformers in the process of what Max Weber would call *Entzauberung*, the demystification of the world. 'Among other things Reformation simplified worship and swept out a great mass of superstitious ceremonial... The Baptists, and all those bodies with whom we are historically connected, marched in the vanguard of Protestantism... Baptists are, in fact, more Protestant than the great reformers on some points. The Reformers all retained infant baptism. But infant baptism was part and parcel of that very paganizing tendency which I have tried to describe. It grew out

---

[37] This is how Rauschenbusch, *Christianity and the Social Crisis*, pp. 119-20, sees the original shape of primitive Christian churches: 'The churches of the first generation were not churches in our sense of the word. They were not communities for the performance of a common worship, so much as communities with a common life. They were social communities with a religious basis. A common religious experience and hope brought them together, but the community of life extended to far more than that. They prayed together, but they also ate together. They had no church buildings, but met in the homes of their members. That in itself was an influence against ecclesiasticism and for social intimacy. They had a rudimentary organization, as every human society is sure to have, but they had no official clergy distinct from the laity. They were democratic organizations of plain people.'

[38] *WB*, p. 24.

[39] *WB*, p. 25.

[40] *WB*, p. 25: 'It can make many mistakes in receiving too quickly and in excluding too slowly, but at least it tries to keep its membership clean and homogenious.'

[41] 'Our churches are Christian democracies', *WB*, p. 25. Rauschenbusch, *Christianity and the Social Crisis*, p. 127: '[R]eligious utterence was the common right of all Christians.'

[42] *WB*, p. 26; Rauschenbusch, *Christianity and the Social Crisis*, pp. 198, 295.

of a double root: the belief that original sin damns even infants to hell; and the belief that baptism regenerates.' But 'it was an alien element in Protestantism'.[43] The Rochester theologian is happy to see that 'Holy places, holy times, holy formulas, holy experts are all left behind, and the only thing God asks for is love for himself and love for our fellowmen.'[44]

Let us now look more closely at his view of gospel ordinances.

> Christianity had only two religious acts in which form counted for anything, baptism and the Lord's Supper. One was a bath, the other a meal. These two simple acts of daily life were used to express great spiritual thoughts. But men with pagan habits of mind seized on these and saw in them just what they were looking for. Baptism was to them a mystic cleansing which washed away guilt and defilement, a magic bath from which a man rose regenerate as a new man with the past all cleaned away. When they heard the words 'This is my body, this is my blood', they felt that in some mysterious way Christ was really present in the bread and wine, and when they swallowed the elements, his divine life entered into them and gave them the assurance and power of immortality. These superstitious ideas became ever more powerful and concrete as time passed; they were adopted by theologians and defended as part of the essence of Christianity.[45]

To be clear about Rauschenbusch's stance on baptism I will quote only one more statement, but one which is definitive: '[the] baptism of believers is an outward sign'.[46]

---

[43] *WB*, p. 28.

[44] *WB*, p. 27, cf. Rauschenbusch, *Christianity and the Social Crisis*, p. 94.

[45] *WB*, p. 27. Rauschenbusch, *Christianity and the Social Crisis*, p. 177: 'Christianity in the heathen world rapidly relapsed toward the pre-prophetic stage of religion. The material furnished by Christianity was worked over into a new ceremonialism, essentially like the magic ritual of the Greek mysteries and Oriental cults, only more wonderful and efficacious. Baptism was a bath of regeneration, cleansing the guilt of all prebaptismal sins, and making the soul like that of a new-born child. In the sacrament of the eucharist in some mysterious way the very body and blood of the Lord were present, and the divine could be physically eaten and its powers received to transform the material into the spiritual and immortal. The formulas of baptism and the Lord's supper were frought with magic powers. Worship became a process of mystagogic initiation into the divine mysteries. All the old essentials of pagan religion were reproduced in Christian form, but with scarcely a break in their essence: the effort to placate God by sacrifice, the amulets, vows, oracles, festivals, incense, candles, pictures and statues. It was like a tropical jungle sprouting again after it is cut down.'

[46] *WB*, p. 22. Rauschenbusch, *A Theology for the Social Gospel*, p. 197, recognizes also dangers of the traditional Baptist tendency to emphasize the individualistic aspect of baptism of believers: 'Baptists have always been dogged by superstitions and thrust down into paganism. The individualistic interpretation of it as an escape from damnation tainted it with selfishness.'

The Bible Alone is the Sufficient Authority for Faith and Practice

Interestingly enough, Rauschenbusch places his treatment of the rule of faith at the end of his treatise. One can take this as a proof that he relegates the Bible to the position of a marginal element in the Christian life. That would perfectly fit the simplistic picture of Rauschenbusch as an uncritical confessor of a liberal theological creed. However, the theologian from Rochester had in fact a high regard for scripture as the necessary and primary guide in Christian belief and conduct. Emphasizing this role of the Bible,[47] Rauschenbusch questions the ultimately binding character of other standards of Christian faith. He refers especially to the phenomenon of rigid creedalism. Therefore, he is combating the promotion of, as he calls it, a 'dead authority'.[48] He finds it to be a Baptist distinctive which must be maintained that '[W]e Baptists have no authoritative creed... [T]his freedom from creeds has left Baptists free to grow without jars and struggles.'[49] Attaching an absolute value to any standard other than the Bible Rauschenbusch perceives as a form of dangerous enslavement. He compares such absolute extra-biblical standards to hoops: 'hoops are good around barrels, but I should not advise putting nice, tightly fitting hoops around the body of a growing child'.[50]

Christian faith and Christians themselves, he argues, need a real freedom to exercise their gifts and to serve needy humanity accordingly. While creeds and similar formulae conserve in an abstract way certain perceptions, the Bible being existentially orientated directs us to the living experience of God: 'Creeds record ideas in their abstract profile, Bible records life in its richness'; 'Human nature with its love and hate and fear and hope and sin and passion is always the same, and what was true in the days of Ramses II under the shadows of the pyramids, is true in the days of Roosevelt I under the shadow of the sky scrapers. Hence creeds are dead and the Bible is alive.'[51] Rauschenbusch is aware of the fact that Baptists do not always resist the temptation to introduce strict doctrinal or theological uniformity. He speaks about those who dream about an 'iron-clad Baptist creed with a thousand points'.[52] Then, in the context of creedal danger, Rauschenbusch describes Baptist ways of misusing the Bible: 'There are, indeed, many Baptists who have tried to use the Bible just as other denominations use their creed. They have turned the Bible into one huge creed, and practically that meant: "You must believe everything which we think the Bible means and says." They have tried to impose on us their little interpretation of the great Book. But fortunately the Bible is totally different from a creed. A creed contains sharply defined and abstract theology; the Bible contains a record of concrete and glowing religious life...'.[53] Elsewhere he refers to the obvious

---

[47] On his understanding of inspiration of the scriptures, see Rauschenbusch, *A Theology for the Social Gospel*, pp. 189ff.

[48] *WB*, p. 30.
[49] *WB*, p. 30.
[50] *WB*, p. 30.
[51] *WB*, p. 31.
[52] *WB*, p. 23.
[53] *WB*, p. 31.

errors of Protestant/evangelical—including Baptist—biblicism: 'We have paralyzed the Bible by turning it into law book and a collection of proof texts... We have fusses about trifles in it and have missed the greatest things. We have reduced it all to a single level, as if Esther was equal to Isaiah, and Old Testament to the New, and Zephaniah or Jude to our Lord Jesus Christ.'[54]

An Analysis of Rauschenbusch's View of Baptist Identity

After such an overview of the main tenets of Baptist identity as seen by Rauschenbusch, we may attempt to draw some conclusions, unveiling the strengths and weaknesses of his perception of Baptist distinctives. Looking at strengths and weaknesses, trends and opportunities, may help the future inheritors of Rauschenbusch's legacy to embrace the valuable elements of his thought about Baptist identity. The text from the *Rochester Baptist Journal* is not a thoroughly systematic exposition of Baptist distinctives. As we know, the preparation of a series of articles for a periodical has its own logic. They are usually written *ad hoc*, and an author is normally under the pressure of time and the magazine's editor, so very often she or he cannot develop and form her/his thought as would be the case in a different context. So it appears proper to dig deeper in the soil of Rauschenbusch's thought, discovering at least some solid aspects of Baptist identity for the next generations of Baptists.

Weaknesses

Let us start with weaknesses. I will point out four of them.

REMNANTS OF PLATONISM

With his passion for Christians' social involvement, Rauschenbusch cannot be accused of being a subjective idealist. However, he seems to be an inheritor of that strand of Baptist mentality which built its worldview on tenets of old Calvinistic/Reformed, scholastic Platonism or Neoplatonism. The 'spiritual' is for some within that tradition the only 'real' and the only worthy matter. Earthly reality is only a reflection of an ideal world to which we are heading. So Rauschenbusch probably unintentionally falls into the trap of speaking of 'spiritual' Christianity as the real Christianity.[55] He encourages us to go through the 'simpler and more *spiritual* way',[56] to 'be simple, truthful, *spiritual*';[57] he says that 'The Christian faith as Baptists hold it, sets *spiritual* experience boldly to the front as the one great thing in religion',[58] confesses that he 'claim[s] such a purely *spiritual* religion',[59]

---

[54] *WB*, p. 31.

[55] See his criticism of the Platonic influence on early Christianity, Rauschenbusch, *Christianity and the Social Crisis*, p. 162nn.

[56] *WB*, p. 21.

[57] *WB*, p. 29.

[58] *WB*, p. 21.

and speaks of 'simple, ethical, *spiritual* worship'.[60] Of course there is nothing bad in being 'spiritual', as long as it is not set in opposition to the 'existential', to the daily, to the 'down to earth' existence of Christians.

THE INCARNATIONAL DIMENSION OF CHRISTIANITY IS UNDERVALUED

Remnants of Platonism in the Rauschenbusch's thought can also be noticed and observed in his reduced Christology. Here we approach the most problematic aspect of his theology. As an ally of the *Leben-Jesu-Forschung* school he seems to stand on the side of nineteenth-century radical reinterpretations of the doctrine of Christ. In other words, in his writings the Godhead of Christ is not sufficiently identified. This may lead us to the opinion that, according to the theologian of Rochester, in meeting Christ we do not meet God himself, but we meet only his inferior—although impressive—agent.[61] This seems to be the Rauschenbusch's way to preach the precious Baptist tenet of 'the Lordship of Christ over the soul'.[62] Yet, if Jesus is not God himself, God incarnate, than he cannot exercise this Lordship over the soul and he cannot save us. And if we share the view that Jesus is not God himself, if we strip him of his God-like stance and power, we as Christians are still only a sect of Judaism. Two last weaknesses we observe here are of lesser importance, but we must note them.

AN EXAGGERATED BELIEF IN THE PROMISE OF EVOLUTION

Almost until the outbreak of World War I, Rauschenbusch identified himself with nineteenth-century optimism about civilization. As a social evolutionist he believed in the gradual improvement of the human community. He seems to find a similar paradigm in the history of religions. Thus, in describing certain religious phenomena he recognizes in them the 'lower stages of religion',[63] or a 'higher stage of religious development',[64] or identifies certain elements of religious reality as being in accord with—as he says—the 'noblest tendencies of our age'.[65] Elsewhere he speaks about the 'capacity for growth in religious thought. It is fatal to make the religious thought of one age binding for a higher age.'[66] Although in certain contexts these kinds of statements can be quite innocent, they can suggest that Christianity is

---

[59] *WB*, p. 23.

[60] *WB*, p. 28. Italics added.

[61] In Rauschenbusch's famous 'Prayers for the Social Awakening' of 1910, which are characterized by an awesome beauty, Christ is addressed unusually seldom. On the theology of those prayers, see Philip LeMasters, 'Walter Rauschenbusch on Prayer and Social Action', in Gary Furr and Curtis W. Freeman (eds), *Ties That Bind: Life Together in the Baptist Vision* (Macon GA: Smyth and Helwys, 1994), pp. 191-204.

[62] Rauschenbusch preferes to speak about 'direct personal relation with God', *WB*, p. 22 (note that 'God', and not Jesus is mentioned).

[63] *WB*, p. 26.

[64] *WB*, p. 27.

[65] *WB*, p. 21.

[66] *WB*, p. 29.

merely another stage in the evolutionary development of religion, not a divinely established reality in Christ. Reading these statements we may also gain an impression that through evolutionary development we will see the emergence of a better form of the human race or of new ways of coping with our human predicament. But until *consummatio* occurs we will have both the 'old-time problems' and the 'old-time gospel'.

EN BLOC CRITICISM OF OTHER FORMS OF CHRISTIANITY

It seems to me that in his *Rochester Journal* article Rauschenbusch gave himself freedom to criticize some Christian denominations, or even Judaism,[67] in a way which has the danger that it continues an old Baptist tradition of using a 'hate language' while speaking about those with whom we do not agree. Although the theologian from Rochester was an ecumenical Christian and a kind spirit, I think he fell here into a common trap. When a person speaks or writes to their own people they are inclined to be less disciplined in their statements about those outside; they are more outspoken, and so less just. But there are strengths as well as weaknesses.

Strengths

As stated earlier, it may be said that in his 'Why I Am a Baptist' article Rauschenbusch did not present his Baptist convictions in a systematic way. Even the structure of his treatise does not convey the whole richness of thought that one can find there. Thus, I would like to offer my own key to the understanding of his perception of Baptist identity. I hope it will lead us to the bedrock principles of Rauschenbusch's statements on Baptist distinctives.

THE UNDENIABLE VALUE OF THE HUMAN PERSON

Throughout all his theological discourses, Rauschenbusch shows his concern for every human being, especially oppressed people, the neglected, the needy and the weak.[68] This anthropological concentration is motivated by his conviction that this is the attitude of God himself: to care for and to respect humans. Rauschenbusch's anthropology is ultimately God-orientated, because he wants to understand each of us *vis-à-vis* God. Only in having a relationship with God will humanity find its lost wholeness. But God is the God of real love, so he respects us and our autonomy: 'nothing has any value in the sight of God that is not the free outflow of the man's life. What would we care for the compulsory love of a wife or child?'.[69] Rauschenbusch would not be himself if he did not speak of the universal scope and, let us say, the egalitarian character of God's tenderness. Thus he says, 'Experience of God is open to the simplest mind.'[70] Here, in the way he understands God-given human dignity, he seems to see the deepest reasons for freedom of religion for

---

[67] See, e.g., *WB*, pp. 22, 25.

[68] See Rauschenbusch, *The Social Principles of Jesus, passim.*

[69] *WB*, p. 23.

[70] *WB*, p. 23.

everybody, for religious voluntarism,[71] and for democratic rule in the church[72] and in the state.[73] As we already noted, Rauschenbusch emphases his conviction that full human existence is almost impossible without social participation.

DIRECT ACCESS TO GOD

For the theologian of Rochester, God is the God who speaks: *Deus dixit*! Such a God invites each of us to dine with him: '[W]e want every man to go into that inner solitude of his own soul where no man can follow him, to hear the still small voice of the Eternal and to settle the past and the future with the great Father of his spirit.'[74] Hence, he says, Baptists 'confront the soul with God'.[75] Thus, Rauschenbusch calls for a relational understanding of Christianity, in terms of the 'I—Thou' relationship, where there should not be any interference and mediation: 'Christianity...is just a new life with God and a new life with men'.[76] This is why he opposes every kind of ceremonialism, sacramentalism and traditionalism, which he perceives rather as obstacles than as helps in religious life:[77] 'The great mass of men take their religion at second hand. Some strong religious soul in the past has had a real experience with God. He tells others about it; they believe it and then take their belief in his experience as a substitute for having any such experience themselves... It is no more religion than moon-light is sunlight.'[78]

RESTORATIONISM

This is one way to describe Rauschenbusch's desire to *restore* the proper shape of Christianity. He believes there is in fact something like 'genuine Christianity'[79] or 'true Christianity'.[80] For him there is no doubt that this can be found in 'primitive Christianity',[81] 'apostolic Christianity',[82] or 'original Christianity'.[83] So he calls us to 'go back' to it. This is his Protestant and Baptist call, *ad fontes*. The theologian of Rochester encourages us to return to the, as he calls it, 'least adulterated form' of Christianity. Practically, he finds this in the Bible, since he clearly believes in the irreplaceable role of the scriptures. For Rauschenbusch, 'These books are the deposit

---

[71] *WB*, p. 22: 'Experimental religion is necessarily free and voluntary.'
[72] *WB*, p. 25: 'Our people are sovereign in them [churches].'
[73] *WB*, p. 25.
[74] *WB*, p. 24.
[75] *WB*, p. 22.
[76] *WB*, p. 23.
[77] *WB*, p. 21: '[S]ome religious bodies...hinder the soul from finding God more than they help it'; *WB*, p. 28: '[B]ut the saving power was largely in spite of what was called Christian worship, and not by means of it.'
[78] *WB*, p. 22.
[79] *WB*, p. 21.
[80] *WB*, p. 28.
[81] *WB*, p. 25.
[82] *WB*, p. 25.
[83] *WB*, p. 23.

of the purest and freshest form of Christianity. It is the mountain-brook before it had grown muddy in the plain by the inflow of other waters…. [The Bible] is still calling us up higher today beyond traditional Christianity to the religion of Christ… Baptists, in tying to the New Testament, have hitched their chariot to a star, and they will have to keep moving.'[84] Let us carefully note that for him the focus is the New Testament, since he offers only New Testament restorationism.

UNITY IN ESSENTIALS AND LIBERTY IN MATTERS OF SECONDARY IMPORTANCE

As Rauschenbusch sought to discern the development of the revelatory deeds of God, differentiating between the role of the Old and New Testaments for Christians, so he set out a hierarchy of truths and values. Therefore, he speaks about essentials and matters of secondary importance. We find that in his article he stipulates 'what is essential in the religious and ethical life',[85] what he perceives as 'fundamental',[86] as the 'most essential and abiding thing',[87] and as 'the only essential thing in religion'.[88] He advocates freedom in secondary concerns, freedom which was demanded by the dignity of the individual, who has the right to be different also in indifferent matters. As someone who was the subject of fiery attacks from opponents, he was practically expressing an early Christian conviction that 'in the primary matters let there be unity, in the secondary liberty, but in everything love'.

THE INSTRUMENTAL ROLE OF THE BIBLE, OF THE ELEMENTS OF CHURCH LIFE AND OF DENOMINATIONAL IDENTITY

Since Rauschenbusch stresses the relational nature of Christianity, that is communion between persons, he sees the scriptures, church structures, offices, ordinances and denominational values as designed to support our direct and lively relationship with God. All these institutions should point beyond themselves to what has ultimate worth: God and human beings bound together in the bonds of love. Nothing besides that has ultimate and absolute importance. 'The Christian Church…is not an end in itself. It is always a means to an end. It is to create and foster the religious life in the individual…'.[89] Or, 'The Bible merely helps us to see if it [the church] is Christian.'[90] Also our Baptist identity is a temporary help to keep us on the proper track of discipleship.

Knowing all this, Rauschenbusch suggests, we can be constructively critical about Baptist identity: 'I do not want to foster Baptist self-conceit, because thereby I should grieve the spirit of Christ. I do not want to make Baptists shut themselves up in their little clam shells and be indifferent to the ocean outside them. I am a Baptist, but I am more than a Baptist… The old Adam is a strict denominationalist; the new

---

[84] *WB*, p. 31.
[85] *WB*, p. 21.
[86] *WB*, p. 21: '[E]xperience…it is fundamental in our church life.'
[87] *WB*, p. 23.
[88] *WB*, p. 23: '[P]ersonal religion as the only essential thing in religion.'
[89] *WB*, p. 24.
[90] *WB*, p. 25.

Adam is just a Christian.'[91] Thus, Rauschenbusch puts into practice a tenet that Paul Tillich later called 'A Protestant Principle'.[92] However, we must clearly state that this kind of approach is attractive only to a person or to communities certain that they are in possession of greater riches than the holy books, local church structures or denominations. They know that they prize most highly a relationship with God, who gave the Bible, who uses the church, and who ministers through humble and self-reforming denominations. And if they have such a God they have everything in its place: the Bible, churches and denominational identity. This God who came to the world in Christ is the 'canon in the canon', the 'core of the core', the 'heart of the heart'—whether in the Bible, in the church and in denominational identity.

Conclusion

For Rauschenbusch, 'Baptists have a magnificent body of truth—free, vital, honest, spiritual and wholly in line with the noblest tendencies of our age.'[93] This truth had to do with the value of the individual and personal experience, and with the value of the community. Thus, Baptists should fight for maintaining the interrelation between individual freedom and trans-personal solidarity that combats evil and egoistic individualism within an ordered and democratic society. Rauschenbush believed there must be an ethical verification of religious life.[94] Central to Baptist principles, in Rauschenbusch's thought, was a strong identification with the 'ethical passion of primitive Christianity'.[95] He believed that there could not be a real Christian life without the empirical manifestation of that in the daily life. Positive moral attitudes, he believed, provide ethical legitimization to one's religion. This could lead to theological weaknesses, as I have argued, but it has to be seen in the context of a focus on Christ. Here is one final, moving thought from Rauschenbusch:

> [T]he only thing that God really cares for, is a Christ-like life. To live all the time in the consciousness of the love and nearness of God, to merge all our desires and purposes in His will to walk humbly before him and justly and lovingly with all men this is the real Christian worship... A loving and pure life is the true liturgy of Christian worship. The life of Jesus was as full of religion as a nightingale is full of song or a rose full of fragrance.[96]

---

[91] *WB*, p. 31.

[92] See Paul Tillich, *The Protestant Era* (Chicago, IL: The Univeristy of Chicago Press, 1948).

[93] *WB*, p. 21.

[94] Rauschenbusch, *The Social Principles of Jesus*, p. 38.

[95] Rauschenbusch, *Christianity and the Social Crisis*, p. 177.

[96] *WB*, p. 28.

CHAPTER 13

Baptists in Black and White: Evangelical Diversity during the Montgomery, Alabama, Bus Boycott

Wayne Flynt

Many factors separate Baptists worldwide into diverse religious communities. Theology, nationality, language, education, gender, and class all operate to shape a denominational family that appears to be sometimes anarchical, often times chaotic, and continuously dysfunctional. What I propose to do is add a racial dimension to this discussion.

The setting for my story is a familiar one: Montgomery, Alabama, in 1955–56, at the point of origin for the modern American Civil Rights Movement. At that time, two of every three church members, in this most Bible-oriented of all Bible Belt American states, was Baptist, either black or white. Once upon a time, before the Civil War, they worshipped in the same churches. After the war, blacks left white Baptist churches en masse, seeking congregations that promoted black leadership, worship styles, music, and expression.

For both the state's white and black Baptists, Montgomery became an unofficial capital. From earliest settlement, the central Alabama plantation belt produced the state's most affluent white Baptists. Their leaders played a major role in the campaigns to defend slavery, promote missions and public education, and to establish a separate Southern Baptist Convention. Montgomery's First Baptist Church, located only a few blocks west of the state capitol, was arguably the state's leading white congregation during the nineteenth century, several times hosting national meetings of the Southern Baptist Convention. Its membership drew heavily from influential public employees, state officials, and leading politicians.

Equi-distant from the capitol to the north was First Colored Baptist Church, which furnished both the venue and leadership for the 1880 establishment of the National Baptist Convention, Inc., which would eventually become the nation's largest African American religious organization. As the black migrations of 1915–1930 and 1940–1960 spread African Americans from the deep South into the Great Lakes industrial states, the church essentially replicated itself in Chicago, Cleveland, and a dozen other midwestern cities.

Even closer to the capitol, Dexter Avenue Baptist Church afforded elite blacks a congenial home. Historically pastored by the denomination's intellectual and social stars, Dexter Avenue never rivaled First Colored Baptist in size, but greatly exceeded it in influence. Many of Dexter's members were black professionals or were faculty and administrators at nearby Alabama State University. Among the church's pastors in the 1950s was Vernon Johns, a graduate of Virginia College and Seminary and Oberlin School of Theology. At Oberlin, Johns had come under the influence of Social Gospel professors and ideas. From the pulpit of the Dexter Avenue church, he preached a gospel of militant activism, black economic solidarity, and strong aversion to black class divisions. Until his departure from Montgomery, on the eve of the Brown decision, Johns stayed in trouble either with his congregation or local whites for his outspoken sermons boldly advertised on the bulletin board in front of the church such as: 'Will There Be Segregation in Heaven?' and 'It is Safe to Murder Negroes in Montgomery'. Twice Johns provoked racial incidents: once when he refused to give up his seat on a city bus when ordered to do so; and again when he entered a white restaurant and ordered a sandwich.

Despite some qualms about Johns' confrontational ideology, some members of the congregation were as determined as their pastor to initiate change. Dr Mary Fair Burks, chair of the English department at Alabama State, led a group of Dexter Avenue church women to organize the Women's Political Council, which sought to register black voters.

Of course, it is not the Rev. Johns or Dexter's church women who are best remembered in this story. It is Martin Luther King, Jr, a young graduate student who became pastor of the church in 1954. But even King conceded that Johns had done the hard work of raising the consciousness of his congregation about racial injustice and the obligation of the church to confront it.

The central role of black Baptist pastors in the unfolding Civil Rights Movement has theological, ecclesiastical, and social explanations. Pastors were almost alone within the black community in their independence from white control. Congregations provided their livelihood and insisted they be responsive to black aspirations. And black Baptist pastors had no bishops or hierarchy through which whites could influence them.

African American theology centered on the exodus event: God was a deliverer of his people from bondage. For a half-million black Baptists living in oppression within the state's borders, this message had immediate and current relevance. The bondage was no longer slavery in Egypt but segregation in the American South.

Separate from theology, black and white Baptists developed separate civil religions. Both groups of Baptists were biblicists who sought individual conversion, supported missions, and shared similar beliefs about church polity. Both also emphasized personal sin, guilt, repentance, being born again, and the need to demonstrate repentance by righteous living.

But whereas proof of new birth to black Baptists was social justice linked to personal righteousness, white Baptists were quite content to define righteousness exclusively in terms of personal conduct.[1] Thus, the black church proclaimed a prophetic message of liberation and social transformation, while the white church

---

[1] Andrew M. Manis, *Southern Civil Religions in Conflict: Black and White Baptists and Civil Religion, 1947–1957* (Athens, GA: University of Georgia Press, 1987), p. 27.

proclaimed a message of resisting change and endorsing the political, economic, and social status quo. Alabama Baptists used conflicting civil religions both to legitimatize racist Alabama society and to subvert it.

Among black Baptists in Montgomery differences in class, race, gender, theology, and even personal ambition played roles in the unfolding Civil Rights drama.

No better evidence of the divergence of these sharply contrasting biblical visions can be found than in the events in Montgomery during the decade between 1955 and 1970. After Rosa Parks' arrest for violating a city ordinance restricting black seating on city buses, the Women's Political Council called for a boycott of the bus system. A mass meeting on Monday evening, 5 December 1955, at Holt Street Baptist Church, finalized plans for the boycott. Holt Street's pastor, A.W. Wilson, was also vice president of the black Alabama Baptist State Convention. At that meeting, black Baptists sang an anthem not of the movement, but of the historic church, 'Leaning on the Everlasting Arms'; lyrics that spoke of unity, confidence in God, and ultimate vindication:

> What a fellowship, what a joy divine,
> Leaning on the everlasting arms;
> What a blessedness, what a peace is mine,
> Leaning on the everlasting arms;
> What have I to dread, what have I to fear,
> Leaning on the everlasting arms?
> I have blessed peace with my Lord so near,
> Leaning on the everlasting arms.

Ralph Abernathy, an Alabama native, graduate of Alabama State University, and pastor of First Colored Baptist Church, with a mainly working-class membership, spoke at Holt Street and at many subsequent mass rallies. His recurring theme was straight out of the New Testament on the power of redemptive suffering: '[Jesus] suffered the indignities of persecution by secular authority and eventually he suffered the humiliation and final agony of the cross. We, too, could suffer, and in so doing, share his martyrdom and rejoice in his resurrection. Whatever happened to us would happen to him. If we were killed, our blood would cry out from the earth for justice.'[2]

This vision permeated the black masses. When a bomb destroyed Abernathy's church, the pastor stood heart-broken before his historic building, now reduced to rubble: windows shattered, beams splintered, walls caved in. Physically ill over destruction that he believed his activism had wrought on his congregation, Abernathy preached the following Sunday. When he finished, a female parishioner, Susie Beasley, sensed her pastor's distress and responded in the grand tradition of 'holding up' the pastor ('amen', 'uh huh,' 'that's right'):

---

[2] Ralph D. Abernathy, *And the Walls Came Tumbling Down: An Autobiography* (New York: Harper and Row, 1989), p. 157.

'The pastor appears to be burdened this morning, and no pastor can lead if he's burdened. So I want to reassure the pastor. When we were building this church, the forces that opposed us used to pass these grounds and say, "When unborn generations pass this spot, they will look at this hole in the ground where the First Baptist Church was supposed to have stood." They didn't think we could build such a church in the black community. But we built it!

And I want you to know pastor, that we will build it again. And if the Klan bombs it again, we are going to build it again. And again and again. God's church is going to stand.

So lead on, pastor. Don't be afraid. We are with you always.'[3]

It is debatable how Martin Luther King would have reacted to such a traditional black 'rousement'. Arriving in Montgomery as a twenty-five-year-old equipped with an exceptionally fine education at Atlanta's Morehouse College, Crozier Theological Seminary, and Boston University, King continued Dexter Avenue's heritage of cerebral Christianity. While a student at Morehouse, he had pondered whether the 'emotionalism' in Negro churches could be intellectually respectable, as well as emotionally satisfying.[4]

The influence of the Social Gospel and neo-orthodox theology had become central to his theology. As King wrote,

a religion true to its nature must also be concerned about man's social conditions. Religion deals with both earth and heaven, both time and eternity... It seeks not only to integrate men with God but to integrate men with men and each man with himself... Any religion that professes to be concerned with the souls of men and is not concerned with slums that damn them, the economic conditions that strangle them, and the social conditions that cripple them is a dry-as-dust religion. Such a religion is the kind the Marxists like to see—an opiate of the people.[5]

Election as president of the newly formed Montgomery Improvement Association (MIA) and regular participation in the 1955–56 mass meetings put King back in touch with the folk roots of black Baptist religion. Historians are nearly unanimous in attributing the success of the Civil Rights Movement to its capacity to generate and sustain a mass movement within black churches. From among such pastors of these churches, King found lieutenants who established the Southern Christian Leadership Conference (SCLC). Although King could be profound when occasion demanded, as when speaking on the mall in Washington or writing his letter from the Birmingham jail, he increasingly recognized the power of emotional religion to

---

[3] Abernathy, *And the Walls Came Tumbling Down*, p. 187.
[4] Taylor Branch, *Parting the Waters: America in the King Years, 1954–63* (New York: Simon and Schuster, 1988), p. 62.
[5] Martin Luther King, Jr, *Stride Toward Freedom: The Montgomery Story* (New York: Harper and Brothers, 1958), pp. 38, 91, 208.

rally a people and make God a personal combatant in a great cosmic struggle for justice.

Although they never occupied as prominent a platform, black Baptist women played a significant role in the bus boycott. Jo Ann Robinson, an English professor at Alabama State and a fervent Christian, served as president of the Women's Political Council. Zecozy Ausborn Williams worked on voter registration drives and the boycott. As an active member of Mount Calvary Baptist Church and a field worker for a regional grouping of twenty-seven black Baptist churches, she applied the organizing skills she learned in the church to Civil Rights activities.[6]

Not only were black Baptists divided along class lines, as the histories of First Colored Baptist and Dexter Avenue demonstrate, they also quarreled about tactics. Increasing militancy by King, Abernathy, Robinson and their colleagues, alienated more conservative and accommodationist leaders within the National Baptist Convention, USA (NBC). Jealousy over King's growing celebrity exacerbated the old grievances; and for some time moderizers within the NBC had challenged the long tenure and tight reign of the denomination's president, Joseph H. Jackson. Reformers, led by King, lost the power struggle for control of the convention. As a result, they organized the Progressive National Baptist Convention in 1961. Central to the ideology of the new group were term limits for convention officers and vigorous advocacy of civil rights.[7]

Such differences were just as pronounced among white Baptists in the capital city. Montgomery was not only the political capital of Alabama, it was also the capital of white Alabama Baptists. The State Baptist headquarters were located on the outskirts of the city, and prominent denominational officials were scattered among Montgomery's numerous Baptist churches. The denomination roundly denounced the bus boycott and urged gradualism in implementing the Brown Decision, which desegregated public schools. As the Southern Baptist Convention drifted toward increasing support of integration, Alabama Baptists directed their criticism at liberalizing forces within the denomination by threatening to withhold cooperative program contributions unless denominational leaders relented in their efforts to desegregate.

Of course, not all white Baptists were of one mind about race. Substantial numbers of pastors, professors at the state's two Baptist colleges, and lay people took a more moderate stance. In 1961, state headquarters hired Dr H.O. Hester to head a new department of special missions. Bringing a strong commitment to social justice to the job, Hester quietly began bi-racial meetings and projects. He urged

---

[6] Zecozy Ausborn Williams, 'Oral history by Louisa Weinrib', 31 August 1989, Montgomery League of Women Voters Oral History Project, Auburn University Archives, Auburn, Alabama.

[7] Wilson Fallin, Jr, 'Civil Rights Movement and Reorganization, 1954–1970' from a forthcoming chapter of a book on black Alabama Baptists, provisionally entitled *Uplifting the People: Black Baptists in Alabama, 1701–2000* (Tuscaloosa, AL: University of Alabama Press, forthcoming). I am grateful to the author, who is the historian of the National Baptist Convention, USA, for sharing these insights with me.

white Baptists to avoid racial stereotypes and insisted that bi-racial work be truly cooperative, not paternalistic. He persuaded the state convention and the SBC Home Mission Board to employ A.W. Wilson, who, as vice president of the Colored Baptist State Convention, had been one of King's key lieutenants during the bus boycott.[8]

By no means did most white Baptists share Hester's moderate racial opinions. Henry L. Lyon, Jr, pastor of Montgomery's Highland Avenue Baptist Church, built his congregation to more than 3,000 members by 1961, making the church the largest in the capital city. His success resulted in his election as president of the state convention in 1955 and re-election the following year. He was among the state denomination's most influential leaders and certainly one of its premier segregationists. He spoke frequently at Citizens' Council rallies and proudly wore the sobriquet, 'High Priest of Segregation'.

Lyon used his popular radio program to mount a full-scale assault on integration. According to his account, he had received a call from God to defend segregation as he was poised to preach a sermon during the bus boycott. He interpreted his election as convention president as confirmation of this calling. God's message had been clear: segregation 'was good and morally right for humanity in every respect' and was the 'commandment and law of God'. In a 1957 television interview, Lyon proclaimed racial segregation to be 'one of the principal teachings of the Holy Bible', and urged Christians to use 'every legal means' to preserve it and the states' rights. If all else failed, he urged Alabamians to close public schools because integration would lead inevitably to racial amalgamation.

Lyon quickly enlarged his following beyond Montgomery. He helped organize the segregationist Baptist Laymen of Alabama, and newly-elected governor, George C. Wallace, invited Lyon to offer the invocation at his January 1963 inauguration. The prayer was a classic expression of southern white civil religion, invoking the Confederacy, southern ancestry, states' rights, nationalism, and the US Constitution:

Almighty God...we thank thee for this glorious occasion which brings us to this sacred place, the cradle of the Confederacy—where in the yesterdays, our ancestors dedicated themselves to the cause of states' rights and freedom for the souls of men.

We beseech thee for strength as sons and daughters of the sovereign state of Alabama that we may pledge anew our allegiance to the flag of the United States of America. Fill our souls with unflinching courage as we join hand and heart with all friends of democracy to preserve the Constitution of our great nation. May we rather die than surrender this God-given heritage.[9]

---

[8] 'Report to Administration Committee and Executive Board', Alabama Baptist State Convention, 9-10 December 1965, from Department of Special Missions, Samford University Archives; *Alabama Baptist*, 28 September 1961, 4 July 1968.

[9] Henry Lyon, Jr, 'Is Racial Segregation Christian? What Is the Position of the Minister of the Gospel?', *Alabama Bible Society Quarterly* 14 (July, 1958), pp. 21-23; Dr Henry L. Lyon, Jr, interview by WSFA-TV, transcript copy in Hudson Baggett Papers,

Just to make sure God was fully informed about current events in America, Lyon added a prayerful postscript: 'Our Father, in our day formal public prayers in public schools have been declared unconstitutional. Take us back to the example set by the framers of our Constitution.' In its own way, Lyon's prayer was as much a gesture of spiritual defiance as Wallace's more famous political proclamation that cold January inaugural day of 'segregation today, segregation tomorrow, segregation forever'.[10] Wallace was delighted with the prayer. A few months later, he congratulated Lyon for helping rescue Alabama churches 'from the hands of preachers who are brainwashing the people with their message of racial integration'.[11]

Whether because of Lyon's influence or contiguous to it, an incident at Montgomery's Normandale Baptist Church put a tragically personal face on the city's racial divisions. A young black woman settled in the capital after living in the Midwest. She had visited Normandale several times with her baby and decided to join because it was more like her previous church than the city's African American congregations. The embarrassed pastor visited her and explained that the congregation did not want her. Deacons subsequently presented a resolution denying membership to blacks and allowing no debate on the matter. The motion carried by a small majority. As a result, some church members left to join other parishes. Some state convention staff decided to remain, in fear of possibly losing their jobs, others perhaps because they hoped slowly to change church policy. Lifetime relationships were damaged and the congregation divided.[12] It would not be the last time white Baptist churches fought and split over issues of race. But the tragedy was no less real for its increasing frequency.

So deeply did Montgomery's black and white Baptists divide, that even the nation's most famous evangelist could not bring them together. Billy Graham hoped his appearance in the city during the turmoil of the 1965 Selma-to-Montgomery march could help heal racial wounds. As with all his urban rallies, Graham insisted this one in the cradle of the Confederacy be integrated. Many white Baptists resented this condition as much as they admired Graham personally. The local white ministerial association did not issue an invitation to Graham, usually a requirement for his rallies, and many state officials boycotted his appearance. Leon Macon, segregationist editor of the *Alabama Baptist*, the state's second largest circulating newspaper, publicly praised Graham (he 'stuck to preaching the Gospel'), but privately complained that the world-famous evangelist reduced his influence by

---

Samford University (3 November 1957); Henry L. Lyon, Jr, 'Racial Agitation in Montgomery', *Alabama Bible Society Quarterly* 17 (July, 1961), pp. 60-61.

[10] Henry L. Lyon, Jr, to Leon Macon, 12 January 1963, Leon Macon Papers, Samford University.

[11] Stephan Lesher, *George Wallace: American Populist* (New York: Addison-Wesley, 1994), p. 206.

[12] Wendell F. Wentz diary and 'It Happened in Alabama', manuscript by Wendell F. Wentz both in Wendell F. Wentz papers, Samford University Archives. Earl Hall, who pastored the church during the 1970s, disputes some details of the incidents Wentz describes.

public statements on 'political and social situations'. Macon advised his twenty-year-old son not to attend Graham's integrated services. Although the convention's executive secretary appeared on the platform to welcome Graham, he did so uneasily, privately complaining that President Lyndon Johnson had engineered the invitation. A Billy Graham crusade designed to bring Baptists and Montgomerians together may well have driven them farther apart.[13]

The moral of this story is a sad one. People who share the name Baptist can act in such contradictory ways that the name of the denomination seems to be all they share. Although Baptists often act as if theology is the defining characteristic of their identity, here is a case where two groups of Baptists who share fundamentalistic theology fiercely differed. Clearly, in Montgomery during the 1950s and 1960s, race trumped all other issues, leaving a legacy of bitterness and schism that remains unhealed to this day.[14]

[13] *Alabama Baptist*, 24 June 1965; Leon Macon to Mrs P.D. Gates, 10 May 1965 and Macon to K.G. Purcell, 9 February 1965 both in Leon Macon papers, Samford University Archives; George E. Bagley, *Four Decades with Alabama Baptists: An Oral History Memoir* (Birmingham: Alabama Baptist Historical Commission), p. 204.

[14] For more about this subject, see Wayne Flynt, *Alabama Baptists: Southern Baptists in the Heart of Dixie* (Tuscaloosa, AL: University of Alabama Press, 1998).

CHAPTER 14

Women, Ministry and Identity: Establishing Female Deacons at First Baptist Church, Waco, 1996

William L. Pitts, Jr

Introduction

Numerous factors contribute to understanding Baptist identity, including theology, ethnicity, class, region, and political environment. This chapter focuses on changing gender roles in Baptist leadership as part of the evolving identity of Baptists. In 1996 First Baptist Church, Waco, Texas, ordained its first women deacons—Doris Smith and Amanda Smith (not related). The church, once seen as socially conservative, has moved rapidly to elect many more women to this leadership position. In 2003 twenty-four of the 130 deacons of the church were women.[1] Additional women have been selected as deacons every year since the process began.

Thesis and Sources

This chapter documents a major change in one local Baptist church. The research relies primarily on interviews with six key participants—four women deacons (Doris Smith, Amanda Smith, Doriss Hambrick and Anita Rolf), the pastor (Dr Scott Walker), and a former deacon chairman (Alton Pearson). The author also cites other participants in the process, as well as records of deacons' meetings and policy papers adopted by the church. The story not only addresses a significant change at First Baptist Church, Waco; it may also be viewed as a case study important to current Baptist identity—a change other Baptist churches today face: to adopt, to reject, or to avoid including women deacons. Significant new opportunities opened for women in the United States in the 1960s.[2] Acceptance of women in church leadership roles was part of that social change.[3] On the other hand, it is a change which still seems

---

[1] The church has both active and inactive deacons. In April 2004 ninety of the deacons were active. The church membership at the same time was about 2,000 members.

[2] The ideas of the women's movement are most frequently traced to Betty Friedan's *The Feminine Mystique* (New York: Dell, 1962).

[3] The movement in the churches gathered much momentum in the 1980s. See E.A. Livingstone (ed.), *Concise Dictionary of the Christian Church* (Oxford: Oxford University press, 2000), s.v. 'Feminist Theology'.

---

novel in the practice of most Baptist churches in the southern states of the United States.

Precedents

Precedents for women deacons at First Baptist, Waco, may be found in the church well over 100 years ago. In 1877, B.H. Carroll, pastor of the church, not only argued that women deacons were biblical, he also supported the office of women deacons in the church. They served in several capacities, but they served without ordination. Members now regularly cite this precedent. In addition, several Waco churches—both Baptist and non-Baptist—began to ordain women as deacons in the 1960s and following. In 1975, Lake Shore Baptist Church elected women deacons; Seventh and James Baptist Church followed in 1980.[4] Several of the interviewees cited the importance of this precedent in their thinking; others reported influence from female family members and friends who were serving as deacons in other cities.

Discussing New Directions

In order for the change to occur, the idea first had to be planted. Doris Smith remembers that one Wednesday night former pastor Peter McLeod asked members to think about possibilities for the future of the church. One of the possibilities he suggested was women deacons. Doris remembers a member who was terribly upset. She and her husband followed him out to the car to reassure him that this was just a possibility, not a proposal. Yet this member left and immediately joined Columbus Avenue Baptist Church.[5] Alton Pearson mentioned that an example of the church's growing consciousness of the issue was a discussion in his Sunday School class led by Dr Bob Patterson, who teaches theology in the Department of Religion at Baylor University.[6] When she first heard the proposal to include women as deacons, Doriss Hambrick said she 'didn't think it would happen'.[7] She was surprised and sceptical about its implementation. And, ironically, Doris Smith, one of the first women elected, said it would 'never happen'.[8]

Why the high level of scepticism? Doriss Hambrick believes the answer lies in the influence of a traditional view of Southern culture and of Baptists in the South, both generally seen as socially conservative. In the church where she grew up, near

---

[4] Carol Crawford Holcomb has thoroughly examined the beginning of the story at Seventh and James in 'Coming into a New Awareness: Women Deacons at Seventh and James Baptist Church', *Texas Baptist History* 18 (1988), pp. 1-26.

[5] Doris Smith, interview by author, 15 February 2001, tape recording, Oral History Memoir, Baylor University Institute for Oral History, Waco.

[6] Alton Pearson, interview by author, 27 February 2001, tape recording, Oral History Memoir, Baylor University Institute for Oral History, Waco.

[7] Doriss Hambrick, interview by author, 15 February 2001, tape recording, Oral History Memoir, Baylor University Institute for Oral History, Waco.

[8] D. Smith interview.

Amarillo, Texas, 'women didn't speak in church'. Moreover, 'they didn't ask to' do so.[9] They would sing in the choir and play instruments in church, and they would work in the Sunday School. But they took no formal leadership positions. This situation prevailed despite the fact that there were not enough men to carry out the tasks of the church. This understanding of Southern culture recurs in the interviews. It served to explain why women were not a part of the deacon body in the Baptist churches of the South.[10] The culture of male leadership in the churches prevailed. It was not challenged—by either men or women. Thus changing the church's practice and thought on this issue represents a decisive shift—a new model of leadership, authority, power and ministry in the local Baptist churches in the South. From the broad perspective of church history, it appears that over the past half century we have been witnessing and are participating in a major revolution in the organization and identity of Christian churches. This revolution is now influencing some Baptist churches in the southern United States.

The Pastor

The role of a new pastor was decisive in extending the diaconate to include women. Anita Rolf remembered exactly when the idea first dawned on her. She was part of the Pastor Search Committee that interviewed Scott Walker. In the process of the interviews, he indicated that he would support such a change. As she recalls it, this interview seems to have planted a seed in the minds of several church leaders and opened the door to change.[11] Walker accepted the invitation of the church to become its pastor in 1994. Several experiences had made him welcome women deacons. He grew up as a missionary child in the Philippines, where he experienced what he calls a 'macho' culture which was nevertheless greatly dependent on strong roles for women in the home. Moreover, in the fledgling Protestant churches in this Catholic society, the missionaries relied heavily on women to carry out church work. His seminary training (Southern Baptist Theological Seminary) supported women who were preparing for the ministry. F.F. Bruce, the British biblical scholar, had resolved the scriptural question for him: Bruce argued that there was no doubt that men and women both served as deacons in the early New Testament church.[12] Finally, Walker's earlier pastorates were carried out in congregations in Athens, Georgia and Charleston, South Carolina, which had included women deacons.[13] Thus by training, practice and conviction the new pastor was prepared to support the change.

---

[9] Hambrick interview.

[10] Pearson interview; also see Anita Rolf interview by author, 13 February 2001, tape recording, Oral History Memoir, Baylor University Institute for Oral History, Waco.

[11] Rolf interview.

[12] See, e.g., F.F. Bruce, *Answers to Questions* (Exeter: Paternoster Press, 1972), p. 184.

[13] Scott Walker, interview by author, 8 February 2001, tape recording, Oral History Memoir, Baylor University Institute for Oral History, Waco.

Scott Walker was apprehensive about the issue.[14] While supportive of a gender inclusive team of deacons, Walker says he did not want to appear to be pushing an agenda. The issue was being seriously discussed within eighteen months of his arrival. He did worry about timing.[15] In Amanda Smith's view, the new 'vision' brought to the church by the pastor was essential for the change to occur. Someone had to have the idea and to provide leadership in the process. She says that Walker was the initiator and the driving force.[16] Walker, on the other hand, attributes the shift to lay leadership.[17] Lay leadership did, in fact, prove to be critical to the process.

Committee and Deacons

In order to move from idea to practice, the proposal would have to be developed and accepted in three stages: committee, deacons and church. In 1994 the deacon chair, Kent Starr, appointed a committee to re-examine criteria for deacon selection. The issue had been debated repeatedly in the preceding two decades. The same criteria surfaced with each new group nominated. Does the candidate drink alcoholic beverage? Does the candidate tithe? Has the candidate ever been divorced? The committee always came back to a traditional list of criteria.

The Committee Report

Kent Starr appointed Clyde Hart to chair the committee. Former deacon chair, Alton Pearson, thought this was an ideal choice since Hart, Baylor track coach, was accustomed to working in compliance with 'a lot of regulations'. Clyde Hart, Pearson thought, could be objective in applying the guidelines of the church. Clyde's father was a Baptist minister, now in his 90s, who supported women deacons.[18] The committee met for eighteen months. When the committee redrew the deacon selection policy document it did not focus on the specifics of alcohol, the tithe or divorce. The document says that the purpose of the deacon is to be a servant, and it cites, instead of particulars, the general biblical criteria of 'good reputation, full of the Spirit and of wisdom' (Acts 6.3). The policy makes specific mention of women deacons. In the section on transfer deacons the document reads, 'A deacon who has been ordained by another Baptist church and has transferred his or her membership to First Baptist Church of Waco may also be recommended to the

---

[14] Pearson interview.

[15] Walker interview.

[16] Amanda Smith, interview by author, 22 February 2001, tape recording, Oral History Memoir, Baylor University Institute for Oral History, Waco. She credits Larry Maddox, the church's assistant pastor, with a key leadership role. She believes, moreover, that general staff support of the idea was essential for the change to occur.

[17] Walker interview.

[18] Pearson interview.

Deacon Selection Committee.'[19] Thus the issue had already been discussed in committee: women as well as men were envisaged in the deacon transfer process, thereby opening the way for electing women as deacons.

The Deacons

Alton Pearson, retired president of Hillcrest Baptist Hospital, became chairman of the deacons during this period. He is credited by many interviewees with providing leadership essential in leading the church through the process of creating women deacons. Pearson took a broad view of deacon selection. He says bluntly, 'We needed new blood. I looked at that crowd, and they were old. We needed young men, and we needed women.' Thus he presented a pragmatic argument which included women. He also provided practical procedural advice when he suggested that the church survey the practice of other churches. Third, he noted that he had worked with women in hospital/healing roles and found them capable. 'Deacons', he said, 'are for service, not to run the church'; he resisted the image of a board of deacons that exists merely to make financial decisions. Fourth, he resolved the hermeneutical question. When looking to the Bible for guidance, he held strongly to the sentiment that people should not sit in judgment of one another. He noted that divorce is now common in American society, and that we have many people who, although divorced, can serve well. Fifth and finally, he noted that the committee had created a provision for active and inactive deacons, thereby allowing people to remain deacons in name but withdraw from active service if they disapproved of the change.[20]

Debate in Deacons' Meeting

The new policy proposal came before the deacons on 13 May 1996. Chairman Clyde Hart recommended adoption of the policy. One deacon asked for the inclusion of the traditional biblical texts, Acts 6.16 and 1 Timothy 3.8-13. The deacons accepted his amendment.[21] Another deacon gave the minority report from the committee. He thought it was a mistake to emphasize broad general criteria. He said this policy would open the way to selection of 'mediocre people'. A third deacon read out the Timothy passage and simply said, 'My Bible tells me these are the requirements'. The pastor spoke to the issue, emphasizing that although the committee members did not all agree, they were seeking to find common ground in order 'to give a unified direction to the church'.[22] The deacons voted on the deacon policy document; it passed forty-one to seventeen. The minutes do not record any discussion of women. A two-thirds majority was required for policy changes. The drafters included the biblical texts but chose the broader requirement of 'good reputation' for deacons,

---

[19] Policy for the Election and Tenure of Deacons, First Baptist Church of Waco, Texas, 22 May 1966, p. 2.
[20] Pearson interview.
[21] Deacon Minutes, 13 May 1996, p. 1.
[22] Deacon Minutes, 13 May 1996, p. 3.

thereby shifting qualifications from specific disqualifiers to service as the key criterion, and in so doing opened the way for women to serve as deacons. The church and the deacon selection committee would immediately turn to women to serve—but not before public airing of the issue.

Response of the Church

The final stage in the process was acceptance by the entire church.

Public Hearing

Since the new policy specifically mentioned the possibility of women deacons for the church, the pastor resolved to have an open public discussion of the issue. He said that creating an appropriate review process was critical for acceptance of change. He was especially concerned that the church stay together through this process.[23] The church devoted a Sunday evening service to discussion. Microphones were placed in the aisles of the church, and the pastor encouraged everyone who desired to speak to do so. Many people remarked on the open character of the hearing; Pearson and others believe that it was the key to the church's acceptance of the new policy.[24]

Support Expressed

When the proposal was read, long-time First Baptist member Emmy Parrish said in a very audible aside, 'It's about time!' Amanda Smith recalled that the meeting was 'never a contested thing'.[25] Pearson recalls positive support for the document from retired religion professor Eddie Dwyer.[26] Doris Smith says that 'everyone who wanted to stood and talked'.[27] Most of the public comment was favourable.

Resistance Expressed

Resistance to the proposal which had surfaced in the deacon's meeting, however, carried over into the public discussion. Now occurred what seemed to all of the interviewees the most surprising development in the course of the process. Voiced opposition came from young people in the church, chiefly those in their 30s.[28] They were typically young marrieds with children. The rationale for objecting to the proposed policy centered on two issues according to Amanda Smith: biblical

---

[23] Walker interview. The concern to preserve unity and peace in the church directly affected this research: interviewees refused to name opponents of the new policy or families that left the church.

[24] See Pearson, Rolf, and D. Smith interviews.

[25] A. Smith interview.

[26] Pearson interview.

[27] D. Smith interview.

[28] See Pearson, A. Smith and D. Smith interviews.

interpretation and belief in the tradition of the subservience of the wife.[29] Pearson used slightly different language: 'It was just the idea that the man is the head of the house.'[30] Doris Smith reflected on the biblical issue. She said, 'They quoted the Bible. But you know you can make your point on both sides from the Bible. They didn't make me mad because they were honest about it [their convictions].'[31] Pearson also observed that the opposition expressed was 'not ugly'.[32]

Four issues clearly emerged in analyzing the dynamics of this public forum. First, how will scripture be used? Over and over in the history of the church an interpretation shapes thought and practice only to be challenged; reformers have always sought biblical justification for their reinterpretations. Second, the cultural traditions of male dominance were at issue. The highly committed active young members had apparently seen only male leadership in their home churches as they grew up. No other model had been considered. Third, the older church members had wider exposure to a variety of practices and were willing to support the proposal. The debate was centred, then, not only on scripture and gender; it was also shaped by age differences. Fourth, it was especially important to participants that the church preserve as much unity and harmony as possible. Thus decorum prevailed in the meeting despite strong convictions held on both sides.

Walker says that when the vote was taken about 90% voted for it and 10% against it. He thought that the church lost only two families as a result of adopting the new policy.[33]

Women Selected as Deacons

The inclusive new policy was implemented at once. The procedure for deacon selection allowed for any church member to nominate any other church member. In the next round of nominations two women's names surfaced repeatedly: Doris Smith and Amanda Smith. These two women were nominated by the committee, approved by the deacons, and elected and ordained by the church.

Doris Smith had worked in the church all her life. She enjoyed young children and had spent years working with four-year olds. In the 1960s she and other women of the church created what has since been known as the 'Sewing Class', an inner city ministry. Doris' sister and her daughter were both in churches with women deacons. Her attorney husband, Vernon, had served as chair of the deacons. When asked to serve as a deacon, she had reservations. She thought younger women should have the opportunity. She believed that they would attract others to the church. She was pressed by the pastor to serve and said, 'All right, but I can't be as energetic as I

---

[29] A. Smith interview.
[30] Pearson interview.
[31] D. Smith interview.
[32] Pearson interview.
[33] Walker interview.

used to be. But maybe it's good to have an older person because no one is going to get mad at me.'[34]

Amanda Smith recalls that when she was asked to serve she was shocked and humbled. Her memory of her interview with the pastor was important. They talked about qualifications but especially about a new programme in which every deacon would be asked to pick an area of active service and participate in a particular ministry. He convinced her that she was needed, especially for ministry to women.[35]

Consequences

The church experienced both immediate and long term consequences of this important decision.

Immediate Consequences

How would this change affect the unity of the church? What specific roles for women were available? What personal impact would ordination have on these women?

CHURCH UNITY

The most obvious evidence of discontent in church is whether members leave in protest. Interviewees remembered only one or two families who left. Amanda Smith said that the greatest regret she has is that 'we lost a very strong family'. Yet she also emphasized a point that no one else made. She said that earlier First Baptist Church had also lost a family by *not* having women deacons. Her neighbours had moved from First Baptist to St Paul's Episcopal Church because they wanted full participation opportunities for their young daughters. Amanda was also aware that 'we lost a few active deacons to inactive status as a result [of the policy change]'. She also recalls that when she served communion, one man changed places with another, apparently to avoid serving on the same row with her.[36] On the other hand, all of the women deacons interviewed named men who spoke a word of encouragement to them. There is no doubt that this change was marked by strong feelings. People adjusted one way or another, but no one could ignore the change that transpired.

INFLUENCE ON THE OTHER WOMEN IN THE CHURCH

Several interviewees said women church members expressed special appreciation for the fact that other women were now involved in serving them communion. This was perhaps the change most regularly commented on by general members of the congregation.[37]

---

[34] D. Smith interview.
[35] A. Smith interview.
[36] A. Smith interview.
[37] A. Smith interview.

PERSONAL IMPACT ON THE NEW DEACONESSES
The author was interested in the personal feelings of these new deacons. Doris Smith said that her Sunday night ordination was very moving—precisely the description I have heard from men for many years.[38]

Longer Term Consequences: Present and Future
Including women deacons meant that the church established important new patterns of governance, worship and service which would influence its practice for many years ahead.

WOMEN ADDRESSING WOMEN'S ISSUES
Doris Smith says that now when she hears a complaint or rumour from other women in Sunday School, such as 'They are spending on things we don't need', she intervenes to set the record straight. She is now able to defuse potential problems created by hearsay by simply reporting the facts because she has been present in the deacons' meeting where all the proposals are discussed.[39]

NURTURING
All of the interviewees talked about the newly adopted structured deacon ministry programme in which each deacon selects one of five ministries (hospital, bereavement, visitation, hospitality or missions). Each deaconess interviewed had developed a strong sense of vocational service through participation in one of these activities.

WOMEN IN MINISTRY
Clearly women will have a visible and vital role in deacon ministry in the future of First Baptist Church, Waco. Women have served on staff for a long time. They now have a fresh source of support in leadership from women deacons. When asked about a woman as chair of the deacons, Amanda Smith said that the idea should not be pushed for now. 'Give it time', she advised. People need time to get used to the current change.[40] When asked about this experience as a case study or example for other churches, Doriss Hambrick said that she would not have supported it if it had been highly divisive. She believed that it would still be a divisive issue for many Southern Baptist churches.[41] Women have been added to each class of deacons since 1996. Everyone interviewed believes the pattern will continue. The process also paved the way for the first ordination of a female minister in the church's history. In the autumn of 2000, the church ordained Rebecca Reynolds.[42]

---

[38] D. Smith interview. Laying on of hands and personal affirmation by many friends can hardly fail to make a powerful impression on the candidate.
[39] D. Smith interview.
[40] A. Smith interview.
[41] Hambrick interview.
[42] Pearson interview.

WOMEN IN WORSHIP

Part of women's increased role is their high visibility in worship. Women were already leading in worship by praying and reading scripture. Doriss Hambrick observed that since women have been ordained they now provide additional leadership by giving the welcome to the service, taking the offering, serving communion, and greeting guests at the end of the service. 'They're everywhere', she said.[43] Ordination has legitimated many new forms of leadership.

EMPOWERMENT

When asked to become a deacon, Doriss Hambrick exclaimed, 'O, my soul! I'll have to think about it.'[44] Her teenage daughter voted against the new policy, but Doris was influenced by Sally Firmin, her friend, who said, 'It's such a shame not to be able to serve in your own church.'[45] Doris said that she had two daughters, and that she wanted them to have a choice. The world was changing, and she was prepared to change with it—especially for the sake of the next generation of women, her daughters.[46]

When asked about other women who qualify but choose not to serve, the response is that some older women have too many responsibilities, especially care of their own mothers. And many younger women still resist accepting the role of deacons for cultural or biblical reasons.[47]

Doriss Hambrick observed that including a woman's perspective meant that some programmes important to women, such as daycare, now get more input and support. 'Women now know that money is available. Experience in the deacons' meetings helps them make decisions more readily.' She said that the older, limited vision was that 'we can only do what the earnings of the cookie sale will bring in'. Now they understood 'that they could help shape and approve the budget'.[48]

When the women deacon option was broached, Anita Rolf remembered thinking, 'I appreciate that; I'm not there.' However, when asked to serve she repeated to herself, 'You are being called by the church to serve. It may be wrong theologically, but you are being called.'[49] She accepted after a struggle. She served on the Deacon Selection Committee in 2000 and was delighted to see not only women but also the church's first Hispanic and first Black elected deacons. 'That was important to me', she concluded. Empowering women has paved the way to empowering others.[50] Liberation is at work at First Baptist Church, Waco.

Finally, women achieved a fuller level of empowerment in Waco Baptist churches when Julie Pennington-Russell was called as pastor of Calvary Baptist Church in

---

[43] Hambrick interview.
[44] Hambrick interview.
[45] Hambrick interview.
[46] Hambrick interview.
[47] A. Smith interview.
[48] Hambrick interview.
[49] Rolf interview.
[50] Rolf interview.

1998. She was the first woman to serve as senior pastor among Baptists in the state. Dorisanne Cooper followed only eighteen months later as senior pastor of Lake Shore Baptist Church.[51]

Conclusion
Causes of Change

Many factors were involved in bringing about this change. Leadership was critical—both clerical and lay. Concern for unity coupled with willingness to change were essential. A new hermeneutic had to be accepted by a large consensus of people. The new policy would not have been accepted if the people thought it was non-biblical.[52] The classic texts were reinterpreted and placed in a larger theological context that adopted the model of deacons as servants. This made it' much easier for women who were being asked to accept the new assignment. A fourth influence was the new programme for deacons which gave women and men specific opportunities for active service. A fifth factor was the pragmatic one. The older men may have earned their spurs years ago, but many were inactive and had finished their effective leadership of the church. The church needed new blood for many ministries it envisioned. Sixth, cultural forces were at work. Traditional roles which limited women's leadership in the South had been undergoing steady erosion for a generation, and other progressive churches had long since made the change.

An Evolving Identity

Levels of change are difficult to assess. Few people left the church. Yet everyone was forced to confront the issue and work through it. It is probably not a reversible issue; the policy is likely set for the future. To judge from the assessment of interviewees, substantial change has occurred, creating not merely a surface perception of change, but a profound shift in the lives of women and men in understanding the nature of this church. The women's revolution of the past generation has been one of the decisive shifts of modern history. It has many expressions, not least of which are the changes in identity we are experiencing in the churches.[53] First Baptist, Waco, was twenty years behind her sister church at Lake Shore in ordaining women as deacons. Other denominations had ordained women as deacons and ministers long before, and many have now moved to the question of gay ordination. From this perspective the church seems far behind the curve of social

---

[51] Terry Jo Ryan, 'Waco Native to Lead Church', *Waco Tribune Herald*, 4 December 2001, p. 1B.

[52] A. Smith interview.

[53] Many of the same issues surfaced in 1981–83 when First Baptist, Oklahoma City, made the decision to open the diaconate to women. See Gene Garrison, 'Our Process of Ordaining Women Deacons', *Folio* 3.1: *A Newsletter for Southern Baptist Women in Ministry* (Summer, 1985), pp. 3-4.

changes. On the other hand, relatively few Baptist churches in the South have taken the step to ordain women. From the perspective of ordained women deacons, First Baptist, Waco, is now clearly in the progressive camp, having affirmed leadership roles for women. This action took courage; members had to rethink the nature of the church—and their identity as Baptists.

PART 3

Global Baptist Identities

CHAPTER 15

Naga Baptists: A Brief Narrative of their Genesis[1]

Robert Eric Frykenberg

'one catches an elephant with an elephant and a quail with a quail'[2]
Vedanayakam Shastriar

High atop a peak on a projecting spur of a range of 'hills'—so called because all mountain ranges in South Asia pale in significance beside the mighty, snow-clad Himalayan peaks and ranges to the north—the tiny new village of New Molung came into being. Two thousand six hundred feet above the Assam Valley (nearly sea level) its inhabitants had a commanding view. Westward, just below freshly hewn log houses, a massive log gate, log palisades, and dry-moats full of up-turned spikes (*pongis*), were newly cleared fields for planting and grazing, lookout nests, dark and deep forests and ravines. These plunged downward over lesser hillocks and rushing streams to the valley floor where, on a bright day, corrugated iron roofs of tea estates could be seen glittering in the sun. Beyond these, across the shimmering bright green rice fields and waving belts of grasses, bamboos, and orchards, the mighty Brahmaputra resembled a vast ribbon of molten shining silver flowing hundreds of miles to the sea. And beyond this great river, more plains led to hill ranges, each mounting higher toward the skyline where, on a clear day, snow-clad peaks and ridges of the mighty Himalayas themselves glinted. If one turned south-eastwards behind the village, further mountain ridges could be seen, mounting rank on rank in the sun. Behind Molung eastward were more deep ravines, covered by wildly dense, never-ending forests that stretched all the way to the Chin and Kachin hills of Burma.[3]

---

[1] Credit is due to two of my former students, Richard M. Eaton and Christopher R. King, for superb research on this subject, begun as members of the South Asian History Seminar at the University of Wisconsin–Madison, many years ago.

[2] 'Twelve Arguments of the Divine Songsters', in D. Dennis Hudson (ed.), *Protestant Origins in India: Tamil Evangelical Christians, 1706–1835* (London: RoutledgeCurzon; Grand Rapids, MI: Eerdmans, 2000), p. 155.

[3] Mary Mead Clark, *A Corner of India* (Philadelphia, PA: American Baptist Publication Society, 1907/Gauhati: Christian Literature Society, 1978), 'Among the Clouds', pp. 35-39, a vivid description also of flora and fauna, both colourful and wild.

The year was 1876. Molung[4] was the very first wholly Christian community ever to be formed among Naga peoples. More than that, the colony was a 'Village of Refuge' (in a biblical sense). Its members, due to persecution, had recently left their homes in the much larger, sturdier and better defended village of Molung-kimong, and moved to an empty, uninhabited hilltop, three hours walk away.[5] But, to understand the significance of what had just happened one must glance back to a chain of events that had begun many years earlier.

I

The story of New Molung begins with Godhula. Godhula was a venturesome Assamese Christian evangelist who, along with his wife Lucy, a teacher, had for years held positions within the American Baptist mission. The eldest son of Koliber, a washerman (*dhobi*) of Shibsagar, seems to have come from a low-caste, disadvantaged background. Baptized Godhula Rufus Brown and educated at the Christian Orphan School in Nowagong, we may be justified in presuming that he owed much to the influence of Nathan Brown (1807–86),[6] and Miles Bronson (1812–83).[7] In early 1836, Nathan Brown, the very first American Baptist missionary to enter Assam (1835–55), had begun pioneer work in Sadiya, the uppermost point where the Brahmaputra disgorges from the Himalayas into the Assam Valley. But, after suffering many tragedies that ended, at last, with the Khampti uprising and massacre of the East India Company's garrison in 1839, the Sadiya mission had been abandoned. He had moved to Jaipur, and then to Sibsagar, where he had established Assam's first printing press and its first periodical publication, *Orunodoi*.[8] But a mission deputation from America, led by Dr Solomon, had made disruptive decisions that, in due course, had provoked Brown's resignation (after twenty years and many brilliant contributions) and Bronson's return to America (ostensibly on furlough), after having had to shut the Nowagong

---

[4] The full name of this village was Molung-yimsen (or 'New Molung'). See Joseph Puthenputakal, *Baptist Missions in Nagaland* (Calcutta: Firma KLM, 1984), p. 209 nn.1-2.

[5] Sources vary on whether the distance was three kilometers or three miles. In any case, one consequence for the new colony was that the mother village thereafter came to be known Molung-ymchen ('Old Molung'), as against Molung-yimsen ('New Molung').

[6] Eliza Whitney Brown, *The Whole World Kin: A Pioneer Experience Among Remote Tribes, and Other Labors of Nathan Brown* (Philadelphia, PA: Hubbard Brothers [1890]), pp. xvi, 607.

[7] Harriette Bronson Gunn, *In A Far Country: A Story of Christian Heroism and Achievement* (Philadelphia, PA: American Baptist Publication Society, [c.1911]), p. 244. Miles Bronson, an American Baptist Missionary, and his wife, Lucy.

[8] See Jayeeta Sharma, 'Missionaries and Print Culture in Nineteenth Century Assam: The *Orunodoi* Periodical of the American Baptist Mission', in Robert Eric Frykenberg (ed.), *Christians and Missionaries in India* (London: RoutledgeCurzon/Grand Rapids, MI: Eerdmans, 2003), pp. 256-73, for further understanding about the remarkable influence of this publication on the culture of modern Assam.

Orphan Institution he had established in 1843. Godhula and his wife, both of whom had been trained at Nowagong, the first co-educational institution to have been established in north-east India, owed much to these earliest missionaries. That the American Baptist missionaries had even entered Assam at all also owed much, in turn, to the Serampore (British Baptist) mission which, due to internal staff and funding problems, had agreed to relinquish work in Assam and Arracan to the American Baptists.[9]

II

It was in the river town of Shibsagar[10] that Godhula met Subongmeren. Subongmeren was an Ao Naga who had regularly come down into the valley to barter. There he was befriended and invited to live in the home of Godhula and his wife. Blessed and impressed by the hospitality of this Christian home, he had learned about the redeeming love of the almighty and everlasting God and of Jesus Christ as his personal Redeemer, Saviour and Master. Within a few months, he had accepted the gospel and become a baptized believer. His decision was no less pivotal for Godhula. Thereafter, as he heard Subongmeren speak about his own people in the hilltop village of Molung-kimong, as he learned about the fears and troubles of the village, and as he realized how much other Ao Nagas could benefit from hearing the gospel, Godhula thought that he himself, and perhaps even his wife, might be able to go up into the hills and live in the village of their Ao Naga friend.

For many months, Godhula worked with Subongmeren, endeavouring to learn as much as possible of the Ao Naga language. In October 1871, after finally convincing himself that he had acquired a sufficient mastery of the strange new tongue, Godhula embarked upon his venture.[11] With the blessing of Dr Edward Winter Clark and his wife Mary, American Baptist missionaries under whom he worked, he and his Ao Naga friend set out for the tea gardens at Amguri. There he met other Ao Nagas, several of them from Subongmeren's home village. But when these Ao Nagas learned of his wish to accompany them into the hills, to visit and perhaps even to live in their village, they tried to dissuade him. None of them were

---

[9] *Missionary Register* (1839), p. 139; and *Missionary Magazine* 19 (1839), pp. 3, 16. Victor Sword, *Baptists in Assam: A Century of Missionary Service, 1836-1936* (Chicago, IL: Conference Press, 1935), pp. 34-40. As early as 1819, William Carey had translated the New Testament, and by 1833, the whole Bible. Carey's first convert, Krishna Chandra Pal, had been the first missionary to go into Khasia Hills of Assam and through his efforts the first converts were baptized.

[10] 'Siva's Lake' (or 'Shiva's Ocean'), from which the town took its name, was a huge, square, man-made temple tank or reservoir, roughly a thousand yards on each side, around which streets, bazaars, and houses for inhabitants were built.

[11] People of Assam were, on the whole, terrified of Nagas, whom they associated with 'head-cutting' and the demons and devils inhabiting the dark unknown of the forest-clad mountains. Moreover, for centuries Assamese peoples had suffered countless predatory raids from Naga warriors, sometimes as many as four or five a year.

village officers (*tartars*), and they did not feel that they had the authority to bring a total stranger into the midst of their fortified village. Centuries of experience, and instincts for self-preservation, had taught Ao Nagas to be suspicious of all strangers. Most Ao Nagas had never submitted to alien rule, and were extremely jealous of their independence. But, when other Ao Nagas informed Godhula that they could not vouch for his safety, and did not know what might happen if they brought him to their village, Godhula persisted. Imploring them with pleas both compelling and importunate, they eventually agreed to take the 'foreigner' along. They even promised to guard him along the way and to take him to their village, but only on the condition that all of them would abide by whatever decisions the village officers might make.

The journey took two days. It required one night of sleeping in the forest, with campfires burning and guards standing watch. The following day, Godhula found himself clambering up slopes that 'no elephant or horse' could ever climb. After his arrival at Molung-kimong, he was immediately taken before the village elders and leaders. Despite his careful and deferential explanations, the village lords were not at all happy. For all they knew, he was a (British) 'Company' spy, someone who by guile had managed to talk his way into the village, someone who, after now having had an opportunity to assess defensive arrangements within the village, on which they depended for their very lives, could take such information to their enemies. As a consequence, Godhula was immediately placed in custody within a small hut, where guards stood watch, day and night, to make sure that he would not to escape.

Parenthetically, it may be appropriate to mention, at this point, the first missionaries to come into contact with Nagas in 1835–37. The Browns, Bronsons, and Cutters had come to the frontier town of Sadiya at the prior (1836) invitation of Captain (later Major) Francis Jenkins, the newly appointed Political Officer (Commissioner and Agent to the Governor-General) for Assam. Miles Bronson, having found Namsung Nagas more friendly than the Kamptis and Singpos, had spent a whole day at their village. But he had never assuaged suspicions that he was an agent of the ever-encroaching Company and its forces. On 28 January 1839, Kamptis had attacked Sadiya and slain the Company's officers together with eighty sepoys and servants. The missionaries had managed to survive by hiding in boats along the riverbank. Sadiya had then been abandoned and missionaries had moved to Jaipur, on the edge of the Naga hills. The lesson was clear: missionaries had to remain discreetly removed and separate from being too closely identified with the Raj.

Godhula, in short, had to be extremely careful not to suggest any possible links with the government. Yet, despite his confinement and the ominous circumstances, the prisoner lifted up his voice and started to sing. With a deep and melodious voice, he loudly sang songs of praise and thanksgiving to God, and prayed for his captors. Little could he have known how much Nagas loved music, especially vocal music. Two years earlier, Edward Payson Scott, an American Baptist missionary, had been suddenly surrounded by the poised spears of Naga warriors as he attempted to approach their village. To counter their fears that belonged to the Maharani ('the

Great Queen [of England]'), or that he was coming to steal and make slaves of children, he had taken out his violin and begun to sing, 'Am I a soldier of the Cross' and 'Alas, and did my Saviour bleed, and did my sovereign die? Would he devote that sacred head, for such a worm as I.' Entranced by what they heard, his listeners had driven their spear points into the ground and asked for more. [12]

Each day, people came and listened to Godhula. Each day, they stood just outside his 'jail' so that they could hear the tones, tunes, and tempos of his songs. Each day, in response to amiable comments, and conversation about things both mundane and spiritual, his fluency in the Ao Naga language improved. The influence of his personality, the friendship and goodwill he exuded, impressed more and more villagers, especially women and children. They responded to his words with respect. His calm assurance, his good humour, his insights and his understandings charmed them. As numbers of hearers increased, he found opportunities to share his faith, to teach the good news of the gospel. He sought for ways to connect Naga understandings of their unseen world, where concepts of a distant high god collided with personal fears of malevolent local demons, with biblical concepts of an almighty God of creation—of things both seen and unseen. He attempted to turn their belief structures upside down, arguing that God was not distant, indifferent and uncaring, but that he loved them. God could and would surely defeat and destroy all local devils and demons.

At last, after he had been released from confinement and allowed to live freely in the village, he informed the villagers that he would need to return to his home and his wife, down in Shibsagar. He also made a point of declaring that he had never intended to bring distress or harm to the village. Even now he did not wish to disturb the well-being of the community, and would be leaving as soon as they allowed him to go. His listeners heard these words with distress. Over the weeks of his incarceration, they had become so attached to him that they did not want him to leave. Finally, when the day of his departure arrived, many wept and begged him to return and to live with them. Forty armed warriors, spears and axes in hand, were sent to escort him personally all the way back to Shibsagar.

When Godhula arrived at Shibsagar, the district officer and missionaries stared at him. They could hardly believe their eyes. Having all but given him up for lost, certain that by then he would have 'lost his head', his return in such a grand fashion, with a full retinue of ceremonially dressed armed guards, became a matter for astonishment and wonder!

---

[12] Robert C. Torbet, *Venture of Faith* (Philadelphia, PA: Judson Press, 1955), p. 218; *The Baptist Missionary Magazine* (1913), p. 53; also described in Puthuvail Thomas Philip, *The Growth of Baptist Churches in Nagaland* (Guwahati, Assam: Christian Literature Centre, 2nd edn, 1983), p. 49. Nowadays, Naga Christian choirs, singing Bach cantatas and Swedish Baptist hymns, make occasional international tours.

III

From that time onwards, Godhula continued to make more and more trips to and from Molung-kimong (or Dekha-haimong as it was called by the Assamese). In due course, his wife, Lucy, joined him, working alongside him as a teacher. As the native missionary couple became settled, and became accepted as members within the community, their boldness and courage, along with their musical skills and winsome ways, inspired increasing admiration, affection, and confidence. Godhula's message—that the great God of All Creation was neither distant nor indifferent to the plight of any Naga individual, whether man, woman or child and whatever age a person might be; that God had redeemed humanity by means of the substitutionary atonement of the sacrificial blood of his Son (Yesu); and that God could and would send his powerful Spirit to enter into the life of any person who turned to him in the name of Yesu—stirred minds and won hearts. The idea that this was a God who was indeed not only more caring but also more powerful than all the malevolent local demons and gods that surrounded them, and that faith in Yesu could bring greater security than anything they had previously known, made an impact.[13] In due time, at Godhula's bidding, a small bamboo chapel, as a place both for worship and learning, was erected by the Nagas themselves. Six months later, when Godhula went down to Shibsagar, he was accompanied by nine newly converted Ao Naga Christians of Molung-kimong. There in Shibsagar, on 11 November 1872, they were baptized and formed the nucleus of the world's first Naga Christian congregation.

Yet these were not the very first Nagas to become Christians. As already mentioned, between 1838 and 1840, Miles Bronson, his wife Ruth, and his sister Rhoda had moved beyond Sadiya, up river to Namsang, at the farthest point of the valley near where the Brahmaputra emerges from the Himalayas. After one or two became Christians, he had started a tiny school and prepared a simple Naga spelling or wordbook, together with a catechism. But constant illness, the death of his sister, and other tragedies ending in the massacre at Sadiya, had prompted his move to Nowgong in 1841. The converts were among the massacre victims. A decade later, in 1851, Ao Naga men from the village of Merangkong living in Shibsagar had been baptized by S.M. Whiting, but had then been killed. Thus, all previous individual Naga converts had lost their lives, either from war or from disease.[14]

At this point, Edward Winter Clark, the American Baptist missionary in Shibsagar with whom and under whom Godhula had worked, decided that he himself would personally return with Godhula to the new Ao Naga Christian community of

---

[13] For more on concepts of God and cosmologies linked thereto, together with citations of pertinent literature, a good place to start is with Richard M. Eaton, 'Comparative History as World History: Religious Conversion in Modern India', *Essays on Islam and Indian History* (Oxford and New Delhi: Oxford University Press, 2000), pp. 60-72. An earlier rendition of this essay is found in *The Indian Economic and Social History Review*, 21.1 (1984), pp. 1-44.

[14] H.K. Barpujari, *The American Missionaries and North-East India, 1836–1900 AD* (Guwahati: Spectrum Publications, 1986), pp. xvi-xvii; letters from pp. 231-67. Clark, *A Corner in India*, p. 5.

Molung-kimong. When Clark arrived, the villagers immediately erected a special house to accommodate him. This simple structure, made of woven bamboo walls, was ready for habitation by nightfall. A few days later, on 23 December 1872, fifteen more Ao Nagas of Molung-kimong who had already openly and publicly professed their faith in Christ were baptized.

For Clark himself the trip into Naga country was a life-changing event. On his return to Shibsagar the following month, the British district officer, Colonel Campbell, quipped that the American had somehow managed 'to keep his head'. Clark responded, 'I believe that I have found my life-work.'[15] Both men, one an American missionary and the other a British official, well understood how stubbornly Naga peoples had always clung to their independence, and how tenaciously they still resisted all attempts to bring them under any kind of outside rule. Naga war bands were still making frequent raids and forays on to the lowlands of the Assam valley taking captives and heads; and when Company troops launched punitive expeditions into the hills, they often suffered losses. Thus, for Clark to venture into the Naga Hills was to go beyond the protection (or jurisdiction) of the Raj, into areas where no Union Jack had as yet been hoisted. But, even so, three more years would pass before Clark finally managed to make a permanent move up the ravines, across the swift-flowing streams, and up to his new hilltop abode in Molung-kimong village. During all that time, Godhula and his able wife Lucy continued to provide the pastoral care and the steady daily instruction necessary to consolidate and strengthen the small community they had helped to bring into being. He taught the boys and young men, while she set up a school for girls, women and children. From among the best and brightest of these would emerge the first elements of an expanding pool of local leaders, known as 'Helpers'. These were patiently trained in how to take responsibility for the welfare of the flock. Thus it was that, out beyond the reach of the imperial government and almost exclusively by means of local and native agency, a community of Naga Christians began to grow. Stemming from such events, foundations were laid and a pattern set for the subsequent expansion of Christian faith among other Naga tribes.

IV

But all did not go smoothly for the new community of Ao Naga believers. There were cultural, social, economic, and political difficulties and troubles. By the time of Clark's arrival, the rapidly growing little community of new believers within Molung-kimong had already begun to arouse serious opposition and resentment. This became increasingly vocal among those who saw the spreading new faith and its culture as a threat to the old ways, if not to the very survival of the village itself. Especially offensive and provocative, for example, was the setting aside of one day in every seven as a sabbath day for rest and worship. This disturbed the political economy of the village. It took workers away from their assigned tasks, whether

---

[15] Clark, *A Corner in India*, pp. 15 and 26.

tilling soil, herding livestock, standing guard, doing essential household work, caring for children, or performing other important tasks.[16] Among disruptions that would disturb long-established customs, was the attempt do away with the *morung*. This, as we shall see, was an institutionalized system of segregating rambunctious young men and teenage youths, housing them in special quarters (long-houses), where they could partake in activities that prepared them for war or in celebrations that involved intoxicants.

Matters more mundane, beyond village preservation and security, had already bothered the more astute leaders for some time. Molung-kimong faced deeper troubles. Amounts of tillable lands were becoming too limited; soils were all but exhausted from over-cropping; and timber lines were moving farther and farther away, in places that were less secure and more risky. Prospects of poverty loomed for weaker elements of the village. Indeed, the possibility of moving the whole village to a new site had already been considered. Yet, it was only after increasing numbers within the old village turned Christian that internal pressures and tensions began seriously to undermine civic coherence and tranquillity.

What disturbed others was the very presence of a 'white face' in their midst. Such a presence seemed to foreshadow a greater, yet unseen threat. Most Naga peoples, as such, had never before been subject to alien rule. To make sure this never happened, each 'village-state' had to be constantly vigilant. Jealously guarding their autonomy, and boasting about the freedom in which they had gloried for so long, Ao Nagas were determined not to compromise their independence. The 'white face' represented danger.[17] This foreigner, this missionary, might well be a spy, an agent of the Raj that had only recently established its dominion in the lowlands of Assam. These new teachings, spreading like wildfire, might just be a ploy. The pen that was reducing their language to written form for the first time ever might store information about them that might someday be used against them. Even the Christian message, about love and peace for all mankind, could be construed as undermining the old ways, as weakening defensive preparedness and military strength. All these things portended the possibility that someday 'good' wars, skull houses, and other means of gaining personal glory, honour, and booty would cease.

Matters finally came to a head when two young warriors of the *morung*, whose prowess and skills made them potential future leaders of the village, became Christians. Not only this, but the same two gifted youths began to initiate actions and policies that could be seen as compromising, if not actually stifling, the warlike spirit and strength of the village. And when these same two young leaders

---

[16] Among other disruptions that would eventually disturb long-established customs, was the doing away with the *morung*, an institutionalized system of segregating rambunctious young men and teenage youths, housing them in special quarters (long-houses), where they could partake in activities that prepared them for war or in celebrations that involved intoxicants, and so forth.

[17] Many opposed Clark's continued residence, predicting that sooner or later this foreigner would be found to have been a 'disguised agent of "The Company"'. Clark, *A Corner in India*, p. 17.

themselves began to lift their own voices, vigorously evangelizing among the non-Christian elements of the village, some began to resist all Christian activities, doing so by means both covert and overt. And when various forms of harassment, petty vexation, and persecution failed to halt the radical movement in their midst, opponents decided to resort to more direct forms of protest. A war party within the *morung* was organized and then launched on a 'head-hunting' expedition, with the hope that a new collection of freshly cut human heads might not only bring honour to the village but also act as a deterrent to further conversions. Surely such actions, they felt, might discourage Christians, and weaken the Christian influence that was disrupting the village. But when this party returned empty-handed and racked with fevers, sores, and wounds, and when their various maladies merely provided means for new medical skills, the opposition found itself defeated.

Even so, covert hostility and dissension within the village continued. The exact sequence of what happened next seems somewhat confusing. But one thing remains certain. Something happened that brought about a major crisis in Naga affairs, and became a defining moment in Naga history. Some of the Christians in Molung-kimong, having met together and organized, quietly decided that the time had come to move away to some other location. So as to defuse domestic tensions and restore peace and harmony, they would depart from Molung-kimong and establish an entirely new village colony. They would create their own settlement—a 'Village of Refuge'—where they might henceforth live according to Christian principles without being disturbed. But, of course, as soon as they gathered and began to pack their belongings, meagre as these were, their actions quickly became known. Strenuous attempts were made first to dissuade them and then to prevent them from leaving. On the day of their departure, as loud objections, insults and threats were being hurled at them from above, a number of whole families, together with their livestock and possessions, walked out of the great gate of Molung-kimong and began their trek towards an uncertain future.

The empty peak to which these families climbed, soon to become New Molung (Molung-yimsen), was thickly forested. It was the wilderness haunt of elephants, tigers, leopards, serpents, and lesser foes. Arriving late in the afternoon of 24 October 1876, they spent their first two nights with nothing but the starry sky for their canopy. They dared not risk being discovered by villages that crowned the other peaks that surrounded them. The biggest immediate danger for the hapless little community lay in the possibility that some adventurous young warriors wanting to enlarge their village's skull-house might make a raid before it could erect a bastion of essential defences—palisades, a main gate, and a dry moat armed with sharp, spike-poisoned bamboo stakes. They dared not light fires that might emit smoke or burn too brightly. For that reason, as work progressed, slant-roofed shelters were open solely toward the Assam plain. Even so, it could only be a matter of a few days before the clearing away of forests on the peak, along with the erection of a new stockade and the clearing of fields for cultivation and grazing, would be noticed. Even so, the new little hamlet of New Molung remained very fragile and vulnerable. Its chances for survival, depending upon circumstances and forces that were beyond its control, seemed remote. That the colony was not immediately destroyed was viewed as a miracle. It was seen as a sign of protection by the Almighty in whom they had only recently, and all too imperfectly, come to put their trust.

Meanwhile, back in Molung-kimong, or Molung-ymchen ('Old Molung') as it was soon to be called, consternation increased. The enraged village chief or head (*tartar*) and other rulers did all in their power to defeat the new colony and to bring the secessionists to their senses. The loss of so much manpower was seen, in itself, as a blow to village resources — with economic, political, and military implications. No less serious were less tangible losses. Village pride and prestige had been cut to the quick, and replaced by lowered self-esteem and public shame. For such reasons alone, the village rulers turned to other Ao Naga villages for help. They wanted to punish the deserters and force their return to the fold. Their own version of what had happened was spread in all directions, with the aim of instigating assaults against the tiny new colony.

According to time-honoured local traditions among Naga tribes, the founding of any new village required consultation and approval from some larger and older 'parent' village. Well-established villages tended to resist any moves that might, thereby, reduce their resources and weaken their defences. Thus, assertions were circulated indicating that, so far, this 'parent' village had already long disapproved of such a move and that it had tried to prevent previous plans for resettlement. Admitting that consultation had long been a necessary pre-condition for the establishment of a new settlement, Ao Naga protocol required approval not only from those who ruled Old Molung, but also, more importantly, from those who ruled the much larger, and the still more powerful 'foster-parent' village that had founded Molung-kimong. This village was Sungdia. Sungdia was 'war village'. As such, it was one of the most powerful of all Ao Naga villages. It had never before, at least in its memory, known military defeat.

Whether or not proper protocols had been observed before the founding of New Molung is difficult to determine. In any case, rumours about the secession and strife linked thereto had been rife for months. Thus, when appealed to by Old Molung, Sungdia sent a message indicating its disapproval of building any new village and commanding secessionists to desist immediately and to return to their old homes. In justifying this command, Sungdia pointed out that the long-term costs to Ao-Nagas would not be worth the effort: blood would flow and skulls would be lost, so that Ao Nagas might be weakened in relation to other great war tribes. Sungdia's war record was such that any village receiving such a message could well be expected to tremble. Sungdia's words made it clear that leaders of the Christian village had little or no option but to comply with such a dire communication. They faced a terrible choice: desist or be destroyed. In the despair of that dark hour, members later told how the community turned their faces to the ground and lifted their voices to heaven in cries for help, strength and wisdom.

At last, after much careful thought and discussion, a consensus was reached and words of a highly courteous, deferential and delicately phrased reply were drafted and sent to the lords of Sungdia. The import of this message from the New Molung community was bold, courageous, and sagacious:

> We remember, Sungdia, with much gratitude your kindness to the Dekha-haimong [Molung-kimong] people, of whom we are a part. Time and again you have fought for us when in peril; we have only thankful hearts to you-ward. We desire most earnestly to perpetuate the pleasant relations of the past, and to remain under your parental watch-care. A little handful of us have come off from Dekha haimong to form a new community, where we may worship in peace and quiet the one true God, of whom we have so recently heard. He is the great God who made heaven and earth and all things. Heretofore success has ever crowned your arms, but you cannot fight against the great Jehovah. Beware, we as your loving children entreat you. The white man's object here is to give you the very richest of blessings; for this only has he come. Believe this![18]

With bated breath, the Christian families at New Molung waited for a reply. At Sungdia, a three-day conference took place. During vigorous discussions that ensued, leaders in Sungdia learned that false rumours had been spread, and misrepresentations had led to misunderstandings of the situation. In their reply to the new colony, the lords of Sungdia not only avowed strong bonds of friendship but also gave their pledge that the war village would support the new venture.

Many in both villages, Old Molung as well as New Molung, were enormously relieved by this peaceful resolution to the conflict. The courage and firmness of the missionaries, both Godhula and Clark, had also made a strong impression on observers. Here were strangers who had been prepared to risk their own lives for the sake of their Naga friends. More and more permanent houses went up, more forest lands were cleared, and rice cultivation went forward. One family after another among those who, from fear, had remained behind in Old Molung, now decided to join the new village. Other Christians elected to remain behind in the old village. Soon after these events, Clark's wife Mary herself decided to join her husband. Her travel into the hills required her sometimes being carried on the back of an Ao Naga Christian, sitting in a especially constructed 'back-chair' (or 'back palanquin'). She whimsically called it her 'pull-man'. Her arrival, seen as a significant symbol of commitment, prompted villagers to enlarge the house that they had built for her husband. This home, while possessing an unheard of 'three rooms' divided by flimsy bamboo and rattan walls, doors, and windows, was sparse in furnishings. Modern conveniences and belongings were kept in tin boxes and trunks.

V

From this time onwards, a whole new order began to come into being—not only within the village of New Molung itself, but thereafter within other Naga villages. No longer were great and expensive ceremonies and rituals, with blood offerings to

---

[18] Clark, *A Corner of India*, p. 23.

propitiate village deities and demons, encouraged; nor, as time went on, were these even tolerated. No longer did campaigns of aggressive warfare, with the customary hunting of heads, find favour. Rather, Christian communities became known as champions of peace, committed to spreading tranquillity. While no law or rule prevented those who settled in the village from worshiping as they chose, neither was there any law requiring residents to be Christians. The pervasive culture and spiritual ethos of the village became increasingly Christian. This was symbolized by the erection of a cross in a prominent place where all could see it and understand the commitments made by Christians within the village.

Meanwhile, with the establishing of New Molung important institutions also arose. Some were entirely traditional and others entirely new or modern; but many, in one way or another, were a blending of old and new, with old forms tending to cloak new content. By tradition, New Molung, like any Naga village, was entirely self-governing. Domestic tranquillity was founded upon village consensus, generated through elemental forms of 'democratic' decision-making by an 'elected' ruling council and its officers. The village chose its own 'headmen' (*tartars*), with one man often becoming predominant as chief. Other leaders served as civil magistrates or military commanders, either for limited terms or for life. All sat together as members of a common council. These officers had powers of 'taxation', by which they could commandeer such labour or materials as might be requisite for the well-being of whole community. They were paid for their efforts by perquisites of office in much the same way. All higher offices—whether civil, military, priestly or whatever—were supposed to be held by the more experienced and mature members of the community. Younger persons were selected and trained, being taken either from the *morung* (a common residence for as yet unmarried young men) or from among younger householders. Great oratorical power, along with rhetorical gifts and skills, were required if one was to be influential or prominent. On public occasions an officer was decked out in distinctive tribal regalia with a colourfully decorated blanket gracefully flowing over his right shoulder in such a way as to enable his other hand to make dramatic or eloquent gestures (sign language being essential when an alien tongue could not be understood). At the same time, the right hand would grasp a long, decorated spear, which could be banged on the ground to give emphasis to the words being spoken. On some occasions, spears of all who met within a council hall might be ceremonially thrust into the ground outside the door, thereby symbolizing peace and harmony within the village.[19] Nothing seems to have mattered more to a Naga than fame, glory and honour. Symbols of public recognition ranked bravery and courage at the top. This was why heads were hunted and skull houses enlarged. Since Nagas had, from time immemorial, lived in a Hobbesian 'state of nature', where war of every tribe against every tribe, often made life 'nasty, brutish, and short', and where every village (*sang*) saw itself as being

---

[19] Similarly also, visitors who called might thrust their spear into the ground, like a 'calling-card', indicating arrival.

potentially at war with most other villages, all members of a village community had to be ready, on the instant, for armed combat.

It was for this reason that village locations on hilltops were selected, planned, and built with defence in mind. Watchtowers were placed at strategic points, with guards and sentinels posted everywhere. Whenever or wherever men cultivated their fields, weapons and shields were stacked close at hand. Women and children, when going outside the stockade to fetch water or firewood from down the slopes, never went alone. Mothers going into fields for work left older children to watch over little ones, with instructions on what to do in an emergency and how to hide. When alarms sounded, whether by drums or shouts, all were expected to know exactly where to go and what to do. Safety in travel outside the village depended on how large and well-protected the group of travellers was. Nagas, when talking to missionaries, recalled that during times of raging hostilities they had slept with their knees bent and axes in hand.[20]

The most important new institution of New Molung was the schoolhouse. It was precisely at this point that the pioneer American Baptist missionaries, Edward and Mary Clark, began to play a more crucial role in building up the cultural infrastructure of the new Christian community. What they did would have profoundly important long-term implications for the future of all Nagas. They laid the foundations of Naga literacy. This began when, as Mary herself put it, 'two of the most intelligent men of the village were chosen to come...morning by morning to talk with us, rather to permit us to pick from their mouths, or throats it seemed, their unwritten language'.[21] Each man was given one rupee (worth 33 cents US at that time) for each series of eight sessions, with accounts being kept on a rattan piece stuck into the bamboo wall. By this means, following procedures calling for constant and disciplined conversation and consultation, checking and cross-checking with local people for verification, making sure that various meanings, nuances and idiomatic expressions were more fully understood and that mistakes were corrected. By this means, the missionaries acquired increasing mastery of the Ao Naga language—an on-going and never-ending process that continued for years. By this means also, they compiled an Ao Naga dictionary and an Ao Naga grammar. By this means, most important of all, they reduced Ao Naga language to written form and, in the process, made a momentous decision, that would have far-reaching implications, both for Nagas and for the history of India: namely, they decided to use Roman script and fonts, rather than Sanskrit (Deva-Nagari) script.

---

[20] In non-Christian/pre-Christian villages, all heads counted, especially the heads of women which, with their long black hair, were prized as trophies of war. Such trophies, with tufts died red or yellow, adorned spear shafts and axe-handles; boar-tusk or cowrie-shell necklaces also bespoke valour or wealth. Men were 'cows' or 'women' until they contributed to a skull-house; and their women would lift their voices to trill over such prizes. Slaves taken in war were used to pay off indemnities. Clark, *A Corner of India*, pp. 45-48.

[21] Clark, *A Corner of India*, p. 84.

The fact that, prior to the coming of Clark into the hills, Christians had received most of the information that undergirded their new faith from the mouths of Godhula and his wife Lucy, who were literate mainly in Assamese, meant that, initially and inadvertently, their knowledge had been conveyed, and received, in a Sanskritized idiom. But due to Naga prejudices this idiom had never had a strong appeal. To understand this, it is important to remember that during 600 years of living in unhappy proximity to the Sanskritized culture of the Ahom civilization, Nagas had remained, both deliberately and amazingly, impervious to and all but insulated from that culture. But now, as Ao Nagas became better acquainted with these two missionary couples, one Assamese and one American, who as individuals unstintingly gave of themselves, even at the risk of their own lives, they were open to new ideas—to spiritual understandings brought from totally alien civilizations. American Baptist missionaries who, after forty years, had found the Assamese so impervious to the gospel, with only tiny numbers becoming Christians, were now amazed to find so many Naga hearts and minds open to their message.

Literacy in their own mother tongue, together with literacy in English as a second language (and Assamese as a third), was the cultural dynamite that exploded, catapulting Nagas from the stone age into modernity.[22] Fully realizing the strategic significance of literacy for the still infant Christian community, the Clarks set about teaching as many as possible, young and old alike, how to gain access not only to scripture but also to modern knowledge in all its forms by means of the written word. They especially emphasized practical knowledge, aiming to provide tools for good health and well-being. The entirely new system of learning that was launched linked what boys and girls, and their parents, already knew to worlds of ideas hitherto never dreamt of. From simple ABCs, simple words and simple Arabic numerals and sums, they moved to increasingly complex phrases and sentences. An almost entirely new Ao Naga language was grafted on to the old language. Then, for those whose literacy advanced to higher levels, English was introduced. For the very first time, a Naga could thumb through an issue of *Harper's* magazine or look at an advertisement for new farm tools, and ask questions about what the pages contained. Working long hours day and night, aiming first to produce a simple dictionary and a grammar, and then to provide more and more sophisticated translations of scripture and textbooks (eventually by means of a hand-press sent out from Boston), missionaries gradually brought about an intellectual revolution among the Naga peoples.

---

[22] Cf. Lamin Sanneh, *Translating the Message: The Missionary Impact on Culture* (Maryknoll, NY: Orbis Books, 1992). See also, Brör Tiliander, *Christian and Hindu Terminology: A Study of their Mutual Relations with Special Reference to the Tamil Area* (Uppsala: Skrifter Religionshist. Inst. Uppsala 12, 1974), for comparative insights into problems of translating concepts and how indigenous meanings are transformed.

VI

The new colony of Molung prospered and grew rapidly. Families from other villages came and settled, bringing their old beliefs and rituals with them, so that soon there were more than a hundred houses. Other villages, seeing this prosperity, invited the missionaries to visit them, and then asked for teachers to come and live among them. To begin with, there not being enough Ao Nagas with training sufficiently advanced to meet such requests, some Assamese Christians had to be recruited for the work. Outstanding among these new 'Helpers' were Zilli and his wife Jointa. Memorable among Zilli's early accomplishments was a full-fledged school concert in which the bamboo chapel, lit by lamps and lanterns, they gave recitations and sang hymns. Among the first Ao Naga teachers to take up tasks in other villages was Tungbangla, a young woman who, with her friend Noksangla, had been among the first schoolgirls of Molung. After her marriage, she and her husband moved to Yazang where she started a small school. This then grew into a congregation which called an elderly Christian from Molung to be its pastor. For him a chapel and house were built. Among the first Ao Naga preachers was Edeeba who, in his orations, held listeners spellbound, taking them from the story of creation, step by step, down to the story of the great atonement for all sin made by 'Yesu Kreestu', and then to the Resurrection and Pentecost. There were times of near disaster when, in going from one village to another, oath-bound warriors plotted against Clark and Godhula, only to have their plans foiled by the arrival of sturdy young men who were friendly to the old and new villages of Molung.

But again, as before, political troubles among the villages began to disturb the progress of Christian expansion. Messengers appeared bringing news that two Molung men had been speared while on their way to Old Molung. At this point, an appeal was made to the British Chief Commissioner asking for protection. The Deputy Commissioner in Shibsagar, Colonel Campbell, whose authority now extended to the foot of the Naga hills, was asked to settle the affair. Officers of Templu, the offending village, eventually paid a heavy fine and signed (with thumb prints) an agreement indicating that depredations on Molung paths would cease. In celebration of this victory, Molung's bodyguard turned out in their full regalia to express their gratitude and to celebrate the vindication of their cause.

This trouble and events that followed in its wake led to circumstances that, in turn, seemed to be a catalyst for the rapid expansion of Christian influence among other Ao Naga villages. Notable among large and prosperous Ao Naga villages was Merangkong, the village that had seen the very first Naga conversion some twenty-five years earlier. One day, a leader from that village came to the Christian congregation in Molung and publicly announced, 'In Merangkong on Sundays, hundreds of people, men, women, and children, come together to hear what I can tell them about the Christian religion.'[23] An imposing figure, whose deeply resonant voice and fiery enthusiasm would one day bring him renown as a preacher, this person's name was Imrong.

---

[23] Clark, *A Corner of India*, p. 105.

Imrong seems to have liked grand public displays. Not long after this, he marched to Molung with 250 men at his back, all dressed in ceremonial regalia, with war axes rattling in their sheaths, shields on their shoulders, and long spears in their hands. His only purpose for coming, he said, was to express affection. Imrong's coming to Molung in this manner, being largely a matter of ceremonial display, seems to have been an important event. Diplomatic protocol required that, in turn, there would be a full-scale return visit to Merangkong by the notables of Molung. What lay behind this event was an earlier incident, namely, fear inspired by the discovery at the gateway of Old Molung (Molung-kimong, New Molung's mother village), of a broken *pongee* (sharpened bamboo spike, normally poisoned) and an extinguished firebrand. This event, comparable to 'flinging down a gauntlet', had been nothing less, in other words, than a full declaration of war by the people of Templu. Failure to respond to this challenge or to provoke armed response had, in turn, led to the killing of the two warriors of Old Molung several months earlier.

The large delegation that went from Old Molung to Merangkong, accompanied by a full retinue of warriors in ceremonial regalia, included Clark and Godhula. Its purpose, quite apparently, was to declare an imminent outbreak of war between Old Molung and Templu. Ostensibly repenting of their actions, especially after their confrontation with British authority in Shibsagar, Templu's head men had sent invitations asking for Clark and Godhula to visit them. These invitations had become ever more insistent. Thus, after consultations in Merangkong with those who had come from Molung, a decision was made that Clark and Godhula, accompanied this time by a small body-guard of only twenty men from Merangkong, would go to Templu.

The action was fraught with danger. At any point along the dark path—a veritable tunnel of creepers, vines, and overhanging boughs—they could run into an ambush of flying arrows and spears. Indeed, the party had hardly gone four miles or so before a halt was called. Tell-tale signs of danger lurked on every hand, with forebodings of trouble lying ahead. Deciding to move ahead in a solid phalanx, the order was given for a gun to be fired. Almost immediately, shouts and calls came from hidden Templu men. Claiming to have been surprised and frightened at the appearance of such a formidable procession, they claimed that they had merely been preparing to defend themselves. Whatever the case, with matters so explained, both parties marched together toward Templu. There, at the base of Templu hill, an advance party went ahead to inform the village officers. In response, the entire leadership of the village, including its chief officer and other notables, rushed down the hill with as much dignity as such haste would allow, to welcome the delegations from Molung and Merangkong. The entire entourage was then escorted up through the gate and into the main street of the village. In the consultations that followed, Templu officials confessed to having ambushed and killed the two Molung men. But they also insisted that what they had done had been instigated by false reports from yet another village, which was still treacherously trying to use false reports for its own ends. After further expressions of regret, Templu sued for peace and forgiveness. Yet, even as these expressions were exchanged, men from the accused 'treacherous' village, that had long been at odds with Merangkong and had instigated the entire affair, suddenly appeared in Templu. Knowing full well that these enemies could go home and return with enough men to launch an attack on Templu, Clark, Godhula and the Merangkong delegation quickly left the village, hoping to reach Merangkong before dark. There, Clark's wife waited, surrounded by an armed guard of fifteen warriors.

This whole experience was frightening, not just for the missionaries, but for all the Ao Naga Christians. It reminded them again, as if they needed reminding, that their very lives were precariously balanced. In the midst of an environment of the big 'war-villages' of the Ao Naga tribe, life was becoming increasingly hazardous. Each journey into a village, with its gate adorned by skulls and beset by evidences of ritual blood-sacrifices to evil spirits, served to remind Naga Christians of the ever-present dangers around them; and every time someone was carried off by a tiger, the event would be attributed to the work of demons. Deft diplomacy was required of the Ao Naga Christians in order for them to survive.

By 1878, and often thereafter, Clark was called upon to serve as a neutral arbiter or broker whose task it was to negotiate between Ao Naga villages or to represent Ao Naga villages, Christian and non-Christian alike, in their dealings with other tribes or with colonial authorities. By that time, after years of living in a simple bamboo-and-thatch hut, surrounded by their Christian community and supported by helpers, friends, and villages far and near, the Clarks had become increasingly beloved and respected throughout the entire Ao Naga tribe. Ao Naga tribal leaders recognized the important contributions made by the missionaries to the maintenance of tranquility and the growth of prosperity throughout Ao tribal lands, peoples and villages. On several occasions, when called upon to do so, they had been able to send messengers to the Deputy Commissioner (soon to be District Magistrate) in Shibsagar, warning of an impending attack on some local village or sending information about hostilities that were about to break out. When special permission was obtained for some Ao Naga Christians to obtain firearms and ammunition so that they could defend themselves against foes, both human and non-human, the prestige of the Clarks increased even more.

Word suddenly came in late 1879, signaled from hilltop to hilltop almost as quickly as the telegraph, that a really big war had finally broken out between the Angami Nagas and the Raj. Messages then came from British magistrates urging the Clarks to flee. The Clarks never hesitated over their decision: they would remain with their own people. Wars and rumours of wars every year had become such a regular part of life that they could find no reason to alter their ways. They decided to wait quietly on events, praying that they and their people would be spared, and that the war would soon end.

VII

What was at issue was a shift in policy by the Government of India. After years of vacillating, between a 'forward' policy and a policy of withdrawal, leaving the tribes to themselves, authorities in Calcutta had finally decided to enter the hills and take control. Angami Nagas were one of the most fierce, powerful and warlike of all Naga tribes, much feared by other tribes and dreaded on the plains, where they were much given to looting, carrying off livestock, and taking slaves and human heads. To put a stop to such chronic depredations, a political agent had taken up residence in Samaguting, the strategic gateway to the plains, and then established his headquarters in Kohima, stationing troops there. This action, penetrating right into the very heart of the Angami tribe, with large war villages all around them, was a direct affront—a threat to Naga freedom. Aroused war villages in the interior, especially in the stronghold of Khonoma, soon organized a general uprising. When C.B. Damant, the Political Agent, endeavoured to stop the uprising, he and his entire escort were killed. Kohima was attacked and besieged. Holding out for thirteen days, it was finally relieved by fresh forces from Assam. The campaign that followed lasted until March of the following year (1880), when Khonoma was destroyed and the Angamis were forced to surrender firearms and pay indemnities. Thereafter, all of Angami country was occupied and a strong military force was stationed permanently in Kohima. British authority was extended over the Lotha tribe, whose villages covered much of the area between the Angamis and the Ao Nagas. While direct rule over Angami and Ao Naga villages was not imposed, so that a large measure of local autonomy continued, war between villages and raids against villages of Assam proper were outlawed under the threat of heavy penalties.

Having watched as these events unfolded, and anticipating the final outcome, Clark had wasted no time in taking advantage of the situation. At his request, a young couple, C.D. King and his wife, had already been sent out from America. But these new missionaries, having hardly arrived in Assam before the hostilities broke out, were obliged to take refuge at Samaguting until peace was re-established in Kohima. The village of Kohima, at an elevation of 4,000 feet, would eventually become the headquarters for government administration and the capital of Nagaland. Five years later, in 1885, the imperial government also extended its authority to the whole the Ao Naga peoples. This it did by a ceremonial show of force, with troops marching and counter-marching the length and breadth of Ao Naga territories to the sound of bagpipes and drums, carrying the flag and publicly declaring at every village it approached that henceforth there would be no more spilling of blood, nor head-hunting or plundering raids, and no more toleration for inter-tribal wars. Like the Angamis and Lothas before them, the Ao Nagas could not believe what they heard. To them the British action seemed to be nothing more than another raid, albeit a huge one. They went on as before—ambushing, pillaging, and taking heads.

By that time, Edward and Mary Clark, exhausted and ill after their years of constant strain, had decided to return to America for a furlough. Summing up achievements during their years in Molung, they could claim that the fifty-one Ao Nagas whom they counted as baptized believers did not begin to reflect the true number of Christians whose gatherings for worship were now occurring in several other villages. One year later, when the Clarks returned from America, they discovered that twenty-four more believers had been baptized during their absence. But even the larger figure of seventy-nine does not accurately reflect the number of Ao Naga Christians. All these early missionaries, especially Baptists, were very careful about administering baptism prematurely. There were many who were enrolled in schools and involved in worship who would not be baptized until they could meet minimum standards of understanding, faithfulness and witness. Hence many others who were not yet baptized were part of the Christian community. Christians of Merangkong, meanwhile, soon received a literate and well-trained young Naga couple as their pastor and teacher. In the years that followed, Merangkong produced a steady stream of talented Christian leaders. (In 1904, Merangkong hosted the Annual Meeting of the Ao Naga Association of Baptist Churches.)

Among other accomplishments during their years among the Ao Nagas, Edward and Mary Clark produced an Ao-Naga–English dictionary, a grammar, a catechism, translations of two Gospels, Matthew and John, the story of Joseph (taken from Genesis), a gospel hymnbook, other portions of the New Testament, and several school textbooks. A simple 'hand-press' that had been sent out to them from Philadelphia had enabled them to print all of these works themselves, with each page being printed as soon as it was ready. Later, Mary Clark was to publish a full grammar of the Ao Naga language, a work that is still in print.[24] In 1898, a special school for training Ao Naga pastors and teachers was established at Impur. The new settlement located on a huge, flat-topped elevation further up into the hills.

VIII

From the 1880s and 1890s onwards, a steadily accelerating growth of Naga Baptist Christian congregations and villages occurred. In due course, what had begun with the Ao Nagas spread to the Angami Nagas, Lotha Nagas and Sema Nagas; and, ultimately thereafter, to more and more of the fifty plus tribes that could be described as Naga (spreading across down into the princely state of Manipur and across the ravines of northern Burma, where Kachins, Chins, and Karens were also being reached with the Christian gospel). Baptist missionaries followed along the wake of the advance of Christianity, establishing and strengthening educational and other infrastructures.

To understand the accelerating proliferation of Christian conversions among Naga tribes, with numbers of converts and congregations doubling and tripling in every decade and among ever-widening circles of Naga peoples, qualitative and quantitative distinctions can be made. Conversions among the extremely aggressive and warlike Angami Nagas, for example, came much more slowly than among the Ao Nagas or

---

[24] Mrs E.W. (M.M.) Clark, *The Ao-Naga Grammar: With illustrations, Phrases, and Vocabulary* (Delhi: Gian Publications, 1981 [1893]), p. 181.

the Sema Nagas. Ao Nagas, over the years, also had more than twice as many missionaries (seventeen) as the Angamis (seven).

Initially, and not surprisingly, Ao Nagas had far more trained leaders, both pastors and teachers, with much higher numbers of Christians, both men and women, as well as children, who were literate, both in their 'mother tongue' and English than other Naga tribes. Ao Naga Impur to the north and Angami Kohima to the south of the Sema Nagas became and remained the two most important centres for training young Naga evangelists, preachers, and teachers, both male and female.

Sema Nagas turned Christian with virtually no direct missionary contact. J.H. Hutton, studying them in the years 1915–20, found one small Christian village and a few scattered households. Just a few years later, during the 1920s, a missionary traveling among the Sema Nagas, en route from Impur to Kohima, discovered many Christian groups who regularly came together for worship and did so in their own meeting houses, albeit without any apparent leadership. A decade later, J.E. Tanquist, the senior missionary at Kohima who reported on this seemingly spontaneous movement, described 'marvels of spiritual transformation the likes of which I have never seen before'.[25]

With astonishing swiftness, a mass movement swept through Sema Naga villages. This reflected a remarkable symbiosis of conceptual and cultural categories. The existing Sema Naga vocabulary was easily adapted to 'Christian' meanings. The result was a metamorphosis that, at the same time, was adapted to new socio-political realities on the ground. The abolition of incessant warfare, of every tribe and village against every other as a ritualized institution of aggrandizement among Sema Naga village lords, coincided with a rejection of dependency among lower level warriors and weaker villages. Turning Christian became a means both of preserving domestic security and of enhancing local authority. Thus, instead of head-hunting and war, competitive efforts were made to obtain Christian institutions, with newly trained preachers and teachers (trained in Kohima or Impur) which, in turn, helped to bring about new kinds of prosperity, security, and status. Finally, partly as a result of their involvement and sufferings during the Japanese invasion of World War II, Sema Nagas turned to the Christian faith more rapidly, more massively, and more thoroughly than any other Naga people. So much was this so that, within a short time, they themselves spearheaded missionary efforts among all the remaining unreached Naga tribes.

Actions and attitudes of imperial rulers (district officers and political agents) who established the new governing institutions in the wake of the Angami War were often ambivalent. While initially not dismayed to find a readily available supply of reliable and well-trained young Nagas to fill clerical and administrative needs, and while such positions, in due course, also provided increasing employment and brought prosperity to an ever-widening circle of Naga villages,[26] some British

---

[25] Tanquist Papers MSS (1936), pp. 240-41, held at Bethel Theological Seminary Archives, St Paul, Minnesota.

[26] Naga peoples themselves resented Assamese (or other kinds of Indian) officials. They retained an especially strong antipathy against the employment of Assamese

officials, from the 1920s onwards, eventually turned against conversion movements and, therewith, against missionary activities. These they blamed for disrupting and even destroying the cultures and traditions of a proud indigenous antiquity. Thus, with occasional exceptions, especially during earlier years when British rule had not yet been extended into the Naga hills, relations between missionaries and imperial officials became increasingly ambiguous and uneasy.

From the 1920s onward, despite seeing advantages in employing educated Nagas, almost all of whom were Christians, for lower level positions within the civil or police services, antipathy toward Christianization increased. While no formal steps to expel missionaries were taken, British magistrates and judges frowned upon events that divided a village community between Christians and non-Christians. Many of them, as dedicated ethnologists, sought to preserve traditional cultures and time-honoured institutions. Baptist prohibitions against drinking rice beer, against 'heathen' or 'lewd' songs and dances, against reckless consumption at Feasts of Merit, and against working on the Sabbath were viewed as disruptive and destructive. The wearing of western forms of clothing and adoption of modern elements, styles or technologies were also seen as undermining tribal cultures. Many years later (1950), when they established themselves in Nagaland, Catholic missionaries from South India took a more relaxed approach to drinking, dancing, and tribal traditions. Finally, twentieth-century officials and scholars, almost all of whom were anthropologists, ethnologists, or sociologists, were so secular in their attitudes that constantly sought for ways to explain, if not to explain away, Christian conversions—often in pseudo-scientific or socio-scientific terms. They themselves rarely took religion itself seriously, preferring to see all elements of supernatural religion as epiphenomenal or false consciousness that could be accounted for in rational terms.

IX

Two countervailing, contradictory, or dialectically opposed processes can be observed as having occurred that, in the long run, were to lead to much misery, suffering and war. One was the hybridizing integration or 'nationalization' that led to the emergence of a pan-Naga consciousness. Another was the alienation of Nagas from Indian nationalism and their rejection of it in all its forms. Both processes were complex and need to be understood, at least in brief measure. In terms of relations with India, if not the wider world, one impulse remained separatist and the other integrationist. The results, both for Nagas and for India, led to tragedy and on-going armed hostilities.

---

intruders, whether officials or merchants, who came and settled in Kohima and other newly burgeoning towns. Ahom rulers, after all, were ancient enemies who had through the ages tried to conquer and dominate Naga peoples. They viewed bankers, merchants, and money-lenders as tricksters who had always tried to defraud them and to ensnare them in debt-bondage.

The socio-political emergence of a strong 'Naga' consciousness gathered momentum as a direct consequence of World War I. Nagas returning from military service in France, where 2,000 or more had been in a volunteer labour group, formed a Naga Club in 1919. Composed of local officials and village lords, all of whom had gone to Baptist missionary schools, especially around Kohima and Mokochung, the club met regularly for discussions and also ran a cooperative store. In 1929, when the Simon Commission came to Kohima to obtain local opinions about the future of India, the Club formally submitted a memorandum. Signed by leaders from twenty tribes, its words were sagely ominous and prescient:

> We pray that the British Government will continue to safeguard our rights against all encroachments from other people who are now more advanced than us, by withdrawing our country from the reformed [sic] and placing directly under its own protection. If the British Government, however, want to throw us away, we pray that we should not be thrust to the mercy of the people [i.e. of India] who could never have conquered us themselves, and to whom we are never subjected; but to leave us alone to determine for ourselves as in ancient time.[27]

Yet, the main driving force behind the social mobilization of all Naga peoples and what eventually brought them together and made them into a single society was the building up of individual tribal Baptist (church) associations. The first of these, naturally, was the Ao Baptist Association. Founded in 1897, this association met annually to build solidarity, deal with common problems, increase the number of schools, and find inspiration in attractive musical and preaching programmes. Almost inevitably, and invariably, these associations served political ends, both for dealing with internal disputes between Ao Baptist individuals or between Ao Baptist congregations, and for dealing with Ao Baptist disputes with or pressures from non-Christian Ao leaders and villages. Thus, for example, when non-Christian rulers of several villages tried to compel Christian minorities within villages to pay for feasts (e.g. Feasts of Merit) and festivals or 'forbidden actions on days of prohibition', called '*gennas*', by levying heavy fines against the Christians, their demand was overruled on appeal to government officials on the grounds that 'the religious scruples of the Christians must be properly respected'.[28]

While growth of congregations within the Ao Baptist Association was initially quite slow until 1920, thereafter its upward trajectory was spectacular at least until 1971, when the centennial of the Ao Naga Baptists was celebrated. Indeed, in subsequent reports of the association, Ao Naga Baptists emphasized the strength of their missionary work among the Sema Nagas, thereby indicating that while foreign

---

[27] M. Alemchiba Ao, *A Brief Historical Account of Nagaland* (Kohima: Naga Institute of Culture, 1970), p. 164, quoted in Julian Jacobs, *et al.*, *The Nagas, Hill Peoples of Northeast India: Society, Culture, and the Colonial Encounter* (London: Thames and Hudson, 1990), pp. 151-52.

[28] *Ao Baptist Association Annual Report for 1906*, p. 156, as found in Philip, *Growth of Baptist Churches in Nagaland*, p. 71

(American Baptist) missionaries did little among the Sema Nagas, Ao Nagas were playing a more predominant role than was shown in missionary reports to America. At the time of their centennial, according to Frederick S. Downs, Ao Nagas were reaching out to seventy percent of the entire Nagaland population.[29]

In due course, as predictably as clockwork, another thirteen tribal church associations came into being. The second of these was the Angami Baptist Association, founded in 1912. Growth remained extremely slow, from the founding of the first Angami Baptist Church in Kohima, until the 1920s and 1930s. Growth became rapid after 1939 and accelerated into a 'people movement' in the period between 1951 and 1971. The third association to be formed was the *Sema Baptist Kughakulu* (Sema Baptist Convention). This, with its centre at Mokochung, was started in 1922. Under the relentless efforts of Inaho and Kiyevi, and other local evangelists, converts and congregations multiplied until, in 1938, there were seventy-eight churches, twenty-four schools and over 8,000 Semas who were baptized believers. When funds for building a training school could not be raised, 7,753 days of volunteer work enabled the completion of ten buildings within a twenty-five-acre campus compound at Aizuto. The fourth assembly of local deacons, elders, pastors and teachers was the Lotha Baptist Association, founded in 1926, with its centre in Wokha. Names of other Naga Christian organizations that formed are the Kuki (1926), Rengma (1940), Chakhesang (1949), Zeliangrong (1953), Sangtam, Chang, Konyak, Phom, Yimchunger, and Kheamungan Baptist Associations.[30] What these integrating events show, beyond all doubt, is a spirit of adventure, exploration, and expansion that was driven by indigenous Naga missions to yet unreached Naga tribes and that contributed to the social mobilization that, in turn, gave rise of Naga 'national' consciousness.

It should hardly be surprising, in the light of such events, that separate tribal councils should have been formed for the purpose of local self-government. Each of the first two, the Lotha Council (1923) and the Ao Council (1928), can be seen as almost natural projections of the Baptist association which, in many respects, paralleled it, so that many of the same leaders served in each. The value of Naga contributions to the Allied cause during the Second World War led to the formation of an over-all Naga District Council which, in 1946, was turned into the Naga National Council. That body was to make demands for total independence.

---

[29] Frederick S. Downs, *The Mighty Works of God: A Brief History of the Council of Baptist Churches in North East India: The Mission Period, 1836–1950* (Gauhati: CLS, 1971), p. 113; Philip, *Growth of Baptist Churches in Nagaland*, p. 75.

[30] These are listed and described by Philip, *Growth of Baptist Churches in Nagaland*, pp. vi-viii, 67-125, 126-63, who went to each centre, examined records, and consulted with local leaders.

Conclusion

Naga peoples have experienced 'the most massive movement to Christianity in all of Asia, second only to the Philippines'.[31] Well over ninety percent of all Nagas are Christian. Moreover, while most Naga Christians are Baptist, since 1950, when Catholic missionaries were first admitted into Naga territories, a small but growing number have become Catholics. Significantly, the most dramatic transformation to Christian identity occurred only *after* the ending of imperial rule and the subsequent expulsion of foreign missionaries by the national government of India.[32]

It would be a mistake to conclude that the growth of Christian faith among the Nagas was an alien imposition upon a hapless people. While both colonial rule and missionary efforts played significant roles, neither can be said to have been the primary instruments of the conversion of Nagas to Christianity. Most conversions took place in areas well beyond either missionary or colonial control, in languages that local people could understand because it was their mother tongue. As one anonymous Naga put it,

> Europeans do not have a monopoly on Christianity... Christianity came to Europe from Asia and some Indians were Christians 500 years before the Europeans. When Europeans became Christians, they made it a European indigenous religion. They changed their names and founded festivals in relation to their cultures. Now I, like many Nagas, am a Christian, but I am not a European. I have a relationship with my God. Now my God can speak to me in dreams, just as happened to my Angami ancestors. I don't have to be like Anglicans or Catholics and go through all those rituals. I don't need them. What I am talking about is Naga Christianity—an indigenous Naga Christianity.[33]

It is this indigenous culture and this fiercely independent spirit that have, since time immemorial, especially since the Indian Empire moved into Assam after the first Burma War in 1826, and finally since it had to confront Indian nationalism in both its secularist and its sectarian modes, precipitated the troubles that have continued, even despite the formation of a separate State of Nagaland in 1963. Similarly, among forest peoples in the hills across a wide belt of interior and exterior frontiers, from Kanya Kumari at the southernmost tip of the Indian peninsula, up through the badlands of Central India, into areas surrounding the Brahmaputra Valley, and across the mountainous regions of Burma, even to the Thai border, conversions of this nature occurred among hundreds of separate peoples such as Badigas, Chenchus, Yerrakulas, Bheels, Khonds (Gonds), Mundas, Santals, Khasis, Mizos, Nagas, Chins, Kachins, Karens, and many, many more than can be named here. All of these were peoples who, for ages untold, had never been

---

[31] Eaton, 'Comparative History', p. 47.
[32] Eaton, 'Comparative History', p. 48.
[33] International Work Group for Indigenous Affairs [IWGIA], *The Naga Nation and Its Struggle Against Genocide* (Copenhagen: International Work Group for Indigenous Affairs, 1986), pp. 106-107.

Sanskritized or Islamicized and who were only too eager to escape from conditions of brutality and insecurity. This having been so, Christianity has simply become an accepted and vital part of a Naga ethnic identity, as this was 'constructed' (or 'invented') during the past century. As such, it separates them from peoples from whom they fervently want to be separated, namely, Hindus and Muslims. It is this sense of common heritage that also drives them to discover the antiquity of their own culture. Underlying all, therefore, is a sense of a common Christianity. And this, for the most part, has been and still is Baptist.

Beyond the scope of this study, a study that is needed is the role of Naga Baptists in larger political processes. As already suggested, this followed at least two parallel courses: the one aimed at complete separation from India, and the other attempting to integrate Nagas into the body politic of India. Initially, the weight of Naga sentiments favoured total independence. This attitude was strengthened in reaction to Assamese attempts to incorporate the whole of the Naga peoples and territories into the State of Assam and, at the same time, to rescind provisions for autonomous self-government that had been progressively accorded to Naga peoples in return for their desisting from predatory attacks into the Assam valley, as a device for achieving pacification of the Naga tribes. When Nagas loudly protested, Nehru himself went up to Kohima to 'lecture' the Nagas on their duties as patriotic citizens of India. When his public address to a huge gathering of Nagas at or near the Kohima railway station took on a condescendingly paternalistic air, insomuch that Nagas were severely scolded for their failure to submit to the dictates of New Delhi, the entire crowd turned their backs on him *en masse* and silently walked away.[34] Nehru, an extremely proud person, never forgot this affront and became even more unbending in his attitude and policy towards the Nagas. They, in turn, would not accept Indian rule. Being well-armed, with masses of modern weapons accumulated during hostilities against the Japanese (and soon able to acquire armaments from Maoist China), Nagas were able to launch a full-scale 'war of independence'—or an 'insurgency'—depending upon which rhetorical slant one gives to the violence that followed and that, though much diminished, is still on going.

Since 1963, when statehood was granted to a self-governing but not independent or sovereign Nagaland, Nagas have remained divided in their loyalties, either pragmatically accepting local autonomy as 'the next best thing' or retaining a fierce devotion to a totally independent nation. The Naga government in exile, proclaimed in 1956 as the Naga Federal Government (NFG) has continued the often bloody struggle as an armed opposition movement.[35]

---

[34] This unforgettable anecdote has remained in my memory ever since the late 1940s when, as a student at Bethel College, St Paul, Minnesota, it was told to me by Bengt Anderson, and later corroborated by J.E. Tanquist. It still needs to be checked out in local or national newspapers of India, something I have not yet been able to do.

[35] This struggle, in many uncanny ways, can be compared with the parallel struggle that has been going on in Kashmir, in which many Kashmiris, despite allegations of Pakistani sympathy, have also struggled for a totally independent state.

The literature on events of the last half-century or more is vast, with polemics and studies attempting careful detachment arrayed on both sides. Further analysis on this matter being beyond the scope of this essay, what remains pertinent are questions concerning roles played by Naga Baptists in the struggles. But, even this subject, is too large to attempt here. Suffice it to say that Baptists, of one sort or another, seem to have fallen on both sides of the divide. Phizo, one of the early Naga nationalist leaders, came out of Kohima where he had been one of Tanquist's students. (Tanquist told me that he was not a good student due to his 'opportunistic' political activities).[36] Many, whom one might call 'Maoist Baptists', were engaged in hostilities against India. Many others became part of modern India, taking part in the Legislative Assembly, the Government of Nagaland, and in various branches of the administrative services. Interestingly, there often seems to have been a rather close correlation between Members of the Legislative Assembly (MLAs) in Nagaland and the Nagaland Baptist Church. Nevertheless, a much closer analysis of this subject is needed.

Sources: Archival and Bibliographic

Research Materials and Historiographic Concerns

History, like any scholarly discipline, undergoes constant and continuous revision. This occurs when historians gain access to new data drawn from hitherto unused source materials or apply new, or hitherto unused tools of analysis. The historian's work is always, therefore, contingent. It depends upon varieties of infrastructures that are determined by available resources or by circumstances of access to archives or artifacts. Letters, records and reports relating to American Baptist missionaries in the Naga Hills are located in at least three places outside of India: (1) Archives of the American Baptist Historical Society (hitherto preserved at the Colgate School of Divinity, Rochester, New York); (2) the Archives of the American Baptist International Ministries (formerly known as the American Baptist Foreign Mission Society, Valley Forge, Pennsylvania); and (3) Archives of the Baptist General Conference (formerly known as the Swedish Baptist Conference, preserved at Bethel Theological Seminary, St Paul, Minnesota). Official materials predominate in the first two locations; and private collections of Swedish–American Baptist missionaries can be found in the third location.[37]

---

[36] One of Phizo's nephews, I was also informed (many years ago), was a professor of medicine at the University of Pennsylvania; and a diaspora of other Naga researchers, scholars, and technicians were scattered across North America.

[37] A considerable body of Swedish–American Baptist missionaries, starting with Joseph Tanquist, worked among different Naga tribes during the twentieth century. The Swedish Baptist Conference, from whence they came, was one of several ethnically distinct conferences that were branches of the mainline Northern Baptist (subsequently American Baptist) Convention. These branches, tending to be, on the whole, theologically much more conservative and evangelical (and less 'modernist' or liberal)

A large collection of nineteenth-century documents, letters and reports from American Baptist missionaries (taken from archives in Rochester and Valley Forge), together with Material and Moral Improvement reports, from Selections of Records, Government of Bengal (for Assam), have been edited and published by H.K. Barpujari. This work, entitled *The American Missionaries and North-East India: A Documentary Study* (Guwahati-Delhi: Spectrum Publications, 1986), with its extensive introduction and biographical notes, is an extremely useful goldmine of primary source materials. Another such work, albeit much more difficult to obtain, is the volume edited by Esama Murray, *Thus Saith the Missionaries: A Collection of Valuable Records from the Writings of the American Baptist Missionaries on the Early Naga Church in General, and the Lotha Church in Particular, 1874* (Wokha, Nagaland: Examo Murryl, 1979).

Church or missionary records and papers located in India can be found in library archives of such institutions as the Naga Christian Council (in Kohima, Nagaland), the Council of the Baptist Churches of North East India (in Guwahati, Assam), Eastern Theological College (Jorhat, Assam), Serampore College (Hoogly, West Bengal), and also (on microfilm) in Union Theological College (Bangalore, Karnataka). Frederick S. Downs, one of the leading authorities on this subject, indicated that 'only a few of the churches and associations have kept historical records...[or] to have preserved even official documents like minutes, annual reports, etc., which are of such great value to historians'.[38] Puthuvail Thomas Philip, on the other hand, personally visited ten out of fourteen local (or tribal) Naga Baptist associations and was able both to collect written raw materials and to conduct oral interviews. Field directors, along with assemblies of elders, deacons, and their associates, opened up their facilities and provided him with interviews detailing activities of Naga Christians within each tribe.[39] No less extensive, or thorough, has been the research of Joseph Puthenpurkal, a Catholic scholar in Shillong, whose work, based on a doctoral dissertation submitted to the Urban University, Rome, gives a thorough and descriptive listing of the letters and reports of Baptist missionaries from the Naga hills.[40]

Concerning difficulties to be encountered when studying the history of Christianity in any part of North-East India, as also of India, the foremost are difficulties of language and literacy. Not only are there dozens, if not scores, of separate Naga languages, but there are perhaps more than one hundred different local

---

than the larger Convention, and hence able to recruit more missionaries, finally split off and became separate denominations during the 1940s.

[38] Quoted by H.K. Barpujari, *The American Missionaries and North-East India, 1836–1900 AD* (Guwahati: Spectrum Publications, 1986), preface, as taken from Frederick S. Downs, *Christianity in North East India: Historical Perspectives* (Delhi: Indian Society for Promoting Christian Knowledge/ Gauhati: Christian Literature Centre, 1983).

[39] Philip, *Growth of Baptist Churches in Nagaland*, pp. viii-ix.

[40] Joseph Puthenputakal, *Baptist Missions in Nagaland: A Study in Historical and Ecumenical Perspective* (Calcutta: Firma KLM, 1984).

languages among the many other tribal groups of North-East India. Moreover, with literacy among these groups dating only from when Christianity was first introduced, often hardly more than a century ago—with literary materials, as a consequence, having begun to increase only a few generations ago, and with hardly any systematic work of collecting, cataloguing, or preserving written or printed materials having been done, or even begun—many if not most of the primary sources for historical understanding remain either in the memories and oral traditions of Naga Christians. Beyond that, one must fall back upon such missionary sources, both manuscript and printed, private or unofficial and official described above as exist.

Finally, between 1939 and 1976, renowned anthropologists published a number of noteworthy monographs on the Nagas: Christoph von Fürer-Haimendorf, *The Naked Nagas* (London: Methuen, 1939/Calcutta: Firma KLM, 2nd edn, 1962) and *The Konyak Nagas: An Indian Frontier Tribe* (New York: Reinhart & Winston, 1969), and Verrier Elwin (ed.), *The Nagas in the Nineteenth Century* (Bombay: Oxford University Press, 1969). Thereafter, secular literature on Nagas and Nagaland has continued to thicken.

CHAPTER 16

From Southern Baptist Identity to Chinese Baptist Identity, 1850–1950

Li Li

What is Chinese Baptist life and how has it been developed? In general, Chinese Baptist life is a form of Baptist Christianity with a strong Chinese identity to reflect its social and cultural reality. Chinese Baptist experience had its root in Western Baptist missions in China. Through Western missionaries' adaptation to China and Chinese Baptists' innovations in formulating the Christian message, Baptist churches in China grew to be a Baptist expression that combined both its Christian essence and Chinese context to form an independent denomination of Christianity in China.

The transformation of the Southern Baptist identity to the Chinese Baptist identity is of particular importance. The post-bellum American South and post-Opium War China shared the same tragedy of being defeated by stronger military powers. Both thus searched for ways to revive themselves. Facing material obstacles, claims of high spirituality became easy ways in which to raise self-confidence. The Southern Baptists went to China in part to prove their religious capability of spreading the gospel. After receiving the 'good news', the Chinese Baptists creatively made their inputs in a way which demonstrated their religious ingenuity. As a result, while many Southern Baptist missionaries established themselves in a new home in China, the Chinese Baptists found a new faith that connected together their own experience and the wider society.[1]

The Beginnings of Southern Baptist Missions in China

The American Baptist interest in China started in the early nineteenth century. In 1831, the American Baptists organized the 'General Convention of the Baptist Denomination in the United States of America for Foreign Missions', which became known more popularly as the 'Triennial Convention' for Baptists. From the beginning Asia was a major focus because the Triennial Convention was initiated by

---

[1] Foreign Mission Board (SBC), *A Century for Christ in China, 1836–1936* (Richmond, VA: Foreign Mission Board, 1936); A.R. Gallimore, *Brief Sketches of Baptist Mission in China, 1836–1936* (Shanghai: China Baptist Publication Society, 1936).

two American congregational missionaries to India, Adoniram Judson and Luther Rice, who later chose to become Baptists. At a time when China was the largest mission ground for most American foreign missionaries, American Baptists, too, soon shifted their attention to China.[2] The possible spread of the Christian faith in a country with such a rich history and with the largest population in the world was a challenging dream and one not to be overlooked.

The American Baptist work among the Chinese people began among the overseas Chinese in South and South-East Asia and was followed by mission inside China. In Siam and Malaya in the early nineteenth century some American Baptist missionaries organized Bible translation from English into Chinese. Beginning in 1806, the well-known British Baptist missionary, William Carey, directed a project in Serampore, India, to translate the Bible into Chinese. The task was completed in 1823 and resulted in the first formal production of the Chinese Bible. This became the foundation for any future Chinese biblical publication. Between 1830 and 1835, the American Baptist Triennial Convention joined the American Board of Commissioners for Foreign Missions and the Protestant Episcopal Church in sending ten missionaries to work with the first ordained Chinese Protestant worker, Liang A-fah, in Malacca, Malaya. In December 1835, with the help of the American Baptist missionary, William Dean, the first Chinese Baptist church opened its door in Bangkok.

The first American Baptist missionary couple arrived in Macao in September 1836 and thus officially opened the new chapter of American Baptist mission in China's homeland. The Revd John Lewis Shuck and his wife, Henrietta Hall Shuck, of Richmond, Virginia, came to Macao with great enthusiasm. In 1837, Issachar J. Roberts, an independent Baptist missionary from Tennessee, joined them in Macao. For seven years, during 1836–42, the three missionaries laboured vigorously in house to house missions and created a school in Macao. Their goal was to go to Guangzhou (Canton), but this proved to be impossible because the Manchu Court would not allow missionaries to come into China.[3]

The Opium War (1840–42) finally enabled the Shucks to go to China. Unable to compete with the overwhelming military power of Great Britain, the Chinese lost the war and were forced to sign the first unequal treaty—the Treaty of Nanjing. This treaty specifically guaranteed rights for Western Christian missionaries to conduct their missions in China. Because of the war, the British were able to acquire Hong Kong as their colony in China. As a result, the Shucks moved to Hong Kong in March 1842. In October, William Dean arrived in Hong Kong from Thailand. Shortly after, Issachar Roberts also came to Hong Kong. In May 1842, the first Chinese Baptist church was established in Hong Kong.[4] In the summer of 1844,

---

[2] G. Winfred Hervey, *The Story of Baptist Missions in Foreign Lands* (St Louis, MO: Chancy H. Barns, 1888), p. 499.

[3] Winston Crawley, *Partners Across the Pacific: China and the Southern Baptists. Into the Second Century* (Nashville, TN: Broadman Press, 1986), pp. 28-32.

[4] Paul Yat-Keung Wong, 'The History of Baptist Missions in Hong Kong' (PhD dissertation, Southern Baptist Theological Seminary, 1974), pp. 57-60.

Roberts moved to Guangzhou. After the death of Henrietta in November 1844, John Lewis Shuck went to Guangzhou, accompanied by nine Chinese assistants. Upon arrival at Guangzhou in April 1845, the small group immediately organized the First Baptist Church of Canton (Guangzhou). Finally the American Baptists had realized their goal of having evangelical missions in mainland China.[5]

By this time, the missionaries were under the sponsorship of the American Baptist Board of Foreign Missions, affiliated with the Triennial Convention. However, the domestic situation began to change in America and this change gave birth to independent Southern Baptist Missions worldwide. Along with the growing political tensions between the South and the North in the United States on the issue of slavery, the Southern Baptists wanted to separate themselves from the North by establishing their own organization. Outraged by the refusal of the Triennial Convention to appoint Southern slave owners as missionaries, the Southerners held their first Southern Baptist Convention (SBC) in 1845 in Augusta, Georgia. In the meantime, the SBC created its own Foreign Mission Board (FMB) and instructed the Board to 'correspond with the Baptist Missionaries in China, and propose to them to come under the patronage of this board'.[6] John Lewis Shuck and Issachar Roberts accepted the offer. Shuck actually came back and attended the Foreign Mission Board meeting in March 1846 in Richmond, Virginia. He was officially received as a Southern Baptist missionary to China. At the same time, his long time Chinese helper and preacher, Yeung Hing (or Yong Seen-Song), was also appointed as preacher among his own Chinese people. Shuck and Song returned to China in 1847. This time they went directly to Guangzhou and then to Shanghai. As a result, Southern Baptist mission in China began. 'Let us assume four hundred millions as the population of the empire', the SBC declared, thinking of the great evangelical potential in China; 'let us assume them to pass before us'.[7]

The Southern Baptists made Guangzhou the first strategic location for their Christian missions. One by one, the SBC Foreign Mission Board appointed to Guangzhou a number of missionaries, including Samuel Clopton, George Pearcy, and Francis C. Johnson. In 1849, the FMB sent to Guangzhou its first single woman missionary, Harriet Baker, to open a girls' school there. By 1861, there were five missionaries and their families working in the Guangzhou station. The American Civil War disrupted the Southern Baptist operation in China for about a decade. In the early 1870s, another three missionaries, including a single woman, were sent to Guangzhou.[8] Due to their hard work, reports to the FMB in 1900 showed 1,800 Chinese Baptists in Guangzhou.[9]

After the Opium War, the Southern Baptists also moved northward to start their missions in Shanghai. Matthew Yates and his wife, missionaries from North

---

[5] *SBC Annual Report* (1845), p. 7.

[6] Baker J. Cauthen, *Advance: A History of Southern Baptist Foreign Missions* (Nashville, TN: Broadman Press, 1970), p. 79.

[7] *SBC Annual Report* (1870), Foreign Mission Board Annex, 4.

[8] *Baptist Missionary Magazine* 53 (1873), p. 277.

[9] Data collected from the China section in *SBC Annual Report* (1900).

Carolina, arrived in Shanghai in September 1847. Another couple, Thomas W. Tobey and his wife, joined them two weeks later. Quickly, the Southern Baptists established solid ground in Shanghai by constructing the First Baptist Church of Shanghai in 1850. In 1881, the Southern Baptist missionaries helped create the Shanghai Baptist Association, the first local Baptist alliance in China. In 1895, the organization evolved to become Kiangsu (Jiangsu) Baptist Association, to cover the entire province centered in Shanghai. By the end of the nineteenth century there were twenty Southern Baptist missionaries and more than 1,000 Chinese Baptists in the Shanghai region.

Moreover, the Southern Baptists kept pushing their missions into North China. This became possible after Yantai (Chefoo) became a treaty port through the Treaty of Tianjin in 1858. In December 1860, J. Landrum Holms and Sally Holms settled down in Yantai while Jesse Boardman Hartwells and his wife went to Dengzhou. In October 1861, J.L. Holms was killed by Taiping forces, but Sally Holms, his widow, continued her mission for another twenty years. In 1862, Sally helped organize the First Baptist church in Dengzhou. In 1863, Tarleton Perry Crawfords came to join the Shangdong mission after eleven years of service in East China. In 1870, the first Chinese Baptist pastor in the area, Mr Woo Tsun-chau, was ordained and became the pastor of the First Baptist Church of Dengzhou. In 1873, Charlotte (Lottie) Moon arrived in Dengzhou and eventually became a legend for Southern Baptist missions in China. By 1890, there were fourteen Southern Baptist missionaries in Shandong and they formed the North China Baptist Association. By the end of the nineteenth century there were about 1,000 Chinese Baptists in North China.[10]

From Southern Baptist Identity to China Missionary Identity

Living in China, many Southern Baptist missionaries changed dramatically to adjust to the social and cultural environment. They had to struggle to survive at first. They then had to modify their evangelism in order to accommodate to the Chinese people. Conducting their work in China, the Southern Baptist missionaries creatively developed their own Christian theology to allow them to continue their missions in many different and difficult circumstances. As a result, they began to form a unique religious identity that was different from their originally American-based Southern Baptist identity. As they became inter-cultural people, so did their faith.

Most of the missionaries initially had little preparation for living in China beyond their limited and vague knowledge of Chinese history and culture. Many did not even have the ability to speak or to write Chinese. Lottie Moon stated that she

---

[10] Regarding Lottie Moon, see Keith Harper (ed.), *Send the Light: Lottie Moon's Letters and Other Writings* (Macon, GA: Mercer University Press, 2002); Irwin T. Hyatt, *Our Ordered Lives Confess: Three Nineteenth-Century American Missionaries in East Shantung* (Cambridge, MA: Harvard University Press, 1976); Jerry Rankin and Don Ruthledge, *A Journey of Faith and Sacrifice: Retracing the Steps of Lottie Moon* (Birmingham, AL: New Hope, 1996).

received very little briefing about China before she left America for the new country where she would serve. She knew almost nothing about China; nor did she understand any of the Chinese languages. She later confessed that she had found herself totally lost in her early years in China: 'Opportunities are coming everyday and we are unable to grasp them because of no trained women workers.'[11] She had to spend more time in familiarizing herself with the local community than in conducting any mission to the Chinese.

The missionaries had to learn about China first. All of them attended language schools in order to learn the Chinese language. To their surprise, the missionaries found out that there were so many dialects spoken, especially in southern China, that people could hardly understand each other from place to place. It was a frustration to the missionaries because, as one missionary said, 'missionaries learning one dialect often feel their limitations because of their inability to serve other than their immediate field'.[12] In addition to language, the missionaries also had to get to know the Chinese culture, in particular its religious systems. 'The Chinese systems of religion', recorded in the SBC annual report of 1868, 'teach morality according to their ideas of a healthy state of public sentiment. They often commended the morality of the Bible.'[13] Therefore, it became the consensus among the Southern Baptist missionaries that the nature of the Chinese people was religious. Such an understanding constituted the fundamental assumption in the continuation of the Southern Baptist missions in China.[14]

Living in China, the Southern Baptist missionaries began to develop a personal identity that was different from their original American Southerners' identity. They wore Chinese clothes, ate Chinese food, stayed in Chinese houses, and spoke Chinese languages. They gradually became emotionally attached to China. Over time, many viewed China not only as their mission site but also, or more importantly, their second home. The missionaries also regarded themselves as local residents in the places where they were living. Their letters to the FMB often confirmed their desire to stay in China permanently. As a result, they were more and more and more assimilated into Chinese society. While they were evangelizing the Chinese, the missionaries were at least partially converted into the Chinese culture.[15]

The transformation of the missionaries' identity from purely American to a new understanding through a growing Chinese influence had a tremendous impact upon

---

[11] Hyatt, *Our Ordered Lives Confess*, p. 108.

[12] Margaret McRae Lackey, *'Laborers Together': A Study of Southern Baptist Missions in China* (New York: Fleming H. Revell, 1921), p. 22.

[13] *SBC Annual Report* (1868), p. 47.

[14] Winston Crawley, *Global Mission, A Story to Tell: An Interpretation of Southern Baptist Foreign Missions* (Nashville, TN: Broadman Press, 1985), pp. 31-32.

[15] For more discussion on the missionaries' cultural transformation, see Patricia Hill, *The World Their Household: The American Women's Foreign Mission Movement and Cultural Transformation* (Ann Arbor, MI: University of Michigan Press, 1985); Jane Hunter, *The Gospel of Gentility: American Women in Turn-of-the-Century China* (New Haven, CT: Yale University Press, 1984).

Southern Baptist missions in China. The missionaries initially went to China to respond to God's call and satisfy their own American-based evangelical dream of Christianizing China. After they became part of Chinese society, their goal changed. Although the missionaries still aimed at Christianizing the Chinese, they also wanted to serve the people. Accordingly, they modified their mission strategy to accommodate the need to help the Chinese in real ways.[16] Such a new approach opened the door to a new missionary identity that was grounded in the Chinese context.

In order to understand the transformation of the missionaries' identity, it is necessary to examine the historical development of the mission operation. The Southern Baptist missions in China started mainly as an evangelistic mission that emphasized converting the Chinese people. The Shanghai mission reported in 1851 that 'The preaching of the Gospel has constituted the chief work at which our brethren in this great city have aimed.'[17] The missionaries employed many tactics to advance their evangelical cause. They first tried to be friends to the Chinese people. They then used their personal connections to preach the gospel. Personal evangelism was, as reported by the SBC missions in China, the 'most important kind of "women's work for women" in China. All lady missionaries do more or less of it.'[18] In addition to personal evangelism, the missionaries also engaged in public preaching. Sometimes they preached to people on the streets. At other times, the missionaries went to market towns and started preaching amid the crowds. Many missionaries gave away Christian literature aboard buses and ferries. Others visited Chinese tea houses where large numbers of Chinese often gathered. A few missionaries launched activities inside Chinese prisons.

Despite the tremendous work of the missionaries before 1895 successes were small in terms of the number of the converts. In the decade 1856–65, Southern Baptist missions only attracted forty-seven Chinese converts. The numbers for the next three decades were not much better. In 1866–75, there were 289 Chinese Baptist converts; in 1876–85, there were 568; and in 1886–95, there were 808.[19] Many Southern Baptist missionaries began to wonder what to do next. Their growing Chinese identity made a difference and it was this which rescued Southern Baptist missions in China. The missionaries realized that they had to become missionaries for the Chinese people rather than missionaries for the Southern Baptist Foreign Mission Board. In practice, they should adopt methods that were more appealing to the Chinese people rather than to the FMB. As a result, the social gospel, using social services such as schools and hospitals to help evangelism, developed into the predominant method of evangelism.[20]

---

[16] Marvin Mayers, *Christianity Confronts Culture: A Strategy for Crosscultural Evangelism* (Grand Rapids, MI: Zondervan, rev. edn, 1987), pp. 34-41.

[17] *SBC Annual Report* (1851), p. 35.

[18] *SBC Annual Report* (1898), Appendix A, p. vi.

[19] Data collected from *SBC Annual Reports* of various years.

[20] Foreign Mission Board, *Southern Baptists in China* (Richmond, VA: Foreign Mission Board of the Southern Baptist Convention, 1940), pp. 45-52.

Following Baptist tradition, education became the first area of social gospel activities conducted by the Southern Baptists in China. As early as 1850, the report of the Shanghai mission indicated that there were three schools: 'The three schools under the direction of the mission are continued with prospects of much good... These schools afford favourable methods of access to youthful minds.'[21] Eventually the schools in Shanghai grew to be the well-known Eliza Yates School for girls and the Ming Jung School for boys. In 1863, the Southern Baptists created a small boarding school in Dengzhou, Shandong. In 1888, missionary Emma Young started Pooi To School for girls in Guangzhou. The Pui Ching School for boys began the next year.[22]

In addition to the regular education offered, the spiritual effects of these Baptist schools were very strong. Similar to schools in America, the students in mission schools took courses in mathematics, English, science, history, and sports. Of course, being schools for the Chinese, students had to take Chinese language courses. On top of the common curriculum, the students were required to take Bible courses. They also had to participate in campus Christian fellowships. It was the hope of the missions that these students would grow up in a Christian environment and in future would serve as seeds to spread the gospel to their family members and friends.[23] The SBC annual reports recorded the tremendous impact of the Christian religion upon the Chinese students: 'Our schools have had an influence in impressing divine truth upon the pupils. Some of the children, in spite of the opposition of idolatrous parents, persist in returning thanks to God when they eat.'[24] The religious teaching at the schools, and the outworking of that, was becoming part of the students' daily behaviour.

Southern Baptist missions in China were briefly interrupted by the Chinese Boxer Movement in 1899–1900. More than a half century after China was forced to open its doors to the West, many Chinese, especially the peasants, saw their lives deteriorating to a point where it was becoming unbearable. The annual war indemnity payments from China to the Western countries exhausted China's national treasury. Floods of Western industrialized goods were imported into China that completely destroyed traditional Chinese household manufacturing. Yet the Manchu Court was still living in luxury. Natural disasters in the forms of drought and famine took a heavy toll on ordinary people's life. Starting in Shandong Province in mid-1899, poor Chinese peasants rose up to save themselves. They mainly channeled their anger towards Westerners. In particular, Western missionaries became easy targets because the missionaries often lived among the Chinese people throughout China with little Western military protection. Between 1899 and 1900, more than

---

[21] *SBC Annual Report* (1851), p. 23.

[22] Data collected from *SBC Annual Reports* of various years.

[23] Chester Miao and Frank W. Price, *Religion and Character in Christian Middle School* (Shanghai: Chinese Christian Education Association, 1929), p. 55.

[24] *SBC Annual Report* (1874), p. 36.

350 Western missionaries were killed by the Chinese Boxers. The Western mission movement in China suffered a major blow.[25]

After the defeat of the Boxer Movement by Western troops, Western missions in China, especially the Southern Baptist missions, entered a golden age of growth. In July 1900, the joint Western army thoroughly conquered China and for the first time captured the Forbidden City. Relying upon Western military power, Christian missions very quickly revived themselves. The Southern Baptists had some advantages in this new beginning. Throughout the nineteenth century, Southern Baptist missions were concentrated in southern China, mainly Guangzhou and Shanghai, where the Boxer Movement had little influence. During the movement, the missionaries in Shandong retreated back to Shanghai. As a result, no Southern Baptist missionaries died. After the end of the Boxer Movement, Southern Baptist missionaries were ready to start their missions once again.

This time, Southern Baptist missionaries were more conscious of Chinese needs in their attempt to revive their missions. Responding to the lack of modern medical care in many parts of China, Southern Baptists began to create mission hospitals. In the first decade of the twentieth century, Southern Baptists created many hospitals throughout China: The Warren Memorial Hospital in Huang Xian, Shandong Province (1902); The Stout Memorial Hospital in Wuzhou, Guangxi Province (1904); The Zhengzhou Hospital in Henan Province (1905); The James Pollard Bagby Memorial Hospital in Yangzhou, Jiangsu Province (1907); The Czner-Alexander Memorial Hospital in Pingdu, Shandong Province (1909); The Mayfield-Tyzzer Hospital and the Kathleen Mallory Hospital in Laizhou, Shandong Province (1910). On average, each of these hospitals annually treated 3,000-5,000 Chinese patients and performed several hundred operations. Very often, the hospitals grew to be centres of the cities where they were located.[26]

The fact that hospitals were closely connected with the Southern Baptist missionaries, and in turn connected them with the Chinese people, greatly helped evangelistic work. Ordinary Chinese came to the hospitals and could feel the true spirit of love. As recorded in the SBC annual report for 1902: 'The medical work...has increased our church attendance; it has brought to hear the gospel a number...who had heretofore never entered a chapel... It has helped to allay prejudice against the missionaries and against Christianity; it has brought decided blessings to at least some who have been treated.'[27] After overcoming their prejudice and suspicion towards the missions, it became easier for more Chinese people to pay attention to Baptist preaching. The reports sent by the missionaries in China to the FMB often indicated large conversion rates among Chinese patients, sometimes reaching half of the patient population. Furthermore, the medical missions enabled the Southern Baptists to attract some very enthusiastic Chinese Christian workers.

[25] Robert Coventry Forsyth, *The China Martyrs of 1900* (New York: Fleming H. Revell), 1904.
[26] Data collected from *SBC Annual Reports* of various years.
[27] *SBC Annual Report* (1902), Appendix A, p. 97.

The increased reliance on Chinese Christian workers led to the necessity of offering better training to them so that the Chinese workers could be more effective in helping the Southern Baptist missions. Many missionaries recognized 'The great multitudes of China must be evangelized by Chinese. The churches can never be really strong until they are self-supporting, self-governing and self-propagating; and this means that they must be manned with an efficient native ministry. Here, then, is the peculiar sphere of the missionary—to train pastors and evangelists.'[28] At the request of the missionaries, the Southern Baptist FMB sponsored several theological seminaries, including the Bush Theological Seminary in Shangdong (1904), the Graves Theological Seminary in Guangzhou (1906), and the Shanghai Baptist College and Theological Seminary (1909).[29] Beginning with theological training, the Southern Baptist educational mission entered into the field of higher education. Eventually, the Baptist Shanghai College developed into a top university in China.

The Southern Baptist seminaries helped change the nature of the relationship between the missionaries and the Chinese Christian workers. The training at the seminaries enabled the growth of Chinese Christian leaders. Many Chinese graduates of the seminaries took over the leadership of the Baptist churches all over China. As Chinese workers demonstrated more and more competence, the role of the missionaries changed from domination of the mission to sharing power and responsibilities. The two sides thus became partners in promoting Baptist mission in China. The position of the missionaries shifted from one in which they were seen as superior to the Chinese Christian workers to one in which they became equal alongside the new, fully-trained Chinese Christian leaders.

In an effort to get their message across to a larger Chinese audience, the Southern Baptists devoted tremendous energy to the publication of Christian literature. Understanding the traditional Chinese Confucian emphasis on learning and reading, the missionaries realized the power of Christian literature in reaching ordinary Chinese. Traditionally, the Chinese people valued highly the printed word because of the influence of Confucianism. 'These feelings', according to the missionaries' observations, 'tend to give the printed page a permanence which it does not have in other lands, and makes the difference between the spoken word and the written character all the more marked.'[30] Responding to China's unique situation, the Southern Baptists launched the largest organized publication agency in foreign lands, The China Baptist Publication Society. It was first created in Guangzhou in 1899 and moved to Shanghai in 1907. The society's purpose was the publication and distribution of Bibles, Christian books and tracts, and Sunday School literature. The missionaries reported to the FMB, 'The press is to wield a greater power for the

---

[28] S.J. Porter, *Southern Baptist Missions in China* (Richmond, VA: Foreign Mission Board, Southern Baptist Convention, 1936), p. 18.

[29] Data collected from *SBC Annual Reports* of various years. Also see Jessie G. Lutz, *China and the Christian Colleges* (Ithaca, NY: Cornell University Press, 1971).

[30] R.H. Graves, *Forty Years in China* (Baltimore, MA: H.H. Woodward Co., 1895), p. 254.

spread of the Gospel than ever before in China.'[31] The wide availability of Christian literature through publications by the society made it easy for Chinese Christians to study and understand the Christian message. This literature also attracted many Chinese who otherwise would not have had contact with Christianity.

As the missionaries made themselves more fully part of Chinese society, the Chinese people responded to the Christian call more enthusiastically. In the early twentieth century, Christian missions in general enjoyed a significant revival after the downturn during the Boxer Movement. As the Chinese people witnessed the extraordinary services in education and medicine offered by the Christian missions, they also came to listen to the religious message behind the services. The number of churchgoers rose sharply, as did the number of converts. The most outstanding revival was the Shandong Revival, in the birthplace of the Boxer Movement. People became conscious of personal sin and had a genuine desire for wholehearted change. Southern Baptist missionaries reported to the FMB, 'The most telling and sure evidence that the Revival is from God is the evidence of changed lives; opium given up, idols torn down, quarrels of years standing made up, village hoodlums turned into humble men of prayer and soul winning.'[32]

Similar revivals throughout China led to a significant increase in the number of Chinese Baptists. In 1886–95, there were 808 Baptists in China. In 1896–1905, the total number of Chinese Baptists reached 4,160. The number tripled in 1906–15 to 15,375. By the end of the next decade, 1925, China had 26,425 Baptists under the auspices of the Southern Baptist missions.[33] Southern Baptist missionaries' adjustment to China's social context produced great results. After the missionaries became more closely associated with Chinese society, more Chinese responded to the call of Baptist missionaries and of local Baptist Christians.

From China Missionary Identity to Chinese Baptist Identity

With the increasing Chinese participation in the Southern Baptist missions, the nature of the missions began to change to become more and more a service for the Chinese. Superficial adaptation was no longer enough. The increasing number of Chinese Baptists demanded qualitative transformation to make Baptist faith and practice more fully a Chinese faith. Gradually, the Chinese Baptists took control of the leadership, the finance, and the operation of Baptist work. As a result, a Chinese Baptist identity was established.

The increasing number of Chinese Baptists demanded Chinese Baptist leadership. By the beginning of the twentieth century, many Chinese Baptists attended the theological seminaries created by the Southern Baptist missions. After completing

---

[31] *SBC Annual Report* (1901), p. 95.

[32] Mary K. Crawford, *The Shantung Revival* (Shanghai: The China Baptist Publication Society, 1933), p. 102. See also Daniel H. Bays, 'Christian Revivals in China, 1900–1937', in Edith L. Blumhofer and Randall Balmer (eds), *Modern Christian Revival* (Urbana and Chicago, IL: University of Illinois Press, 1993).

[33] Data collected from *SBC Annual Reports* of various years.

their studies, these Chinese seminary graduates became active in their churches, many becoming pastors and deacons. In southern China, Pastor Cheung Lap-tsoi was a prominent Chinese Baptist leader in Guangzhou. In central China, Pastor Wong Ping San and Deacon Wong Yuk San were instrumental in operating the famous North Gate Church in Shanghai. In North China, the missionaries reported to the FMB in 1917, 'Years ago the work was carried out by missionaries and native helpers. Now, it is carried on by Chinese and foreign helpers.'[34]

Furthermore, Chinese Baptists gradually took over the leadership in the theological seminaries and publication societies. In the most prestigious institution, the University of Shanghai (formerly the College of Shanghai), Professor Tong Tsing-en became the first Chinese professor in 1906. In 1915, he became the Vice President. During 1917–18, Professor Tong was the Acting President. In 1928, the American educated Chinese Baptist, Dr Herman C.E. Liu, served with distinction as the President of the University of Shanghai until his assassination by the Japanese on 7 April 1938. In the publication field, Mr Chang Wen-kai became the editor of *True Light* magazine, which was circulated throughout China as well as to twenty-two foreign countries. The South China Mission reported to the FMB that 'This is the way it should be... We can no long differentiate between missionaries and Chinese. We are one with them; and with one mind and one heart we are all working for our great constructive Baptist Program.'[35]

The participation in the mission leadership by the Chinese Baptists greatly increased the level of contextualization of Baptist life in China. A major innovation in Chinese Baptist activity from the beginning was the close association between the faith itself and its established institutions, such as the mission compounds, the churches, the mission schools and the mission hospitals. To Chinese Baptists their religion would not be real if it existed without these practical elements. The religious institutions made Baptist life part of the Chinese social structure and thus constituted the actual symbols to demonstrate that Baptist belief was in China to stay.[36] Chinese Baptists thus viewed churches, schools and hospitals not only as the tools of the social gospel but also as the gospel itself. Without the existence of these institutions, there would be no faith for them.

Therefore, the primary goal for Chinese Baptists was to keep alive mission institutions such as churches, schools, and hospitals. Dr Herman C.E. Liu once said, 'The Baptists have promoted several lines of work, chiefly evangelistic work, educational work, medical work, and the production and circulation of Christian literature. We have made a worthy record.'[37] Baptist missions would not have survived without these real contributions. As long as Baptists maintained their devotion to concrete works, Liu insisted, 'there is really no limit to what Baptists in

---

[34] *SBC Annual Reports* (1917), p. 86.

[35] Crawley, *Partners Across the Pacific*, p. 76.

[36] Wang Zhixin, *Zhongguo jidujiao shigang* [*A History of Chinese Christianity*] (Shanghai: Qinnianhui shuju, 1940), pp. 24-35.

[37] Herman C.E. Liu, 'How Can Baptists Now Best Serve the Cause of Christ in China?', *The New East*, 24.4 (June, 1930), p. 5.

China may accomplish for the cause of Christ'.[38] Working at the University of Shanghai, President Liu committed himself fully to the continuing existence of the University. He often had to make concessions to the changing Chinese social context to make the University more acceptable to the Chinese public. He knew, nonetheless, that Baptists would survive in China as long as he could ensure its smooth operation. He declared, 'We want to make the college...more Chinese, to meet the needs of Chinese social life.'[39] The University of Shanghai was the leading Christian higher educational institution to register with the Chinese government in the Nationalist Revolution. Although it might appear secular, it was the most practical and effective way to ensure the presence of Baptists in China.

The experience of Herman Liu and the University of Shanghai exemplified an important new aspect of the identity of Chinese Baptist life: it was a patriotic and nationalistic expression of religion in China. Amid rising Chinese nationalism, Christians of any denomination had to acquire a political identity in order to stay in China. Patriotism thus offered a convenient vehicle. Indigenization of Christianity as a Chinese religion was also a process designed to unite Christianity with Chinese nationalism. Facing the constant revolutions in twentieth-century China, the politicization of Christianity became unavoidable in order for the Christian faith to demonstrate its Chinese identity.

A major step towards the politicization of Baptist life in China was to ally Baptist faith with Chinese nationalism. In order to make their expression of Christianity more Chinese, the Chinese Baptists wanted to construct a strong linkage between their faith and their patriotism. They claimed that the purpose of Baptists was not to Westernize Chinese society. Instead, the Baptist faith was meant to serve China's interest by making her stronger. T.L. Shen, a prominent Chinese Baptist, stated in 1928, 'China *must* meet the requirements of the modern world, but she must also be *permitted* to meet them with her own resources and plans.'[40] In this process, Baptists could make a corporate contribution to China's path towards modernization. Chinese Baptists also emphasized that individually they were Chinese first and Baptists second. They stressed that their baptism was not intended to detach them from Chinese society. Instead, their faith allowed them to serve China wholeheartedly because it made them firm believers in using Western genius to fulfill the Chinese goals to make the country stronger.

The desire of Chinese Baptists to demonstrate their patriotism and nationalism gave rise to the independent movement within the Baptist churches. In time, many Baptist churches came under the control of the Chinese Baptists. By the early twentieth century most churches had Chinese pastors. The Southern Baptist regional missions also developed, becoming Chinese-controlled area Baptist organizations, such as the Kiangsu (Jiangsu) Baptist Association and the Two Kwang (Guang)

---

[38] Liu, 'How Can Baptists Now Best Serve', p. 7.

[39] Herman Chan-en Liu, 'Shanghai College and Baptist Churches', *The New East*, 22.6 (May, 1928), p. 5.

[40] T.L. Shen, 'Religious Liberty in China', *The China Christian Year Book* (1928), p. 49.

Baptist Association. The Chinese Baptists were becoming leaders in their own kind of Baptist life, which was very much a Chinese faith. An important sign of Chinese independence was reflected in their attempt to organize their own missions without the involvement of the American missionaries. In the Southern Baptist South China Mission, there were fifty-five Chinese men and seventeen Chinese women working as missionaries among their fellow Chinese people. Although most of them were funded by Southern Baptist missions, thirteen of them were supported by their own Chinese Baptist churches.[41]

As a result of the growing Chinese influence in the Baptist missions, the relationship between the Chinese Baptists and the Southern Baptist missionaries also changed from student–teacher to equal partners. In all the missions—evangelical, educational, and medical—the Chinese workers were replacing the missionaries. Pastor Cheung San-kei in Guangzhou, Pastor Wu Gi-djung in Shanghai, and Pastor Li Show-ting in Dengzhou all served as fine examples of Chinese leadership capability, because the churches under their control quickly doubled their membership. Chinese Bible women, such as Wang The-lu in Henan, were especially successful in promoting Baptist beliefs among Chinese women. The Southern Baptist missionaries acknowledged the fact that the Chinese workers were often more effective in developing more Chinese converts and church members. The missionaries were deeply impressed by the devotion demonstrated by Chinese workers. A missionary reported from South China, 'Our native medical assistant refused the offer of $1,300 a year and continued with us at a salary of $480. It was only faithfulness to Christ that caused him to do so.'[42]

The Chinese input into the Southern Baptist missions had a major impact upon one fundamental element in Baptist theology—the relationship between the Baptists and the government. One important doctrine held by the Southern Baptists, stated by the famous Edgar Young Mullins, was that 'to be responsible, the soul must be free…a free church in a free state'.[43] Southern Baptists struggled hard to maintain their independence from government control. Chinese Baptists, however, realized that the relationship between the Baptist missions and the Chinese government had to be a friendlier one in order for Baptist beliefs to survive, otherwise rising Chinese nationalism would destroy Christianity altogether. Therefore, Chinese Baptists decided to cooperate fully with the Chinese government by ensuring that Baptist thinking was more in line with Chinese nationalism and by personally participating in Chinese politics as well.

The first political action of the Chinese Christians, including the Baptists, was to denounce the unequal treaties that had been the symbol of the unity between Christianity and Western imperialism. Many Chinese Baptist leaders openly called for the abolition of the unequal treaties and the end of all foreign privileges, including Western settlements, extra-territoriality, and the protection of the Christian

---

[41] Crawley, *Partners Across the Pacific*, pp. 72-79.

[42] Porter, *Southern Baptist Missions in China*, p. 26.

[43] Albert McClellan, *Meet Southern Baptists* (Nashville, TN: Broadman Press, 1978), p. 38.

missions. A group of Chinese Baptists published a declaration in 1925 stating, 'We
do not want to build Christianity upon the basis of the gunboat policy. Neither do
we want to have the protection from the unequal treaties that will destroy our
nation.'[44]

As part of their effort to eliminate imperialistic elements of being Baptist,
Chinese Baptists started a massive movement to nationalize the religion.
Throughout the country they took over the full administrative responsibility for their
churches' operation. Now the missionaries became church workers in subordination
to Chinese leadership. Chinese Baptists affirmed their goal of making the entire
Baptist operation 'self-dependent, self-financed, and self-propogated'. The late 1920s
thus became the turning point in transforming the Baptist missions from a Southern
Baptist endeavour to an independent Chinese institution.

The most extreme action taken by the Chinese was in response to the
government's requirement of the registration of Christian institutions. In November
1925 the Chinese government started the 'Movement to Recover Educational
Rights'. It required all the Christian schools to establish a Chinese board of trustees,
appoint Chinese principals, and register with the Chinese authorities. In the
meantime, the Chinese government also demanded that all the Christian hospitals
comply with similar requirements. By doing so, administrative control of the
Christian organizations would pass from Western to Chinese control. Furthermore,
the Chinese government demanded all Christian institutions to severe their
relationships with Western mission boards.[45]

The period of the late 1920s was a real test for the Southern Baptist missions in
China. The Southern Baptist FMB, based upon the traditional Baptist belief in the
complete freedom of the church from any government control, ordered the Baptist
institutions in China not to register with the Chinese government. In fact, the Board
was prepared to close its institutions if the Chinese government should force them to
register. Chinese Baptists, however, kept petitioning the Board that the struggle for
religious liberty in China was not to be fought in the same way as in America.
'Religion to the Chinese', stated by T.L. Shen, 'actually meant "living" the way'.[46]
Chinese Baptists argued that if the government gave them no other alternative, the
Baptist missions should comply with the demand for registration. In August 1930,
Chinese Baptists created the China Baptist Alliance so that they could take
independent decisions. At its inaugural meeting, the Alliance decided to cooperate
with the Chinese government on the issue of registration because it was the only

[44] Crawley, *Partners Across the Pacific*, p. 76.

[45] Alice H. Gregg, *China and Educational Autonomy: The Changing Role of the
Protestant Educational Missionary in China, 1807–1937* (Syracuse, NY: Syracuse
University Press, 1946); Tatsuro Yamamoto and Sumiko Yamamoto, 'The Anti-Christian
Movement in China, 1922–1927', *Far Eastern Quarterly*, 12 (February, 1953), pp. 140-
45; Ka-che Yip, *Religion, Nationalism and Chinese Students: The Anti-Christian
Movement of 1922–1927* (Bellingham, WA: Center for East Asian Studies, Western
Washington Universities, 1980).

[46] Shen, 'Religious Liberty in China', p. 50.

way to maintain Baptist life in China. Indeed, by the end of 1930 all Baptist institutions, including schools and hospitals, had registered with the Chinese government. In the meantime, the Baptist churches began to preach the message that patriotism was essential in creating a Chinese Baptist theology.[47]

The nationalization of Christianity in China actually inspired the rise of a new Baptist theology that was based upon Baptist adaptation to the extremely politicized Chinese social environment. Despite the opposition from the Southern Baptist FMB, the new Chinese Baptist theology considered the survival of the Baptist institutions like schools and hospitals more important than the continuation of evangelism. It also stressed that a good Baptist should first be a true patriot of China and that an indigenized theology was also a nationalist theology. Building a strong alliance with Chinese nationalism, Baptists became a part of modern China that would not go away. It was in China to stay.

By the time of the Baptist Centennial Conference held in Guangzhou in 1936, the Chinese Baptists had completely taken over the entire operation of the Southern Baptist missions in China. Following orders from the Chinese government, the Chinese Baptists became leaders of the Baptist missions in China while the missionaries could only serve as ordinary workers in the missions. All of the Baptist churches claimed to be self-supporting. In their preaching, Chinese pastors also tried to include Chinese nationalist ideology, especially Sun Yat-sen's Three Peoples' Principles. The Baptist Centennial Conference gave an opportunity for Chinese Baptists to demonstrate to the government that they were now truly in charge of Baptist life. Only the Chinese Baptist leaders sat on the stage. The conference formally abolished the Southern Baptist divisions of South, Central, North, and Interior China Missions and in their place the conference created Baptist conventions based on Chinese provinces with local Chinese Baptists as trustees and administrators. Finally, the Southern Baptist missions in China had been transformed into Chinese Baptist institutions.[48]

The Sino-Japanese War of 1937–45 testified to the Chinese nature of Baptist belief and practice in China. Chinese Baptists were among the first to protest against the Japanese invasion. Relying upon their international connections, they revealed to the world Japanese atrocities and Chinese sufferings. They helped China win international sympathy and support. For this, Herman C.E. Liu, the best-known Chinese Baptist leader, finally paid with his own life when he was assassinated by Japanese spies in 1939. The other important contribution by Chinese Baptists during

---

[47] Editorial, 'Jiaohui yijiao xingzhenquan zhuquan zhi wenti' ['The problem for the church to turn over power to the new government'], *China Christian Education Quarterly*, 4 (June, 1928), pp. 43-52.

[48] For more information of nationalist rule, see Lloyd E. Eastman, *The Abortive Revolution: China under the Nationalist Rule, 1927–1937* (Cambridge, MA: Harvard University Press, 1974); Lancelot Forster, *The New Culture in China* (New York: Frederick A. Stokes, 1936); Zhongyan wenhua gongzuo weiyuanhui [Central Commission on Cultrual Work], *Zhongguo guomindang yu wenhua jiaoyu* [*The GMD and Culture and Education*] (Taibei: Zhengzhong shuju, 1984).

wartime was their efforts to preserve hope for China through education. During 1937–41, in the Western settlements in Shanghai, the Baptist University of Shanghai continued its operation. In the meantime, Baptists also combined all the Baptist schools that had been lost in the Japanese occupation and created the Baptist Union Middle School. It enrolled 405 students in 1938, 530 in 1939, and 1,050 in 1940. The school also proved the viability of Chinese theology: Baptist faith would survive as long as Baptist institutions continued in China. At the Middle School an evangelistic meeting in September 1940 produced 167 student converts, while a week of Bible courses in March 1941 led to 130 converts. By the end of 1941, the majority of the students had become Christians.[49] The Japanese attack on Pearl Harbor ended the Western settlements in China and forced the Baptist schools into closure. The Baptist expression of Christianity, however, remained in the minds of many Chinese.[50]

It was this strong Chinese identity that firmly made Baptists part of postwar Chinese society. Recognizing the tremendous wartime Christian contribution, the Chinese government now fully acknowledged the existence of all kinds of Christianity, including the Baptist form. Baptist institutions were reopened in the formerly Japanese controlled territories. The number of churchgoers rose constantly. Chinese Baptist life had the best environment in which to grow. The Communist triumph in 1949, however, destroyed such a prospect. Under Communist leadership, atheism has since ruled over China.[51]

Conclusion

The history of the development of Chinese Baptist life clearly demonstrates the identity of Baptist faith to be a combination of Chinese nationalism and Baptist theology. Throughout its existence in China, Baptist commitment has been viable only when it has fully integrated itself into Chinese society. As a result, it has created new religious interpretations that are quite different from its Southern Baptist roots. In the process, however, as noted by T.L. Shen, it has assumed 'a liberal attitude of humility, tolerance, and sympathy'.[52] Eventually, Chinese Baptist life became much more an expression of a faith professed and further developed by the Chinese themselves rather than a somewhat alien religion imposed on the Chinese by missionaries. It became a new and independent Christian denomination in China.

---

[49] Tstsu Chen, 'The Baptist Union Middle School', in Papers of the Baptist Union Middle School, Southern Baptist Historical Archives and Library, Nashville, TN.

[50] Arch Carey, *War Years at Shanghai, 1941–45–48* (New York: Vintage Press, 1967); Tao Juyin, *Gudao jianwen—Kangzhan shiqi de shanghai* [*Reports from the Solitary Island—Shanghai in the War of Resistance*] (Shanghai: Shanghai renmin, 1979).

[51] Lionel M. Chassin, *The Communist Conquest of China: A History of the Civil War, 1945–1949* (Cambridge, MA: Harvard University Press, 1965).

[52] Shen, 'Religious Liberty in China', p. 56.

CHAPTER 17

Globalization as Local Phenomenon: Philippine Baptists and the Creation of Community at the End of the Twentieth Century

Brian M. Howell

The Southern Baptist mission to the Philippines unofficially began during World War II, when several missionaries were brought to Baguio from China by the conquering Japanese army. Interred for several years, at least one of these missionaries later wrote that she left Baguio in 1945 'hoping to never see the Philippines again'.[1] But that wish would not come true, for in 1949 these missionaries were again brought to Baguio, this time to escape the advancing Communist Revolution of Mao Ze Dong. Thinking they would return to China within a few years, this group of American missionaries continued their Chinese language study with the small but prosperous Chinese community in the so-called American Simla, the Northern Philippine mountain retreat of Baguio City. Within a year, they had launched an official mission to this Chinese community and founded the first Southern Baptist church in 1950. This church, Baguio Chinese Baptist Church, was pastored by an American missionary for several years as they waited out their exile, but even then they planned for the assumption of leadership by Chinese–Filipinos, creating the Chinese-language based Philippine Baptist Theological Seminary in 1952.

When it became clear that the communist government of China would not fall any time soon, these missionaries decided to launch work among the Filipino populations of Baguio and the nearby city of San Fernando. In 1953 the first American missionaries arrived to learn Philippine languages and classes began to be taught at the seminary in English, to accommodate those Filipinos who had been educated under the American colonial regime. Within ten years, Southern Baptist missionaries were spread throughout the island of Luzon and a number of churches had been founded.

Although there were, according to Robert Orr, two distinct phases of missionary method and philosophy between 1954 and his research in 1986, one thing that remained constant for these Southern Baptists was a commitment to turn over

---

[1] Fern Harrington Miles, 'God's Call to the Philippines', in Jan Hill (ed.), *Let the Philippine Island Be Glad* (Fort Worth, TX: Bundok Press, 1999), p. 3.

leadership of new congregations to Filipinos as quickly as they felt possible.[2] Thus, most Filipino congregations founded by the Southern Baptists never had more than a few years in which American missionaries served as leaders.

Even many of the newer congregations, dating back to the 1980s, are now in their second generation of leadership in which young members have gone to seminary and either returned to serve in the church or gone to pastor other congregations. This leads us to an interesting moment in understanding Baptist identity in the Philippines as well as the development of Protestantism generally in a post-missionary era. While much of the anthropological and historical research of Philippine Christianity has focused on the interaction of missionary and missionized, the questions now concern how these believers are re-imagining their Christian identity as a movement no longer flowing from the West, but firmly planted in Filipino soil.

Unfortunately, this process of creating a Christian identity that is manifestly local has often been cast as clash between orthodox, 'missionary' theology and non-Christian, local beliefs.[3] Identifying so-called local Christianity, then, becomes an effort to uncover the indigenous beliefs lurking behind Christian forms. In other words, localization implies theological syncretism, distinctive practices and unique ritual forms. The intrusion of the local into the universal religion of Christianity is taken to refer to the adaptation, or, depending on one's point of view, corruption, of traditional orthodox theology and/or practice.

In the case of the Baguio Baptists, this dichotomy does not capture what it means for these Christians to localize their religion. In fact, by the syncretist logic, Philippine Baptists have not localized their religion much, if at all. Certainly, to identify as a Southern Baptist is clearly to claim an identity that is not 'local'. Indeed, the convention of congregations founded by the Southern Baptists has chosen to retain the name of 'Southern Baptist' to distinguish themselves from the General Baptists, and signal their historic connection to American missionary efforts. Strongest in the northern Philippines, the convention is still officially known as the Luzon Conventions of Southern Baptist Churches. The issue is regularly raised whether they should perhaps change the name, dropping 'Southern'. But at the annual national conference I attended in 1998, the motion was dropped rather quickly as people argued for their 'tradition', their 'historical background', and their connection with 'Southern Baptists around the world'.

But it would be a mistake to think that these Baptists are rejecting locality or their Filipino particularity in favor of some non-local 'Other'. As we begin to

---

[2] Robert Allen Orr, 'Social Change among Religious Change Agents' (PhD dissertation, Columbia University, 1986).

[3] See, e.g., Charles Keyes, 'Christianity as an Indigenous Religion', *Social Compass* (1991), pp. 177-85; also Lorraine V. Aragon, 'Reorganizing the Cosmology: The Reinterpretation of Deities and Religious Practice by Protestants in Central Sulawesi, Indonesia', *Journal of Southeast Asian Studies* 27.2 (1996), pp. 350-73; cf. Joel Robbins, ''God Is Nothing but Talk': Modernity, Language, and Prayer in a Papuan New Guinea Society', *American Anthropologist* 103.4 (2001), pp. 910-12.

explore the history and contemporary ethnographic reality we find that far from being a lonely outpost of American Christianity, the congregations studied represent sites of local production in which the global flow of a transnational religion is brought into meaningful and profound contact with the daily lives of believers on the ground. This case is a challenge to concepts used in interpreting religion as indigenization and contextualization by problematizing ideas of 'culture', 'the Philippines', and the idea of 'context' itself. These issues are perhaps best brought to the fore in recent work on theories of locality.

Producing Baptist Localities

Arjun Appadurai's notion of the 'production of locality' is particularly useful in interpreting the recent history of Baptists in the Philippines.[4] Appadurai notes that locations are inherently social, as opposed to scalar or spacial, implying that locality, like culture, is always in flux, fragile and vulnerable to the agency of actors who would remake the social world either inadvertently or by design.[5] Those attempting to understand locality, he argues, should focus not on a history of community *per se*, but on the techniques by which those communities are produced.[6] Grounding this production in 'local knowledge', Appadurai forces us to consider the very notions of culture and context. If the production of these Baptist communities seems grounded in the non-local knowledge of a theologically informed Baptist identity, does that suggest that 'Philippine culture' has been pushed out in favor of non-local practices? The flaw in this question remains the dichotomy of a particular, distinctive, 'local' Philippines contrasted to the Anglo-American, western, 'global' Christianity practiced. The fundamental insight of Appadurai's theory, that 'locality-producing activities are not only context-driven but are also context-generative', argues that in the world of transnational flows, understanding 'the Philippines' is not to find the unchanged essence of traditional culture, but to find the techniques whereby a Filipino context is produced.[7]

One of the most important ways in which Christians everywhere generate a sense their local identity is through their Christian ritual, in particular, worship.[8] Music, embodied practices, speech forms and liturgy reflect choices made to symbolically associate with or produce particular communities and religious identities. In this chapter, I will look at worship and debates around the propriety of worship within several congregations of Southern Baptist churches in the Northern Philippine city of Baguio. These discussions are illustrative of the processes of identity construction

[4] Arjun Appadurai, *Modernity at Large: Cultural Dimensions of Globalization* (Minneapolis, MN: Public Worlds, University of Minnesota Press, 1996), ch. 9.

[5] Appadurai, *Modernity at Large*, ch. 9.

[6] Appadurai, *Modernity at Large*, p. 182.

[7] Appadurai, *Modernity at Large*, p. 186.

[8] See, e.g., Nancy Tatom Ammerman, *Congregation and Community* (Brunswick, NJ: Rutgers University Press, 1997); Penny Edgell Becker, *Congregations in Conflict: Cultural Models of Local Religious Life* (Cambridge: Cambridge University Press, 1999).

and community formation in which members negotiate their position as part of a global community of Baptists and Christians while self-consciously situating themselves in a local frame. In following the contours of these practices and discussions, I found that although denominationalism has historically been derived from theological distinctions, in the Philippines these theological discussions largely fall away in the face of practice. Distinguishing their practice of Christianity from Christian and non-Christian groups around them, particularly Pentecostalism, these Philippine Baptists engage in the production of a globally informed locality.[9]

Meaningful Worship: Practice and Context

When I asked the question, 'What is your favorite part of the Sunday service?,' all but one of my informants told me 'the message'.[10] The spoken work is privileged in the Protestant setting, and hearing the word and learning about the Bible is, throughout the world, considered the highest duty of the Protestant or evangelical Christian. But none of those I interviewed would say that the other elements of the service were unimportant. Although elsewhere I discuss the place of preaching in the production of locality and community, within each congregation, the worship ritual (primarily meaning congregational singing, individual musical performance, testimonies and other oratory apart from the sermon) consumed considerable resources in terms of time spent preparing, the number of people involved and staff dedicated to the task.[11] The differences in practice between the congregations were not dramatic, but they were significant. Within the debates, decisions and discussions around worship practices, I found a rich source towards understanding the techniques of locality production.

These data are based on eighteen months of research on four congregations of Southern Baptists in the Northern Philippine city of Baguio. Although each congregation has a particular history, they are strongly linked, institutionally and socially, through common association in Baptist conventions, affiliations with the local Philippine Baptist Theological Seminary, and historical roots in the American-based missionary efforts that gave rise to each group. The first congregation, Baguio Chinese Baptist Church (BCBC) was the first Southern Baptist congregation in the Philippines, founded in 1950 by the aforementioned missionaries exiled from China.

---

[9] It might seem strange to focus on the divergence between Pentecostalism and denominational Protestantism in a nation that is 85% Catholic. However, because Catholicism is much further from the Baptist idea of ideal Christian practice (when it is considered true Christianity at all) it is not as powerful nor as frequent a foil in the production of locality undertaken by these Baptist congregations.

[10] This was asked on a survey distributed over several months (November 1999–January 2000).

[11] Brian Howell, 'Practical Belief and the Localization of Christianity: Pentecostal and Denominational Christianity in Global/Local Perspective', *Religion* (in press). See also Brian Howell, 'At Home in the World: Philippine Baptists and the Creation of Context' (PhD dissertation, Washington University, 2002). pp. 264-82.

Here religious practice had a specifically ethnic orientation in which the main morning service was conducted in Chinese, while those members born in the Philippines, who were fluent in English and Tagalog, had an English-speaking service in the evening. Although this congregation, like most Chinese-Filipino churches, had looked hard to find an ethnically Chinese pastor who could preach in Chinese and English, the music director was the Filipino wife of the pastor. She had a bachelor's degree from the University of the Philippines' main campus in Metro Manila and also taught music part-time at the seminary. Her primary responsibility was to organize the choir and play piano during the services, including the main Chinese language service.

The second group, University Baptist Church (UBC), was founded more recently as a student ministry near one of the many universities of Baguio. Since its inception in 1971, this congregation has continued to attract professionals, university graduates and generally upper-class people as the majority of members. When I arrived in 1998, this congregation had recently hired an Indian who was a graduate of the local seminary with a degree in music. With a larger-than-average budget, UBC was able to support a significantly larger staff to manage various aspects of their church as well as provide their 'music pastor' with funds to supplement his worship materials.

Finally, La Trinidad Baptist Church, located in the adjacent city of La Trinidad, had something of a ethnic-minority identity, as most of the members were affiliated with one of the main upland minority groups of the northern Philippines. However, unlike the Chinese church, they did not explicitly mark their identity as an 'ethnic' congregation, and brought few symbols of mountain ethnicity into their congregation. While many of the leaders of this congregation were college-educated professionals, unlike UBC, the congregation was quite heterogeneous in terms of class and education. Partway through my research, a significant group of leaders broke away from TBC over long-simmering conflicts, to start a new congregation that came to be known as Faith Community Church. In terms of worship resources, TBC staffed their music posts with two part-time positions. The first was the accompanist, a member of their congregation who played professionally, gave lessons, and had even been the professional musician of other congregations. The second was primarily responsible for the congregational choir, but who also began leading the Sunday morning worship. Faith Community Church did not even have a full-time pastor by the time I left in 2000, but in the early days of their organization, they spent a fair amount of their time discussing the specific issues of worship practices and musical styles.

Walking into any of these congregations on a Sunday morning, anyone familiar with American Evangelicalism or traditional Baptist Christianity would feel right at home. With the exception of the Chinese congregation who often sang hymns and praise choruses translated into Chinese, all the congregations used English-language music, most of it produced in places like Australia and the United States. And even the Chinese congregation followed a style of worship common among American congregations. Bulletins in every congregation gave the order of the service from the welcome, through a time of singing, the collection of the offering, sermon and benediction. Preaching was as likely to refer to James Dobson and Charles Swindoll as to public figures in the Philippines, and sermon illustrations frequently sounded like they were recently downloaded from sermons.com. Differences between the congregations could not be classified according to which were 'more local' or authentically 'Filipino', but rather the extent to which each relied on traditional western hymns towards those that used so-called contemporary Christian music. That is, whereas the Chinese congregation was more likely to sing traditional hymns, UBC utilized a full worship band of electronic instruments and drum set, while TBC employed a mix of the two. However, after spending time with these congregations, I soon realized that this seeming hegemony of western worship practices (from traditional to contemporary) was not simply the result of a neo-colonial mentality or rejection of locality. Rather, the decisions that gave rise to these differences were made to create a locality in which each congregation could occupy a specific place in the social and religious landscape of the Philippines while indexing membership in a non-local community of faith.

Unlike the practices of preaching, there was a flexibility and openness to worship practices that made them particularly responsive to the process of locality production among lay members. Whereas only professional clergy, distinguished guests, and respected lay leaders were ever invited to preach, young people and new members of the church could easily become involved in the 'music ministry' if they had any ability to sing or play an instrument. At TBC, in fact, there was one young man who joined about the same time I began my research in 1998. Within six months he was a member of the choir and singing 'special music' during the service. Such a young, unknown member was never asked to speak from the front the entire time I was attending the various congregations. Indeed, this particular fellow was thought to be somewhat slow and odd; he would likely never be qualified for preaching or teaching, but his involvement in music was never questioned.

In the case of UBC, the musicians and worship leaders were often young people who had learned to play contemporary electronic instruments. The worship leader, a position present in every congregation, was likely to be a young person with some natural singing talent and a familiarity with both the style of music and specific contemporary Christian songs. Worship style had become something that was not only given over to young people but was also seen as a function of youth culture. That is, the music and other issues of 'worship form' had become, in the minds of these Christians, linked with the generational changes they witnessed in the society as a whole. To the extent that these changes occurred, it was not an effort to conform to an externally imposed pattern, but a response to the perception of a particular, generationally defined subculture and the tastes and values of middle-class youth.

Most of those I spoke with had definite preferences when it came to music and musical styles. Somewhat predictably, the older people overwhelmingly expressed a preference for hymns and more 'traditional' music, as opposed to the hand-clapping, 'rock-and-roll' style of the newer music. But their preferences were rarely voiced as a desire to return to more traditional hymnody. Most expressed sentiments such as this member of UBC:

> BH: When...when you first started coming *was the service a somewhat more traditional Baptist service*—hymns and the like...and that was good for you? *You like the hymns?*
> LC: I like them also. Yes. I very much prefer hymns.
> BH: And when they changed to contemporary music *that was OK with you?*
> LC: *That was OK also, yes...because* my children are growing up already and they like the kind of music also.
> BH: So *its not it is not very important to you,* what kind of music...?
> LC: *Not important.* We should grow with time...grow with time...grow with each generation...[12]

Even those most reluctant to see musical forms moving towards contemporary styles seemed resigned to the inevitability of change. One of the leaders of the Chinese congregation, a well-respected businessman who was known for his cultural and religious conservatism, put it this way:

> MA: I do not think it is so much important what we sing. We cannot just forget all the old, but the young people, they like this [new music]. Why not? Let them sing. Not only [their music] but some hymns, but they are used to this, so we can let them sing [them]. The most important is they stay [within the church].
> BH: Do you like their music?
> MA: I do not like [it.] It is better for me just to sing the hymn... Songs I know. But it is OK.

Perhaps the most reluctance came from the widow of a former lay leader of TBC who had objected to the use of any instruments other than the piano. For many years, this influential leader had banned drums from the service and otherwise kept TBC from adopting more contemporary styles of music. It was only after his untimely death in a car accident in 1997 that musical forms began to change. Yet, even for his widow, while she felt there was a need to balance the changes in the service with a respect for tradition, she expressed this change as a generational difference that would have to be recognized.

> I can tolerate drums as long as it is subdued... Yeah as long as it is not making you associate it with the outside way of music. Young people need to hear what they know, maybe. Just as long as it is properly guided towards worship. Then it is ok. There has to be a line. We should not...there should always be guidance for these young people, so they will not stray.

---

[12] This conversation, like most transcribed interviews in this chapter, is translated from the original mix of English and Tagalog known as 'Taglish'. The italicized words represent sections translated from the Tagalog by the author. Throughout, I have left the English as it was spoken, with words added in square brackets '[−]' for clarity. In both cases, I hope to convey the original voice of the informant as faithfully as possible.

The idea, espoused by all these informants along with many others, that the specific form of worship was less important than the greater concern with attracting and retaining members and converts, was perhaps most graphically demonstrated by the discussions about worship style among the members of the TBC breakaway group that would become Faith Community Church.

In one of the earliest meetings of the breakaway group, the question was raised as to the form of worship to be used. Although the eventual musical and liturgical forms were virtually identical to those practised at other Baptist churches in the area, there was an explicit openness to the forms preferred by 'the people of the community'. 'We should have country music', commented one of the worship leaders. 'That is what the people like.' The comment was met with knowing laughter. No-one in the discussion suggested the use of forms explicitly identified with a particular denominational or 'cultural' tradition (i.e., hymns or a traditional hymnody, traditional Filipino music, or Pentecostal/Charismatic worship). It was clear that worship style and musical forms should, like other aspects of church practice, appeal to the tastes and preferences of 'local' people, meaning a popular and non-Christian background. American-style 'country' music is popular throughout the Philippines, but there is a common stereotype of the mountain people as being particularly drawn to images, music and clothing reminiscent of the American West.[13] The suggestion of using 'country music' immediately brought to mind this locally proscribed identity of the modern, even transnational, mountain person distinct from lowland culture.

This willingness to innovate, to attract or retain a particular membership, was evident in every group. One of my earliest contacts with the congregations came in a meeting of the worship committee of UBC. This committee met weekly to plan the elements of each Sunday's worship (selecting songs, asking various members to read scriptures or lead prayers), as well as planning year-long themes and monthly foci for the sermons and scriptures. In this first meeting, the members of the committee included a single woman in her 30s who worked as an administrator at Texas Instruments, the young Indian music pastor, two college-aged women who served as vocal leaders in worship and a college-age man who played electric bass in the worship band. As this group discussed plans for an upcoming Sunday service, they evaluated the efficacy of practices from the previous service and thought through the elements, discussing their relative merits; they searched through a variety of sources suggesting a great deal of freedom in their ability to think and change the practices of the congregation towards their goals as a committee. The music pastor led the discussion.

---

[13] Kenny Rogers and other US country singers are widely popular in the Philippines. Baguio residents, however, are particularly known for their love of country music. A decades old 'country-western' music club is a landmark in the business district. Many of the local jeepneys are decorated with cowboy paraphernalia and images. Historically, it is thought that one of the reasons the mountain peoples accepted the presence of American colonialists was due to the 'cowboy' image of those early colonial administrators: riding in on horse back, 'straight shooters' who were not like the 'sneaky' lowlanders.

Leader:	What do we think about last week? If I were to ask you to remember the worship, what do you remember?
Member:	Did we have a response song? [murmurs] I think we had, but then we did not have the last song.
Member 2:	It was the hymn. *Kuya* Arnold [the deacon presiding over the previous week's service] did not announce it.
Member 3:	Hymns still grab the hearts of the people. It is good to have the hymn that connects to the message
Member 2:	We need to be sure the emcee knows [to announce the last song]. It is good to have a hymn there.
Leader:	Did people worship? Could we see if they were worshipping like that, or were they just...
Member 3:	I think they were.
Member 2:	I think we did too many new songs. Maybe four? [murmurs of assent] It's too many. I think we can plan two, but four is too many. People do not really worship.

This sort of critical evaluation continued throughout the meeting, with the members raising the concerns of other leaders who wanted to see the order of the service clearly printed in the bulletin or others who felt the services were getting into a 'rut'. The committee took all these suggestions into account, and brought a great many resources (photocopied chapters from Christian books on worship and a number of songbooks published in the United States, Australia, and the Philippines) to bear on their efforts to 'improve' their services. Overall, they were looking to innovate and improve the experience of the Sunday service for the members. Even in the references to the hymns as still 'grabbing the hearts of the people', there was no suggestion that tradition was sacrosanct or essential to their identity as Christians. It was simply in their ability to connect to peoples' current emotions that they were raised as important.

All this freedom and willingness to innovate was somewhat surprising to me, given the number of stories I had been told, particularly by American missionaries, of young leaders clashing with older clergy or lay leaders over issues of worship. A number of well-known church splits had occurred, they told me, over these issues. As I watched members of these congregations planning worship the patterns described above—the feelings of relative freedom and a desire to innovate—were very much the norm. Furthermore, few of my informants ever expressed a strong preference, let alone commitment to not changing aspects of worship. It seemed expected that worship forms would change over time and be reflective of a youth culture. Even in the Chinese church, where traditions were more staunchly defended by the influential leadership, their decision to hire the pastor's wife, a young Filipino woman trained in the modern forms of music and worship, as their music director signaled their willingness, if not desire, to see their worship also move in the direction of the other congregations. I began to wonder if, unlike those congregations where matters of worship had led to splits and schisms, these congregations represented some anomalous example in the larger picture of Philippine Protestantism.

But regardless of peoples' assertions that specific issues of worship style were relatively unimportant to them, the general conformity of these congregations to a similar type of ritual, in the face of the cultural and social difference among the membership and 'target groups', suggested that there were limits to how they would practice their religion. What I found was that the changes in these congregations, from hymns to contemporary songs and moving from 'traditional' instrumentation to a service led by Christian rock bands, did not threaten basic issues of identity within the landscape of Philippine and religious life. Indeed, to the extent that they connected the congregations with a middle-class youth culture, the changes served to act as a positive experience of social and economic place.

The controversies came with the practices associated with Pentecostalism. Though many of the changes present in the congregations of this study, in terms of worship practices, might seem to have led or be leading these groups towards the more (anthropologically) well-known faiths of Pentecostal and Charismatic Christianity, in the minds of most of these church members, Pentecostalism was not defined by raucous music or emotional worship; Pentecostalism was synonymous with the 'gifts of the Spirit' (particularly glossolalia, or 'speaking in tongues'). By excluding practices that would take them into the community of Pentecostalism, these congregations drew a social and religious boundary that marked them off from a social identity in which they would not live, and connected them to a particular community of Christianity that was broader than their own form of Baptist Christianity, but specific nonetheless. Those congregations that had split, I would learn later, did so over these issues of Pentecostal practice, not changes in music style. I would learn that there was, in fact, a congregation connected to UBC that did experience the tension caused by the threatened inclusion of Pentecostalism in a Baptist context.

Putting Pentecostalism in its Place, or The Story of Pastor Mangawang

West Baguio Baptist Church (WBBC) originally began in the same way as TBC: an American missionary saw the geographic area as lacking access to a Baptist congregation so he started one as a Bible study. Soon after he initiated the group, UBC was brought in as the 'mother church', helping the small and struggling congregation with financial and staff support. Some ten years later, WBBC was a small but lively congregation with a budget capable of supporting a part-time pastor. Several years prior to my research, a young graduate of the local Baptist seminary had been hired as their pastor. After two years he was dismissed, using an unusual provision in the charter of this particular church that allowed the congregation to renew (or, in this case, not renew) the contract of a pastor biennially. This was a very unusual move in that, according to informants from throughout the Philippines, churches rarely dismiss a pastor. Pastors would not infrequently leave a congregation, often taking a segment of the congregation with them to start a new congregation, and pastors had been known to resign in the face of dissatisfaction and conflict with members, but the shortage of seminary-trained pastors was such that congregations, particularly small ones that could not pay the larger salaries of UBC or TBC, were loathe to fire a pastor without another waiting in the wings. But even more intriguing about the case of this small church was the reason this pastor was dismissed. He had introduced Pentecostal–style worship.

This pastor, along with hundreds of other Philippine clergy from a number of different Protestant groups, had participated in a 'worship conference' sponsored by Laurence Ko, the leader of a very large, Charismatic-style Baptist church in Singapore. His church had pioneered the use of 'cell groups' as a way of organizing the congregation and bringing many new members into the church through the use of a pyramid hierarchy. This was controversial among many more traditional Baptists who held to the importance of congregational control and equality within church polity. But in the case of WBBC, none of those with whom I spoke about the controversy brought up the issue of church organization; it was all about practice.

Although Lawrence Ko does not advocate Pentecostalism *per se*, the success of his congregation and his prominence as an international church leader have led many to adopt more than his organizational scheme, advocating the worship style he practices as well. The young pastor of WBBC had become enamored with the 'gifts of the Spirit' (i.e., speaking in tongues) and a generally emotive worship style. He pursued relationships with Pentecostal pastors in the area, many of whom had some of the most rapidly growing congregations in the city. As I investigated the circumstances of the controversy and his eventual dismissal, there were few who were able or willing to speak about the details; the pastor still lived in the area and it was a something of an embarrassment to him and members of the congregation who would continue to see him at other Baptist functions. But I spoke with him and with one of the leaders of the congregation who was, at the time of my research, a senior member of the faculty at the seminary. What I learned from this case confirmed what I had heard from the members of the other congregations as they spoke in more abstract terms about the difference between Baptists and Pentecostals.

From the perspective of the pastor, the reluctance of people to participate in more Pentecostal/Charismatic styles of worship reflected their subservience to American missionary Christianity and their reluctance to break with their past. In particular, he believed members of the church were of a 'lower class' and therefore more deferential to 'the whites'. 'They are still impressed with the foreigners', he sighed. 'They are not the *rich/upper-class* (*mayaman*). They are not really ready.' For this pastor, the introduction of a Pentecostal-type worship, based on influences from Asian leaders and pastors of non-missionary founded congregations, represented a break with a western tradition to which Filipinos were subservient.

But the lay leaders of the congregation clearly saw it differently. Dr Ellen Dag-an, a professor at the seminary and widow of a former pastor of the congregation, put it this way: 'The people were not really ready, you know? They are…used to a way, this way. It is the way we have done. Baptist is not so much like Pentecostals. They do not like, you know? Perhaps it is they like already the higher way. It is too loud, they say. Too much shouting. It is better just more quiet.'

I asked her what she personally felt about the changes. Laughing, she replied, 'Oh, I don't know. I am...well...I like the more Baptist-style, you know? It is not so *crazy/wild* (*magulo*). I think for some people, maybe for those who are not so educated or younger, they like [Pentecostal worship styles]. But for me, I am already old. I like more this way.' She went on to explain that there was no theological problem, *per se*, with the idea of speaking in tongues or practising a 'more lively' form of worship, although she emphasized the biblical idea that speaking in tongues should be accompanied by interpretation (i.e., if one person speaks in tongues, which is by definition unintelligible, then either that person or another should 'translate' what was said into a comprehensible form for the entire congregation).[14] 'I believe there must be interpretation, as Paul commands', she stated.

This emphasis on interpretation echoes strongly with the traditional theology and historic roots of Southern Baptist orientations to scripture and orality in general. Although few of those I got to know in these congregations could be called 'Fundamentalists' in the prevailing academic meaning of the term, there is an emphasis on the referential meaning of words in the need for interpretation and understanding that precludes much of the experientially-based practices of Pentecostals and Charismatics.[15] That is, the issue of interpretation is not about literalism, as the members of these congregations have great capacity for biblical interpretation and in every congregation members would study the Bible with the aid of study guides and Bible commentaries reflecting the more sophisticated hermeneutics of Evangelicalism. Where Fundamentalists use a biblical literalism to create an anti-modern view of the world, Evangelicals are comfortable with a variety of hermeneutical tools, so long as those approaches keep the text and the referential word at the center of analysis. Certainly for Christians in the West, how the Bible is approached and the way in which scripture stands *vis-à-vis* experience is a defining characteristic of their faith against the 'Other' of Fundamentalism, Pentecostalism or Liberalism. For the Baptists of Baguio, this emphasis of interpretation and referentialism became a similar defining feature.

The requirement of interpretation was echoed by many of the leaders of every congregation in this study and other seminary faculty as an essential accompaniment to practices of glossolalia. Effectively, this means that the vast majority of speaking in tongues as it is practised in the Pentecostal and Charismatic churches throughout Baguio (and, indeed, throughout the world) would be considered 'unbiblical' and, in the eyes of those holding this doctrine of interpretation, illegitimate. Surprisingly, there were a number of lay people, without seminary training of any kind, who

---

[14] This is seen primarily in 1 Corinthians 14.13, although it is not a command, as J. Abugan stated to me.

[15] See, e.g., Nancy Tatom Ammerman, *Bible Believers: Fundamentalists in the Modern World* (New Brunswick: Rutgers University Press, 1987); also Susan Harding, 'Convicted by the Holy Spirit: The Rhetoric of Fundamentalist Conversion', *American Ethnologist* 14 (1987), pp. 127-81.

offered similar doctrinal explanations for how they thought speaking in tongues should and should not be practised, but for the majority of Baptists with whom I spoke, the main differences between Baptists and Pentecostals—the reason they believed there to be this significant difference in the practice of Pentecostalism and their own form of Christianity—were social. Thus, just as Dr Dag-an felt it was the 'wildness' of Pentecostalism the kept most WBBC members from embracing Pastor Mangawang's reforms, practices became the visible boundaries of what was understood as a social distinction. One member of UBC put it this way:

> Why are Pentecostals popular? *I think it is*...we have to look at it as the need of these people, especially if...let's just say this one group. You know the El Shaddai thing? They have some sort of strategy reaching out to the people, having to join the Catholic and the Christian thing in their worship. They're trying to include that in their worship and most of their members are from the poor family and they kind of want...they have this need to be like...it seems like their lives are already hopeless and they want to be a member of a congregation which will give them hope. Instead of focusing on that, we try to focus on the people who seek God. Two congregations, I think, that is the Jesus Miracle Crusade and the El Shaddai, they tend to focus more on their leaders, rather than to God because they believe that He can do a miracle, [so] they can do a miracle.[16]

When asked what she thought of a Pentecostal service she had attended several years ago at the invitation of a neighbor, a TBC member had this to say:

> They say so many different things [in the service]. *It is as if...as if they were* speaking in tongues, but actually we don't understand what they were telling. So uh...uh...uh...something like that. It is like they are just mumbling, but you cannot hear any...*it is without* meaning. They were just mumbling, singing some words, but not in Ilokano or English or Tagalog. *It was like it was* magic; *I think like* 'abracadabra.' *Something like that.* Maybe people from the poor areas, they don't have much education. They don't know if it is good. They like to do this, *but* I want to study the Bible, hear good sermons.

Another member of TBC gave this interpretation of Pentecostal worship practices:

> They have a very emotional service. *I have not seen every kind of worship*, but I have seen some Pentecostals, *like* Assemblies of God and their own praise and worship. Praise and worship *where they already will cry; they can laugh, they can clap; they can dance; they can do everything*. You know that the Filipinos, *they are a very emotional people* and they have their own way that they appeal to the

---

[16] 'El Shaddai' refers to a Catholic charismatic movement led by 'Brother' Mike Velarde, a lay Catholic businessman who has used his radio network to promote a mass movement of Catholics. They are well-known for lively revival-style meetings in public places such as parks and public squares, complete with electronic bands, charismatic preachers, and ecstatic emotional worship.

emotions. *That's why* [Pentecostalism] *is so popular*. But their service is becoming too high emotionally. *It is like they believe/know* [alam] is it really blessing them at their service *but actually it is just emotion*. It is bringing them down lower. It does not touch their life deeper *if there is a problem*. It cannot touch their spiritual life, [but] will just scratch their emotions. *But for me, it is too much.*

The common theme that emerged as these and many other informants spoke about either their experiences or beliefs about Pentecostalism, was that it reflected something lower—socially, spiritually, and culturally. The practices of Baptist Christianity, then, were seen to be socially 'higher', less emotional (thus more intellectual) and spiritually 'deeper' or more sophisticated. While there is certainly a theological component to these interpretations, the contrast was never framed as Christian versus non-Christian as it often was when people spoke about the various new religious movements and quasi-Christian such as Mormonism, Jehovah's Witnesses, and *Iglesia ni Kristo*, that have gained in recent years. Instead, the salient differences were defined by practices and social group.

Baptist worship practices, as they had come to be defined and experienced in these congregations, marked the congregations as different from the Pentecostal Christianity that represented the other major non-Catholic Christian movement in the country. Even when members were aware of doctrinal differences between themselves as Baptists and other Protestant groups, members of these congregations were likely to see the difference as minor or not distinctive if the worship practices of that group were familiar.

This was most evident in the case of the Chinese church. Among Chinese Protestants, the religious landscape was relatively less cluttered. Although there are undoubtedly many Filipinos of Chinese ancestry attending every sort of religious group, the only religions in the Philippines specifically identifying themselves as 'Chinese' movements are certain Catholic churches, Buddhist temples, an indigenous religious movement based on Buddhist and Confusionist teachings called the 'Bell Church', the Southern Baptists and the United Evangelical Church. According to those who could speak about Chinese communities throughout northern Luzon, Manila and even in the southern islands, Pentecostalism had never attracted those for whom Chinese identity remained very important. There were not, as far as anyone I spoke with knew, any Pentecostal churches conducting their services in Chinese. In terms of religious practice and doctrine, then, the Baptists were very different from all the other Chinese religious movements, except the Presbyterian-based United Evangelical Church.

Those knowledgeable in the two denominations provided me with a basic understanding of the difference between the groups. Whereas the Baptists conformed to the basic Baptist traditions of congregationalism, believer's baptism, and local autonomy, the United Evangelical Church organized itself according to a presbytery system of hierarchically arranged leadership organized according to geographically defined space, and practiced infant baptism. Historically, these issues were the basis of bloody wars throughout Europe, church schisms in the West and elsewhere, and have been the focus of centuries of theological debate. In the contemporary

Philippines, however, these issues seem to have become minor concerns for a religious minority defined largely by practice and an ethnic/cultural identity.

Hard national membership statistics are difficult to come by for any religious body in the Philippines and the Chinese denominations are no exception. Most of those Baguio Baptists with whom I spoke believed the Evangelical Church to have a larger national membership than the Baptists, though the Baptist church was more prominent in Baguio. This seems plausible given the presence of a large Chinese-language seminary in Manila, operated by the United Evangelical Church. (The Chinese Baptist denomination does not operate its own seminary, but relies on the English-speaking Baguio Seminary to train their clergy.) But among those Baptists and Evangelicals with whom I spoke, there never seemed to be a sense of competition or clash between the denominations. In fact, I met both Chinese Baptist clergy who had attended the Evangelical seminary as well as students at the Baptist seminary from United Evangelical churches. Doctrinal distinctions were not ignored nor were they unacknowledged, but these were not considered barriers given that the practices of the two denominations were generally quite similar. Differences in *practice* were largely confined to occasional rituals (i.e., baptism), while the 'everyday' practices of worship and preaching were such that the denominations could easily mingle and even merge when circumstances warranted.

In Baguio, both the Baptists and the United Evangelicals had their own buildings, although the Baptist church was larger and more socially prominent in the Chinese community due to their history as one of the oldest Protestant churches of any kind in the city and their successful Mandarin-learning school. In the nearby lowland city of San Fernando, the United Evangelical Church held the more prominent position, although a tiny (four member) Chinese Baptist congregation did exist. In the larger lowland town of Dagupan, the Chinese Baptist church was the only expressly Chinese congregation in the city and those Chinese Christians from the United Evangelical background attended with relatively few problems. The current leader of that congregation, a Bible woman studying in Baguio, said of the Evangelicals attending the Baptist congregation, 'They feel at home, because we are very much the same. We have no problem and they can join. We have a lot [of Evangelical members] because they do not have a church [in Dagupan], so they come.' She did note that as a leader, she was aware of the different views on baptism. When I pressed her to explain how exactly these problems were worked out, she was reluctant to say that these non-Baptists were holding leadership positions, although she would not state categorically that they were excluded either. Undoubtedly, she felt some tension between the practice of essentially ignoring these differences and her position as a representative of the Baptist denomination, in which the very name reflected the historical importance of the doctrine of baptism. But in practice, this central doctrine had clearly become de-emphasized in the face of the commonalities of practice the two groups shared. She explained:

RT: We don't talk about [the doctrine of baptism] very much. It is a difference you know. They do the infant baptism, and we do not do. But there is no problem for them to come and be in our church.

BH: Can they serve as leaders?
RT: They can serve, but not just all the way. We are a Baptist church and we only have the baptism for adults so it is hard. But they can serve and we just do not really discuss [baptism].
BH   Could a United Evangelical be a deacon?
RT: Ummm...I...it cannot really be, but I don't know. They are like other members, but it is a difference. We have the adult baptism, so they cannot really be all the way as leaders. But they can serve in the committees and are like all members.

In Baguio, where the United Evangelicals had their own congregation and building, the division was visible, yet there was a great deal of contact between the two congregations. The pastor of the Evangelical congregation was a student at the Baptist seminary, and virtually every member of the Baptist church personally knew the more involved members of the Evangelical church as well.

Among the Filipino congregations the blurring of denominational distinctions between those with whom they shared a common practice was evident as well. At TBC, the issue of denominational distinction eventually arose in the face of conflicts between various lay leaders and a pastor hired out of a wealthy, Conservative Baptist church in Manila. Prior to those controversies, the differences between his Conservative Baptist background and the background of TBC were thought to be negligible; it was only once he began to clash with members of the lay leadership over the direction the congregation should take in spending priorities, ministry emphasis and administrative procedure that these same leaders suggested that this pastor was 'insufficiently Southern Baptist' and did not respect 'their traditions'.

At UBC, discussions about the future direction of the congregation periodically included the suggestion that the congregation change its name from 'University Baptist Church' to something less denominationally distinctive. During meetings of an *ad hoc* 'visioning committee' known as the 'Dream Team', one deacon voiced this view several times. 'Maybe there are some', he said, 'who do not feel comfortable with "Baptist." Many churches now they just say "community" or "fellowship." We can perhaps be more like that. More inclusive.' Certainly the choice of names for the TBC breakaway group, eventually settling on the name 'Faith Community Church' reflected this so-called trend. Faith Community's reluctance, or lack of concern, about finding a denominational home further emphasized the relative unimportance of a denominational label or association for the formation of their religious identity.

In worship practices, and the debates about worship practices, we see one of the techniques for the production of locality and identity. In the first place, these practices define the other elements of the religious landscape—Pentecostal, Catholic, non-Christian. Second, the attitude of flexibility, a youth-centered discourse and utilitarianism in changing the practices to effectively attract particular people to the congregation serves to orient the members toward the values of evangelism and outreach while defining who they believe themselves to be and emphasizing a particular constituency as their own. Finally, these practices become the boundaries by which others are excluded. This is particularly important in the case of those with whom they share a relatively undifferentiated theological commitment, yet represent a social and religious place from which these congregations would differentiate themselves.

But clearly, these practices, like those other elements of congregation life, also serve to direct the attention of the members to a community of Christians beyond their own shores, in the global realm of the universal church. At first glance (certainly at my first glance), it might appear that the English-language music, driven by a modern rock beat reflects the most obvious element of 'globalization' (i.e., westernization) in the local congregation. But in the context of worship specifically, the majority of those participating in these rituals do not think of their worship as driven by so-called foreign practices, but as reflecting local realities and modern Philippine life. At the same time, none of these people are oblivious to the connections between their own religious life and those of others outside their specific locale, culture, and nation. There are a great many aspects to religious life that specifically serve to connect these believers to these transnational communities and distinguish them from a locally bound notion of place. It is in the tension of these two aspects of Baptist identity that these communities are created.

Conclusion

Thus, while the case here is particular it is also reflective of general processes of global flows and transnational dynamics. As Massey reminds us, 'localities are about the intersection of social activities and social relations [which are] necessarily...dynamic, changing...they have to be constructed through sets of social relations which bind them inextricably to wider arenas, and other places'.[17] This is particularly true for a transnational religion such as Christianity in which the very nature of the faith is to transcend the local while positioning oneself firmly within localized social bonds, to be 'in the world, but not of the world'. It is very much like what Hsin-Yi Lu, in her study of Taiwanese national identity, calls 'mapping the local in a global terrain'.[18] It is in these processes of negotiation, debate, practice and decision making that we can identify the techniques of community creation and the production of locality.

Certainly, these processes, whether in Baguio or elsewhere, are multifaceted, historically particular and irreducibly complex. The story here has only provided part of the picture. However, worship is a powerful instrument in the project of context-creation. The acts of worship create the bodily postures towards certain ideas, social relations, and theologies that make identity more than cognitive assent or personal conviction; worship practices create communities.[19] American scholars of religion

[17] Doreen Massey, *Space, Place and Gender* (Cambridge: Polity Publishing, 1994). p. 136-42.

[18] Hsin-Yi Lu, *The Politics of Locality: Making a Nation of Communities in Taiwan* (New York: Routledge, 2002), ch. 1.

[19] This is perhaps best expressed in Bourdieu's concept of 'practical belief' in which he argues that particular experiences combine bodily posture with views of history and/or

have noted that historically and contemporaneously, worship practices have both reflected wider social change and served to define distinct communities.[20] But these studies have also frequently privileged theological issues as driving identity, as opposed to practices.[21] For the Baptists of Baguio no such priority seems to have emerged. In the practices of the community, the transcendent has merged with the global to create communities where theologies are not so much learned as lived, and the creation of context flows from local social interactions to globally imagined communities and back again.

In this understanding, these communities are not simply created *de novo* in a-historical or ungrounded space. There is, as clearly seen in the distinctions of Pentecostal and Baptist practice, dynamics of differentiation in which people respond to the local by means of the global. Thus, to paraphrase Marx, people make their own local community, although not entirely of their own choosing. As Lu points out in the case of contemporary Taiwanese nationalism, the processes of defining, describing and inhabiting these localities is always political, contested and competitive. Although the narrative of worship above has emphasized some of the more quiet and subtle negotiations of locality among these Baptists, it is those productive (and, at times, destructive) tensions that keep the process dynamic. As these Baptists continue to look to their locality as ranging across their daily social lives and their eternal, transcendent membership in a community of heaven, they will undoubtedly continue to find surprising and creative ways to live in the now and the not yet.

---

the future in such as way as to 'internalize' their history. See Pierre Bourdieu, *Distinction: A Social Critique of the Judgment of Taste* (trans. Richard Nice; Cambridge: Harvard University Press, 1984), p. 56.

[20] Donald Miller, *Reinventing American Protestantism: Christianity in the New Millennium* (Berkeley and Los Angeles, CA: University of California Press, 1997). See also several of the essays in Mark Noll, David Bebbington, and George Rawlyk (eds), *Evangelicalism: Comparative Studies of Popular Protestantism in North America, the British Isles, and Beyond, 1700–1990* (New York: Oxford University Press, 1994).

[21] See, e.g., Dean Hoge, *Division in the Protestant House* (Philadelphia, PA: Westminster Press, 1976).

CHAPTER 18

'Our own church in our own land':
The Shaping of Baptist Identity in Australia

Ken R. Manley

On Tuesday evening, 17 September 1918, a large number of South Australian Baptists crowded into the Flinders Street Baptist Church, Adelaide, for a Home Mission rally. Adelaide, known as the 'city of churches', was capital of 'the Paradise of Dissent', where Baptists for much of their history enjoyed a status not found in the other Australian colonies. The Flinders Street church building was one of the grandest Baptist chapels in the nation; built in 1863, its Gothic 'cathedral' lines made a striking statement in stone of Baptist presence and ambition. One of the speakers at the meeting was H. Estcourt Hughes (1869–1951), a locally born and trained pastor, who, it was said, delivered 'a stirring utterance' on the theme 'Our own Church in our own Land'.[1] His phrase captures a widespread Australian Baptist sentiment of the time and provides a framework for our exploration of the shaping of Australian Baptist identity.[2]

The date is significant, being just weeks before the end of the First World War which ushered in a critical time for the young nation, founded in 1901. In retrospect, 1918 was also roughly halfway in the history of the Baptist movement in Australia, between the unplanned and unpromising beginnings of the early 1830s and the early years of the third millennium, a convenient vantage point from which to look backwards to trace beginnings and then to advance across the subsequent years to see how far this hope has been realised.

To consider Hughes' vision of 'Our own church in our own land' both emphasises the importance of context for denominational history and raises issues of identity, both for Baptists and the nation.[3] For Australians the task of defining

---

[1] *Australian Baptist*, 24 September 1918, p. 2.

[2] For a history of Australian Baptists offering a national perspective, see Ken R. Manley, *From Woolloomooloo to 'Eternity': A History of Baptists in Australia* (Studies in Baptist History and Thought, 16.1 and 16.2; 2 vols; Milton Keynes: Paternoster, 2006).

[3] Discussions about 'identity' seem to date from the work of Erik Erikson, 'architect of identity in the modern West' in the 1950s; see M. Dixson, *The Imaginary Australian: Anglo-Celts and Identity—1788 to the Present* (Sydney: University of New South Wales Press, 1999), pp. 4, 40-42.

national identity, or identities, has become challenging and divisive as historians, cultural theorists, politicians, social commentators (and advertisers) compete to define the quintessential 'Aussie'. For Baptists in Australia, and in many other places, identity has become an urgent issue. One question of this chapter will be whether current discussions about Australian identity can assist us in our understanding of Baptist identity.

'Our own land'

Hughes' sermon, as summarised in *The Australian Baptist*, illustrates a range of contemporary Anglo–Australian Protestant feelings about Australia:

> He said there was no better land in the world than Australia. Fifty-four thousand Australians had died for it. It was the biggest island in the world, spoke one language, flew one flag, acknowledged one Sovereign. It abounded in every form of pastoral, agricultural, horticultural and mineral wealth, and a catalogue of metals and precious stones was given. God had kept this land for England and for Protestantism. It was the freest land in the world, and no other land made such provision for the needs of its people. This land must be won for Christ, its cities and its country districts.

Hughes demonstrates a typical white, male, Anglo-centric, Protestant pride in the young nation, which, considering its unusual foundation, should be noted. After all, it was only 130 years since the first European settlers had arrived at Port Jackson (Sydney) to establish a remote penal society on the 'Fifth Continent'. Although a harsh and brutal society by any standards, 'Australia' began as an experiment in human engineering and was the product of the European Enlightenment.[4]

By 1918, however, convict origins were not prominent in the nation's memory, though Australiahs have faced a long struggle to deal with the sordid beginnings of settlement and it has been a deeper problem in the national psyche than many people would admit.[5] Perhaps this lies behind the Australian national obsession with sport, especially in beating England at cricket or anything else.[6]

---

[4] J. Gascoigne, *The Enlightenment and the Origins of European Australia* (Cambridge: Cambridge University Press, 2002), pp. 1-16. As Alan Atkinson has observed, 'the very fact that this was to be a community of convicts and ex-convicts raised, almost by accident, profound questions about the common rights of the subject, the responsibilities of power and the possibility of imaginative attachment to a land of exile'. See A. Atkinson, *The Europeans in Australia: A History* (Melbourne: Oxford University Press, 1997), p. x.

[5] See P. Kelly, 'A Nation Reborn', *Australian*, 25 January 1997, as cited by Dixson, *The Imaginary Australian*, p. 106.

[6] G. Blainey, 'Not as the Song of Other Lands', in H. Bolitho and C. Wallace-Crabbe (eds), *Approaching Australia: Papers from the Harvard Australian Studies Symposium* (Cambridge, MA: Harvard University Press, 1998), p. 132.

Sadly, the dispossession of the Aboriginal population was even more comprehensively and shamefully blotted from the nation's memory, only to be recovered in recent decades. Not forgotten was the exciting gold rush of the 1850s which ushered in a period of unprecedented change and growth in the Australian colonies, bringing thousands of immigrants from Britain, Europe, America, China and numerous other places. The dramatic economic growth of the ensuing decades, temporarily halted during the depression of the 1890s, was accompanied by exciting political and social developments. The sentiment of 'a nation for a continent and a continent for a nation', as Edmund Barton, Australia's first Prime Minister, put it, led to the significant achievement in 1901 of six independent colonies forming one nation, without a revolution or use of force, but by popular agreement. Inevitably there were cynics and later critics who judged that federation represented 'less the birth of a nation and the culmination of patriotic feeling, than a readjustment of colonial relations, a somewhat shabby deal among the colonies based on deep suspicions and self-interested manoeuvring'.[7] Regionalism was to remain a powerful force in the new nation.

Hughes enunciated one sense in which Baptists understood Australia to be 'a land of our own': 'God had kept this land for England and Protestantism'. This theme was regularly repeated in Baptist (and Protestant) statements. But the question strikes us forcefully as we hear Hughes' sermon: a land of whose 'own'? There is no awareness of the Catholic Irish who were a powerful force in shaping Australian identity. Even more fundamentally and sadly, the Aborigines' claim for their land is ignored. But Baptists wanted to assert that they had their place in 'a land of our own'.

The strength of feeling 'Australian' was matched completely by an equal sense of being British. To be an 'independent Australian Briton', as future Prime Minister Alfred Deakin had put it, was a source of national pride. Estcourt Hughes would have felt no tension in both praising Australia and affirming 'One Sovereign': nationalism and imperialism were in a state of equilibrium.[8] Accordingly, Australians rushed to volunteer for the Great War, and out of a population of about 4.5 million, some 400,000 were recruited. About 60,000 were killed and Australia had the highest casualty rate (64.95%) of any participating nation. But the question of conscription divided the nation on sectarian lines. Protestants, like T.E. Ruth, the Baptist preacher at Collins Street, Melbourne, advocated compulsion and disputed with the Roman Catholics, led by his more famous and fierce rival, the Irish Archbishop Daniel Mannix. Baptist preacher and essayist, F.W. Boreham, wrote in the Hobart *Mercury* that the idea of compulsion was consistent with 'the spirit of

---

[7] R. White, *Inventing Australia: Images and Identity 1688–1980* (Sydney: Allen & Unwin, 1981), p. 111.

[8] G. Souter, *Lion and Kangaroo: The Initiation of Australia* (Melbourne: Text Publishing, 2000), p. ix.

our Imperial traditions'.[9] Though some few Baptists had opposed the war and conscription, most would have supported T.E. Ruth's position and strongly supported the war as loyal imperialists. Although conscription was defeated in two referenda in 1916 and 1917, sectarian tensions continued for decades.[10]

It was universally affirmed that the nation had 'come of age' through the sacrifices of the war. Anzac Day, which commemorated the fateful landing of Australians and New Zealanders at Gallipoli on 25 April 1915, was destined to become the major national day and to become a form of Australian civil religion.[11] Boreham reflected on Anzac Day in a newspaper editorial in 1956:

> About Anzac Day, as it is celebrated in Australia, there is something startlingly unique. It is the commemoration, not of the great military victory, or of the final struggle of a long and memorable campaign, but of the birth of a young nation and of its baptism of blood. Anzac marks the solemn self-recognition of the Australian people. For the first time since the pioneers blazed the first trails across the continent, Australia knew herself for what she was. The world has never known anything remotely resembling Anzac Day. It was a festival of proud, pathetic memories, and by those memories, all life is touched to finer issues.[12]

Remarkably, Anzac Day has continued to grow in support, especially among young people, and does not now focus on the 'glorification of war', as critics had habitually complained. Influential social commentator Hugh Mackay (the son of a Baptist family) has observed that Anzac Day is 'about sacrifice and hope' and prompts us to answer 'some curly questions': 'Who are we, these people for whom so many others gave up their lives? What are we making of this way of life for which people were once prepared to die? Are we building the kind of nation that justifies the sacrifice of so many, not only those who died, but those who thought our ideals were worth fighting for?'[13]

---

[9] *Mercury*, 3 June 1916, as cited by G. Pound, 'F.W. Boreham the Public Theologian: The interplay of faith and life as expressed in the newspaper editorials of F.W. Boreham, 1912-1959' (DTheol thesis, Melbourne College of Divinity, 2003), p. 88.

[10] K.R. Manley, 'Defending "the freest land in the world": Australian Baptists and Political Protestantism, 1918–32', in G.R. Treloar and R.D. Linder (eds), *Making History for God: Essays on Evangelicalism, Revival and Mission in Honour of Stuart Piggin* (Sydney: Robet Menzies College, 2004), pp. 133-50; M. McKernan, *Australian Churches at War: Attitudes and Activities of the Major Churches, 1914–18* (Sydney: Catholic Theological Faculty, 1980); R.D. Linder, *The Long Tragedy: Evangelical Christians and the Great War, 1914–18* (Adelaide: Open Book, 2000).

[11] From a large literature, see especially K.S. Inglis, *Sacred Places: War Memorials in the Australian Landscape* (Melbourne: Melbourne University Press, 1998), pp. 458-71; R.D. Linder, 'Civil Religion in America and Australia', *Lucas* 3 (June, 1988), pp. 6-23; R.V. Pierard, 'The Anzac Day Phenomenon: A Study in Civil Religion', in Treloar and Linder (eds), *Making History for God*, pp. 239-54.

[12] *Mercury*, 21 April 1956, as cited by Pound, 'F.W. Boreham', p. 145.

[13] H. Mackay, *Turning Point: Australians Choosing their Future* (Sydney: Pan Macmillan, 1999), p. 8.

Anzac Day is a part of the larger issue of Australian identity. Russell Ward, in *The Australian Legend* (1958), argued that since the 1890s the rough, easy-going bushman, laconic, resourceful, loyal to his mates, uncomfortable with parsons and women, and facing adversity with a stoical joke, has become an appealing stereotype for a nation at least three-quarters of whom live in substantial cities. This legend of the bush, it was suggested, merged with the legend of the Anzacs and became a controlling picture of the 'true' Australian. Though this myth has received extensive criticism as being male chauvinist, racist and historically flawed it has remained a powerful self-image.[14]

But, of course, all stereotypes are inadequate. As novelist Rolf 'Boldrewood' expressed it in 1901: 'Know, O friendly generalizer, that there be tall Australians and short Australians...faint or fierce, feeble-clinging or deathless strong...speculative, rash Australians; also cautious, very wary Australians... There is no generic native Australian.'[15] A hundred years after Boldrewood, Australia is more diverse in far more substantial ways. At the beginning of the new millennium Australia is multi-cultural, multi-racial and has as many Buddhists as Baptists.[16] We now recognise several identities.[17] At a simple level, one can be an Australian in an English way, an Aboriginal way, a Jewish way, a Polish, German, Greek, Italian, Chinese, Vietnamese way, and so on, although a range of multiple identities has always been available in Australia.[18] The ties with Britain were gradually broken, one decisive moment coming during the Second World War with the fall of Singapore, which one historian has controversially described as 'The Great Betrayal'.[19] With the conscious determination to turn to America for assistance, Australia moved into a new era. After the Second World War, with thousands of migrants coming not only from Europe but from the 1970s also from Asia, Australia has moved beyond attachment to either a 'British grandmother' or an 'American uncle' to become a nation 'of our own' with multiple identities (and a certain confusion as a result).

Despite our 'national obsession' with identity, Richard White has insisted, however, that national identity is only ever an invention, a mental construct, and a

---

[14] A useful overview of these issues will be found in G. Whitlock and D. Carter (eds), *Images of Australia: An Introductory Reader in Australian Studies* (St Lucia, Qld: University of Queensland Press, 1992).

[15] As cited by White, *Inventing Australia,* p. 63.

[16] In 2001 there were 357,813 Buddhists, about 50,000 more than Baptists: *Sydney Morning Herald,* 18 June 2002, p. 7.

[17] J.J. Smolicz, 'Who is an Australian? Identity, Core Values and the Resilience of Culture', in C.A. Price (ed), *Australian National Identity* (Canberra: Academy of the Social Sciences in Australia, 1991), pp. 41-66.

[18] See especially, K.S. Inglis, 'Multiculturalism and National Identity', in C. Wilcox (ed.), *Observing Australia 1959 to 1999* (Melbourne: Melbourne University Press, 1999), pp. 186-218.

[19] D. Day, *The Great Betrayal: Britain, Australia and the Onset of the Pacific War, 1939–42* (North Ryde, NSW: Angus & Robertson, 1988); for a rebuttal of Day's thesis, see M. Davie, *Anglo-Australian Attitudes* (London: Pimlico, 2001), pp. 131-41.

product of European history. The crucial questions about ideas of national identity deal with 'what their function is, whose creation they are, and whose interests they serve'.[20] This modern post-structuralist approach reflects much international scholarship on nationality and ethnicity. However, as Miriam Dixson has recently argued, 'Anglo–Celtic Australia' (a term which of course includes not only English, but Scottish, Welsh and Irish heritage) continues to play its traditionally central part in civil society. Her intelligent analysis insists on the need to develop forces of cohesion within Australia. Diversity is to be valued and welcomed, but there are numerous examples in recent history of the dangers of a social unravelling—in Russia, the former Yugoslavia, Afghanistan or Indonesia. Her insistence on the value, indeed the necessity, of affirming the core culture with its complex ethnic dynamic is important as a factor in preventing inevitable differences leading to fragmentation. She seeks an integrated debate around identity.[21] Charles Price reached a similar conclusion: 'Though ethnic and religious diversity trouble some Australians, the real task is…to ignore the great diversity that prevails on peripheral matters and to make sure that the over-arching framework of core values is sound, strong, and flexible. Then, whatever our ethnic and religious origins, we can all feel that sense of identification within Australia.'[22] Increasingly, the challenge in this era of globalisation is to understand how Australians fit into a larger world community. As Gregory Hywood has recently observed, Australians have shared in the creation of an open global economy that is driving social and cultural change: 'we are forging a global culture—harder to find than a national identity, but where we chose to be'.[23]

It is here, perhaps, that some parallels with Baptist discussions about identity may be suggested. Baptists, in Australia as elsewhere, have welcomed and prize diversity but in days of fading identity awareness and faced with the possibility of total fragmentation, Baptists need to be clear about their base beliefs and values and use these as a 'holding' core for maintaining an authentic denominational identity and loyalty.

'Our own church'

The place of religion in Australian culture is still debated and it has often been claimed that its influence has been rather weak, though—if this is true, and I am not sure that it is—it still constitutes a historical phenomenon of interest that is only

---

[20] White, *Inventing Australia*, p. viii.

[21] Dixson, *The Imaginary Australian*, p. 162.

[22] Price, *Australian National Identity*, p. 161. One oft-cited attempt to identify core values of Australia was the Fitzgerald Report on immigration policy (1988) which listed parliamentary democracy, the rule of law and equality before the law, freedom of the individual, freedom of speech, freedom of the press, freedom of religion, equality of women, universal education. See Smolicz, 'Who is an Australian?' pp. 53-54.

[23] G. Hywood, 'Australia: a nation in search of an identity', *The Age*, 3 July 2003, p. 13.

now receiving extensive attention from historians.[24] Certainly, there is a long Australian journalistic tradition of depicting religion in hostile and negative terms: wowserish, divisive, reactionary. The *Bulletin*, a radical but influential paper at the end of the nineteenth century when much Australian identity was being shaped, always depicted the clergyman in cartoons with a tight black suit and rolled umbrella, a spoilsport in a land of informality, warmth and optimism.[25]

What did Estcourt Hughes mean by 'Our own church'? At least two issues were being constantly raised at that time. First, how far had the Baptist message and ethos been transplanted into the Australian environment? Was it truly an 'Australian' Baptist Church or was it still essentially 'English'? Beyond the spoken accent and other incidentals, what would the difference actually be? Secondly, could Baptists resolve the tension between the regionalism of the separate states and the growing national sentiment to achieve federation, to establish a Baptist Union of Australia? Linked with this was awareness that although each state had a fierce loyalty to the Baptist faith, at times different groups tended to appeal to different elements from that heritage and developed strong tensions among themselves. To envision 'our own' truly Australian church in our own land, then, included these basic aspects of identity, as it seems to have been for other denominations.[26]

Baptists generally supported the country's federation: Baptist editor A.W. Webb declared, 'Today we claim as our unifying appellation the euphonious name "Australians". We have ceased to be "Colonials"... Seventy-five years ago we were known under the generic term of Botany Bay, and the ill-savour of the name attached to everything Australian', but now Australia was 'an integral part' of the British Empire.[27] Samuel Pearce Carey, great-grandson of the famous missionary (and so one with 'a pedigree it would be an unpardonable sin not to be proud of'), was pastor of Collins Street Baptist Church, Melbourne, when, on 9 May 1901, the first Commonwealth Parliament was inaugurated in Melbourne. Carey declared: 'We are members of the freest, the most broad-based Commonwealth this earth has ever seen. It is the Lord our God who has won us this unexampled freedom. It is the greatest political triumph He has won in all the annals of the world.'[28] Of course no

---

[24] See, e.g., R. Thompson, *Religion in Australia* (Melbourne: Oxford University Press, 1994); H.M. Carey, *Believing in Australia: A Cultural History of Religions* (St Leonards, NSW: Allen & Unwin, 1996); I. Breward, *A History of the Churches in Australasia* (Oxford: Oxford University Press, 2001).

[25] P. O'Farrell, 'The Cultural Ambivalence of Australian Religion', in S.L. Goldberg and F.B. Smith (eds), *Australian Cultural History* (Cambridge: Cambridge University Press, 1988), p. 8.

[26] It is striking that similar points have been noted in a recent discussion about Anglican identity in Australia: see B. Kaye (ed.), *Anglicanism in Australia: A History* (Melbourne: Melbourne University Press, 2002), pp. 170-71.

[27] *Southern Baptist*, 3 January 1901, p. 7.

[28] S.P. Carey, 'The Fundamental Laws', in H.F. Tucker (ed.), *The Church and the Commonwealth* (Melbourne: Melville and Mullen, 1901), p. 120. For Carey in Australia, see K.R. Manley, 'Preaching the Social Gospel: Samuel Pearce at Collins Street Baptist

one asked what Aborigines, estimated to number at least 90,000 — but excluded from citizenship — thought of this 'freest' and 'most broad-based Commonwealth'. This blot on the 'freedom' of a new nation, not to be corrected until 1967, did not at the time attract the attention of any Baptist prophetic voices.

The first substantial legislation of the new parliament was the Immigration Restriction Act that enshrined the White Australia policy. About this there were Baptist criticisms. Carey, for example, in his last address to the Baptist Union of Victoria before leaving to return to England, condemned the White Australia policy:

> I think I understand the patriotic impulse and the idea of the noblest who would keep Australia for the white... But Australia is in peril of a most un-Christlike contemptuousness towards people of the brown and yellow skins. Our Parliaments and Administrations have more than put us to crimson shame by un-British severity and discourtesy towards those of another facial colour than our own. Our Labour press, though it once a year proclaims the sacred brotherhood of men, makes my blood boil with indignation at the tone of its habitual treatment of China and Japan. We need to be baptized into a wider comradeship by Christ... His blood must wash out the blood-lines that divide. To Him, a Syrian of a brown skin, we owe our very souls.[29]

But would people listen to Australian Baptists who have always been a minority group: 2.10% of the population in 1881 to 1.6% in 2001 with a peak of 2.37% in 1901?[30] The census figures (2001) of 309,262 have to be compared with official denominational membership figures (2000) of 62,579 with 823 churches. This minority status of Baptists in Australia contains an important clue for our history. The reasons for this are complex and involve the foundation of Australia and the developed nature of Australian society. David Bollen has argued that Baptists, as a minority, struggled with their identity in Australia: at times of prosperity, they adopted a confident and liberal denominational outlook; at times of pressure, they reverted to a closed sectarian stance.[31] As Henry Coombs comforted NSW Baptists in 1886, smallness was an 'infallible sign of the true church'.[32] Often Baptist attitudes to baptism and open or closed church membership issues reflected this tension. Whilst the details of Bollen's thesis may be debated, it is true that Australian Baptists have often shown either a sectarian outlook or a more open denominationalism, and at times have tried to do both at the same time!

Church, Melbourne (1900–1908)', in D. Neville (ed.), *Prophecy and Passion: Essays in Honour of Athol Gill* (Hindmarsh, SA: Australian Theological Forum, 2002), pp. 346-82.

[29] S.P. Carey, *The Heart-blood of Paul and of the Gospel* (Melbourne: Victorian Baptist Ministers' Fraternal, 1908), unnumbered pages.

[30] Much useful statistical detail is in P. Hughes, *The Baptists in Australia* (Canberra: Australian Government Publishing Service, 1996).

[31] J.D. Bollen, *Australian Baptists: A Religious Minority* (London: Baptist Historical Society, 1975).

[32] *Banner of Truth*, February 1886, pp. 39-40.

Moreover, the minority status dictated that much Baptist energy was devoted to engaging in vigorous debates with other Protestants, defending their position about believer's baptism by immersion. Their feeling of inferiority led them for a time to embrace the extremes of the Baptist successionist theory which saw them making large claims about their apostolicity going back to the first church in Jerusalem, and, of course, even Jesus was a Baptist. In this, of course, they drew heavily on the apologetics of Baptists in the USA.[33] Indeed, they looked wistfully at the rapid growth of Baptists in North America, arguing that Australia's time would come if they too could only be as evangelistic and as organised as their American cousins. Numerous denominational leaders all through the twentieth century made inquiring pilgrimages to see these huge Baptist churches and institutions and divine their secrets. But they were often obliged to reflect that size isn't everything, and treasured the tributes of men like Pearce Carey who told British Baptists in 1909 that Australian Baptists should not be judged statistically: 'In evangelical witness, in spiritual force, in evangelistic enthusiasm, in missionary enterprise, in Protestant values, and in civic leadership, the Australian Baptists are by no means "the least among the princes of Judah".'[34]

But Australian Baptists reflected not only the relative minority status of British Baptists but also the mix of British Baptists who established the first churches in the different Australian colonies. The end of the eighteenth century was a time of dramatic change in British Baptist churches. An outpouring of undenominational evangelical religion had caused many Baptists to re-think their theology of church and mission; new organisations for mission among the 'heathen' and at home emerged. Tensions back in England, as these new movements were developing, proved to be disastrous when shipped to Australia. Thus the early Australian Baptist story is of unplanned beginnings, successive schisms (often over Calvinism or terms of membership and communion), problems of distance, lack of leadership and resources. A sense of frustration and neglect from 'home', rightly or wrongly, dominated earliest memories.

Leading historian of evangelicalism in Australia, Stuart Piggin, has suggested that the history of Australian Baptist churches 'has not been so much that of a single, continuous tradition, but more of a series of implantations some of which have taken root and grown'.[35] A strong case can be made for this only in the early years (say 1831–51), although even then the importance of continuity should not be minimised. He is right, however, in his observation that for a small denomination in a vast land with a sparse population, Baptists 'offered too many options'. This, of course, reflected the various British Baptist traditions.

Indeed, those who know the Baptist story in Britain, the USA and other settler colonies will recognise much that is familiar among Australian Baptists who have

---

[33] See, e.g., J.E. McGoldrick, *Baptist Successionism* (Metuchen, NJ: Scarecrow Press, 1994).

[34] *Southern Baptist*, 15 June 1909, p. 145.

[35] S. Piggin, 'The Role of Baptists in the History of Australian Evangelicalism', *Lucas* 11 (April, 1991), p. 7.

naturally been impacted by developments in Protestant evangelicalism and Baptist life elsewhere. It was invariably remarked by visiting British Baptist leaders in the nineteenth and early twentieth centuries, for example, that developments in Britain were followed as closely in Australia as at 'home'. The 'Downgrade Controversy' of C.H. Spurgeon is a notable example of this phenomenon. Indeed, the issues perhaps had a longer life in Australia. J.G. Greenhough, thought to be one of those whom Spurgeon suspected of unorthodoxy, visited Australia in 1901 and thought Australians a little out of date and (rather over confidently) added:

> We have long since buried and well-nigh forgotten the down grade controversy. Here it is still very much alive… The churches and the ministers are somewhat sharply divided into the old school and the new and the religious journals are full of hot debate on the subject.[36]

The origins of Baptist tensions may be seen in the beginnings of Baptist work in the first three colonies in the 1830s. To recall the outlines of this story is perhaps necessary.

As far as is known, there were no Baptists in the first batch of convicts, although one Baptist prisoner, Richard Boots, arrived in 1810.[37] The first Baptist preacher in Australia, however, ended his career by becoming a convict, or at least being imprisoned for debt. John McKaeg, an eccentric Scottish Baptist whose training at the Horton Academy had been restricted by his inability to speak English, had served as a missionary in Ireland with the Baptist Irish Society (1822–25) and then totally divided the church at Bingley in Yorkshire where there were serious questions raised about his sanity. This unusual specimen of the British Baptist ministry then turned up in Sydney, unheralded and unknown, and conducted the first Baptist service in Australia at the Rose and Crown Inn in Sydney on 24 April 1831. The first baptismal services were held in Woolloomooloo Bay in 1832, much to the amusement of vulgar crowds. McKaeg gathered a mixed group of sympathisers, received a grant of land (being quite untroubled by any scruples about state aid) and 50,000 bricks were bought for a chapel by public subscription before McKaeg's debts from his failed 'tobacco, snuff and cigar manufactory' and alcoholism led to his disgrace and attempted suicide. Apart from the extremes of his moral failure, McKaeg does represent a type of maverick Baptist preacher who occasionally appears in early Australian Baptist history: an impassioned self-appointed evangelist, with a kind of earthy appeal but who cannot sustain a church, becomes a divisive force and prompts the more sober Baptist leaders to establish clear guidelines for the acceptance of preachers by the churches.[38]

---

[36] Reprinted from the *Christian World* in the *Southern Cross*, 21 February 1902, p. 206, and 7 March 1902, pp. 272-73.

[37] K.R. Manley and M. Petras, *The First Australian Baptists* (Eastwood, NSW: Baptist Historical Society of NSW, 1981), pp. 25-26. It should be noted that most convicts declared themselves simply as either Catholic or Protestant.

[38] Manley and Petras, *First Australian Baptists*, pp. 38-52.

McKaeg's successor and the effective founder of our churches in Australia was John Saunders (1806–59) who was a thoughtful and educated solicitor, an evangelical, missionary in outlook, liberal in churchmanship and deeply involved in the social issues of his society. He came in response to a request from a few Baptists in Sydney who were disenchanted with McKaeg. Encouraged and commissioned, though not supported, by the Baptist Missionary Society, Saunders arrived in 1834 and became the first pastor of the Bathurst Street church that was founded in 1836.[39] Saunders happily received the grant of land originally granted to McKaeg but did not receive support from Governor Bourke who established the Church Act in 1836 which materially strengthened the main denominations. Saunders 'reinvented' the Baptist cause, being widely honoured for his work as a temperance leader in a society almost destroyed by the excesses of alcohol. Saunders was also active in protests against the barbarities of the convict system and participated vigorously in the debates over education in the settlement. His missionary commitment was well known and he demonstrated a deep compassion for Aborigines. Late in 1838, prior to the trial and execution of seven white stockmen following the massacre of several Aborigines at Myall Creek, when public clamour was reaching fever pitch, Saunders was outspoken. Historian Henry Reynolds describes Saunders' sermon at this time as 'one of the most eloquent presentations of humanitarian doctrine' from the period. In the context of the times Saunders made a humane and courageous stand.[40]

A different and old-fashioned Protestant tradition was represented by the Strict and Particular Baptist Henry Dowling (1780–1869) who arrived in Hobart, Van Diemen's Land (later Tasmania) on 2 December 1834, the day after Saunders landed in Sydney. He represents those who retained their more rigid Calvinism, and had strict or 'closed' views about communion and church membership.[41] Dowling established services in Launceston and Hobart and also received government funding to act as a religious instructor to penal gangs. Others, such as Daniel Allen who developed a vigorous anti-Roman polemic, continued this tradition, but these preachers stood for the remoteness and rigidity of high-Calvinism at a time when Australian Baptists were generally moving towards evangelical tolerance and unity. Only a few tiny Strict and Particular congregations linger on today.[42]

[39] For Saunders, see B. Dickey (ed.), *The Australian Dictionary of Evangelical Biography* (Sydney: Evangelical History Association, 1994) [hereafter *ADEB*], pp. 330-31; Manley and Petras, *First Australian Baptists*, pp. 53-64.

[40] H. Reynolds, *This Whispering in our Hearts* (St Leonards, NSW: Allen & Unwin, 1998), p. 24. For an edited text of the sermon, see J. Sutton (ed.), *Rev. John Saunders: A Beacon of Light and some Baptist Reflections* (Canberra: Baptist Union of Australia, 2001), pp. 6-9.

[41] For Dowling, see *ADEB*, pp. 96-97.

[42] See M. Chavura, 'Attitudes towards Calvinism among Baptists of New South Wales, 1831–1914', Working Papers, Series 1 (2), Centre for the Study of Australian Christianity, North Ryde; and his 'A history of Calvinism in the Baptist churches of New South Wales, 1831–1914' (PhD thesis, Macquarie University, 1994). R. Humphreys and

There were few General Baptists among the earliest Baptists in Australia, but one sect well represented was the Scotch Baptist. This, of course, was not simply a national description, but rather a set of beliefs, emphases and practices which differed from 'English' Baptists: leadership by a plurality of lay elders, weekly observance of the Lord's Supper (commonly led by a lay leader), prayers and exhortation by 'brethren' during worship.[43] David McLaren (1785–1850), father of the famous preacher Alexander, was manager from 1837 of the SA Colonization Company in Adelaide for George Fife Angas. McLaren, humourless and driven by an overwhelming sense of duty, a 'Scotch' Baptist and the first Baptist preacher in Adelaide, wrote the first tract arguing for believer's baptism in Australia.[44] In the early years of Baptist work there were many Scotch Baptists, especially in Adelaide and Melbourne. Many happily joined the Churches of Christ movement when it was established in Australia.

This rich mix, of open 'English' Particular Baptists, Strict Calvinists, Scotch Baptists, a few General Baptists, to say nothing of Plymouth Brethren, all came together under the hot Australian sun. Traditional differences were not simply transported but translated in the new context, gradually absorbed into a rich diversity of belief and life in one Baptist denomination expressed in state Unions and by 1926 in a national Union. But elements of all these founding traditions shaped the Australian Baptist movement: the rough evangelist, the liberal evangelical, the doughty Calvinist, and the grim, unsmiling but dutiful lay leader.

In two areas Australian Baptists may be thought to have modified their British Baptist heritage. One major source of tension in the early years was the acceptance of state aid by some few pioneers and, indeed, as late as the 1860s in Melbourne James Taylor and Collins Street were for a time alienated from other Baptists over this question.[45] There was no theological justification for this variation of principle, beyond the peculiar circumstances of the colony (as with Dowling in Tasmania), but rather a pragmatic and (in some cases) perhaps an ignorance of the Nonconformist

---

R. Ward, *Religious Bodies in Australia* (Wantirna, New Melbourne Press, 3rd edn, 1995), p. 126, lists four Particular Baptist churches with a total membership of about fifty.

[43] For Scotch Baptists, see D.B. Murray, 'The Scotch Baptist Tradition in Great Britain', *Baptist Quarterly* 33.4 (October, 1989), pp. 186-98.

[44] David McLaren, *An inquiry into the nature and meaning of Christian Baptism* (Adelaide, 1840). For McLaren, see D. Pike, B. Nairn, G. Serle and J. Ritchie (eds), *Australian Dictionary of Biography* (15 vols; Carlton: Melbourne University Press, 1966–2000) [hereafter *ADB*], 2, pp. 176-77 and D. Pike, *Paradise of Dissent* (Melbourne: Melbourne University Press, 1957), *passim*. Manning Clark, *A History of Australia* (5 vols; Melbourne: Melbourne University Press, 1979), 3, p. 64, commented that McLaren was one of the 'high minded' and preached in various chapels 'because in all he had the opportunity to praise liberty of conscience and condemn cards, dancing, theatres, drinking and fornicating'. For a fuller assessment of McLaren, see B.R. Talbot, '"Sharp Shrewd Scotchman": David McLaren (1785–1850)', *Baptist Quarterly* 41.2 (April, 2005), pp. 103-12; Manley, *From Woolloomooloo to 'Eternity'*, pp. 42-47.

[45] K.R. Manley, 'A Colonial Evangelical Ministry and a "Clerical Scandal": James Taylor in Melbourne (1857–1868)', *Baptist Quarterly* 39.2 (April, 2001), pp. 56-79.

'sin' they were committing. This issue disappeared after the 1860s; though it might be observed how easily modern Baptists of the twentieth century accept funding for Baptist schools, aged care homes and various institutions. The other difference, as some thought it to be, was a modification of the autonomy of the local church. There were regular tirades against the danger of 'unbridled Congregationalism'. Home Mission churches were under strict denominational control, circuits were established in rural areas, and in South Australia a highly centralised structure for ministerial movements and salaries ('just a wholesome bit of Presbyterian Church government', as one described it[46]) was developed in the early twentieth century. Ordinations were always arranged and controlled by state Unions, closely linked with accreditation of ministers. In all these cases there was generally an overarching pragmatic concern rather than any tightly reasoned justification, though a theology of ordination was developed to support the centralised practice.[47]

However, an oft-remarked feature of Australian religious life was its imitative quality. The desire to reproduce in a strange environment the remembered security of 'home' is understandable, but certainly the reliance on the 'home' churches for preachers, educators, hymnbooks and most aspects of institutional life was remarkable. Whilst this may suggest a lack of originality, the need of this generation was not originality but reassurance.[48] This tension between an old culture and a new environment, the 'complex fate' of the exile as Henry James once called it, is a strong element in the Australian Baptist story.[49]

But for how long was this reassuring dependence on 'home' to last? In the last decade of the nineteenth century there were more urgent signs of wanting a clearer Australian identity. In 1888, visiting preacher Dr Alexander McLaren (son of our Scotch Baptist pioneer David) visited Melbourne to help celebrate the Jubilee of services in that colony. He urged churches to develop a 'Congregationalism redolent of the soil'. Establishment of the Victorian Baptist Fund, a remarkable achievement of raising £50,000 (including an anonymous gift of £25,000) and the appointment of W.T. Whitley as the foundation principal of the Victorian College were the first signs of this.[50] But in 1902 J.G. Greenhough detected not only a 'self-assertive

---

[46] Unsigned letter in *Southern Baptist*, 27 February 1901, p. 57.

[47] K.R. Manley, 'Ordination among Australian Baptists', *Baptist Quarterly* 28.4 (October, 1979), pp. 159-83. More recently, there have been changes in the practice of ordination by the Union in both Western Australia and NSW.

[48] H. Jackson, *Churches and People in Australia and New Zealand 1860–1930* (Sydney: Allen & Unwin, 1987), p. 47.

[49] H. James, as cited by David Malouf, *A Spirit of Play: The Making of Australian Consciousness* (Sydney: Australian Broadcasting Commission, 1998), p. 25.

[50] B.S. Brown, *Members One of Another: The Baptist Union of Victoria 1862–1962* (Melbourne: Baptist Union of Victoria, 1962), p. 77. For the Fund, see D.M. Himbury, *Centenary History of the Victorian Baptist Fund* (Melbourne: VBF Fund, 1988). I have recently identified the donor as a wealthy grazier, Silas Harding (1816–94): see *Our Yesterdays* 10 (2002), p. 152. For Whitley in Australia, see K.R. Manley, '"The Right

individuality' but also a 'pathetic affection' for British Baptists, 'a sort of gentle, reproachful tone', like a 'daughter forgotten by an absent mother'.[51] Political federation and establishment of national structures among Presbyterians and Methodists stimulated the Baptist dream of federation. What it meant to be an Australian church was, however, never quite as clearly defined as the intensity with which the need for it was proclaimed. To have locally born and trained leaders was one thing, certainly; a national as distinct from a state Union was another, but what else?

Perhaps it was in the 'Bush' that Baptists, like their fellow Australians, imagined themselves coming closest to realising this quest to be Australian. Thus there was a passionate commitment to work 'in the outback'.[52] Certainly F.J. Wilkin, the outstanding leader of Home Missions in Victoria, insisted in 1896 that Home Missions were a 'test of the patriotism' of Baptists.[53] Pioneers of Home Mission became heroes in Baptist eyes; men like George Slade and Wilkin in Victoria; Thomas Llewellyn and T.H. Jaggers in New South Wales; David Badger in South Australia; and William Kennedy in Western Australia—the latter's achievement being quite outstanding.[54] Interestingly, the term 'Bush Baptist' is a colloquial expression (still remembered by older Baptists) whose origin is lost. *The Macquarie Dictionary* defines it as 'a person of doubtful religious persuasion', or 'a person of vague but strong religious beliefs, not necessarily associated with a particular denomination'.[55] Why would a tiny minority denomination like the Baptists be gifted with this phrase? Is this another case of the Australian love of irony? Is it that few really knew what this small sect believed? A colourful former Quaker turned Baptist and self-appointed evangelist, J.J. Westwood, may offer us a clue. Visiting a woolshed in the Riverina, he not only sold ten pounds of tracts but also received three pounds in donations from the shearers. One shearer told his boss, 'Give this

---

Man in the right place": W.T. Whitley in Australia (1891–1901)', *Baptist Quarterly* 37.4 (October, 1997), pp. 174-92.

[51] *Southern Baptist,* 11 June 1902, p. 135.

[52] On the same night as Hughes spoke in Adelaide, Sandford Fleming, recently appointed as Home Mission organizer and evangelist, spoke on 'Our Task Outback'. Fleming, an Australian who had studied at Yale, later returned to the USA and eventually became President of Berkeley Baptist Divinity School (one of a small number of Australians who became significant theological educators in America).

[53] *Southern Baptist*, 18 June 1896, p. 127.

[54] For Wilkin, Badger, and Kennedy, see *ADEB*; for Slade, see B.S. Brown, *A Cloud of Witnesses* (Hawthorn, Vic: Baptist Union of Victoria, 1999), pp. 123-24; for Llewellyn and Jaggers, see A.C. Prior, *Some Fell on Good Ground: A History of the Beginnings and Development of the Baptist Church in New South Wales, Australia, 1831–1965* (Sydney: Baptist Union of NSW, 1966), pp. 156-62.

[55] *The Macquarie Dictionary* (Dee Why: Macquarie Library, rev. edn, 1985); S.J. Baker, *The Australian Language* (Milsons Point: Currawong Press, 1978), p. 75.

gentleman, sir, one pound on my account; I like the Baptists and was brought up amongst them.'[56]

As Stuart Piggin has noted:

> A missionary with the Bush Missionary Society (formed in 1857) reported in 1871 that Spurgeon's sermons were more popular in the Australian bush than any others: they created most interest and seemed to do most good, perhaps because they were cast in an earthy style which would presumably appeal to bush folk. These sermons...were read at house meetings in bush settlements every Lord's Day morning.[57]

Were Spurgeon's sermons, and the informal groups of readers found scattered through the bush, the origins of 'Bush Baptist'?

But Australia was destined to become one of the most urbanised populations in the modern world and it was in the cities that powerful denominational leaders, both ministers and lay people, were generally located. During the nineteenth century Australian Baptists produced many successful businessmen, especially in South Australia and Victoria, whose wealth and generosity contributed to the denomination's expansion. But the strength of Baptist congregational life was to be in the suburbs of the large cities, a pattern recognisable from the last two decades of the nineteenth century and even more clearly seen in the development of 'Bible belts' in the capital cities where the largest Baptist churches have always been located. Anti-suburbanism has long been a fashionable sport among Australia's intellectuals, but this is where most Australians live.[58] Australia is a nation of ordinary people and 'the quiet suburban life has been the stem culture in Australia'; in ordinary churches like the Baptists, true originality and variety are also found.[59] Of course there is thoughtless uniformity, ugliness and self-centredness in the suburbs as well, and Baptists also have often grappled with renewing their mission in the inner-urban and high-density communities.

Many women have found a place in the ordinariness of Baptist life. In the earliest times of settlement the role of women was clearly limited. A few representative women may be noted. One way women could have an impact was as a teacher or a writer. In South Australia, Matilda Jane Evans (1827–86) combined these two roles after the death of her pastor-husband in 1863. Using the pseudonym of Maud Jeanne

---

[56] *The Journal of J.J. Westwood (Evangelist)* (Melbourne, 1865), p. 359; see A.M. Grocott, *Convicts, Clergymen and Churches* (Sydney: Sydney University Press, 1980), p. 192.

[57] S. Piggin, *Evangelical Christianity in Australia: Spirit, Word and World* (Melbourne: Oxford University Press, 1996), p. 58.

[58] A. Gilbert, 'The Roots of Australian Anti-Suburbanism', in Goldberg and Smith (eds), *Australian Cultural History*, pp. 33-49; T. Rowse, 'Heaven and a Hills Hoist: Australian Critics on Suburbia', *Meanjin Quarterly* 37.1 (1978), pp. 3-13.

[59] J. McCalman, 'The Originality of Ordinary Lives', in W. Hudson and G. Bolton (eds), *Creating Australia: Changing Australian History* (St Leonards: Allen & Unwin, 1997), pp. 86-95.

Franc she wrote fourteen novels, numerous poems and essays. The power of these and similar stories to influence a church's identity should not be underestimated.[60] There were, of course, the pioneer women missionaries, the 'five barley loaves' who constituted the first Australian Baptist missionaries. The best remembered is the redoubtable Ellen Arnold (1858–1931), the first missionary to serve with an Australian Baptist society. These women established Baptist mission work and their successors have created a remarkable story of mission work conducted by Australian Baptist women.[61] Equally remarkable was the evangelistic ministry of Emilia Baeyertz (b.1842), a converted Jewess. Baptised in the Aberdeen Street church, Geelong, she preached to large evangelistic meetings with considerable success in Victoria and South Australia before embarking on an international ministry.[62] Perhaps the most remarkable woman of them all, ordinary in so many ways, was Cecilia Downing (1858–1952). Active on Baptist committees, she was also interested in national and international affairs, served as a long-term member of the Woman's Christian Temperance Union (president, 1912–15) and of the Travellers' Aid Society, but was best known to Melbourne as the president of the Housewives' Association. Mrs Downing has been described as 'unquestionably one of the most influential women of her time in Australia'.[63] In the twentieth century, the question of the ordination of women has proved divisive, though since Marita Munro was ordained in Victoria in 1978, women have now been ordained or accredited in five states.

Of course in a small denomination with a familial tone to its life, especially in the first century or so, key ministers exerted a strong influence. Silas Mead (1834–1909), foundation pastor at Flinders Street from 1861 to 1897, acquired a quasi-episcopal authority in South Australia. In Victoria, Collins Street led denominational life and its succession of ministers from the 1860s to the end of the century, the evangelist but disgraced James Taylor (1814–96), the scholarly but revered James Martin (1821–77) and then, most loved of all, Samuel Chapman (1831–99), became outstanding evangelical influences.[64] Sydney struggled during the

---

[60] See *ADEB*, and B. Wall, *Our Own Matilda* (Kent Town, SA: Wakefield Press, 1994). For a study of the role of story and Baptist identity, see K.R. Manley, 'When Harry met Molly: Story and Baptist Identity, c.1887', *Our Yesterdays* 5 (1997), pp. 5-20.

[61] R.M. Gooden, '"We Trust them to Establish the Work": Significant Roles for Early Australian Baptist Women in Overseas Mission, 1864–1913', in M. Hutchinson and G. Treloar (eds), *This Gospel Shall be Preached* (Sydney: Centre for the Study of Australian Christianity, 1998), pp. 126-46.

[62] See *ADEB*.

[63] J. Smart, 'A Sacred Trust: Cecilia Downing, Baptist Faith and Feminist Citizenship', *Our Yesterdays* 3 (1995), pp. 21-50.

[64] For Taylor, Mead, Martin and Chapman, see *ADEB*. Chapman was the basis of the character of the Rev. Stephen Moore in the novel *Swayed by the Storm* (Melbourne: Thomas C. Lothian, 1911), by Marion Downes, a member of Collins Street: see K.R. Manley, 'From Assurance through Depression to Optimism: Baptists in Victoria 1880–1914', *Our Yesterdays* 10 (2002), p. 38.

nineteenth century, but in Brisbane William Whale (1842–1903) gave a positive and striking lead to the churches, becoming the leading Nonconformist clergyman of the period. Journalists used to joke about going to the Baptist aquarium to hear the Whale 'spout', but his leadership in several industrial disputes earned him universal respect.[65]

However, an oft-repeated theme was that whilst these English imports were greatly appreciated, the need for Australian born and trained men to occupy significant pulpits was felt. Chapman, who was among the best-loved preachers in Victoria's history, outlined his strategy, 'To the Australians I am become an Australian'.[66] In 1910, F.C. Spurr at Collins Street recalled the advice of W.H. Holdsworth, principal of the Baptist College of Victoria, 'not to treat people as the chief of sinners because they are not English'.[67] Of course Australians also had an impact on English ministers who served in their country. W.D. Jackson, when leaving Collins Street in 1935, made a dramatic confession: 'All that I am today, I owe to you, to Australia.' He had undergone a remarkable spiritual experience in Victoria, which altered the direction of his ministry, and he claimed to have been enriched in evangelism and missions work: 'everything he counted worthwhile in his ministry had been the gift of Australia'.[68]

By the end of the nineteenth century Baptist work was established in each state, after having begun quite late in Western Australia in 1895. But differences among Baptists across the nation were already well entrenched. Ironically, it was the moves towards establishing a national body which highlighted these tensions, delayed the formation of the Baptist Union of Australia and restricted the effectiveness of a national programme.

The main problem as far as the eastern states were concerned was South Australia which had a strong tradition of open membership churches and by the end of the century was confidently 'broad, liberal and modern in its times', as J.H. Sexton, a colleague of Hughes, expressed it in 1901.[69] Conversely, the South Australian problem with the eastern states was their conservatism and narrowness and they complained about the lack of liberal viewpoints in the denominational paper, *The Southern Baptist*, which since 1895 had served South Australia, Victoria and Tasmania. Tasmania, under the influence of a succession of Spurgeon-trained men, was deeply conservative whilst Victoria was more broadly evangelical though with many conservatives, including the paper's editor, Allan Webb. Fear that Baptist principles would be diluted by the open membership practice and by the liberalism of South Australia occasioned a strong clash in 1901 when a respected South Australian minister being considered for a Tasmanian church found himself under close scrutiny about his beliefs by the Baptist Union of Tasmania. This caused great

---

[65] For Whale, see *ADEB*; for the 'aquarium' and 'spout', see *Australian Baptist*, 26 August 1924, p. 3; 7 August 1934, p. 4.

[66] *Truth and Progress*, September 1882, p. 105

[67] *Southern Baptist*, 9 June 1910, p. 374.

[68] *Australian Baptist*, 4 June 1935, p. 3.

[69] *Southern Baptist*, 31 July 1901, p. 170.

offence in South Australia: 'It is a reflection on a State, when its credentials are not received in good faith.' At one point letters to the editor about the issue were listed under the heading 'TASMANIA v. SOUTH AUSTRALIA'.[70]

One matter that was raised in this dispute was the place of creeds in Baptist life, just as happened in the Downgrade Controversy in England. South Australia vigorously rejected any creed being imposed whilst Victoria did have a statement of belief, as it had been required to provide one for legal reasons when trustees were appointed for the Victorian Baptist Fund. Their 'creed' was broadly evangelical, in fact was adapted slightly from the (British) Evangelical Alliance statement.[71]

These tensions illustrate the way in which various Australian Baptists drew from different aspects of the Baptist heritage. All had drawn on the traditions of missions as exemplified in 'Our Heroic Carey', as Allan Webb called William Carey in 1892 and his influence was seen in the establishment of Australian Baptist mission societies, first in South Australia in 1864, then in Victoria, New South Wales, Tasmania and Queensland, as well as in the selection of India as the field of service.[72]

But if Carey represented one aspect of Baptist heritage that was a source of unity, there were other points of tension. When Dr H. Wheeler Robinson agreed that 'Spurgeon and Clifford together sum up the Baptist denomination', he meant that 'true evangelism and true liberty', as epitomised in these two contemporaries, were complementary in any 'adequate view of the Baptist faith'.[73] It is striking how often these two emphases recurred at this time in Australian Baptists' depiction of the essentials of Baptist belief, but these two aspects of Baptist identity were often in conflict in Australia.

C.H. Spurgeon (1834–92) had extensive influence in Australia.[74] Spurgeon's printed sermons were widely distributed, often becoming the sermon in many an outback gathering, as we have noted. Spurgeon in this tabloid form had a remarkable impact. But a major source of his influence was through pastors trained in his college. By 1887, some forty-four Spurgeon's men had come to Australasia, by far the largest group from any British college. In 1885, a Spurgeon's man occupied every church in Tasmania. Australians did not generally follow Spurgeon's Calvinism or even his general Puritan theology, and the 'Spurgeonic' tradition among Australian Baptists largely came to mean unashamed and powerful evangelistic preaching.

---

[70] *Southern Baptist,* 31 July 1901, pp. 169-70; 2 October 1901, p. 228.

[71] Brown, *Members One of Another,* pp. 79-81.

[72] *Victorian Baptist,* January 1892, p. 11. See K.R. Manley, '"Our Heroic Carey": William Carey and Australian Baptists', *Our Yesterdays* 1 (1993), pp. 5-22.

[73] H. Wheeler Robinson, *The Life and Faith of the Baptists* (London: Methuen, 1927), p. 165.

[74] M. Petras, 'Charles Haddon Spurgeon: His Influence upon Australia', *Our Yesterdays* 1 (1993), pp. 55-70; K.R. Manley, '"The Magic Name": Charles Haddon Spurgeon and the Evangelical Ethos of Australian Baptists. Part 1', *Baptist Quarterly* 40.3 (July, 2003), pp. 173-84; 'Part 2', 40.4 (October, 2003), pp. 215-29.

But the influence of John Clifford (1836–1923), a convinced Baptist and Free Church leader, was also important.[75] The leading exponent of the social gospel among British Baptists, Clifford was President of the Baptist Union at the time of 'the Downgrade Controversy' (1887–88), and became the first President of the Baptist World Alliance (1905–11). During his Australian tour (1897) most Baptists enthusiastically honoured Clifford, but in Tasmania, where Spurgeon's influence was dominant, Baptists had been notably absent from public welcomes.[76] Socialism and liberalism, as represented by Clifford, were twin evils to many Australian Baptists. Samuel Pearce Carey was once called 'the Dr Clifford of Australia' in South Australia, an exaggerated but well intended tribute. Certainly Carey was deeply influenced by Clifford in theology and was heavily involved in attempts to link churches with the labour movement.[77] Many other Australian Baptists consistently identified themselves with Clifford's position. Whilst the influence of Spurgeon on Australian Baptists has been long lasting and frequently noted, Clifford's influence on Australian Baptists was much greater than seems to have been generally recognised.

So with all these tensions, could Baptist federation be achieved? In 1897 representatives from all the colonies and New Zealand gathered in Melbourne but there were serious problems in agreeing about federation. The key proposals involved a federated missionary society, a national Baptist paper, a federal theological college and uniform 'ministerial standards'. New South Wales proved to be highly suspicious of the whole idea, but eventually in 1913 a national paper, *The Australian Baptist* (based in Sydney), began and the Australian Foreign Mission Board was established (a merger of the state societies). Hopes of a federal college in Melbourne were eventually dashed when it was insisted that the legal requirements of the Victorian Baptist Fund prevented its resources being used to support anything other than a Victorian college. War intervened and it was not until 1926 that the Baptist Union of Australia (BUA) was formed in Sydney.[78] This was a union of the state unions and provided a framework for co-operation.[79]

---

[75] A good modern biography of Clifford is needed, but see the entry by J.H.Y. Briggs in T. Larsen (ed.), *Biographical Dictionary of Evangelicals* (Leicester: Inter-Varsity Press, 2003), pp. 148-50; D. Thompson, 'John Clifford's Social Gospel', *Baptist Quarterly* 31.5 (January, 1986), pp. 199-217.

[76] *Southern Baptist*, 1 July 1897, p. 145. See J. Clifford, *God's Greater Britain* (London: James Clarke, 1899).

[77] Manley, 'Preaching the Social Gospel', pp. 366-79.

[78] B.S. Brown, *Baptised into One Body: A Short History of the Baptist Union of Australia* (Hawthorn, Vic: BUA, 1987).

[79] The first president was J.H. Goble (1863–1923) who exercised a remarkable ministry in Footscray (Melbourne) for almost thirty-six years. He represented an authentic Australian Baptist minister in almost every way: locally born, with working class loyalties, a dedicated pastoral worker, a preacher with the common touch, warmly compassionate and generous, outspoken against unemployment, attacking jingoism and compulsory military training, a supporter of his local football club, a leading Freemason, a committed denominationalist. After his death the citizens erected a life-

In retrospect, although the BUA was inaugurated with great pride and hope, and at times has accomplished much in terms of Christian education and publications, extra-mural education for isolated ministers, home missions, evangelism and ministerial annuity funds, its role has been gradually reduced until today it has a very limited function. Local churches, if they have any strong sense of denominational identity, would see their loyalties and resources linked with the state Baptist Unions. The federal vision has scarcely been maintained. Indeed, with the cessation of *The Australian Baptist* in 1991 the only really national ministries of Australian Baptists are found in Global interAction (the successor to the missionary society) and in Baptist World Aid Australia, both bodies being administered quite separately from the BUA. The marginalisation of this federal vision means that today, although there are cordial relations and regular meetings of key leaders from each state, each Baptist Union produces its own paper, develops its own structures and acts with only a limited awareness of Baptists in other states. 'Our own church' in 'our own State' would be closer to the reality today. Whether we have lost a great deal by this is problematic.

The 'Face' of Baptists

In 1914, the Rev. W.G. Taylor, a Methodist leader in Sydney, suggested that different creeds produced different faces. This prompted the *Bulletin* to prepare a suitable cartoon with twelve faces.[80] The Baptist face is, as Baptist editor J.A. Packer put it, 'the least uncomplimentary of the lot': a bespectacled man with stovepipe hat, droopy moustache and beard, looks every inch a suburban businessman.[81]

What is the 'face' of Baptists today? Church life surveys give us some raw data for an Australian Baptist 'Identikit' picture (such as police artists used to draw). For example, our current profile largely matches the general population in age and education, though 8.7% of Baptists are university educated compared with 7.7% of the general population. There are fewer Baptists earning high incomes compared with the total population and as to occupations Baptists are over represented in the areas of wholesaling, retailing and community services.[82] A typical Aussie Baptist, we might claim, whilst informal or 'laid back' in style, is theologically and socially conservative, evangelistic (at least in theory), with a deep commitment to global missions. The same conservative Aussie can be innovative, pragmatic and adaptable, but may also be insular and independent. This Baptist is likely to be generous and compassionate, a good neighbour but ready to mock the 'tall poppies' in our church

---

sized statue that still stands on the Geelong Road, Footscray, a unique tribute for a Baptist pastor in our country. See *ADB* and *ADEB*.

[80] *Bulletin*, 28 May 1914, p. 13.

[81] *Australian Baptist*, 29 September 1914, p. 13.

[82] Details in Hughes, *The Baptists in Australia*. For the Church Life Surveys, see P. Kaldor *et al*, *Winds of Change* (Homebush West: Lancer, 1994); and P. Kaldor and R. Powell, *Views from the Pews* (Adelaide: Open Book, 1995).

or society. Yet, as these characteristics are listed, innumerable exceptions suggest themselves. Regional variants are greater today than ever before, many Baptists are far more sophisticated than this portrait implies; in other words, Australian Baptists are representative of the global community of those Baptists found in the developed world.

Deeper issues of identity remain elusive. Of course Baptists have changed both regionally and over time and there is no simple way to tell this complex story of a dynamic movement. For example, Baptists in NSW during the twentieth century became a powerful evangelical force and by far the largest Baptist Union. Stuart Piggin has suggested that for the period 1914–59 Baptists in NSW were in the 'vanguard of Australian evangelicalism' where they possessed what he calls 'a glorious trinity in (G.H.) Morling, the archetypal college principal, C.J. Tinsley, the archetypal pastor and John Ridley, the archetypal evangelist'.[83] There is, of course, another side to this. Several talented pastors left for the Presbyterian ministry during this era, in part because of a perceived anti-intellectualism among Baptists. Both the principals before and after Morling's long tenure of forty years left in unhappy circumstances and both were obliged to find a place in other denominations.

The last four decades have witnessed the most remarkable changes. Though there were many regional differences, there was at least a clearly discerned common identity as Baptists. The Billy Graham Crusade in 1959 was a great success; perhaps Australia was as close to genuine revival as it has ever been.[84] But the Graham Crusade proved to be the end rather than the beginning of church renewal and the 60s quickly proved to be a challenge for all churches as they were in North America and Europe.[85]

Five features of these decades, which have shaped the modern 'face' or 'faces' of Australian Baptists, may briefly be noted.

(1) Americanisation has continued to shape much of our culture generally, not least in our churches. As early as 1900, when Samuel Pearce Carey was preparing to come to Melbourne in 1900, William McLean, a wealthy deacon of the Collins Street church, arranged for him first to visit America:

Australians are a people standing midway between the English and the Americans, more American than the English, and more English than the Americans... If you get some practical insight into the American view point, you will be wiser to guide us under the Southern skies.[86]

---

[83] Piggin, 'The Role of Baptists', p.14.

[84] Piggin, *Evangelical Christianity in Australia*, pp. 154-71.

[85] D. Hilliard, 'The Religious Crisis of the 1960s: The Experience of the Australian Churches', *Journal of Religious History* 21.2 (1997), pp. 209-27.

[86] S.P. Carey, 'The Conspiracy of Circumstances', in W.E. Geil (ed.), *Ocean and Isle* (Melbourne: W.T. Pater, 1902), p. 244. For McLean (1845–1905), see *ADEB*.

Across the ensuing century Baptists have become less English and even more like the Americans. In 1957 architect Robin Boyd coined the word 'Austerica' to describe the Americanization of the post war Australian landscape.[87] Among Baptists, there has been a demonstrable shift from a British Protestant culture to an American Protestant culture.[88] Popular theology is now largely disseminated through American publishing houses and this is linked with American-produced music, film, radio and television. Youth programmes, theological teacher and evangelist exchanges, church growth approaches and Christian education have all been influential. Certainly every state was attracted for a decade or so to Southern Baptist models of education in the All Age Sunday School, and in co-operative budgets. Whilst there is much contemporary seeking after a 'dinkum' Aussie theology and practice and an increasing disenchantment with many aspects of American Protestant and political culture, it is probably true that much of our church life remains imitative, especially of 'successful' North American evangelical churches. Of course all this is but a part of American cultural hegemony, although any American will ask us: which America are we talking about, for is not America also a nation of multiple identities? Australian Baptists must assume responsibility for our part in the emergence of a global Western evangelicalism.

(2) In part because of extreme conservative American Protestant influence, fundamentalism has also continued to have some impact; or perhaps it would be clearer to say, the tensions among American evangelicals have had their echoes here. Independent Baptist churches, exported from the USA, have been with us from the 1960s and are self-avowedly fundamentalist.[89] The impact of conservative Bible colleges, independent 'faith' missions and fundamentalist-type literature on our churches is significant. Fundamentalism has shaped the identity of at least some significant parts of our Baptist community, especially in Queensland. This is to say that militant anti-liberalism, insistence on biblical inerrancy, millenarianism, anti-ecumenism are part of our identity as Australian Baptists, though they have not produced the divisions experienced in other parts of the Baptist world.

(3) Moves for church unity have, ironically, been especially divisive for Baptists, as they have often been for other evangelical movements. Australian Baptists have generally rejected participation in conciliar expressions of the ecumenical movement.[90] Yet in other ways many barriers have been broken down and most

---

[87] R. Boyd, *The Australian Ugliness* (Melbourne: Penguin, 1960), pp. 78-79; first in the *Age*, 21 September 1957, as cited in G. Davison, 'Driving to Austerica: The Americanization of the Postwar Australian City', in Bolitho and Wallace-Crabbe (eds), *Approaching Australia*, pp. 159-83.

[88] See N. Buch, 'American Influence on Protestantism in Queensland since 1945' (PhD thesis, University of Queensland, 1995).

[89] See D. Parker, 'Fundamentalism and Conservative Protestantism in Australia 1920–1980' (PhD thesis, University of Queensland, 1982).

[90] For details, see K.R. Manley, 'Australian Baptists Today', in M. Petras (ed.), *Australian Baptists Past and Present* (Eastwood, NSW: Baptist Historical Society of NSW, 1988), pp. 55-57. Baptist migrants from Eastern Europe or Latin America,

Baptists evidence a 'pragmatic ecumenism' which leads to co-operation in a wide range of activities: in theological education; in exploring traditions of worship and spirituality; in evangelism and in action on social issues.

(4) Evangelicalism has many faces and to distinguish differing aspects of its influence on Australian Baptists is problematic. For example, many Australian Baptists, like other evangelicals, have reclaimed their heritage of commitment to social justice as being integral to our mission. In all denominations there has been change in attitude towards social ethical issues. A wider range of issues has been addressed, touching on more than alcohol and gambling, although the current gambling opposition has seen the churches working closely with other community groups. Questions such as war and conscription, racial discrimination, Aboriginal rights, overseas aid, immigration policy, child abuse, public housing, treatment of illegal refugees have all been studied, often in concert with other denominations. Sexuality has been a source of division, with vigorous discussion on topics such as the family law and divorce, abortion, and homosexuality. Baptists have shared in a new concentration on research and preparing papers on social ethical issues, which can be placed in the public forum.

The 60s and 70s was the time when 'radical discipleship' came to be part of our vocabulary. The influence of communities like the House of the New World in Sydney, the House of Freedom in Brisbane and the House of the Gentle Bunyip in Melbourne, all essentially Baptist in foundation, was important.[91] People like Athol Gill and John Hirt inspired a large number of Baptists with an emphasis on a Christian counter-culture. This embraced critical appraisal of economic and political life as well as denominational structures, a renewal of committed community life, a praxis-model of learning and a deep commitment to practical working for social justice that could be local or extend to countries like El Salvador. A rich liturgical approach to worship and an openness to new forms of spirituality in part derived from these movements. Thus today Baptists have some centres for spirituality, drawing on many traditions but clearly Baptist, such as the semi-monastic community at Breakwater (Geelong) where Eastern Orthodoxy has been a major influence. Also from the radical movement came a strong push to be authentically Australian, free of any ecclesiastical imperialism, British or American, to develop a 'gum-leaf' theology, to be a 'fair dinkum' church.

Relatively few Baptist politicians have achieved leadership in political life, though at least two have been State premiers (Digby Denham in Queensland and Tom Playford [a kind of Baptist] in South Australia) and one Prime Minister (J.M. Bruce) was the son of a Baptist deacon. Two Liberal political leaders, John Hewson (a former leader of the party) and the Federal Treasurer Peter Costello (brother of Tim, a leading Baptist minister with a high media profile) come from Baptist backgrounds.

---

recalling the oppression of their own experiences, have been extremely vocal on this issue.

[91] M.R. Munro, 'A History of the House of the Gentle Bunyip (1975–90): A Contribution to Australian Church Life' (MA thesis, University of Melbourne, 2002).

(5) The global impact of charismatic renewal has affected all denominations in Australia, not least Baptists, where our large degree of congregational freedom has facilitated change. This has probably been the most dramatic difference in the last two decades with the impact being felt in various ways including theology, worship, patterns of church life, ministry and leadership.

Thus the most obvious changes in Baptist life have come in worship and nowhere is the current diversity of our life more apparent. 'Soft' charismatic style may dominate but is not the only form. A mix of global and Australian influences is seen in the 'Hillsong' style of worship but some churches have a liturgical structure, printed prayers, follow a lectionary, and use Taize prayers. There may be banners, candles, drama, modern hymns and songs, many of Australian composition: is this mix at last an 'Australian' Baptist church at worship?

These issues raise a last and basic question about identity. Is there a future for Australian Baptists? The day of denominationalism may well be fading in Australia, though I think Baptists do have a future, even if we will be reinvented yet again in the process.[92] To identify 'core Baptist values' and strengthen these is an urgent challenge for our Baptist leaders and thinkers. We rightly affirm diversity but in the bewildering range of Baptist identities now present the need for focal points of cohesion as Baptists is even more apparent. This is why Australian Baptists are interested participants in international Baptist discussions about our identity.

To know our own story is to recognise what holds us together with other Christians as well as what characterises our way of being church. As Miriam Dixson has observed about Australian society generally, 'Historians can help, steering a path between the tendency of modernity to dismiss the past and that of fundamentalism to cling to it.'[93] To such a vocation Baptist historians in Australia—and elsewhere— are called.

How, then, shall we face our future as Baptists with 'our own church in our own land'? Another Australian historian, Inga Clendinnen, gives us a clue:

> I am not suggesting that we shuffle backwards into the twenty-first century. I would recommend a crabwise approach, eyes swivelling sideways, backwards, forwards, with equal intensity, because while the past is past, it is not dead. Its hand is on our shoulder. As for what has to be done—I end with the words of the great British historian E.P. Thompson: 'This is not a question we can ask of history. It is, this time, a question history asks of us'.[94]

---

[92] For a discussion of possibilities, see K.R. Manley (ed.), *Future Church: A Baptist Discussion* (Hawthorn, Vic.: Baptist Union of Victoria, 1996).

[93] Dixson, *The Imaginary Australian*, p. 92.

[94] I. Clendinnen, *True Stories* (Sydney: Australian Broadcasting Commission, 1999), p. 103.

CHAPTER 19

Theological Education and the Quest for Identity in the Baptist Convention of Zimbabwe

Henry Mugabe

This study seeks to discuss the quest for identity by the Baptist Convention of Zimbabwe in general and the role played by theological education in that quest. The first part will discuss the historical development of the Baptist Convention of Zimbabwe, especially the role played by the women through the Women's Missionary Union (WMU). This study will also discuss the history of formal theological education; the role played by the Bible, and some of the creative ways that Baptists dialogue with African traditional religions. There are four Baptist groups in Zimbabwe; all of them are members of the All Africa Baptist Fellowship and the Baptist World Alliance.[1] The focus of this exploration and analysis is the Baptist Convention of Zimbabwe and its emerging identity, an identity that has become distinct from that of the Southern Baptist missionaries who were its founders.

The identity of any people is not neutral. It is always something that is rooted in the politics of its place and time. According to Mazrui and Shariff, identity is a relative and dynamic concept that is shaped by the vicissitudes of the politics and socio-economic conditions of the place and time. Identity is, in fact, a process by which power and status are negotiated, disinheritance and oppression legitimized, and liberation struggles waged. Intellectual debates on the identity of a peculiar people, therefore, are not free of political underpinnings revolving around struggles of dominance and liberation, of subjection and autonomy.[2]

For African churches, like the Baptist Convention of Zimbabwe, the question of identity is a crucial one, because the history of Christian missions in Africa has been inextricably bound up with the history of colonialism. Furthermore, in Africa missionaries tend to keep within their authority some areas of power, especially the control of institutions or fixed properties. Quite often these have been or are used to control the young convention. Handing over responsibility to the national

---

[1] The four Baptist Groups in Zimbabwe are the Association of the United Baptist Churches of Zimbabwe, Baptist Convention of Zimbabwe, Baptist Union of Zimbabwe, and National Baptist Convention of Zimbabwe.

[2] A.M. Mazrui and I.N. Shariff, *The Swahili: Idiom and Identity of an African People* (Trenton, NJ: Africa World Press, 2001), p. 5.

convention by the Foreign Mission Board has been a continuous problem in African countries. The issue of identity is about allowing others to make their own choices, control their own destiny and live in their own home in their own way. Africans want a Christianity with an African face.

The Baptist Convention of Zimbabwe

The Baptist Convention of Zimbabwe grew out of the missionary efforts of Southern Baptist Missionaries from the USA. The first missionaries to be appointed were Clyde and Hattie Dotson who had come to the country as missionaries of one of the faith missions, the South Africa General Mission. Sometime in 1949, after a disagreement with some of his colleagues at Rusitu Mission, where he was working, Dotson resigned. He then became an independent missionary.[3] In September 1950, the Foreign Mission Board of the Southern Baptist Convention (SBC) voted to accept responsibility for mission work in Rhodesia. Consequently, the Dotsons were appointed as contract workers in southern Rhodesia *in absentia*.[4] They were later designated as special appointees.[5] Other missionaries, including two medical doctors, Giles and Wana Ann Fort, from the hospital at Sanyati soon joined the Dotsons.[6] In the meantime, Dotson had made contact with Joseph Nyathi, who had trained and worked with Baptists in South Africa and was now seeking for a Baptist group to be associated with in southern Rhodesia. By the end of 1952 the missionaries reported that they had organized five churches with a membership of 204, with three ordained pastors and seventeen lay pastors.[7]

The various churches that had been founded by the Mission used to meet for an annual evangelistic conference. A committee was chosen to look into the matter of forming a convention. In January 1963, the committee recommended a model constitution to a meeting of church representatives who then formally organized themselves into a convention, elected their own officers and planned for their own first annual convention meeting, which met in Gwelo, 6–9 July 1963. The Revd Abel Nziramasanga, who was to become one of the stalwarts of the Convention, was elected as the first president.[8] Thirty-nine churches were represented at that first annual meeting. In those early years the mission paid the pastors. After a short period of time a decision was taken by the Evangelistic Worker's Committee of the

---

[3] For a biography of Clyde J. Dotson, see Davis L. Saunders, 'Clyde J Dotson: Pioneer Missionary to Southern Rhodesia', *Baptist History and Heritage* 23 (1988), pp. 51-59.

[4] Davis L. Saunders, 'A History of Baptists in East and Central Africa' (ThD dissertation, The Southern Baptist Theological Seminary, Louisville, Kentucky, 1973), p. 76.

[5] Saunders, 'Baptists in East and Central Africa', p. 77.

[6] Michael Gelfand, *Godly Medicine in Zimbabwe* (Gweru: Mambo Press, 1988), pp. 207-208.

[7] Saunders, 'Baptists in East and Central Africa', p. 83.

[8] The Revd Abel Nziramasanga was in the first group of students who enrolled at the African Baptist Theological Seminary in 1955.

Foreign Mission Board to present a ten-year master plan whereby all organized churches were gradually to assume the responsibility of paying the salary of their pastors within a period of ten years. The Mission would reduce their subsidy by ten per cent every year. This matter caused a lot of tension between the young Convention and the Mission. The Convention's contention was that the Mission, without any prior consultation, unilaterally imposed the matter. Relations between the Convention and the Mission were very strained, especially between 1965 and 1967. In 1965 the evangelistic conference was cancelled and the Convention had to arrange its meetings without a Mission subsidy. In 1966, the Convention elected new leaders, who told the missionaries to 'plan with them and not for them' in future.[9] It was difficult for pastors, who were previously paid by the Mission, to be paid now by the poor churches. Yet money from the Mission had too many strings attached to it. The process of supporting themselves put in motion the forming of an identity for the young Convention churches. Years later one of the pastors remarked that after the Mission had stopped paying their salaries, they were free to speak their minds in meetings openly.[10]

Convention pastors were also unhappy that none of them could participate fully during Mission meetings and yet the Convention constitution required that the Convention have two foreign missionary advisors. The fact that the missionaries did not have a national person as an advisor was a reflection of paternalism on the part of the Mission. Only they (the missionaries) could act as advisors to the nationals; the nationals could not reciprocate. Naturally such an attitude would cause tension in a context where there was a rise of African nationalism. This was the period of the 'winds of change' blowing across the continent of Africa, when many countries were fighting for independence from colonialism.

The Mission continued to expand its ministries as more Southern Baptist missionaries arrived on the scene. The ministries included a theological seminary, women's ministry, publications, Bible Way Correspondence, Baptist bookstores, education and medical services. The Mission and Convention operated like two parallel organizations until 1971, when the Mission recommended that the Mission and Convention appoint boards of directors for all institutions. In 1978 there were recommendations to come up with One Baptist Programme of Work so that there could be co-ordination between the ministries of the Mission and Convention. Even under the One Baptist Programme of Work model, the Convention continued to be a junior partner, with the Mission calling the tune because it provided the funding. With the decrease of funding from the Mission, the Convention became more and more independent.

With the coming of national independence in 1980, the new African government of Zimbabwe required that missionaries only come into the country at the invitation of indigenous religious bodies. This meant that the Convention had to apply for

---

[9] Saunders, 'Baptists in East and Central Africa', p. 100.

[10] The sentiments were expressed to me by the late Revd N.C. Nyatoro, then pastor of Mucheke Baptist Church, in 1975.

missionary permits according to the government of Zimbabwe's criteria for personnel requirements.[11] Missionaries found it hard to accept the new situation.

Women's Ministry: The Women's Missionary Union

Right from the beginning of their work in Zimbabwe, missionaries realized that women were the majority in the churches they had just planted; therefore they found it necessary to create special structures for women through the WMU. The visit of the Revd and Mrs T.J. Ariyonde from Nigeria in 1952 helped in the organization of the WMU. The first WMU convention was held at Sanyati in 1954. Initial leadership was in the hands of missionary wives, but was eventually turned over to pastors' wives.[12] Full members of the WMU were eligible to wear the cherished uniform, a navy blue skirt, purple trimmed with navy blue jacket, and a purple headscarf. Before they could wear the uniform (*kupfeka*, which means 'to dress up'), they needed to meet certain qualifications.[13] They had to learn certain things and had to be of a certain character to wear the uniform worthily. These include being married according to western customs (the so-called Christian marriage). At first missionaries had strong reservations about women having a uniform. Their reluctance was based on the fact that the custom was foreign to the WMU group in North America. In spite of the missionary reservations about uniforms, the African women insisted that uniforms were necessary in their particular context because they were in keeping with other women's groups organized by other denominations. Furthermore, their uniform would mean that people would recognize them as they gave a distinctive Baptist witness in their respective areas.

The WMU has a manual which tells women all they need to know about their movement. The manual covers topics on spiritual growth, which includes knowing about the world, praying, Bible study, witnessing, sharing of possessions (stewardship), and home living. Other topics cover such areas as the organization of the WMU, materials for WMU meetings, and WMU awards.

---

[11] The government of Zimbabwe was interested in missionaries who came to impart skills and not just preachers.

[12] Some of the early leaders of the women were Mrs Tabitha Ndhlovu and Mrs Joan Nyathi, who were both wives of pastors.

[13] *WMU Manual* (Baptist Churches of Rhodesia Zimbabwe, 1979), pp. 37-38. The manual lists the following seven items as the qualifications for wearing the WMU uniform: she must be a baptized member of a Baptist church; she must be faithful to her church and must attend Sunday School, church services, and prayer meetings; she must be faithful in her Christian life; she must be properly married, by Christian marriage—by marriage by the DC, or marriage by the civil courts; if a woman is divorced through no fault of her own and remains faithful to God and her church the local WMU will encourage her to continue to wear the uniform; in a polygamous marriage, the first wife is the only one who is entitled to wear the uniform. The other wives should be encouraged to participate as associate members; she must not smoke tobacco or drink beer.

The spontaneity and joy that accompany the worship of God during the Baptist women's meetings usually surprise outsiders. The women give testimonies, play drums, sing, clap and dance. The WMU hymn is part of their weekly meetings. Women wear their uniforms on special occasions such as weddings and funerals. In Zimbabwe funerals and weddings are very important communal events. Women put on their uniforms as a witness to their faith in Jesus Christ on such occasions. The women also wear their uniforms when visiting the sick in homes, hospitals and villages. Other activities women are involved in include income generating projects to raise funds for church buildings and charitable programmes, such as feeding the hungry, paying school fees and buying school uniforms for orphans and children from poor families. The women point out that Jesus did not just preach but also had concern for the hungry, thirsty, sick, naked and those in prison (Mt. 25.31-46).

Ironically, though women are by far the majority in the churches and are more active members of the churches than their male counterparts, leadership by and large is in male hands. This is in line with the approach of Southern Baptist missionaries, whose Convention denies women a leadership position as ministers in local churches.

Nevertheless, the winds of change cannot be stopped. Consequently, one woman was ordained to the pastoral ministry. Three women are pastors of churches, which they inherited from their late husbands who were pastors before them. A few women have been ordained as deacons in some of the churches. Local churches are autonomous and they hold different views about what the role of women should be. The majority of the churches are against the ordination of women, a position strongly advocated by all Southern Baptist missionaries today.[14]

The Baptist Theological Seminary of Zimbabwe

In April 1953, ten Southern Baptist missionaries meeting at Sanyati voted to begin 'a standardized programme for training evangelists and ministers'. A special committee was formed to locate a suitable site for the seminary. In 1954, the Baptist Mission in Southern Rhodesia, on behalf of the Foreign Mission Board of the SBC, purchased a 100 hectare plot, plot number 4, Traveller's Rest, about twenty kilometers outside Gweru, just off the old main road to Harare. The African Baptist Theological Seminary of the Rhodesia Baptist Mission, the seminary's original name, was opened in January 1955. Eight men were enrolled in the three-year, English-speaking course and four were enrolled in the two-year vernacular course. Only six of these original students completed their courses. By 1958, English became the only language of instruction, and in that same year eleven men and ten women entered the seminary. That became the largest single class for the next fifteen

---

[14] All Southern Baptist missionaries have to sign the 2000 *Baptist Faith and Message* which denies women leadership positions as ordained ministers in a local church. However, this new condition, among others, caused one of the former missionaries to Zimbabwe and lecturer at the Baptist Seminary to leave after refusing to sign.

years. In 1964, the enrolment was fifteen students—six came from Zambia, four from Malawi and only five from Rhodesia.

The tension caused by the souring of relationships between the Convention and the Mission, together with the political tension in the country caused by Ian Smith's unilateral declaration of Independence, affected enrolment at the seminary. In 1967 and 1968 only one student was enrolled and he was from Malawi. Later on the situation improved, and in 1972 the total enrolment was thirteen men and eight women who were wives of married male students. The seminary had no national teacher even at this late stage. The first national teacher was employed only in 1978 during the liberation war.

For the first seventeen years of the seminary's existence, the principal was responsible for the administration of the seminary and the Foreign Mission Board wholly funded the seminary. In 1972, a seven-member Board of Directors composed of three members each from the Convention churches and the Mission became the governing authority for the institution. The seventh member was the principal, who was *ex officio*. In 1986, board membership was enlarged to include nine members elected by the Convention and three by the Mission. At first the Mission resisted the change, which was a requirement from the Accrediting Council for Theological Education in Africa.[15] Out of frustration that they had lost control of the institution by having more representation from the Convention than the Mission, between 1986 and 1991 the Mission took a unilateral decision not to elect representatives to serve on the seminary board. However, the Convention went ahead and elected some missionaries to the board as representatives from the churches. When the Mission finally decided to elect the three members they were entitled to, there were missionaries on the seminary board who represented the Convention and others who represented the Mission.

The Foreign Mission Board of the SBC, now called the International Mission Board (IMB), remains the proprietor of the seminary. Over the years and on a number of occasions the Convention was promised the title deeds to the seminary farm upon the fulfillment of certain conditions over a period of time. The conditions included fidelity to Baptist doctrines and the ability of the seminary to raise more than fifty per cent of its annual budget with the difference coming from the Mission. But because the goal posts have been and are changing the hand-over has not happened up to now.[16] For example, the Baptist Theological Seminary of Zimbabwe met all the requirements by 1996, but the title deeds were not handed over to the National Convention. There seems to be an attempt to use the issue of title deeds to try and control the kind of theology taught at the seminary—a kind of ecclesiastical colonialism. The Dutch missiologist, Johannes E. Verkuyl, defines ecclesiastical colonialism as 'the urge of missionaries to impose the model of the mother church

[15] The Accrediting Council for Theological Education in Africa wanted the local churches to have more representation than missionaries, specifically on the Board of Directors.

[16] From the time of the planning and development council in the early 1980s to today, the goal posts have been shifted each time there is a new IMB mission leader.

on the native churches among whom they are working rather than give people the freedom to shape their own churches in response to the gospel'.[17] It is unheard of for Africans to impose their theologies on churches in America or Europe and yet missionaries from the West continue to impose theirs on African churches, and even to use unethical methods to do so. It is clear that the IMB representatives are not going to hand over the property without a fight. It is difficult for the leaders of the Baptist Convention of Zimbabwe to know what is required of them in order for the IMB to give them title deeds to the seminary.

The second national person to be employed by the seminary had a doctorate from the Southern Baptist Southwestern Theological Seminary in the USA. Missionaries were not ready, however, to deal with a national who was more qualified than they were. Out of frustration because of the treatment he received, he resigned from the seminary to go and be the founding dean of an evangelical graduate school of theology in Kenya. The seminary was left with no meaningful contribution from national teachers.

The seminary was temporarily relocated to Gweru town itself during the liberation war in 1979. Missionaries were the first to move, leaving the only national teacher staying at the seminary with other national workers. With the end of the war and the advent of Independence the seminary moved back to its original site. From the early 1980s the seminary applied for accreditation with the Accrediting Council for Theological Education in Africa (ACTEA). Seeking accreditation with ACTEA made the seminary deliberately seek to Africanize, upgrade standards and contextualize the curriculum. ACTEA insists that the majority of board members and teaching staff for an African theological institution should be Africans. The curriculum of the seminary became more relevant to the Zimbabwean context by intentionally wanting to meet the needs of the church in Zimbabwe. There was a move away from the temptation to reproduce curricula from elsewhere. It is Jesse Mugambi's contention that contextualization of curricula for ministerial formation is essential for training effective church leadership, both clerical and lay. Such contextualization can be accomplished only if local theologians are encouraged to reflect on the relevance of the gospel in local situations and cultures.[18]

In 1986, the seminary was accredited by ACTEA at secondary level. By the late 1980s it was enrolling more and more high school graduates from countries like Angola, Malawi, Zambia and Mozambique. It also sought in this period to become an Associate College of the University of Zimbabwe.[19] A telling illustration of the theology that was being taught at the seminary is the story of Akim and Martha Chirwa, who graduated from the seminary and went back to their country of Malawi to pastor Soche Baptist Church in Blantyre. While in Malawi they became involved

---

[17] Johannes Verykyl, *Contemporary Missiology: An Introduction* (Grand Rapids, MI: Eerdmans, 1978), p. 173.

[18] Jesse Mugambi, 'Theological method in African Christianity', *Theology and the Transformation of Africa* (Tangaza Occasional Papers, 10; 2000), pp. 69-100.

[19] In 2002 the Seminary officially became an Associate College of the University of Zimbabwe although it had started operating as such in 1994.

with a political pressure group fighting for an end to oppression and dictatorship in their country. The Revd Chirwa attributed his involvement in the pressure group to the theological training he had received at the seminary in Gweru where he had studied liberation theology, black theology and African theology. His studies enabled him to understand that sin was not only personal and individual but also structural. He is of the opinion that the church must concern itself with issues of injustice and oppression.[20]

In 2000, the seminary also became a member of ZIMTEE, which stands for Zimbabwe Theological Education by Extension.[21] ZIMTEE is an ecumenical enterprise comprising all the mainline denominations in Zimbabwe.[22]

The Bible in the Seminary and the Convention

The Bible plays a very important role in the life and ministry of Baptist believers in Zimbabwe. Most of them, if not all, would refer to themselves as 'people of the book'. Just like many African Christians, the ability to re-read the Bible in the vernacular brought a very important change to the lives of Baptist believers. For Baptist believers the Bible became an independent standard of reference on a number of issues. Like other African Christians, Baptists in Zimbabwe began to realize that certain things in the Bible were different from what the missionaries had interpreted them. The Bible was silent on other matters. For example, there was the discovery that salvation of the soul tended to be emphasized over against issues of justice. Moreover, missionaries tended to give polygamy more of a focus than divorce.[23] However, the Bible speaks strongly against divorce and is silent about polygamy. It is not an exaggeration that some scriptural teachings were exaggerated by a large number of missionaries.

Although the Baptist Convention of Zimbabwe is not a member of the Evangelical Fellowship of Zimbabwe, its members consider themselves to be evangelicals.[24] They consider the Bible to be the word of God, the supreme authority

---

[20] Klaus Fiedler, 'The "Smaller" Churches and Big Government', in M.S. Nzunda and Kenneth R. Rose (eds), *Church, Law and Political Transition in Malawi 1992–94* (Gweru: Mambo Press, 1995), pp. 161-62.

[21] ZIMTEE offers a Diploma in Theology through the Joint Board for the Diploma in Theology.

[22] The main line churches included are the Anglicans, the Methodist Church in Zimbabwe, and the Reformed Church in Zimbabwe. However, the students who are enrolled through ZIMTEE come from the cross section of denominations of Zimbabwe.

[23] Inus Daneel, *Quest for Belonging* (Gweru: Mambo Press, 1987), pp. 68-101. When the Bible was translated into the vernacular for the first time it was possible for African believers to distinguish between the missionary and Scripture. Scripture became an independent standard of judging issues.

[24] Many of the Baptist pastors were suspicious about the call by some evangelicals to have Zimbabwe declared a Christian nation. Separation of church and state is strongly upheld by most pastors of the Baptist Convention of Zimbabwe.

and record of God's revelation. Baptist believers carry their Bibles with them, and they read and quote from Scripture quite often. During church services or Bible studies they take notes and underline certain sections of the Bible to mark important passages, which are often memorized.

Reading the Bible often leads African believers to develop an analysis of what, in their view, are the shortcomings of western Christianity. For instance, they discovered that the great heroes of faith in the Bible, namely Abraham, Moses, David, Solomon, and many others, were polygamous. Consequently, African believers discovered that the Bible has been misinterpreted on many occasions.

It is quite interesting to note that the Old Testament has appealed to most African believers. For example, during the colonial era, one of the Rhodesian police asked the first national teacher at the Baptist Seminary of Zimbabwe, the late Revd Saul Nyemba, why he always liked to preach from the Old Testament. His reply was that there messages of justice were to be found. This incident happened when he was still a pastor.[25]

It is no secret that the Bible has served in the past both as a liberating and an oppressive document. The best example of the oppressiveness of the Bible is the issue of women. Some of the teachings about women have been quite oppressive. The Pauline teaching women to be submissive to men, which serves to reinforce the domesticity of women, is a case in point.[26]

Consequently, Douglas Waruta and Zablon Nthamburi have identified several basic principles upon which Africans have built their reverence for the Bible. These include: emphasizing the Bible as a community document, the applicability of the message of the Bible to the life of the current African communities, and obeying and taking seriously the Bible as a message from God; the practicality of the biblical message; the basic biblical message as saving people from impending catastrophes—physical, political, economic, social and religious—as well as giving counsel and enlightening people on all matters affecting their lives; the power of the Bible to bring about the outcome of God's warnings and promises; and the frankness of the Bible in saying what needs to be said. They also concern the necessity of receiving the biblical message in its basic or literal sense before one tries to allegorize its message.[27]

The above principles from Waruta and Nthamburi are not exhaustive, but what they have found out in Kenya is applicable to Baptist life in Zimbabwe. There is, however, a great danger in simplistic biblicism, which is promoted by some fly-by-night foreign preachers who have little knowledge of the Bible but plenty of enthusiasm. Some Baptist preachers have tended to imitate such preachers to the detriment of serious biblical teaching, which liberates and promotes life. For

---

[25] The Revd Saul Nyemba was the first national to teach full-time at the Baptist Theological Seminary of Zimbabwe.

[26] In most cases the Bible has been used to silence women in the churches.

[27] See Douglas Waruta and Zablon Nthamburi, 'Biblical Hermenuetics in Africa Instituted Churches', in Hannah Kinoti and John Waliggo (eds), *Bible in African Christianity* (Nairobi: Action Publishers, 1997), pp. 52-55.

instance, any serious scholarship of the Bible is looked upon with suspicion. The Bible is literally interpreted. Some preachers even believe that the Genesis account of the serpent speaking is literal.

Consequently, the Baptist Seminary of Zimbabwe has taken critical biblical studies seriously. However, the various 'critical' or 'scientific' methods of biblical studies from the West have not been value-neutral. Some of those methods were used to further European colonial interests and propagated by persons who believed in the supremacy of European cultures, labeling Africans as primitive creatures.[28] There is a need to conceptualize them for the Zimbabwean context. The Baptist Seminary and Convention of Zimbabwe seriously continue to wrestle with issues of biblical interpretation for their particular context. Merely repeating certain Bible phrases does not help African Christians understand Scripture in a clear and meaningful way. Both formal and informal aspects of theological education must take the Bible seriously.

Dialogue with African Culture

Dialogue between Christianity and African traditional religions has not taken place in conferences but in the very lives of African Christians as they try to come to terms with the meaning of their faith in an African context. Both missionaries and colonial administrators adopted a negative attitude towards African traditional religions. W.R. Peaden, who lived at this time, reported the situation as follows: 'The missionaries adopted hostile pastures towards any aspects of Shona [Shona is the term which refers to six clusters of ethnic groups in Zimbabwe] by calling them evil... These methods of these early missionaries were to lead to rejection, dependency, or worst of all, to try to hold two cultures in parallel separate compartments.'[29]

Baptist missionaries were no different. African Christians, said the missionaries, had to distance themselves from things African. The lack of dialogue between traditional African religion and the Christian faith led to parallelism, the practice of two religions at the same time without even trying to reconcile them. The negative attitude adopted by both Christianity and colonialism was bent on eradicating the religious and cultural structures that provided the ideological underpinnings for an indigenous African philosophy. It made Africans want to identify with that which was furthest removed from themselves; for instance the widespread tendency to identify with other people's (western) cultures rather than their own.

Real dialogue involves acceptance, rejection and modification. One area where serious dialogue has taken place is the area of death, mortuary and funeral rites. Ignoring missionary fears of syncretism, a number of African pastors transformed a Shona rite of *Kugadzira* (bringing back the spirit of the deceased) to *Manyaradzo*, a ceremony of consolation. The traditional view is that ancestors are in a state of

---

[28] See Frans J. Verstraelen, *Zimbabwean Realities and Christian Responses* (Gweru: Mambo Press, 1998), pp. 82-84.

[29] As quoted in T.L. Presler, *Transfigured Night* (Pretoria: Unisa, 1999), p. 334.

consciousness where they can intervene in human affairs, exerting power over human affairs. Benefits bestowed by ancestors include children, fertility, good health, wealth, and protection from danger and general well being. The rite of *Kugadzira* usually takes place about a year after a person has died. During the ceremony the deceased is installed as an ancestor.[30] Baptist missionaries, among others, have generally condemned the practice as a form of ancestor worship. However, the church's condemnation of the practice has pushed it underground. Many Christians secretly take part in these rites with the result that the old and new faiths exist side by side in the lives of many Zimbabwean Christians, including Baptists, without any meaningful dialogue or clear-cut exposition.

Many Baptists have devised the consolation service called *Manyaradzo*, with the unveiling of the tombstone as part of its ceremonies, and this is held after the customary lapse of time after death, to replace the *kurova guva* rites, which are usually considered as form of ancestor worship.[31] The *Manyaradzo* ceremony offers both continuity and discontinuity with the traditional rites. The Shona and Ndebele (Ndebele is another ethnic group, which is different from Shona) longing to remember and care for the departed is met, and yet the church leaders stress during the ceremony that they are commemorating the departed and are not appeasing their spirits. The departed is commended to Christ rather than installed to become an ancestor. The prayers offered are clearly directed to the triune God, who is thanked for the life of the deceased, and not to the spirit of the deceased. Thus, the *Manyaradzo* ceremony both builds on the traditional rite and also transforms it into something Christian.[32] Sermons and testimonies given at the *Manyaradzo* service make references to the contribution made by the deceased to both church and society, their exemplary lifestyle and the like. Thus, the traditional 'living with ancestors' is transformed to a Christian focus of an awareness of the 'cloud of witnesses' (Heb. 12.1). Christians are to be inspired by the way the deceased lived their life before God and the community of faith.[33]

Manyaradzo is one of the positive ways to dialogue with traditional culture. It was not initiated by missionaries but was an innovation from African pastors. There is a quest by Africans to be in a church where they feel they belong and have an African identity. A decent burial is important in African cultures and the dead need to be remembered by the living. *Manyaradzo* would be classified among the mourning rites, which are those customs which are followed by the bereaved during the period in which the dead pass from this life to the next. The rite also has a pastoral value in that it helps the bereaved to deal with death. *Manyaradzo*, therefore, embodies an African theology of death from a Christian perspective.

---

[30] The deceased persons can only function as ancestors after the ceremony has been performed.

[31] Some scholars object to the use of the term ancestor worship.

[32] Inus Daniel, *The Quest for Belonging* (Gweru: Mambo Press, 1991), pp. 235-38.

[33] Daniel, *Quest for Belonging*, p. 238.

Conclusion

Although the Baptist Convention of Zimbabwe grew out of the mission efforts of the Southern Baptists' missionary enterprise, they have sought to express their allegiance to Christ as Lord within their own Zimbabwean culture, using Zimbabwean cultural categories and symbols. Likewise, the WMU developed its own identity in ways which were never envisaged by the missionaries who started it. Despite missionary protests, the Baptist women decided to have a uniform like the women of other denominations in Zimbabwe. Thus, the Baptist women affirmed their own identity by being Baptist in their own way, which was meaningful to them in their context.

Some tensions continue. The IMB is still holding on to the title deeds to the farm on which the seminary is built. The Convention rejected the conditions set by the representatives of the IMB, refusing to be treated like perpetual children. Theological development needs freedom to take its own course, otherwise it becomes a carbon copy of overseas theologies on African soil. Creative theology goes beyond the mere repetition of the church's inherited statements of faith and traditions; it also challenges the church to rethink its position in the light of the contemporary understandings of the Christian faith. No theology is ever final. Christians always need to understand and express their faith in new ways, which are in tune with their time and context. The Baptist Theological Seminary does not have to sacrifice its theological sanity, when doing theology in its Zimbabwe context, in order to accommodate certain material resources from outside. There is the need to respect each other's identity on the part of all Christians, and this happens when there is a realization that all Christians are equal participants in God's mission regardless of who they are and the material possessions at their disposal.

The Baptist Convention in Zimbabwe has reached a stage where either the Mission has to change its way of working with it or the Mission witness will die. At the present moment, the Convention–Mission relationship is not at all healthy. For its part, the Baptist Convention is determined to seek to mould its own identity and is determined that it will never be colonized again.

CHAPTER 20

Baptists, Religious Liberty and Evangelization: Nineteenth-Century Challenges

William H. Brackney

Introduction

The course of Baptist advocacy of religious liberty is more complex than it would appear at first glance.[1] All Baptists have not been advocates of the ideal in the same way (or at all!) and the contexts and thrust of religious liberty have evolved over the four centuries of Baptist life and thought. This essay is a beginning attempt to define an important transition in Baptist thinking as the nineteenth century dawned and new opportunities for Baptist witness emerged, especially outside the North American Baptist context. First, we shall summarize the state of Baptist witness at the conclusion of the eighteenth century and then look at the meaning of religious liberty as mission contexts opened in Asia, Africa, Europe, and South America.

To begin with, there is an important semantic issue. What did Baptists mean by 'religious liberty' and its cognates? Was there a consistent usage across 200 years? One of the pioneers of the tradition, Thomas Helwys, put it this way in his now classic work, *A Mistery of Iniquity*: 'For men's religion to God is between God and themselves. The king shall not answer for it. Neither may the king be judge between God and man. Let them be heretics, Turks, Jews, or whatsoever, it appertains not to the earthly power to punish them in the least measure.'[2] Helwys was speaking out of the vivid experience of persecution for matters of conscience, and what he strove for was freedom from government interference in matters of the Spirit. His focus was the freedom of the individual. His claim was truly radical in assuming the universal right to personal freedom of religion, regardless of one's persuasion, Christian or otherwise. While he did not use the precise term, Helwys was addressing what later

---

[1] So argued John Coffey in his essay, 'From Helwys to Leland: Baptists and Religious Toleration in England and America, 1612–1791', in David Bebbington (ed.), *The Gospel in the World: International Baptist Studies* (Studies in Baptist History and Thought, 1; Carlisle: Paternoster Press, 2002), pp. 13-14.

[2] Thomas Helwys, *A Short Declaration of the Mystery of Iniquity* (ed. Richard Groves Macon, GA: Mercer University Press, 1998 [1612]), p. 53.

writers would call 'religious freedom'.[3] The Baptist movement can be rightly proud that such a theoretical position was taken from the outset.

Another writer who spent only a brief time as a Baptist, but delivered much to their lore of religious freedom, was Roger Williams. He said in 1644, 'It is the will and command of God, since the coming of his Son the Lord Jesus, a permission of the most paganish, Jewish, Turkish, or anti-Christian consciences and worships be granted to all men in all nations and countries...'.[4] Here, then, was the essence of a related position, 'religious toleration'.[5] Note his use of the term 'permission'. Early in the past century, J.E.E. (Lord) Acton and W.K. Jordan noted that religious liberty is a positive right of religious communities that they may practice their duties under the protection of the law that assumes the independence of all such communities.[6] Religious 'toleration' was a term much in vogue in seventeenth- and eighteenth-century England and the Colonies.

The terminology 'liberty of conscience' and 'soul liberty' enter the vocabulary of libertarian thought mostly in the context of theological and philosophical writers. Both apply to individual rights and have powerful implications. Early Baptists who used these terms drew upon earlier sixteenth-century writers in Puritan, Separatist, and Independent traditions. The use of 'conscience' and 'soul' conjured up images of separate spiritual spheres belonging to individuals over which civil magistrates had no authority or power.[7] As time went on among Baptist writers, these last two terms became more or less archaic, mostly reminders of the seventeenth century, like John Clarke's use of the term 'freedom in religious concernments' in the charter of

---

[3] I delineate between 'religious liberty' and 'religious freedom' in this way: 'religious liberty' implies that there is a context in which religious matters or beliefs are not entirely free or have been freed from denial of some sort. 'Religious freedom' is the matured, generic concept of religious belief or practice free of any control or interference, that is, completely free in theory or praxis—what Leon McBeth has referred to as 'absolute or complete' liberty: H. Leon McBeth, *English Baptist Literature on Religious Liberty to 1689* (New York: Arno Press, 1980), pp. 276-77. Religious 'freedom' is terminology especially associated with the United Nations Declaration on Human Rights (1948) and human rights discourse. Many writers now interchange these terms.

[4] Roger Williams, *The Bloudy Tenent of Persecution for Cause of Conscience* (ed. Richard Groves; Macon, GA: Mercer University Press, 2001), p. 3.

[5] Some British writers prefer the cognate term 'tolerance', for instance Coffey, 'Baptists and Religious Liberty', pp. 21-28.

[6] J.E.E. Acton, 'The History of Freedom in Antiquity' and 'The History of Freedom in Christianity', both in J. Rufus Fears (ed.), *Selected Writings of Lord Acton. Volume I: Essays in the History of Liberty* (Indianapolis, IN: The Liberty Fund, 1985), pp. 7 and 35 respectively; W.K. Jordan, *The Development of Religious Toleration in England: Volume 1. From the Beginning of the English Reformation to the Death of Queen Elizabeth* (London: George Allen and Unwin, 1932), p. 18.

[7] Jordan, *Religious Toleration*, pp. 251-53. See especially the 1573 sermon of Edward Dering on the limitations of magisterial power.

Rhode Island.[8] In this essay, we shall note the use of 'toleration', 'liberty', and 'freedom' in various contexts, not necessarily interchangeably.

In the realm of external religious liberty, Baptists in the United States had reason to be pleased with the achievements of their various levels of government with respect to cessation of persecution, growing toleration, and later with the doctrines of religious liberty and the separation of church and state. This amounted to a history of religious freedom. The 1663 charter of Rhode Island was the work of Newport Baptist pastor John Clarke and provided for full religious liberty in 'religious concernments'. Eighteenth-century writers Isaac Backus and John Leland produced major polemics on the subject and raised a considerable debate around the Continental Congress and later in the Constitutional Convention of 1787. What they called for was liberty to worship according to their own conscience and complete freedom from government interference in religion. Religious liberty generally had become a Baptist distinctive by the 1790s from Virginia to New England. Baptists had directly influenced public policymakers if one is to believe the indirect evidence of Alvah Hovey, L.F. Greene, T.B. Maston, W.G. McLoughlin, E.S. Gaustad,[9] and others. At the conclusion of the eighteenth century there was much experience to report, but no textbook on religious freedom, no clear definitions, and much reliance upon the discourse of American constitutional documents and British anti-establishment themes.

New challenges emerged, however, in the new century.[10] In Britain, the issue of religious liberty was revisited in the 1830s and 1840s in the resurgence of the Nonconformist agenda. Baptists were among the most vocal advocates of a voluntary system and helped to form organizations like the Religious Freedom Society (1839), the Evangelical Voluntary Church Association (1840), the Anti-State Church Association (1844), and the Evangelical Alliance (1846). Much of this effort coalesced later in the century as the 'Free Church movement'. In the United States,

---

[8] Isaac Backus and John Leland, for instance, commonly use liberty and freedom interchangeably. See Edwin S. Gaustad, 'The Backus-Leland Tradition', *Foundations* 2:2 (April, 1959), pp. 147-148.

[9] Alvah Hovey, *A Memoir of the Life and Times of the Rev. Isaac Backus* (Boston, MA: Gould and Lincoln, 1859); L.F. Greene (ed.), *The Writings of the Late Elder John Leland, Including Some Events of His Life, Written by Himself, with Additional Sketches, &c* (New York: Arno Press and The New York Times, 1969 [1845]); Thomas B. Maston, *Isaac Backus, Pioneer of Religious Liberty* (Rochester, NY: American Baptist Historical Society, 1962); William G. McLoughlin, *Isaac Backus and the American Pietistic Tradition* (Library of American Biography; Boston, MA: Little, Brown, 1967); Gaustad, 'The Backus-Leland Tradition'.

[10] The nineteenth century is a key era in both Baptist development and the emphasis upon Christian missions. For differing perspectives on 'The Great Century', see Kenneth Scott Latourette, 'A Historian Looks Ahead; The Future of Christianity in Light of Its Past', *Church History* 15 (1946), pp. 3-16; and Franklin H. Littell, 'The Anabaptist Theology of Mission', and Wilbert R. Schenk, 'The 'Great Century' Reconsidered', in Wilbert R. Schenk (ed.), *Anabaptism and Mission* (Scottdale, PA: Herald Press, 1984), pp. 13-23 and 158-177 respectively.

however, religious toleration and religious liberty came to be reinterpreted and applied in missionary work and evangelism. In British North America (later the Dominion of Canada) a hybrid of British and American Baptists produced a libertarian position from a particular understanding of 'voluntarism'.

But all of this discussion of philosophical tolerance and the intellectual and political fine points of liberty of conscience and religious liberty were not for Baptists ends in themselves. Unbelievers were hardly converted by argumentation or Aristotelian logic. Rather, Baptists, like other evangelicals, held that conversion was a work of grace, without which humans were destined to perdition. Winning converts solely to the principle and practice of religious freedom could result in indifference to religion in general or skepticism as it had in the West. How then would Baptists reconcile their historic commitment to liberty of conscience and the urgency they felt about the call to missions and evangelism among non-Christian cultures?

It was left to the first 'overseas' missionaries sent out from England, the United States and Canada to confront the situations, reflect from their theological orientations, and respond with modifications to historic ideals of religious freedom. Indeed, 'liberty of conscience' as an individual attribute came first, then religious toleration became a first priority in missionary endeavor; later, upon reflection, one can see the emerging sophistication of the meaning of 'religious freedom'. The first generation of Baptist missionaries confronted the challenge in each instance.

English Baptist Antecedents

Among Baptists, missionary efforts commenced with the Carey mission from England in 1792. This project played heavily and well in the Baptist press in the United States and numerous churches and individuals rose to support William Carey. Carey's achievement of toleration (spelled permission) for his presence and work in India was no small or quick accomplishment, as Penny Carson has shown in her significant essay.[11] The British government needed to ensure stability and profit from its Crown Company in India, and this depended upon a policy of toleration of Hindu and other Indian religious practices. Christianity did not enjoy toleration *per se*, especially Dissenter versions, because it was seen as an attempt to convert the Indian peoples to English religion. Moreover, what the Dissenters preached in various forms of egalitarianism was held to be potentially subversive of the social order the British wished to maintain over a subject population. As a contemporary observer noted, 'an extreme fear of creating political disturbances…seems to have possessed the Company's government from the beginning…the countenance and support given

---

[11] Penny Carson, 'The British Raj and the Awakening of the Evangelical Conscience: The Ambiguities of Religious Establishment and Toleration, 1698–1833', in Brian Stanley (ed.), *Christian Missions and the Enlightenment* (Grand Rapids, MI: Eerdmans, 2001), pp. 45-70. Carson has filled in quite astutely the lacunum that has long existed in understanding British government policy and the interplay of Establishment and Dissenters in mission context in the first decade of the new century.

by government to the prevailing forms of religion, is a weighty subject and calls for the solemn consideration of British Christians'.[12]

Carey and his colleagues found out the hard way that licenses were not granted to Dissenter missionaries; they simply moved to India, and the Company for the most part came to tolerate them as long as the Bible was not used in schools, tracts contained nothing offensive to Hindu or Muslim sensibilities, and missionaries were not to travel in sensitive border areas. Throughout the early years in Bengal, Carey was many times called before the authorities and forbidden to preach or publish materials, only to have policy eased sufficiently to allow the work to continue. His temperament being assertive and disliking secrecy, he was at one point prepared to demand work permits of the Court of Directors or even to take the overland route to India! His biographer observed 'they were prepared to take faith's kingdom by violence'.[13]

What the British East India Company wanted was not proselytism, but 'instilling the virtuous and moral principles of the religion of the Church of England' among the natives in a manner that involved 'long, cautious and pacific negotiations'.[14] Carey and his community of Dissenting missionaries changed all of that by relocating to the Danish commercial sector at Serampore and starting their mission anyway. Despite setbacks in 1800–02 when the British overtook the Danish colony on occasion and Carey was warned not to circulate his tracts or to engage in 'preachings', Carey used his tutorship at Fort William College to expansive effect. This situation of dismissive toleration changed materially in 1813. As the result of a campaign in Britain in general to extend toleration, the charter of the Company was revised to include among other provisions, a 'pious clause' whereby an Anglican episcopate was approved for India, the Church of Scotland was granted an establishment status, and Dissenters were no longer refused licenses. Carson has well stated, 'The right of a Christian country to propagate Christianity in her colonies had been publicly acknowledged.'[15] At the outset of American Baptist overseas missions, the English Baptists in India were about to enjoy unprecedented toleration by government authorities.

It was quickly and widely known that William Carey and Joshua Marshman had baptized the Judsons and Luther Rice upon their arrivals in India, and American Baptist missions were thus seen as the spiritual offspring of the Serampore Trio. Carey's mission was in fact an inspiration for domestic missionaries of the American West as well: Isaac McCoy named his school and station in Kansas Territory after Carey.

What, in fact, were American Baptists doing in mission work? Within their immediate context in North America they were engaged in four types of evangelical

---

[12] Howard Malcolm, *Travels in South-Eastern Asia: Embracing Hindustan, Malaya, Siam and China, with Notices of Numerous Missionary Stations, and a Full Account of the Burman Empire* (Philadelphia, PA: American Baptist Publication Society, 1853), p. 272.

[13] S. Pearce Carey, *William Carey* (New York: Doran Company, 1923), p. 124.

[14] Carey, *William Carey*, pp. 56, 64.

[15] Carey, *William Carey*, p. 67.

work. First was domestic church planting and the organization of associational life. This was a response to the moving frontier from Nova Scotia to Alabama. Baptist pastors felt a special urgency to conduct preaching tours in the vast reaches of the interior to start churches, lest Methodists and Presbyterians should carry the West. John Mason Peck, the venerable apostle of the West, feared that 'Paedos, College folk, and Antinomians' would predominate in Illinois Territory: 'You must devote yourself to the cause in the West', he wrote in 1831. 'Now is the crisis, tomorrow will be too late.'[16] Second was preaching and church planting among indigenous peoples. This had been a Baptist interest since Elkanah Holmes had opened a mission to the Indians on the New York frontier in 1796 and pastors from the Shaftsbury (Vermont) Baptist Association made forays into Lower Canada in the 1790s. Indian missions were added to the agenda of the General Missionary Convention in 1817, and men like Isaac McCoy, Humphrey Posey, and James Welch were dispatched to the Ohio and Mississippi valleys to meet the challenge. Third was literature development and distribution. Eventually this gave rise to the Baptist General Tract Society, founded by Luther Rice in 1824. Fourth was a kind of humanitarian endeavor among select groups. Mary Webb of Boston best illustrated this approach in her witness of providing food, clothing, and housing for indigent peoples of Boston. It would not be long, at the urgings of men like William Staughton, Thomas Baldwin, and William Rogers, before Baptists in the United States would consider how they could engage in overseas missionary work.

God's Sovereignty in Asia

The pioneer overseas circumstance that American Baptists could truly own was in the mission of Adoniram and Ann Judson in Burma. The Judsons, and others in their train—Luther Rice, the Newells, Gordon Hall, and Samuel Nott, Jr—embarked upon their missionary exploits in a cradle of evangelical Calvinism. Their's was a deep sense that God was entering upon a new dispensation and that God had ordained Christian witness to the heathen. For Judson, this was to be a kind of evangelical experimentation. First he sought an appointment with the London Missionary Society. Failing that, he became the catalyst for the formation of the American Board of Commissioners for Foreign Missions, an enterprise of New Light Congregationalists and Presbyterians. That took him to India, where he and Mrs Judson converted to Baptist principles. That in turn rallied Baptists in the United States around his mission as the starting point for their own foreign efforts among the 'heathen'. Being deprived of religious liberty first stung the Judsons in India, where representatives of the monopolistic East India Company forbade the group from settling at India. Doubtless the Judsons naively thought that they might be allowed to remain in India as other English Dissenters had been, a type of religious 'squatters' without licenses but tolerated on their good behavior. With great

---

[16] John Mason Peck to Jonathan Going, 10 January 1832 (Manuscript Collections, Andover Newton Theological School).

disappointment, therefore, Adoniram and Ann heard the decision of Governor General Lord Minto that they could not remain in Bengal or India or any other British colony in the Far East. They were after all, Americans in a British colony during a state of war between the two nations. Thus, as a secondary objective, on the advice of William Carey's son, Felix, the Judsons left for Burma.

What the Judsons found in Burma was yet another form of religious intolerance. In a restricted sense, foreigners were allowed full exercise of their religion. With permission, they could build religious edifices and celebrate religious holidays. But no native Burman could join any foreign sect. Changes in the religious fervor of the ruler, for instance to Buddhism, could result in tighter controls upon the population. A traveler in the 1830s from the United States observed 'the whole population is thus held in chains, as iron-like as caste itself; and to become a Christian openly is to hazard everything, even life'.[17] In 1816, upon arrival, young Judson reflected to his friends back home, 'We know not the designs of God in regard to this country; but I cannot but have raised expectations... [I]s Burmah to remain a solitary instance of the inefficiency of prayer, of the forgetfulness of a merciful and Faithful God?[18] One year later, planted firmly in Rangoon, Judson was more confident: 'I have no doubt that God is preparing the way for the conversion of Burmah to his Son... I know not that I shall live to see a single convert; but notwithstanding, I feel that I would not leave my present situation to be made a king.'[19]

Adoniram served in Burma from 1813–50, and the issue of religious freedom was again sharply focused in 1824–26. When the Judsons arrived in Burma, the country was ruled by an authoritarian regime that gave little place to religions other than Buddhism. The early months of his mission were punctuated with various forms of harassment, the same fate suffered by a small group of Roman Catholic missionaries who escaped at the whim of the viceroy. Judson interpreted the sacrifices in a Christological way: 'Let us remember that the Son of God chose to become incarnate under the most unprincipled and cruel despot that ever reigned. And shall any disciple of Christ refuse to do a little service for his Saviour, under a government where his Saviour would not have refused to live and die for his soul? God forbid.' One by one Judson's converts were accused of heretical teaching and the mission's very survival in 1819 was threatened by the installation of a new emperor who was much connected with Buddhism. Judson decided to bring clarification to their status by meeting with the emperor to solicit toleration for Christians. The petition, no doubt Adoniram's work, used the United States as an example of 'sustaining the character of teachers and explainers of the contents of the Sacred Scriptures of our religion'. Judson went on to reason that when such teachers traveled elsewhere, preaching and propagating Christian truths, goodwill resulted and

---

[17] Malcolm, *Travels in Asia*, p. 212.

[18] Adoniram Judson to Thomas Baldwin, 5 August 1816, printed in Francis Wayland (ed.), *A Memoir of the Life and Labors of the Rev. Adoniram Judson, D.D.* (2 vols; Boston, MA: Phillips, Sampson, 1853), I, p. 181.

[19] Adoniram Judson to Thomas Baldwin, 26 August 1817, printed in Wayland (ed.), *A Memoir*, I, p. 192.

those who heard would be freed from 'future punishment'. Consequently, he asked that royal permission be given so that missionaries could 'take refuge in the royal power' to preach to both foreigners and Burmans, 'exempt from government molestation'.[20] In a bit of a rage, however, the emperor read part of the petition, refused it and dismissed the efforts of Judson and his company. He reminded them that the English, Portuguese, Musselmans, and members of other religions could freely practice their rites in Burma, but there was no purpose served in granting more. In essence, Judson was prohibited from propagating the Christian religion and Burmans were banned from receiving instruction. He continued to hold worship services, engage in language instruction, and relate to those who came to his home.

A pawn in the worsening struggle between the British and the Burman Empire, and in the midst of the Burmese War with Siam, Judson looked for every opportunity to improve his lot for Christian witness. What he sought was religious toleration. In a second and more favorable audience at court in 1823, the emperor granted the Judsons permission to use a piece of property and there they could construct a 'zayat', or place of recreation, and a residence. Back in the United States, the Baptist Board recognized the growing problem with respect to toleration and agreed with its premier missionary. They pondered the feasibility of sending a special ambassador to the Court at Ava with an objective of obtaining toleration of Christianity in the Burman Empire. Initially the Board agreed in February 1823 to depute Dr Elnathan Judson, a physician, to go in this capacity.[21] A more practical solution was later found in authorizing Dr Jonathan Price to accompany Adoniram to the Court at Ava, bound with a petition from the General Missionary Convention and gifts for the emperor. This petition was prepared in the context of negotiations between the Board and US president James Monroe regarding the establishment of an institution of higher learning at the nation's capital. That exchange revealed much about the cultural dimensions then prevailing among Baptists about religious liberty: !

> We thankfully feel that we are not approaching a monarch, the bend of whose eye, shall control the tenors or the transports of our bosoms... [I]t is your felicity to look down on a flourishing and approving community where liberty dreads no oppression, where Religion moves beautiful and free as an Angel of light; where the useful and finer arts are prevailing and science advancing with the silent resplendence of the morning... You are waited upon, Sir, by a denomination of

---

[20] Years later the editor of Judson's memoirs, the esteemed Francis Wayland, commented, 'Can we thus properly ask one man to permit another man to obey God?' He doubted that the petition should have ever been sought and viewed the situation as a classic Baptist confrontation of earthly powers who pretended to have authority over spiritual matters. See Wayland (ed.), *A Memoir*, I, pp. 246-49. In a strongly Calvinist assertion, Wayland, p. 249, reasoned, 'The wisdom of God had decreed that the seed of a Christian Church in Burmah should be sown amid persecution unto death.'

[21] Elnathan was Adoniram's brother who volunteered to go and cover his expenses by working as a ship's doctor en route to Calcutta. 'Minutes of the Baptist Board for Foreign Missions', 2 February 1823, p. 81.

Christians, to whom national freedom is dear as the 'current of the soul', whose ecclesiastical government is interwoven with its dictates, and whose ardent desires and endeavours embrace the victories of patriotism and piety from the Potomac to the ends of the earth.[22]

Out of a context of religious freedom established by public legislation, the Baptist leadership in Boston requested toleration for the efforts of their missionaries. The sustained efforts of Judson with the Board's support led to an allowance of a site and residence granted by the emperor as a temporary personal concession to the American missionary.

The Judsons used the openness toward them to great advantage until 8 June 1824 when Adoniram was arrested as a spy and imprisoned for two years at Oung-Pen-La, the infamous 'death prison'. (Ironically the same emperor authorized Judson's incarceration.) Thereafter, he helped to negotiate the peace treaty and focused especially upon religious toleration for Christianity.[23] His efforts in this regard were thwarted by both sides which reduced the issues to military and commercial articles. Judson, under strong influence of his wife and the Baptist Board, declined positions in the British and Burman governments and withdrew to the Tenasserim Provinces in Burma and the security of British law. For the remainder of his career Adoniram would become a devoted missionary evangelist and translator, sometimes traveling among the isolated tribes. In 1826 after his harrowing, torturous prison experience, he would write of his contribution to achieving a change in public policy in Burma: 'So far as I had a view to the attainment of religious toleration in accompanying the embassy, I have entirely failed. I feel the disappointment more deeply on account of the many tedious delays which have already occurred...in consequence of which [I] have been absent from my wife's dying bed...'.[24] Steeped in an evangelical Calvinist mindset, mildly critical of both creeds and establishments, he wrote to his friend Archibald Campbell in Burma, 'true religion is a very different thing from all that you have probably been acquainted with. True religion is seldom to be found among mitered prelates and high dignitaries. It consists not in attachment to any particular church, nor in the observance of any particular forms of worship. Nor does it consist in a mere abstinence from flagrant crimes, a mere conformity to the rules of honesty and honor. True religion consists in a reunion of the soul to that great, omnipresent, infinite Being from whom we have all become alienated, in consequence of the fall.'

---

[22] 'Minutes of the Baptist Board', 6 May 1823, pp. 103-104.

[23] *The Missionary Jubilee: An Account of the Fiftieth Anniversary of the American Baptist Missionary Union, at Philadelphia May 24, 25, & 26 1864, with Historical Papers and Discourses,* edited by American Baptist Foreign Mission Society (New York: Sheldon, 1865), and Joan Jacobs Brumberg, *Mission for Life: The Story of the Family of Adoniram Judson, The Dramatic Events of the First American Foreign Mission, and the Course of Evangelical Religion in the Nineteenth Century* (New York: The Free Press, 1980), pp. 95-101.

[24] Judson to Lucius Bolles, 7 December 1826, printed in Wayland (ed.), *A Memoir,* I, 416.

Here he exhibited, from his own personal experience, the foundational liberty of conscience.

Adoniram Judson thus represents an early phase of American Baptist understanding of religious toleration and liberty in the mission context. Without the training or upbringing of Baptists, Judson fell back upon his Hopkinsian[25] theological orientation from Andover Theological Seminary. A strong devotion to the eternal purposes of God in human affairs led him to assume that the success or failure of the Burman mission depended upon God's willingness to have the Burman people hear the gospel. Judson lacked a full-blown case for religious freedom in a non-Christian culture and was unsure that presenting one beyond the normal petition process requesting toleration was appropriate. What he sought was liberty to live in the Burman Empire, practice Christian beliefs, witness both to foreigners and Burmans, and continue his translation work. Whether his mission succeeded or not, God would determine: 'all that we can say is, "It is not in man that walketh to direct his steps".'[26] Even in light of a golden opportunity to be the agency perhaps by which Burma accepted greater religious liberty, Judson 'emphatically wished to know nothing among them save Jesus Christ and him crucified'.[27]

African Americans and the Limits of Baptist Toleration

Early in the development of overseas missions from North America, Baptists were confronted with the prospect of African Americans in their midst who desired to live with at least toleration, if not liberty, practicing their faith according to Baptist principles, and building churches. This circumstance represented a unique challenge to the otherwise libertarian ideals of Baptists in America. The earliest of these, according to Mechal Sobel, were found in the slave communities among the Tidewater plantations in colonial Virginia in the 1750s.[28] While slave worship was noticed, slaves' ability to organize and create sustained congregations was sharply curtailed by prevailing customs and laws of racial slavery and segregation. Well into the nineteenth century, particularly after the Nat Turner Rebellion, slave congregations were seen as a threat to the security of the White community. Moreover, White Baptists were silent in addressing the obvious deprivation of rights. Thus, it is not too strong an assertion to say that the intersection of Baptist libertarian ideals with racial servitude did not produce religious toleration, let alone

---

[25] A reference to Samuel Hopkins, a pivotal thinker in the evolution of New England Calvinism who placed slightly more stress upon human ability than his predecessors. See Frank Hugh Foster, *A Genetic History of New England Theology* (New York: Garland, 1987 [1907]), pp. 162-86; and Joseph Haroutunian, *Piety Versus Moralism: The Passing of the New England Theology* (New York: Harper Torchbooks, 1970 [1932]), pp. 50-58.

[26] Wayland (ed.), *A Memoir*, I, p. 372.

[27] Wayland (ed.), *A Memoir*, I, p. 395.

[28] Mechal Sobel, *Trabelin On: The Slave Journey to an Afro-Baptist Faith* (Princeton, NJ: Princeton University Press, 1988), p. 102.

religious freedom. It probably did not even allow for complete freedom of conscience for African Americans.

An interesting example of the struggle among African Americans for religious toleration in mission context was in the case of David George (1743–1810). George was a freed slave from South Carolina who left the lower colonies in 1782 to join the Loyalists in Nova Scotia. There he planned to settle a community of former slaves at the town of Shelburne. He built a church and enjoyed wide response to his preaching. It was not long before racial antagonisms flared up and in 1784 ruffians interrupted his preaching and resident soldiers harassed most Blacks out of the community. Beaten with sticks and driven into a nearby swamp, George returned to his home and meeting house for Christmas, only to find that the meeting house had been turned into an unlicensed tavern. He made several valiant attempts to recover his ministry, starting as many as seven preaching places in Nova Scotia and New Brunswick. Ultimately shortage of land and racial prejudice led George in 1792 to organize a group and buy passage to join Granville Sharp in the Sierra Leone Company in West Africa. George lost many of his cohorts either on the voyage or later, but managed to start a church which he served under duress until 1810. The transplanted Nova Scotians were prone to division and several were accused of subjugating Africans to their personal service. George himself protested the establishment behavior of Church of Scotland chaplains and he became embroiled in theological controversy. For a brief time the English Baptists supported a mission in the African colony, but withdrew in 1797.[29]

Next in the African American experience was the mission of Lott Cary to Africa. The Richmond (Virginia) Baptist Missionary Society promoted the work of Cary, a gifted freed slave and the General Missionary Convention appointed him and Colin Teague to Africa in 1821, serving until 1828, when he was killed in a military accident. What is often glossed over in Cary's appointment was the connection with the American Colonization Society. This group, founded in 1816 by prominent Americans like Henry Clay, Bushrod Washington, Daniel Webster, and W.H. Wilmer, an Episcopal theological educator, proposed to send Africans back to Africa to re-colonize a haven for freed persons of color. The work of the Society, as long as it survived, was premised upon racial inferiority of African Americans and their preferred 'design' for the climate and societies of Africa. It was also built upon a scheme of 'sincere missionary efforts from morally committed Churches and Christian believers', of which Baptists were one willing group.[30] The cooperative scheme proved to be politically loaded.

---

[29] See James W. Walker, *The Black Loyalists: The Search for a Promised Land in Nova Scotia and Sierra Leone, 1783–1870* (New York: Africana, 1976); Richard West, *Back to Africa: A History of Sierra Leone and Liberia* (New York: Holt, Rinehart and Winston, 1970); and Grant Gordon, *From Slavery to Freedom: The Life of David George, Pioneer Black Baptist Minister* (Hantsport, NS: Lancelot Press, 1992).

[30] Cf. Charles Morrow Wilson, *Liberia: Black African Microcosm* (New York: Harper and Row, 1971), p. 7, with G.E. Saigbe Boley, *Liberia: The Rise and Fall of the First Republic* (New York: St Martin's Press, 1983), p. 12.

Four factors ultimately militated against the Colonization Society's plan: lack of sufficient funds, competing state societies, the breakdown of efforts to plant a successful colony in Africa, and the emergence of the antislavery movement in the United States in the 1830s. Lott Cary himself suffered from insufficient support from the Baptist community, forcing him to engage in military and political affairs.[31] African Americans would have to wait until the establishment of congregations in the Free States in the antebellum period and no surviving mission to Africa by Baptists was forthcoming until the 1880s. Africans and African American Baptists would remain a painful reminder of the limits of Baptist thinking about religious toleration, let alone religious freedom, although some made the ideological pilgrimage that Brian Stanley describes as 'the politically sensitive ideology of human rights and brotherhood to reinforce their claims of missionary and humanitarian obligation'.[32]

European Baptists and the Politics of Religious Freedom

Perhaps the most colorful confrontation challenge to Baptist ideals of religious liberty was seen in the German states as Johann Gerhard Oncken (1801–84) began his evangelical work. He reflected both British and American perspectives on religious liberty issues. Oncken became an appointee of the American Baptist Board from 1834 to 1874.[33] His American biographer stated he lived in England during his youth where he became a Christian and joined an Independent (Congregational) church. Interested in Christian literature, he learned the bookselling business and returned to Germany engaged in evangelical work for the British Continental Society (1823–28) and from 1828 for the Edinburgh Bible Society. Some time before 1834 he met an American sea captain who shared with him Baptist principles and connected him with two prominent American Baptist ministers, J.L. Dagg of Philadelphia and Spencer H. Cone of New York. At length, Professor Barnas Sears, on sabbatical leave from the Hamilton Literary and Theological Institution in upstate New York, found Oncken in Hamburg, organized a local church, baptized him and others, and ordained him.[34] Reporting to the Baptist Board, Sears recommended

---

[31] A review of the annual payments to Cary's mission in this era shows that the money was spasmodic and well behind other priorities like the Judson Mission, J.M. Peck and Isaac McCoy in the West, and Columbian College.

[32] Brian Stanley, 'Christianity and Civilization in English Evangelical Mission Thought', in Stanley (ed.), *Christian Missions*, p. 172.

[33] Hans Luckey, *Johann Gerhard Oncken und die Unfange des deutschen Baptismus* (Kassel: Oncken Verlag, 1934), pp. 63-81; Gunter Balders, *Theure Bruder Oncken: Das Leben Johann Gerhard Onckens in Bildern und Dokumenten* (Kassel: Oncken Verlag, 1978), pp. 22-47.

[34] The ordination was a highly unusual act, predicated upon Sears' authority from First Baptist, Hamilton, New York. There is no record this was ever ratified by the local church. For a connection with the Hudson River Baptist Association, see Balders, *Bruder Oncken*, p. 45.

immediate appointment for Oncken and this was achieved. While evidence to be more theologically definitive is lacking, several general comments may be made. First, Oncken was clearly converted under the influence of evangelical Calvinists in Britain. Upon his return to Germany he was united with a congregation of the Reformed faith. He later recounted the work of 'sovereign grace' in his early life.[35] His association with leading Baptists of the Regular or Calvinistic Baptist community of the north-eastern states signaled his continuation along an evangelical path. Finally, the encounter and doubtless friendly interrogation of Barnas Sears, a professor in a Regular Baptist evangelical theological school in the United States, led to his being theologically acceptable for ordination. What Sears did was to accredit J.G. Oncken for missionary service on behalf of the Hudson River Baptist Association and the American Baptist Board of Missions, both recognized, mainstream Baptist bodies.

Barnas Sears, to be recalled fondly as 'brother Sears', made a long-lasting impression upon Oncken and the beginnings of the Baptist witness in Europe. His views of the Established Church in the German states were typical of the American evangelical community and gibed with Oncken's experience: Lutheran pastors were considered 'Rationalists', leading a corrupt Church that united Lutherans and Reformed churches 'where every shade of Pantheism, Deism, Supernaturalism, Arminianism, Calvinism, etc. are pronounced to be indivisibly one'.[36] Oncken's charge from Sears was to be pastor of the newly constituted church at Hamburg, to itinerate among the different sections of Germany and elsewhere preaching, constituting churches, 'distributing the Word of God in tracts and disseminating the doctrines of the Cross'.[37]

Dissenter evangelism and church planting were threats to German Lutheran authorities. Early in his work for the Baptists, Oncken encountered two types of resistance, those local persons within the Lutheran and Roman Catholic communities that opposed his preaching and baptizing, and those in government circles who pursued him relentlessly. In September 1837, for instance, following a baptism in the River Elbe, he recounted, 'we were disturbed by a man landing with one or two others. He began to employ the most abusive language; threatened to drown me, and took hold of Dr. Lange's ears. We suffered all this quietly, in order to prevent the interference of the authorities, and got into our boats as soon as possible.'[38] Much later in his career, he was still harassed as in Copenhagen where

---

[35] J.G. Warren, 'Origin and Progress of the Mission in Germany', *The Missionary Magazine* 42:2 (February, 1867), p. 473. He continued to enjoy the support of churches in England and Scotland.

[36] Letter from Barnas Sears to the Board in 'Mission to Europe', 10 November 1834, in *American Baptist Magazine* 15.6 (June, 1835), p. 232.

[37] Letter from Barnas Sears to the Board in 'Germany', *American Baptist Magazine* 16.1 (January, 1836), p. 135.

[38] 'Journal of Mr. Oncken', *The/Baptist Missionary Magazine* 18.3 (March, 1838), p. 90.

children and adults peered in the windows and laughed and 'when the blinds were closed they pounded on the windows and stoned the building'.[39]

Severe prohibitions were enacted against evangelical work by various governments, urged on by Lutheran clergy. Sometimes this involved Baptist workers who refused to work on the Sabbath, a common practice in many German industries.[40] 'Conventicle Laws' forbade more than a handful of persons meeting for religious purposes unless a Lutheran pastor was present. The Senate of the City of Hamburg passed a resolution authorizing the chief of police to inform Oncken that it viewed the Baptist church as a criminal schism, of which he was the sole author. He was summarily prohibited from all ministerial functions, the administration of sacraments, from evangelism, and from meeting in his conventicles. Members of his congregation were likewise forbidden to meet as such,[41] though Oncken frequently continued meeting in spite of the fear of police intervention. He maintained that his meetings were for the purposes of household devotions only. To thwart police capture, Oncken resorted to a Baptist practice from the English Restoration, meeting and baptizing in the dark of night.[42] Sometimes, as in May 1840, he was strip-searched, interrogated for as long as six hours, and imprisoned for several weeks, and assessed the charges for his incarceration.[43] His fate was shared by colporters Lange, Peter Monster, Julius Köbner and G.W. Lehmann.[44] In Marburg, an infant was sprinkled against the will of Baptist parents and the parents were fined.[45] Often, when Oncken was brought before the magistrate, his responses were clever, calm, and convincing. In Oldenburg he told a magistrate that no delineation could be made between missionary personnel and membership, because 'every Baptist was a missionary'.

---

[39] *The/Baptist Missionary Magazine* 42.3 (March, 1862), p. 81.

[40] 'Germany', in *The/Baptist Missionary Magazine* 18.6 (June, 1838), p. 146; 18.9 (September, 1838), p. 297; and 19.11 (November, 1839), p. 268.

[41] 'Religious Freedom Infringed by the Hamburg Senate', in *The/Baptist Missionary Magazine* 19.8 (August, 1839), p. 195; 20.5 (May, 1840), p. 163. On the 'Conventicle Laws', see Wayne Alan Detzler, 'Johann Gerhard Oncken's Long Road to Toleration', *Journal of the Evangelical Theological Society* 36.2 (June, 1993), pp. 229-40, esp. p. 237.

[42] 'Mission to Germany', *The/Baptist Missionary Magazine* 40.7 (July, 1860), p. 261; 50.2 (February, 1870), p. 58.

[43] *The/Baptist Missionary Magazine* 20.11 (November, 1840), pp. 258, 260; 21.8 (August, 1841), p. 266. He reported that two watchmen were placed over the Baptist meeting house and 'five Jews were employed by these Christians to take away my property for preaching the gospel of Christ'. For another account of the same ill treatment, see *The/Baptist Missionary Magazine* 35.7 (July, 1855), p. 323, and 37.2 (February, 1857), p. 44, where reports were made from Mecklenburg, Hesse, Cassel, Schaumburg-Lippe, and Schleswig.

[44] 'Mission to Germany and Denmark', *The/Baptist Missionary Magazine* 21.6 (June, 1841), p. 180.

[45] 'Letter from Mr. Oncken', *The/Baptist Missionary Magazine* 23.4 (April, 1843), p. 75.

The influence of J.G. Oncken on the spread of the principles of religious toleration and ultimately religious liberty can hardly be overestimated.[46] Not only were his labors transformative in Germany, but he also traveled widely in Poland, Austria-Hungary, Switzerland, Russia and Ukraine. Yet Oncken's position on religious liberty has never been carefully analyzed. Essentially a self-taught, but widely read person, he was informed by history. As a German, he much extolled Martin Luther's religious contributions. Standing before a Luther monument at Worms in 1861 he mused, 'I rejoiced to think that the spirit of Martin Luther can never be quite extinguished, while the Word of God, which he gave us in our native tongue, shall exist. Yes, we Baptists owe him our best treasure and we shall do well ever to keep before us Luther's heroic example of non-submission to worldly power in matters of religion.'[47] An inherent German love for the scriptures transformed Oncken into a spiritual and social democrat, at whose foundation lay freedom of conscience. At the cornerstone laying of the new chapel in Hamburg in 1866, he observed

As long as Germany refuses to return to the living God and the word of his truth, it will never attain to that true freedom with which Christ blesses all who submit to Him as their Redeemer. It is only where the word of God has struck its roots deep in the hearts of the people, that men enjoy the highest political freedom. The Bible, and the Bible alone, is the guaranty of freedom to an emancipated world.[48]

With respect to religious toleration in Germany, the examples of the United States and England in this regard were especially poignant to Oncken. As he observed it, these nations enjoyed the highest freedoms because there the Bible ruled and 'the men whom the Son of God has made free from sin and the dominion of evil passions are fitted to rear the edifice of national freedom'.[49] Not only were these nations examples of a high order of gospel freedom to Oncken, but he also worked through their diplomatic channels when it served his purposes.[50]

---

[46] It has been argued that Oncken was essentially an autocratic administrator while his colleague Julius Köbner was the theorist of religious liberty. This is based primarily upon Köbner's preparation of 'Manifest des frien Urchristentums an das deutsche Volk' in 1848. While this document was indeed a far-reaching piece of libertarian thought, it was silenced by the authorities and virtually destroyed. Köbner himself went to a pastorate in Denmark. See Erich Geldbach, 'Julius Köbner's Contribution to Baptist Identity' in the present volume.

[47] 'Letter from Mr. Oncken', *The/Baptist Missionary Magazine* 41.1 (January, 1861), p. 6.

[48] 'Letter from Mr. Oncken', *The/Baptist Missionary Magazine* 41.6 (June, 1866), p. 177.

[49] 'Letter from Mr. Oncken', *The/Baptist Missionary Magazine* 41.6 (June, 1866), p. 177.

[50] While this worked within European communities it was not successful when Oncken attempted to gain access with the Russian Czar. See 'Mr. Oncken's Visit to St. Petersburg', *The/Baptist Missionary Magazine* 45.2 (June, 1865), p. 182.

A second important point in Oncken's position was his opposition to creeds. Knowledge of the scriptures was a sure antidote for creedal summaries. He spent a good portion of his life in the service of the Bible Society distributing portions of scripture, teaching the Bible and sponsoring the publication of tracts on evangelical truths. In the larger realm of the political implications of Oncken's liberal views, he may well be credited with being a major catalyst toward separation of church and state in Germany. The struggles of Oncken and the German Baptists came to the attention of the Evangelical Alliance 1847–53 and through Oncken's influence it joined voices with the Protestant Alliance and the Hombourg Conference against the better judgment of the Lutherans.[51] His personal leadership in this regard can be seen in his mission to the King of Prussia in January 1855 where he, Lehmann, Köbner,[52] and others met in the Council Chamber with Frederick William IV to present their concerns over persecution of Baptists and the hope that the undefined position in Prussia with respect to toleration might be changed. The king acknowledged Oncken's leadership and interviewed him carefully about his work. This important overture did secure a personal affirmation of religious toleration (strengthened later under William I) as well as leaving the impression that Prussia could influence a number of other German states in the direction of toleration, if the king were so disposed.[53]

In 1858 the tide began to turn as news arrived that the Hamburg government had recognized the Baptist church there and certified their right to solemnize marriages and register births.[54] On 1 January 1866 the Senate and Burgerschaft of Hamburg passed legislation that ended state support of the Lutheran Church.[55] Hamburg thus became the first state in Germany to disestablish the Church, where, as Oncken put it, 'perfect religious liberty has become law'. For religious Dissenters it meant registration of births and marriages became a civil matter and all public funding committed to the Church ceased. Oncken theologically interpreted this unspeakably joyful event as public testimony to the inherent right of every person to worship God in accordance with the dictates of their conscience and without human legislation. Here was the Baptist principle realized in public experience. Oncken

---

[51] On the role of the Evangelical Alliance and its interest in common action in the German situation, see Ian Randall and David Hilborn, *One Body in Christ: The History and Significance of the Evangelical Alliance* (Carlisle: Paternoster Press, 2001), pp. 90-92.

[52] The three were known as the 'Kleeblat', roughly translated 'cloverleaf'.

[53] *The/Baptist Missionary Magazine* 35.2 (February, 1855), pp. 100-103. The other states Oncken hoped to move toward toleration were Schleswig, Holstein, Mecklenburg-Schwerin, Buckeburg, and Hesse. Frederick's first response was to have the Baptists join the Mennonites and form a united movement, but Oncken demurred on the reluctance of Mennonites to understand believer's baptism as did the Baptists. Unfortunately, Oncken's personal relationship with the king diminished in 1857, when the king became mentally incapacitated.

[54] *The/Baptist Missionary Magazine* 38.8 (August, 1858), p. 299.

[55] Hamburg was a self-governing city among the German states.

reflected that his and others' imprisonment for truth, the spoiling of his goods, had not been in vain. His triumph was personal: 'for forty-three years I have preached Christ almost in every hole and corner of this city; but the glorious event...surely is a call from that God who has loosened our bonds and set the captives free'.[56]

The hinge in Oncken's thinking, though, was the nature of his evangelical witness.[57] He saw the preaching of Baptists in Germany as a 'bright and shining light in a dark place'. This meant that Baptists were contradicting the theology and praxis of the State Church who made baptism 'the gate of heaven', and who in his mind could not differentiate between true and nominal Christianity. He described the content of his message as 'preaching Christ and a free and full salvation through faith in him and His finished work'. In Calvinistic terms, the effects of preaching were God's work—'the ingathering of vast numbers of souls to Christ', as preachers were faithful to the Word.[58] Another noticeable element was the support Oncken gave to 'revivals'. In the milieu of the 1840s to the 1860s, a revival was both an evangelistic means from which baptisms of believers resulted, as well as a renewal opportunity of churchly association in a hostile environment where believers could be threatened back into the established churches (to use his phrase, 'some have returned to the bosom of the Lutheran Church').[59] No sacramentarian or strict confessionalist, Oncken believed firmly in the priority of religious experience. 'A religion which does not feel the obligation to bear a living testimony to Christ', he told his Hamburg congregation, 'is not worthy of the name.'[60] The liberty of movement, assembly and preaching that legislation on religious liberty brought was directly tied to missions: 'streams of God's truth have gone forth through the labors of eighty-one missionaries, the circulation of fully one million copies of the Holy Scriptures in different languages...'. But most of all, he reckoned that about 50,000 precious souls had been converted, baptized, and gathered into New Testament churches. Prussian victories in the wars with Austria and Bavaria had extended liberty even further, for Lutheran clergy in Saxony and Mecklenburg no longer could exclude Baptists from preaching tours there. He was particularly full of praise for the constitution of Bismarck's North German Confederation that promised full religious

---

[56] 'Letter from Mr. Oncken', *The/Baptist Missionary Magazine* 41.5 (May, 1866), p. 136.

[57] This is the theme of Detzler's article ('Oncken's Long Road', pp. 231-232) where Oncken's evangelical pilgrimage is re-traced as is his 'endorsement' from conservative German university theologians Hengstenberg, Hahn, and Tholuck.

[58] 'Letter from Mr. Oncken', *The/Baptist Missionary Magazine* 44.11 (November, 1869), p. 411.

[59] 'Letter from Mr. Oncken', *The/Baptist Missionary Magazine* 41.2 (February, 1866), p. 54.

[60] 'The Ceremonies at Hamburg', *The/Baptist Missionary Magazine* 41.6 (June, 1866), p. 176.

liberty there also.[61] Observers in the larger evangelical community embraced Oncken and his mission, especially the members of the Evangelical Alliance that met in Württemburg in 1861 at the invitation of Philip Paulus.[62]

Baptism was of course crucial to Oncken's theological identity. His understanding of baptism introduced a new doctrine of the church, essentially that taught by Baptists in England and the United States, and even earlier by Anabaptist sects. Baptism followed a sovereign work of grace that was identifiable in a person's experience, vividly for some, less so for others. Following catechism in the faith, each person seeking believer's baptism was to request the rite voluntarily. There are numerous letters in which Oncken recounted the examination he put candidates through in order to determine the authenticity of their faith in Christ. He conducted the ordinance as a memorial of the gospel, as in Romans 6. Administered to believers only, he used a trinitarian formula for immersion.[63] The scene of Oncken's baptisms was often a river where he recorded the public witness, and he used familiar metaphors such as the 'silent grave' to describe the rite. Sometimes he overstated his claim for the validity of believers' baptism, arguing that Jesus was a Baptist and that there was a connection between the apostolic era and modern Baptists. In this regard he exhibited an American tendency toward 'successionism'.[64]

There was additionally a social concern inherent in Oncken's theology of religious liberty, as he observed, 'in many hitherto wretched families, Christianity has worked the happiest results—sobriety for drunkenness, industry for laziness, and that best gift of the gospel, peace and good will for clamor and strife'. One must 'see' these transformations in order to be able fully to appreciate the 'moral power of gospel truth'.[65] Here one notices what recent historians of missions have described as 'Christianity over civilization' where the gospel became the 'great engine of social change'.[66]

J.G. Oncken's understanding of religious toleration evolved to full religious liberty, and in so doing he developed a political theology. In his early years of ministry in Hamburg and its immediate regions, he was content to contend for toleration for his Baptist brethren. He was slow to articulate a full-blown case for

---

[61] 'Letter from Mr. Oncken', *The/Baptist Missionary Magazine* 42.2 (February, 1867), pp. 47-48. On the rise of the Confederation, see R.R. Palmer and Joel Colton, *A History of the Modern World* (New York: A.A. Knopf, 1967), pp. 524-25.

[62] 'Germany—Letter from Mr. Oncken', *The/Baptist Missionary Magazine* 41.1 (January, 1861), p. 4. The Alliance was formed in 1846 and welcomed Oncken's Christological emphases.

[63] 'Letter from Mr. Oncken', *The/Baptist Missionary Magazine* 54.12 (December, 1874), pp. 426-27.

[64] Detzler, 'Oncken's Long Road', pp. 235-full range, speaks of Oncken's 'irreconcilable ecclesiology' and adduces various Germans opposed to the practice as immoral or unnecessary. But he misses the longstanding antagonism to both re-baptism and immersion that Lutherans felt for Anabaptists. Oncken was seen in that context.

[65] 'Germany', *The/Baptist Missionary Magazine* 43.12 (December, 1863), p. 428.

[66] Stanley, 'Christianity and Civilization', p. 177.

religious liberty, in part because of his evangelical witness that circumscribed religious toleration. But in the revolutions of 1848, Oncken moved to a position he called 'free course' to the gospel. 'Civil and religious despotism, always linked together, must also fall together: thus it is in Germany and Austria, and the priestly power, under which we groaned so long, is destroyed.' Clearly a 'revolutionary', he boldly asserted, 'We can now move freely and fearlessly in every direction, circulate the Holy Scriptures among the adherents of Rome, supply the millions with tracts, and preach the blessed gospel in regions where Satan reigned in undisturbed repose.'[67] His efforts were thus directed at no less than two adversaries: the malevolent established churches and the government forces that had carried out persecutions and punishments upon him and his co-workers. Legally banished from nearly every state in Germany, he wanted to bring both down in the face of civil and religious freedom. He wrote that it was a shame for any country to persecute a man on account of his faith. 'Surely the principles of toleration ought to be proclaimed in Germany from the housetops', he boldly asserted.[68] Historians well note that after 1848 the Lutheran Church in the German states was no longer a '*Staatskirche*' but a '*Landeskirche*'. Thanks to Oncken and the Kleeblat, it would be joined by a powerful '*Volkskirche*'.[69]

In Oncken's mission to Germany, then, one sees the elements of an historic Baptist libertarian understanding first of religious toleration, then of religious liberty, and still further the separation of church and state, religious voluntarism and the nature of the church as a gathered people of God. As he put it in 1858, there was a decided difference between 'orthodox' Christianity and 'true' Christianity, and the latter necessitated the principles of toleration.[70] Additionally, Oncken was clearly an evangelical who saw God's purpose as essentially salvation-oriented, and he took every opportunity to press for the permission of religious freedom to extend his evangelistic and colporterage missions. In the midst of revolutions and denominational schisms in the mid-1840s, he reminded his followers, 'We have just one work to do, and whatever convulsions may shake the earth, we must have our eye and heart fixed on this: to preach Christ, become all things to all men, that we may save some, and restore apostolic churches.'[71] Further, Oncken was engaged in a major way in extending Baptist principles into the European contexts against the established Lutheran, Catholic, Orthodox, and Reformed Churches. He was so convinced of the biblical bases of Baptist egalitarianism that he could not separate

---

[67] 'Germany-Letter of Mr. Oncken', *The/Baptist Missionary Magazine* 28.10 (October, 1848), p. 387.

[68] 'The Church at Hamburg', *The/Baptist Missionary Magazine* 38.8 (August, 1858), p. 299.

[69] *Annual Report of the American Baptist Missionary Union* (1848), p. 86; Detzler, 'Oncken's Long Road', p. 239.

[70] 'Letter from Mr. Oncken', *The/Baptist Missionary Magazine* 38.8 (August, 1858), p. 299.

[71] 'Extracts of a Letter from Mr. Oncken', *The/Baptist Missionary Magazine* 26.12 (December, 1846), p. 359.

gospel truths from sectarian principles and practices. Finally, he saw the desired pattern in the recent histories of the United States and Britain and this would create a definite cultural profile for his ideas of religious freedom in Germany.

A Chinese Bible and the Freedom of the Scriptures

Yet another important challenge to religious liberty in the mission context is taken from the Far East, the field of William Dean (1807–95) in Siam and China. Dean arrived in Bangkok in 1835 and spent the next two decades between Siam and China translating the scriptures into a Baptist-sensitive version. Like Judson and Oncken, in Siam Dean initially faced initial restrictions upon religious liberty, including laws against foreigners traveling in the interior of the country and the ever-present ridicule of foreign teachers. Dean overcame those obstacles and gathered in Bangkok the first Protestant church among the Chinese in 1835. In this regard, Judson was a model. Dean later developed a close friendship with the Siamese royal family and received favored treatment and permission for his work.[72] Health concerns, the death of his first wife, Matilda, and advice from friends led him in the 1840s to move to Singapore and then Macao, settling at Hong Kong in 1842. In the Hong Kong context he enjoyed the benefits of a British Crown Colony with a liberal policy toward missionary work.

In China Dean encountered much more openness by government authorities. The longstanding public posture of the Chinese government toward westerners and their missionaries was forcibly altered. After an incident in 1759, Governor-General Li Ssu-yao promulgated 'Five Regulations' that essentially confined foreigners to the channel of the Cohong in Canton, made it unlawful to learn the Chinese language or to converse with Chinese, and prohibited the distribution of literature. Another restriction was laid down in 1835 when the Chinese Emperor issued an edict against the distribution of foreign books, 'designing to seduce men with lies'.[73] Larger events would open opportunities for Christian missions: following military operations between the British and Chinese, in 1842 the Cohong monopolistic system was abolished, five ports were opened to trade and residence of British consuls, and Hong Kong was ceded to the British who subsequently organized it as a Crown Colony. Finally, in 1858 in the Treaty of Tientsin foreigners were granted travel privileges in the interior and more ports were opened to trade.

But, undercurrents of opposition to Christianity in China were deep and historic and these provided the real challenge. A seventeenth-century work, *An Anthology of Writings Exposing Heterodoxy* (1639; republished in 1855) reproduced an anti-foreign and anti-Christian literary tradition in China. Joyce Chan, in her study of

---

[72] Francis Wayland Goddard, *Called to Cathay* (New York: Baptist Literature Bureau, 1948), pp. 22-23.

[73] On the restrictions, see Immanuel C.Y. Hsu, *The Rise of Modern China* (New York: Oxford University Press, 2000), pp. 144-51; Jonathan D. Spence, *God's Chinese Son: The Taiping Heavenly Kingdom of Hong Xiuquan* (New York: W.W. Norton, 1996), pp. 20-21.

Dean's translation efforts, has listed the blossoming of new anti-Christian polemics in the 1850s and 1860s. The move toward a potentially 'nationalized' form of Christianity under the Taiping 'Heavenly Kingdom' further entrenched traditional Confucian scholars against the foreign religion.[74] Debt, opium, and military defeats added more to this ideology. Additionally, Paul Cohen has shown that Christianity was seen as an evil religion, with its practitioners guilty of various types of immorality.[75]

William Dean's evangelism, church planting, and Bible translation efforts were staged against this background. He used the freedom of Hong Kong to establish a base of ministry from which he interacted with Chinese and intensively studied the language. In order to meet the intellectual rigor of Chinese religious and scholarly heritage, he studied the filial piety of Chinese society, the political monarchianism, and the religious ideological idioms. To convince the literati of the validity and substance of Christian texts, he worked in a tradition of classical scholarship and language, within the literary achievements of the *Kangxi Dictionary* (1727) and the more recent Qing textual methods. But his efforts to contextualize, as Chan has shown, failed in the end because his exclusively monotheistic theology clashed with native polytheism and China itself moved away from classical linguistics to the more practical and colloquial Mandarin.[76]

Dean, however, faced a second, even less predictable form of religious intolerance. This time it came from Christians of other denominations and through the interdenominational Bible societies. As Adoniram Judson and William Carey before him, he emulated their efforts to translate the scriptures into indigenous languages. He took up translation work as his mission emphasis along with preaching and evangelistic efforts, and this really dominated his ministry for over half a century. Where he ran into difficulties was in his Baptist-specific choices of terminology for 'God' and 'baptize'. In the context of the Taiping Rebellion (1851–64) and the attempts of translators to produce a version of the Bible that was acceptable to classic Chinese philosophy, what emerged was a Bible that was produced under state auspices and which supported in many ways a theology of the divine right of kings. It was destined to become the established text. This was unacceptable to William Dean and he produced not only a version with a more egalitarian view of God, but also one that captured the original biblical tradition of baptism by immersion. He also broke with the dominant Bible Society rule ('without notes or comments') and added both notes and comments to his translations in the hope of a greater comprehension of the Bible among new Chinese converts. In this later regard he joined a struggle being fought between Baptists in Britain and the United States, as

---

[74] Chung-Yan Joyce Chan, 'Beating the Rock with the Hammer of God's Word: William Dean and Denominational Identity in Cross-cultural Context' (PhD dissertation, Baylor University, 2003).

[75] Chan, 'Beating the Rock', p. 282; Paul Cohen, 'The Anti-Christian Tradition in China', *Journal of Asian Studies* 20 (February, 1961), p. 169.

[76] Chan, 'Beating the Rock', pp. 284-86.

well as in the mission context over the proper ground rules for scripture translation.[77]

The 'Term Question' (name of God) and the proper translation of βαπτίζω created a significant rift between Baptists and other Christians. Non-Baptists took the position that the Baptist translation was sectarian and benefited only the Baptists. Largely in control of the original Bible societies, the 'paedo-baptists' rejected the Baptist effort as unnecessary and unhelpful. As the secretary of the British and Foreign Bible Society put it, 'If the Baptists refuse all reasonable considerations such as Christian principles claim of us for them, we must regretfully act without them in the way we can.'[78] What that meant was that Baptist translation work, long disrespected by the other denominations, would be ostracized and no major printer of Bibles would touch the overly sectarian efforts.[79] Baptists, on the other side, became increasingly unwilling to cooperate in a translation effort that supported a monarchical idea of God and society, and that obscured the true meaning of baptism as a rite for adults and one's profession of faith. In the United States, eventually a new organization was formed in 1850, the American Bible Union, to produce a faithful rendition of the scriptures and this carried the approbation of overseas missionaries like Adoniram Judson and William Dean.[80] Here Dean in particular encountered intense opposition and a subtle form of intolerance from what has been labeled a 'pseudo-establishment' comprised of other Christian missionaries and ecclesiastical leaders.[81]

Denouement in Latin America

In many ways, the mission of Canadian Baptist Archibald Reekie in Bolivia, and later Cuba, portrays the finale of challenges to a century of ideological expansion of religious liberty in the mission context. Reekie (1862–1942) was originally an appointee of the Canadian Baptist Foreign Mission Board based in Ontario and Quebec, which was heavily influenced by the American Baptist Missionary Union. He was educated at McMaster University in the liberal American tradition of Rochester Seminary and Colgate University professors. Especially prominent among his mentors was Albert H. Newman, noted historian of Baptists and their drive for freedom of conscience. Reekie was the pioneer Baptist (and evangelical) missionary to Bolivia, the last of the Republics to be evangelized by non-Catholics. At the

---

[77] Goddard, *Called to Cathay*, p. 31.

[78] Quoted in Chan, 'Beating the Rock', p. 292.

[79] For this reason in 1898 American and Southern Baptists formed the China Baptist Publication Society to produce literature reflective of their nuances and scholarship.

[80] The outworking of this controversy is seen in *Judson's Burmese Bible: Correspondence Between the British and Foreign Bible Society and the Baptists* (Rangoon: American Baptist Mission Press, 1900), pp. 6-15.

[81] This is Chan's terminology, 'Beating the Rock', p. 292, and I think aptly descriptive.

outset of his mission to Bolivia he saw himself as an apostle of religious liberty, opening the opportunity for other evangelicals to follow.

Reekie learned his lessons well about the relationships of religious liberty to missionary witness. No longer was it a matter of assuming that one might wait upon God's providence and possibly be thwarted or disappointed by human obstacles; God's clear intention was to build his kingdom from sea to sea. On an initial fact-finding trip to Bolivia in 1897, Reekie ascertained how he would go about his plan in a country that was locked in what he called 'the darkness of papal control'. He proposed to enter Bolivia as a teacher of English, settling in the newly organized mining regions of the Altiplano. He planned to generate sufficient income from his teaching to support himself and devote the Canadian home funds directly to evangelical purposes.

Reekie took up residence at Oruro in 1898. A mining center far removed from Potosi and Sucre where the Conservative Party and the Catholic Church were ensconced, Oruro was open, progressive and identified with the Liberal politics of La Paz. He set up his school and began to organize a congregation of Scottish emigres and Aymara/Quechua converts. He understood the value of getting the scriptures into the hands of the common people and used Bible Society materials already prepared in Spanish. It was unlawful to hold Protestant church services, to distribute religious literature, or to preach publicly, but there were few enforcement agents in Oruro and Reekie took advantage of the situation. With additional personnel, Baptist churches sprang up in Cochabamba, Santa Cruz and around the shores of Lake Titicaca.

Within one year, the Liberal Party was swept into power in general in Bolivia. The issue was seemingly the location of a national capital and La Paz was the choice. Reekie sought the favor of the local prefect and then began a Protestant mission effort in La Paz. Further, he reached out to Catholic priests and attended Roman Catholic services. His display of a broad-minded evangelical witness did not go unnoticed and when the Freedom of Worship Act passed the new legislature in 1899, with other measures allowing for civil marriages to be registered, it was obvious that Baptists had made a distinct contribution to the creation of public policy along with establishing their churches across the strategic centers of Bolivia. One member of the Bolivian National Congress acknowledged to Reekie that Baptists had helped Bolivians to achieve religious liberty.[82]

From Individual Rights to Denominational Doctrine

The intersection of evangelical witness and gospel imperative with religious toleration and ultimately religious liberty and religious freedom, formed a significant challenge for the North American Baptist community in 1800. It was not unexplored territory in light of British Baptist experience antedating that of North Americans and

---

[82] Archibald Reekie to the Board, 14 October 1908 (Reekie Papers, Canadian Baptist Archives). Reekie later served as an appointee of the American Baptist Home Mission Society in Cuba during World War II.

continuing throughout the century. A transformation took place in Baptist theological and evangelization priorities. The old Calvinistic views of salvation for an elect gradually gave way to an evangelical thrust aimed at heathen peoples. Similarly, the instrumentality of missionaries and means supplemented and reinterpreted the doctrine of the sovereignty of God. Baptists came to believe God willed that the whole world should be saved through the means of preaching and evangelism. And underlying these transitions was another perhaps even more significant, namely the change from understanding the heathen as incapable and depraved, to an anthropology that stressed the autonomy and capacity of the human will.[83] If humans were religiously free, they could and would respond favorably to the invitation of the gospel. This would ensue either because of the power of truth to overcome error or the conviction of the Holy Spirit, or both. Thus the course of Baptist libertarian thought ran concurrently: freedom of conscience for the individual, religious toleration in social practice, and religious freedom as a political ideology. Who could miss the inevitable 'slide in the direction of the Baptist position', as one editor observed, 'who more than any other group have advanced the race'.[84]

There are several factors that play into this ideological transformation among North American Baptists and those in their extended spheres of influence. Some were theoretical/theological and others very practical. First was the Enlightenment emphasis upon individualism and the Baptist stress upon freedom of conscience or soul liberty.[85] It is surprising that this theme has received so little attention in studies of mission and the Enlightenment, even by Baptist scholars. It is surely an area of very fruitful enquiry. Next was the nineteenth-century trend in Europe and the Americas toward democratization and republican forms of government. This began with revolutions in the United States and France and continued in Latin America in the 1820s and Europe at mid-century. Third was the disestablishment of state churches as the voluntary principle took root. Examples of this are seen in the United States, the British Isles, Germany, and the growth of plurality of Christian denominations in mission and colonial contexts. Americans were especially bullish on their record of disestablishment: 'Step by step it progressed until it found its enunciation in the national Constitution and expunged from the codified laws of every state the last vestige of any assertion of its authority to control in matters of faith. It has been an arduous struggle.'[86] Some American Baptist writers were prepared almost to canonize the constitution: 'The article in the American Constitution guaranteeing the free exercise of religion to all is by far the most

---

[83] Stanley, 'Christianity and Civilization', p. 179. The Enlightenment notion of the unity of humankind was at work in this formulation.

[84] J.B. Gambrell, 'Baptists and the Twentieth Century', in A.H. Newman (ed.), *A Century of Baptist Achievement* (Philadelphia, PA: American Baptist Publication Society, 1901), p. 450.

[85] In 1898 E.Y. Mullins would refer to this 'axiom' as 'soul competence'. See E.Y. Mullins, *Axioms of the Christian Religion* (Nashville, TN: Sunday School Board, rev. edn, 1978), pp. 76-77.

[86] Mullins, *Axioms*, pp. 76-77.

important writing since the canon of inspiration was closed and the seal of deity stamped on it.'[87]

By the 1860s American (and Canadian!) Baptist missionaries and their policy-making boards understood their principles of religious *freedom* as co-equal with principles of civil justice, a voluntary church, and equalitarianism: the natural equality of all men before the law, as before God; the right to self-government through constitutions, laws and magistrates; ordained by a majority of the people; government existing by the will of God and for the good of the governed; the right of every one to the blessings of liberty and knowledge.[88] As one Canadian Baptist put it, the Baptist doctrine of soul liberty broadened into the conception of personal liberty and found expression in the ordinances of civil liberty, ultimately bringing forth the political emancipation of mankind.[89] Evangelical Baptist individualism and ecclesiology were wedded to Enlightenment political theory. It was as though the Bible, the English Bill of Rights, and the American Declaration of Independence had been fused to create a divinely ordained, enlightened social order.

But there were the practical matters as well. Baptists entertained no inclination toward persecution or martyrdom, as their Anabaptist cousins.[90] Following the lead of the phraseology in the US Bill of Rights, missionaries required the 'free exercise of religion', unhindered by any government.[91] When missionaries were placed in jeopardy, as in the case of the Judsons, they repaired to the nearest form of American or British diplomatic presence to buttress their case and protect their interests and property. Oncken repeatedly reminded his hearers and adversaries of the examples of republicanism in the United States. Dean enjoyed the protection of a British Crown Colony in Hong Kong and he served as a quasi-diplomat between the United States and Siam. Archibald Reekie was in continual contact with the American and British consuls in Peru and Bolivia. Each relied upon necessary political ideology and supportive institutions to open the mission fields to evangelical workers. It was not hard to conceive how the rhetoric of an aggressive libertarian theology in an age of American and British expansionism could reinforce the missionary enterprise. The

[87] Gambrell, 'Baptists and the Twentieth Century', p. 448.

[88] William Crowell, 'Literature of American Baptists from 1814 to 1864', in *The Missionary Jubilee: An Account of the Fiftieth Anniversary of the American Baptist Missionary Union, with Commemorative Papers and Discourses* (New York: Sheldon, 1865), p. 436.

[89] J.D. Freeman, 'The Place of Baptists in the Christian Church', *The Baptist World Congress. London, July 11–19, 1905. Authorised Record of Proceedings* (London: Baptist Union Publication Department, 1905), p. 26.

[90] Franklin H. Littell, 'The Anabaptist Theology of Mission', in Wilbert R. Schenk (ed.), *Anabaptism and Mission*, p. 22. In contrast, among Anabaptists in the same era no form of compulsion was to be used, the triumph of true faith by the 'Pauline method'.

[91] This is a vital point for US constitutional scholars who distinguish between 'disestablishment' and 'free exercise' in their doctrine of the separation of church and state. From an American perspective, disestablishment had been won in the United States, but the mission context was a continual reminder of the lack of 'free exercise' elsewhere.

redoubtable Augustus H. Strong of Rochester Seminary asserted, 'Let us believe that Christ can and will convert the mightiest and most arbitrary monarch on earth, so that he shall be willing to give his people civil justice and constitutional liberty.'[92]

The nineteenth century, then, was pre-eminently a Baptist century. What emerged from the nineteenth century for the denomination was a 'doctrine' or formal teaching on religious freedom. At its foundation was liberty of conscience for individuals, which is realized not just in expressed freedom of belief, but also in responding to the truth of the Bible and the invitation of the gospel, again either through the work of the Holy Spirit or the overwhelming evidence of reason. Upon that foundation was built an interpretation of the United States (and to a slightly lesser extent, Great Britain) as the political state embodiment of free exercise of religion, and even more the practice of pure democracy over absolutism in government. Finally, the 'doctrine' involved a missionary imperative in the direction of the Baptist position. As J.B. Gambrell, a Southern Baptist, put it in 1901,

> In America, the Protestant communions have come so completely to the Baptist position as regards liberty of conscience, separation of church and state, etc., that their people do not know they ever held other views. Toleration has been greatly broadened in Britain. The Irish disestablishment bill passed and there is steady progress toward entire freedom. France has become a republic and there is large liberty there. Rome has opened her doors to the Bible... The gospel can be preached nearly anywhere on the earth's surface today, and the great nations of the earth will protect the missionaries... [T]he spirit of the age abhors religious persecution... [T]he call reaches us from every quarter of the globe, 'Come over and help us...'.[93]

If the first meeting of the Baptist World Alliance in 1905 may be used as a summation of the evolving course of mainstream Baptist libertarian ideology, the international Baptist community had achieved a fairly comprehensive understanding of a doctrine of religious freedom at the turn of the twentieth century. Various mission contexts had re-shaped an eighteenth-century idea. In one of the major addresses, a Toronto Baptist pastor exclaimed,

> Individuality in relation to God and Christ and salvation conducts an irresistible sequence to freedom of thought and speech and Press, to popular government, to unfettered scientific investigation, to universal education. Soul liberty cannot be dissevered from civil freedom. All modern reforms in government, broadening from the few to the many, can be traced to the requisite more or less of this great principle.[94]

---

[92] A.H. Strong, 'The Congress Sermon: The Greatness and the Claims of Christ', *Baptist Congress Proceedings*, p. 63.
[93] Gambrell, 'Baptists and the Twentieth Century', pp. 450, 453.
[94] Freeman, 'The Place of Baptists in the Christian Church', p. 27.

General Index

Studies in Baptist History and Thought

(All titles uniform with this volume)
Dates in bold are of projected publication
Volumes in this series are not always published in sequence

David Bebbington and Anthony R. Cross (eds)
Global Baptist History
(SBHT vol. 14)
This book brings together studies from the Second International Conference on Baptist Studies which explore different facets of Baptist life and work especially during the twentieth century.
__2006__ / 1-84227-214-4 / approx. 350pp

David Bebbington (ed.)
The Gospel in the World
International Baptist Studies
(SBHT vol. 1)
This volume of essays from the First International Conference on Baptist Studies deals with a range of subjects spanning Britain, North America, Europe, Asia and the Antipodes. Topics include studies on religious tolerance, the communion controversy and the development of the international Baptist community, and concludes with two important essays on the future of Baptist life that pay special attention to the United States.
2002 / 1-84227-118-0 / xiv + 362pp

John H.Y. Briggs (ed.)
Pulpit and People
Studies in Eighteenth-Century English Baptist Life and Thought
(SBHT vol. 28)
The eighteenth century was a crucial time in Baptist history. The denomination had its roots in seventeenth-century English Puritanism and Separatism and the persecution of the Stuart kings with only a limited measure of freedom after 1689. Worse, however, was to follow for with toleration came doctrinal conflict, a move away from central Christian understandings and a loss of evangelistic urgency. Both spiritual and numerical decline ensued, to the extent that the denomination was virtually reborn as rather belatedly it came to benefit from the Evangelical Revival which brought new life to both Arminian and Calvinistic Baptists. The papers in this volume study a denomination in transition, and relate to theology, their views of the church and its mission, Baptist spirituality, and engagements with radical politics.
__2007__ / 1-84227-403-1 / approx. 350pp

Damian Brot
Church of the Baptized or Church of Believers?
A Contribution to the Dialogue between the Catholic Church and the Free Churches with Special Reference to Baptists
(SBHT vol. 26)
The dialogue between the Catholic Church and the Free Churches in Europe has hardly taken place. This book pleads for a commencement of such a conversation. It offers, among other things, an introduction to the American and the international dialogues between Baptists and the Catholic Church and strives to allow these conversations to become fruitful in the European context as well.
2006 / 1-84227-334-5 / approx. 364pp

Dennis Bustin
Paradox and Perseverence
Hanserd Knollys, Particular Baptist Pioneer in Seventeenth-Century England
(SBHT vol. 23)
The seventeenth century was a significant period in English history during which the people of England experienced unprecedented change and tumult in all spheres of life. At the same time, the importance of order and the traditional institutions of society were being reinforced. Hanserd Knollys, born during this pivotal period, personified in his life the ambiguity, tension and paradox of it, openly seeking change while at the same time cautiously embracing order. As a founder and leader of the Particular Baptists in London and despite persecution and personal hardship, he played a pivotal role in helping shape their identity externally in society and, internally, as they moved toward becoming more formalised by the end of the century.
2006 / 1-84227-259-4 / approx. 324pp

Anthony R. Cross
Baptism and the Baptists
Theology and Practice in Twentieth-Century Britain
(SBHT vol. 3)
At a time of renewed interest in baptism, *Baptism and the Baptists* is a detailed study of twentieth-century baptismal theology and practice and the factors which have influenced its development.
2000 / 0-85364-959-6 / xx + 530pp

Anthony R. Cross and Philip E. Thompson (eds)
Baptist Sacramentalism
(SBHT vol. 5)
This collection of essays includes biblical, historical and theological studies in the theology of the sacraments from a Baptist perspective. Subjects explored include the physical side of being spiritual, baptism, the Lord's supper, the church, ordination, preaching, worship, religious liberty and the issue of disestablishment.
2003 / 1-84227-119-9 / xvi + 278pp

Anthony R. Cross and Philip E. Thompson (eds)
Baptist Sacramentalism 2
(SBHT vol. 25)
This second collection of essays exploring various dimensions of sacramental theology from a Baptist perspective includes biblical, historical and theological studies from scholars from around the world.
2006 / 1-84227-325-6 / approx. 350pp

Paul S. Fiddes
Tracks and Traces
Baptist Identity in Church and Theology
(SBHT vol. 13)
This is a comprehensive, yet unusual, book on the faith and life of Baptist Christians. It explores the understanding of the church, ministry, sacraments and mission from a thoroughly theological perspective. In a series of interlinked essays, the author relates Baptist identity consistently to a theology of covenant and to participation in the triune communion of God.
2003 / 1-84227-120-2 / xvi + 304pp

!   Stanley K. Fowler
More Than a Symbol
The British Baptist Recovery of Baptismal Sacramentalism
(SBHT vol. 2)
Fowler surveys the entire scope of British Baptist literature from the seventeenth-century pioneers onwards. He shows that in the twentieth century leading British Baptist pastors and theologians recovered an understanding of baptism that connected experience with soteriology and that in doing so they were recovering what many of their forebears had taught.
2002 / 1-84227-052-4 / xvi + 276pp

Steven R. Harmon
Towards Baptist Catholicity
Essays on Tradition and the Baptist Vision
(SBHT vol. 27)
This series of essays contends that the reconstruction of the Baptist vision in the wake of modernity's dissolution requires a retrieval of the ancient ecumenical tradition that forms Christian identity through rehearsal and practice. Themes explored include catholic identity as an emerging trend in Baptist theology, tradition as a theological category in Baptist perspective, Baptist confessions and the patristic tradition, worship as a principal bearer of tradition, and the role of Baptist higher education in shaping the Christian vision.
2006 / 1-84227-362-0 / approx. 210pp

Michael A.G. Haykin (ed.)
'At the Pure Fountain of Thy Word'
Andrew Fuller as an Apologist
(SBHT vol. 6)
One of the greatest Baptist theologians of the eighteenth and early nineteenth centuries, Andrew Fuller has not had justice done to him. There is little doubt that Fuller's theology lay behind the revitalization of the Baptists in the late eighteenth century and the first few decades of the nineteenth. This collection of essays fills a much needed gap by examining a major area of Fuller's thought, his work as an apologist.
2004 / 1-84227-171-7 / xxii + 276pp

Michael A.G. Haykin
Studies in Calvinistic Baptist Spirituality
(SBHT vol. 15)
In a day when spirituality is in vogue and Christian communities are looking for guidance in this whole area, there is wisdom in looking to the past to find untapped wells. The Calvinistic Baptists, heirs of the rich ecclesial experience in the Puritan era of the seventeenth century, but, by the end of the eighteenth century, also passionately engaged in the catholicity of the Evangelical Revivals, are such a well. This collection of essays, covering such things as the Lord's Supper, friendship and hymnody, seeks to draw out the spiritual riches of this community for reflection and imitation in the present day.
2006 / 1-84227-149-0 / approx. 350pp

Brian Haymes, Anthony R. Cross and Ruth Gouldbourne
On Being the Church
Revisioning Baptist Identity
(SBHT vol. 21)
The aim of the book is to re-examine Baptist theology and practice in the light
of the contemporary biblical, theological, ecumenical and missiological context
drawing on historical and contemporary writings and issues. It is not a study in
denominationalism but rather seeks to revision historical insights from the
believers' church tradition for the sake of Baptists and other Christians in the
context of the modern–postmodern context.
2006 / 1-84227-121-0 / approx. 350pp

Ken R. Manley
From Woolloomooloo to 'Eternity': A History of Australian Baptists
Volume 1: Growing an Australian Church (1831–1914)
Volume 2: A National Church in a Global Community (1914–2005)
(SBHT vols 16.1 and 16.2)
From their beginnings in Australia in 1831 with the first baptisms in
Woolloomooloo Bay in 1832, this pioneering study describes the quest of
Baptists in the different colonies (states) to discover their identity as Australians
and Baptists. Although institutional developments are analyzed and the roles of
significant individuals traced, the major focus is on the social and theological
dimensions of the Baptist movement.
2 vol. set 2006 / 1-84227-405-8 / approx. 900pp

Ken R. Manley
'Redeeming Love Proclaim'
John Rippon and the Baptists
(SBHT vol. 12)
A leading exponent of the new moderate Calvinism which brought new life to
many Baptists, John Rippon (1751–1836) helped unite the Baptists at this
significant time. His many writings expressed the denomination's growing
maturity and mutual awareness of Baptists in Britain and America, and exerted a
long-lasting influence on Baptist worship and devotion. In his various activities,
Rippon helped conserve the heritage of Old Dissent and promoted the
evangelicalism of the New Dissent
2004 / 1-84227-193-8 / xviii + 340pp

Peter J. Morden
Offering Christ to the World
Andrew Fuller and the Revival of English Particular Baptist Life
(SBHT vol. 8)
Andrew Fuller (1754–1815) was one of the foremost English Baptist ministers of his day. His career as an Evangelical Baptist pastor, theologian, apologist and missionary statesman coincided with the profound revitalization of the Particular Baptist denomination to which he belonged. This study examines the key aspects of the life and thought of this hugely significant figure, and gives insights into the revival in which he played such a central part.
2003 / 1-84227-141-5 / xx + 202pp

Peter Naylor
Calvinism, Communion and the Baptists
A Study of English Calvinistic Baptists from the Late 1600s to the Early 1800s
(SBHT vol. 7)
Dr Naylor argues that the traditional link between 'high-Calvinism' and 'restricted communion' is in need of revision. He examines Baptist communion controversies from the late 1600s to the early 1800s and also the theologies of John Gill and Andrew Fuller.
2003 / 1-84227-142-3 / xx + 266pp

Ian M. Randall, Toivo Pilli and Anthony R. Cross (eds)
Baptist Identities
International Studies from the Seventeenth to the Twentieth Centuries
(SBHT vol. 19)
These papers represent the contributions of scholars from various parts of the world as they consider the factors that have contributed to Baptist distinctiveness in different countries and at different times. The volume includes specific case studies as well as broader examinations of Baptist life in a particular country or region. Together they represent an outstanding resource for understanding Baptist identities.
2005 / 1-84227-215-2 / approx. 350pp

James M. Renihan
Edification and Beauty
The Practical Ecclesiology of the English Particular Baptists, 1675–1705
(SBHT vol. 17)
Edification and Beauty describes the practices of the Particular Baptist churches at the end of the seventeenth century in terms of three concentric circles: at the centre is the ecclesiological material in the Second London Confession, which is then fleshed out in the various published writings of the men associated with these churches, and, finally, expressed in the church books of the era.
2005 / 1-84227-251-9 / approx. 230pp

Frank Rinaldi
'The Tribe of Dan'
A Study of the New Connexion of General Baptists 1770–1891
(SBHT vol. 10)
'The Tribe of Dan' is a thematic study which explores the theology, organizational structure, evangelistic strategy, ministry and leadership of the New Connexion of General Baptists as it experienced the process of institutionalization in the transition from a revival movement to an established denomination.
2006 / 1-84227-143-1 / approx. 350pp

Peter Shepherd
The Making of a Modern Denomination
John Howard Shakespeare and the English Baptists 1898–1924
(SBHT vol. 4)
John Howard Shakespeare introduced revolutionary change to the Baptist denomination. The Baptist Union was transformed into a strong central institution and Baptist ministers were brought under its control. Further, Shakespeare's pursuit of church unity reveals him as one of the pioneering ecumenists of the twentieth century.
2001 / 1-84227-046-X / xviii + 220pp

Karen Smith
The Community and the Believers
A Study of Calvinistic Baptist Spirituality in Some Towns and Villages of
Hampshire and the Borders of Wiltshire, c.1730–1830
(SBHT vol. 22)
The period from 1730 to 1830 was one of transition for Calvinistic Baptists. Confronted by the enthusiasm of the Evangelical Revival, congregations within the denomination as a whole were challenged to find a way to take account of the revival experience. This study examines the life and devotion of Calvinistic Baptists in Hampshire and Wiltshire during this period. Among this group of Baptists was the hymn writer, Anne Steele.
2005 / 1-84227-326-4 / approx. 280pp

Martin Sutherland
Dissenters in a 'Free Land'
Baptist Thought in New Zealand 1850–2000
(SBHT vol. 24)
Baptists in New Zealand were forced to recast their identity. Conventions of communication and association, state and ecumenical relations, even historical divisions and controversies had to be revised in the face of new topographies and constraints. As Baptists formed themselves in a fluid society they drew heavily on both international movements and local dynamics. This book traces the development of ideas which shaped institutions and styles in sometimes surprising ways.
2006 / 1-84227-327-2 / approx. 230pp

Brian Talbot
The Search for a Common Identity
The Origins of the Baptist Union of Scotland 1800–1870
(SBHT vol. 9)
In the period 1800 to 1827 there were three streams of Baptists in Scotland: Scotch, Haldaneite and 'English' Baptist. A strong commitment to home evangelization brought these three bodies closer together, leading to a merger of their home missionary societies in 1827. However, the first three attempts to form a union of churches failed, but by the 1860s a common understanding of their corporate identity was attained leading to the establishment of the Baptist Union of Scotland.
2003 / 1-84227-123-7 / xviii + 402pp

Philip E. Thompson
The Freedom of God
Towards Baptist Theology in Pneumatological Perspective
(SBHT vol. 20)
This study contends that the range of theological commitments of the early Baptists are best understood in relation to their distinctive emphasis on the freedom of God. Thompson traces how this was recast anthropocentrically, leading to an emphasis upon human freedom from the nineteenth century onwards. He seeks to recover the dynamism of the early vision via a pneumatologically-oriented ecclesiology defining the church in terms of the memory of God.
2006 / 1-84227-125-3 / approx. 350pp

Philip E. Thompson and Anthony R. Cross (eds)
Recycling the Past or Researching History?
Studies in Baptist Historiography and Myths
(SBHT vol. 11)
In this volume an international group of Baptist scholars examine and re-examine areas of Baptist life and thought about which little is known or the received wisdom is in need of revision. Historiographical studies include the date Oxford Baptists joined the Abingdon Association, the death of the Fifth Monarchist John Pendarves, eighteenth-century Calvinistic Baptists and the political realm, confessional identity and denominational institutions, Baptist community, ecclesiology, the priesthood of all believers, soteriology, Baptist spirituality, Strict and Reformed Baptists, the role of women among British Baptists, while various 'myths' challenged include the nature of high-Calvinism in eighteenth-century England, baptismal anti-sacramentalism, episcopacy, and Baptists and change.
2005 / 1-84227-122-9 / approx. 330pp

Linda Wilson
Marianne Farningham
A Plain Working Woman
(SBHT vol. 18)
Marianne Farningham, of College Street Baptist Chapel, Northampton, was a household name in evangelical circles in the later nineteenth century. For over fifty years she produced comment, poetry, biography and fiction for the popular Christian press. This investigation uses her writings to explore the beliefs and behaviour of evangelical Nonconformists, including Baptists, during these years.
2006 / 1-84227-124-5 / approx. 250pp

Other Paternoster titles
relating to Baptist history and thought

George R. Beasley-Murray
Baptism in the New Testament
(Paternoster Digital Library)
This is a welcome reprint of a classic text on baptism originally published in 1962 by one of the leading Baptist New Testament scholars of the twentieth century. Dr Beasley-Murray's comprehensive study begins by investigating the antecedents of Christian baptism. It then surveys the foundation of Christian baptism in the Gospels, its emergence in the Acts of the Apostles and development in the apostolic writings. Following a section relating baptism to New Testament doctrine, a substantial discussion of the origin and significance of infant baptism leads to a briefer consideration of baptismal reform and ecumenism.

2005 / 1-84227-300-0 / x + 422pp

Paul Beasley-Murray
Fearless for Truth
A Personal Portrait of the Life of George Beasley-Murray
Without a doubt George Beasley-Murray was one of the greatest Baptists of the twentieth century. A long-standing Principal of Spurgeon's College, he wrote more than twenty books and made significant contributions in the study of areas as diverse as baptism and eschatology, as well as writing highly respected commentaries on the Book of Revelation and John's Gospel.

2002 / 1-84227-134-2 / xii + 244pp

David Bebbington
Holiness in Nineteenth-Century England
(Studies in Christian History and Thought)
David Bebbington stresses the relationship of movements of spirituality to changes in their cultural setting, especially the legacies of the Enlightenment and Romanticism. He shows that these broad shifts in ideological mood had a profound effect on the ways in which piety was conceptualized and practised. Holiness was intimately bound up with the spirit of the age.

2000 / 0-85364-981-2 / viii + 98pp

Clyde Binfield
Victorian Nonconformity in Eastern England 1840–1885
(Studies in Evangelical History and Thought)
Studies of Victorian religion and society often concentrate on cities, suburbs, and industrialisation. This study provides a contrast. Victorian Eastern England—Essex, Suffolk, Norfolk, Cambridgeshire, and Huntingdonshire—was rural, traditional, relatively unchanging. That is nonetheless a caricature which discounts the industry in Norwich and Ipswich (as well as in Haverhill, Stowmarket and Leiston) and ignores the impact of London on Essex, of railways throughout the region, and of an ancient but changing university (Cambridge) on the county town which housed it. It also entirely ignores the political implications of such changes in a region noted for the variety of its religious Dissent since the seventeenth century. This book explores Victorian Eastern England and its Nonconformity. It brings to a wider readership a pioneering thesis which has made a major contribution to a fresh evolution of English religion and society.
2006 / 1-84227-216-0 / approx. 274pp

Edward W. Burrows
'To Me To Live Is Christ'
A Biography of Peter H. Barber
This book is about a remarkably gifted and energetic man of God. Peter H. Barber was born into a Brethren family in Edinburgh in 1930. In his youth he joined Charlotte Baptist Chapel and followed the call into Baptist ministry. For eighteen years he was the pioneer minister of the new congregation in the New Town of East Kilbride, which planted two further congregations. At the age of thirty-nine he served as Centenary President of the Baptist Union of Scotland and then exercised an influential ministry for over seven years in the well-known Upton Vale Baptist Church, Torquay. From 1980 until his death in 1994 he was General Secretary of the Baptist Union of Scotland. Through his work for the European Baptist Federation and the Baptist World Alliance he became a world Baptist statesman. He was President of the EBF during the upheaval that followed the collapse of Communism.
2005 / 1-84227-324-8 / xxii + 236pp

Christopher J. Clement
Religious Radicalism in England 1535–1565
(Rutherford Studies in Historical Theology)
In this valuable study Christopher Clement draws our attention to a varied assemblage of people who sought Christian faithfulness in the underworld of mid-Tudor England. Sympathetically and yet critically he assess their place in the history of English Protestantism, and by attentive listening he gives them a voice.
1997 / 0-946068-44-5 / xxii + 426pp

July 2005

Anthony R. Cross (ed.)
Ecumenism and History
Studies in Honour of John H.Y. Briggs
(Studies in Christian History and Thought)
This collection of essays examines the inter-relationships between the two fields in which Professor Briggs has contributed so much: history—particularly Baptist and Nonconformist—and the ecumenical movement. With contributions from colleagues and former research students from Britain, Europe and North America, *Ecumenism and History* provides wide-ranging studies in important aspects of Christian history, theology and ecumenical studies.
2002 / 1-84227-135-0 / xx + 362pp

Keith E. Eitel
Paradigm Wars
The Southern Baptist International Mission Board
Faces the Third Millennium
(Regnum Studies in Mission)
The International Mission Board of the Southern Baptist Convention is the largest denominational mission agency in North America. This volume chronicles the historic and contemporary forces that led to the IMB's recent extensive reorganization, providing the most comprehensive case study to date of a historic mission agency restructuring to continue its mission purpose into the twenty-first century more effectively.
2000 / 1-870345-12-6 / x + 140pp

Ruth Gouldbourne
The Flesh and the Feminine
Gender and Theology in the Writings of Caspar Schwenckfeld
(Studies in Christian History and Thought)
Caspar Schwenckfeld and his movement exemplify one of the radical communities of the sixteenth century. Challenging theological and liturgical norms, they also found themselves challenging social and particularly gender assumptions. In this book, the issues of the relationship between radical theology and the understanding of gender are considered.
2005 / 1-84227-048-6 / approx. 304pp

David Hilborn
The Words of our Lips
Language-Use in Free Church Worship
(Paternoster Theological Monographs)
Studies of liturgical language have tended to focus on the written canons of Roman Catholic and Anglican communities. By contrast, David Hilborn analyses the more extemporary approach of English Nonconformity. Drawing on recent developments in linguistic pragmatics, he explores similarities and differences between 'fixed' and 'free' worship, and argues for the interdependence of each.

2006 / 0-85364-977-4

Stephen R. Holmes
Listening to the Past
The Place of Tradition in Theology
Beginning with the question 'Why can't we just read the Bible?' Stephen Holmes considers the place of tradition in theology, showing how the doctrine of creation leads to an account of historical location and creaturely limitations as essential aspects of our existence. For we cannot claim unmediated access to the Scriptures without acknowledging the place of tradition: theology is an irreducibly communal task. *Listening to the Past* is a sustained attempt to show what listening to tradition involves, and how it can be used to aid theological work today.

2002 / 1-84227-155-5 / xiv + 168pp

Mark Hopkins
Nonconformity's Romantic Generation
Evangelical and Liberal Theologies in Victorian England
(Studies in Evangelical History and Thought)
A study of the theological development of key leaders of the Baptist and Congregational denominations at their period of greatest influence, including C.H. Spurgeon and R.W. Dale, and of the controversies in which those among them who embraced and rejected the liberal transformation of their evangelical heritage opposed each other.

2004 / 1-84227-150-4 / xvi + 284pp

Galen K. Johnson
Prisoner of Conscience
John Bunyan on Self, Community and Christian Faith
(Studies in Christian History and Thought)
This is an interdisciplinary study of John Bunyan's understanding of conscience across his autobiographical, theological and fictional writings, investigating whether conscience always deserves fidelity, and how Bunyan's view of conscience affects his relationship both to modern Western individualism and historic Christianity.

2003 / 1-84227- 151-2 / xvi + 236pp

R.T. Kendall
Calvin and English Calvinism to 1649
(Studies in Christian History and Thought)
The author's thesis is that those who formed the Westminster Confession of Faith, which is regarded as Calvinism, in fact departed from John Calvin on two points: (1) the extent of the atonement and (2) the ground of assurance of salvation.

1997 / 0-85364-827-1 / xii + 264pp

Timothy Larsen
Friends of Religious Equality
Nonconformist Politics in Mid-Victorian England
During the middle decades of the nineteenth century the English Nonconformist community developed a coherent political philosophy of its own, of which a central tenet was the principle of religious equality (in contrast to the stereotype of Evangelical Dissenters). The Dissenting community fought for the civil rights of Roman Catholics, non-Christians and even atheists, on an issue of principle which had its flowering in the enthusiastic and undivided support which Nonconformity gave to the campaign for Jewish emancipation. This reissued study examines the political efforts and ideas of English Nonconformists during the period, covering the whole range of national issues raised, from state education to the Crimean War. It offers a case study of a theologically conservative group defending religious pluralism in the civic sphere, showing that the concept of religious equality was a grand vision at the centre of the political philosophy of the Dissenters.

2007 / 1-84227-402-3 / x + 300pp

Donald M. Lewis
Lighten Their Darkness
The Evangelical Mission to Working-Class London, 1828–1860
(Studies in Evangelical History and Thought)
This is a comprehensive and compelling study of the Church and the complexities of nineteenth-century London. Challenging our understanding of the culture in working London at this time, Lewis presents a well-structured and illustrated work that contributes substantially to the study of evangelicalism and mission in nineteenth-century Britain.
2001 / 1-84227-074-5 / xviii + 372pp

Stanley E. Porter and Anthony R. Cross (eds)
Semper Reformandum
Studies in Honour of Clark H. Pinnock
Clark Pinnock has clearly been one of the most important evangelical theologians of the last forty years in North America. Always provocative, especially in the wide range of opinions he has held and considered, Pinnock, himself a Baptist, has recently retired after twenty-five years of teaching at McMaster Divinity College. His colleagues and associates honour him in this volume by responding to his important theological work which has dealt with the essential topics of evangelical theology. These include Christian apologetics, biblical inspiration, the Holy Spirit and, perhaps most importantly in recent years, openness theology.
2003 / 1-84227-206-3 / xiv + 414pp

Meic Pearse
The Great Restoration
The Religious Radicals of the 16th and 17th Centuries
Pearse charts the rise and progress of continental Anabaptism – both evangelical and heretical – through the sixteenth century. He then follows the story of those English people who became impatient with Puritanism and separated – first from the Church of England and then from one another – to form the antecedents of later Congregationalists, Baptists and Quakers.
1998 / 0-85364-800-X / xii + 320pp

Charles Price and Ian M. Randall
Transforming Keswick
Transforming Keswick is a thorough, readable and detailed history of the convention. It will be of interest to those who know and love Keswick, those who are only just discovering it, and serious scholars eager to learn more about the history of God's dealings with his people.
2000 / 1-85078-350-0 / 288pp

Jim Purves
The Triune God and the Charismatic Movement
A Critical Appraisal from a Scottish Perspective
(Paternoster Theological Monographs)
All emotion and no theology? Or a fundamental challenge to reappraise and realign our trinitarian theology in the light of Christian experience? This study of charismatic renewal as it found expression within Scotland at the end of the twentieth century evaluates the use of Patristic, Reformed and contemporary models (including those of the Baptist Union of Scotland) of the Trinity in explaining the workings of the Holy Spirit.

2004 / 1-84227-321-3 / xxiv + 246pp

Ian M. Randall
Evangelical Experiences
A Study in the Spirituality of English Evangelicalism 1918–1939
(Studies in Evangelical History and Thought)
This book makes a detailed historical examination of evangelical spirituality between the First and Second World Wars. It shows how patterns of devotion led to tensions and divisions. In a wide-ranging study, Anglican, Wesleyan, Reformed and Pentecostal-charismatic spiritualities are analysed.

1999 / 0-85364-919-7 / xii + 310pp

Ian M. Randall
One Body in Christ
The History and Significance of the Evangelical Alliance
In 1846 the Evangelical Alliance was founded with the aim of bringing together evangelicals for common action. This book uses material not previously utilized to examine the history and significance of the Evangelical Alliance, a movement which has remained a powerful force for unity. At a time when evangelicals are growing world-wide, this book offers insights into the past which are relevant to contemporary issues.

2001 / 1-84227-089-3 / xii + 394pp

Ian M. Randall
Spirituality and Social Change
The Contribution of F.B. Meyer (1847–1929)
(Studies in Evangelical History and Thought)
This is a fresh appraisal of F.B. Meyer (1847–1929), a leading Free Church minister. Having been deeply affected by holiness spirituality, Meyer became the Keswick Convention's foremost international speaker. He combined spirituality with effective evangelism and socio-political activity. This study shows Meyer's significant contribution to spiritual renewal and social change.

2003 / 1-84227-195-4 / xx + 184pp

Geoffrey Robson
Dark Satanic Mills?
Religion and Irreligion in Birmingham and the Black Country
(Studies in Evangelical History and Thought)
This book analyses and interprets the nature and extent of popular Christian belief and practice in Birmingham and the Black Country during the first half of the nineteenth century, with particular reference to the impact of cholera epidemics and evangelism on church extension programmes.
2002 / 1-84227-102-4 / xiv + 294pp

Alan P.F. Sell
Enlightenment, Ecumenism, Evangel
Theological Themes and Thinkers 1550–2000
(Studies in Christian History and Thought)
This book consists of papers in which such interlocking topics as the Enlightenment, the problem of authority, the development of doctrine, spirituality, ecumenism, theological method and the heart of the gospel are discussed. Issues of significance to the church at large are explored with special reference to writers from the Reformed and Dissenting traditions.
2005 / 1-84227330-2 / xviii + 422pp

Alan P.F. Sell
Hinterland Theology
Some Reformed and Dissenting Adjustments
(Studies in Christian History and Thought)
Many books have been written on theology's 'giants' and significant trends, but what of those lesser-known writers who adjusted to them? In this book some hinterland theologians of the British Reformed and Dissenting traditions, who followed in the wake of toleration, the Evangelical Revival, the rise of modern biblical criticism and Karl Barth, are allowed to have their say. They include Thomas Ridgley, Ralph Wardlaw, T.V. Tymms and N.H.G. Robinson.
2006 / 1-84227-331-0

Alan P.F. Sell and Anthony R. Cross (eds)
Protestant Nonconformity in the Twentieth Century
(Studies in Christian History and Thought)
In this collection of essays scholars representative of a number of Nonconformist traditions reflect thematically on Nonconformists' life and witness during the twentieth century. Among the subjects reviewed are biblical studies, theology, worship, evangelism and spirituality, and ecumenism. Over and above its immediate interest, this collection provides a marker to future scholars and others wishing to know how some of their forebears assessed Nonconformity's contribution to a variety of fields during the century leading up to Christianity's third millennium.

2003 / 1-84227-221-7 / x + 398pp

Mark Smith
Religion in Industrial Society
Oldham and Saddleworth 1740–1865
(Studies in Christian History and Thought)
This book analyses the way British churches sought to meet the challenge of industrialization and urbanization during the period 1740–1865. Working from a case-study of Oldham and Saddleworth, Mark Smith challenges the received view that the Anglican Church in the eighteenth century was characterized by complacency and inertia, and reveals Anglicanism's vigorous and creative response to the new conditions. He reassesses the significance of the centrally directed church reforms of the mid-nineteenth century, and emphasizes the importance of local energy and enthusiasm. Charting the growth of denominational pluralism in Oldham and Saddleworth, Dr Smith compares the strengths and weaknesses of the various Anglican and Nonconformist approaches to promoting church growth. He also demonstrates the extent to which all the churches participated in a common culture shaped by the influence of evangelicalism, and shows that active co-operation between the churches rather than denominational conflict dominated. This revised and updated edition of Dr Smith's challenging and original study makes an important contribution both to the social history of religion and to urban studies.

2006 / 1-84227-335-3 / approx. 300pp

David M. Thompson
Baptism, Church and Society in Britain from the Evangelical Revival to
Baptism, Eucharist and Ministry
The theology and practice of baptism have not received the attention they
deserve. How important is faith? What does baptismal regeneration mean? Is
baptism a bond of unity between Christians? This book discusses the theology of
baptism and popular belief and practice in England and Wales from the
Evangelical Revival to the publication of the World Council of Churches'
consensus statement on *Baptism, Eucharist and Ministry* (1982).
2005 / 1-84227-393-0 / approx. 224pp

Martin Sutherland
Peace, Toleration and Decay
The Ecclesiology of Later Stuart Dissent
(Studies in Christian History and Thought)
This fresh analysis brings to light the complexity and fragility of the later Stuart
Nonconformist consensus. Recent findings on wider seventeenth-century
thought are incorporated into a new picture of the dynamics of Dissent and the
roots of evangelicalism.
2003 / 1-84227-152-0 / xxii + 216pp

Haddon Willmer
Evangelicalism 1785–1835: An Essay (1962) and Reflections (2004)
(Studies in Evangelical History and Thought)
Awarded the Hulsean Prize in the University of Cambridge in 1962, this
interpretation of a classic period of English Evangelicalism, by a young church
historian, is now supplemented by reflections on Evangelicalism from the
vantage point of a retired Professor of Theology.
2006 / 1-84227-219-5

Linda Wilson
Constrained by Zeal
Female Spirituality amongst Nonconformists 1825–1875
(Studies in Evangelical History and Thought)
Constrained by Zeal investigates the neglected area of Nonconformist female
spirituality. Against the background of separate spheres, it analyses the
experience of women from four denominations, and argues that the churches
provided a 'third sphere' in which they could find opportunities for
participation.
2000 / 0-85364-972-3 / xvi + 294pp

Nigel G. Wright
Disavowing Constantine
Mission, Church and the Social Order in the Theologies of
John Howard Yoder and Jürgen Moltmann
(Paternoster Theological Monographs)
This book is a timely restatement of a radical theology of church and state in the
Anabaptist and Baptist tradition. Dr Wright constructs his argument in dialogue
and debate with Yoder and Moltmann, major contributors to a free church
perspective.
2000 / 0-85364-978-2 / xvi + 252pp

Nigel G. Wright
Free Church, Free State
The Positive Baptist Vision
Free Church, Free State is a textbook on baptist ways of being church and a
proposal for the future of baptist churches in an ecumenical context. Nigel
Wright argues that both baptist (small 'b') and catholic (small 'c') church
traditions should seek to enrich and support each other as valid expressions of
the body of Christ without sacrificing what they hold dear. Written for pastors,
church planters, evangelists and preachers, Nigel Wright offers frameworks of
thought for baptists and non-baptists in their journey together following Christ.
2005 / 1-84227-353-1 / xxviii + 292

Nigel G. Wright
New Baptists, New Agenda
New Baptists, New Agenda is a timely contribution to the growing debate about
the health, shape and future of the Baptists. It considers the steady changes that
have taken place among Baptists in the last decade – changes of mood, style,
practice and structure – and encourages us to align these current movements and
questions with God's upward and future call. He contends that the true church
has yet to come: the church that currently exists is an anticipation of the joyful
gathering of all who have been called by the Spirit through Christ to the Father.
2002 / 1-84227-157-1 / x + 162pp

Paternoster
9 Holdom Avenue,
Bletchley,
Milton Keynes MK1 1QR,
United Kingdom   July 2005
Web: www.authenticmedia.co.uk/paternoster